FOURTH

EDITION

CONSUMER BEHAVIOR

BUYING, HAVING, AND BEING

Michael R. Solomon

Auburn University

...tional, Inc.

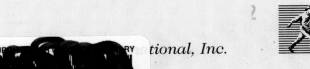

CONSUMER BEHAVIOR
BUYING, HAVING, AND BEING

FOURTH
EDITION

Michael R. Solomon
Auburn University

Prentice Hall,
Upper Saddle River, New Jersey 07458

TO GAIL, AMANDA, ZACHARY, AND ALEX—STILL MY FAVORITE CONSUMERS!

Acquisitions Editor:	Whitney Blake
Editorial Assistant:	Michele Foresta
Editor-in-Chief:	Natalie Anderson
Marketing Manager:	Shannon Moore
Associate Managing Editor:	Linda DeLorenzo
Permissions Coordinator:	Jennifer Rella/Monica Stipanov
Managing Editor:	Dee Josephson
Manufacturing Buyer:	Kenneth J. Clinton
Manufacturing Supervisor:	Arnold Vila
Manufacturing Manager:	Vincent Scelta
Designer:	Ann France
Design Manager:	Patricia Smythe
Interior Design:	John Romer
Photo Research Supervisor:	Melinda Lee Reo
Image Permission Supervisor:	Kay Dellosa
Photo Researcher:	Teri Stratford
Cover Design:	Cheryl Asherman
Illustrator (Interior):	Alexander Teshin Associates
Cover Illustration:	Tom Herzberg
Production/Composition:	Monotype Composition, Inc.

Credits and acknowledgments for materials borrowed from other sources and reproduced, with permission, in this textbook appear on page vi.

ISBN 0-13-081255-2

Prentice-Hall International (UK) Limited, London
Prentice-Hall of Australia Pty. Limited, Sydney
Prentice-Hall Canada, Inc., Toronto
Prentice-Hall Hispanoamericana, S.A., Mexico
Prentice-Hall of India Private Limited, New Delhi
Prentice-Hall of Japan, Inc., Tokyo
Simon & Schuster Asia Pte. Ltd., Singapore
Editora Prentice-Hall do Brasil, Ltda., Rio de Janeiro
Prentice-Hall, Upper Saddle River, New Jersey

Printed in the United States of America

10 9 8 7 6 5 4 3 2 1

ABOUT THE AUTHOR

MICHAEL R. SOLOMON, Ph.D. is Human Sciences Professor of Consumer Behavior in the Department of Consumer Affairs, School of Human Sciences, at Auburn University. Prior to joining Auburn in 1995, he was Chairman of the Department of Marketing in the School of Business at Rutgers University, New Brunswick, New Jersey. Professor Solomon began his academic career at the Graduate School of Business Administration at New York University, where he also served as Associate Director of NYU's Institute of Retail Management. He earned B.A. degrees in Psychology and Sociology *magna cum laude* at Brandeis University in 1977, and a Ph.D. in Social Psychology at the University of North Carolina at Chapel Hill in 1981. He was recently named to the Fulbright/FLAD Chair in Market Globalization, and in fall served as Distinguished Lecturer in Marketing in the M.B.A. program at the Technical University of Lisbon.

Professor Solomon's primary research interests include consumer behavior and lifestyle issues, the symbolic aspects of products, the psychology of fashion, decoration, and image, and services marketing. He has published numerous articles on these and related topics in academic journals, and has delivered invited lectures on these subjects at universities in the United Kingdom, Scandinavia, and Australia. He sits on the editorial boards of the *Journal of Consumer Research* and the *Journal of Retailing.*

Professor Solomon received the Cutty Sark Men's Fashion Award in 1981 for his research on the psychological aspects of clothing. He is the editor of *The Psychology of Fashion* and coeditor of *The Service Encounter: Managing Employee/Customer Interaction in Services Businesses,* both published by Lexington Books.

In addition to his academic activities, Professor Solomon is a frequent contributor to mass media. His feature articles have appeared in *Psychology Today, Gentleman's Quarterly,* and *Savvy.* He has been quoted in numerous national magazines and newspapers, including *Allure, Elle, Glamour, Mademoiselle, Mirabella, Newsweek,* the *New York Times, Self, USA Today,* and the *Wall Street Journal.* He has been a guest on *The Today Show, Good Morning America,* CNBC, Channel One, *Inside Edition, Newsweek on the Air,* and National Public Radio. He recently appeared in a video on fashion and image produced and distributed by Kayser-Roth.

Professor Solomon has provided input as an advisor and an expert witness to a variety of organizations on issues related to consumer behavior, services marketing, retailing, and advertising. His consultancies have included Armstrong World Industries, Celanese, Hakuhodo Advertising (Tokyo), Johnson & Johnson, Kayser-Roth, Levi-Strauss, Prudential Securities, and United Airlines. He has spoken before many business groups, including The Association of Fashion and Image Consultants; Burson-Marsteller, Inc.; Color Me Beautiful, Inc.; The Cosmetics, Toiletries, and Fragrances Association; Credit Agricole Mutuel; The Image Industry Council International; The Institut für Kommunikations-Forschung (Hamburg), The International Furnishings and Design Association; The Japanese Financial Services Council; The National Kitchen and Bath Association; The Fragrance Foundation; the Napier Company; Southmark Corporation; The Textile Rental Services Association; The Fashion Group International; and The International Apparel Federation (Milan). He currently lives in Auburn, Alabama with his wife Gail, their three children, Amanda, Zachary, and Alexandra, and Chloe, their golden retriever.

Photo Credits

Brief Contents

Contents

PREFACE

I wrote this book because I'm fascinated by the everyday activities of people. The field of consumer behavior is, to me, the study of how our world is influenced by the action of marketers. Because I'm a consumer myself, I have a selfish interest in learning more about how this process works—and so do you.

In many courses, students are merely passive observers, learning about topics that affect them indirectly only, if at all. Not everyone is a plasma physicist, a medieval French scholar, or even an industrial marketer. We are, however, all consumers. As a result, many of the topics dealt with in this book have both professional and personal relevance to the reader, whether he or she is a student, professor, or marketing practitioner. Nearly everyone can relate to the trials and tribulations associated with last-minute shopping, primping for a big night out, agonizing over an expensive purchase decision, fantasizing about a week in the Caribbean, celebrating a holiday, or commemorating a landmark event, such as a graduation, getting a driver's license, or (dreaming about) winning the lottery.

BEYOND CANNED PEAS: BUYING, HAVING, AND BEING

As the book's subtitle suggests, my version of this field goes beyond looking at the act of buying to having and being as well. Consumer behavior is more than buying things, such as a can of peas; it also embraces the study of how having (or not having) things affects our lives and how our possessions influence the way we feel about ourselves and about each other—our state of being.

In addition to understanding why people buy things, we also try to appreciate how products, services, and consumption activities contribute to the broader social world we experience. Whether shopping, cooking, cleaning, playing basketball, hanging out at the beach, or even looking at ourselves in the mirror, our lives are touched by the marketing system. As if these experiences were not complex enough, the task of understanding the consumer multiplies geometrically when a multicultural perspective is taken. This book not only probes the psyche of the American consumer, but also attempts wherever possible to consider the many other consumers around the world whose diverse experiences with buying, having, and being are equally vital to understand. In addition to the numerous examples of marketing and consumer practices relating to consumers and companies outside the United States that appear throughout the book, chapters contain boxes called "Multicultural Dimensions" that highlight cultural differences in consumer behavior. I developed the models of consumer behavior that appear at the beginning of text sections to underscore the complex—and often inseparable—interrelationships between the individual consumer and his or her social realities.

THE REVELANCE OF CONSUMER RESEARCH

The field of consumer behavior is young, dynamic, and in flux. It is constantly being cross-fertilized by perspectives from many different disciplines. I have tried to express the field's staggering diversity in these pages. Consumer researchers represent virtually every social science discipline, plus a few represent the physical sciences and the arts for good measure. From this melting pot has come a healthy "stew" of research perspectives, viewpoints regarding appropriate research methods, and even deeply held beliefs about what are and what are not appropriate issues for consumer researchers to study in the first place.

The book also emphasizes the importance of understanding consumers in formulating marketing strategy. Many (if not most) of the fundamental concepts in marketing are based on the practitioner's ability to know people. After all, if we don't understand why people behave as they do, how can we identify their needs? If we can't identify their needs, how can we satisfy their needs? If we can't satisfy people's needs, we don't have a marketing concept, so we might as well fold our tents and go home! To illustrate the potential of consumer research to inform marketing strategy, the text contains numerous examples of specific applications of consumer behavior concepts by marketing practitioners as well as of windows of opportunity in which such concepts could be used (perhaps by alert strategists after taking this course!). Many of these possibilities are highlighted in special features called "Marketing Opportunities."

THE GOOD, THE BAD, AND THE UGLY

The strategic focus is, however, tempered by an important qualification: Unlike some contemporary treatments of consumer behavior, this book does not assume that everything marketers do is in the best interests of consumers or of their environment. Likewise, as consumers, we do many things that are not positive either. People are plagued by addictions, status envy, ethnocentrism, racism, sexism, and other "isms" and, regrettably, there are times when marketing activities—deliberately or not—encourage or exploit these human flaws. This book deals with the totality of consumer behavior, warts and all. Marketing mistakes or ethically suspect activities are also highlighted in special features labeled "Marketing Pitfalls."

On the other hand, marketers have helped to create many wonderful (or at least unusual) things, such as holidays, comic books, the music industry, "pet rocks," and the many stylistic options available to us in the domains of clothing, home design, the arts, cuisine, and so on. I have also taken pains to acknowledge the sizable impact of marketing on popular culture. Indeed, the final section of this book reflects very recent work in the field that scrutinizes, criticizes, and sometimes celebrates consumers in their everyday worlds. I hope you will enjoy reading about such wonderful things as much as I enjoyed writing about them.

ACKNOWLEDGMENTS

I am grateful for the many helpful comments on how to improve the fourth edition that were provided by my peer reviewers. Special thanks go to the following people:

Paul Chao, University of Northern Iowa
Peter L. Gillett, University of Central Florida
Douglas Hausknecht, University of Akron
Carol Kaufman, Rutgers University—Camden
Donna Tillman, California State Polytechnic University—Pomona
Gail Tom, California State University—Sacramento
Stuart Van Auken, California State University—Chicago

Many colleagues made significant contributions to this edition. I would like to thank, in particular, the following people who made constructive suggestions and/or who provided me with a "sneak peek" at their research materials and manuscripts now in press or under review:

Jennifer Aaker, Stanford University
Linda Alwitt, DePaul University
Craig Andrews, Marquette University
Søren Askegaard, Odense University (Denmark)
Stacy Baker, Texas A&M University
Siva Balasubramanian, Southern Illinois University
Gary Bamossy, Vrije Universiteit (Netherlands)
Sharon Beatty, University of Alabama
Russell Belk, University of Utah
Paula Bone, West Virginia University
Stephen Brown, University of Ulster (Northern Ireland)
Cindy Clark, C.D. Clark, Ltd.
Bettina Cornwell, University of Memphis
Janeen Costa, University of Utah
Joseph Cote, Washington State University—Vancouver
Robin Higie Coulter, University of Connecticut
Margaret Craig-Lees, University of New South Wales (Australia)
Pam Scholder Ellen, Georgia State University
Richard Elliott, Oxford University (U.K)
Basil Englis, Berry College
Eileen Fischer, York University (Canada)
Susan Fournier, Harvard University
Stephen Gould, Baruch College
Guliz Gër, Bilkent University (Turkey)
Kent Grayson, London Business School (U.K)
Ron Groves, Edith Cowan University (Australia)
Pola Gupta, University of Northern Iowa
William Havlena, Fordham University
Elizabeth Hirschman, Rutgers University
Margaret Hogg, Manchester School of Management (U.K.)
Susan Holak, City University of Staten Island
Morris Holbrook, Columbia University
Rebecca Holman, The Wirthlin Group

Marty Horn, DDB Needham
Douglas Holt, University of Illinois
Lynn Kahle, University of Oregon
James Kellaris, University of Cincinnati
Michel Laroche, Concordia University (Canada)
Stephen La Tour, Auburn University
Kenneth Lord, Niagara University
Roger Marshall, Nanyang Technological University (Singapore)
Mary Martin, University of North Carolina at Charlotte
Mary Ann McGrath, Loyola University of Chicago
Damien McLoughlin, University College Dublin (Ireland)
Stephanie O'Donohoe, University of Edinburgh (U.K.)
Anna Olofsson, Gazoline Advertising (Sweden)
Lisa Penalõza, University of Colorado
Greta Pennell, University of Indianapolis
Dennis Rook, University of Southern Carolina
Greg Rose, University of Mississippi
Herbert Rotfeld, Auburn University
Margaret Rucker, University of California at Davis
Shay Sayre, California State University at Fullerton
Jonathan Schroeder, University of Rhode Island
David Schumann, University of Tennessee
John Sherry, Northwestern University
Jagdish Sheth, Emory University
Elnora Stuart, Winthrop University
Darach Turley, Dublin City University Business School (Ireland)
Alladi Venkatesh, University of California at Irvine
Melanie Wallendorf, University of Arizona
Dan Wardlow, San Francisco State University
Judy Zaickhowsky, Simon Fraser University (Canada)
Gerald Zaltman, Harvard University

Extra special thanks are due to the preparers of the ancillary materials: John R. Brooks, Jr. from Houston Baptist University for preparation of the Instructor's Manual and Test Item File, Kellye Brooks for preparation of the Powerpoint file, and Beverlee Anderson for preparation of the new video case/Internet exercises.

I would also like to thank the good people at Prentice Hall who have done yeoman service on this edition. In particular I am indebted to my tenacious editor, Whitney Blake, for helping me to navigate the sometimes treacherous waters of publishing. Thanks also to Gabrielle Dudnyk, Rachel Falk, Michele Foresta, Steven Deitmer, Janet Ferruggia, and John "The Chill" Chillingworth for their support and great work.

My friends and colleagues have been fantastic since this project began. Without their support and tolerance, I would never have been able to sustain the "illusion" that I was still an active researcher during the two years I worked on this edition. I am grateful to my department chair, Carol Warfield, and to Dean June Henton for their continuing support. Special thanks go to Lei Zhou for her assistance throughout. I am also particularly indebted to Basil Englis for his intellectual and emotional support—he personifies my image of what a good colleague and friend should be.

Also, I am grateful to my students, who have been a prime source of inspiration, examples, and feedback. The satisfaction I have garnered from teaching them about consumer behavior motivated me to write a book I felt they would like to read.

Last but not least, I would like to thank my family and friends for sticking by me during this revision. They know who they are, since their names pop up in chapter vignettes throughout the book. My apologies for "distorting" their characters in the name of poetic license! My gratitude and love go out to my parents, Jackie and Henry, and my in-laws, Marilyn and Phil. My super children, Amanda, Zachary, and Alexandra, always made the sun shine on gray days. Finally, thanks above all to Gail, my wonderful wife, friend, and occasional research assistant: I still do it all for you.

M.R.S.
Auburn, AL
July 1998

ANCILLARY MATERIALS AVAILABLE FOR INSTRUCTORS

Adopters of the fourth edition will be provided with a useful set of resources, many of which are new to this edition. The improvements to the teaching package include full Web support for professor and students through our PHLIP Web site (www.prenhall.com/phbusiness), a new video library with internet exercises, and a secondary set of overhead transparencies featuring advertisements. The following items comprise the support package for Consumer Behavior 4/E:

INSTRUCTOR'S MANUAL

This manual includes chapter summaries, chapter outline with annotations for video cases and internet exercises, answers to end of chapter discussion questions, field projects, and notes for Powerpoint transparencies and ad transparencies.

TEST ITEM FILE:

For each chapter of the text, this file includes 50 multiple choice, 25 true/false and applications questions. These test items are page referenced to the text.

3.5″ IBM TEST MANAGER

This powerful computerized testing package, available for DOS and Windows-based computers, allows instructors to create their own personalized exams using questions from the Test Item File. It offers full mouse support, complete question edition, random test generation, graphics, and printing capabilities.

POWERPOINT FILES

Prepared in PowerPoint 4.0, these files provide lecture slides for each chapter, important figures/concepts from the text, and transitional notes to move from one concept to another within a lecture.

COLOR TRANSPARENCIES

The complete set of PowerPoint files are available on acetate transparencies. In addition, a second set of ad transparencies are available featuring current ads (with teaching notes) and ads from the video/video cases.

CONSUMER BEHAVIOR VIDEO LIBRARY

The 1999 video library consists of 18 segments featuring such companies as Nike, Starbucks, Dupont, Intel, and Levi Strauss. In addition, the latest reel from NY Festivals is included featuring current award winning advertisements. The Consumer Behavior Video Library is updated annually to keep the segments very current. Teaching notes and video cases are available in the Instructor's Manual and through PHLIP. (See below for a description of PHLIP.)

PHLIP-PRENTICE HALL LEARNING ON THE INTERNET PARTNERSHIP
WWW.PRENHALL.COM/PH BUSINESS/PHLIP

Visit the best Web site for Principles of Marketing-for both professors and students! Go to www.prenhall.com/phbusiness and click on PHLIP. This Web site features bi-weekly updates of articles from a large number of periodicals, Web links which update the material in the text, student study resources, faculty resources, and much more. The Instructor's Manual and PowerPoint files can also be downloaded from this site.

1

CONSUMERS IN THE MARKETPLACE

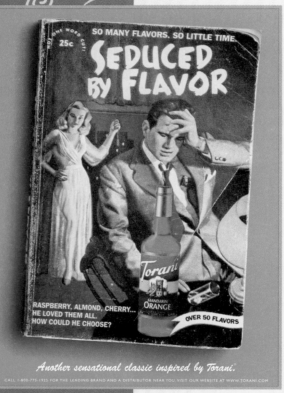

This introductory section provides an overview of the field of consumer behavior. Chapter 1 looks at how the field of marketing is influenced by the actions of consumers and also at how we as consumers are influenced by marketers. It describes the discipine of consumer behavior and some of the different approaches to understanding what makes consumers tick. It also highlights the importance of the study of consumer behavior to such public policy issues as addiction and environmentalism.

1

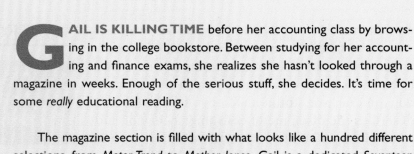

GAIL IS KILLING TIME before her accounting class by browsing in the college bookstore. Between studying for her accounting and finance exams, she realizes she hasn't looked through a magazine in weeks. Enough of the serious stuff, she decides. It's time for some *really* educational reading.

The magazine section is filled with what looks like a hundred different selections, from *Motor Trend* to *Mother Jones*. Gail is a dedicated *Seventeen* reader, but as she scans the many titles, she is struck by the glamorous models featured on the covers of other women's magazines. She thinks maybe it's time to expand her horizons a bit. After all, she's a college junior now—time to listen to her sorority sisters and remake her somewhat girlish image.

Looking over the many choices, Gail considers buying a copy of *Vogue*. No, that seems a bit too old and stodgy for her, even though she knows from her consumer behavior class that the magazine's editors are trying hard to reposition it as a more "with it" alternative to *Elle* and *Glamour*. *Cosmopolitan* is full of pictures of slightly older working women in revealing dresses. Well, she's not quite ready to go that far! *Allure* and *McCall's* look like magazines her mother (a stylish "mature" woman) would read, and she can look at *Family Circle* and *Ladies' Home Journal* anytime she visits her Aunt Margie and the kids in the suburbs—as if she'd want to read about endless diets and home decorating ideas.

Finally, Gail is intrigued by a magazine called *Marie Claire*—the cover model has a new hairstyle that she's been thinking about trying for herself. Gail overheard two of her sorority sisters talking about this magazine. It's popular in France and publishes editions in 22 countries. *Marie Claire* is now trying to make it in America[1] (http://www.hearstcorp.com/mag8.html). As Gail flips through the pages, her attention is caught by the many ads showing cute clothes, and she catches a whiff of that new perfume her friend Monica just bought. Yeah, this magazine is just what the doctor ordered to help create the New Gail. Monica and the other sisters will be proud of her. . . .

An Introduction to Consumer Behavior

CONSUMER BEHAVIOR: PEOPLE IN THE MARKETPLACE

This book is about people like Gail. It concerns the products and services they buy and use, and the ways these fit into their lives. This introductory chapter describes some important aspects of the field of consumer behavior and some of the reasons it's essential to understand how people interact with the marketing system.

For now, though, let's return to one "typical" consumer: Gail, the business major. This brief story allows us to highlight some aspects of consumer behavior that will be covered in the rest of the book.

● As a consumer, Gail can be described and compared to other individuals in a number of ways. For some purposes, marketers might find it useful to categorize Gail in terms of her age, gender, income, or occupation. These are some examples of descriptive characteristics of a population, or *demographics.* In other cases, marketers would rather know something about Gail's interests in clothing or music, or the way she spends her leisure time. This sort of information comes under the category of *psychographics,* which refers to aspects of a person's lifestyle and personality. Knowledge of consumer characteristics plays an extremely important role in many marketing applications, such as defining the market for a product, or deciding on the appropriate techniques to employ when targeting a certain group of consumers.

● Gail's purchase decisions are heavily influenced by the opinions and behaviors of her sorority sisters. A lot of product information, as well as recommendations to use or avoid particular brands, is transmitted by conversations among real people, rather than by way of television commercials, magazines, or billboards. The bonds among Gail's group are cemented by the common products they use. There is also pressure on each group member to buy things that will meet with the group's approval, and a consumer often pays a price in the form of group rejection or embarrassment when he or she does not conform to others' conceptions of what is good or bad, "in" or "out."

● As members of a large society, such as the United States, people share certain *cultural values,* or strongly held beliefs about the way the world should be structured. Other values are shared by members of *subcultures,* or smaller groups within the culture, such as Hispanics, teens, Midwesterners, or even "Valley Girls" and "Hell's Angels." The people who matter to Gail—her *reference group*—value the idea that women in their early twenties should be innovative, style conscious, independent, and daring (at least a little).

- When examining magazines, Gail was exposed to many competing "brands." Numerous magazines did not capture her attention at all, whereas others were noticed and rejected because they did not fit the "image" with which she identified or to which she aspired. The use of *market segmentation strategies* means targeting a brand only to specific groups of consumers rather than to everybody—even if it means that other consumers who don't belong to this *target market* are turned off by that product.

- Brands often have clearly defined images or "personalities" created by product advertising, packaging, branding, and other marketing strategies that focus on positioning a product a certain way. The purchase of a magazine in particular is very much a lifestyle statement: It says a lot about what a person is interested in, as well as something about the type of person she would like to be. People often choose a product because they like its image, or because they feel its "personality" somehow corresponds to their own. Moreover, a consumer may believe that by buying and using the product or service, its desirable qualities will magically "rub off" onto him or her.

- When a product succeeds in satisfying a consumer's specific needs or desires, as *Marie Claire* did for Gail, it may be rewarded with many years of *brand loyalty;* a bond between product and consumer that is very difficult for competitors to break. Often a change in one's life situation or self-concept is required to weaken this bond. Brand loyalty can also be affected when a brand's image is altered, or repositioned. For example, *Vogue* devoted an entire issue to fashion items that could be bought for under $500; although these clothes are still very expensive by many women's standards, they are still a radical departure from the magazine's usual emphasis on *haute couture* apparel with price tags that could cover tuition at many universities.

- Consumers' evaluations of products are affected by their appearance, taste, texture, or smell. We may be swayed by the shape and color of a package, as well as by more subtle factors, like the symbolism used in a brand name, in an advertisement, or even in the choice of a cover model for a magazine. These judgments are affected by—and often reflect—how a society feels that people should define themselves at that point in time. For example, Gail's choice of a new hairstyle says something about the type of image women like her want to project in the late 1990s. If asked, Gail might not even be able to say exactly why she considered some magazines and rejected others. Many product meanings are hidden below the surface of the packaging and advertising, and this book will discuss some of the methods used by marketers and social scientists to discover or apply these meanings.

- *Marie Claire* has an international image that appealed to Gail. A product's image often is influenced by its *country of origin,* which helps to determine its "brand personality." In addition, our opinions and desires increasingly are shaped by input from around the world, which is becoming a much smaller place due to rapid advancements in communications and transportation systems. In today's global culture, consumers often prize products and services that "transport" them to different places and allow them to experience the diversity of other cultures.

MULTICULTURAL DIMENSIONS

The "Cosmo Girl" is an image that is carefully cultivated by the editors of *Cosmopolitan*. The magazine is read by 2.7 million Americans each month. The American "Cosmo Girl," as described by founding editor Helen Gurley Brown, expects to get married but is not in any hurry. She may wait until her late thirties to have children. Sex is ". . . very important, but not on the first date." She owns at least one long black skirt with a slit, owns many pairs of shoes, and wears big jewelry.

Although the American Cosmo Girl is well defined, the magazine also publishes 25 international editions, most of which are separate entities with their own editorial staffs. In some cases local cultures conflict with the Cosmo Girl's liberated image. Latin American editors, for instance, face problems created by a more macho society that often has a double sexual standard for men and women. Advertisers are sometimes reluctant to buy into a magazine they see as "perverted," and some parts of the magazine are censored. In countries such as Hong Kong, the American image fits well, since women are expected to be more independent and ambitious.[2] In late 1997, the Indonesian version of *Cosmopolitan* debuted—analysts are divided as to whether the country that is home to the world's largest Muslim population, where most women do not leave home without their heads and bodies completely covered, will be ready for the Cosmo Girl.[3]

The "Cosmo Girl" takes on many different faces around the world.

WHAT IS CONSUMER BEHAVIOR?

The field of **consumer behavior** covers a lot of ground: It is the study of the processes involved when individuals or groups select, purchase, use, or dispose of products, services, ideas, or experiences to satisfy needs and desires. Consumers take many forms, ranging from an eight-year-old child begging her mother for Gummi Bears candy to an executive in a large corporation deciding on a multimillion-dollar computer system. The items that are consumed can include anything from canned peas, a massage, democracy, rap music, or hoopster rebel Dennis Rodman. Needs and desires to be satisfied range from hunger and thirst to love, status, or even spiritual fulfillment.

CONSUMERS ARE ACTORS ON THE MARKETPLACE STAGE

The perspective of **role theory** takes the view that much of consumer behavior resembles actions in a play.[4] As in a play, each consumer has lines, props, and costumes that are necessary to put on a good performance. Because people act out many different

Finely-tuned segmentation strategies allow marketers to reach only those consumers likely to be interested in buying their products.

roles, they sometimes alter their consumption decisions depending on the particular "play" they are in at the time. The criteria they use to evaluate products and services in one of their roles may be quite different from those used in another role.

CONSUMER BEHAVIOR IS A PROCESS

In its early stages of development, the field was often referred to as *buyer behavior,* reflecting an emphasis on the interaction between consumers and producers at the time of purchase. Most marketers now recognize that consumer behavior is an ongoing *process,* not merely what happens at the moment a consumer hands over money or a credit card and in turn receives some good or service.

The **exchange,** a transaction where two or more organizations or people give and receive something of value, is an integral part of marketing.[5] While exchange remains an important part of consumer behavior, the expanded view emphasizes the entire consumption process, which includes the issues that influence the consumer before, during, and after a purchase. Figure 1–1 illustrates some of the issues that are addressed during each stage of the consumption process.

CONSUMER BEHAVIOR INVOLVES MANY DIFFERENT ACTORS

A **consumer** is generally thought of as a person who identifies a need or desire, makes a purchase, and then disposes of the product during the three stages in the consumption process. In many cases, however, different people may be involved in this sequence of events. The *purchaser* and *user* of a product might not be the same

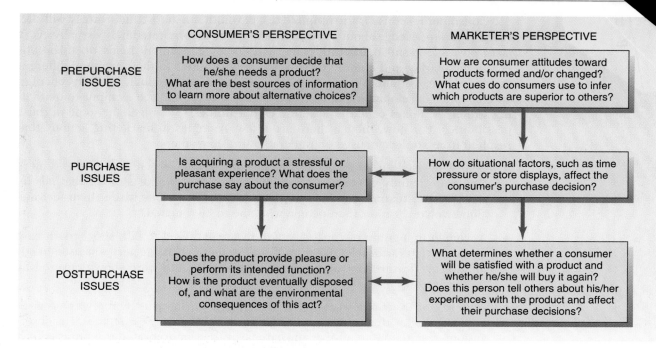

FIGURE 1–1 ■ Some Issues that Arise during Stages in the Consumption Process

person, as when a parent picks out clothes for a teenager (and makes selections that can result in "fashion suicide" in the view of the teen). In other cases, another person may act as an *influencer,* providing recommendations for or against certain products without actually buying or using them. For example, a friend's grimace when one tries on a new pair of pants may be more influential than anything a mother or father might do.

Finally, consumers may be organizations or groups, in which one person may make the decisions involved in purchasing products that will be used by many, as when a purchasing agent orders the company's office supplies. In other organizational situations, purchase decisions may be made by a large group of people—for example, company accountants, designers, engineers, sales personnel, and others—all of whom will have a say in the various stages of the consumption process. As we'll see in Chapter 12, one important type of organization is the family, where different family members play pivotal roles in decision making regarding products and services used by all.

CONSUMERS' IMPACT ON MARKETING STRATEGY

Talking about buying magazines or other products can be a lot of fun (almost as much fun as actually making the purchases!). But, on the more serious side, why should managers, advertisers, and other marketing professionals bother to learn about consumer behavior?

Very simply, understanding consumer behavior is good business. A basic marketing concept states that firms exist to satisfy consumers' needs. These needs can only be satisfied to the extent that marketers understand the people or organizations that will use the products and services they are trying to sell, and that they do so *better* than their competitors.

Consumer response is the ultimate test of whether a marketing strategy will succeed. Thus, knowledge about consumers should be incorporated into virtually every facet of a successful marketing plan. Data about consumers helps organizations define the market and identify threats and opportunities in their own and different countries that will affect consumers' receptivity to the product. In every chapter, we'll see how developments in consumer behavior can be used as input to marketing strategies. Boxes called "Marketing Opportunities" will highlight some of these possibilities. For now, though, here are a few examples of marketing actions that resulted from studies focused on understanding consumers:

- Schick devised an ad for its razors showing a woman gently stroking a man's face after a study of consumer perceptions of rival brands showed that ads by rival Gillette featuring men in rugged, outdoor situations made them feel like "lone wolves," rather than people who like to be touched.[6]

- A woman in a group of consumers who were gathered to talk about tooth care observed that tartar felt "like a wall" on her teeth. This imagery was used in ads for Colgate Tartar Control, in which room-sized teeth were shown covered by walls of tartar.[7]

- An account executive working on a campaign for Pioneer Stereo was assigned to "hang out" with guys who were likely prospects to buy car stereos. His observations resulted in an advertising campaign that incorporated the phrases they used to describe their cars: "My car is my holy temple, my love shack, my donutmaker, my drag racer of doom. . . ."[8] This campaign helped Pioneer overtake Sony in this market.

- A Danish firm wanted to introduce a new cigarette brand targeted at blue-collar American males. Unfamiliar with American consumers, it sent researchers to interview men in Arkansas, where the brand was to be test-marketed. In-depth interviews found that many of the potential customers felt sexually frustrated and powerless and that they responded to these deep feelings by getting together with their buddies and smoking cigarettes. The company used an ad depicting a brash, confident smoker and challenged these frustrated men to "Make your move."[9]

- Researchers for a manufacturer of Swiss chocolate found that many chocolate lovers hide secret "stashes" around their houses. One respondent even confessed to hiding candy bars inside her lingerie drawer. The result was an ad campaign theme of "The True Confessions of Chocaholics."[10]

SEGMENTING CONSUMERS

The process of **market segmentation** identifies groups of consumers who are similar to one another in one or more ways, and then devises marketing strategies that appeal to one or more groups—even at the expense of excluding other segments from the firm's target market. There are many dimensions that can be used to slice up a larger market.

Demographics are statistics that measure observable aspects of a population, such as birth rate, age distribution, and income. The U.S. Census Bureau is a major source of demographic data on families, but many private firms gather additional data on specific population groups as well. The changes and trends revealed in demographic studies are of great interest to marketers, because the data can be used to locate and predict the size of markets for many products, ranging from home mortgages to brooms and can openers. Imagine trying to sell baby food to a single male, or an around-the-world vacation to a couple making $15,000 a year!

Table 1–1 provides a statistical snapshot of the "typical" American consumer, based on data compiled by the 1990 Census and additional information from marketing surveys and opinion polls. As you go down this list, you will quickly see that

---

TABLE 1-1 ■ A Statistical Snapshot of the "Typical" American Consumer

Basics
- The typical American is a white woman who is 32.7 years old.
- She is married and is a mother.
- She graduated from high school.
- Her family income was $35,225 in 1989.

Home
- The typical American family owns a home.
- It is in the suburbs.
- The house is mortgaged. The total monthly ownership cost is $737.
- The house has three bedrooms.
- The house is 11 to 20 years old. The family has been living in it for 2 to 5 years.
- The house is heated with natural gas.

Work
- The typical American drives to work alone.
- She works for a private company or corporation. She is a clerical worker. The company is in manufacturing.

Possessions
- The house has two telephones. There is no answering machine. The phone carries 3,516 local and long-distance calls a year.
- The house has two or more television sets. There is a VCR. Cable television is available.
- The typical American does not own a gun.
- She expected to spend about $375 on Christmas gifts last year.
- She owed $2,317 on her credit cards at the end of 1991.
- She does not have a will.
- She generates about 3 pounds of garbage every day.

Characteristics
- The average American male is 5 feet 9.4 inches tall and weighs 172 pounds. The average female is 5 feet 3.7 inches tall and weighs 144 pounds.
- They think this current weight is just about right.
- The typical American is Protestant. She belongs to a church but did not attend services last week.
- The typical American is a Democrat and considers herself moderate.
- She considers herself an environmentalist.

Health
- The typical American lost 5.1 days of work or school in the last year because of illness.
- She was in contact with a doctor 5.5 days in the last year.
- Medical bills account for 14% of the average family's spending.
- The typical American doesn't smoke.
- She does not know anyone who has contracted AIDS.

Activities
- The typical American spent 1 or 2 hours driving yesterday.
- She read a newspaper today.
- She watched 28 hours and 13 minutes of television last week, about one-quarter of her waking hours.

Source: Anne Cronin, "A Statistical Portrait of the 'Typical' American," *New York Times* (July 26, 1992):ES5. Copyright © 1992 The New York Times Company. Reprinted by permission.

many of his/her characteristics do not apply directly to you. How different are you from this mythical consumer?

In this book, we'll explore many of the important demographic variables that make consumers the same or different from others. We'll also consider other important characteristics that are a bit more subtle, such as differences in consumers' personalities and tastes that can't be objectively measured yet may be tremendously important in influencing product choices. For now, let's summarize a few of the most important demographic dimensions, each of which will be developed in more detail in later chapters.

AGE

Consumers of different age groups obviously have very different needs and wants. Although people who belong to the same age group differ in many other ways, they do tend to share a set of values and common cultural experiences that they carry throughout life.[11] Levi Strauss, for example, has been successful in positioning itself as a "brand for life" by introducing products such as Dockers to meet the needs of its loyal consumers as they age. A Levi's marketing executive explained, "In the 1960s, growth [in the jeans market] was due to adoption of jeans by 15- to 18-year olds. . . . Now these people are 25–49, and Dockers meshes perfectly with what the Levi brand image is about for them."[12]

GENDER

Many products, from fragrances to footwear, are targeted to either men or women. Differentiating by gender starts at a very early age—even diapers are sold in pink versions for girls and blue for boys. Consumers take these differences seriously: Market research shows that most parents refuse to put male infants in pink diapers![13]

One dimension that makes segmenting by gender so interesting is that the behaviors and tastes of men and women are constantly evolving. For example, in the past most marketers assumed that men were the primary decision makers for automobile purchases, but this perspective is changing with the times: Now more than six out of ten new car buyers under the age of 50 are women.[14]

Marketers like Saturn are attracting large numbers of female buyers.

FAMILY STRUCTURE

A person's family and marital status is yet another important demographic variable, because this has such a big effect on consumers' spending priorities. Young bachelors and newlyweds are the most likely to exercise, go to bars, concerts, and movies, and to consume alcohol. Families with young children are big purchasers of health foods and fruit juices, while single-parent households and those with older children buy more junk food. Home maintenance services are most likely to be used by older couples and bachelors.[15]

SOCIAL CLASS AND INCOME

Social class indicates people who are approximately equal in terms of their incomes and social standing in the community. They work in roughly similar occupations, and they tend to have similar tastes in music, clothing, art, and so on. They also tend to socialize with one another, and they share many ideas and values regarding the way one's life should be lived.[16] The distribution of wealth is of great interest to marketers, because it determines which groups have the greatest buying power and market potential.

RACE AND ETHNICITY

African Americans, Hispanic Americans, and Asian Americans are the three fastest-growing ethnic groups in the United States. As our society becomes increasingly multicultural, new opportunities develop to deliver specialized products to racial and ethnic groups and to introduce other groups to these offerings.

Sometimes this adaptation is just a matter of putting an existing product into a different context. An African American product manager at Pillsbury realized that the company had overlooked the importance of baking as a cultural activity for many African American and Hispanic American consumers. At her urging, small changes were made to appeal to these groups. The company's cornbread twists had been promoted as going with chili, but in packages delivered to African American areas a recipe for corn muffins—the perfect "go-with" for greens—was included instead. The company also added Spanish-language advertising, and detailed preparation instructions for Hispanics who were not used to baking with mixes. Even the "white-bread" Pillsbury Dough Boy now appears in some commercials as a blues singer or a rap star.[17]

GEOGRAPHY

Many national marketers tailor their offerings to appeal to consumers who live in different parts of the country. Heileman Distilleries operates 10 breweries across the United States, and its position in each of its markets is backed up with sponsorship of major local events and other regional promotions. As the company's marketing vice president explained, "The primary objective of being a regional brand is to make the consumer think that 'this product is mine.' . . . People tend to think positively about their hometowns, and a product strongly identified with this aura is likely to strike a responsive chord. . . ."[18] Some of Heileman's successful regional brands include Old Style, Colt 45, Lone Star, Rainier, and Samuel Adams.

RELATIONSHIP MARKETING: BUILDING BONDS WITH CONSUMERS

Marketers are carefully defining customer segments and listening to people in their markets as never before. Many of them have realized that a key to success is building relationships between brands and customers that will last a lifetime. Marketers

MARKETING OPPORTUNITY

Marketers have come up with so many ways to segment consumers—from the overweight to overachievers—that we might ask whether they have run out of segments. Hardly. Changes in lifestyles and other characteristics of the population are constantly creating new opportunities. The following are some "hot" market segments.

● *The military:* Major marketers like General Motors, AT&T, and Kraft General Foods are making special efforts to tailor marketing campaigns specifically to military personnel and their families. Military commissaries sell about $7.5 billion of merchandise a year, making them the equivalent of the nation's sixth-largest supermarket chain. Enlisted personnel are often young and impressionable, so marketers hope to create brand loyalty that will endure after they return to civilian life. In addition, many soldiers are married, and the average family size of 3.5 children is much larger than in the civilian population. Specialized magazines such as *Off Duty, Military Lifestyle,* and *Military Grocery* have sprung up to meet this demand, often featuring specially prepared advertisements depicting men and women in uniform.[19]

● *The disabled:* Along with new legislation furthering the rights of the disabled, some marketers are starting to take notice of the estimated 43 million Americans with physical handicaps. A Budweiser commercial features an athlete competing in a wheelchair marathon; an Eddie Bauer catalog includes a skier with an artificial leg. The Target clothing store chain was one of the pioneers of this approach—the company features children with disabilities in its advertising.[20]

● The imprisoned: A magazine called Prison Life is even targeting consumers behind bars. There are almost 1 million people in prison, and this number is expanding by 7 percent a year. Convicts have an average income of over $1,000 a year—and plenty of time to read! Although some advertisers are reluctant to buy space in a periodical where the premiere issue had mass-murderer Charles Manson on the cover, the publisher expects to sell 200,000 copies of each bimonthly issue.[21]

who believe in this philosophy, called **relationship marketing,** are making an effort to interact with customers on a regular basis, and giving them reasons to maintain a bond with the company over time. In many places throughout this book, a handshake icon will indicate that a relationship marketing strategy is being highlighted.

Some companies build these ties by returning value to the community. The Hanna Andersson company, which sells children's clothing via catalog, runs a program called "Hannadowns," which gives a 20 percent credit toward new purchases when customers return used clothes bought from them previously. The returned clothing is then distributed to charities. The company also donates 5 percent of its pretax profits to charities and shelters benefiting women and children.[22] This return of value to the community cements the relationship by giving customers an additional reason to continue buying the company's products year after year.

Another revolution in relationship building is being brought to us courtesy of the computer. **Database marketing** involves tracking consumers' buying habits very closely, and crafting products and messages tailored precisely to people's wants and needs based on this information. For example, the Ritz-Carlton hotel chain trains associates to enter detailed information into its database, so that if a guest orders decaf coffee from room service he or she will also receive decaf on the next visit.[23] Sophisticated companies such as American Express, General Motors, and Kraft General Foods are combining and constantly updating information from public records and marketing research surveys—with data volunteered by consumers themselves when they return warranty cards, enter sweepstakes, or purchase from catalogs—to build a complex database that fine-tunes their knowledge of what people are buying and how often.[24]

Keeping close tabs on their customers allows database marketers to monitor people's preferences and communicate with those who show an interest in their products or services. Here are just a few examples of the ways marketers have found to stay in touch with their customers:

- Revenues from legal gambling top $30 billion a year—more than the combined take for movies, books, recorded music, park and arcade attractions.[25] To further encourage the droves of Americans flocking to casinos to become regular customers and even bigger bettors, sophisticated "player-tracking systems" are being developed. Although casinos have always tried to keep track of the action among heavy bettors at the roulette or blackjack tables, now they are even monitoring the behavior of the nickel-and-dime set. Slots players can join clubs that reward them with free dinners and shows based on how much change they throw into the "one-armed bandits." When club members insert a membership card in a machine, the casino knows their favorite drink and how much they typically spend on a casino outing. In addition, machines that are getting a lot of use can flag managers, who then send someone to greet the gambler with the offer of a free drink and a club membership.[26]

- Rusted Root, a Pittsburgh-based alternative band, used bounceback cards packaged in the band's CD and sign-up sheets at concerts to compile information about its fans. These techniques yielded a list of 2,000 names, to whom were mailed tour information and ordering forms to buy Rusted Root merchandise. The band also used the data collected about characteristics of its following to develop a profile of the type of person most likely to get into its music, so additional people matching this profile could also be sent promotional mailings.[27]

- Levi Strauss is compiling a customer database by asking jeans buyers to register each new pair of pants. The company used a similar tactic when it launched its newer Slates line, including asking whether a girlfriend or wife had been involved in the buying decision.[28]

- When Johnson & Johnson prepared to launch its Acuvue disposable contact lenses, the marketing strategy was based on the belief that no patient would switch to disposables without the encouragement of an optometrist. So the program was driven by two linked databases: registered eye care professionals who carried Acuvue, and the names of contact lens wearers who had earlier responded to disposable lens advertising. The database tracked customers as they moved from expressions of interest, through an appointment with an optometrist, and on to successive purchases. Johnson & Johnson actually coordinated the appointment process for the optometrists and communicated with lens users by delivering incentive coupons and other material.[29]

MARKETING'S IMPACT ON CONSUMERS

For better or for worse, we all live in a world that is significantly influenced by the actions of marketers. We are surrounded by marketing stimuli in the form of advertisements, stores, and products competing for our attention and our dollars. Much of what we learn about the world is filtered by marketers, whether through the affluence depicted in glamorous magazine advertising or the roles played by family members in commercials. Ads show us how we should act with regard to recycling, alcohol consumption, and even the types of houses and cars we might wish to own. In many ways we are also "at the mercy" of marketers, because we rely on them to sell us products that are safe and perform as promised, to tell us the truth about what they are selling, and to price and distribute these products fairly.

MARKETING AND CULTURE

Popular culture, consisting of the music, movies, sports, books, celebrities, and other forms of entertainment consumed by the mass market, is both a product of and an inspiration for marketers. Our lives are also affected in more far-reaching ways, ranging from how we acknowledge cultural events such as marriage, death, or holidays to how we view social issues such as air pollution, gambling, and addictions. Whether it's The Super Bowl, Christmas shopping, presidential elections, newspaper recycling, body piercing, cigarette smoking, in-line skating, or Barbie dolls, marketers play a significant role in our view of the world and how we live in it.

This cultural impact is hard to overlook, although many people do not seem to realize how much their views—their movie and musical heroes, the latest fashions in clothing, food and decorating choices, and even the physical features that they find attractive or ugly in men and women—are influenced by marketers. For example, consider the product icons that companies use to create an identity for their products. Many imaginary creatures and personalities—from the Pillsbury Doughboy to the Jolly Green Giant—have been at one time or another central figures in popular culture. In fact, it is likely that more consumers could recognize such characters than could identify past presidents, business leaders, or artists. Although these figures never really existed, many of us feel as if we "know" them, and they certainly are effective *spokescharacters* for the products they represent (www.toymuseum.com).

Companies often create *product icons* to develop an identity for their products. Many made-up creatures and personalities, such as Mr. Clean, Bibendum, the Michelin tire man, and the Pillsbury Doughboy, are widely-recognized (and often beloved) figures in popular culture. Bibdenum, one of the oldest icons, dates back to the 1890s. He was born at a time when the "machine age" was dawning, so a man constructed of auto parts truly caught the spirit of the times. Kirk Varnedoe and Adam Gopnik, *High and Low: Modern Art and Popular Culture* (New York: The Museum of Modern Art, 1990).

THE MEANING OF CONSUMPTION

One of the fundamental premises of the modern field of consumer behavior is that people often buy products not for what they *do,* but for what they *mean.* This principle does not imply that a product's basic function is unimportant, but rather that the roles products play in our lives go well beyond the tasks they perform. The deeper meanings of a product may help it to stand out from other, similar goods and services—all things being equal, a person will choose the brand that has an image (or even a personality!) consistent with the purchaser's underlying needs.

For example, although most people probably couldn't run faster or jump higher if they were wearing Nikes versus Reeboks, many die-hard loyalists swear by their favorite brand. These archrivals are largely marketed in terms of their images—meanings that have been carefully crafted with the help of legions of rock stars, athletes, slickly produced commercials—and many millions of dollars. So, when you buy a Nike "swoosh" you may be doing more than choosing shoes to wear to the mall—you may also be making a lifestyle statement about the type of person you are or wish you were. For a relatively simple item made of leather and laces, that's quite a feat!

Our allegiances to sneakers, musicians, or even soft drinks help us define our place in modern society, and these choices also help each of us to form bonds with others who share similar preferences. This comment by a participant in a focus group captures the curious bonding that can be caused by consumption choices: "I was at a Super Bowl party, and I picked up an obscure drink. Somebody else across the room went 'yo!' because he had the same thing. People feel a connection when you're drinking the same thing."[30]

Heard any Volkswagen jokes lately?

Remember the one about the lady who looked under her front hood and thought somebody stole her engine?

Or the one about the guy at the gas station who didn't know where the gas went? Or the water?

Today, the gas station attendants know enough to put the gas in front. And they don't

bother checking your water or trying to sell you some anti-freeze.

(After all, they've seen enough VWs to know that our engine's in the rear, and that it's cooled by air, not water.)

The point is this: People used to make fun of our car, now they have fun with it.

Which helps explain why our joke file's

been getting a bit low. So, if you've heard any good VW quips or sayings or jokes, why not send them on?

...st write to John Stanley, Volkswagen of America, Englewood Cliffs, N. J.

He'll start them on their rounds.

After all, nobody enjoys a good VW joke better than we do.

An interpretative framework to understanding marketing communications can be illustrated by an analysis of one of the best-known and longest-running (1959–1978) advertising campaigns of all time: The work done by the advertising agency Doyle Dane Bernbach for the Volkswagen Beetle. This campaign, widely noted for its self-mocking wit, found many ways to turn the Beetle's homeliness, smallness, and lack of power into positive attributes at a time when most car ads were emphasizing just the opposite. An interpretive analysis of these messages used concepts from literature, psychology, and anthropology to ground the appeal of this approach within a broader cultural context. The image created for the humble car was connected to other examples of what scholars of comedy call the "Little Man" pattern. This is a type of comedic character that is related to a clown or a trickster; a social outcast who is able to poke holes in the stuffiness and rigidity of bureaucracy and conformity. Other examples of the "Little Man" character include Hawkeye in the TV sitcom "M.A.S.H.," the comedian Woody Allen, and Charlie Chaplin. When one looks at the cultural meaning of marketing messages this way, it is perhaps not coincidence that IBM chose the Charlie Chaplin character some years later to help it "soften" its stuffy, intimidating image as it tried to convince consumers that its new personal computer products were user-friendly.

As we have already seen, a trademark of marketing strategies in the late 1990s is an emphasis on building relationships with customers. The nature of these relationships can vary, and these bonds helps us to understand some of the possible meanings products have to us. Here are some of the types of relationships a person might have with a product:

- *Self-concept attachment*—the product helps to establish the user's identity.
- *Nostalgic attachment*—the product serves as a link with a past self.
- *Interdependence*—the product is a part of the user's daily routine.
- *Love*—the product elicits emotional bonds of warmth, passion, or other strong emotion.[31]

One consumer researcher recently developed a classification scheme in an attempt to explore the different ways that products and experiences can provide meaning to people. This *consumption typology* was derived from a two-year analysis of spectators at Wrigley Field who were attending Chicago Cubs baseball games (of course, studying the hapless Cubbies is bound to produce some unique and frustrating experiences!).[32]

This perspective views consumption as a type of action where people make use of consumption objects in a variety of ways. Focusing on an event like a ball game also is a useful reminder that when we refer to consumption, we are talking about *intangible* experiences, ideas, and services (the thrill of a home run hit out of the park or the antics of a team mascot) in addition to *tangible* objects (the hot dogs eaten at the ball park). This analysis identified four distinct types of consumption activities:

Consuming as experience—an emotional or aesthetic reaction to consumption objects. This would include reactions such as the pleasure derived from learning how to mark a scorecard, or appreciating the athletic ability of a favorite player.

Consuming as integration—learning and manipulating consumption objects to express aspects of the self or society. For example, some fans wear Cubs jerseys to express their solidarity with the team. Attending ball games in person rather than watching them on TV allows the fan to more completely integrate his or her experience with that of the team.

Consuming as classification—the activities that consumers engage in to communicate their association with objects, both to self and to others. For example, spectators might buy souvenirs to demonstrate to others that they are die-hard fans, or the more hard core might throw the opposition team's home run ball back onto the field as a gesture of contempt.

Consuming as play—consumers use objects to participate in a mutual experience and merge their identities with that of a group. For example, happy fans might scream in unison and engage in an orgy of "high fives" when one of their team's players hits a home run—this is a different dimension of shared experience than just watching the game at home by oneself.

SEMIOTICS: THE SYMBOLS AROUND US

When we try to "make sense" of a marketing stimulus, whether a distinctive package, an elaborately staged television commercial, or perhaps a model on the cover of a magazine, we do so by interpreting its meaning in light of associations we have with these images. For this reason, much of the meaning we take away is influenced by what we make of the symbolism we perceive. After all, on the surface many marketing images have virtually no literal connection to actual products. What does a cowboy have to do with a bit of tobacco rolled into a paper tube? How can a celebrity such as basketball star Michael Jordan enhance the image of a soft drink or a fast-food restaurant?

For assistance in understanding how consumers interpret the meanings of symbols, some marketers are turning to a field of study known as **semiotics,** which examines the correspondence between signs and symbols and their role in the assignment of meaning.[33] Semiotics is important to the understanding of consumer behavior because consumers use products to express their social identities. Products have learned meanings, and we rely on marketers to help us figure out what those meanings are. As one set of researchers put it, ". . . advertising serves as a kind of culture/consumption dictionary; its entries are products, and their definitions are cultural meanings."[34]

From a semiotic perspective, every marketing message has three basic components: an object, a sign or symbol, and an interpretant. The **object** is the product that is the focus of the message (e.g., Marlboro cigarettes). The **sign** is the sensory imagery that represents the intended meanings of the object (e.g., the Marlboro cowboy). The **interpretant** is the meaning derived (e.g., rugged, individualistic, American). This relationship is diagrammed in Figure 1–2.

According to semiotician Charles Sanders Peirce, signs are related to objects in one of three ways: They can resemble objects, be connected to them, or be conventionally tied to them.[35] An *icon* is a sign that resembles the product in some way (e.g., Bell Telephone uses an image of a bell to represent itself). An *index* is a sign that is connected to a product because they share some property (e.g., the pine tree on some of Procter & Gamble's Spic and Span cleanser products conveys the shared property of fresh scent). A *symbol* is a sign that is related to a product through either

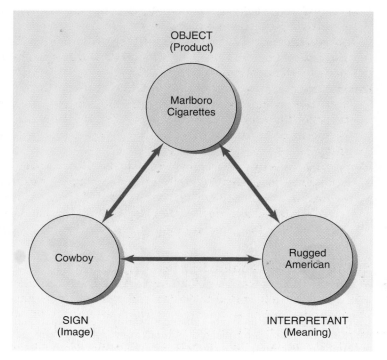

FIGURE 1–2 ■ Relationships of Components in Semiotic Analysis of Meaning

conventional or agreed-upon associations (e.g., the lion in Dreyfus Fund ads provides the conventional association with fearlessness and strength that is carried over to the company's approach to investments). As we shall see in later chapters, these relationships are often culturally bound; that is, they only make sense to a person who is a member of a particular culture. Marketers who forget that meanings do not automatically transfer from one cultural context to another do so at their peril.

One of the hallmarks of modern advertising is that it creates a condition that has been termed **hyperreality.** Hyperreality refers to the becoming real of what is initially simulation of "hype." Advertisers create new relationships between objects and interpretants by inventing new connections between products and benefits, such as equating Marlboro cigarettes with the American frontier spirit.[36] To a large extent, over time the true relationship between the symbol and reality is no longer possible to discern, and the "artificial" associations between product symbols and the real world may take on lives of their own. For example, Tasters' Choice coffee presents an ongoing series of "soap opera" commercials where a romantic relationship is slowly cultivated between two actors—over time, many viewers become so absorbed in this drama that they forget these supposed lovers in reality are just actors in a coffee campaign.

THE GLOBAL CONSUMER

One highly visible—and controversial—by-product of sophisticated marketing strategies is the movement toward a *global consumer culture,* in which people around the world are united by their common devotion to brand name consumer goods, movie stars, and musical celebrities.[37] Some products in particular are associated with a coveted American lifestyle. Levi's jeans, for example, are a status symbol among upwardly mobile Asian and European consumers, who snap them up even though they retail at over $80 in many countries. The company sells its jeans

Levi's jeans are a status symbol among upwardly mobile Asian and European consumers, who snap them up even though they retail at over $80 in many countries. The company is beginning to sell the jeans in India, Hungary, Poland, South Korea, and Turkey.

in such far-flung places as India, Hungary, Poland, South Korea, and Turkey.[38] This book will pay special attention to the good and bad aspects of this cultural homogenization. Each chapter features boxes called "Multicultural Dimensions" that spotlight some international aspect of consumer behavior, and this issue will also be explored in depth in chapter 17.

BLURRED BOUNDARIES: MARKETING AND REALITY

Marketers and consumers coexist in a complicated, two-way relationship. On the one hand, businesspeople try to anticipate buyers' tastes by monitoring evolving preferences and activities and then shaping their actions to "ride the wave" of consumer behavior. When Spelling Entertainment Group found out about spontaneous *Melrose Place* parties happening in bars, the company alleged trademark infringement and sent cease-and-desist letters to bar owners. Then the firm licensed Hiram Walker & Sons' Kahlúa Royal Cream to develop an official *Melrose Place* promotion—bar owners were sent a marketing kit for a sanctioned party, complete with life-size cutouts of the cast and Kahlúa knickknacks.[39]

On the other hand, customers modify products to suit their own needs, and even devise uses for them that were never imagined by the company. The General Cigar Co. recently announced it would drop the word "blunts" from its White Owl Blunts and Garcia y Vega Blunts brands. The company wants nothing to do with the fad of "blunting," a practice especially popular in the inner city in which kids hollow out cheap cigars and fill them with marijuana. This practice is so widespread that the recent boom in sales of inexpensive cigars appears to be fueled largely by what the industry euphemistically terms the "alternative use" market.[40]

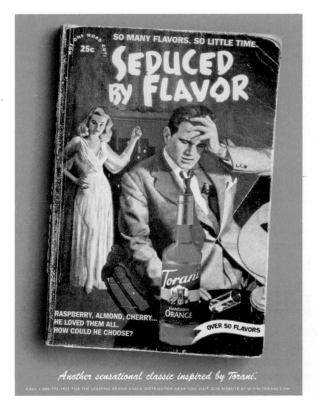

Marketing messages often borrow imagery from other forms of popular culture to connect with their audience. This line of syrups adapts the "look" of a pulp detective novel to make its point.

To what degree is the world of popular culture—and even consumers' perceptions of reality—shaped by the efforts of marketers? More than many of us believe, and this influence is increasing dramatically in recent times. Consider the following examples of this blurring of boundaries between marketing and culture:[41]

- During the O. J. Simpson murder trial, a computer monitor in the courtroom featured a large Sony logo. The company eventually had to replace this with a more discrete design after objections were raised about the free exposure Sony was receiving on news coverage of the proceedings.[42]

- A TV commercial paid for by Honda features a glowing review of its CR-V sport utility vehicle by *USA Today*. The spot, which features close up shots of the newspaper, was produced with the cooperation of the paper.[43]

- The pink Energizer bunny is being portrayed in documentary-style commercials in which "Bunny Spotters" track his movements. According to an agency account director, "The bunny has sort of crossed the line from Hollywood and gone into the real world."[44]

- The Continental Indoor Soccer League includes a team called the Detroit Neon, named after Chrysler's successful compact car. Similarly, the Hooters restaurant chain now sponsors both an arena football team (the Miami Hooters) and the Jacksonville Hooters of the United States Basketball League.[45]

- Several deaths of young men were reported following the release of the movie *The Program* by Touchstone Pictures. In the movie, students lie down in the center of a busy highway to prove their courage. In real life, it's not as easy to get up and walk away at the end of the scene.[46]

- The Walt Disney Co. sparked an uproar when it announced plans to build a theme park near Manassas, Virginia, a major Civil War battleground. The idea behind "Disney's America" was to allow visitors to "experience" the Civil War era through rides and other attractions, including simulations of slavery. After a pitched battle among historians, politicians, and concerned citizens, Disney finally scrapped the project.[47]

- In the United Kingdom, Unilever's Van den Bergh Foods Ltd. distributes a video game starring its snack sausage, Peperami. The character battles evil snack-food foes Carlos the Carrot and the Terminutter.[48]

- Some of the most popular episodes of the comedy hit *Seinfeld* are built around products, including Jerry's car (a Saab), Elaine's favorite candy (JuJuBees), Kenny Rogers' Roasters restaurant, Snapple, Junior Mints, and Colombo frozen yogurt. Kramer drinks Diet Coke even though he has appeared in Pepsi commercials. On the other hand, George can be seen snacking on Rold Gold Pretzels, which he has also been paid to endorse.[49]

MARKETING ETHICS AND PUBLIC POLICY

In business, conflicts often arise between the goal to succeed in the marketplace and the desire to maximize the well-being of consumers by providing them with safe and effective products and services. Unfortunately, merely giving lip service to the importance of appropriate activities may not be sufficient. For example, a 1997

Advertising Age study of beer ads on MTV showed that the major brewers often ran commercials in time slots that violated their own voluntary Beer Institute code.[50]

BUSINESS ETHICS

Business ethics are essentially rules of conduct that guide actions in the marketplace—the standards against which most people in a culture judge what is right and what is wrong, good or bad. These universal values include honesty, trustworthiness, fairness, respect, justice, integrity, concern for others, accountability, and loyalty. Sometimes, ethical decisions can be costly—in the short term—when they result in lost business. For example, despite robust sales of a video game called *Night Trap* made by Sega, executives at Toys "Я" Us decided to pull the product from store shelves. This action came after complaints from parents about the game, in which players defend a group of barely dressed sorority sisters against zombies, who suck out the students' blood with a giant syringe if they win.[51]

Notions of right and wrong do differ among people, organizations, and cultures. Some businesses, for example, believe it is all right for salespeople to persuade customers to buy, even if it means giving them false information; other firms feel that anything less than total honesty with customers is terribly wrong. Because each culture has its own set of values, beliefs, and customs, ethical business behaviors are defined quite differently around the world. Giving "gifts" in exchange for getting business from suppliers or customers is common and acceptable in many countries, for example, even though this may be considered bribery or extortion in the United States.

Whether intentionally or not, some marketers do violate their bond of trust with consumers. In some cases, these actions are actually illegal, as when a manufacturer deliberately mislabels the contents of a package or a retailer adopts a "bait-and-switch" selling strategy, whereby consumers are lured into the store with promises of inexpensive products with the sole intent of getting them to switch to higher-priced goods.

In other cases, marketing practices have detrimental effects on society even though they are not explicitly illegal. Some companies erect billboards for alcohol and tobacco products in low-income neighborhoods; others sponsor commercials depicting groups of people in an unfavorable light to get the attention of a target market. Recently, many people complained that Coors's "Swedish bikini team" advertising campaign demeaned women in an attempt to appeal to young male beer drinkers.

Industry is increasingly coming to realize that ethical behavior is also good business in the long run, since the trust and satisfaction of consumers translates into years of loyalty from customers whose needs have been met. However, many problems remain. Throughout this book, ethical issues related to the practice of marketing are highlighted. Special boxes called "Marketing Pitfalls" feature questionable practices by marketers or the possible adverse effects on consumers of certain marketing strategies.

NEEDS AND WANTS:
DO MARKETERS MANIPULATE CONSUMERS?

One of the most common and stinging criticisms of marketing is that marketing techniques (especially advertising) are responsible for convincing consumers that they "need" many material things and that they will be unhappy and somehow inferior people if they do not have these "necessities." The issue is a complex one, and

This ad was created by the American Association of Advertising Agencies to counter charges that ads create artificial needs. Courtesy of American Association of Advertising Agencies.

is certainly worth considering: Do marketers give people what they want, or do they tell people what they should want?

DO MARKETERS CREATE ARTIFICIAL NEEDS?

The marketing system has come under fire from both ends of the political spectrum. On the one hand, some members of the religious right believe that marketers contribute to the moral breakdown of society by presenting images of hedonistic pleasure, thus encouraging the pursuit of secular humanism. On the other hand, some leftists argue that the same deceitful promises of material pleasure function to buy off people who would otherwise be revolutionaries working to change the system.[52] The marketing system creates demand that only its products can satisfy.

A Response: A *need* is a basic biological motive; a *want* represents one way that society has taught us that the need can be satisfied. For example, thirst is biologically based; we are taught to want Coca-Cola to satisfy that thirst rather than, say,

MARKETING PITFALL

The charge that businesses create artificial needs is relevant in the case of gasoline marketing. Oil companies have attempted to convince consumers of the need for premium gasolines, even though this need has been questioned by many people. As one automotive engineer noted, "Oil company advertising has led people to the conclusion that more expensive fuels will make their cars start easier, get more gas mileage, and last longer. . . . But in most cases this is untrue. . . . Your engine has to be designed to use that extra octane. . . . Otherwise, . . . the extra cost is just lining the pockets of the oil companies."[53] The Federal Trade Commission estimates that 80 percent to 90 percent of the cars on the road run well on regular, unleaded gasoline. However, nearly a third of all motorists use midgrade or premium gasoline in their automobiles. As part of a 1997 settlement with the federal government over advertising claims about its gasoline, Exxon agreed to run television commercials in 18 markets informing motorists that most cars don't need premium grades.[54]

goat milk. Thus, the need is already there; marketers simply recommend ways to satisfy it. A basic objective of marketing is to create awareness that needs exist, not to create them.

ARE ADVERTISING AND MARKETING NECESSARY?

As social critic Vance Packard wrote over 40 years ago, "Large-scale efforts are being made, often with impressive success, to channel our unthinking habits, our purchasing decisions, and our thought processes by the use of insights gleaned from psychiatry and the social sciences."[55] The economist John Kenneth Galbraith charged that radio and television are important tools to accomplish this manipulation of the masses. Because virtually no literacy is required to use these media, they allow repetitive and compelling communications to reach almost everyone.

Many feel that marketers arbitrarily link products to desirable social attributes, fostering a materialistic society in which we are measured by what we own. One influential critic even argued that the problem is that we are not materialistic enough—that is, we do not sufficiently value goods for the utilitarian functions they deliver but instead focus on the irrational value of goods for what they symbolize. According to this view, for example, "Beer would be enough for us, without the additional promise that in drinking it we show ourselves to be manly, young at heart, or neighborly. A washing machine would be a useful machine to wash clothes, rather than an indication that we are forward-looking or an object of envy to our neighbors."[56]

A Response: Products are designed to meet existing needs, and advertising only helps to communicate their availability.[57] According to the *economics of information* perspective, advertising is an important source of consumer information.[58] This view emphasizes the economic cost of the time spent searching for products. Accordingly, advertising is a service for which consumers are willing to pay, because the information it provides reduces search time.

DO MARKETERS PROMISE MIRACLES?

Consumers are led to believe through advertising that products have magical properties; products will do special and mysterious things for consumers in a way that will transform their lives. They will be beautiful, have power over others' feelings, be successful, be relieved of all ills, and so on. In this respect, advertising functions as mythology does in primitive societies: It provides simple, anxiety-reducing answers to complex problems.

A Response: Advertisers simply do not know enough about people to manipulate them. Consider that the failure rate for new products ranges from 40 percent to 80 percent. In testimony before the Federal Trade Commission, one advertising executive observed that although people think that advertisers have an endless source of magical tricks and/or scientific techniques to manipulate people, in reality, the industry is successful when it tries to sell good products and unsuccessful when selling poor ones.[59]

PUBLIC POLICY AND CONSUMERISM

Concern for the welfare of consumers has been an issue since at least the beginning of the twentieth century. Partly as a result of consumers' efforts, many federal agencies have been established to oversee consumer-related activities. These include the Department of Agriculture, the Federal Trade Commission, the Food and Drug Administration, the Securities and Exchange Commission, and the Environmental Protection Agency. After Upton Sinclair's 1906 book *The Jungle* exposed the awful

This cartoon lampoons the widely held belief that marketers manipulate consumers by making us feel inadequate about ourselves. Then they bombard us with products and services we don't *really* want or need with the promise that we will be better people, more attractive, more successful, and so on if only we will buy them. How valid is this criticism? Copyright © 1994 by Bill Watterston. Courtesy of Universal Press Syndicate.

conditions in the Chicago meat-packing industry, Congress was prompted to pass important pieces of legislation—the Pure Food and Drug Act in 1906 and the Federal Meat Inspection Act a year later—to protect consumers. A summary of some important consumer legislation since that time appears in Table 1–2.

CONSUMERISM AND CONSUMER RESEARCH

President John F. Kennedy ushered in the modern era of consumerism with his *Declaration of Consumer Rights* in 1962. These include the right to safety, the right to be informed, the right to redress, and the right to choice. The 1960s and 1970s were a time of consumer activism as consumers began to organize to demand better-quality products (and to boycott companies that did not provide them). These movements were prompted by the publication of books such as Rachel Carson's *Silent Spring* in 1962, which attacked the irresponsible use of pesticides, and Ralph Nader's *Unsafe at Any Speed* in 1965, which exposed safety defects in General Motors' Corvair automobile. Consumers themselves continue to have a vigorous interest in consumer-related issues, ranging from environmental concerns, such as pollution caused by oil spills, toxic waste, and so on, to excessive violence and sex on television or in the lyrics of popular rock and rap songs.

The field of consumer behavior can play an important role in improving our lives as consumers.[60] Many researchers play a role in formulating or evaluating public policies such as ensuring that products are labeled accurately, that people can comprehend important information presented in advertising, or that children are not exploited by program-length toy commercials masquerading as television shows.

Many firms are making the choice to protect or enhance the natural environment as they go about their business activities, a practice known as **green marketing**. The Park Plaza in Boston markets itself as "Boston's Eco-Logical Travel Alternative;" the hotel uses a recycling system that cut laundry water use by more than half, installed Thermopane windows to reduce heating costs, and recycles enough paper to save 300 trees a year.[61] Other have focused their efforts on reducing wasteful packaging. Gillette has eliminated the outer boxes on some deodorants, Kodak's Ektar films are no longer packaged in cardboard boxes, and Procter & Gamble introduced refillable containers for Downy fabric softener.[62]

TABLE 1–2 ■ Sampler of Federal Legislation Intended to Enhance Consumer's Welfare

YEAR	ACT	PURPOSE
1951	Fur Products Labeling Act	Regulates the branding, advertising, and shipment of fur products.
1953	Flammable Fabrics Act	Prohibits the transportation of flammable fabrics across state lines.
1958	National Traffic and Safety Act	Creates safety standards for cars and tires.
1958	Automobile Information Disclosure Act	Requires automobile manufacturers to post suggested retail prices on new cars.
1966	Fair Packaging and Labeling Act	Regulates packaging and labeling of consumer products. (Manufacturers must provide information about package contents and origin.)
1966	Child Protection Act	Prohibits sale of dangerous toys and other items.
1967	Federal Cigarette Labeling and Advertising Act	Requires cigarette packages to carry a warning label from the Surgeon General.
1968	Truth-in-Lending Act	Requires lenders to divulge the true costs of a credit transaction.
1969	National Environmental Policy Act	Established a national environmental policy and created the Council on Environmental Quality to monitor the effects of products on the environment.
1972	Consumer Product Safety Act	Established the Consumer Product Safety Commission to identify unsafe products, establish safety standards, recall defective products, and ban dangerous products.
1975	Consumer Goods Pricing Act	Bans the use of price maintenance agreements among manufacturers and resellers.
1975	Magnuson-Moss Warranty-Improvement Act	Creates disclosure standards for consumer product warranties and allows the Federal Trade Commission to set policy regarding unfair or deceptive practices.
1990	The Nutrition Labeling and Education Act	Reaffirms the legal basis for the Food and Drug Administration's new rules on food labeling and establishes a timetable for the implementation of those rules. Regulations covering health claims became effective May 8, 1993. Those pertaining to nutrition labeling and nutrient content claims went into effect May 8, 1994.

Other companies feel that the best way to serve their communities is through *cause marketing,* where marketing efforts are linked to a charitable cause. Nissan, for example, sponsors a neighborhood program called "Food from the Hood" that encourages entrepreneurship by getting inner-city kids to produce and sell food products.[63] According to a Cone/Roper survey of 2,000 American adults, 84 percent believe that cause marketing creates a positive image of a company and 78 percent say they would be more likely to buy a product associated with an important cause. In addition, 66 percent say they would switch brands, 62 percent would switch retailers, and 54 percent would pay more for the product.[64]

In addition, there is a growing movement in the field to develop knowledge about **social marketing,** which attempts to encourage such positive behaviors as increased literacy and to discourage negative activities such as drunk driving (see Chapter 7).[65] A current project in Sweden aimed at curbing adolescent drinking is typical of this perspective. The Swedish Brewer's Association is investing 10 million Skr (about $7.5 million dollars) in a cooperative effort with the Swedish Non-Violence Project to change teens' attitudes about alcohol consumption.

Consumer researchers working on the project discovered that adolescents freely admit that they "drink in order to get drunk" and enjoy the feeling of being intoxicated, so persuading them to give up alcohol is a formidable task. However, they also are afraid of losing control over their own behavior, especially if there is a risk for them to be exposed to violence. And, while worries about the long-term health effects of drinking don't concern this group (after all, at this age many believe they will live forever . . .), female adolescents report a fear of becoming less attractive as a result of prolonged alcohol consumption. Based on these findings, the group commissioned to execute this project decided to stress a more realistic message of "drink if you want to, but within a safe limit. Don't lose control, because if you do, you might get yourself into violent situations." They made up the motto, "Alco-hole in your head" to stress the importance of knowing one's limits. This message is being emphasized along with strong visual images that will appear on billboards, in video spots that depict situations involving young drinkers getting out of control, and in school presentations given by young people who will be credible sources for teens.[66]

THE DARK SIDE OF CONSUMER BEHAVIOR

Despite the best efforts of researchers, government regulators, and concerned industry people, sometimes consumers' worst enemies are themselves. Individuals are often depicted as rational decision makers, calmly doing their best to obtain products and services that will maximize the health and well-being of themselves, their families, and their society. In reality, however, consumers' desires, choices, and actions often result in negative consequences to the individual and/or the society in which he lives. Some consumer activities stem from social pressures, such as excessive drinking or cigarette smoking, and the cultural value placed on money can encourage activities such as shoplifting or insurance fraud. Exposure to unattainable ideals of beauty and success can create dissatisfaction with the self. Many of these issues will be touched on later in the book, but for now let's review some dimensions of what has been called "the dark side" of consumer behavior.

ADDICTIVE CONSUMPTION

Consumer addiction is a physiological and/or psychological dependency on products or services. While most people equate addiction with drugs, virtually any product or service can be seen as relieving some problem or satisfying some need to the point where reliance on it becomes extreme. Indeed, some psychologists are even raising concerns about "Internet addiction," where people (particularly college students!) become obsessed by on-line chat rooms to the point that their "virtual" lives take priority over their real ones.[67]

COMPULSIVE CONSUMPTION

For some consumers, the expression "born to shop" is taken quite literally. These consumers shop because they are compelled to do so, rather than because shopping is a pleasurable or functional task. **Compulsive consumption** refers to repetitive shopping, often excessive, as an antidote to tension, anxiety, depression, or boredom. "Shopaholics" turn to shopping much the way addicted people turn to drugs or alcohol.[68]

Compulsive consumption is distinctly different from impulse buying, which will be discussed in chapter 10. The impulse to buy a specific item is temporary, and it centers on a specific product at a particular moment. In contrast, compulsive buying is an enduring behavior that centers on the process of buying, not the purchases themselves. As one woman who spent $20,000 per year on clothing confessed, "I was possessed when I went into a store. I bought clothes that didn't fit, that I didn't like, and that I certainly didn't need."[69]

In some cases, it is fairly safe to say that the consumer, not unlike a drug addict, has little to no control over consumption. Whether alcohol, cigarettes, chocolate, or diet colas, the products control the consumer. Even the act of shopping itself is an addicting experience for some consumers. Much negative or destructive consumer behavior can be characterized by three common elements:[70]

1. The behavior is not done by choice.
2. The gratification derived from the behavior is short lived.
3. The person experiences strong feelings of regret or guilt afterwards.

Gambling is an example of a consumption addiction that touches every segment of consumer society. Whether it takes the form of casino gambling, playing the "slots," betting on sports events with friends or through a bookie, or even buying lottery tickets, excessive gambling can be quite destructive. Taken to extremes, gambling can result in lowered self-esteem, debt, divorce, and neglected children. According to one psychologist, gamblers exhibit a classic addictive cycle: They experience a "high" while in action and depression when they stop gambling, which leads them back to the thrill of the action. Unlike drug addicts, however, money is the substance that hard-core gamblers abuse.[71]

CONSUMED CONSUMERS

People who are used or exploited, willingly or not, for commercial gain in the marketplace can be thought of as **consumed consumers.** The situations in which consumers themselves become commodities can range from traveling road shows that feature dwarfs and midgets to the selling of body parts and babies. Some examples of consumed consumers include the following.

- *Prostitutes:* Expenditures on prostitution in the United States alone are estimated at $20 billion annually. These revenues are equivalent to those in the domestic shoe industry.[72]
- *Organ, blood, and hair donors:* In the United States, over 11 million people per year sell their blood (not including voluntary donations).[73] A lively market also exists for organs (e.g., kidneys), and some women sell their hair to be made into wigs.
- *Babies for sale:* Several thousand surrogate mothers have been paid to be medically impregnated and carry babies to term for infertile couples.[74]

ILLEGAL ACTIVITIES

A recent survey conducted by the McCann Erickson advertising agency revealed the following tidbits:[75]

- Ninety-one percent of people say they lie regularly. One in three fibs about their weight, one in four about their income, and 21 percent lie about their age. Nine percent even lie about their natural hair color.
- Four out of ten Americans have tried to pad an insurance bill to cover the deductible.

- Nineteen percent say they've snuck into a theater to avoid paying admission.
- More than three out of five people say they've taken credit for making something from scratch when they have done no such thing. According to Pillsbury's CEO, this ". . . behavior is so prevalent that we've named a category after it—speed scratch."

Many consumer behaviors are not only self-destructive or socially damaging, they are illegal as well. Crimes committed by consumers against businesses have been estimated at more than $40 billion per year. These include shoplifting, employee pilferage, arson, and insurance fraud. Arson alone causes $2 billion per year in damages and its incidence is growing by 25 percent annually.[76]

CONSUMER THEFT

A retail theft is committed every five seconds. **Shrinkage** is the industry term for inventory and cash losses from shoplifting and employee theft. This is a massive problem for businesses that is passed onto consumers in the form of higher prices (about 40 percent of the losses can be attributed to employees rather than shoppers). A family of four spends about $300 extra per year because of markups to cover shrinkage.[77] The problem is not unique to the United States. For example, shrinkage losses in Great Britain are estimated at more than a million pounds per day.[78]

Shoplifting is America's fastest-growing crime. The large majority of shoplifting is *not* done by professional thieves or by people who genuinely need the stolen items.[79] About three-quarters of those caught are middle- or high-income people who shoplift for the thrill of it or as a substitute for affection. And, shop-

Adbusters Quarterly is a Canadian magazine devoted to culture jamming.

lifting is common among adolescents. Research evidence indicates that teen shoplifting is influenced by factors such as having friends who also shoplift. It is also more likely to occur if the adolescent does not believe that this behavior is morally wrong.[80]

ANTICONSUMPTION

Some types of destructive consumer behavior can be thought of as **anticonsumption,** whereby products and services are deliberately defaced or mutilated. Anticonsumption can range from product tampering, by which innocent consumers are hurt or killed, to graffiti on buildings and subways. Anticonsumption can also take the form of political protest, in which activists alter or destroy billboards and other advertisements that promote what they feel to be unhealthy or unethical acts—a practice that has been termed **culture jamming.** For example, some members of the clergy in areas heavily populated by minorities have organized rallies to protest the proliferation of cigarette and alcohol advertising in their neighborhoods.

In some cases these acts are a form of **cultural resistance,** whereby consumers who are alienated from mainstream society (e.g., juvenile delinquents) single out objects that represent the values of the larger group and modify them as an act of rebellion or self-expression.[81] In the hippie culture of the 1960s and 1970s, for example, many antiwar protestors began wearing cast-off military apparel, often replacing insignias of rank with peace signs and other symbols of "revolution."

CONSUMER BEHAVIOR AS A FIELD OF STUDY

By now it should be clear that the field of consumer behavior encompasses many things, from the simple purchase of a carton of milk to the selection of a complex networked computer system, from the decision to donate money to a charity to devious plans to rip off a company or store. There's an awful lot to understand, and many ways to go about it.

Although people have certainly been consumers for a long time, it is only recently that consumption per se has been the object of formal study. In fact, although many business schools now require that marketing majors take a consumer behavior course, most colleges did not even offer such a course until the 1970s.

MARKETING PITFALL

Some companies choose to profit by appealing to people's baser instincts. This strategy is now finding its way to the World Wide Web. To promote an on-line game, SegaSoft created a fictional cult called the Cyber Diversion movement that encourages the primal urge to kill. The imaginary founder of the so-called "New Christian Cyberdiversionists" proclaims, "We kill. It's OK. It's not our fault any more than breathing or urinating." According to a company vice-president, "It's a marketing campaign, but there is some validity to the concept [that] you need an outlet for aggressive urges. If it becomes a movement, all the better. Starting a movement is a good way to market a product." Thirteen separate Web sites, each crafted to look "homemade," were created about the "movement."[82]

INTERDISCIPLINARY INFLUENCES ON THE STUDY OF CONSUMER BEHAVIOR

Consumer behavior is a very young field, and as it grows, it is being influenced by many different perspectives. Indeed, it is hard to think of a field that is more interdisciplinary. People with training in a very wide range of fields—from psychophysiology to literature—can now be found doing consumer research. Consumer researchers are employed by universities, manufacturers, museums, advertising agencies, and governments. Several professional groups, such as the Association for Consumer Research, have been formed since the mid-1970s. A summary of career opportunities in consumer behavior can be found in appendix I on the PHLIP website.

To gain an idea of the diversity of interests of people who do consumer research, consider the list of professional associations that sponsor the field's major journal, the *Journal of Consumer Research:* The American Home Economics Association, The American Statistical Association, The Association for Consumer Research, The Society for Consumer Psychology, The International Communication Association, The American Sociological Association, The Institute of Management Sciences, The American Anthropological Association, The American Marketing Association, The Society for Personality and Social Psychology, The American Association for Public Opinion Research, and The American Economic Association.

So, with all of these researchers from diverse backgrounds interested in consumer behavior, which is the "correct" discipline to look into these issues? You might remember a children's story about the blind men and the elephant. The gist of the story is that each man touched a different part of the animal, and as a result, the descriptions each gave of the elephant were quite different. This analogy applies to consumer research as well. A given consumer phenomenon can be studied in different ways and at different levels depending on the training and interests of the researchers studying it.

Figure 1–3 provides a glimpse at some of the disciplines working in the field and the level at which each approaches research issues. These diverse disciplines can be roughly characterized in terms of their focus on micro versus macro consumer behavior topics. The fields closer to the top of the pyramid concentrate on the individual consumer (micro issues), and those toward the base are more interested in the aggregate activities that occur among larger groups of people, such as consumption patterns shared by members of a culture or subculture (macro issues). To demonstrate that the same marketing issue can be explored at different levels, Table 1–3 lists research issues that might be of interest to each contributing discipline and provides examples of how these might be applied in the marketing of women's magazines. In addition, Appendix II found on the PHLIP website provides an overview of the many different research techniques available to study these issues. Appendix III presents some sources of consumer data that can be used by researchers.

THE ISSUE OF STRATEGIC FOCUS

Many regard the field of consumer behavior as an applied social science. Accordingly, the value of the knowledge generated should be judged in terms of its ability to improve the effectiveness of marketing practice. Recently, though, some researchers have argued that consumer behavior should not have a strategic focus at all; the field should not be a "handmaiden to business." It should instead focus on

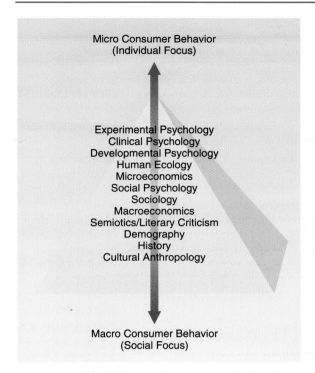

Micro Consumer Behavior
(Individual Focus)

Experimental Psychology
Clinical Psychology
Developmental Psychology
Human Ecology
Microeconomics
Social Psychology
Sociology
Macroeconomics
Semiotics/Literary Criticism
Demography
History
Cultural Anthropology

Macro Consumer Behavior
(Social Focus)

FIGURE 1–3 ■
The Pyramid of
Consumer Behavior

the understanding of consumption for its own sake, rather than because the knowledge can be applied by marketers.[83]

This rather extreme view is probably not held by most consumer researchers, but it has encouraged many to expand the scope of their work beyond the field's traditional focus on the purchase of consumer goods such as food, appliances, cars, and so on to embrace social problems such as homelessness or preserving the environment. Certainly, it has led to some fiery debates among people working in the field!

THE ISSUE OF TWO PERSPECTIVES ON CONSUMER RESEARCH

One general way to classify consumer research is in terms of the fundamental assumptions the researchers make about what they are studying and how to study it. This set of beliefs is known as a **paradigm.** As in other fields of study, consumer behavior is dominated by a paradigm, but some believe it is in the middle of a *paradigm shift,* which occurs when a competing paradigm challenges the dominant set of assumptions.

The basic set of assumptions underlying the dominant paradigm at this point in time is called **positivism** (or sometimes *modernism*). This perspective has significantly influenced Western art and science since the late sixteenth century. It emphasizes that human reason is supreme, and that there is a single, objective truth that can be discovered by science. Positivism encourages us to stress the function of objects, to celebrate technology, and to regard the world as a rational, ordered place with a clearly defined past, present, and future.

The emerging paradigm of **interpretivism** (or *postmodernism*) questions these assumptions. Proponents of this perspective argue that there is too much emphasis

TABLE 1–3 ■ Interdisciplinary Research Issues in Consumer Behavior

DISCIPLINARY FOCUS	MAGAZINE USAGE SAMPLE RESEARCH ISSUES
Experimental Psychology: product role in perception, learning, and memory processes	How specific aspects of magazines, such as their design or layout, are recognized and interpreted; which parts of a magazine are most likely to be read
Clinical Psychology: product role in psychological adjustment	How magazines affect readers' body images (e.g., do thin models make the average woman feel overweight?)
Microeconomics/Human Ecology: product role in allocation of individual or family resources	Factors influencing the amount of money spent on magazines in a household
Social Psychology: product role in the behavior of individuals as members of social groups	Ways that ads in a magazine affect readers' attitudes toward the products depicted; how peer pressure influences a person's readership decisions
Sociology: product role in social institutions and group relationships	Pattern by which magazine preferences spread through a social group (e.g., a sorority)
Macroeconomics: product role in consumers' relations with the marketplace	Effects of the price of fashion magazines and expense of items advertised during periods of high unemployment
Semiotics/Literary Criticism: product role in the verbal and visual communication of meaning	Ways in which underlying messages communicated by models and ads in a magazine are interpreted
Demography: product role in the measurable characteristics of a population	Effects of age, income, and marital status of a magazine's readers
History: product role in societal changes over time	Ways in which our culture's depictions of "femininity" in magazines have changed over time
Cultural Anthropology: product role in a society's beliefs and practices	Ways in which fashions and models in a magazine affect readers' definitions of masculine versus feminine behavior (e.g., the role of working women, sexual taboos)

on science and technology in our society, and that this ordered, rational view of behavior denies the complex social and cultural world in which we live. Others feel that positivism puts too much emphasis on material well-being, and that its logical outlook is dominated by an ideology that stresses the homogenous views of a culture dominated by white males.

Interpretivists instead stress the importance of symbolic, subjective experience, and the idea that meaning is in the mind of the person—that is, we each construct our own meanings based on our unique and shared cultural experiences, so there are no right or wrong answers. In this view, the world in which we live is composed of a *pastiche,* or mixture of images.[84] The value placed on products because they help us to create order in our lives is replaced by an appreciation of consumption as offering a set of diverse experiences. The major differences between these two perspectives on consumer research are summarized in Table 1–4.

TABLE 1–4 ■ **Positivist versus Interpretivist Approaches to Consumer Behavior**

ASSUMPTIONS	POSITIVIST APPROACH	INTERPRETIVIST APPROACH
Nature of reality	Objective, tangible Single	Socially constructed Multiple
Goal	Prediction	Understanding
Knowledge generated	Time free Context independent	Time bound Context dependent
View of causality	Existence of real causes	Multiple, simultaneous shaping events
Research relationship	Separation between researcher and subject	Interactive, cooperative with researcher being part of phenomenon under study

Source: Adapted from Laurel A. Hudson and Julie L. Ozanne, "Alternative Ways of Seeking Knowledge in Consumer Research," *Journal of Consumer Research* 14 (March 1988): 508–21. Reprinted with the permission of The University of Chicago Press.

TAKING IT FROM HERE: THE PLAN OF THE BOOK

This book covers many facets of consumer behavior, and many of the research perspectives briefly described in this chapter will be highlighted in later chapters. The plan of the book is simple: It goes from micro to macro. Think of the book as a sort of photograph album of consumer behavior: Each chapter provides a "snapshot" of consumers, but the lens used to take each picture gets successively wider. The book begins with issues related to the individual consumer and expands its focus until it eventually considers the behaviors of large groups of people in their social settings. The topics to be covered correspond to the wheel of consumer behavior presented in Figure 1–4.

Section II, " Consumers as Individuals," considers the consumer at his or her most micro level. It examines how the individual receives information from his or her immediate environment and how this material is learned, stored in memory, and used to form and modify individual attitudes—both about products and about oneself. Section III, " Consumers as Decision Makers," explores the ways in which consumers use the information they have acquired to make decisions about consumption activities, both as individuals and as group members. Section IV, " Consumers and Subcultures," further expands the focus by considering how the consumer functions as a part of a larger social structure. This structure includes the influence of different social groups with which the consumer belongs and/or identifies, including social class, ethnic groups, and age groups. Finally, Section V, "Consumers and Culture," completes the picture as it examines marketing's impact on mass culture. These effects include the relationship of marketing to the expression of cultural values and lifestyles, how products and services are related to rituals and cultural myths, and the interface between marketing efforts and the creation of art, music, and other forms of popular culture that are so much a part of our daily lives.

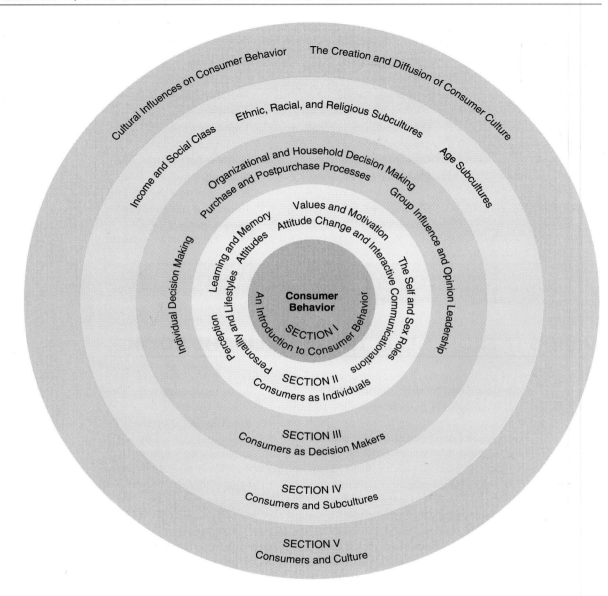

FIGURE 1–4 ■ The Wheel of Consumer Behavior

- Consumer behavior is the study of the processes involved when individuals or groups select, purchase, use, or dispose of products, services, ideas, or experiences to satisfy needs and desires.

- A consumer may purchase, use, and/or dispose of a product, but these functions may be performed by different people. In addition, consumers may be thought of as role players who need different products to help them play their various parts.

- Market segmentation is an important aspect of consumer behavior. Consumers can be segmented according to many dimensions, including product usage, demographics (the objective aspects of a population, such as age and sex), and psychographics (psychological and lifestyle characteristics). Emerging developments, such as the new emphasis on relationship marketing and the practice of database marketing, mean that marketers are much more attuned to the wants and needs of different consumer groups.

- Marketing activities exert an enormous impact on individuals. Consumer behavior is relevant to our understanding of both public policy issues (e.g., ethical marketing practices) and of the dynamics of popular culture.

- Marketers try to communicate with consumers by creating relationships between their products or services and desired attributes. A semiotic analysis involves the correspondence between stimuli and the meaning of signs. The intended meaning may be literal (e.g., an icon such as a street sign with a picture of children playing). The meaning may be indexical; it relies on shared characteristics (e.g., the red in a stop sign means danger). Finally, meaning can be conveyed by a symbol, in which an image is given meaning by convention or by agreement of members of a society (e.g., stop signs are octagonal, while yield signs are triangular).

- Although textbooks often paint a picture of the consumer as a rational, informed decision maker, in reality many consumer activities are harmful to individuals or to society. The "dark side" of consumer behavior includes addiction, the use of people as products (consumed consumers), and theft or vandalism (anticonsumption).

- The field of consumer behavior is interdisciplinary; it is comprised of researchers from many different fields who share an interest in how people interact with the marketplace. These disciplines can be categorized by the degree to which their focus is micro (the individual consumer) or macro (the consumer as a member of groups or of the larger society).

- There are many perspectives on consumer behavior, but research orientations can roughly be divided into two approaches: The positivist perspective emphasizes the objectivity of science and the consumer as a rational decision maker. The interpretivist perspective, in contrast, stresses the subjective meaning of the consumer's individual experience and the idea that any behavior is subject to multiple interpretations rather than to one single explanation.

KEY TERMS

Anticonsumption p. 29
Business ethics p. 21
Database marketing p. 12
Compulsive consumption
p. 26
Consumed consumers p. 27
Consumer p. 6
Consumer addiction p. 26
Consumer behavior p. 5
Cultural resistance p. 29

Culture jamming p. 29
Demographics p. 8
Exchange p. 6
Green marketing p. 24
Hyperreality p. 18
Interpretant p. 17
Interpretivism p. 31
Object p. 17
Market segmentation p. 8
Paradigm p. 31

Popular culture p. 14
Positivism p. 31
Relationship marketing
p. 12
Role theory p. 5
Semiotics p. 17
Shrinkage p. 28
Sign p. 17
Social marketing p. 25

CONSUMER BEHAVIOR CHALLENGE

1. This chapter states that people play different roles and that their consumption behaviors may differ depending on the particular role they are playing. State whether you agree or disagree with this perspective, giving examples from your personal life. Try to construct a "stage set" for a role you play—specify the props, costumes, and script that you use to play a role (e.g., job interviewee, conscientious student, party animal . . .).

2. Some researchers believe that the field of consumer behavior should be a pure, rather than an applied, science. That is, research issues should be framed in terms of their scientific interest rather than their applicability to immediate marketing problems. Give your views on this issue.

3. Name some products or services that are widely used by your social group. State whether you agree or disagree with the notion that these products help to form group bonds, supporting your argument with examples from your list of products used by the group.

4. Although demographic information on large numbers of consumers is used in many marketing contexts, some people believe that the sale of data on customers' incomes, buying habits, and so on constitutes an invasion of privacy and should be stopped. The chapter notes that even people's gambling activities are now being monitored by casino personnel. Is Big Brother watching? Comment on this issue from both a consumer's and a marketer's point of view.

5. List the three stages in the consumption process. Describe the issues that you considered in each of these stages when you made a recent important purchase.

6. State the differences between the positivist and interpretivist approaches to consumer research. For each type of inquiry, give examples of product dimensions that would be more usefully explored using that type of research over the other.

7. What aspects of consumer behavior are likely to be of interest to a financial planner? to a university administrator? to a graphic arts designer? to a social worker in a government agency? to a nursing instructor?

8. Critics of targeted marketing strategies argue that this practice is discriminatory and unfair, especially if such a strategy encourages a group of people to buy a product that may be injurious to them or that they cannot afford. For example, community leaders in largely minority neighborhoods have staged protests against billboards promoting beer or cigarettes in these areas. On the other hand, The Association of National Advertisers argues that banning targeted marketing constitutes censorship, and thus is a violation of the First Amendment. What are your views regarding this issue?

9. Do marketers have the ability to control our desires or the power to create needs?

10. Find an ad that is rich in symbolism and perform a semiotic analysis of it. Identify each type of sign used in the ad and the product qualities being communicated by each. Comment on the effectiveness of the signs that are used to communicate the intended message.

11. Construct a ritual script for a wedding in your culture. How many artifacts can you list that are contained in this script?

NOTES

1. Deirdre Carmody, "Hearst Finds Unexpected Success in a Magazine for Dreamers," *New York Times* (September 12, 1994): D6.
2. Suzanne Cassidy, "Defining the Cosmo Girl: Check Out the Passport," *New York Times* (October 12, 1992): D8.
3. Fara Warner, "Advertising: Cosmopolitan Girl Dresses up for Summer Debut in Indonesia," *Wall Street Journal Interactive Edition* (April 9, 1997).
4. Erving Goffman, *The Presentation of Self in Everyday Life* (Garden City, NY: Doubleday, 1959); George H. Mead, *Mind, Self, and Society* (Chicago: University of Chicago Press, 1934); Michael R. Solomon, "The Role of Products as Social Stimuli: A Symbolic Interactionism Perspective," *Journal of Consumer Research* 10 (December 1983): 319–29.
5. Michael R. Solomon and Elnora W. Stuart, *Marketing: Real People, Real Choices* (Englewood Cliffs, NJ: Prentice Hall, 1997), pp. 15–16.
6. Ronald Alsop, "Agencies Scrutinize Their Ads for Psychological Symbolism," *Wall Street Journal* (June 11, 1987): 27.
7. Jeffrey F. Durgee, "On Cezanne, Hot Buttons, and Interpreting Consumer Storytelling," *Journal of Consumer Marketing* 5 (Fall 1988): 47–51.
8. Leslie Kaufman, "Enough Talk," *Newsweek* (August 18, 1997): 48–49.
9. Joshua Levine, "Desperately Seeking Jeepness," *Forbes* (May 15, 1989): 134; Anthony Ramirez, "New Cigarettes Raising Issue of Target Market," *New York Times* (February 18, 1990): 28; Howard Schlossberg, "Segmenting Becomes Constitutional Issue," *Marketing News* (April 16, 1990): 1.
10. Annetta Miller, "You Are What You Buy," *Newsweek* (June 4, 1990): 59.
11. Natalie Perkins, "Zeroing in on Consumer Values," *Advertising Age* (March 22, 1993): 23.
12. Quoted in March Magiera, "Levi's Broadens Appeal," *Advertising Age* (July 17, 1989): 1 (2 pp.).
13. Jennifer Lawrence, "Gender-Specific Works for Diapers—Almost Too Well," *Advertising Age* (February 8, 1993) S10 (2 pp.).
14. Julie Candler, "Woman Car Buyer—Don't Call Her a Niche Anymore," *Advertising Age* (January 21, 1991): S8.
15. Charles M. Schaninger and William D. Danko, "A Conceptual and Empirical Comparison of Alternative Household Life Cycle Models," *Journal of Consumer Research* 19 (March 1993): 580–594; Robert E. Wilkes, "Household Life-Cycle Stages, Transitions, and Product Expenditures," *Journal of Consumer Research* 22, 1 (June 1995): 27–42.
16. Richard P. Coleman, "The Continuing Significance of Social Class to Marketing," *Journal of Consumer Research* 10 (December 1983): 265–280.
17. Linda Keene, "Making a Stale Business Poppin' Fresh," *Sales & Marketing Management* (April 1992): 38–9.
18. Quoted in George Rathwaite, "Heileman's National Impact with Local Brews," *Marketing Insights* (1989; premier issue): 108 (7 pp.).
19. Cyndee Miller, "Military Market Considered Strong Despite Troop Cuts," *Marketing News* (August 3, 1992)2: 1; Eben Shapiro, "Consumers in the Military Require Precision Marketing," *New York Times* (May 26, 1992): D10.
20. Elizabeth Roberts, "This Ad's For You," *Newsweek* (February 24, 1992): 40.
21. Jolie Solomon, "Putting the 'Con' in Consumer," *Newsweek* (October 26, 1992): 49.
22. Kevin Gudridge, "High Prices Wear Well for Cataloger," *Advertising Age* (August 23, 1993): 10.
23. Alice Z. Cuneo, "Tailor-Made Not Merely 1 of a Kind," *Advertising Age* (November 7, 1994): 22.
24. Robert C. Blattberg and John Deighton, "Interactive Marketing: Exploiting the Age of Addressability," *Sloan Management Review* 331 (Fall 1991)1: 5–14.
25. Gerri Hirshey, "Gambling Nation," *New York Times Magazine* (July 17, 1994): 36 (14 pp.).
26. Bruce Orwall, "Like Playing Slots? Casinos Know All About You," *New York Times* (December 20, 1995): B1 (2 pp.).
27. "Old Data, New Tricks," *PROMO* (April 1996): DB6.
28. Jane Hodges and Alice Z. Cuneo, "Levi's Registration Program Will Seek to Build Database," *Advertising Age* (February 24, 1997): 86.
29. Robert C. Blattberg and John Deighton, "Interactive Marketing: Exploiting the Age of Addressability," *Sloan Management Review* 331 (Fall 1991)1: 5–14.
30. Quoted in "Bringing Meaning to Brands," *American Demographics* (June 1997): 34.
31. Susan Fournier, "Consumers and Their Brands. Developing Relationship Theory in Consumer Research," *Journal of Consumer Research* 24 (March 1998): 343–373.
32. Douglas B. Holt, "How Consumers Consume: A Taxonomy of Consumption Practices," *Journal of Consumer Research* 22 (June 1995)1: 1–16; personal communication, August 27, 1997.
33. See David Mick, "Consumer Research and Semiotics: Exploring the Morphology of Signs, Symbols, and Significance," *Journal of Consumer Research* 13 (September 1986): 196–213.
34. Teresa J. Domzal and Jerome B. Kernan, "Reading Advertising: The What and How of Product Meaning," *Journal of Consumer Marketing* 9 (Summer 1992): 48–64.
35. Arthur Asa Berger, *Signs in Contemporary Culture: An Introduction to Semiotics* (New York: Longman, 1984); David Mick, "Consumer Research and Semiotics: Exploring the Morphology of Signs, Symbols, and Significance," *Journal of Consumer Research* 13 (September 1986): 196–213; Charles Sanders Peirce, in eds. Charles Hartshorne, Paul Weiss, and Arthur W. Burks, *Collected Papers* (Cambridge, MA: Harvard University Press, 1931–1958).
36. Jean Baudrillard, *Simulations* (New York: Semiotext(e), 1983); A. Fuat Firat and Alladi Venkatesh, "The Making of Postmodern Consumption," in *Consumption and Marketing: Macro Dimensions,* eds. Russell Belk and Nikhilesh Dholakia (Boston: PWS-Kent, 1993); A. Fuat Firat, "The Consumer in Postmodernity," in *Advances in Consumer Research* 18, eds. Rebecca H. Holman and Michael R. Solomon

(Provo, UT: Association for Consumer Research, 1991): 70–6.

37. For a recent discussion of this trend, see Russell W. Belk, "Hyperreality and Globalization: Culture in the Age of Ronald McDonald," *Journal of International Consumer Marketing,* 8 (3&4 1995):23–38.

38. Nina Munk, "The Levi Straddle," *Forbes* (January 17, 1994): 44 (2 pp.).

39. Mary Kuntz and Joseph Weber, "The New Hucksterism," *Business Week* (July 1, 1996): 75 (7 pp.).

40. Alix M. Freedman and Suein L. Hwang, "Cigar Maker Exposes Dirty Secret of 'Blunting'," *Wall Street Journal* (April 8, 1996): B1 (2 pp.).

41. "Goodbye Johnny, Hello Tic Tac," *Advertising Age* (May 25, 1992): 22; Cleveland Horton, "Hyundai Pulls Planned Ad in L.A. Beating Aftermath," *Advertising Age* (April 22, 1991): 2; Randall Rothenberg, "Does Integration Lead to Segregation?: The Ethical Problems of Integrated Marketing," paper presented at the 11th annual Advertising and Consumer Psychology Conference, Chicago, 1992.

42. Fara Warner, "Why It's Getting Harder to Tell the Shows from the Ads," *Wall Street Journal* (June 15, 1995): B1 (2 pp.).

43. Sally Goll Beatty, "Advertising: USA Today Rides Free in Ad That Toots Horn for Honda," *Wall Street Journal Interactive Edition* (March 11, 1997).

44. Quoted in David Barboza, "Advertising: A Campaign that Keeps 'Going and Going and Going' is now Going in Some New Directions," *New York Times* (December 26, 1996): D7.

45. Randall Lane, "The Ultimate Sponsorship," *Forbes* (March 14, 1994): 106.

46. Michael DeCourcy Hinds, "Not Like the Movie: 3 Take a Dare, and Lose," *New York Times* (October 19, 1993): A1 (2 pp.).

47. Tony Horwitz and Richard Turner, "Disney and Academics Escalate Battle over the Entertainment Value of History," *Wall Street Journal* (June 21, 1994): B1 (2 pp.).

48. Mary Kuntz and Joseph Weber, "The New Hucksterism," *Business Week* (July 1, 1996): 75 (7 pp.).

49. Warner, "Why It's Getting Harder to Tell the Shows from the Ads." T. L. Stanley, "You Want It Where,?" *PROMO Magazine* (May 1997): S4 (4 pp.).

50. Chuck Ross and Ira Teinowitz, "Beer Ads Had Wide Underage Reach on MTV," *Advertising Age* (January 6, 1997): 4, 36.

51. Joseph Pereira, "Toys 'R' Us Says It Decided to Pull Sega's *Night Trap* from Store Shelves," *Wall Street Journal* (December 17, 1993): B5F.

52. William Leiss, Stephen Kline, and Sut Jhally, *Social Communication in Advertising: Persons, Products, & Images of Well-Being* (Toronto: Methuen, 1986); Jerry Mander, *Four Arguments for the Elimination of Television* (New York: William Morrow, 1977).

53. Matthew L. Wald, "Looking for Savings as Gas Prices Rise," *New York Times* (May 27, 1989): 48.

54. David Ivanovich, "Exxon to Run Commercials Saying Most Cars Don't Need Premium," *Houston Chronicle* (1997), accessed via *Newslink,* August 15, 1997.

55. Packard (1957), quoted in Leiss et al., *Social Communication,* p. 11.

56. Raymond Williams, *Problems in Materialism and Culture: Selected Essays* (London: Verso, 1980).

57. Leiss et al., *Social Communication.*

58. George Stigler, "The Economics of Information," *Journal of Political Economy* (1961): 69.

59. Quoted in Leiss et al., *Social Communication;* 11.

60. For consumer research and discussions related to public policy issues, see Paul N. Bloom and Stephen A. Greyser, "The Maturing of Consumerism," *Harvard Business Review* (November–December 1981): 130–39; George S. Day, Assessing the Effect of Information Disclosure Requirements," *Journal of Marketing* (April 1976): 42–52; Dennis E. Garrett, "The Effectiveness of Marketing Policy Boycotts: Environmental Opposition to Marketing," *Journal of Marketing* 51 (January 1987): 44–53; Michael Houston and Michael Rothschild, "Policy-related Experiments on Information Provision: A Normative Model and Explication," *Journal of Marketing Research* 17 (November 1980): 432–49; Jacob Jacoby, Wayne D. Hoyer, and David A. Sheluga, *Misperception of Televised Communications* (New York: American Association of Advertising Agencies, 1980); Gene R. Laczniak and Patrick E. Murphy, *Marketing Ethics: Guidelines for Managers* (Lexington, Lexington Books, 1985), 117–23;

Lynn Phillips and Bobby Calder, "Evaluating Consumer Protection Laws: Promising Methods," *Journal of Consumer Affairs* 14 (Summer 1980): 9–36; Donald P. Robin and Eric Reidenbach, "Social Responsibility, Ethics, and Marketing Strategy: Closing the Gap between Concept and Application," *Journal of Marketing* 51 (January 1987): 44–58; Howard Schutz and Marianne Casey, "Consumer Perceptions of Advertising as Misleading," *Journal of Consumer Affairs* 15 (Winter 1981): 340–57; Darlene Brannigan Smith and Paul N. Bloom, "Is Consumerism Dead or Alive? Some New Evidence," in ed. Thomas C. Kinnear, *Advances in Consumer Research* 11 (Provo, UT: Association for Consumer Research, 1984); 369–73.

61. L.C. Noechowicz, "America's Hotels Going Green," *Montgomery Advertiser* (September 19, 1996): 4A.

62. "Concerned Consumers Push for Environmentally Friendly Packaging," *Boxboard Containers* (April 1993): 4.

63. Joshua Levine, "Badass Sells," *Forbes* (April 21, 1997): 142 (6).

64. Arnott, Nancy, "Marketing With a Passion," *Sales & Marketing Management* (January 1994): 64–71.

65. Cf. Philip Kotler and Alan R. Andreasen, *Strategic Marketing for Nonprofit Organizations,* 4th ed., Englewood Cliffs, NJ: Prentice Hall, 1991; Jeff B. Murray and Julie L. Ozanne, "The Critical Imagination: Emancipatory Interests in Consumer Research," *Journal of Consumer Research* 18 (September 1991): 192–44; William D. Wells, "Discovery-Oriented Consumer Research," *Journal of Consumer Research* 19 (March 1993): 489–504.

66. Bertil Swartz, " 'Keep Control:' The Swedish Brewers Association Campaign to Foster Responsible Alcohol Consumption Among Adolescents," paper presented at the 1997 ACR Europe Conference, Stockholm, June; Anna Oloffson, Ordpolen Informations AB, Sweden, personal communication, August 1997.

67. "Psychologist Warns of Internet Addiction," *Montgomery Advertiser* (August 18, 1997): 2D.

68. Thomas C. O'Guinn and Ronald J. Faber, "Compulsive Buying: A Phenomenological Explanation,"

Journal of Consumer Research 16 (September 1989): 154.

69. Quoted in Anastasia Toufexis, "365 Shopping Days Till Christmas," *Time* (December 26, 1988): 82; see also Ronald J. Faber and Thomas C. O'Guinn, "Compulsive Consumption and Credit Abuse," *Journal of Consumer Policy* 11 (1988): 109–21; Mary S. Butler, "Compulsive Buying—It's No Joke," *Consumer's Digest* (September 1986): 55; Derek N. Hassay and Malcolm C. Smith, "Compulsive Buying: An Examination of the Consumption Motive," *Psychology & Marketing* 13 (December 1996): 741–52.

70. Georgia Witkin, "The Shopping Fix," *Health* (May 1988): 73; see also Arch G. Woodside and Randolph J. Trappey III, "Compulsive Consumption of a Consumer Service: An Exploratory Study of Chronic Horse Race Track Gambling Behavior" (working paper #90-MKTG-04, A. B. Freeman School of Business, Tulane University, 1990); Rajan Nataraajan and Brent G. Goff, "Manifestations of Compulsiveness in the Consumer-Marketplace Domain," *Psychology & Marketing* 9 (January 1992): 31–44; Joann Ellison Rodgers, "Addiction: A Whole New View," *Psychology Today* (September/October 1994): 32 (11 pp.).

71. James Barron, "Are We All Really Losers with Gambling, a Spreading Social Addiction?" *New York Times* (May 31, 1989): A18.

72. Helen Reynolds, *The Economics of Prostitution* (Springfield, IL.: Thomas, 1986).

73. "Precious Drops," *The Economist* (October 14, 1989): 28.

74. Barbara Katz Rothman, "Cheap Labor: Sex, Class, Race and 'Surrogacy'," *Society* 25 (March–April 1988): 21.

75. "Advertisers Face up to the New Morality: Making the Pitch," (Bloomberg), accessed vis SS *Newslink* (July 8, 1997).

76. Paul Bernstein, "Cheating—The New National Pastime?" *Business* (October–December 1985): 24–33.

77. "Shoplifting: Bess Myerson's Arrest Highlights a Multibillion-Dollar Problem that Many Stores Won't Talk About," *Life* (August 1988): 32.

78. Roy Carter, "Whispering Sweet Nothings to the Shop Thief," *Retail & Distribution Management* (January/February 1986): 36.

79. Catherine A. Cole, "Deterrence and Consumer Fraud," *Journal of Retailing* 65 (Spring 1989): 107–20; Stephen J. Grove, Scott J. Vitell, and David Strutton, "Non-Normative Consumer Behavior and the Techniques of Neutralization," in eds. Terry Childers, et al., *Marketing Theory and Practice*, (1989 AMA Winter Educators' Conference; Chicago: American Marketing Association, 1989); 131–35.

80. Anthony D. Cox, Dena Cox, Ronald D. Anderson, and George P. Moschis, "Social Influences on Adolescent Shoplifting—Theory, Evidence, and Implications for the Retail Industry," *Journal of Retailing* 69 (Summer 1993)2: 234–46.

81. Julie L. Ozanne, Ronald Paul Hill, and Newell D. Wright, "Culture as Contested Terrain: The Juvenile Delinquents' Use of Consumption as Cultural Resistance" (unpublished manuscript, Virginia Polytechnic Institute and State University, 1994).

82. Quoted in Alice Z. Cuneo, "SegaSoft Online Games Tap into Cultlike Mind-Set," *Advertising Age* (April 7, 1997): 3 (2 pp.).

83. Morris B. Holbrook, "The Consumer Researcher Visits Radio City: Dancing in the Dark," in eds. Elizabeth C. Hirschman and Morris B. Holbrook, *Advances in Consumer Research* 12 (Provo, UT: Association for Consumer Research, 1985): 28–31.

84. Alladi Venkatesh, "Postmodernism, Poststructuralism and Marketing" (paper presented at the American Marketing Association Winter Theory Conference, San Antonio, February 1992); see also A. Fuat Firat, "Postmodern Culture, Marketing and the Consumer," in eds. T. Childers et al, *Marketing Theory and Application* (Chicago: American Marketing Association, 1991); 237–42; A. Fuat Firat and Alladi Venkatesh, "The Making of Postmodern Consumption," in eds. Russell W. Belk and Nikhilesh Dholakia, *Consumption and Marketing: Macro Dimensions* (Boston: PWS-Kent, 1993).

CONSUMERS AS INDIVIDUALS

Whatever you do, don't get them mixed up.

The bunny on the right is one of 12 Dung Buddies — lovable miniatures made with Zoo Doo fertilizer that dissolves in soil over time. But remember, they go in your garden, not in your mouth. **DUNG BUDDY**

In this section, we focus on the internal dynamics of consumers. While "no man is an island," each of us is to some degree a self-contained receptor for information about the outside world. We are constantly confronted with advertising messages, products, other people persuading us to buy something, and even reflections of ourselves that make us happy or sad. Each chapter in this section will consider a different aspect of the individual that is "invisible" to others—but of vital importance to ourselves.

Chapter 2 describes the process of perception, in which information from the outside world about products and other people is absorbed and interpreted. Chapter 3 focuses on the way this information is mentally stored and how it adds to our existing knowledge about the world during the learning process. Chapter 4 discusses our reasons or motivations for absorbing this information and how it is influenced by the values to which we subscribe as members of a particular culture.

Chapter 5 explores how our views about ourselves—particularly our sexuality and our physical appearance—affect what we do, want, and buy. Chapter 6 goes on to consider how people's individual personalities influences these decisions, and how the choices we make in terms of products, leisure activities, and so on help to define our lifestyles.

Chapters 7 and 8 discuss how our attitudes—our evaluations of all these products, messages, and so on—are formed and (sometimes) changed by marketers, and how we as individual consumers engage in our ongoing dialogue with these businesspeople by virtue of our responses to these messages.

SECTION OUTLINE

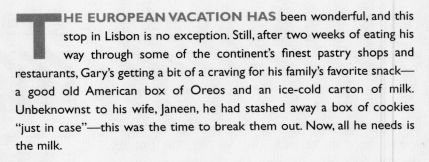

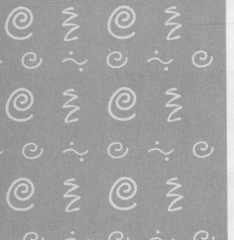

THE EUROPEAN VACATION HAS been wonderful, and this stop in Lisbon is no exception. Still, after two weeks of eating his way through some of the continent's finest pastry shops and restaurants, Gary's getting a bit of a craving for his family's favorite snack— a good old American box of Oreos and an ice-cold carton of milk. Unbeknownst to his wife, Janeen, he had stashed away a box of cookies "just in case"—this was the time to break them out. Now, all he needs is the milk.

On an impulse, Gary decides to surprise Janeen with a mid-afternoon treat. He sneaks out of the hotel room while she's napping, and finds the nearest *grosa*. When he heads to the small refrigerated section, though, he's puzzled—no milk here. Undaunted, Gary asks the clerk, "*leite, por favor?*" The clerk quickly smiles and points to a rack in the middle of the store piled with little white square boxes. No, that can't be right— Gary resolves to work on his Portuguese. He repeats the question, and again he gets the same answer. Finally, he investigates and sure enough he sees the boxes, labeled with the brand name Parmalat, contain something called ultra heat treated (UHT) milk. Nasty! Who in the world would drink milk out of a little box that's been sitting on a warm shelf for who knows how long? Gary dejectedly returns to the hotel, his snacktime fantasies crumbling like so many stale cookies . . .

Perception

2

INTRODUCTION

Actually, Gary would be surprised to learn that many people in the world drink milk out of a box every day. UHT is Grade A pasteurized milk that has been heated until the bacteria causing spoilage are destroyed, and it can last for five to six months without refrigeration if its aseptic container is unopened. Its main manufacturer, the Parmalat Group, is one of the largest dairy companies in the world. In 1996, in fact, the company sold over $4 billion dollars' worth of the stuff in 21 countries. Shelf-stable milk is particularly popular in Europe, where refrigerator space in homes and stores tends to be more limited than in the United States. Seven out of ten Europeans drink it routinely.

The company is trying to crack the American market as well, though analysts are dubious about its prospects. To begin with, milk consumption in the United States is declining steadily as teenagers choose soft drinks instead. The Milk Industry Foundation pumped $44 million into an advertising campaign to promote milk drinking.

But enticing Americans to drink milk out of a box is another thing. In focus groups, American consumers say they have trouble believing the milk is not spoiled or unsafe. They consider the square, quart-sized boxes more suitable for dry food, and some even feel the name "Parmalat" sounds too much like baby formulas such as Enfamil or Similac. The company spent $2 million to introduce the product in New York and is stressing its convenience and its healthful aspects as it contains no preservatives.[1] Still, it's going to be a long, uphill battle to change Americans' perceptions about the proper accompaniment to a bag of Oreos.

We live in a world overflowing with sensations. Wherever we turn, we are bombarded by a symphony of colors, sounds, and odors. Some of the "notes" in this symphony occur naturally, such as the loud barking of a dog, the shades of the evening sky, or the heady smell of a rose bush. Others come from people: The person sitting next to you in class might sport tinted blonde hair, bright pink pants, and enough nasty perfume to make your eyes water.

Marketers certainly contribute to this commotion. Consumers are never far from advertisements, product packages, radio and television commercials, and billboards, all clamoring for our attention. Each of us copes with this bombardment by paying attention to some stimuli and tuning out others. The messages to which we do choose to pay attention often wind up differing from what the sponsors intended, as we each put our "spin" on things by taking away meanings consistent with our own unique experiences, biases, and desires. This chapter focuses on the process of perception, in which sensations are absorbed by the consumer and then are used to interpret the surrounding world.

Sensation refers to the immediate response of our sensory receptors (eyes, ears, nose, mouth, fingers) to basic stimuli such as light, color, sound, odors, and textures. **Perception** is the process by which these sensations are selected, organized, and interpreted. The study of perception, then, focuses on what we add to or take

This ad for a luxury car emphasizes the contribution made by all of our senses to the evaluation of a driving experience. In addition to the five channels of sight, sound, touch, smell, and taste, the ad mentions the "sixth sense" of intuition in its treatment of the "power of perception."

away from these raw sensations as we choose which to notice, and then go about assigning meaning to them.

The perceptual process is illustrated by Gary's encounter with milk in a box. He had learned to equate the temperature of milk with freshness, so he experienced a negative physical reaction when confronted with a product that contradicted his expectations. Gary's evaluation of Parmalat was affected by factors such as the design of the package, the brand name, and even by the area in the grocery store in which it was displayed. He accessed a portion of the raw data available and processed it to be consistent with his needs. These expectations are largely affected by a consumer's cultural background; Europeans do not necessarily have the same perceptions of milk, and as a result their reactions to the product are quite different.

Like computers, people undergo stages of information processing in which stimuli are input and stored. Unlike computers, though, we do not passively process whatever information happens to be present. In the first place, only a very small number of the stimuli in our environment are ever noticed. Of these, an even smaller number are attended to. The stimuli that do enter consciousness might not be processed objectively. The meaning of a stimulus is interpreted by the individual, who is influenced by his or her unique biases, needs, and experiences. As shown in Figure 2–1, these three stages of *exposure, attention,* and *interpretation* make up the process of perception. Before considering each of these stages, let's step back and consider the sensory systems that provide sensations to us in the first place.

SENSORY SYSTEMS

External stimuli, or *sensory inputs,* can be received on a number of channels. We may *see* a billboard, *hear* a jingle, *feel* the softness of a cashmere sweater, *taste* a new flavor of ice cream, or *smell* a leather jacket. The inputs picked up by our five senses constitute the raw data that begin the perceptual process. For example, sensory data emanating from the external environment (e.g., hearing a tune on the radio) can generate internal sensory experiences when the song triggers a young man's memory of his first dance and brings to mind the smell of his date's perfume

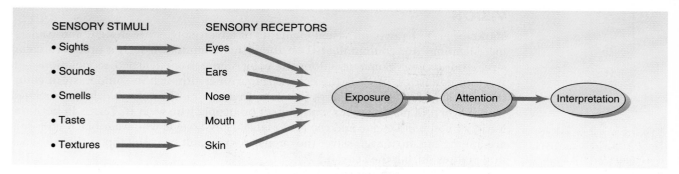

FIGURE 2–1 ■ An Overview of the Perceptual Process

or the feel of her hair on his cheek. These responses are an important part of **hedonic consumption,** or the multisensory, fantasy, and emotional aspects of consumers' interactions with products.[2]

The unique sensory quality of a product can play an important role in helping it to stand out from the competition, especially if the brand creates a unique association with the sensation. The Owens-Corning Fiberglass Corporation was the first company to trademark a color, when it used a bright pink for its insulation material and adopted the Pink Panther cartoon character as its spokescharacter. Harley-Davidson actually trademarked the distinctive sound made by a "hog" revving up.[3] Hedonic consumption plays a central role in many marketing strategies that emphasize fantasy aspects of products. For example, ads for Toyota's RAV4 sport utility vehicle features the vehicle in people's dreams, and the "I Can't Believe It's Not Butter" margarine brand portrays hunk star Fabio as a sculpture which comes to life.[4]

This Brazilian toothpaste ad uses vivid perceptual imagery to communicate a product benefit.

VISION

Marketers rely heavily on visual elements in advertising, store design, and packaging. Meanings are communicated on the visual channel through a product's color, size, and styling. Some reactions to color come from learned associations—in Western countries, black is the color of mourning; although in some Eastern countries, notably Japan, white plays this role. In addition, the color black is associated with power and may even have an impact on people who wear it. Teams in both the National Football League and the National Hockey League who wear black uniforms are among the most aggressive; they consistently rank near the top of their leagues in penalties during the season.[5]

Colors may also influence our emotions more directly. Evidence suggests that some colors (particularly red) create feelings of arousal and stimulate appetite, and others (such as blue) are more relaxing. Products presented against a backdrop of blue in advertisements are better liked than when a red background is used.[6] Maybe that explains why blue-colored products, from pasta and juice to tortilla chips and Jell-O, have been introduced in the last few years.[7]

Color frequently is a key issue in package design. These choices used to be made casually. For example, the familiar Campbell's soup can was produced in red and white because a company executive liked the football uniforms at Cornell University! Now, however, color is a serious business, and many companies realize that their color choices can exert a big influence on consumers' assumptions about what is inside the package. This "package" includes automobiles, where consumers' preferences for exterior hues change with the tides of fashion. That's why DuPont, which is a leader in the car paint industry, invests heavily in efforts to predict car buyers' tastes in exterior colors a year, three years, and five years down the road.

As this Dutch ad for Dreft detergent illustrates ("Flowery orange fades without Dreft"), vivid colors are often an attractive feature.

MULTICULTURAL DIMENSIONS

Cultural differences in color preferences create the need for marketing strategies tailored to different countries. Procter & Gamble, for example, uses brighter colors in makeup it sells in Latin countries.[8] P&G and other cosmetics companies have found that women in Mexico and South America are willing to pay a premium for bold-colored nail polishes with names such as "Orange Flip." Latina homemakers typically get dressed up in high heels tinted in tropical colors to go to the supermarket. For these women, the natural look is out. As one legal secretary in Mexico City explained, "When you don't wear makeup, men look at you like you are sick or something."[9]

These decisions help to "color" our expectations of what's inside the package. When introducing a white cheese as a "sister product" to an existing blue "Castello" cheese, a Danish company launched it in a red package under the name of Castello Bianco. The red package was chosen to provide maximum visibility on store shelves. Although taste tests were very positive, sales were disappointing. A subsequent semiotic analysis of consumer interpretations showed that the red packaging and the name gave the consumers wrong associations with the product type and its degree of sweetness. Danish consumers had trouble associating the color red with the white cheese. Also the name Bianco connoted a sweetness that was incompatible with the actual taste of the product. It was relaunched in a white package and given the name "white Castello," and almost immediately sales more than doubled.[10]

Some color combinations come to be so strongly associated with a corporation that they become known as the company's *trade dress,* and the company may even be granted exclusive use of these colors. For example, Eastman Kodak has successfully protected its trade dress of yellow, black, and red in court. As a rule, however, trade dress protection is granted only when consumers might be confused about what they are buying because of similar coloration of a competitor's packages.[11]

SMELL

Odors can stir emotions or create a calming feeling. They can invoke memories or relieve stress. Some of our responses to scents result from early associations that call up good or bad feelings, and that explains why businesses are exploring connections between smell, memory, and mood. For example, one study found that consumers who viewed ads for either flowers or chocolate and who also were exposed to flowery or chocolatey odors spent more time processing the product information and were more likely to try different alternatives within each product category.[12]

Fragrance is processed by the limbic system, the most primitive part of the brain and the place where immediate emotions are experienced. One study even found that the scent of fresh cinnamon buns induced sexual arousal in a sample of male medical students![13] At least to some extent consumers' reactions to odors depends on their cultural background: Vidal Sassoon products sold in Asia include a pine aroma that smells like floor cleaner to Americans.[14]

Smell is a direct line to feelings of happiness, hunger, and even memories of happy times. This explains why "plain" vanilla has of late become so widely used in scented products, from perfumes and colognes to cake frosting, coffees, and ice creams (e.g., Coty sold $25 million worth of its Vanilla Fields cologne spray in a four-month period). An industry executive explains that vanilla ". . . evokes memories of home and hearth, warmth and cuddling."[15]

Scented advertising (now a $90 million business) is taking new turns, as marketers are experimenting with scents such as cigarettes, pizza, beer, and vodka. A study by the market research department of the *New York Times* found that when choosing between two similar food or beverage products, 81 percent of consumers would choose one they could both smell and see over one they could only see. Samuel Adams beer was one of the first non-perfume products to be advertised with a scent strip that smelled of hops, and Rolls Royce distributed ads scented with the smell of leather.[16] However, a note of caution: This technique adds at least 10 percent to the cost of producing an ad, so marketers will need to watch their dollars and scents.[17]

SOUND

Music and sound are also important to marketers. Consumers buy millions of dollars' worth of sound recordings each year, advertising jingles maintain brand awareness, and background music creates desired moods.[18] Many aspects of sound may affect people's feelings and behaviors. Two areas of research that have widespread applications in consumer contexts are the effects of background music on mood and the influence of speaking rate on attitude change and message comprehension.

BACKGROUND TUNES: THE SOUND OF MUZAK

The Muzak Corporation estimates that its recordings are heard by 80 million people every day. This so-called "functional music" is played in stores, shopping malls, and offices to either relax or stimulate consumers. Research shows that workers tend to slow down during midmorning and midafternoon, so Muzak uses a system it calls "stimulus progression," in which the tempo increases during those slack times. Muzak has been linked to reductions in absenteeism among factory workers, and even the milk and egg output of cows and chickens is claimed to increase under its influence.[19]

This ad for Everlast sports apparel pokes fun at the proliferation of scented ads.

MARKETING OPPORTUNITY

Approximately 26 million Americans are deaf or have difficulty hearing. As marketers become more sensitive to the needs of this market segment, sign language in advertising is increasing. Anheuser-Busch, McDonald's, and American Airlines are using sign language in commercials. Advertisers feel this tactic delivers a double benefit: It meets the needs of a consumer group, and it breaks through the clutter of spoken ads—people tend to stop and watch the spot more carefully.

Most advocates for the deaf community are also pleased. As the director of the National Association of the Deaf commented, these ads help to show the general population that the deaf are "regular" consmers who buy products like everyone else. A commercial for Kellogg's Corn Flakes won an award from the National Easter Seal Society for its portrayal of a deaf woman, who uses sign language in her enthusiastic endorsement of the cereal.[20]

TIME COMPRESSION

Time compression is a technique used by broadcasters to manipulate perceptions of sound. It is a way to pack more information into a limited time by speeding up an announcer's voice in commercials. The speaking rate is typically accelerated to about 120 percent to 130 percent of normal. This effect is not detectable by most people; in fact, some tests indicate that consumers prefer a rate of transmission that is slightly faster than the normal speaking rate.[21]

Evidence for the effectiveness of time compression is mixed. It has been shown to increase persuasion in some situations and to reduce it in others. One explanation for a positive effect is that the listener uses a person's speaking rate to infer whether the speaker is confident; people seem to think that fast talkers must know what they are talking about.[22] Another, more plausible explanation is that the listener is given less time to elaborate in his or her mind on the assertions made in the commercial. The acceleration disrupts normal responses to the ad and changes the cues used to form judgments about its content. This change can either hinder or facilitate attitude change, depending on other conditions.[23]

TOUCH

Although relatively little research has been done on the effects of tactile stimulation on consumer behavior, common observation tells us that this sensory channel is important. Moods are stimulated or relaxed on the basis of sensations of the skin, whether from a luxurious massage or the bite of a winter wind. Touch has even been shown to be a factor in sales interactions. In one study, for example, diners who were touched by waitpeople gave bigger tips, and food demonstrators in a supermarket who lightly touched customers had better luck in getting shoppers to try a new snack product and to redeem coupons for the brand.[24]

People associate the textures of fabrics and other surfaces with product qualities. The perceived richness or quality of the material in clothing, bedding, or upholstery is linked to its "feel," whether rough or smooth, flexible or inflexible. A smooth fabric such as silk is equated with luxury, although denim is considered practical and durable. Some of these tactile/quality associations are summarized in Table 2–1. Fabrics that are composed of scarce materials or that require a high degree of processing to achieve their smoothness or fineness tend to be more expensive and thus are seen as being higher class. Similarly, lighter, more delicate textures are assumed

TABLE 2–1 ■ Tactile Oppositions in Fabrics

PERCEPTION	MALE	FEMALE	
High class	Wool	Silk	Fine
Low class	Denim	Cotton	↕
	Heavy ←——→	Light	Coarse

to be feminine. Roughness is often positively valued for men, and smoothness is sought by women.

TASTE

Our taste receptors obviously contribute to our experience of many products. Specialized companies called "flavor houses" keep busy trying to develop new concoctions to please the changing palates of consumers. For example, consumers' greater appreciation of different ethnic dishes has contributed to increased desires for spicy foods, so the quest for the ultimate pepper sauce is a hot taste trend. More than 50 stores in the United States now specialize in supplying fiery concoctions with names such as Sting and Linger, Hell in a Jar, and Religious Experience (comes in Original, Hot, and Wrath).[25]

Flavor houses also have been busy coping with demands for good-tasting foods that are also low in calories and fat. When the Quaker Oats Company decided to capitalize on this trend by buying a small rice cake manufacturer, consumers complained that the cakes tasted like styrofoam, and sales were disappointing. A flavor house was hired to develop a rice cake that tasted like buttered popcorn. This new taste was perfected along with several others, and industry-wide sales of rice cakes now exceed $100 million a year.[26]

Food companies go to great lengths to ensure that their products taste as they should. Consider, for example, the procedure used by Nabisco as it monitors the quality of its cookies. The company uses a group of "sensory panelists" as cookie tasters. These consumers are recruited because they have superior sensory abilities,

MARKETING PITFALL

The Clearly Canadian beverage company recently introduced Orbitz—a "texturally enhanced" drink with numerous "flavored gel spheres" floating in the bottle. The company spent more than a year developing the technology that would keep the edible jelly balls floating in the drink. The company learned from the mistake of a competitor, Mistic Brands: When Mistic launched a similar product called "Jumpin Gems," the balls settled on the bottom, and consumers thought the drink had just gone bad.

Clearly Canadian appears to face long odds of success. One industry consultant commented, "It's gross. It's like, when you drink a glass of milk, do you want to find lumps?" He adds, ". . . basically, people are taught not to drink things floating in their glass." But, the company is banking on the product's weirdness to appeal to rebellious teens. It points to the success of Goldschalger, a spicy liquor with real bits of gold floating in it, and to (some) consumers' affection for tequila brands featuring worms in the bottom of the bottle (which is taken as a sign of authenticity). Some drinks sold in Southeast Asia feature bursting malt balls or chunks of fruit, but only time will tell if Western consumers will prefer to chew rather than sip their drinks.[27]

and they are then given six months of training. In a *blind taste test,* the panelists rate the products of Nabisco and its competitors (the specific types and brands being tested are kept secret) on a number of features. These include "rate of melt," "fracturability and density," "molar packing" (the amount of cookie that sticks to the teeth), and the "notes" of the cookie, such as sweetness, saltiness, or bitterness. A typical evaluation session takes the group eight hours to rate just one sample of cookies.[28]

EXPOSURE

Exposure is the degree to which people notice a stimulus that is within range of their sensory receptors. Consumers concentrate on some stimuli, are unaware of others, and even go out of their way to ignore some messages. An experiment by a Minneapolis bank illustrates consumers' tendencies to miss or ignore information in which they are not interested. After a state law was passed that required banks to explain details about money transfer in electronic banking, the Northwestern National Bank distributed a pamphlet to 120,000 of its customers at considerable cost to provide the required information, which was hardly exciting bedtime reading. In 100 of the mailings, a section in the middle of the pamphlet offered the reader $10.00 just for finding that paragraph. Not a single person claimed the reward.[29] Before we consider what people may *choose* not to perceive, let's consider what they are capable of perceiving.

SENSORY THRESHOLDS

If you have ever blown a dog whistle and watched pets respond to a sound you cannot hear, you know that there are some stimuli that people simply are not capable of perceiving. Of course, some people are better able to pick up sensory information than are others, whose sensory channels may be impaired by disabilities or age. The science that focuses on how the physical environment is integrated into our personal, subjective world is known as **psychophysics.**

THE ABSOLUTE THRESHOLD
When we define the lowest intensity of a stimulus that can be registered on a sensory channel, we speak of a *threshold* for that receptor. The **absolute threshold** refers to the minimum amount of stimulation that can be detected on a given sensory channel. The sound emitted by a dog whistle is too high to be detected by human ears, so this stimulus is beyond our auditory absolute threshold. The absolute threshold is an important consideration in designing marketing stimuli. A billboard might have the most entertaining copy ever written, but this genius is wasted if the print is too small for passing motorists to see it from the highway.

THE DIFFERENTIAL THRESHOLD
The **differential threshold** refers to the ability of a sensory system to detect changes or differences *between* two stimuli. The mimimum difference that can be detected between two stimuli is known as the **j.n.d.** (just noticeable difference).

    The issue of when and if a difference between two stimuli will be noticed by consumers is relevant to many marketing situations. Sometimes a marketer may want to ensure that a change is observed, as when merchandise is offered at a discount. In other situations, the fact that a change has been made may be downplayed, as in the case of price increases or when a product is downsized.

A consumer's ability to detect a difference between two stimuli is *relative*. A whispered conversation that might be unintelligible on a noisy street can suddenly become public and embarrassingly loud in a quiet library. It is the relative difference between the decibel level of the conversation and its surroundings, rather than the absolute loudness of the conversation itself, that determines whether the stimulus will register.

In the nineteenth century, a psychophysicist named Ernst Weber found that the amount of change that is necessary to be noticed is systematically related to the original intensity of the stimulus. The stronger the initial stimulus, the greater the change must be for it to be noticed. This relationship is known as **Weber's Law**, and is expressed in the following equation:

$$K = \frac{\Delta I}{I}$$

where

K = *a constant (this varies across the senses)*
ΔI = *the mimimal change in intensity of the stimulus required to produce a j.n.d.*
I = *the intensity of the stimulus where the change occurs*

For example, consider how Weber's Law might work with respect to a product that has had its price decreased for a special sale. A rule-of-thumb used by some retailers is that a markdown should be at least 20 percent for this price cut to make an impact on shoppers. If so, a pair of socks that retails for $10 should be put on sale for $8 (a

Campbell's soup has been gradually modifying its label for the last 125 years. In perhaps the most dramatic packaging change to date, Campbell's unveiled new cans in 1994 that feature a photograph of a bowl of soup in the center. Each can carries a label proclaiming "New look same great soup!"[1]
1. "Campbell Soups Up Its Old Label," *Sacramento Bee* (April 22, 1994): F1 (2).

$2 discount). However, a sports coat selling for $100 would not benefit from a "mere" $2 discount—it would have to be marked down to $80 to achieve the same impact.

Many companies choose to update their packages periodically, making small changes that will not necessarily be noticed at the time. When a product icon is updated, the manufacturer does not want people to lose their identification with a familiar symbol. A recent *corporate identity campaign*—in which a company tries to build a distinctive image for a line of products—illustrates the importance of phasing in an identity image by making incremental changes over time. When IBM sold its line of desktop printers, typewriters, and related supplies to an investment firm, the new company needed a new name and logo because the sales agreement stipulated that it would lose the rights to the IBM name in 1996.

The new company wanted consumers to simultaneously perceive its product line as being new but also connected with the more familiar IBM image. A new name, Lexmark International, was selected from an initial list of 200 candidates, and a four-stage timetable was developed to phase in the Lexmark name over the five-year period in which the new company was entitled to use the IBM logo. A corporate advertising image campaign, initiated to assist in the transition, included an ad asking consumers to "Imagine a brand-new company with more than 50 years of experience." The successive changes in the logo are shown in Figure 2–2.[30]

FIGURE 2–2 ■ **Evolution of the Lexmark Logo. The four stages illustrate the company's attempt to phase in the new identity by relying on the more familiar IBM image for as long as possible.**

SUBLIMINAL PERCEPTION

Most marketers are concerned with creating messages above consumers' thresholds so they will be noticed. Ironically, a good number of consumers appear to believe that many advertising messages are, in fact, designed to be perceived unconsciously, or *below* the threshold of recognition. Another word for threshold is *limen,* and stimuli that fall below the limen are termed *subliminal.* **Subliminal perception** occurs when the stimulus is below the level of the consumer's awareness.

Subliminal perception is a topic that has captivated the public for over 30 years, despite the fact that there is virtually *no proof* that this process has any effect on consumer behavior. A survey of American consumers found that almost two-thirds believe in the existence of subliminal advertising, and over one-half are convinced that this technique can get them to buy things they do not really want![31]

In fact, most examples of subliminal perception that have been "discovered" are not subliminal at all—they are quite visible. Remember, if you can see it or hear it, it is *not* subliminal, because the stimulus is above the level of conscious awareness! Nonetheless, the continuing controversy about subliminal persuasion has been important in shaping the public's beliefs about advertising and marketers' ability to manipulate consumers against their will.

SUBLIMINAL TECHNIQUES

Subliminal messages supposedly can be sent on both visual and aural channels. *Embeds* are tiny figures that are inserted into magazine advertising by using high-speed photography or airbrushing. These hidden figures, usually of a sexual nature, supposedly exert strong but unconscious influences on innocent readers. To date, the only real impact of this interest in hidden messages is to sell "exposés" written by a few authors, and to make some consumers (and students of consumer behavior) look a bit more closely at print ads—perhaps seeing whatever their imaginations lead them to see.

Many consumers also are fascinated by the possible effects of messages hidden on sound recordings. An attempt to capitalize on subliminal auditory perception techniques is found in the growing market for self-help cassettes. These tapes, which typically feature the sound of waves crashing or some other natural sound, supposedly contain subliminal messages to help the listener stop smoking, lose weight, gain confidence, and so on. Despite the rapid growth of this market, there is little evidence that subliminal stimuli transmitted on the auditory channel can bring about desired changes in behavior.[32]

Along with the interest in hidden self-help messages on recordings, some consumers have become concerned about rumors of satanic messages recorded backward on rock music selections. The popular press has devoted much attention to such stories, and state legislatures have considered bills requiring warning labels about these messages. These backward messages do indeed appear on some albums, including Led Zeppelin's classic song "Stairway to Heaven," which contains the lyric ". . . there's still time to change." When played in reverse, this phrase sounds like "so here's to my sweet Satan."

The novelty of such reversals might help to sell records, but the "evil" messages within have no effect.[33] Humans do not have a speech perception mechanism operating at an unconscious level that is capable of decoding a reversed signal. On the other hand, subtle acoustic messages such as "I am honest. I won't steal. Stealing is dishonest" are broadcast in more than 1,000 stores in the United States to prevent shoplifting and do appear to have some effect. Unlike subliminal perception, though, these messages are played at a (barely) audible level, using a technique known as

NOTHING ELSE IS A PEPSI

Ice cubes and liquids are a prime culprit for accusations of subliminal persuasion; critics often focus on ambiguous shapes in drinks that supposedly spell out words like S E X as evidence for the use of this technique. This Pepsi ad, while hardly subliminal, gently borrows from this "supposed" practice.

threshold messaging.[34] After a nine-month test period, theft losses in one six-store chain declined almost 40 percent, saving the company $600,000. Some evidence indicates, however, that these messages are effective only on individuals who are predisposed to suggestion. For example, someone who might be thinking about taking something on a dare but who feels guilty about it might be deterred, but these soft words will not sway a professional thief.[35]

DOES SUBLIMINAL PERCEPTION WORK? EVALUATING THE EVIDENCE

Some research by clinical psychologists suggests that people can be influenced by subliminal messages under very specific conditions, though it is doubtful that these techniques would be of much use in most marketing contexts. Effective messages must be very specifically tailored to individuals, rather than the mass messages required by advertising.[36] They should also be as close to the liminal threshold as possible. Other discouraging factors include the following issues.

- There are wide individual differences in threshold levels. In order for a message to avoid conscious detection by consumers who have a low threshold, it would have to be so weak that it would not reach those who have a high threshold.

- Advertisers lack control over consumers' distance and position from a screen. In a movie theater, for example, only a small portion of the audience would be in exactly the right seats to be exposed to a subliminal message.
- The viewer must be paying absolute attention to the stimulus. People watching a television program or a movie typically shift their attention periodically and might not even be looking when the stimulus is presented.
- Even if the desired effect is induced, it operates only at a very general level. For example, a message might increase a person's thirst, but not necessarily for a specific drink. Because basic drives are affected, marketers could find that after all the bother and expense of creating a subliminal message, demand for competitors' products increases as well!

Clearly, there are better ways to get our attention—let's see how.

ATTENTION

As you sit in a lecture, you might find your mind wandering (yes, even you!). One minute you are concentrating on the instructor's words, and in the next, you catch yourself daydreaming about the upcoming weekend. Suddenly, you tune back in as you hear your name being spoken. Fortunately, it's a false alarm—the professor has called on another "victim" who has the same name. But, she's got your attention now . . .

Attention refers to the extent to which processing activity is devoted to a particular stimulus. As you know from sitting through both interesting and less interesting lectures, this allocation can vary depending on both the characteristics of the stimulus (i.e., the lecture itself) and the recipient (i.e., your mental state at the time).

Although we live in an "information society," we can have too much of a good thing. Consumers often are in a state of *sensory overload,* exposed to far more information than they can or are willing to process. In our society, much of this bombardment comes from commercial sources, and the competition for our attention is increasing steadily. The average adult is exposed to about 3000 pieces of advertising information every single day.[37]

PERCEPTUAL SELECTION: BARRIERS TO RECEPTION OF MARKETING MESSAGES

Because the brain's capacity to process information is limited, consumers are very selective about what they pay attention to. The process of **perceptual selection** means that people attend to only a small portion of the stimuli to which they are exposed. Consumers practice a form of "psychic economy," picking and choosing among stimuli to avoid being overwhelmed. How do they choose? Both personal and stimulus factors help to decide.

PERSONAL SELECTION FACTORS

Experience, which is the result of acquiring and processing stimulation over time, is one factor that determines how much exposure to a particular stimulus a person accepts. *Perceptual filters* based on our past experiences influence what we decide to process.

Perceptual vigilance is one such factor. Consumers are more likely to be aware of stimuli that relate to their current needs. A consumer who rarely notices car ads will become very much aware of them when he or she is in the market for a new car. A newspaper ad for a fast-food restaurant that would otherwise go unnoticed becomes significant when one sneaks a glance at the paper in the middle of a five o'clock class.

The flip side of perceptual vigilance is **perceptual defense.** This means that people see what they want to see—and don't see what they don't want to see. If a stimulus is threatening to us in some way, we may not process it—or we distort its meaning so that it's more acceptable. For example, a heavy smoker may block out images of cancer-scarred lungs because these vivid reminders hit a bit too close to home.

Still another factor is **adaptation,** the degree to which consumers continue to notice a stimulus over time. The process of adaptation occurs when consumers no longer pay attention to a stimulus because it is so familiar. A consumer can become "habituated" and require increasingly stronger "doses" of a stimulus for it to be noticed. For example, a consumer *en route* to work might read a billboard message when it is first installed, but after a few days, it just becomes part of the passing scenery. Several factors can lead to adaptation:

- *Intensity:* Less-intense stimuli (e.g., soft sounds or dim colors) habituate because they have less sensory impact.
- *Duration:* Stimuli that require relatively lengthy exposure in order to be processed tend to habituate because they require a long attention span.
- *Discrimination:* Simple stimuli tend to habituate because they do not require attention to detail.
- *Exposure:* Frequently encountered stimuli tend to habituate as the rate of exposure increases.
- *Relevance:* Stimuli that are irrelevant or unimportant will habituate because they fail to attract attention.

STIMULUS SELECTION FACTORS

In addition to the receiver's "mind-set," characteristics of the stimulus itself play an important role in determining what gets noticed and what gets ignored. These factors need to be understood by marketers, who can apply them to their messages and packages to boost their chances of cutting through the clutter and commanding attention. In general, stimuli that differ from others around them are more likely to be noticed (remember Weber's Law). This *contrast* can be created in several ways:

- *Size:* The size of the stimulus itself in contrast to the competition helps to determine if it will command attention. Readership of a magazine ad increases in

MARKETING PITFALL

The advent of the VCR has allowed consumers armed with remote control fast-forward buttons to be much more selective about the television messages to which they are exposed. By "zipping," viewers fast-forward through commercials on recorded tapes of their favorite programs. A VCR marketed by Mitsubishi in Japan even distinguishes between the different types of TV signals used to broadcast programs and commercials and automatically pauses during ads so they are not recorded at all.[38]

How big an issue is "zipping" for marketers? The jury is still out on this question. In one survey, 69 percent of VCR owners said that they had increased their television viewing time, so overall exposure to commercials might actually be increased as people continue to purchase VCRs.[39] Still, widespread zipping has enhanced the need for advertising creativity, as interesting commercials do not get zipped as frequently. In addition, longer commercials and those that keep a static figure on the screen (such as a brand name or a logo) appear to counteract the effects of zipping.[40] In an effort to hold viewers' attention, NBC recently eliminated station breaks after the network's research showed that 15 to 25 percent of viewers switched channels during these times. NBC now features "value-added entertainment moments," such as a brief final scene from a show, trivia questions, bloopers, and so on, to discourage channel surfing or trips to the kitchen during program breaks.[41]

proportion to the size of the ad.[42] Drink sizes are even becoming a marketing tool, as companies scramble to eliminate anything "small" from their offerings. McDonald's offers only regular, large, and supersize drinks, and 7-Eleven boasts that it makes America's biggest drink, the 64-ounce double gulp. (Note: The idea that "more is better" is largely American. The chain's international stores don't sell this version, as the company feels that in Europe and Japan small is often interpreted as luxurious and precious rather than just less of a good thing!)[43]

- *Color:* As we've seen, color is a powerful way to draw attention to a product or to give it a distinct identity. For example, Black & Decker inaugurated a new line of tools, called DeWalt, targeted to the residential construction industry. The new line was colored yellow instead of black, which made them stand out against other "dull" tools.[44]

- *Position:* Not surprisingly, stimuli that are in places we're more likely to look stand a better chance of being noticed. That's why the competition is so heated among suppliers to have their products displayed in stores at eye level. In magazines, ads that are placed toward the front of the issue, preferably on the right-hand side, also win out in the race for readers' attention. (Hint: The next time you read a magazine, notice which pages you're more likely to spend time looking at).[45]

One recent study found that the noticeability of warning labels on alcoholic beverages was improved by placing the message on the front label in a horizontal position and by reducing surrounding clutter.[46] Another study that tracked consumers' eye movements as they scanned telephone directories also illustrates the importance of a message's position. Consumers scanned listings in alphabetical order, and they noticed 93 percent of quarter-page display ads but only 26 percent of plain listings. Their eyes were drawn to color ads first, and these were viewed longer than black-and-white ones. In addition, subjects spent 54 percent more time viewing ads for businesses they ended up choosing, which illustrates the influence of attention on subsequent product choice.[47]

- *Novelty:* Stimuli that appear in unexpected ways or places tend to grab our attention. Another solution has been to put ads in unconventional places, where there will be less competition for attention. These places include the backs of shopping carts, walls of tunnel, floors of sports stadiums, and even before movies.[48] More obscure places where advertisements can be found these days are public toilets,[49] gasoline pump handles, and on steps in the London

MULTICULTURAL DIMENSIONS

Familiar packages and product designs get our attention, but this strategy can backfire when imitators illegally exploit the recognition value of well-known brands. Federal surveys indicate that American annual losses due to product forgery are now $200 billion, and it's been estimated that 5 percent of the products sold worldwide are phony, as underground operations in countries such as South Korea, Vietnam, and Russia churn out fake versions of many products. A senior FBI official has called brand piracy "the crime of the 21st century."[50] Consider that Chinese compact-disk factories produced 3 million legitimate disks in 1994—and 70 million pirated ones, says the Recording Industry Association of America. The International Anticounterfeiting Coalition estimates that 70 percent of medicines sold in Third World countries are knockoffs. An attorney for Microsoft says, "We refer to some countries in Asia as one-disk markets. More than 99 percent of the software is illegitimate copies."[51]

Underground.[52] An executive at Campbell's Soup, commenting on the company's decision to place ads in church bulletins, noted, "We have to shake consumers up these days in order to make them take notice. . . . We have to hit them with our ads where they shop and play and on their way to work."[53] Some advertisers, including Clorox, McDonald's, and Quaker Oats, have even taken to printing part of their ads upside down to get the reader's attention.[54]

INTERPRETATION

Interpretation refers to the meaning that we assign to sensory stimuli. Just as people differ in terms of the stimuli that they perceive, the eventual assignment of meanings to these stimuli varies as well. Two people can see or hear the same event, but their interpretation of it can be as different as night and day depending on what they had expected the stimulus to be. For example, Vernor's ginger ale did poorly in a taste test against leading ginger ales. When the research team instead introduced it as a new type of soft drink with a tangier taste, it won handily. An executive noted, "People hated it because it didn't meet the preconceived expectations of what a ginger ale should be."[55]

Consumers assign meaning to stimuli based on the **schema,** or set of beliefs, to which the stimulus is assigned. In a process known as *priming,* certain properties of a stimulus typically will evoke a schema, which leads us to evaluate the stimulus in terms of other stimuli we have encountered that are believed to be similar. Identifying and evoking the correct schema is crucial to many marketing decisions, because this determines what criteria will be used to evaluate the product, package, or message. That helps to explain Gary's revulsion at the thought of warm milk. Similarly, when Toro introduced a lightweight snow thrower, it was named the "Snow Pup." Sales were disappointing because the word "pup" called up a schema that grouped small, cuddly things together—not the desirable attributes for a snow thrower. When the product was renamed the "Snow Master," sales went up markedly.[56]

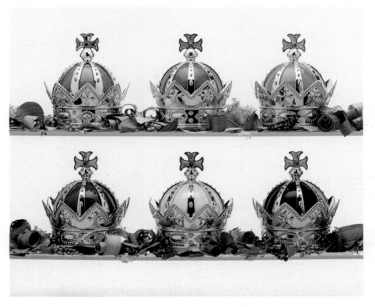

Crown Air Freshener's ". . . widespread popularity illustrates how a product can be interpreted differently by different consumers. American Auto Accessories of Corona, N.Y. sells more than 10 million a year, but the company is not sure why they appeal to diverse groups, ranging from urban cab drivers to Southern truckers. Some are bought by church deacons or cabbies who view them as a religious symbol. Others see the product as a symbol of gang membership and prostitution.. . ." From Michael A. Keating, "A Crowning and Mysterious Achievement", *American Demographics* (March 1995): 13.

STIMULUS ORGANIZATION

One factor that determines how a stimulus will be interpreted is its assumed relationship with other events, sensations, or images. When RJR Nabisco introduced a version of Teddy Grahams (a children's product) for adults, restrained packaging colors were used to reinforce the idea that the new product was for grown-ups but sales were disappointing. The box was then changed to a bright yellow to convey the idea that this was a fun snack, and buyers' more positive association between a bright primary color and taste led adults to start buying the cookies.[57]

Our brains tend to relate incoming sensations to others already in memory based on some fundamental organizational principles. These principles are based on *Gestalt psychology,* a school of thought that maintains that people derive meaning from the *totality* of a set of stimuli, rather than from any individual stimulus. The German word **gestalt** roughly means whole, pattern, or configuration, and this perspective is best summarized by the saying "the whole is greater than the sum of its parts." A piecemeal perspective that analyzes each component of the stimulus separately will be unable to capture the total effect. The gestalt perspective provides several principles relating to the way stimuli are organized

The **closure principle** states that people tend to perceive an incomplete picture as complete. That is, we tend to fill in the blanks based on our prior experience. This principle explains why most of us have no trouble reading a neon sign even if one or two of its letters are burned out or filling in the blanks in an incomplete message. The principle of closure is also at work when we hear only part of a jingle or theme. Utilization of the principle of closure in marketing strategies encourages audience participation, which increases the chance that people will attend to the message.

The **principle of similarity** tells us that consumers tend to group together objects that share similar physical characteristics. Green Giant

This ad for Colombian coffee illustrates Gestalt principles of perception, in which the individual parts (the colored circles) are seen as a whole (the familiar symbol used to promote Colombian coffee).

Obviously, an honor student.

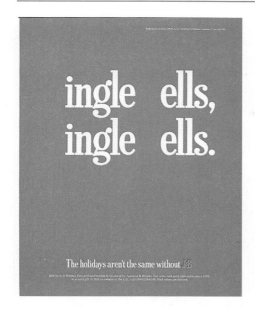

ingle ells,
ingle ells.

The holidays aren't the same without J&B

This J&B ad illustrates use of the principle of closure, in which people participate in the ad by mentally filling in the gaps.

relied on this principle when the company redesigned the packaging for its line of frozen vegetables. It created a "sea of green" look to unify all of its different offerings.

The **figure-ground principle** states that one part of a stimulus will dominate (the *figure*), while other parts recede into the background (the *ground*). This concept is easy to understand if one thinks literally of a photograph with a clear and sharply focused object (the figure) in the center. The figure is dominant, and the eye goes straight to it. The parts of the configuration that will be perceived as figure or ground can vary depending on the individual consumer as well as other factors. Similarly, in marketing messages that use the figure-ground principle, a stimulus can be made the focal point of the message or merely the context that surrounds the focus.

THE EYE OF THE BEHOLDER: INTERPRETATIONAL BIASES

The stimuli we perceive are often ambiguous—it's up to us to determine the meaning based on our past experiences, expectations, and needs. The process of "seeing what you want to see" was demonstrated in a classic experiment in which students at Princeton and Dartmouth viewed a movie of a particularly rough football game between the two schools. Although everyone was exposed to the same stimulus, the degree to which students saw infractions and the blame they assigned for those they did see, was quite different depending on which college they attended.[58]

As this experiment demonstrates, consumers tend to project their own desires or assumptions onto products and advertisements. This interpretation process can backfire for marketers, as occurred in these recent cases:

● A Detroit woman mistakenly packed a can of Anheuser-Busch's Bud Ice beer in her grandson's lunch, confusing it with a package of Hawaiian Punch. A Seattle mother thought the brew was a holiday-style can of Pepsi. Her daughter was on the losing end: She got hit with a five-day suspension for bringing beer to school.[59]

UNITED COLORS
OF BENETTON.

The subjective nature of perception is demonstrated by a controversial advertisement developed for Benetton by a French agency. Because a black man and a white man were handcuffed together, the ad was the target of many complaints about racism after it appeared in magazines and on billboards around the United States, even though the company has a reputation for promoting racial tolerance. People interpreted it to depict a black man who had been arrested by a white man; their prior assumptions distorted the ad's meaning.[1]
1. Kim Foltz, "Campaign on Harmony Backfires for Benetton," *The New York Times* (November 20, 1989): D8.

- When Ocean Spray introduced its Cranberry Juice Cocktail Refill in concentrated form, the new product came in an 8-ounce carton with a picture of the more familiar 48-ounce bottle on it. Many confused consumers thought the concentrate package was a single-serving juice carton, and many nasty surprises occurred until the company hastily added the word *refill* to the bottle.[60]

- In 1992, Planters Lifesavers Company introduced a vacuum-packed peanuts package called Planters Fresh Roast. The idea was to capitalize on consumers' growing love affair with fresh roast coffee by emphasizing the freshness of the nuts in the same way. A great idea—until irate supermarket managers began calling to ask who was going to pay to clean the peanut gook out of their stores' coffee grinding machines.[61]

Whatever you do, don't get them mixed up.

The bunny on the right is one of 12 Dung Buddies – lovable miniatures made with Zoo Doo fertilizer that dissolves in soil over time. But remember, they go in your garden, not in your mouth. **DUNG BUDDY**

People often use characteristics of a package to infer its contents. Sometimes, this strategy can backfire—as this ad for a fertilizer product called Dung Buddy reminds us. As the ad points out, ". . . they go in your garden, not in your mouth."

PERCEPTUAL POSITIONING

As we've seen, a product stimulus often is interpreted in light of what we already know about a product category and the characteristics of existing brands. Perceptions of a brand comprise both its functional attributes (e.g., its features, its price, and so on) and its symbolic attributes (its image, and what we think it says about us when we use it). We'll look more closely at issues such as brand image in later chapters, but for now it's important to keep in mind that our evaluation of a product typically is the result of what it *means* rather than what it *does*. This meaning—as perceived by consumers—constitutes the product's *market position,* and it

MARKETING PITFALL

Some European alcohol manufacturers are trying to tap a new generation of young drinkers by camouflaging their products as nonalcoholic and giving them names like Lemonhead and Mrs. Pucker's. Hooper's Hooch, a lemony alcoholic beverage from Bass PLC, is one of a dozen different brands known as "alcopops" recently launched in the United Kingdom. The drink's slogan is "One taste and you're Hooched," and it's being test marketed in the United States in lemonade, cola, and orange flavors. The sweet drinks contain 4 to 5.5 percent alcohol, and appeal to teenagers. In Britain, alcohol laws are looser than in the United States—those under 18 can't purchase an alcoholic drink, but they are allowed to consume one in certain restaurants and in their homes. Though industry executives maintain that the drinks are clearly labeled, critics argue that this strategy is a deliberate attempt to appeal to kids who grew up drinking Coke, Orangina, and other soft drinks.[62]

Not to be outdone, Stroh Brewery now is testing its new St. Ides Special Brew Freeze and Squeeze, an ice cold fruit-flavored malt liquor in five urban markets. The new drink is appearing in deli freezer bins, sporting colorful packages with logos that look like a line of nonalcoholic drinks called Crooked I juices and teas. The difference is that these drinks have the same alcohol content as a 40-ounce bottle of St. Ides malt liquor. Although the company maintains that it is the responsibility of retailers to keep the drink away from kids, one alcohol treatment expert describes the concoction as ". . . training wheels for the big stuff."[63]

FIGURE 2–3 ■ **HMV Perceptual Map**

How does a marketer determine where a product actually stands in the minds of consumers? One technique is to ask them what attributes are important to them, and how they feel competitors rate on these attributes. This information can be used to construct a perceptual map; a vivid way to paint a picture of where products or brands are "located" in consumers' minds. GRW Advertising created this perceptual map for HMV music stores, a British client that operates stores in large American cities. The agency wanted to know more about how its target market, frequent buyers of CDs, perceived the different stores they might patronize. GRW plotted perceptions of such attributes of competitors as selection, price, service, and hipness on an imaginary street map to show "the lay of the land." For example, Tower Records is located where Selection Street runs past Hip Highway and the High Awareness Interstate, while small independent stores are at a point where Local Taste Alley goes past Hip Highway and Customer Service Court. Based on this research, the firm determined that HMV's strengths were service, selection, and the stores' abilities to cater to local taste because store managers can order their own stock. This map was used in the strategic decision to specialize in music products as opposed to competing by offering other items sold by the competition, such as video games, fragrances, and computer CD-ROM's.

Source: Stuart Elliott, "Advertising: A Music Retailer Whistles a New Marketing Tune to Get Heard Above the Cacophony of Competitors," *The New York Times* (July 2, 1996): D7; personal communication, GRW Advertising, April 1997.

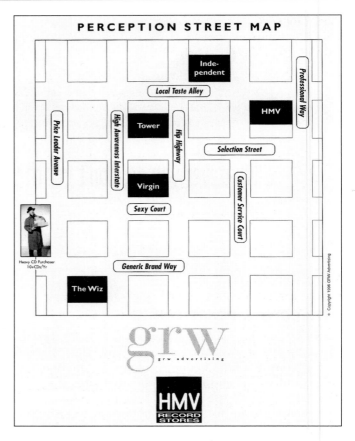

may have more to do with our expectations of product performance as communicated by its color, packaging, or styling than with the product itself. For example, when the background color on Barrelhead Sugar-Free Root Beer was changed from blue to beige, consumers said it tasted more like old-fashioned root beer served in a frosty mug.[64]

A **positioning strategy** is a fundamental part of a company's marketing efforts as it uses elements of the marketing mix (i.e., product design, price, distribution, and marketing communications) to influence the consumer's interpretation of its meaning. For example, although consumers' preference for the taste of one product over another are important, this functional attribute is only one component of product evaluation. Coca-Cola found this out the hard way when it committed its (in)famous New Coke marketing blunder in the 1980s. New Coke was preferred to Pepsi in blind taste tests (in which the products were not identified) by an average of 55 percent to 45 percent in 17 markets, yet New Coke ran into problems when it replaced the older version—consumers' impassioned protests and letter-writing campaigns eventually forced the company to bring back "Classic Coke." People do not buy a cola for taste alone; they are buying intangibles such as brand image as well.[65] Coca-Cola's unique position as part of an American, fun-loving lifestyle is based on years of marketing efforts that involve a lot more than taste alone.

POSITIONING DIMENSIONS

There are many dimensions that can be used to establish a brand's position in the marketplace. These include:[66]

- *Lifestyle:* Grey Poupon mustard is a "higher class" condiment.
- *Price leadership:* L'Oréal's Noisôme brand face cream is sold in upscale beauty shops, while its Plenitude brand is available for one-sixth the price in discount stores—even though both are based on the same chemical formula.[67]
- *Attributes:* Bounty paper towels are "the quicker picker upper."
- *Product class:* The Mazda Miata is a sporty convertible.
- *Competitors:* Northwestern insurance is "the quiet company."
- *Occasions:* Wrigley's gum is an alternative at times when smoking is not permitted.
- *Users:* Levi's Dockers are targeted primarily to men in their twenties to forties.
- *Quality:* At Ford, "Quality is Job 1."

REPOSITIONING

Repositioning occurs when a brand's original market position is modified. In some cases, a marketer may decide that a brand is competing too closely with another of its own products, so sales are being *cannibalized* (i.e., the two brands are taking sales away from each other, rather than from competing brands). This was the reason for the decision by Cadbury Beverages to reposition Crush, an orange soda. The brand was targeted to the teen market when it was acquired from Proctor & Gamble. However, Cadbury already marketed Sunkist to this segment, so it is taking steps to move Crush toward an all-family position.[68]

Another reason for repositioning crops up when too many competitors are stressing the same attribute. For example, promotional strategies in the airline industry focused on price advantages for several years, but then several airlines including American, TWA, and Virgin Atlantic began stressing comfort instead.[69]

Finally, repositioning can occur when the original market evaporates or is unreceptive to the offering. *Details* magazine was initially launched as an "underground nightlife magazine," but was relaunched as a fashion and lifestyle magazine for twentysomething males. Formerly criticized for being too raw and bold, it now strives to be more sophisticated so that advertisers wishing to reach younger males will encounter a more conducive environment in which to place their advertising.[70]

- Perception is the process by which physical sensations such as sights, sounds, and smells are selected, organized, and interpreted. The eventual interpretation of a stimulus allows it to be assigned meaning. A **perceptual map** is a widely used marketing tool that evaluates the relative standing of competing brands along relevant dimensions.
- Marketing stimuli have important sensory qualities. We rely on colors, odors, sounds, tastes, and even the "feel" of products when forming evaluations of them.

CHAPTER SUMMARY

- Not all sensations successfully make their way through the perceptual process. Many stimuli compete for our attention, and the majority are not noticed or accurately comprehended.

- People have different thresholds of perception. A stimulus must be presented at a certain level of intensity before it can be detected by sensory receptors. In addition, a consumer's ability to detect whether two stimuli are different (the differential threshold) is an important issue in many marketing contexts, such as changing a package design, altering the size of a product, or reducing its price.

- A lot of controversy has been sparked by so-called subliminal persuasion and related techniques, by which people are exposed to visual and aural messages below the threshold. Although evidence that subliminal persuasion is effective is virtually nonexistent, many consumers continue to believe that advertisers use this technique.

- Some of the factors that determine which stimuli (above the threshold level) do get perceived are the amount of exposure to the stimulus, how much attention it generates, and how it is interpreted. In an increasingly crowded stimulus environment, advertising clutter occurs when too many marketing-related messages compete for attention.

- A stimulus that is attended to is not perceived in isolation. It is classified and organized according to principles of perceptual organization. These principles are guided by a *gestalt,* or overall pattern. Specific grouping principles include closure, similarity, and figure-ground relationships.

- The final step in the process of perception is interpretation. Symbols help us make sense of the world by providing us with an interpretation of a stimulus that is often shared by others. The degree to which the symbolism is consistent with our previous experience affects the meaning we assign to related objects.

KEY TERMS

Absolute threshold p. 51	Hedonic consumption p. 45	Principle of similarity p. 60
Adaptation p. 57	Interpretation p. 59	Psychophysics p. 51
Attention p. 56	j.n.d. p. 51	Repositioning p. 65
Closure principle p. 60	Perception p. 43	Schema p. 59
Differential threshold p. 51	Perceptual defense p. 57	Sensation p. 43
Exposure p. 51	Perceptual map p. 64	Subliminal perception p. 54
Figure-ground principle p. 61	Perceptual selection p. 56	Weber's Law p. 52
Gestalt p. 60	Perceptual vigilance p. 56	
	Positioning strategy p. 63	

CONSUMER BEHAVIOR CHALLENGE

1. Many studies have shown that our sensory detection abilities decline as we grow older. Discuss the implications of the absolute threshold for marketers attempting to appeal to the elderly.

2. Interview three to five male and three to five female friends about their perceptions of both men's and women's fragrances. Construct a perceptual map for each set of products. Based on your map of perfumes, do you see any areas that are not adequately served by current offerings? What (if any) gender differences did you obtain regarding both the relevant dimensions used by raters and the placement of specific brands along these dimensions?

3. Assuming that some forms of subliminal persuasion may have the desired effect of influencing consumers, do you think the use of these techniques is ethical? Explain your answer.

4. Assume that you are a consultant for a marketer who wants to design a package for a new premium chocolate bar targeted to an affluent market. What recommendations would you provide in terms of such package elements as color, symbolism, and graphic design? Give the reasons for your suggestions.

5. Do you believe that marketers have the right to use any or all public spaces to deliver product messages? Where would you draw the line in terms of places and products that should be restricted?

6. Using magazines archived in the library, track the packaging of a specific brand over time. Find an example of gradual changes in package design that may have been below the j.n.d.

7. Collect a set of current ads for one type of product (e.g., personal computers, perfumes, laundry detergents, or athletic shoes) from magazines, and analyze the colors employed. Describe the images conveyed by different colors, and try to identify any consistency across brands in terms of the colors used in product packaging or other aspects of the ads.

8. Look through a current magazine and select one ad that captures your attention over the others. Give the reasons.

9. Find ads that utilize the techniques of contrast and novelty. Give your opinion of the effectiveness of each ad and whether the technique is likely to be appropriate for the consumers targeted by the ad.

NOTES

1. Company information accessed from http://www.albury.net.au/~habs/whatsnew.html, August 18, 1997; cf. also Marc E. Babej, "How About a Nice Box of Warm Milk," *Forbes* (August 29, 1994): 86; John Tagliabue, "Unchilled Milk: Not Cool Yet," *New York Times,* Prentice Hall Edition (June 10, 1995): 10.

2. Elizabeth C. Hirschman and Morris B. Holbrook,"Hedonic Consumption: Emerging Concepts, Methods, and Propositions," *Journal of Marketing* 46 (Summer 1982): 92–101.

3. Glenn Collins, "Owens-Corning's Blurred Identity," *New York Times* (August 19, 1994): D4.

4. Leah Haran, "Madison Avenue Visits Dream Land," *Advertising Age* (March 16, 1996): 12.

5. Mark G. Frank and Thomas Gilovich, "The Dark Side of Self- and Social Perception: Black Uniforms and Aggression in Professional Sports," *Journal of Personality and Social Psychology* 54 (1988)1: 74–85.

6. Joseph Bellizzi and Robert E. Hite, "Environmental Color, Consumer Feelings, and Purchase Likelihood," *Psychology & Marketing* 9 (1992): 347–63; Ayn E. Crowley, "The Two-Dimensional Impact of Color on Shopping," *Marketing Letters,* in press; Gerald J. Gorn, Amitava Chattopadhyay, and Tracey Yi, "Effects of Color as an Executional Cue in an Ad: It's in the Shade" (unpublished manuscript, University of British Columbia, 1994).

7. Wendy Bounds, "Mood is Indigo for Many Food Marketers," *Wall Street Journal* (September 23, 1993): B2.

8. Paulette Thomas, "Cosmetics Makers Offer World's Women an All-American Look with Local Twists," *Wall Street Journal* (May 8, 1995): B1 (2 pp.).

9. Dianne Solis, "Cost No Object for Mexico's Makeup Junkies," *Wall Street Journal* (June 7, 1994): B1.

10. "Ny emballage og nyt navn fordoblede salget," *Markedsføring* 12 (1992): 24. Adapted from Michael R. Solomon, Gary Bamossy, and Soren Askegaard, *Consumer Behavior: A European Perspective* (London: Prentice Hall International, 1998).

11. Meg Rosen and Frank Alpert, "Protecting Your Business Image: The Supreme Court Rules on Trade Dress," *Journal of Consumer Marketing* 11 (1994)1: 50–5.

12. Deborah J. Mitchell, Barbara E. Kahn, and Susan C. Knasko, "There's Something in the Air: Effects of Congruent or Incongruent Ambient Odor on Consumer Decision Making," *Journal of Consumer Research* 22 (September 1995): 229–38; for a review of olfactory cues in store environments, see also Eric R. Spangenberg, Ayn E. Crowley, and Pamela W. Henderson, "Improving the Store Environment: Do Olfactory Cues Affect Evaluations and Behaviors?" *Journal of Marketing* 60 (April 1996): 67–80.

13. Maxine Wilkie, "Scent of a Market," *American Demographics* (August 1995): 40–9.

14. Paulette Thomas, "Cosmetics Makers Offer World's Women an All-American Look with Local Twists," *Wall Street Journal* (May 8, 1995): B1 (2 pp.).

15. Quoted in Glenn Collins, "Everything's Coming up Vanilla," *New York Times* (June 10, 1994): D1 (2 pp.).

16. Anthony Ramirez, "Advertising: Bored to the Gills with Trendy New Beers? How Does a Scratch-and-Sniff Magazine Campaign Sound?" *New York Times* (October 31, 1994): D7.

17. Tamar Cherry, "Advertising: New Scented Ads Promise Magazine Readers Aromas Mimicking Toothpaste and Leather," *New York Times* (July 9, 1996): D2.

18. Gail Tom, "Marketing with Music," *Journal of Consumer Marketing* 7 (Spring 1990): 49–53; J. Vail, "Music as a Marketing Tool," *Advertising Age* (November 4, 1985): 24.

19. Otto Friedrich, "Trapped in a Musical Elevator," *Time* (December 10, 1984): 3.

20. Kevin Goldman, "More Advertisers Listen to Sign Language," *Wall Street Journal* (November 10, 1993): B8.

21. James MacLachlan and Michael H. Siegel, "Reducing the Costs of Television Commercials by Use of Time Compression," *Journal of Marketing Research* 17 (February 1980): 52–7.

22. James MacLachlan, "Listener Perception of Time Compressed Spokespersons," *Journal of Advertising Research* 2 (April/May 1982): 47–51.

23. Danny L. Moore, Douglas Hausknecht, and Kanchana Thamodaran, "Time Compression, Response Opportunity, and Persuasion," *Journal of Consumer Research* 13 (June 1986): 85–99.

24. Jacob Hornik, "Tactile Stimulation and Consumer Response," *Journal of Consumer Research* 19 (December 1992): 449–458.

25. Becky Gaylord, "Bland Food Isn't so Bad—It Hurts Just to Think about this Stuff," *Wall Street Journal* (April 21, 1995): B1.

26. Eben Shapiro, "The People Who Are Putting Taste Back on the Table," *New York Times* (July 22, 1990): F5.

27. Robert Frank, "Yum! It's a Bottle of Soda Filled with Big Lumps of Slippery Jelly," *Wall Street Journal* (May 16, 1996): B1.

28. Judann Dagnoli, "Cookie Tasters Chip in for Nabisco," *Advertising Age* (August 21, 1989): 58.

29. "$10 Sure Thing," *Time* (August 4, 1980): 51.

30. Stuart Elliott, "Another Remarkable Story of the Brand-Name Lexicon," *New York Times* (August 13, 1992)

31. Michael Lev, "No Hidden Meaning Here: Survey Sees Subliminal Ads," *New York Times* (May 3, 1991): D7.

32. Philip M. Merikle, "Subliminal Auditory Messages: An Evaluation," *Psychology & Marketing* 5 (1988)4: 355–72.

33. Timothy E. Moore, "The Case against Subliminal Manipulation," *Psychology & Marketing* 5 (Winter 1988): 297–316.

34. Sid C. Dudley, "Subliminal Advertising: What Is the Controversy About?" *Akron Business and Economic Review* 18 (Summer 1987): 6–18; "Subliminal Messages: Subtle Crime Stoppers," *Chain Store Age Executive* (July 1987)2: 85; "Mind Benders," *Money* (September 1978): 24.

35. Timothy E. Moore, "The Case against Subliminal Manipulation," *Psychology & Marketing* 5 (Winter 1988): 297–316.

36. Joel Saegert, "Why Marketing Should Quit Giving Subliminal Advertising the Benefit of the Doubt," *Psychology & Marketing* 4 (Summer 1987): 107–20. See also Dennis L. Rosen and Surendra N. Singh, "An Investigation of Subliminal Embed Effect on Multiple Measures of Advertising Effectiveness," *Psychology & Marketing* 9 (March/April 1992): 157–73; for a more recent review see Kathryn T. Theus, "Subliminal Advertising and the Psychology of Processing Unconscious Stimuli: A Review of Research," *Psychology & Marketing* (May/June 1994): 271–90.

37. James B. Twitchell, *Adcult USA: The Triumph of Advertising in American Culture,* New York: Columbia University Press, 1996.

38. David Kilburn, "Japanese VCR Edits out the Ads," *Advertising Age* (August 20, 1990): 16.

39. Kate Lewin, "Getting around Commercial Avoidance," *Marketing and Media Decisions* (December 1988)4: 116.

40. Craig Reiss, "Fast-Forward Ads Deliver," *Advertising Age* (October 27, 1986)2: 3; Steve Sternberg, "VCRs: Impact and Implications," *Marketing and Media Decisions* 22 (December 1987)5: 100.

41. Bill Carter, "NBC Cancels the Pause between Shows," *New York Times* (October 3, 1994): D6.

42. Roger Barton, *Advertising Media* (New York: McGraw-Hill, 1964).

43. Cynthia Crossen, "Case of the Vanishing Medium: Perpetrator is Large," *Wall Street Journal* (February 26, 1996): B1, B8.

44. Suzanne Oliver, "New Personality," *Forbes* (August 15, 1994): 114.

45. Adam Finn, "Print Ad Recognition Readership Scores: An Information Processing Perspective," *Journal of Marketing Research* 25 (May 1988): 168–77.

46. J. Craig Andrews and Richard G. Netemeyer, "Alcohol Warning Label Effects: Socialization, Addiction, and Public Policy Issues," in ed. Ronald P. Hill, *Marketing and Consumer Research in the Public Interest* (Thousand Oaks, CA: Sage, 1996): 153–75.

47. Gerald L. Lohse, "Consumer Eye Movement Patterns on Yellow Pages Advertising," *Journal of Advertising* XXVI, 1 (Spring 1997): 61–73.

48. Michael R. Solomon and Basil G. Englis (Fall 1994), "Reality Engineering: Blurring the Boundaries Between Marketing and Popular Culture," *Journal of Current Issues and Research in Advertising,* 16 (Fall) 2: 1–18.

49. "Toilet Ads," *Marketing* (December 5, 1996): 11.

50. Quoted in David Stipp, "Farewell, My Logo," *Fortune* (May 27, 1996): 128–40, p. 130.

51. Quoted in Stipp, "Farewell, My Logo," p. 135.

52. "Rare Media Well Done," *Marketing* (January 16, 1997): 31.

53. Quoted in Kim Foltz, *New York Times* (October 23, 1989): D11.

54. Stuart Elliott, "When Up Is Down, Does It Sell?" *New York Times* (February 21, 1992)2: D1.

55. Quoted in Tim Davis, "Taste Tests: Are the Blind Leading the Blind?" *Beverage World* (April 1987) 3: 44.

56. Tom et al., "Cueing the Consumer."

57. Anthony Ramirez, "Lessons in the Cracker Market: Nabisco Saved New Graham Snack," *New York Times* (July 5, 1990): D1.

58. Albert H. Hastorf and Hadley Cantril, "They Saw a Game: A Case Study," *Journal of Abnormal and Social Psychology* 49 (1954): 129–34.; see also Roberto Friedmann and Mary R. Zimmer, "The Role of Psychological

Meaning in Advertising," *Journal of Advertising* 17 (1988)1: 31–40.

59. Gannett News Service, "Grandmother Packs Lunch with 'Punch'," *Montgomery Advertiser* (March 28, 1996): 2A.

60. Thomas Hine, "Why We Buy: The Silent Persuasion of Boxes, Bottles, Cans, and Tubes," *Worth* (May 1995): 78–83.

61. Robert M. McMath, "Chock Full of (Pea)nuts," *American Demographics* (April 1997): 60.

62. Tara Parker-Pope, "Spiked Sodas, an Illicit Hit with Kids in U.K., Head for U.S.," *Wall Street Journal* (February 12, 1996): B1.

63. David M. Halbfinger, "Icy, Fruity Malt Liquor Lures Minors, Critics Say," *New York Times* (July 24, 1997): B1, B6, quoted on B1.

64. Ronald Alsop, "Color Grows More Important in Catching Consumers' Eyes," *Wall Street Journal* (November 29, 1984): 37.

65. See Tim Davis, "Taste Tests: Are the Blind Leading the Blind?" *Beverage World* (April 1987)3: 43–44.

66. Adapted from Michael R. Solomon and Elnora W. Stuart, *Marketing: Real People, Real Choices* (Upper Saddle River, NJ: Prentice Hall, 1997).

67. William Echikson, "Aiming at High and Low Markets," *Fortune* (March 22, 1993): 89.

68. Patricia Winters, "Cadbury Puts Crush Back on TV," *Advertising Age* (February 25, 1991): 16.

69. Adam Bryant, "Competition is Shifting from Fares to Chairs," *New York Times* (March 26, 1993): D15.

70. Scott Donaton, "Magazine of the Year," *Advertising Age* (March 1, 1993): S1 (3 pp.).

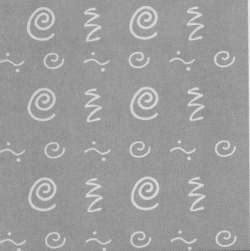

IT'S SATURDAY NIGHT, AND Joe is stylin'! As he saunters into the Club Velvet in Minneapolis, all heads turn to check out his swanky wing-tip shoes, narrow tie, and sharkskin suit—particularly that woman in the corner wearing the red suit with padded shoulders and those elegant white elbow-length gloves. Joe is glad to hear the soothing sounds of Vic Damone crooning on the jukebox and to see the old bubble machine working overtime. He slides onto a bar stool, and without even asking, good ol' Ron the bartender slips him his usual: a dry martini in a highball glass and a smuggled Cuban cigar. As Joe settles in for the evening, he has fond memories of last year when he celebrated his 21st birthday the very same way. This year looks like it'll be even smoother. . . .

3

Learning
and Memory

THE LEARNING PROCESS

In the last couple of years, Lounge Culture became a craze in many urban areas. A nostalgia craze, partly fueled by the movie *Swingers,* sent young people yearning for the simpler times of the 1950s flocking to bars like the Lava Lounge in Los Angeles, Bimbo's in San Francisco, the Electrolush Lounge in Vancouver, and 999999s in New York City (as in "dressed to the . . ."). Retro groups like Combustible Edison became big, and easy-listening hits like Esquivel's "Space-Age Bachelor Pad Music" racked up sales. Bubble machines. The mambo. Tiki bars. Big fat stogies. Denizens of Lounge Culture patterned their behavior after that of stars such as George Peppard in *Breakfast at Tiffany's* and Ursula Andress in *The Tenth Victim* as they aimed to be "swank," a campy version of stylish. There are even new men's magazines, like *Kutie* and *Hollywood Highball,* turning up to cater to this retro crowd.[1] As one young aficionado observed, "Life is very difficult today in many ways, especially sexually. The list of noes is huge. . . . That's why a lot of this has to do with the formality of another time."[2]

Joe learned how to be "swank" mostly by observing others and by absorbing images he sees in old movies. When he patterns his choices of drinks, clothes, and music after what he has seen, he is rewarded by the approval of others who share his tastes. In this chapter, we'll explore how learned associations among feelings, events, and products is an important aspect of consumer behavior.

Learning refers to a relatively permanent change in behavior that is caused by experience. The learner need not have the experience directly; we can also learn by observing events that affect others.[3] We learn even when we are not trying: Consumers recognize many brand names and can hum many product jingles, for example, even for products they themselves do not use. This casual, unintentional acquisition of knowledge is known as *incidental learning.*

Learning is an ongoing process. Our knowledge about the world is being revised constantly as we are exposed to new stimuli and receive ongoing feedback that allows us to modify our behavior when we find ourselves in similar situations at a later time. The concept of learning covers a lot of ground, ranging from a consumer's simple association between a stimulus such as a product logo (e.g., Coca-Cola) and a response (e.g., "refreshing soft drink") to a complex series of cognitive activities (e.g., writing an essay on learning for a consumer behavior exam). Psychologists who study learning have advanced several theories to explain the learning process. These theories range from those focusing on simple stimulus-response connections (*behavioral theories*) to perspectives that regard consumers as complex problem solvers who learn abstract rules and concepts by observing others (*cognitive theories*). Understanding these theories is important to marketers as well, because basic learning principles are at the heart of many consumer purchase decisions.

BEHAVIORAL LEARNING THEORIES

Behavioral learning theories assume that learning takes place as the result of responses to external events. Psychologists who subscribe to this viewpoint do not focus on internal thought processes. Instead, they approach the mind as a "black box" and emphasize the observable aspects of behavior, as depicted in Figure 3–1. The observable aspects consist of things that go into the box (the *stimuli,* or events perceived from the outside world) and things that come out of the box (the *responses,* or reactions to these stimuli).

This view is represented by two major approaches to learning: classical conditioning and instrumental conditioning. According to this perspective, people's experiences are shaped by the feedback they receive as they go through life. Similarly, consumers respond to brand names, scents, jingles, and other marketing stimuli, based on the learned connections they have formed over time. People also learn that actions they take result in rewards and punishments, and this feedback influences the way they will respond in similar situations in the future. Consumers who receive compliments on a product choice will be more likely to buy that brand again, but those who get food poisoning at a new restaurant will not be likely to patronize it in the future.

CLASSICAL CONDITIONING

Classical conditioning occurs when a stimulus that elicits a response is paired with another stimulus that initially does not elicit a response on its own. Over time, this second stimulus causes a similar response because it is associated with the first stimulus. This phenomenon was first demonstrated in dogs by Ivan Pavlov, a Russian physiologist doing research on digestion in animals.

Pavlov induced classically conditioned learning by pairing a neutral stimulus (a bell) with a stimulus known to cause a salivation response in dogs (he squirted dried meat powder into their mouths). The powder was an *unconditioned stimulus* (UCS) because it was naturally capable of causing the response. Over time, the bell became a *conditioned stimulus* (CS); it did not initially cause salivation, but the dogs learned to associate the bell with the meat powder and began to salivate at the

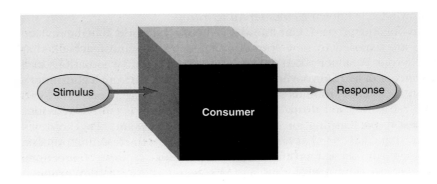

FIGURE 3–1 ■ The Consumer as a "Black Box": A Behaviorist Perspective on Learning

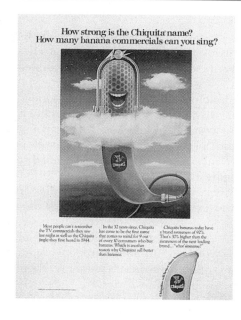

How strong is the Chiquita name?
How many banana commercials can you sing?

Most people can't remember the TV commercials they saw last night as well as the Chiquita jingle they first heard in 1944.

In the 32 years since, Chiquita has come to be the first name that comes to mind for 9 out of every 10 consumers who buy bananas. Which is another reason why Chiquitas sell better than bananas.

Chiquita bananas today have a brand awareness of 92%. That's 30% higher than the awareness of the next leading brand..."what's its name?"

Many classic advertising campaigns consist of product slogans that have been repeated so many times that they are etched in consumers' minds. The ad shown here brags about the high awareness of the Chiquita banana® jingle ("I'm Chiquita banana®, and I'm here to say. . . .")

sound of the bell only. The drooling of these canine consumers over a sound, now linked to feeding time, was a *conditioned response* (CR).

This basic form of classical conditioning demonstrated by Pavlov primarily applies to responses controlled by the autonomic (e.g., salivation) and nervous (e.g., eye blink) systems. That is, it focuses on visual and olfactory cues that induce hunger, thirst, sexual arousal, and other basic drives. When these cues are consistently paired with conditioned stimuli such as brand names, consumers may learn to feel hungry, thirsty, or aroused when later exposed to the brand cues.

Classical conditioning can have similar effects for more complex reactions, too. Even a credit card becomes a conditioned cue that triggers greater spending, especially because it is a stimulus that is present only in situations in which consumers are spending money. People learn they can make larger purchases with credit cards, and they also have been found to leave larger tips than when paying by cash.[4] Small wonder that American Express reminds us, "Don't leave home without it."

REPETITION

Conditioning effects are more likely to occur after the (CS) conditioned and unconditioned (UCS) stimuli have been paired a number of times.[5] Repeated exposures increase the strength of stimulus-response associations and prevent the decay of these associations in memory.

Many classic advertising campaigns consist of product slogans that have been repeated so many times that they are etched in consumers' minds. Conditioning will not occur or will take longer if the CS is only occasionally paired with the UCS. One result of this lack of association may be *extinction,* which occurs when the effects of prior conditioning are reduced and finally disappear. This can occur, for example, when a product is overexposed in the marketplace so that its original allure is lost. The Izod Lacoste polo shirt, with its distinctive crocodile crest, is a good example of this effect—when the once-exclusive crocodile started to appear on baby clothes and many other items, it lost its cachet and was successfully challenged as a symbol of casual elegance by other contenders, such as the Ralph Lauren polo player.[6]

STIMULUS GENERALIZATION

Stimulus generalization refers to the tendency of stimuli similar to a CS to evoke similar, conditioned responses. For example, Pavlov noticed in subsequent studies that his dogs would sometimes salivate when they heard noises that only resembled a bell, such as keys jangling.

People also react to other, similar stimuli in much the same way they responded to the original stimulus. A drugstore's bottle of private brand mouthwash deliberately packaged to resemble Listerine mouthwash may evoke a similar response among consumers, who assume that this "me too" product shares other characteristics of the original. Indeed, consumers in one study on shampoo brands tended to rate those with similar packages as similar in quality and performance as well.[7]

This "piggybacking" strategy can cut both ways: When the quality of the me-too product turns out to be lower than that of the original brand, consumers may exhibit even more positive feelings toward the original. However, if the quality of the two competitors is perceived to be about equal, consumers may conclude the price premium they are paying for the original is not worth it.[8] In addition, consumers' learned associations with a large corporation can influence what they believe about its products. The company's overall reputation has been shown to have a particularly strong impact on brand evaluations, and to a lesser extent its reputation for social responsibility can also affect these individual brand ratings.[9]

STIMULUS DISCRIMINATION

Stimulus discrimination occurs when a stimulus similar to a CS is *not* followed by a UCS. When this happens, reactions are weakened and will soon disappear. Part of the learning process involves making a response to some stimuli but not to other, similar stimuli. Manufacturers of well-established brands commonly urge consumers not to buy "cheap imitations," because the results will not be what they expect.

MARKETING APPLICATIONS OF BEHAVIORAL LEARNING PRINCIPLES

Many marketing strategies focus on the establishment of associations between stimuli and responses. Behavioral learning principles apply to many consumer phenomena, ranging from the creation of a distinctive brand image to the perceived linkage between a product and an underlying need.

The transfer of meaning from an unconditioned stimulus to a conditioned stimulus explains why "made-up" brand names like Marlboro, Coca-Cola, or IBM can exert such powerful effects on consumers. The association between the Marlboro Man and the cigarette is so strong that in some cases the company no longer even bothers to include the brand name in its ads. When nonsense syllables (meaningless sets of letters) are paired with such evaluative words as beauty or success, the meaning is transferred to the fake words. This change in the symbolic significance of initially meaningless words shows that even complex meanings can be conditioned by fairly simple associations.[10] These associations are crucial to many marketing strategies that rely on the creation and perpetuation of **brand equity,** where a brand has strong positive associations in a consumer's memory and commands a lot of loyalty as a result.[11] We'll be returning to the important concept of **brand loyalty** in the following chapters.

APPLICATIONS OF REPETITION

One advertising researcher argued that more than three exposures to a marketing communication are wasted. The first exposure creates awareness of the product, the second demonstrates its relevance to the consumer, and the third serves as a reminder of the product's benefits.[12] However, even this bare bones approach implies that repetition is needed to ensure that the consumer is actually exposed to (and processes) the message at least three times. As we saw in the last chapter, this exposure is by no means guaranteed because people tend to tune out or distort many marketing communications. Marketers attempting to condition an association must ensure that the consumers they have targeted will be exposed to the stimulus a sufficient number of times in order to make it "stick."

On the other hand, it is possible to have too much of a good thing: Consumers can become so used to hearing or seeing a marketing stimulus that they no longer pay attention to it. This problem, known as *advertising wearout,* can be alleviated by varying the way in which the basic message is presented. For example, the tax preparation firm of H&R Block is famous for its long-standing "Another of the seventeen reasons to use H&R Block . . ." campaign.

APPLICATIONS OF CONDITIONED PRODUCT ASSOCIATIONS

Advertisements often pair a product with a positive stimulus to create a desirable association. Various aspects of a marketing message, such as music, humor, or imagery, can affect conditioning. In one study, for example, subjects who viewed a slide of pens paired with either pleasant or unpleasant music were more likely to later select the pen that appeared with pleasant music.[13]

The *order* in which the conditioned stimulus and the unconditioned stimulus is presented can affect the likelihood that learning will occur. Generally speaking, the unconditioned stimulus should be presented prior to the conditioned stimulus. The technique of *backward conditioning,* such as showing a soft drink (the CS) and then playing a jingle (the UCS) is generally not effective.[14] Because sequential presentation is desirable for conditioning to occur, classical conditioning is not as effective in static situations, such as in magazine ads, in which (in contrast to TV or radio) the marketer cannot control the order in which the CS and the UCS are perceived.

Just as product associations can be formed, they can be *extinguished.* Because of the danger of extinction, a classical conditioning strategy may not be as effective for products that are frequently encountered, as there is no guarantee they will be accompanied by the CS. A bottle of Pepsi paired with the refreshing sound of a carbonated beverage being poured over ice may seem like a good application of conditioning. Unfortunately, the product would also be seen in many other contexts where this sound was absent, reducing the effectiveness of a conditioning strategy.

By the same reasoning, a novel tune should be chosen over a popular one to pair with a product, since the popular song might also be heard in many situations where the product is not present.[15] Music videos in particular may serve as effective UCSs because they often have an emotional impact on viewers, and this effect may transfer to ads accompanying the video.[16]

APPLICATIONS OF STIMULUS GENERALIZATION

The process of stimulus generalization is often central to branding and packaging decisions that attempt to capitalize on consumers' positive associations with an existing brand or company name, as illustrated by a hair-cutting establishment called United Hairlines.[17] In one 20-month period, Procter & Gamble introduced almost 90 new products. Not a single one carried a new brand name. In fact, roughly 80 percent of all new products are actually extensions of existing brands or product lines.[18] Strategies based on stimulus generalization include the following:

MARKETING OPPORTUNITY

The marketing value of an admired stimulus is clearly demonstrated at universities with winning sports teams, where loyal fans snap up merchandise from underwear to toilet seats emblazoned with the school's name—about $2.5 billion a year of college merchandise. This business did not even exist 20 years ago, when schools were reluctant to commercialize their images. Texas A&M was one of the first schools that even bothered to file for trademark protection, and that was only after someone put the Aggie logo on a line of handguns.

Today, it's a different story. Even little-known schools have become merchandising powerhouses, largely due to television exposure of their teams. It hasn't hurt that athletic gear has become part of the fashion landscape, and many people buy team-related merchandise to make a fashion statement rather than an athletic statement. In fact, the University of Michigan's "Fab Five" basketball players had a lot to do with turning long, baggy shorts into a chic item. All this fuss over sweatshirts, drink coasters, and trash cans is welcomed by many college administrators—universities collectively earn about $100 million per year in royalties.[19]

- *Family branding:* a variety of products capitalize on the reputation of a company name. Companies such as Campbell's, Heinz, and General Electric rely on their positive corporate images to sell different product lines.

- *Product line extensions:* related products are added to an established brand. Dole, which is associated with fruit, introduced refrigerated juices and juice bars, whereas Sun Maid went from raisins to raisin bread. Other recent extensions include Woolite rug cleaner, Cracker Jack gourmet popping corn, and Ivory shampoo.[20]

- *Licensing:* well-known names are "rented" by others. This strategy is increasing in popularity as marketers try to link their products and services with well-established figures—licensing has become so commonplace that even imprisoned cult leader Charles Manson received royalties on T-shirts bearing his likeness.[21]

Companies as diverse as McDonald's and Harley-Davidson have authorized the use of their names on products—even Spam lovers can buy underwear, earrings, and other items bearing the logo of the canned "meat product"![22] The movie *Jurassic Park* and its sequel *The Lost World* generated over $1 billion in licensed merchandise sales, with about 5,000 products crawling out of the primordial ooze and onto store shelves. The movie *Forrest Gump* inspired new products ranging from table tennis sets (inspired by his Ping-Pong championships) to shrimp from the Bubba Gump Seafood Company.[23] Japan Airlines licensed the rights to use Disney characters—in addition to painting Mickey Mouse and Donald Duck on several of its planes, the carrier is requiring its flight attendants to wear mouse ears on some domestic flights![24]

Another licensing phenomenon is "The X-Files" television show, which has inspired a cult following around the world. Warner Bros. Records released "Songs in the Key of X," featuring alternative artists such as Soul Coughing, Foo Fighters, Nick Cave, and R.E.M. X-Files fans can buy mouse pads, pinball games, upscale jewelry, and even a mug that reads "The truth is out there" until heat is applied—then it says "Trust no one."[25]

- *Look-alike packaging:* distinctive packaging designs create strong associations with a particular brand. As noted earlier, this linkage often is exploited by mak-

ers of generic or private label brands who wish to communicate a quality image by putting their products in very similar packages.[26]

APPLICATIONS OF STIMULUS DISCRIMINATION

An emphasis on communicating a product's distinctive attributes vis-à-vis its competitors is an important aspect of *positioning,* where consumers learn to differentiate a brand from its competitors (see chapter 2). This is not always an easy task, especially in product categories in which the brand names of many of the alternatives look and sound alike. For example, a recent survey showed that many consumers have a great deal of trouble distinguishing among products sold by the top computer manufacturers. With a blur of names like OmniPlex, OptiPlex, Premmia, Premium, ProLinea, ProLiant, etc., this confusion is not surprising.[27]

Companies with a well-established brand image try to encourage stimulus discrimination by promoting the unique attributes of their brand-hence the constant

MARKETING PITFALL

For a stimulus-response connection to be maintained, a new product must share some important characteristics with the original. Trouble can result if consumers do not make the connection between a brand and its extension. In fact, if attributes of the new products are inconsistent with the consumer's beliefs about the family brand, the overall image of the family brand runs the danger of being diluted.[28]

When Cadillac came out with the smaller Cadillac Cimarron, people who already owned Cadillacs did not regard the new model as a *bona fide* Cadillac. Arm & Hammer deodorant failed, possibly because consumers identified the product too strongly with something in the back of their refrigerators.[29] An extension even has the potential to weaken the parent brand, as the Carnation Company discovered. The company cancelled plans for "Lady Friskies," a contraceptive dog food, after tests indicated it would reduce sales of regular Friskies.[30]

reminders for American Express Traveler's Checks: "Ask for them by name. . . ." On the other hand, a brand name that is used so widely that it is no longer distinctive becomes part of the *public domain* and can be used by competitors, as has been the case for such products as aspirin, cellophane, the yo-yo, and the escalator.

INSTRUMENTAL CONDITIONING

Instrumental conditioning, also known as *operant conditioning,* occurs as the individual learns to perform behaviors that produce positive outcomes and to avoid those that yield negative outcomes. This learning process is most closely associated with the psychologist B. F. Skinner, who demonstrated the effects of instrumental conditioning by teaching pigeons and other animals to dance, play Ping-Pong, and so on by systematically rewarding them for desired behaviors.[31]

Whereas responses in classical conditioning are involuntary and fairly simple, those in instrumental conditioning are made deliberately to obtain a goal and may be more complex. The desired behavior may be learned over a period of time, as intermediate actions are rewarded in a process called *shaping.* For example, the owner of a new store may award prizes to shoppers just for coming in, hoping that over time they will continue to drop in and eventually even buy something.

Also, whereas classical conditioning involves the close pairing of two stimuli, instrumental learning occurs as a result of a reward received following the desired behavior. Learning takes place over a period of time, during which other behaviors are attempted and abandoned because they are not reinforced. A good way to remember the difference is to keep in mind that in instrumental learning, the response is performed because it is instrumental to gaining a reward or avoiding a punishment. Consumers over time come to associate with people who reward them and to choose products that make them feel good or satisfy some need.

HOW INSTRUMENTAL CONDITIONING OCCURS

Instrumental conditioning occurs in one of three ways. When the environment provides **positive reinforcement** in the form of a reward, the response is strengthened and appropriate behavior is learned. For example, a woman who gets compliments after wearing Obsession perfume will learn that using this product has the desired effect, and she will be more likely to keep buying the product. **Negative reinforcement** also strengthens responses so that appropriate behavior is learned. A perfume company might run an ad showing a woman sitting home alone on a Saturday night because she did not use its fragrance. The message to be conveyed is that she could have *avoided* this negative outcome if only she had used the perfume. In contrast to situations in which we learn to *do* certain things in order to avoid unpleasantness, **punishment** occurs when a response is followed by unpleasant events (such as being ridiculed by friends for wearing an offensive smelling perfume)—we learn the hard way *not* to repeat these behaviors.

To help in understanding the differences among these mechanisms, keep in mind that reactions from a person's environment to behavior can be either positive or negative, and that these outcomes or anticipated outcomes can be applied or removed. That is, under conditions of both positive reinforcement and punishment the person receives a reaction after doing something. In contrast, negative reinforcement occurs when a negative outcome is avoided—the removal of something negative is pleasurable and hence is rewarding.

Finally, when a positive outcome is no longer received, **extinction** is likely to occur and the learned stimulus-response connection will not be maintained (as when a woman no longer receives compliments on her perfume). Thus positive and negative reinforcement *strengthen* the future linkage between a response and an outcome because of the pleasant experience. This tie is *weakened* under conditions of both punishment and extinction because of the unpleasant experience. The relationships among these four conditions are easier to understand by referring to Figure 3–2.

An important factor in operant conditioning is the set of rules by which appropriate reinforcements are given for a behavior. The issue of what is the most effective *reinforcement schedule* to use is important to marketers, because it relates to the amount of effort and resources they must devote to rewarding consumers in order to condition desired behaviors. Several schedules are possible:

- *Fixed-interval reinforcement:* After a specified time period has passed, the first response that is made brings the reward. Under such conditions, people tend to respond slowly right after being reinforced, but their responses speed up as the time for the next reinforcement looms. For example, consumers may crowd into a store for the last day of its seasonal sale and not reappear until the next one.

- *Variable-interval reinforcement:* The time that must pass before reinforcement is delivered varies around some average. Because the person does not know exactly when to expect the reinforcement, responses must be performed at a consistent rate. This logic is behind retailers' use of so-called *secret shoppers*;

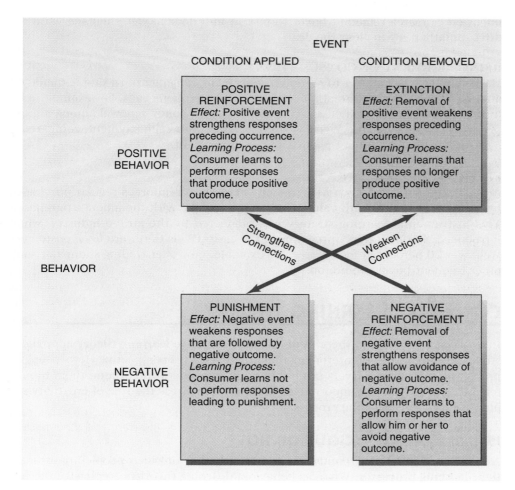

FIGURE 3–2 ■ Four Types of Learning Outcomes

people who periodically test for service quality by posing as a customer at unannounced times. Because store employees never know exactly when to expect a visit, high quality must be maintained constantly "just in case."

- *Fixed-ratio reinforcement:* Reinforcement occurs only after a fixed number of responses. This schedule motivates people to continue performing the same behavior over and over. For example, a consumer might keep buying groceries at the same store in order to earn a prize after collecting 50 books of trading stamps.

- *Variable-ratio reinforcement:* The person is reinforced after a certain number of responses, but he or she does not know how many responses are required. People in such situations tend to respond at very high and steady rates, and this type of behavior is very difficult to extinguish. This reinforcement schedule is responsible for consumers' attraction to slot machines. They learn that if they keep throwing money into the machine, they will eventually win something (if they don't go broke first).

APPLICATIONS OF INSTRUMENTAL CONDITIONING PRINCIPLES

Principles of instrumental conditioning are at work when a consumer is rewarded or punished for a purchase decision. Business people shape behavior by gradually reinforcing consumers for taking appropriate actions. For example, a car dealer might encourage a reluctant buyer to just sit in a floor model, then suggest a test drive, and then try to close the deal.

REINFORCEMENT OF CONSUMPTION

Marketers have many ways to reinforce consumers, ranging from a simple thank you after a purchase to substantial rebates and follow-up phone calls. For example, a life insurance company obtained a much higher rate of policy renewal among a group of new customers who received a thank you letter after each payment, compared to a control group that did not receive any reinforcement.[32]

FREQUENCY MARKETING

A popular technique known as **frequency marketing** reinforces regular purchasers by giving them prizes with values that increase along with the amount purchased. This instrumental learning strategy was pioneered by the airline industry, which introduced "frequent flyer" programs in the early 1980s to reward loyal customers. Well over 20 percent of food stores, for example, now offer trading stamps or some other frequent-buyer promotion.

COGNITIVE LEARNING THEORY

In contrast to behavioral theories of learning, **cognitive learning theory** approaches stress the importance of internal mental processes. This perspective views people as problem solvers who actively use information from the world around them to master their environment. Supporters of this view also stress the role of creativity and insight during the learning process.

IS LEARNING CONSCIOUS OR NOT?

A lot of controversy surrounds the issue of whether or when people are aware of their learning processes. Whereas behavioral learning theorists emphasize the routine, automatic nature of conditioning, proponents of **cognitive learning** argue that

MULTICULTURAL DIMENSIONS

A popular frequency marketing concept in Europe puts an interesting twist on reinforcement—customers actually pay for the privilege of belonging. These programs take the form of "value clubs," to which customers pay dues to receive benefits. The concept began in the 1980s and is particularly popular in Germany where strict regulations limit the use of discounts and other price promotions. Value clubs offer two classes of rewards: (1) "soft benefits," which include premiums such as T-shirts but also the use of travel services and other amenities, and (2) "hard benefits"—actual discounts on products. For example, the IKEA Family is a value club sponsored by the Swedish furniture retailer that offers a vacation home exchange service to its members in nine European countries. The value club concept is beginning to travel across the ocean: Volkswagen and Swatch have now set up American chapters, and more companies will likely follow their lead.[33]

The value club concept reinforces customers' choices. A membership card from the VW Club entitles the bearer to discounts on airfares, hotels, movie tickets, and ski packages.

even these simple effects are based on cognitive factors: Expectations are created that a stimulus will be followed by a response (the formation of expectations requires mental activity). According to this school of thought, conditioning occurs because subjects develop conscious hypotheses and then act on them.

On the one hand, there is some evidence for the existence of nonconscious procedural knowledge. People apparently do process at least some information in an automatic, passive way, which is a condition that has been termed *mindlessness*.[34] When we meet someone new or encounter a new product, for example, we have a tendency to respond to the stimulus in terms of existing categories we have learned, rather than taking the trouble to formulate new ones. Our reactions in these cases are activated by a *trigger feature*, some stimulus that cues us toward a particular pattern. For example, men in one study rated a car in an ad as superior on a variety of characteristics if a seductive woman (the trigger feature) was present, despite the fact that the men did not believe the woman's presence actually had an influence on their evaluations.[35]

Nonetheless, many modern theorists are beginning to regard some instances of automatic conditioning as cognitive processes, especially where expectations are formed about the linkages between stimuli and responses. Indeed, studies using *masking effects,* which make it difficult for subjects to learn CS/UCS associations, show substantial reductions in conditioning.[36] For example, an adolescent girl may observe that women on television and in real life seem to be rewarded with compliments and attention when they smell nice and wear alluring clothing. She figures out that the probability of these rewards occurring is greater when she wears perfume, and so she deliberately wears a popular scent to obtain the reward of social acceptance.

OBSERVATIONAL LEARNING

Observational learning occurs when people watch the actions of others and note the reinforcements they receive for their behaviors—learning occurs as a result of *vicarious* rather than direct experience. This type of learning is a complex process; people store these observations in memory as they accumulate knowledge, perhaps using this information at a later point to guide their own behavior. This process of imitating the behavior of others is called *modeling.* For example, a woman shopping for a new kind of perfume may remember the reactions her friend received on wearing a certain brand several months earlier, and she will base her behavior on her friend's actions.

In order for observational learning in the form of modeling to occur, four conditions must be met:[37]

1. The consumer's attention must be directed to the appropriate model, who for reasons of attractiveness, competence, status, or similarity it is desirable to emulate.
2. The consumer must remember what is said or done by the model.
3. The consumer must convert this information into actions.
4. The consumer must be motivated to perform these actions.

These factors are summarized in Figure 3–3.

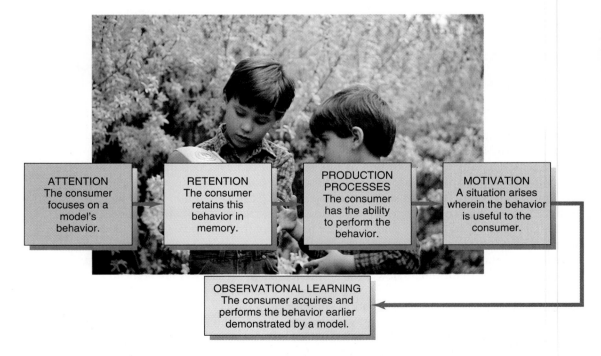

ATTENTION
The consumer focuses on a model's behavior.

RETENTION
The consumer retains this behavior in memory.

PRODUCTION PROCESSES
The consumer has the ability to perform the behavior.

MOTIVATION
A situation arises wherein the behavior is useful to the consumer.

OBSERVATIONAL LEARNING
The consumer acquires and performs the behavior earlier demonstrated by a model.

FIGURE 3–3 ■ Components of Observational Learning

MARKETING PITFALL

The modeling process is a powerful form of learning, and people's tendencies to imitate others' behaviors can have negative effects. Of particular concern is the potential of television shows and movies to teach violence to children. Children may be exposed to new methods of aggression by models (e.g., cartoon heroes) in the shows they watch. At some later point, when the child becomes angry, these behaviors will be imitated.

A classic study demonstrates the effect of modeling on children's actions. Kids who watched an adult stomp on, knock down, and otherwise torture a large inflated "Bobo doll" repeated these behaviors when later left alone in a room with the doll; children who did not witness these acts did not.[38] Unfortunately, the relevance of this study to violent TV shows seems quite clear.

APPLICATIONS OF COGNITIVE LEARNING PRINCIPLES

Consumers' ability to learn vicariously by observing how the behavior of others is reinforced makes the lives of marketers much easier. Because people do not have to be directly reinforced for their actions, marketers do not necessarily have to actually reward or punish them for purchase behaviors (think how expensive or even ethically questionable that might be!). Instead, they can show what happens to desirable models who use or do not use their products, knowing that consumers will often be motivated to imitate these actions at a later time. For example, a perfume commercial might depict a woman surrounded by a throng of admirers who are providing her with positive reinforcement for using the product. Needless to say, this learning process is more practical than providing the same attention to each woman who actually buys the perfume!

Consumers' evaluations of models go beyond simple stimulus-response connections. For example, a celebrity's image elicits more than a simple reflexive response of good or bad.[39] It is a complex combination of many attributes. In general, the degree to which a model will be emulated depends on his or her social attractiveness.

This cosmetics ad illustrates the principle of vicarious reinforcement. The model uses the product and is shown reaping the reward—the approval of her boyfriend.

Attractiveness can be based on several components, including physical appearance, expertise, or similarity to the evaluator.

THE ROLE OF MEMORY IN LEARNING

Memory involves a process of acquiring information and storing it over time so that it will be available when needed. Contemporary approaches to the study of memory employ an information-processing approach. They assume that the mind is in some ways like a computer: Data is input, processed, and output for later use in revised form. In the **encoding** stage, information is entered in a way the system will recognize. In the **storage** stage, this knowledge is integrated with what is already in memory and "warehoused" until needed. During **retrieval,** the person accesses the desired information.[40] The memory process is summarized in Figure 3–4.

Many of our experiences are locked inside our heads, and they may surface years later if prompted by the right cues. Marketers rely on consumers to retain information they have learned about products and services, trusting that it will later be applied in situations in which purchase decisions must be made. During the consumer decision-making process, this *internal memory* is combined with *external memory,* which includes all of the product details on packages, in shopping lists, and other marketing stimuli, to permit brand alternatives to be identified and evaluated.[41]

ENCODING INFORMATION FOR LATER RETRIEVAL

The way information is *encoded,* or mentally programmed, helps to determine how it will be represented in memory. In general, incoming data that are associated with other information already in memory stand a better chance of being retained. For example, brand names that are linked to physical characteristics of a product category (e.g., Coffee Mate creamer or Sani-Flush toilet bowl cleaner) or that are easy to visualize (e.g., Tide detergent or Mercury Cougar cars) tend to be more easily retained in memory than more abstract brand names.[42]

TYPES OF MEANING

A consumer may process a stimulus simply in terms of its *sensory meaning,* such as its color or shape. When this occurs, the meaning may be activated when the person sees a picture of the stimulus. We may experience a sense of familiarity on seeing an ad for a new snack food we have recently tasted, for example. In many cases, though, meanings are encoded at a more abstract level. *Semantic meaning* refers to symbolic associations, such as the idea that rich people drink champagne or that fashionable men wear earrings.

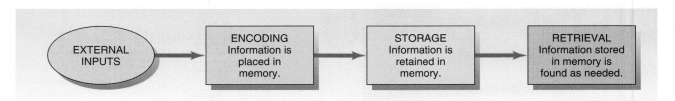

FIGURE 3–4 ■ The Memory Process

PERSONAL RELEVANCE

Episodic memories are those that relate to events that are personally relevant.[43] As a result, a person's motivation to retain these memories will likely be strong. Couples often have "their song" that reminds them of their first date or wedding. The memories that might be triggered on hearing this song would be quite different and unique for them.

Commercials sometimes attempt to activate episodic memories by focusing on experiences shared by many people. Woodstock '94 was a musical extravaganza that owed its success to consumers' episodic memories of the original festival in 1969, where half a million kids partied in the mud for three days on a farm in update New York. Unlike the original festival, though, this one featured product sponsorship by Pepsi, ATM machines, even an official Woodstock '94 condom.[44]

And, recall of the past may have an effect on future behavior. For example, a college fund-raising campaign can get higher donations by evoking pleasant college memories. Some especially vivid associations are called *flashbulb memories*. These are usually related to some highly significant event. As one example, many people claim to remember exactly what they were doing when President Kennedy was assassinated in the early 1960s.

MEMORY SYSTEMS

According to the information-processing perspective, there are three distinct memory systems: sensory memory, short-term memory (STM), and long-term memory (LTM). Each plays a role in processing brand-related information. The interrelationships of these memory systems are summarized in Figure 3–5.

SENSORY MEMORY

Sensory memory permits storage of the information we receive from our senses. This storage is very temporary; it lasts a couple of seconds at most. For example, a person might be walking past a donut shop and get a quick, enticing whiff of something baking inside. Although this sensation would last only for a few seconds, it

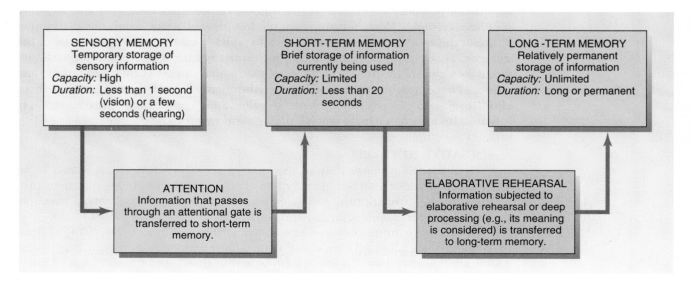

FIGURE 3–5 ■ **Relationships among Memory Systems**

would be sufficient to allow the person to determine if he or she should investigate further. If the information is retained for further processing, it passes through an *attentional gate* and is transferred to short-term memory.

SHORT-TERM MEMORY

Short-term memory (STM) also stores information for a limited period of time, and its capacity is limited. Similar to a computer, this system can be regarded as *working memory;* it holds the information we are currently processing. Verbal input may be stored *acoustically* (in terms of how it sounds) or *semantically* (in terms of what it means).

The information is stored by combining small pieces into larger ones in a process known as *chunking.* A chunk is a configuration that is familiar to the person and can be manipulated as a unit. For example, a brand name can be a chunk that summarizes a great deal of detailed information about the brand.

Initially, it was believed that STM was capable of processing between five to nine chunks of information at a time, and for this reason phone numbers were designed to have seven digits.[45] It now appears that three to four chunks is the optimal size for efficient retrieval (seven-digit phone numbers can be remembered because the individual digits are chunked, so we may remember a three-digit exchange as one piece of information).[46]

LONG-TERM MEMORY

Long-term memory (LTM) is the system that allows us to retain information for a long period of time. In order for information to enter into long-term memory from short-term memory, *elaborative rehearsal* is required. This process involves thinking about the meaning of a stimulus and relating it to other information already in memory. Marketers sometimes assist in the process by devising catchy slogans or jingles that consumers repeat on their own.

STORING INFORMATION IN MEMORY

Relationships among the types of memory are a source of some controversy. The traditional perspective, known as *multiple-store,* assumes that STM and LTM are separate systems. More recent research has moved away from the distinction between the two types of memory, instead emphasizing the interdependence of the systems. This work argues that depending on the nature of the processing task, different levels of processing occur that activate some aspects of memory rather than others. These approaches are called **activation models of memory.**[47] The more effort it takes to process information (so-called "deep processing"), the more likely it is that information will be placed in long-term memory.

ASSOCIATIVE NETWORKS

Activation models propose that an incoming piece of information is stored in an *associative network* containing many bits of related information organized according to some set of relationships. The consumer has organized systems of concepts relating to brands, manufacturers, and stores.

These storage units, known as **knowledge structures,** can be thought of as complex spider webs filled with pieces of data. This information is placed into *nodes,* which are connected by *associative links* within these structures. Pieces of information that are seen as similar in some way are chunked together under some more abstract category. New, incoming information is interpreted to be consistent with the structure already in place.[48]

According to the *hierarchical processing model,* a message is processed in a bottom-up fashion: Processing begins at a very basic level and is subject to increasingly complex processing operations that require greater cognitive capacity. If processing at one level fails to evoke the next level, processing of the ad is terminated and capacity is allocated to other tasks.[49]

An associative network is developed as links form between nodes. For example, a consumer might have a network for "perfumes." Each node represents a concept related to the category. This node can be an attribute, a specific brand, a celebrity identified with a perfume, or even a related product. A network for perfumes might include concepts like the names Chanel, Obsession, and Charlie, as well as attributes like sexy and elegant.

When asked to list perfumes, the consumer would recall only those brands contained in the appropriate category. This group constitutes that person's **evoked set.** The task of a new entrant that wants to position itself as a category member (e.g., a new luxury perfume) is to provide cues that facilitate its placement in the appropriate category. A sample network for perfumes is shown in Figure 3–6.

SPREADING ACTIVATION

A meaning can be activated indirectly; energy spreads across nodes of varying levels of abstraction. As one node is activated, other nodes associated with it also begin to be triggered. Meaning thus spreads across the network, bringing up concepts including competing brands and relevant attributes that are used to form attitudes toward the brand.

This process of *spreading activation* allows consumers to shift back and forth between levels of meaning. The way a piece of information is stored in memory depends on the type of meaning assigned to it. This meaning type will in turn deter-

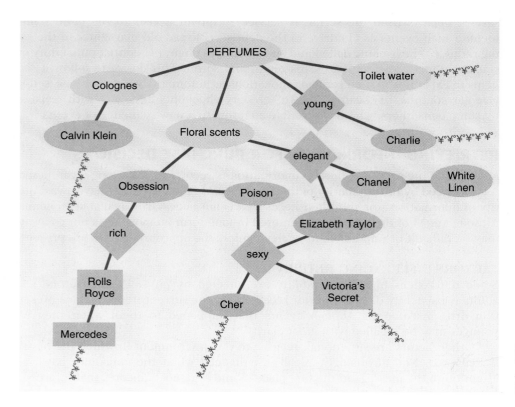

FIGURE 3–6 ■ An Associative Network for Perfumes

mine how and when the meaning is activated. For example, the *memory trace* for an ad could be stored in one or more of the following ways:

- *Brand-specific:* in terms of claims made for the brand
- *Ad-specific:* in terms of the medium or content of the ad itself
- *Brand identification:* in terms of the brand name
- *Product category:* in terms of how the product works or where it should be used, or in terms of experiences with the product
- *Evaluative reactions:* positive or negative emotions, such as "that looks like fun"[50]

LEVELS OF KNOWLEDGE

Knowledge is coded at different levels of abstraction and complexity. *Meaning concepts* are individual nodes (e.g., elegant). These may be combined into a larger unit, called a *proposition* (also known as a *belief*). A proposition links two nodes together to form a more complex meaning, which can serve as a single chunk of information. For example, a proposition might be that "Chanel is a perfume for elegant women."

Propositions are in turn integrated to produce a complex unit known as a *schema,* which as we have already seen is a cognitive framework that is developed through experience. Information that is consistent with an existing schema is encoded more readily.[51] The ability to move up and down among levels of abstraction greatly increases processing flexibility and efficiency. For this reason, young children, who do not yet have well-developed schemas, are not able to make as efficient use of purchase information as are older children.[52]

One type of schema that is relevant to consumer behavior is a *script,* a sequence of events that is expected by an individual. For example, consumers learn *service scripts* that guide their behavior in commercial settings. Consumers learn to expect a certain sequence of events, and they may become uncomfortable if the service departs from the script. A service script for a visit to the dentist might include such events as (1) drive to the dentist, (2) read old magazines in the waiting room, (3) hear name called and sit in dentist's chair, (4) dentist puts funny substance on teeth, (5) dentist cleans teeth, and so on. This desire to follow a script helps to explain why such service innovations as automatic bank machines, self-service gas stations, or "scan-your-own" grocery checkouts have met with resistance by some consumers, who have trouble adapting to a new sequence of events.[53]

RETRIEVING INFORMATION FOR PURCHASE DECISIONS

Retrieval is the process whereby information is recovered from long-term memory. As evidenced by the popularity of the game *Trivial Pursuit,* people have a vast quantity of information stored in their heads that is not necessarily available on demand. Although most of the information entered in long-term memory does not go away, it may be difficult or impossible to retrieve unless the appropriate cues are present.

FACTORS INFLUENCING RETRIEVAL

Some differences in retrieval ability are affected by physiological factors. Older adults consistently display inferior recall ability for current items such as prescription drug instructions, though events that happened to them when they were younger may be recalled with great clarity.[54]

Other factors are situational, relating to the environment in which the message is delivered. Not surprisingly, recall is enhanced when the consumer pays more attention to the message in the first place. Some evidence indicates that information

Trivial Pursuit a popular board game, tests consumers' memories of cultural happenings.

about a *pioneering brand* (the first brand to enter a market) is more easily retrieved from memory than *follower brands* because the first product's introduction is likely to be distinctive and, for the time being, no competitors divert the consumer's attention.[55] In addition, descriptive brand names are more likely to be recalled than are those that do not provide adequate cues as to what the product is.[56]

The viewing environment of a marketing message also can affect recall. For example, commercials shown during baseball games yield the lowest recall scores among sports programs because the activity is stop-and-go rather than continuous. Unlike football or basketball, the pacing of baseball gives many opportunities for attention to wander even during play. Similarly, General Electric found that its commercials fared better in television shows with continuous activity, such as stories or dramas, compared to variety shows or talk shows that are punctuated by a series of acts.[57] Finally, a large-scale analysis of TV commercials found that commercials shown first in a series of ads are recalled better than those shown last.[58]

STATE-DEPENDENT RETRIEVAL

In a process called *state-dependent retrieval,* people are better able to access information if their internal state is the same at the time of recall as when the information was learned. This phenomenon, called the *mood congruence effect,* underscores the desirability of matching a consumer's mood at the time of purchase when

MULTICULTURAL DIMENSIONS

Structural differences in languages can result in recall differences. One study found that Chinese consumers are more likely to recall information when brand names were presented in written form than in spoken form, whereas the opposite pattern was found for American consumers. This suggests that more attention to the use of calligraphy or logos that visually reinforce the brand name will be especially effective for Chinese, but English-speaking consumers might react better to the sound qualities of a brand.[59]

planning exposure to marketing communications. A consumer is more likely to recall an ad, for example, if his or her mood or level of arousal at the time of exposure is similar to that in the purchase environment. By recreating the cues that were present when the information was first presented, recall can be enhanced. For example, Life cereal uses a picture of "Mikey" from its commercial on the cereal box, which facilitates recall of brand claims and favorable brand evaluations.[60]

FAMILIARITY AND RECALL

As a general rule, prior familiarity with an item enhances its recall. Indeed, this is one of the basic goals of marketers who are trying to create and maintain awareness of their products. The more experience a consumer has with a product, the better use he or she is able to make of product information.[61]

However, there is a possible fly in the ointment: As noted earlier in the chapter, some evidence indicates that extreme familiarity can result in inferior learning and/or recall. When consumers are highly familiar with a brand or an advertisement, they may attend to fewer attributes because they do not believe that any additional effort will yield a gain in knowledge.[62] For example, when consumers are exposed to a *radio replay,* in which the audio track from a television ad is replayed on the radio, they do very little critical, evaluative processing and instead mentally replay the video portion of the ad.[63]

SALIENCE AND RECALL

The *salience* of a brand refers to its prominence or level of activation in memory. As noted in chapter 2, stimuli that stand out in contrast to their environment are more likely to command attention, which, in turn, increases the likelihood they will

The Fragrance Foundation is an industry group that promotes the use of perfumes and colognes. One way to do this is by emphasizing that favorite smells have the power to evoke memories of earlier times.

be recalled. Almost any technique that increases the novelty of a stimulus also improves recall (a result known as the *von Restorff Effect*).[64] This effect explains why unusual advertising or distinctive packaging tends to facilitate brand recall.[65]

Introducing a surprise element in an ad can be particularly effective in aiding recall even if it is not relevant to the factual information being presented.[66] In addition, *mystery ads,* in which the brand is not identified until the end of the ad, are more effective at building associations in memory between the product category and that brand—especially in the case of relatively unknown brands.[67]

PICTORIAL VERSUS VERBAL CUES: IS A PICTURE WORTH A THOUSAND WORDS?

There is some evidence for the superiority of visual memory over verbal memory, but this advantage is unclear because it is more difficult to measure recall of pictures.[68] However, the available data indicates that information presented in picture form is more likely to be recognized later.[69] Certainly, visual aspects of an ad are more likely to grab a consumer's attention. In fact, eye-movement studies indicate that about 90 percent of viewers look at the dominant picture in an ad before they bother to view the copy.[70]

Although pictorial ads may enhance recall, they do not necessarily improve comprehension. One study found that television news items presented with illustrations (still pictures) as a backdrop result in improved recall for details of the news story, even though understanding of the story's content does not improve.[71]

FACTORS INFLUENCING FORGETTING

Marketers obviously hope that consumers will not forget about their products. However, in a poll of more than 13,000 adults, over half were unable to remember any specific ad they had seen, heard, or read in the last 30 days.[72] Clearly, forgetting by consumers is a big headache for marketers (not to mention students studying for marketing exams!).

Early memory theorists assumed that memories simply fade with the passage of time: In a process of **decay,** the structural changes in the brain produced by learning simply go away. Forgetting also occurs due to **interference;** as additional information is learned, it displaces the earlier information.

Stimulus-response associations will be forgotten if the consumers subsequently learn new responses to the same or similar stimuli in a process known as *retroactive interference.* Or, prior learning can interfere with new learning, a process termed *proactive interference.* Because pieces of information are stored as nodes in memory that are connected to one another by links, a meaning concept that is connected by a larger number of links is more likely to be retrieved. But, as new responses are learned, a stimulus loses its effectiveness in retrieving the old response.[73]

These interference effects help explain problems in remembering brand information. Consumers tend to organize attribute information by brand.[74] Additional attribute information regarding a brand or similar brands may limit the person's ability to recall old brand information. Recall may also be inhibited if the brand name comprises frequently used words. These words cue competing associations and result in less retention of brand information.[75]

In one study, brand evaluations deteriorated more rapidly when ads for the brand appeared with messages for 12 other brands in the same category than when the ad was shown with ads for 12 dissimilar products.[76] By increasing the salience of a brand, the recall of other brands can be impaired.[77] On the other hand, calling a competitor by name can result in poorer recall for one's own brand.[78]

Finally, a phenomenon known as the *part-list cueing effect* allows marketers to strategically utilize the interference process. When only a portion of the items in a category are presented to consumers, the omitted items are not as easily recalled. For example, comparative advertising that mentions only a subset of competitors (preferably those that the marketer is not very worried about) may inhibit recall of the unmentioned brands with which the product does not favorably compare.[79]

PRODUCTS AS MEMORY MARKERS

Products and ads can themselves serve as powerful retrieval cues. Indeed, the three types of possessions most valued by consumers are furniture, visual art, and photos. The most common explanation for this attachment is the ability of these things to call forth memories of the past.[80]

Products are particularly important as markers when our sense of past is threatened, as when a consumer's current identity is challenged due to some change in role caused by divorce, moving, graduation, and so on.[81] Our possessions often have *mnemonic* qualities that serve as a form of external memory by prompting consumers to retrieve episodic memories. For example, family photography allows consumers to create their own retrieval cues, with the 11 billion amateur photos taken annually forming a kind of external memory bank for our culture.

Researchers are just beginning to probe the effects of *autobiographical memories* on buying behavior. These memories appear to be one way that advertisements create emotional responses; ads that succeed in getting us to think about our own past also appear to get us to like these ads more—especially if the linkage between the nostalgia experience and the brand is strong.[82]

THE MARKETING POWER OF NOSTALGIA

Nostalgia has been described as a bittersweet emotion; the past is viewed with both sadness and longing. References to "the good old days" are increasingly common, as advertisers call up memories of youth—and hope these feelings will translate to what they're selling today. A stimulus is at times able to evoke a weakened response even years after it was initially perceived, an effect known as *spontaneous recovery,* and this reestablished connection may explain consumers' powerful nostalgic reactions to songs or pictures they have not been exposed to in quite a long time. This strategy also may work because over half of adults think things were better in the past than they are today, according to research by Roper Starch Worldwide. Most people view their childhood as the best time of life—particularly if they are less successful in the present than they had hoped: Longing for the past decreases as people's educational achievements increase.[83] That may also help to explain why about 22 million Americans attend some variety of reunion every year.[84]

Many marketers are realizing the appeal nostalgia holds for many consumers. Some companies are continuing to use their old trademark characters, or are even bringing some out of retirement, including the Campbell Soup Kids, the Pillsbury Doughboy, Betty Crocker, and Planters' Mr. Peanut—who recently celebrated his 75th year with the company.[85] The craze for "worn-in" American products is even stronger in Japan, where "vintage" pairs of Adidas, Nike, and Converse sneakers sell for as high as $1,000—the older versions are even more cherished than the current models.[86]

A study of network television commercials found that about 10 percent contained some nostalgic reference, and this appeal was especially prevalent in the food and beverage categories.[87] One trend is "retro marketing"—companies like Ovaltine, Alka-Seltzer, and Shake 'N Bake are going into their vaults and running

To capitalize on consumer nostalgia for an earlier, more glamorous era, Warnaco introduced a new line of intimate apparel inspired by Marilyn Monroe, and the company uses photos from classic Marilyn films like "The Seven Year Itch" to promote the line. According to Warnaco's CEO, nearly 35 years after her death Marilyn is still viewed as this ". . . wonderful icon of all that is beautiful, sexy and glamorous."[1]

1. Jane L. Levere, "Lingerie Maker Hopes Monroe Image Hasn't Lost Sizzle," *The New York Times News Service* (accessed February 10, 1997): [On-line] Available World Wide Web: http://www.ssnewslink.com/college/marilyn.htm.

commercials from the 1950s and 1960s. The risk in this style of advertising is being positioned as "yesterday's brand," so the successful campaigns are presenting classic footage in a fun, tongue-in-cheek way.[88]

Not surprisingly, people in their 40s and 50s are the primary target of these retro appeals. In a survey of baby boomers, Bugs Bunny was the best-remembered cartoon character, Barbie was the favorite toy, and the boomers' favorite ad slogan was M&M's "Melts in your mouth, not in your hand."[89] And, to supply the "soundtrack" for these memories, an increasing number of radio stations are converting to what the industry calls the "adult standards" format, also known as nostalgia radio.[90] No Marilyn Manson music here!

MARKETING PITFALL

Some die-hard fans were not pleased when the Rolling Stones sold the tune "Start Me Up" for about $4 million to Microsoft, which wanted the classic song to promote its Windows 95 launch. The Beach Boys sold "Good Vibrations" to Cadbury Schweppes for its Sunkist soft drink, Steppenwolf's "Born to be Wild" was used to plug the Mercury Cougar, and even Bob Dylan sold "The Times They Are A-Changin'" to Coopers & Lybrand.[91] Other rock legends have refused to play the commercial game, including Bruce Springsteen, the Grateful Dead, Led Zeppelin, Fleetwood Mac, R.E.M., and U2. According to U2's manager, "Rock 'n roll is the last vestige of independence. It is undignified to put that creative effort and hard work to the disposal of a soft drink or beer or car."[92] Singer Neil Young is especially adamant about not selling out; in his song "This Note's For You," he croons, "Ain't singing for Pepsi, ain't singing for Coke, I don't sing for nobody, makes me look like a joke."

MULTICULTURAL DIMENSIONS

Nostalgia for the "bad old days"? Parts of eastern Europe are experiencing nostalgia for the bygone Communist era—a time of shoddy goods but no unemployment. This revival of interest in days gone by has been termed *ostalgie,* an acronym for "East-Nostalgia." Berlin's Humboldt University and the City Museum even staged a fashion show of the 1960s displaying clothes, appliances, and posters from the Communist era. *Ostalgie* is feeding growing consumer interest in the Trabant—a car that was essentially a cardboard box powered by a lawnmower engine. The vehicle was so shoddy that a running joke was that its value could be doubled by filling it with sand. Still, renewed longing for the homely Trabant has resulted in the Son of Trabant, which is being built in the same factory used to construct the original death trap.[93] The Trabant is even being given a statue in the city of Zwickau, where it was born. It will be a life-sized Trabant made of stone with a mother on the hood to symbolize the link between man and machine.[94]

Meanwhile, a West German automaker probably has a better chance of benefitting from fond memories of days gone by. Hoping to win back former buyers—and to lure new ones—Volkswagen unveiled an updated version of the "Bug," the small round shouldered car that became a generational icon in the U.S. in the 1960s and '70s. Back in those days, the "Bug" was cramped and noisy, but was a hit because it was relatively cheap, fuel-efficient, and had symbolic value as a protest against Detroit's "big boats." The VW executive in charge of North America feels "the Beetle is the core of the VW soul. If we put it back in people's minds, they will think of our other products more." Following the re-introduction of the Beetle in the U.S., Volkswagen will also sell the nostalgic Bug in Europe.[95]

MEMORY AND AESTHETIC PREFERENCES

In addition to liking ads and products that remind us of our past, our past experiences also help to determine what we like now. Consumer researchers have created a *nostalgia index* that measures the critical ages during which our preferences are likely to be formed and endure over time. For example, liking for specific songs appears to be related to how old a person was when that song was popular—on average songs that were popular when he or she was 23.5 years old are the most likely to be favored, whereas preferences for fashion models peak at age 33 and for movie stars at age 26 to 27.[96]

MEASURING MEMORY FOR MARKETING STIMULI

Because marketers pay so much money to place their messages in front of consumers, they are naturally concerned that people will actually remember these messages at a later point. It seems that they have good reason to be concerned. In one

This ad for Land O Lakes butter uses "old-fashioned" imagery and is based on the brand's nostalgic appeal— "The Taste That Brings You Back."

study, less than 40 percent of television viewers made positive links between commercial messages and the corresponding products, only 65 percent noticed the brand name in a commercial, and only 38 percent recognized a connection to an important point.[97]

Even more sadly, only 7 percent of television viewers can recall the product or company featured in the most recent television commercial they watched. This figure represents less than half the recall rate recorded in 1965 and may be attributed to such factors as the increase of 30- and 15-second commercials, and the practice of airing television commercials in clusters rather than in single-sponsor programs.[98]

RECOGNITION VERSUS RECALL

One indicator of good advertising is, of course, the impression it makes on consumers. But how can this impact be defined and measured? Two basic measures of impact are *recognition* and *recall*. In the typical recognition test, subjects are shown ads one at a time and asked if they have seen them before. In contrast, free recall tests ask consumers to independently think of what they have seen without being prompted for this information first—obviously this task requires greater effort on the part of respondents.

Under some conditions, these two memory measures tend to yield the same results, especially when the researchers try to keep the viewers' interest in the ads constant.[99] Generally, though, recognition scores tend to be more reliable and do not decay over time the way recall scores do.[100] Recognition scores are almost always better than recall scores because recognition is a simpler process and more retrieval cues are available to the consumer.

Both types of retrieval play important roles in purchase decisions, however. Recall tends to be more important in situations in which consumers do not have product data at their disposal, so they must rely on memory to generate this information.[101] On the other hand, recognition is more likely to be an important factor in a store, where consumers are confronted with thousands of product options and information (i.e., external memory is abundantly available) and the task may simply be to recognize a familiar package. Unfortunately, package recognition and familiarity can have a negative consequence in that warning labels may be ignored, since their message is taken for granted and not really noticed.[102]

THE STARCH TEST

A widely used commercial measure of advertising recall for magazines is called the *Starch Test,* a syndicated service founded in 1932. This service provides scores on a number of aspects of consumers' familiarity with an ad, including such categories as "noted," "associated," and "read most." It also scores the impact of the component parts of an overall ad, giving such information as "seen" for major illustrations and "read some" for a major block of copy.[103] Factors such as the size of the ad, whether it appears toward the front or the back of the magazine, if it is on the right or left page, and the size of illustrations play an important role in affecting the amount of attention given to an ad as determined by Starch scores.

PROBLEMS WITH MEMORY MEASURES

While the measurement of an ad's memorability is important, the ability of existing measures to accurately assess these dimensions has been criticized for several reasons, which we explore now.

RESPONSE BIASES

Results obtained from a measuring instrument are not necessarily due to what is being measured, but rather to something else about the instrument or the respondent. This form of contamination is called a **response bias.** For example, people tend to give "yes" responses to questions, regardless of what is asked. In addition, consumers often have an eagerness to be "good subjects" by pleasing the experimenter. They will try to give the responses they think he or she is looking for. In some studies, the claimed recognition of bogus ads (ads that have not been seen before) is almost as high as the recognition rate of real ads.[104]

MEMORY LAPSES

People are also prone to unintentionally forget information. Typical problems include *omitting* (leaving facts out), *averaging* (the tendency to "normalize" memories by not reporting extreme cases), and *telescoping* (inaccurate recall of time).[105] These distortions call into question the accuracy of product usage databases that rely on consumers to recall their purchase and consumption of food and household items. In one study, for example, people were asked to describe what portion of various foods—small, medium, or large—they ate in a typical meal. However, different definitions of "medium" were used (e.g., 3/4 cup versus 1 1/2 cups). Regardless of the measurement used, about the same number of people claimed they typically ate "medium" portions.[106]

MEMORY FOR FACTS VERSUS FEELINGS

Although techniques are being developed to increase the accuracy of memory scores, these improvements do not address the more fundamental issue of whether recall is necessary for advertising to have an effect. In particular, some critics argue that these measures do not adequately tap the impact of "feeling" ads in which the objective is to arouse strong emotions rather than to convey concrete product benefits. Many ad campaigns, including those for Hallmark cards, Chevrolet, and Pepsi use this approach.[107] An effective strategy relies on a long-term buildup of feeling rather than on a one-shot attempt to convince consumers to buy the product.

Also, it is not clear that recall translates into preference. We may recall the benefits touted in an ad but not believe them. Or, the ad may be memorable because it is so obnoxious and the product becomes one we "love to hate." The bottom line: Although recall is important, especially for creating brand awareness, it is not necessarily sufficient to alter consumer preferences. To accomplish this, more sophisticated attitude-changing strategies are needed. These issues will be discussed in chapters 7 and 8.

CHAPTER SUMMARY

- Learning is a change in behavior that is caused by experience. Learning can occur through simple associations between a stimulus and a response, or via a complex series of cognitive activities.

- Behavioral learning theories assume that learning occurs as a result of responses to external events. Classical conditioning occurs when a stimulus that naturally elicits a response (an unconditioned stimulus) is paired with another stimulus that does not initially elicit this response. Over time, the second stimulus (the conditioned stimulus) comes to elicit the response even in the absence of the first.

- This response can also extend to other, similar stimuli in a process known as stimulus generalization. This process is the basis for such marketing strategies as licensing and family branding, where a consumer's positive associations with a product are transferred to other contexts.

- Operant or instrumental conditioning occurs as the person learns to perform behaviors that produce positive outcomes and avoid those that result in negative outcomes. Whereas classical conditioning involves the pairing of two stimuli, instrumental learning occurs when reinforcement is delivered following a response to a stimulus. Reinforcement is positive if a reward is delivered following a response. It is negative if a negative outcome is avoided by not performing a response. Punishment occurs when a response is followed by unpleasant events. Extinction of the behavior will occur if reinforcement is no longer received.

- Cognitive learning occurs as the result of mental processes. For example, observational learning takes place when the consumer performs a behavior as a result of seeing someone else performing it and being rewarded for it.

- Memory refers to the storage of learned information. The way information is encoded when it is perceived determines how it will be stored in memory. The memory systems known as sensory memory, short-term memory, and long-term memory each play a role in retaining and processing information from the outside world.

- Information is not stored in isolation; it is incorporated into knowledge structures, in which it is associated with other related data. The location of product information in associative networks, and the level of abstraction at which it is coded, help to determine when and how this information will be activated at a later time. Some factors that influence the likelihood of retrieval include the level of familiarity with an item, its salience (or prominence) in memory, and whether the information was presented in pictorial or written form.

- Products also play a role as memory markers; they are used by consumers to retrieve memories about past experiences (autobiographical memories) and are often valued for their ability to do this. This function also contributes to the use of nostalgia in marketing strategies.

- Memory for product information can be measured through either recognition or recall techniques. Consumers are more likely to recognize an advertisement if it is presented to them than to recall one without being given any cues. However, neither recognition nor recall automatically or reliably translate into product preferences or purchases.

KEY TERMS

Activation models of memory p. 86
Behavioral learning theories p. 72
Brand equity p. 74
Classical conditioning p. 72
Cognitive learning p. 80
Cognitive learning theory p. 80
Decay p. 91
Encoding p. 83
Evoked set p. 87
Extinction p. 78

Frequency marketing p. 80
Instrumental conditioning p. 78
Interference p. 91
Knowledge structures p. 86
Learning p. 71
Long-term memory p. 86
Memory p. 83
Negative reinforcement p. 78
Nostalgia p. 92
Observational learning p. 82

Positive reinforcement p. 78
Punishment p. 78
Response bias p. 96
Retrieval p. 83
Sensory memory p. 85
Short-term memory p. 86
Stimulus discrimination p. 74
Stimulus generalization p. 74
Storage p. 83

CONSUMER BEHAVIOR CHALLENGE

1. Identify three patterns of reinforcement and provide an example of how each is used in a marketing context.

2. Describe the functions of short-term and long-term memory. What is the apparent relationship between the two?

3. Devise a "product jingle memory test." Compile a list of brands that are or have been associated with memorable jingles, such as Chiquita Banana or Alka-Seltzer. Read this list to friends, and see how many jingles are remembered. You may be surprised at the level of recall.

4. Identify some important characteristics for a product with a well-known brand name. Based on these attributes, generate a list of possible brand extension or licensing opportunities, as well as some others that would most likely not be accepted by consumers.

5. One troubling aspect of product licensing is when movies targeted to adult audiences spawn tie-ins intended for kids. This resulted in a public relations problem for McDonald's Corporation, which was strongly criticized for its cross-promotional deal with the Warner Bros. movie *Batman Returns*. The movie was rated PG-13, so (in theory at least) it couldn't be seen by the kids who were stockpiling Batman collectors' cups and Happy Meal toys. Similarly, Mattel sells a line of *Beverly Hills, 90210* dolls. An executive explains that these are suitable for little girls because "there is some kind of moral to every story."[108] Do you agree with this reasoning? What, if any, guidelines should be placed on product licensing?

6. Collect some pictures of "classic" products that have high nostalgia value. Show these pictures to consumers, and allow them to free associate. Analyze the types of memories that are evoked, and think about how these associations might be employed in a product's promotional strategy.

NOTES

1. "Cocktail Culture Lives!" *New York Times Magazine* (August 24, 1997): 21.
2. Quoted in Randall Rothenberg, "The Swank Life," *Esquire* (April 1997): 71–9, quoted on p. 73.
3. Robert A. Baron, *Psychology: The Essential Science* (Boston: Allyn & Bacon, 1989).
4. Richard A. Feinberg, "Credit Cards as Spending Facilitating Stimuli: A Conditioning Interpretation," *Journal of Consumer Research* 13 (December 1986): 348–56.
5. R. A. Rescorla, "Pavlovian Conditioning: It's Not What You Think It Is," *American Psychologist* 43 (1988): 151–60; Elnora W. Stuart, Terence A. Shimp, and Randall W. Engle, "Classical Conditioning of Consumer Attitudes: Four Experiments in an Advertising Context," *Journal of Consumer Research* 14 (December 1987): 334–39.
6. "Anemic Crocodile," *Forbes* (August 15, 1994): 116.
7. James Ward, Barbara Loken, Ivan Ross, and Tedi Hasapopoulous, "The Influence of Physical Similarity of Affect and Attribute Perceptions from National Brands to Private Label Brands," in eds. Terence A. Shimp et al., *American Marketing Educators' Conference* (Chicago: American Marketing Association, 1986): 51–6.
8. Judith Lynne Zaichkowsky and Richard Neil Simpson, "The Effect of Experience with a Brand Imitator on the Original Brand," *Marketing Letters* 7 (1996)1: 31–9.
9. Tom J. Brown and Peter A. Dacin, "The Company and the Product: Corporate Associations and Consumer Product Responses," *Journal of Marketing* 61 (January 1997): 68–84.
10. Chris T. Allen and Thomas J. Madden, "A Closer Look at Classical Conditioning," *Journal of Consumer Research* 12 (December 1985): 301–15; Chester A. Insko and William F. Oakes, "Awareness and the Conditioning of Attitudes," *Journal of Personality and Social Psychology* 4 (November 1966): 487–96; Carolyn K. Staats and Arthur W. Staats, "Meaning Established by Classical Conditioning," *Journal of Experimental Psychology* 54 (July 1957): 74–80.
11. Kevin Lane Keller, "Conceptualizing, Measuring, and Managing Customer-based Brand Equity," *Journal of Marketing* 57 (January 1993): 1–22.
12. Herbert Krugman, "Low Recall and High Recognition of Advertising," *Journal of Advertising Research* (February/March 1986): 79–80
13. Gerald J. Gorn, "The Effects of Music in Advertising on Choice Behavior: A Classical Conditioning Approach," *Journal of Marketing* 46 (Winter 1982): 94–101.
14. Calvin Bierley, Frances K. McSweeney, and Renee Vannieuwkerk, "Classical Conditioning of Preferences for Stimuli," *Journal of Consumer Research* 12 (December 1985): 316–23; James J. Kellaris and Anthony D. Cox, "The Effects of Background Music in Advertising: A Reassessment," *Journal of Consumer Research* 16 (June 1989): 113–18.
15. Frances K. McSweeney and Calvin Bierley, "Recent Developments in Classical Conditioning," *Journal of Consumer Research* 11 (September 1984): 619–31.
16. Basil G. Englis, "The Reinforcement Properties of Music Videos: 'I Want My . . . I Want My . . . I Want My . . . MTV'" (paper presented at the meetings of the Association for Consumer Research, New Orleans, 1989).
17. "Giving Bad Puns the Business," *Newsweek* (December 11, 1989): 71.
18. Bernice Kanner, "Growing Pains—and Gains: Brand Names Branch Out," *New York* (March 13, 1989): 22.
19. Dana Rubin, "You've Seen the Game. Now Buy the Underwear," *New York Times* (September 11, 1994): F5.
20. Peter H. Farquhar, "Brand Equity," *Marketing Insights* (Summer, 1989): 59.
21. "Charles Manson Gets Royalties on T-Shirts," *New York Times* (November 25, 1993): A21.
22. John Marchese, "Forever Harley," *New York Times* (October 17, 1993): 10; "Spamming the Globe," *Newsweek* (August 29, 1994): 8.
23. Marcy Magiera, "Promotional Marketer of the Year," *Advertising Age* (March 21, 1994): S1 (2 pp.); Stuart Elliott, "Gump Sells, to Viacom's Surprise," *New York Times* (October 7, 1994): D1 (2 pp.).
24. Valerie Reitman, "Flight Attendants in Japan Follow in Annette Funicello's Footsteps," *Wall Street Journal* (September 1, 1994): B1.
25. Cyndee Miller, "X-Files No Alien to Licensing," *Marketing News* (May 20, 1996): 1 (2).
26. "Look-Alikes Mimic Familiar Packages," *New York Times* (August 9, 1986): D1.
27. Laurie Hays, "Too Many Computer Names Confuse Too Many Buyers," *Wall Street Journal* (June 29, 1994): B1 (2 pp.).
28. Barbara Loken and Deborah Roedder John, "Diluting Brand Beliefs: When Do Brand Extensions Have a Negative Impact?" *Journal of Marketing* 57 (July 1993): 71–84.
29. Kanner, "Growing Pains."
30. Farquhar, "Brand Equity."
31. For a comprehensive approach to consumer behavior based on operant conditioning principles, see Gordon R. Foxall, "Behavior Analysis and Consumer Psychology," *Journal of Economic Psychology* 15 (March 1994): 5–91.
32. Blaise J. Bergiel and Christine Trosclair, "Instrumental Learning: Its Application to Customer Satisfaction," *Journal of Consumer Marketing* 2 (Fall 1985): 23–8.
33. Ian P. Murphy, "Customers Can Join the Club—But at a Price," *Marketing News* (April 28, 1997): 8.
34. Ellen J. Langer, *The Psychology of Control* (Beverly Hills, CA.: Sage, 1983).
35. Robert B. Cialdini, *Influence: Science and Practice,* 2nd ed. (New York: William Morrow, 1984).
36. Chris T. Allen and Thomas J. Madden, "A Closer Look at Classical Conditioning," *Journal of Consumer Research* 12 (December 1985): 301–15; see also Terence A. Shimp, Elnora W. Stuart, and Randall W. Engle, "A Program of Classical Conditioning Experiments Testing Variations in the Conditioned Stimulus and Context," *Journal of Consumer Research* 18 (June 1991): 1–12.
37. Albert Bandura, *Social Foundations of Thought and Action: A Social Cognitive View* (Upper Saddle River, NJ: Prentice Hall, 1986); Baron, *Psychology.*
38. Terence A. Shimp, "Neo-Pavlovian Conditioning and Its Implications for Consumer Theory and Research," in eds. Thomas S. Robertson and Harold H. Kassarjian, *Handbook of*

Consumer Behavior, (Upper Saddle River, NJ: Prentice Hall, 1991).

39. Bandura, *Social Foundations of Thought and Action.*

40. R. C. Atkinson and I. M. Shiffrin, "Human Memory: A Proposed System and Its Control Processes," in eds. K. W. Spence and J. T. Spence, *The Psychology of Learning and Motivation: Advances in Research and Theory* (New York: Academic Press, 1968)2: 89–195.

41. James R. Bettman, "Memory Factors in Consumer Choice: A Review," *Journal of Marketing* (Spring 1979): 37–53. For a study that explores the relative impact of internal versus external memory on brand choice, see Joseph W. Alba, Howard Marmostein, and Amitava Chattopadhyay, "Transitions in Preference over Time: The Effects of Memory on Message Persuasiveness," *Journal of Marketing Research* 29 (November 1992)4: 406–16.

42. Kim Robertson, "Recall and Recognition Effects of Brand Name Imagery," *Psychology & Marketing* 4 (Spring 1987): 3–15.

43. Endel Tulving, "Remembering and Knowing the Past," *American Scientist* 77 (July/August 1989): 361.

44. John Milward, "Field of Dreams," *Rolling Stone* (August 11, 1994): 36 (2).

45. George A. Miller, "The Magical Number Seven, Plus or Minus Two: Some Limits on Our Capacity for Processing Information," *Psychological Review* 63 (1956): 81–97.

46. James N. MacGregor, "Short-Term Memory Capacity: Limitation or Optimization?" *Psychological Review* 94 (1987): 107–8.

47. See Catherine A. Cole and Michael J. Houston, "Encoding and Media Effects on Consumer Learning Deficiencies in the Elderly," *Journal of Marketing Research* 24 (February 1987): 55–64; A. M. Collins and E. F. Loftus, "A Spreading Activation Theory of Semantic Processing," *Psychological Review* 82 (1975): 407–28; Fergus I. M. Craik and Robert S. Lockhart, "Levels of Processing: A Framework for Memory Research," *Journal of Verbal Learning and Verbal Behavior* 11 (1972): 671–84.

48. Walter A. Henry, "The Effect of Information-Processing Ability on Processing Accuracy," *Journal of Consumer Research* 7 (June 1980): 42–8.

49. Anthony G. Greenwald and Clark Leavitt, "Audience Involvement in Advertising: Four Levels," *Journal of Consumer Research* 11 (June 1984): 581–92.

50. Kevin Lane Keller, "Memory Factors in Advertising: The Effect of Advertising Retrieval Cues on Brand Evaluations," *Journal of Consumer Research* 14 (December 1987): 316–33. For a discussion of processing operations that occur during brand choice, see Gabriel Biehal and Dipankar Chakravarti, "Consumers Use of Memory and External Information in Choice: Macro and Micro Perspectives," *Journal of Consumer Research* 12 (March 1986): 382–405.

51. Susan T. Fiske and Shelley E. Taylor, *Social Cognition* (Reading, MA: Addison-Wesley, 1984).

52. Deborah Roedder John and John C. Whitney Jr., "The Development of Consumer Knowledge in Children: A Cognitive Structure Approach," *Journal of Consumer Research* 12 (March 1986): 406–17.

53. Michael R. Solomon, Carol Surprenant, John A. Czepiel, and Evelyn G. Gutman, "A Role Theory Perspective on Dyadic Interactions: The Service Encounter," *Journal of Marketing* 49 (Winter 1985): 99–111.

54. Roger W. Morrell, Denise C. Park, and Leonard W. Poon, "Quality of Instructions on Prescription Drug Labels: Effects on Memory and Comprehension in Young and Old Adults," *The Gerontologist* 29 (1989): 345–54.

55. Frank R. Kardes, Gurumurthy Kalyanaram, Murali Chandrashekaran, and Ronald J. Dornoff, "Brand Retrieval, Consideration Set Composition, Consumer Choice, and the Pioneering Advantage" (unpublished manuscript, The University of Cincinnati, Ohio, 1992).

56. Judith Lynne Zaichkowsky and Padma Vipat, "Inferences from Brand Names" (paper presented at the European meeting of the Association for Consumer Research, Amsterdam, June 1992).

57. Herbert E. Krugman, "Low Recall and High Recognition of Advertising," *Journal of Advertising Research* (February/March 1986): 79–86.

58. Rik G. M. Pieters and Tammo H. A. Bijmolt, "Consumer Memory for Television Advertising: A Field Study of Duration, Serial Position, and Competition Effects," *Journal of Consumer Research* 23 (March 1997): 362–72.

59. Bernd H. Schmitt, Yigang Pan, and Nader T. Tavassoli, "Language and Consumer Memory: The Impact of Linguistic Differences between Chinese and English," *Journal of Consumer Research* 21 (December 1994): 419–31.

60. Keller, "Memory Factors in Advertising."

61. Eric J. Johnson and J. Edward Russo, "Product Familiarity and Learning New Information," *Journal of Consumer Research* 11 (June 1984): 542–50.

62. Eric J. Johnson and J. Edward Russo, "Product Familiarity and Learning New Information," in ed. Kent Monroe, *Advances in Consumer Research* 8, (Ann Arbor, MI: Association for Consumer Research, 1981): 151–5; John G. Lynch and Thomas K. Srull, "Memory and Attentional Factors in Consumer Choice: Concepts and Research Methods," *Journal of Consumer Research* 9 (June 1982): 18–37.

63. Julie A. Edell and Kevin Lane Keller, "The Information Processing of Coordinated Media Campaigns," *Journal of Marketing Research* 26 (May 1989): 149–64.

64. Lynch and Srull, "Memory and Attentional Factors in Consumer Choice."

65. Joseph W. Alba and Amitava Chattopadhyay, "Salience Effects in Brand Recall," *Journal of Marketing Research* 23 (November 1986): 363–70; Elizabeth C. Hirschman and Michael R. Solomon, "Utilitarian, Aesthetic, and Familiarity Responses to Verbal versus Visual Advertisements," in ed. Thomas C. Kinnear, *Advances in Consumer Research* 11, (Provo, UT: Association for Consumer Research, 1984): 426–31.

66. Susan E. Heckler and Terry L. Childers, "The Role of Expectancy and Relevancy in Memory for Verbal and Visual Information: What is Incongruency?" *Journal of Consumer Research* 18 (March 1992): 475–92.

67. Russell H. Fazio, Paul M. Herr, and Martha C. Powell, "On the Development and Strength of Category-Brand Associations in Memory: The Case of Mystery Ads," *Journal of Consumer Psychology* 1 (1992)1: 1–13.

68. Hirschman and Solomon, "Utilitarian, Aesthetic, and Familiarity Responses to Verbal versus Visual Advertisements."

69. Terry Childers and Michael Houston, "Conditions for a Picture-Super-

iority Effect on Consumer Memory," *Journal of Consumer Research* 11 (September 1984): 643–54; Terry Childers, Susan Heckler, and Michael Houston, "Memory for the Visual and Verbal Components of Print Advertisements," *Psychology & Marketing* 3 (Fall 1986): 147–50.

70. Werner Krober-Riel, "Effects of Emotional Pictorial Elements in Ads Analyzed by Means of Eye Movement Monitoring," in ed. Thomas C. Kinnear, *Advances in Consumer Research* 11 (Provo, UT: Association for Consumer Research, 1984): 591–6.

71. Hans-Bernd Brosius, "Influence of Presentation Features and News Context on Learning from Television News," *Journal of Broadcasting & Electronic Media* 33 (Winter 1989): 1–14.

72. Raymond R. Burke and Thomas K. Srull, "Competitive Interference and Consumer Memory for Advertising," *Journal of Consumer Research* 15 (June 1988): 55–68.

73. Burke and Srull, "Competitive Interference and Consumer Memory for Advertising."

74. Johnson and Russo, "Product Familiarity and Learning New Information."

75. Joan Meyers-Levy, "The Influence of Brand Name's Association Set Size and Word Frequency on Brand Memory," *Journal of Consumer Research* 16 (September 1989): 197–208.

76. Michael H. Baumgardner, Michael R. Leippe, David L. Ronis, and Anthony G. Greenwald, "In Search of Reliable Persuasion Effects: II. Associative Interference and Persistence of Persuasion in a Message-Dense Environment," *Journal of Personality and Social Psychology* 45 (September 1983): 524–37.

77. Alba and Chattopadhyay, "Salience Effects in Brand Recall."

78. Margaret Henderson Blair, Allan R. Kuse, David H. Furse, and David W. Stewart, "Advertising in a New and Competitive Environment: Persuading Consumers to Buy," *Business Horizons* 30 (November/December 1987): 20.

79. Lynch and Srull, "Memory and Attentional Factors in Consumer Choice."

80. Russell W. Belk, "Possessions and the Extended Self," *Journal of Consumer Research* 15 (September 1988): 139–68.

81. Russell W. Belk, "The Role of Possessions in Constructing and Maintaining a Sense of Past," in eds. Marvin E. Goldberg, Gerald Gorn, and Richard W. Pollay, *Advances in Consumer Research* 16, (Provo, UT: Association for Consumer Research, 1989): 669–78.

82. Hans Baumgartner, Mita Sujan, and James R. Bettman, "Autobiographical Memories, Affect and Consumer Information Processing," *Journal of Consumer Psychology* 1 (January 1992): 53–82; Mita Sujan, James R. Bettman, and Hans Baumgartner, "Autobiographical Memories and Consumer Judgments" (working paper no. 183, Pennsylvania State University, University Park, 1992).

83. Diane Crispell, "Which Good Old Days," *American Demographics* (April 1996): 35.

84. Paula Mergenhagen, "The Reunion Market," *American Demographics* (April 1996): 30–4.

85. Stuart Elliott, "At 75, Mr. Peanut is Getting Expanded Role at Planters," *New York Times* (September 23, 1991): D15.

86. Jennifer Cody, "Here's a New Way to Rationalize Not Cleaning Out Your Closets," (June 14, 1994): B1.

87. Lynette S. Unger, Diane M. McConocha, and John A. Faier, "The Use of Nostalgia in Television Advertising: A Content Analysis," *Journalism Quarterly* 63 (Fall 1991): 345–53.

88. Joe Marconi, "Retro Marketing Helps Brand Gain New Image," *Marketing News* (October 21, 1996): 10.

89. "For Boomers, These Were a Few of Our Favorite Things," *Adweek* 10 (February 3, 1992): 16.

90. William Dunn, "Sinatra Has the Last Dance," *American Demographics* (July 1994): 39.

91. Thomas F. Jones, "Our Musical Heritage is Being Raided," *San Francisco Examiner,* 1997, accessed via ssnewslink, Newslink, 5/23/97.

92. Quoted in Kevin Goldman, "A Few Rockers Refuse to Turn Tunes Into Ads," *New York Times* (August 25, 1995): B1 (2 pp.), quoted on p. B1.

93. "Ostalgie for the Days When They'd Never Had it so Good," Accessed February 10, 1997, ssnewslink, *The Independent*, London.

94. "Trabant Gets Statue," *Algemeen Dagblad* (Holland) (June 23, 1997): 7.

95. Gabriella Stern, "VW Hopes Nostalgia Will Spur Sales of Retooled Beetle, Fuel US Comeback," *The Wall Street Journal,* Europe edition (May 7, 1997):4.

96. Morris B. Holbrook and Robert M. Schindler, "Some Exploratory Findings on the Development of Musical Tastes," *Journal of Consumer Research* 16 (June 1989): 119–24; Morris B. Holbrook and Robert M. Schindler, "Market Segmentation Based on Age and Attitude toward the Past: Concepts, Methods, and Findings Concerning Nostalgic Influences on Consumer Tastes," *Journal of Business Research* 37 (September 1996)1: 27–40.

97. "Only 38% of T.V. Audience Links Brands with Ads," *Marketing News* (January 6, 1984): 10.

98. "Terminal Television," *American Demographics* (January 1987): 15.

99. Richard P. Bagozzi and Alvin J. Silk, "Recall, Recognition, and the Measurement of Memory for Print Advertisements," *Marketing Science* 2 (1983): 95–134.

100. Adam Finn, "Print Ad Recognition Readership Scores: An Information Processing Perspective," *Journal of Marketing Research* 25 (May 1988): 168–77.

101. Bettman, "Memory Factors in Consumer Choice."

102. Mark A. deTurck and Gerald M. Goldhaber, "Effectiveness of Product Warning Labels: Effects of Consumers' Information Processing Objectives," *Journal of Consumer Affairs* 23 (1989)1: 111–25.

103. Finn, "Print Ad Recognition Readership Scores."

104. Surendra N. Singh and Gilbert A. Churchill Jr., "Response-Bias-Free Recognition Tests to Measure Advertising Effects," *Journal of Advertising Research* (June/July 1987): 23–36.

105. William A. Cook, "Telescoping and Memory's Other Tricks," *Journal of Advertising Research* 27 (February/March 1987): 5–8.

106. "On a Diet? Don't Trust Your Memory," *Psychology Today* (October 1989): 12.

107. Hubert A. Zielske and Walter A. Henry, "Remembering and Forgetting Television Ads," *Journal of Advertising Research* 20 (April 1980): 7–13; Cara Greenberg, "Future Worth: Before It's Hot, Grab It," *New York Times* (1992): C1; S. K. List, "More than Fun and Games," *American Demographics* 4 (August 1992): 44.

108. Marcy Magiera, "Kids, or Young Adult? Tie-Ins Can Be PG-13," *Advertising Age* (February 8, 1993): S14.

AS BASIL SCANS THE menu at the trendy health food restaurant Judy has dragged him to, he reflects on what a man will give up for love. Now that Judy has become a die-hard vegetarian, she's slowly but surely working on him to forsake those juicy steaks and burgers for healthier fare. He can't even hide from tofu and other vegan delights at school; the dining facility in his dorm just started offering "veggie" alternatives to its usual assortment of greasy "mystery meats" and other delicacies he has come to love.

Judy is totally into it; she claims that eating this way not only cuts out unwanted fat, but is good for the environment. Just his luck to fall head-over-heels for a "tree-hugger." As Basil gamely tries to decide between the stuffed artichokes with red pepper vinaigrette and the grilled marinated zucchini, fantasies of a flaming grill loaded with a 24-ounce T-bone dance before his eyes.

Motivation
and Values

4

INTRODUCTION

Judy certainly is not alone in believing that eating green is good for the body, the soul, and the planet. About 15 percent of America's 15 million college students eat vegetarian in a typical day, according to the National Restaurant Association. The proportion of students who are vegetarian is about two to three times greater than the rate found in the overall population, and female students are especially likely to avoid meat. In addition, many consumers who are concerned about where their food comes from have taken to buying organic products that have been grown only with natural pesticides and fertilizers. The organic food market is expected to grow fourfold to $10 billion per year within five years, and in late 1997 the U.S. Department of Agriculture passed regulations to certify which food products can truly be labeled organic. Anticipating a change in food preferences as these vegetarian and vegan college students enter the adult market, some major food companies are working on new products to cater to their needs. Pillsbury is marketing "The Green Giant Harvest Burger," and ConAgra offers a line of meatless meals called "Life Choice."[1]

The forces that drive people to buy and use products are generally straightforward, as when a person chooses what to have for lunch. As hard-core vegans demonstrate, however, even the consumption of basic food products may also be related to wide-ranging beliefs regarding what is appropriate or desirable. In some cases, these emotional responses create a deep commitment to the product. Sometimes people are not even fully aware of the forces that drive them toward some products and away from others. Often these choices are influenced by the person's *values*—his or her priorities and beliefs about the world.

To understand motivation is to understand *why* consumers do what they do. Why do people choose to Bungee jump off a bridge or go white-water rafting in the Yukon, while others spend their leisure time playing chess or gardening? Whether to quench a thirst, kill boredom, or to attain some deep spiritual experience, we do everything for a reason, even if we can't articulate what that reason is. Marketing students are taught from day one that the goal of marketing is to satisfy consumers' needs. However, this insight is useless unless we can discover *what* those needs are and *why* they exist. A popular beer commercial says, "Why ask why?" In this chapter, we'll find out.

THE MOTIVATION PROCESS

Motivation refers to the processes that cause people to behave as they do. It occurs when a need is aroused that the consumer wishes to satisfy. Once a need has been activated, a state of tension exists that drives the consumer to attempt to reduce or eliminate the need. This need may be *utilitarian* (i.e., a desire to achieve some functional or practical benefit, as when a person loads up on green vegetables for nutritional reasons) or it may be *hedonic* (i.e., an experiential need, involving emotional responses or fantasies, as when Basil thinks longingly about a juicy steak sizzling on the grill). The desired end state is the consumer's **goal.** Marketers try to create products and services that will provide the desired benefits and permit the consumer to reduce this tension.

Whether the need is utilitarian or hedonic, a discrepancy exists between the consumer's present state and some ideal state. This gulf creates a state of tension. The magnitude of this tension determines the urgency the consumer feels to reduce the tension. This degree of arousal is called a **drive.** A basic need can be satisfied any number of ways, and the specific path a person chooses is influenced both by his or her unique set of experiences and by the values instilled by the culture in which the person has been raised.

These personal and cultural factors combine to create a **want,** which is one manifestation of a need. For example, hunger is a basic need that must be satisfied by all; the lack of food creates a tension state that can be reduced by the intake of such products as cheeseburgers, double fudge Oreo cookies, raw fish, or bean sprouts. The specific route to drive reduction is culturally and individually determined. Once the goal is attained, tension is reduced and the motivation recedes (for the time being). Motivation can be described in terms of its *strength,* or the pull it exerts on the consumer, and its *direction,* or the particular way the consumer attempts to reduce motivational tension.

The same product can be consumed to achieve utilitarian and hedonic goals. As this ad illustrates, for many drivers an automobile provides much more than simple transportation from Point A to Point B.

This ad for exercise equipment shows men a desired end state (as dictated by contemporary Western culture), and suggests a solution (purchase of the equipment) to attain it.

MOTIVATIONAL STRENGTH

The degree to which a person is willing to expend energy to reach one goal as opposed to another reflects his or her underlying motivation to attain that goal. Many theories have been advanced to explain why people behave the way they do. Most share the basic idea that people have some finite amount of energy that must be directed toward certain goals.

BIOLOGICAL VERSUS LEARNED NEEDS

Early work on motivation ascribed behavior to instinct, the innate patterns of behavior that are universal in a species. This view is now largely discredited. For one thing, the existence of an instinct is difficult to prove or disprove. The instinct is inferred from the behavior it is supposed to explain (this type of circular explanation is called a *tautology*).[2] It is like saying that a consumer buys products that are status symbols because he or she is motivated to attain status, which is hardly a satisfying explanation.

DRIVE THEORY

Drive theory focuses on biological needs that produce unpleasant states of arousal (e.g., your stomach grumbles during a morning class). We are motivated to reduce the tension caused by this arousal. Tension reduction has been proposed as a basic mechanism governing human behavior.

In a marketing context, tension refers to the unpleasant state that exists if a person's consumption needs are not fulfilled. A person may be grumpy if he hasn't eaten, or he may be dejected or angry if he cannot afford that new car he wants. This state activates goal-oriented behavior, which attempts to reduce or eliminate this unpleasant state and return to a balanced one, is called **homeostasis.**

Those behaviors that are successful in reducing the drive by satisfying the underlying need are strengthened and tend to be repeated. (This aspect of the learning process was discussed in chapter 3.) Your motivation to leave class early in order to grab a snack would be greater if you hadn't eaten in 24 hours than if you had eaten only two hours earlier. If you did sneak out and got indigestion after, say, wolfing down a package of Twinkies, you would be less likely to repeat this behavior the next time you wanted a snack. One's degree of motivation, then, depends on the distance between one's present state and the goal.

Drive theory, however, runs into difficulties when it tries to explain some facets of human behavior that run counter to its predictions. People often do things that *increase* a drive state rather than decrease it. For example, people may delay gratification. If you know you are going out for a lavish dinner, you might decide to forego a snack earlier in the day even though you are hungry at that time.

EXPECTANCY THEORY

Most current explanations of motivation focus on cognitive factors rather than biological ones to understand what drives behavior. **Expectancy theory** suggests that behavior is largely pulled by expectations of achieving desirable outcomes—*positive incentives*—rather than pushed from within. We choose one product over another because we expect this choice to have more positive consequences for us. Thus the term *drive* is used here more loosely to refer to both physical and cognitive processes.

MOTIVATIONAL DIRECTION

Motives have direction as well as strength. They are goal oriented in that specific objectives are desired to satisfy a need. Most goals can be reached by a number of routes, and the objective of marketers is to convince consumers that the alternative they offer provides the best chance to attain the goal. For example, a consumer who decides that she needs a pair of jeans to help her reach her goal of being accepted by others can choose among Levi's, Wranglers, Jnco, Calvin Klein, and many other alternatives, each of which promises to deliver certain benefits.

NEEDS VERSUS WANTS

The specific way a need is satisfied depends on the individual's unique history, learning experiences, and cultural environment. The particular form of consumption used to satisfy a need is termed a *want.* For example, two classmates may feel their stomachs rumbling during a lunchtime lecture. If neither person has eaten since the night before, the strength of their respective needs (hunger) would be about the same. However, the ways each person goes about satisfying this need might be quite dif-

MULTICULTURAL DIMENSIONS

Consumer desire has been defined as "a feeling of longing for goods or services not presently enjoyed."[3] Consumers in the former Eastern bloc are now bombarded with images of luxury goods, yet may still have trouble obtaining basic necessities. In one study in which Romanian students named the products they hoped for, their wish lists included not only the expected items such as sports cars and the latest model televisions, but also water, soap, furniture, and food.

Their frustration was summed up by one informant, who explained, "Then [before the democratic revolution] there were few goods on the shelves, but we could afford them. Now there are more goods on the shelves, but no one can afford them."[4] Ironically, these consumers appear to be less happy now, because they are given more to desire but still can't attain these products. This frustration is a result of *relative deprivation*—the gulf between what is available and what one possesses becomes wider.

ferent. The first person may be a vegan like Judy who fantasizes about gulping down a big handful of trail mix, while the second person may be a meat hound like Basil who is aroused by the prospect of a greasy cheeseburger and fries.

TYPES OF NEEDS

People are born with a need for certain elements necessary to maintain life, such as food, water, air, and shelter. These are called *biogenic needs*. People have many other needs, however, that are not innate. *Psychogenic needs* are acquired in the process of becoming a member of a culture. These include the need for status, power, affiliation, and so on. Psychogenic needs reflect the priorities of a culture, and their effect on behavior will vary from environment to environment. For example, an American consumer may be driven to devote a good chunk of his income to products that permit him to display his wealth and status, while his Japanese counterpart may work equally hard to ensure that he does not stand out from his group.

Consumers can also be motivated to satisfy either utilitarian or hedonic needs. The satisfaction of *utilitarian needs* implies that consumers will emphasize the objective, tangible attributes of products, such as miles per gallon in a car; the amount of fat, calories, and protein in a cheeseburger; and the durability of a pair of blue jeans. *Hedonic needs* are subjective and experiential; consumers might rely on a product to meet their needs for excitement, self-confidence, fantasy, and so on. Of course, consumers can be motivated to purchase a product because it provides *both* types of benefits. For example, a mink coat might be bought because of the luxurious image it portrays and because it also happens to keep one warm through the long cold winter.

MOTIVATIONAL CONFLICTS

A goal has *valence,* which means that it can be positive or negative. A positively valued goal is one toward which consumers direct their behavior; they are motivated to *approach* the goal and will seek out products that will be instrumental in attaining it. However, not all behavior is motivated by the desire to approach a goal. As we saw in last chapter's discussion of negative reinforcement, consumers may instead be motivated to *avoid* a negative outcome. They will structure their purchases or consumption activities to reduce the chances of attaining this end result. For example, many consumers work hard to avoid rejection, a negative goal. They will stay away from products that they associate with social disapproval. Products such as deodorants and mouthwash frequently rely on consumers' negative motivation by depicting the onerous social consequences of underarm odor or bad breath.

Because a purchase decision can involve more than one source of motivation, consumers often find themselves in situations in which different motives, both positive and negative, conflict with one another. Because marketers are attempting to satisfy consumers' needs, they can also be helpful by providing possible solutions to these dilemmas. As shown in Figure 4–1, three general types of conflicts can occur: approach–approach, approach–avoidance, and avoidance–avoidance.

APPROACH–APPROACH CONFLICT

In an approach–approach conflict, a person must choose between two desirable alternatives. A student might be torn between going home for the holidays or going on a skiing trip with friends. Or, she might have to choose between two CDs.

The **theory of cognitive dissonance** is based on the premise that people have a need for order and consistency in their lives and that a state of tension is created when beliefs or behaviors conflict with one another. The conflict that arises when choosing between two alternatives may be resolved through a process of cognitive dissonance reduction, in which people are motivated to reduce this inconsistency (or dissonance) and thus eliminate unpleasant tension.[5]

A state of dissonance occurs when there is a psychological inconsistency between two or more beliefs or behaviors. It often occurs when a consumer must make a choice between two products, both of which usually possess both good and bad qualities. By choosing one product and not the other, the person gets the bad qualities of the chosen product and loses out on the good qualities of the unchosen one.

This loss creates an unpleasant, dissonant state that the person is motivated to reduce. People tend to convince themselves after the fact that the choice they made was the smart one by finding additional reasons to support the alternative they chose, or perhaps by "discovering" flaws with the option they did not choose. A marketer can resolve an approach–approach conflict by bundling several benefits

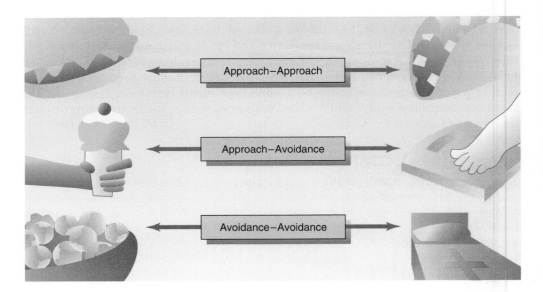

FIGURE 4–1 ■ **Three Types of Motivational Conflicts**

together. For example, Miller Lite's claim that it is "less filling" *and* "tastes great" allows the drinker to "have his beer and drink it too."

APPROACH–AVOIDANCE CONFLICT

Many of the products and services we desire have negative consequences attached to them as well. We may feel guilty or ostentatious when buying a status-laden product such as a fur coat or we might feel like a glutton when contemplating a tempting package of Twinkies. When we desire a goal but wish to avoid it at the same time, an approach–avoidance conflict exists.

Some solutions to these conflicts include the proliferation of fake furs, which eliminate guilt about harming animals to make a fashion statement, and the success of diet foods, such as those produced by Weight Watchers, that promise good food without the calories [http://www.weight-watchers.com]. Many marketers try to overcome guilt by convincing consumers that they are deserving of luxuries (e.g., when the model for L'Oréal cosmetics claims "Because I'm worth it!").

AVOIDANCE–AVOIDANCE CONFLICT

Sometimes consumers find themselves "caught between a rock and a hard place." They may face a choice with two undesirable alternatives, for instance the option of either throwing more money into an old car or buying a new one. Marketers frequently address this conflict with messages that stress the unforeseen benefits of choosing one option (e.g., by emphasizing special credit plans to ease the pain of new-car payments).

CLASSIFYING CONSUMER NEEDS

Much research has been done on classifying human needs. On the one hand, some psychologists have tried to define a universal inventory of needs that could be traced systematically to explain virtually all behavior. One such effort, developed by Henry Murray, delineates a set of 20 psychogenic needs that (sometimes in combination) result in specific behaviors. These needs include such dimensions as *autonomy* (being independent), *defendance* (defending the self against criticism), and even *play* (engaging in pleasurable activities).[6]

SPECIFIC NEEDS AND BUYING BEHAVIOR

Other motivational approaches have focused on specific needs and their ramifications for behavior. For example, individuals with a high *need for achievement* strongly value personal accomplishment.[7] They place a premium on products and services that signify success because these consumption items provide feedback about the realization of their goals. These consumers are good prospects for products that provide evidence of their achievement. One study of working women found that those who were high in achievement motivation were more likely to choose clothing they considered businesslike, and less likely to be interested in apparel that accentuated their femininity.[8] Some other important needs that are relevant to consumer behavior include the following:

- *Need for affiliation* (to be in the company of other people):[9] This need is relevant to products and services that are "consumed" in groups and alleviate loneliness, such as team sports, bars, and shopping malls.
- *Need for power* (to control one's environment):[10] Many products and services allow consumers to feel that they have mastery over their surroundings,

ranging from "hopped-up" muscle cars and loud boom boxes (large portable radios) that impose one's musical tastes on others to luxury resorts that promise to respond to the customer's every whim.

- *Need for uniqueness* (to assert one's individual identity):[11] This need is satisfied by products that pledge to accentuate a consumer's distinctive qualities. For example, Cachet perfume claims to be "as individual as you are."

MASLOW'S HIERARCHY OF NEEDS

One influential approach to motivation was proposed by the psychologist Abraham Maslow. Maslow's approach is a general one originally developed to understand personal growth and the attainment of "peak experiences."[12] Maslow formulated a hierarchy of biogenic and psychogenic needs, in which levels of motives are specified. A hierarchical approach implies that the order of development is fixed—that is, a certain level must be attained before the next, higher one is activated. This universal approach to motivation has been adapted by marketers because it (indirectly) specifies certain types of product benefits people might be looking for, depending on the different stages in their development and/or their environmental conditions.

These levels are summarized in Figure 4–2. At each level, different priorities exist in terms of the product benefits a consumer is looking for. Ideally, an individual progresses up the hierarchy until his or her dominant motivation is a focus on "ultimate" goals, such as justice and beauty. Unfortunately, this state is difficult to achieve (at least on a regular basis); most of us have to be satisfied with occasional glimpses, or peak experiences. Examples of product appeals tailored to each level are provided in Table 4–1.

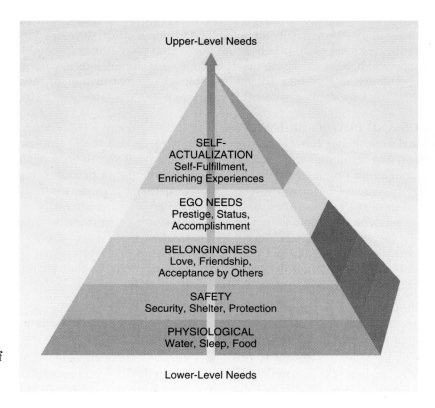

FIGURE 4–2 ■ Levels of Needs in the Maslow Hierarchy

TABLE 4–1 ■ Maslow's Hierarchy and Marketing Strategies

LEVEL OF HIERARCHY	RELEVANT PRODUCTS	EXAMPLE
Self-actualization	Hobbies, travel, education	U.S. Army—"Be all you can be."
Ego needs	Cars, furniture, credit cards, stores, country clubs, liquors	Royal Salute Scotch—"What the rich give the wealthy."
Belongingness	Clothing, grooming products, clubs, drinks	Pepsi—"You're in the Pepsi generation."
Safety	Insurance, alarm systems, retirement investments	Allstate Insurance—"You're in good hands with Allstate."
Physiology	Medicines, staple items, generics	Quaker Oat Bran—"It's the right thing to do."

The implication of Maslow's hierarchy is that one must first satisfy basic needs before progressing up the ladder (i.e., a starving man is not interested in status symbols, friendship, or self-fulfillment). The application of this hierarchy by marketers has been somewhat simplistic, especially as the same product or activity can satisfy a number of different needs. For example, one study found that gardening can satisfy needs at every level of the hierarchy:[13]

- *Physiological:* "I like to work in the soil."
- *Safety:* "I feel safe in the garden."
- *Social:* "I can share my produce with others."
- *Esteem:* "I can create something of beauty."
- *Self-actualization:* "My garden gives me a sense of peace."

Another problem with taking Maslow's hierarchy too literally is that it is culture bound. The assumptions of the hierarchy may be restricted to Western culture. People in other cultures (or, for that matter, in Western culture itself) may question the order of the levels as specified. A religious person who has taken a vow of celibacy would not necessarily agree that physiological needs must be satisfied before self-fulfillment can occur.

Similarly, many Asian cultures operate on the premise that the welfare of the group (belongingness needs) are more highly valued than needs of the individual (esteem needs). The point is that this hierarchy, although widely applied in marketing, should be valued because it reminds us that consumers may have different need priorities in different consumption situations and at different stages in their lives, not because it *exactly* specifies a consumer's progression up the ladder of needs.

CONSUMER INVOLVEMENT

As we have seen, a consumer's motivation to attain a goal influences his or her desire to expend the effort necessary to attain the products or services believed to be instrumental in satisfying that objective. However, not everyone is motivated to the same extent—one person might be convinced he or she can't live without the latest style or modern convenience, whereas another is not interested in this item at all.

Involvement refers to "the level of perceived personal importance and/or interest evoked by a stimulus (or stimuli) within a specific situation."[14] As illustrated in Figure 4–3, this definition implies that aspects of the person, the product, and the

MULTICULTURAL DIMENSIONS

Presumably, a person who has had all of his or her needs satisfied lives in "paradise." Conceptualizations of paradise have implications for the marketing and consumption of any products, such as vacation travel, that seek to invoke an ideal state. However, the definition of just what constitutes paradise appears to differ across cultures. To pursue this idea further, the concept of paradise was compared between groups of American and Dutch college students. Informants in both cultures constructed a collage of images to illustrate their overall concept of paradise, and they wrote an essay to accompany and explain this collage. Some similarities were evident in the two societies; both Americans and Dutch emphasized the personal, experiential aspects of paradise, saying "paradise is different for everyone . . . a feeling . . . a state of being." In addition, individuals in both societies said that paradise must include family, friends, and significant others.

However, the Dutch and Americans differed in important and interesting ways. The Americans consistently emphasized hedonism, materialism, individuality, creativity, and issues of time and space consistent with a society in which time is segmented and viewed almost as a commodity (more on this in chapter 10). Conversely, the Dutch respondents showed a concern for social and environmental responsibility, collective societal order and equality, and a balance between work and play as part of paradise. For instance, one Dutch person said that "Respect for animals, flowers, and plants . . . regenerating energy sources, such as wind, water, and sun" are all important parts of paradise. Marketers should expect that, because concepts of paradise differ somewhat, different images and behaviors may be evoked when Americans and Dutch are confronted with marketing messages such as "Hawaii is Paradise," or "you can experience paradise when you drive this car."[15]

A Dutch respondent's collage emphasizes this person's conception of paradise as a place where there is interpersonal harmony and concern for the environment.

situation all combine to determine the consumer's motivation to process product-related information at a given point in time. When consumers are intent on doing what they can to satisfy a need, they will be motivated to pay attention and process any information felt to be relevant to achieving their goals.

On the other hand, a person may not bother to pay any attention to the same information if it is not seen as relevant to satisfying some need. One person who prides himself on his knowledge of exercise equipment may read anything he can find about the subject, spend his spare time in sports stores, and so on, whereas another person might skip over this information without giving it a second thought.

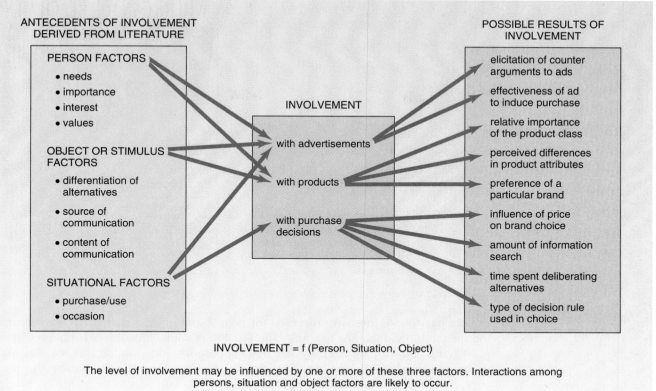

ANTECEDENTS OF INVOLVEMENT
DERIVED FROM LITERATURE

POSSIBLE RESULTS OF
INVOLVEMENT

PERSON FACTORS

- needs
- importance
- interest
- values

OBJECT OR STIMULUS FACTORS

- differentiation of alternatives
- source of communication
- content of communication

SITUATIONAL FACTORS

- purchase/use
- occasion

INVOLVEMENT

with advertisements

with products

with purchase decisions

elicitation of counter arguments to ads

effectiveness of ad to induce purchase

relative importance of the product class

perceived differences in product attributes

preference of a particular brand

influence of price on brand choice

amount of information search

time spent deliberating alternatives

type of decision rule used in choice

INVOLVEMENT = f (Person, Situation, Object)

The level of involvement may be influenced by one or more of these three factors. Interactions among persons, situation and object factors are likely to occur.

FIGURE 4–3 ■ **Conceptualizing Involvement**
Source: Judith Lynne Zaichkowsky, "Conceptualizing Involvement," *Journal of Advertising* 15 (1986)2: 4–14.

Involvement can be viewed as the motivation to process information.[16] To the degree that there is a perceived linkage between a consumer's needs, goals, or values and product knowledge, the consumer will be motivated to pay attention to product information. When relevant knowledge is activated in memory, a motivational state is created that drives behavior (e.g., shopping). As involvement with a product increases, the consumer devotes more attention to ads related to the product, exerts more cognitive effort to understand these ads, and focuses attention on the product-related information in them.[17]

LEVELS OF INVOLVEMENT: FROM INERTIA TO PASSION

The type of information processing that will occur thus depends on the consumer's level of involvement. It can range from *simple processing,* in which only the basic features of a message are considered, all the way to *elaboration,* in which the incoming information is linked to one's preexisting knowledge systems.[18]

A person's degree of involvement can be conceived as a continuum, ranging from absolute lack of interest in a marketing stimulus at one end to obsession at the other. Consumption at the low end of involvement is characterized by **inertia,** in which decisions are made out of habit because the consumer lacks the motivation to consider alternatives. At the high end of involvement, we can expect to find the

This ad for lifestyle magazines targeted to men underscores the strategic value of reaching highly involved consumers.

type of passionate intensity reserved for people and objects that carry great meaning for the individual. For example, the passion of some consumers for famous people (living such as Michael Jordan or—supposedly—dead such as Elvis Presley) demonstrates the high end of the involvement continuum. For the most part, however, a consumer's involvement level with products falls somewhere in the middle, and the marketing strategist must determine the relative level of importance to understand how much elaboration of product information will occur.

THE MANY FACES OF INVOLVEMENT

As previously defined, involvement can take many forms. Involvement can be cognitive, as when a "webhead" is motivated to learn all she can about the latest specs of a new multimedia PC, or emotional, as when the thought of a new Armani suit gives a clotheshorse goosebumps.[19] Further, the very act of buying the Armani may be very involving for people who are passionately devoted to shopping. To complicate matters further, advertisements, such as those produced for Nike or Adidas, may themselves be involving for some reason (e.g., because they make us laugh, cry, or inspire us to work harder).

It seems that involvement is a fuzzy concept, because it overlaps with other things and means different things to different people. Indeed, the consensus is that there are actually several broad types of involvement related to the product, the message, or the perceiver.[20]

PRODUCT INVOLVEMENT

Product involvement is related to a consumer's level of interest in a particular product. Many sales promotions are designed to increase this type of involvement. In a contest sponsored by Dare perfume, for example, women submitted details of their most intimate trysts by letter or by phone to radio talk shows. The winning stories were edited into a romance novel published by Bantam Books. These books, in turn, were given away as a gift with the purchase of the perfume.[21]

MESSAGE-RESPONSE INVOLVEMENT

Message-response involvement (also known as *advertising involvement*), refers to the consumer's interest in processing marketing communications.[22] Television is considered a low-involvement medium, because it requires a passive viewer who exerts relatively little control (remote control "zipping" notwithstanding) over content. In contrast, print is a high-involvement medium. The reader is actively involved in processing the information and is able to pause and reflect on what he or she has read before moving on.[23] The role of message characteristics in changing attitudes is discussed further in chapter 8.

EGO INVOLVEMENT

Ego involvement (sometimes termed *enduring involvement*) refers to the importance of a product to a consumer's self-concept. This concept implies a high level of social risk; the prospect of the product's not performing its desired function may result in embarrassment or damage to the consumer's self-concept. (chapter 5 is devoted to the importance of the self-concept for consumer behavior issues.) This type of involvement is independent of particular purchase situations. It is an ongoing concern related to the self and hedonic experiences (e.g., the emotions felt as a result of using the product).[24]

MEASURING INVOLVEMENT

The measurement of involvement is important for many marketing applications. For example, research evidence indicates that a viewer who is more involved with a television show will also respond more positively to commercials contained in that show, and that these spots will have a greater chance of influencing his or her purchase intentions.[25] The many conceptualizations of involvement have led to some confusion about the best way to measure the concept. The scale shown in Table 4–2 is one widely used method.[26]

TABLE 4–2 ■ **A Scale to Measure Involvement**

	TO ME [OBJECT TO BE JUDGED] IS		
1.	important	_: _: _: _: _: _: _	unimportant*
2.	boring	_: _: _: _: _: _: _	interesting
3.	relevant	_: _: _: _: _: _: _	irrelevant*
4.	exciting	_: _: _: _: _: _: _	unexciting*
5.	means nothing	_: _: _: _: _: _: _	means a lot to me
6.	appealing	_: _: _: _: _: _: _	unappealing*
7.	fascinating	_: _: _: _: _: _: _	mundane*
8.	worthless	_: _: _: _: _: _: _	valuable
9.	involving	_: _: _: _: _: _: _	uninvolving*
10.	not needed	_: _: _: _: _: _: _	needed

Note: Totaling the 10 items gives a score from a low of 10 to a high of 70.

*Indicates item is reverse scored. For example, a score of 7 for item no. 1 (important/unimportant) would actually be scored as 1.

Source: Judith Lynne Zaichkowsky, "The Personal Involvement Inventory: Reduction, Revision, and Application to Advertising," *Journal of Advertising,* 23 (December 1994)4: 59–70.

TEASING OUT THE DIMENSIONS OF INVOLVEMENT

A pair of French researchers devised a scale to measure the antecedents of product involvement. Recognizing that consumers can be involved with a product because it is a risky purchase and/or its use reflects on or affects the self, they advocate the development of an *involvement profile* containing five components:[27]

- The personal interest a consumer has in a product category
- The perceived importance of the potential negative consequences associated with a poor product choice
- The probability of making a bad purchase
- The pleasure value of the product category
- The sign value of the product category

These researchers asked a sample of homemakers to rate a set of 14 product categories on each of the above facets of involvement. The results are shown in Table 4–3. These data indicate that no single component captures consumer involvement, because this quality can occur for different reasons. For example, the purchase of a durable product such as a vacuum cleaner is seen as risky, because one is stuck with a bad choice for many years. However, the vacuum cleaner does not provide pleasure (hedonic value), nor is it high in sign value (i.e., its use is not related to the person's self-concept). In contrast, chocolate is high in pleasure value but is not seen as risky or closely related to the self. Dresses and bras, on the other hand, appear to be involving for a combination of reasons.

TABLE 4–3 ■ **Involvement Profiles for a Set of French Consumer Products**

	IMPORTANCE OF NEGATIVE CONSEQUENCES	SUBJECTIVE PROBABILITY OF MISPURCHASE	PLEASURE VALUE	SIGN VALUE
Dresses	121	112	147	181
Bras	117	115	106	130
Washing machines	118	109	106	111
TV sets	112	100	122	95
Vacuum cleaners	110	112	70	78
Irons	103	95	72	76
Champagne	109	120	125	125
Oil	89	97	65	92
Yogurt	86	83	106	78
Chocolate	80	89	123	75
Shampoo	96	103	90	81
Toothpaste	95	95	94	105
Facial soap	82	90	114	118
Detergents	79	82	56	63

Average product score = 100.

Note the first two antecedents of personal importance and importance of negative consequences are combined in these data.

Source: Gilles Laurent and Jean-Noël Kapferer, "Measuring Consumer Involvement Profiles." *Journal of Marketing Research* 22 (February 1985): 45, Table 3. By permission of American Marketing Association.

SEGMENTING BY INVOLVEMENT LEVELS

A measurement approach of this nature allows consumer researchers to capture the diversity of the involvement construct, and it also provides the potential to use involvement as a basis for market segmentation. For example, a yogurt manufacturer might find that even though its product is low in sign value for one group of consumers, it might be highly related to the self-concept of another market segment, such as health food enthusiasts or avid dieters. The company could adapt its strategy to account for the motivation of different segments to process information about the product. Note also that involvement with a product class may vary across cultures. Although this sample of French consumers rated champagne high in both sign value and personal value, the ability of champagne to provide pleasure or be central to self-definition might not transfer to other countries (e.g., Islamic cultures).

STRATEGIES TO INCREASE INVOLVEMENT

Although consumers differ in their level of involvement with respect to a product message, marketers do not have to just sit back and hope for the best. By being aware of some basic factors that increase or decrease attention, they can take steps to increase the likelihood that product information will get through. A consumer's motivation to process relevant information can be enhanced fairly easily by the marketer who uses one or more of the following techniques:[28]

- Appeal to the consumers' hedonic needs. For example, ads using sensory appeals generate higher levels of attention.[29]
- Use novel stimuli, such as unusual cinematography, sudden silences, or unexpected movements in commercials.
- Use prominent stimuli, such as loud music and fast action, to capture attention in commercials. In print formats, larger ads increase attention. Also, viewers look longer at colored pictures as opposed to black and white.
- Include celebrity endorsers to generate higher interest in commercials. (This strategy will be discussed in chapter 8.)
- Build a bond with consumers by maintaining an ongoing relationship with them. Learn from the actions of Saturn, the subsidiary of General Motors [http://www.saturncars.com]. The car maker has cultivated a group of loyal, even fanatic, consumers. This high involvement level was evident during the company's "homecoming," when 25,000 Saturn owners journeyed to the Saturn factory in Spring Hill, Tennessee for a complimentary weekend of tours, dances, and barbecues.[30]

VALUES

A **value** is a belief that some condition is preferable to its opposite. For example, it's safe to assume that most people place a priority on freedom, preferring it to slavery. Others avidly pursue products and services that will make them look young, believing that this is preferable to appearing old. A person's set of values plays a very important role in consumption activities—many products and services are purchased because people believe these products will help to attain a value-related goal.

Two people can believe in the same behaviors (e.g., vegetarianism) but their underlying belief systems may be quite different (e.g., animal activism versus health concerns). The extent to which people share a belief system is a function of individual, social, and cultural forces. Advocates of a given belief system often seek out others with similar beliefs, so that social networks overlap and as a result believers tend to be exposed to information that supports their beliefs (e.g., "tree-huggers" rarely hang out with loggers).[31]

CORE VALUES

Every culture has a set of values that it imparts to its members.[32] For example, people in one culture might feel that being a unique individual is preferable to subordinating one's identity to the group, whereas another culture may emphasize the virtues of group membership. A study by Wirthlin Worldwide, for example, found that the most important values to Asian executives are hard work, respect for learning, and honesty. In contrast, North American businesspeople emphasize the values of personal freedom, self-reliance, and freedom of expression.[33]

In many cases, however, values are universal. Who does not desire health, wisdom, or world peace? What sets cultures apart is the *relative importance,* or ranking, of these universal values. This set of rankings constitutes a culture's **value system.**[34] To illustrate a difference in value systems, consider the results of a study by Dentsu, a large Japanese advertising agency. Consumers in New York, Los Angeles, and Tokyo were asked to indicate their preferences regarding the goals an ideal society should aim for. There was a high degree of consensus within the American sample: Residents on each coast said their highest ideal is a "society in which people can live safely." In contrast, Tokyo residents ranked first the goal of a "society with a comprehensive welfare system." About 45 percent of the Americans endorsed the idea of a "society which is very competitive, but in which everybody has an equal chance of success," but only 25 percent of Tokyo residents echoed this sentiment.[35]

Every culture is characterized by its members' endorsement of a value system. These end states may not be equally endorsed by every individual, and in some cases, values may even seem to contradict one another (e.g., Americans appear to value both conformity and individuality, and seek to find some accommodation between the two). Nonetheless, it is usually possible to identify a general set of *core values* that uniquely define a culture. These beliefs are taught to us by *socialization*

Values regarding sexuality are constantly evolving. Some younger people have elected to refrain altogether from premarital sex. A highly visible way to express the value of abstinence is offered by the chastity belts available for men and women in a catalog.

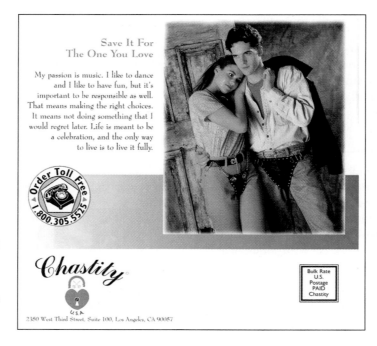

personality

individual

Peperoni

This Swedish shoe ad appeals to the value of individuality.

agents, including parents, friends, and teachers. The process of learning the beliefs and behaviors endorsed by one's own culture is termed **enculturation.** In contrast, the process of learning the value system and behaviors of another culture (often a priority for those who wish to understand consumers and markets in foreign countries) is called **acculturation.**

Core values such as freedom, youthfulness, achievement, materialism, and activity have been claimed to characterize American culture, but even these basic beliefs are subject to change. For example, Americans' emphasis on youth is eroding as the population ages (see chapter 15). Table 4–4 identifies the dominant values underlying a set of American print ads representing the period from 1900 to 1980. The prevalence of product effectiveness as an underlying advertising theme is obvious.

TABLE 4–4 ■ **Cultural Values Frequently Emphasized in American Advertising: 1900–1980**

OVERALL VALUE	THEMES INCLUDED	PROPORTION OF ADS USING VALUE AS CENTRAL THEME
Practical	Effectiveness, durability, convenience	44
Family	Nurturance in family, happy home, getting married	17
New	Modernism, improvement	14
Cheap	Economy, bargain, good value	13
Healthy	Fitness, vigor, athleticism	12
Sexy/vain	Good appearance, glamor, eroticism	13
Wisdom	Knowledge, experience	11
Unique	Expense, value, distinctiveness, rarity	10

Source: Adapted from Richard W. Pollay, "The Identification and Distribution of Values Manifest in Print Advertising, 1900–1980." Adapted with the permission of Lexington Books, an imprint of Macmillan, Inc., from *Personal Values and Consumer Psychology* by eds. Robert E. Pitts Jr. and Arch G. Woodside. Copyright © 1984 by Lexington Books.

APPLICATIONS OF VALUES TO CONSUMER BEHAVIOR

Despite their importance, values have not been as widely applied to direct examinations of consumer behavior as might be expected. One reason is that broad-based concepts such as freedom, security, or inner harmony are more likely to affect general purchasing patterns than to differentiate between brands within a product category. For this reason, some researchers have found it convenient to make distinctions among broad-based *cultural values* such as security or happiness, *consumption-specific values* such as convenient shopping or prompt service, and *product-specific values* such as ease of use or durability.[36] For example, people who value group affiliation and approval have been shown to place more importance on style and brand name when evaluating the desirability of clothing products.[37]

Because values drive much of consumer behavior (at least in a very general sense), it could be said that virtually *all* consumer research is ultimately related to the identification and measurement of values. This section will describe some specific attempts by researchers to measure cultural values and apply this knowledge to marketing strategy.

THE ROKEACH VALUE SURVEY

The psychologist Milton Rokeach identified a set of **terminal values,** or desired end states, that apply to many different cultures. *The Rokeach Value Survey,* a scale used to measure these values, also includes a set of **instrumental values,** which are composed of actions needed to achieve these terminal values.[38] These two sets of values appear in Table 4–5.

TABLE 4–5 ■ **Two Types of Values in the Rokeach Value Survey**

INSTRUMENTAL VALUES	TERMINAL VALUES
Ambitious	A comfortable life
Broadminded	An exciting life
Capable	A sense of accomplishment
Cheerful	A world at peace
Clean	A world of beauty
Courageous	Equality
Forgiving	Family security
Helpful	Freedom
Honest	Happiness
Imaginative	Inner harmony
Independent	Mature love
Intellectual	National security
Logical	Pleasure
Loving	Salvation
Obedient	Self-respect
Polite	Social recognition
Responsible	True friendship
Self-controlled	Wisdom

Source: Richard W. Pollay, "Measuring the Cultural Values Manifest in Advertising," *Current Issues and Research in Advertising* (1983): 71–92. Reprinted by permission of University of Michigan Division of Research.

MULTICULTURAL DIMENSIONS

Japanese culture is well known for its emphasis on cleanliness. The Shinto religion requires a ritual washing of hands and mouth before entering shrines, and people always take off their shoes at home to avoid dirtying the floors. When people give money as a wedding gift, they often iron the bills before placing them in the envelope. Some laundromats even allow customers to rinse out the inside of a machine before using it.

This value has reached new proportions since a food poisoning epidemic in the summer of 1996. Demand for products such as antiseptic bicycle grips, karaoke microphones, and gauze masks is skyrocketing, and a rash of sterilized products ranging from stationery and floppy disks to telephones and dishwashers is invading the market. Pentel makes a germ-free pen decorated with a medical blue cross; the popular brand is advertised with the slogan, "The pen is mightier than the bacterium." Japan's Sanwa Bank literally "launders money" for its customers in specially designed ATM machines, and Tokyo's Mitsubishi Bank opened a "Total Anti-Germ Branch" featuring ATMs with surfaces made of plastics saturated with chemicals that resist bacteria and fungus. A bank spokesman noted the branch is especially popular with young female customers who say they "don't want to touch things handled by middle-aged men."[39]

THE LIST OF VALUES (LOV)

Although some evidence indicates that differences on these global values do translate into product-specific preferences and differences in media usage, the Rokeach Value Survey has not been widely used by marketing researchers.[40] As an alternative, the *List of Values (LOV) Scale* was developed to isolate values with more direct marketing applications. This instrument identifies nine consumer segments based on the values they endorse and relates each value to differences in consumption behaviors. These segments include consumers who place a priority on such values as a sense of belonging, excitement, warm relationships with others, and security. For example, people who endorse the value of sense of belonging are older and more likely to read *Reader's Digest* and *TV Guide*, drink and entertain more, and prefer group activities than people who do not endorse this value as highly. In contrast, those who endorse the value of excitement are younger and prefer *Rolling Stone* magazine.[41]

THE MEANS-END CHAIN MODEL

Another research approach that incorporates values is termed a *means–end chain model*. This approach assumes that very specific product attributes are linked at levels of increasing abstraction to terminal values. The person has valued end states, and he or she chooses among alternative means to attain these goals. Products are thus valued as the means to an end. Through a technique called **laddering**, consumers' associations between specific attributes and general consequences are uncovered. Consumers are helped to climb up the "ladder" of abstraction that connects functional product attributes with desired end states.[42]

To understand how laddering works, consider a woman who expresses a liking for a flavored potato chip. Probing might reveal that this attribute is linked to strong taste (another attribute). A consequence of strong taste is that she eats fewer chips. As a result, she won't get fat, which in turn means that she will have a better figure. Finally, a better figure results in greater self-esteem, a terminal value for this person.[43]

The notion that products are consumed because they are instrumental in attaining more abstract values is central to one application of this technique, called the *Means–End Conceptualization of the Components of Advertising Strategy (MECCAS)*. In this approach, researchers first generate a map depicting relationships between functional product or service attributes and terminal values. This information is then used to develop advertising strategy by identifying elements such as the following:[44]

- *Message elements:* the specific attributes or product features to be depicted
- *Consumer benefit:* the positive consequences of using the product or service
- *Executional framework:* the overall style and tone of the advertisement
- *Leverage point:* the way the message will activate the terminal value by linking it with specific product features
- *Driving force:* the end value on which the advertising will focus

This technique was used to develop advertising strategy for Federal Express [http://www.fedex.com]. The researchers developed a "Hierarchical Value Map" for secretaries, an important group of decision makers in the category of overnight delivery services. As shown in Figure 4–4, concrete attributes of competitive services, such as having a drop box or on-time delivery, were successively related to more abstract benefits, such as "makes me look good" or "saves time." These intermediate levels were then linked, or laddered, to reveal their relationship to the terminal values of peace of mind and self-esteem.

Based on these results, an advertisement was created. Its message elements emphasized Federal Express' satellite communications network. The consumer benefit was the reliability of the service, which made work easier. The executional framework was a humorous one. A secretary is trying to track down an overnight delivery. She and her boss are interrupted and taken to view the Federal Express satellite system. As a result, the secretary sees the benefit of using the company.

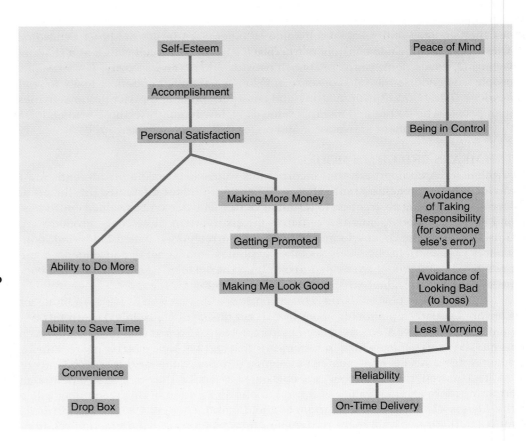

FIGURE 4–4 ■
**Secretaries'
Hierarchical Value Map
for Overnight Delivery
Services**
Source: Adapted from
Thomas J. Reynolds and
Alyce Byrd Craddock, "The
Application of the MECCAS
Model to the Development
and Assessment of
Advertising Strategy: A Case
Study," *Journal of
Advertising Research*
(April/May 1988): 43–54.

The leverage point is that using this service allows her to be in control, which in turn provides peace of mind, the driving force (terminal value).

SYNDICATED SURVEYS

A number of companies track changes in values through large-scale surveys. The results of these studies are then sold to marketers, who pay a fee to receive regular updates on changes and trends. This approach originated in the mid-1960s, when Playtex was concerned about sagging girdle sales. The company commissioned the market research firm of Yankelovich, Skelly & White to see why sales had dropped. Their research determined that sales had been affected by a shift in values regarding appearance and naturalness. Playtex went on to design lighter, less restrictive garments, while Yankelovich went on to track the impact of these types of changes in a range of industries. Gradually, the firm developed the idea of one big study to track American attitudes. In 1970, the Yankelovich Monitor™ was introduced. It is based on two-hour interviews with 4,000 respondents.[45]

For example, the Yankelovich Monitor reports a movement among American consumers in the 1990s toward simplification and away from hype, as people try to streamline their hectic lives and reduce their concerns about gaining the approval of others through their purchases. Subaru incorporated this finding into its advertising strategy: In one TV spot the voice-over proclaims, "I want a car . . . Don't tell me about wood paneling, about winning the respect of my neighbors. They're my neighbors. They're not my heroes . . ."[46] A successful campaign for Sprite tells us that "Image is nothing. Obey your thirst."

Today, many other syndicated surveys also track changes in values; some of these are operated by advertising agencies to allow them to stay on top of important cultural trends and help them to shape the messages they craft on behalf of their clients. These services include VALS 2 (more on this in chapter 6), GlobalScan (operated by the advertising agency Backer Spielvogel Bates), New Wave (the Ogilvy & Mather advertising agency), and the Lifestyles Study conducted by the DDB Needham advertising agency.

MATERIALISM: "HE WHO DIES WITH THE MOST TOYS, WINS . . . "

During World War II, members of "cargo cults" in the South Pacific literally worshiped cargo that was salvaged from crashed aircraft or washed ashore from ships. These people believed that the ships and planes passing near their islands were piloted by their ancestors, and they tried to attract the ships and planes to their villages. They went so far as to construct fake planes from straw in hopes of luring the real ones to their islands.[47]

Although most people don't literally worship material goods in quite this way, things do play a central role in many people's lives. **Materialism** refers to the importance people attach to worldly possessions. Americans inhabit a highly materialistic society in which people often gauge the worth of themselves and others in terms of how much they own (see chapter 13). The popular bumper sticker, "He Who Dies with the Most Toys, Wins" is a comment on this philosophy. A recent study that compared the extent of materialism across 12 countries found Romanians to be the most materialistic, followed by citizens of the United States, New Zealand, Germany, and Turkey.[48]

We sometimes take the existence of an abundance of products and services for granted, until we remember how recent this abundance is. For example, in 1950 two of five American homes did not have a telephone, and in 1940 half of all households still did not possess complete indoor plumbing.

Today, though, many Americans now energetically seek "the good life," which abounds in material comforts. About 40 percent of households have two or more cars, and over $200 billion is spent on vacations in a year.[49] In fact, one way to think about marketing is as a system that provides a certain standard of living to consumers. To some extent, then, our lifestyles are influenced by the standard of living we have come to expect and desire.

Materialists are more likely to value possessions for their status and appearance-related meanings, while those who do not emphasize this value tend to prize products that connect them to other people or that provide them with pleasure in using them.[50] As a result, products valued by high materialists are more likely to be publicly consumed and to be more expensive. A study that compared specific items valued by both types of people found that products associated with high materialists include jewelry, china, or a vacation home, whereas those linked to low materialists included a mother's wedding gown, picture albums, a rocking chair from childhood, or a garden.[51]

Although there is still no shortage of materialistic consumers who relish the race to acquire as much as possible before they die, there are signs that a sizable number of Americans are evolving a different value system. This shift is primarily accounted for by younger people, who appear to be looking for more out of life than furs and Ferraris.

The Brain Waves/Market Facts survey reports that about a quarter of the population is displaying a value system characterized by a rejection of tradition and conformity. Significantly, more than half of this group is under the age of 35. They are still interested in achievement, but they are trying to balance life in the fast lane with an emphasis on developing close personal relationships and having fun.

Through observation and in some cases direct experience, these consumers have come to believe that (unlike the "good old days") a diploma does not guarantee a job, getting a job is no guarantee of keeping a job, retirement may not happen, and marriages often fail. This lack of stability has instilled a value of self-reliance and the desire to build personal networks rather than relying on the government or corporations to take care of them as these institutions did for their parents. Marketing communications like Saab's "Find Your Own Road" and Prudential's "Be Your Own Rock" are designed to appeal to this group.

Very similar findings are reported in a decade-long study by American LIVES of San Francisco, which claims that about one in four Americans—a segment the firm calls Cultural Creatives—is living by a new set of values. Creatives emphasize new and unique experiences. They are altruistic and less concerned with making a lot of money—though most are earning middle to upper-middle incomes. Sixty percent are women. Their key values include:[52]

- *Ecological sustainability:* They are eager to rebuild neighborhoods and believe in voluntarily simplicity.
- *Women's issues:* They are concerned about violence, child abuse, and spouse abuse.
- *Spirituality and self-actualization:* They are into spiritual growth and many are receptive to holistic health products and practices.
- *Social conscience and optimism:* They are willing to devote time and effort to making things better—three quarters are involved in volunteer activities.

This shift away from traditional materialism does not mean the end of marketing! However, different approaches and products are needed to reach this new segment. Cultural Creatives tend to rely more on print and radio media than on TV, and they try to get information from as many different sources as possible. Instead of glitzy ads, they want stories that provide details about the product itself—including where it came from. They look to *Consumer Reports* for purchasing information, they really do read labels, and they are avid consumers of the arts. This segment is looking for ecologically sound, high-mileage cars, and they are also strong purchasers of boutique beers, natural and health foods, exotic vacation travel, and older homes that they can fix up in interesting ways. Marketers who find ways to deliver quality products and at the same time return value to the community will get a warm reception from these "New Age" consumers. One path to success is *cause-related marketing,* where a business teams with a nonprofit organization on a project that benefits both parties. That kind of marriage occurred when Cosmair (which makes Horizon, a men's cologne) partnered with American Rivers, a nonprofit group dedicated to preserving rivers and wild places. Cosmair prepared a Horizon gift box that included the American Rivers logo and supporting literature about the group's efforts. For every box sold, $1 went to American Rivers.[53] This kind of effort creates a current of goodwill for the sponsoring corporation, and quenches the thirst of Cultural Creatives for marketing efforts that make a difference.

CHAPTER SUMMARY

- Marketers try to satisfy consumer needs, but the reasons any product is purchased can vary widely. The identification of consumer motives is an important step in ensuring that the appropriate needs will be met by a product.

- Traditional approaches to consumer behavior have focused on the abilities of products to satisfy rational needs (utilitarian motives), but hedonic motives (e.g., the need for exploration or for fun) also play a role in many purchase decisions.

- As demonstrated by Maslow's hierarchy of needs, the same product can satisfy different needs, depending on the consumer's state at the time. In addition to his or her objective situation (e.g., have basic physiological needs already been satisfied?), the consumer's degree of involvement with the product must be considered.

- Consumer motivations are often driven by underlying values. In this context, products take on meaning because they are seen as being instrumental in helping the person to achieve some goal that is linked to a value, such as individuality or freedom. Each culture is characterized by a set of *core values* to which many of its members adhere.

- *Materialism* refers to the importance people attach to worldly possessions. Although many Americans can be described as being materialists, there are indications of a value shift within a sizable portion of the population.

KEY TERMS

Acculturation p. 119
Consumer desire p. 107
Drive p. 104
Enculturation p. 119
Expectancy theory p. 106
Goal p. 104
Homeostasis p. 106

Inertia p. 113
Instrumental values p. 120
Involvement p. 111
Laddering p. 121
Materialism p. 123
Motivation p. 104
Terminal values p. 120

Theory of cognitive
    dissonance p. 108
Value p. 118
Value system p. 118
Want p. 104

CONSUMER BEHAVIOR CHALLENGE

1. Describe three types of motivational conflicts, citing an example of each from current marketing campaigns.

2. Devise separate promotional strategies for an article of clothing, each of which stresses one of the levels of Maslow's hierarchy of needs.

3. Collect a sample of ads that appear to appeal to consumers' values. What value is being communicated in each ad, and how is this done? Is this an effective approach to designing a marketing communication?

4. What is your conception of paradise? Construct a collage consisting of images you personally associate with paradise, and compare the results with those of your classmates. Do you detect any common themes?

5. Construct a hypothetical means-end chain model for the purchase of a bouquet of roses. How might a florist use this approach to construct a promotional strategy?

6. Describe how a man's level of involvement with his car would affect how he is influenced by different marketing stimuli. How might you design a strategy for a line of car batteries for a segment of low-involvement consumers, and how would this strategy differ from your attempts to reach a segment of men who are very involved in working on their cars?

7. Interview members of a celebrity fan club. Describe their level of involvement with the "product," and devise some marketing opportunities to reach this group.

8. "High involvement is just a fancy term for expensive." Do you agree?

9. "College students' concerns about the environment and vegetarianism are just a passing fad; a way to look 'cool.'" Do you agree?

NOTES

1. Chip Walker, "Meet the New Vegetarian," *American Demographics* (January 1995): 9 (2 pp.); Marilyn Chase, "Pretty Soon the Word 'Organic' on Foods Will Mean One Thing," *Wall Street Journal Interactive Edition* (August 18, 1997).

2. Robert A. Baron, *Psychology: The Essential Science* (Needham, MA: Allyn & Bacon, 1989).

3. Quoted in Russell W. Belk, "Romanian Consumer Desires and Feelings of Deservingness," in ed. Lavinia Stan, *Romania in Transition* (Hanover, NH: Dartmouth Press, 1997): 191–208, quoted on p. 193.

4. Quoted in Belk, "Romanian Consumer Desires and Feelings of Deservingness," p. 200.

5. Leon Festinger, *A Theory of Cognitive Dissonance* (Stanford, CA: Stanford University Press, 1957).

6. See Paul T. Costa and Robert R. McCrae, "From Catalog to Classification: Murray's Needs and the Five-Factor Model," *Journal of Personality and Social Psychology* 55 (1988)2: 258–65; Calvin S. Hall and Gardner Lindzey, *Theories of Personality,* 2nd ed. (New York: Wiley, 1970); James U. McNeal and Stephen W. McDaniel, "An Analysis of Need-Appeals in Television Advertising," *Journal of the Academy of Marketing Science* 12 (Spring 1984): 176–90.

7. See David C. McClelland, *Studies in Motivation* (New York: Appleton-Century-Crofts, 1955).

8. Mary Kay Ericksen and M. Joseph Sirgy, "Achievement Motivation and Clothing Preferences of White-Collar Working Women," in ed. Michael R. Solomon, *The Psychology of Fashion* (Lexington, MA: Lexington Books, 1985): 357–69.

9. See Stanley Schachter, *The Psychology of Affiliation* (Stanford, CA: Stanford University Press, 1959).

10. Eugene M. Fodor and Terry Smith, "The Power Motive as an Influence on Group Decision Making," *Journal of Personality and Social Psychology* 42 (1982): 178–85.

11. C. R. Snyder and Howard L. Fromkin, *Uniqueness: The Human Pursuit of Difference* (New York: Plenum, 1980).

12. Abraham H. Maslow, *Motivation and Personality,* 2nd ed. (New York: Harper & Row, 1970).

13. Study conducted in the Horticulture Department at Kansas State University, cited in "Survey Tells Why Gardening's Good," *Vancouver Sun* (April 12, 1997): B12.

14. John H. Antil, "Conceptualization and Operationalization of Involvement," in ed. Thomas C. Kinnear, *Advances in Consumer Research* 11 (Provo, UT: Association for Consumer Research, 1984): 203–09. The literature offers numerous approaches to the construct of involvement. One recent compilation can be found in a special issue on involvement published in *Psychology & Marketing* 10 (July/August 1993)4. See also Peter H. Bloch, "Involvement beyond the Purchase Process: Conceptual Issues and Empirical Investigation," in ed. Kent Monroe, *Advances in Consumer Research* 8 (Provo, UT: Association for Consumer Research, 1981): 61–5; George S. Day, *Buyer Attitudes and Brand Choice Behavior* (Chicago: Free Press, 1970); Michael J. Houston and Michael L. Rothschild, "Conceptual and Methodological Perspectives on Involvement," in ed. S. C. Jain, *Research Frontiers in Marketing: Dialogues and Directions* (Chicago: American Marketing Association, 1978): 184–7; John L. Lastovicka and David Gardner, "Components of Involvement," in eds. John C. Maloney and Bernard Silverman, *Attitude Research Plays for High Stakes* (Chicago: American Marketing Association, 1979): 53–73; Andrew Mitchell, "Involvement: A Potentially Important Mediator of Consumer Behavior," in ed. William L. Wilkie, *Advances in Consumer Research* 6 (Provo, UT: Association for Consumer Research, 1979): 191–6; Judith Lynne Zaichkowsky, "Conceptualizing Involvement,"

15. Gary J. Bamossy and Janeen Costa, "Consuming Paradise: A Cultural Construction" (paper presented at the Association for Consumer Research Conference, June 1997, Stockholm); Prof. Janeen Costa, personal communication, August 1997.

16. Mitchell, "Involvement."

17. Richard L. Celsi and Jerry C. Olson, "The Role of Involvement in Attention and Comprehension Processes," *Journal of Consumer Research* 15 (September 1988): 210–24.

18. Anthony G. Greenwald and Clark Leavitt, "Audience Involvement in Advertising: Four Levels," *Journal of Consumer Research* 11 (June 1984): 581–92.

19. Judith Lynne Zaichkowsky, "The Emotional Side of Product Involvement," in eds. Paul Anderson and Melanie Wallendorf, *Advances in Consumer Research* 14 (Provo, UT: Association for Consumer Research): 32–5.

20. For a recent discussion of interrelationship between situational and enduring involvement, see Marsha L. Richins, Peter H. Bloch, and Edward F. McQuarrie, "How Enduring and Situational Involvement Combine to Create Involvement Responses," *Journal of Consumer Psychology* 1 (1992)2: 143–53.

21. Laurie Freeman, "Fragrance Sniffs out Daring Adventures," *Advertising Age* (November 6, 1989): 47.

22. Rajeev Batra and Michael L. Ray, "Operationalizing Involvement as Depth and Quality of Cognitive Responses," in eds. Alice Tybout and Richard Bagozzi, *Advances in Consumer Research* 10 (Ann Arbor, MI: Association for Consumer Research, 1983): 309–13.

23. Herbert E. Krugman, "The Impact of Television Advertising: Learning without Involvement," *Public Opinion Quarterly* 29 (Fall 1965): 349–56.

24. Marsha L. Richins and Peter H. Bloch, "After the New Wears Off: The Temporal Context of Product Involvement," *Journal of Consumer*

Research 13 (September 1986): 280–5.

25. Kevin J. Clancy, "CPMs Must Bow to 'Involvement' Measurement," *Advertising Age* (January 20, 1992): 26.

26. For a newer, modified version of this scale, see Edward F. McQuarrie and J. Michael Munson, "A Revised Product Involvement Inventory: Improved Usability and Validity," in eds. John F. Sherry, Jr. and Brian Sternthal, *Advances in Consumer Research* 19 (Provo, UT: Association for Consumer Research, 1992): 108–15.

27. Gilles Laurent and Jean-Noël Kapferer, "Measuring Consumer Involvement Profiles," *Journal of Marketing Research* 22 (February 1985): 41–53; this scale was recently validated on an American sample as well, see William C. Rodgers and Kenneth C. Schneider, "An Empirical Evaluation of the Kapferer-Laurent Consumer Involvement Profile Scale," *Psychology & Marketing* 10 (July/August 1993)4: 333–45.

28. David W. Stewart and David H. Furse, "Analysis of the Impact of Executional Factors in Advertising Performance," *Journal of Advertising Research* 24 (1984)6: 23–6; Deborah J. MacInnis, Christine Moorman, and Bernard J. Jaworski, "Enhancing and Measuring Consumers' Motivation, Opportunity, and Ability to Process Brand Information from Ads," *Journal of Marketing* 55 (October 1991): 332–53.

29. Morris B. Holbrook and Elizabeth C. Hirschman, "The Experiential Aspects of Consumption: Consumer Fantasies, Feelings, and Fun," *Journal of Consumer Research* 9 (September 1982): 132–40.

30. James Bennet, "Saturn Invites the 'Family' to a Party," *New York Times* (June 20, 1994): D1 (2 pp.).

31. Ajay K. Sirsi, James C. Ward, and Peter H. Reingen, "Microcultural Analysis of Variation in Sharing of Causal Reasoning about Behavior," *Journal of Consumer Research* 22 (March 1996): 345–72.

32. Richard W. Pollay, "Measuring the Cultural Values Manifest in Advertising," *Current Issues and Research in Advertising* 6 (1983)1: 71–92.

33. Paul M. Sherer, "North American and Asian Executives Have Contrasting Values, Study Finds," *Wall Street Journal* (March 8, 1996): B12B.

34. Milton Rokeach, *The Nature of Human Values* (New York: Free Press, 1973).

35. *A New Partnership: New Values and Attitudes of the New Middle Generation in Japan and the U.S.A.* (Tokyo: Dentsu Institute for Human Studies, 1989).

36. Donald E. Vinson, Jerome E. Scott, and Lawrence R. Lamont, "The Role of Personal Values in Marketing and Consumer Behavior," *Journal of Marketing* 41 (April 1977): 44–50.

37. Gregory M. Rose, Aviv Shoham, Lynn R. Kahle, and Rajeev Batra, "Social Values, Conformity, and Dress," *Journal of Applied Social Psychology* 24 (1994)17: 1501–19.

38. Quoted in "New Japanese Fads Blazing Trails in Cleanliness," *Montgomery Advertiser* (September 28, 1996): 10A; see also Andrew Pollack, "Can the Pen Really be Mightier than the Germ,?" *New York Times* (July 27, 1995): A4.

39. Milton Rokeach, *Understanding Human Values* (New York: The Free Press, 1979); see also J. Michael Munson and Edward McQuarrie, "Shortening the Rokeach Value Survey for Use in Consumer Research," in ed. Michael J. Houston, *Advances in Consumer Research* 15 (Provo, UT: Association for Consumer Research, 1988): 381–6.

40. B. W. Becker and P. E. Conner, "Personal Values of the Heavy User of Mass Media," *Journal of Advertising Research* 21 (1981): 37–43; Vinson, Scott, and Lamont, "The Role of Personal Values in Marketing and Consumer Behavior."

41. Sharon E. Beatty, Lynn R. Kahle, Pamela Homer, and Shekhar Misra, "Alternative Measurement Approaches to Consumer Values: The List of Values and the Rokeach Value Survey," *Psychology & Marketing* 2 (1985): 181–200; Lynn R. Kahle and Patricia Kennedy, "Using the List of Values (LOV) to Understand Consumers," *Journal of Consumer Marketing* 2 (Fall 1988): 49–56; Lynn Kahle, Basil Poulos, and Ajay Sukhdial, "Changes in Social Values in the United States during the Past Decade," *Journal of Advertising Research* 28 (February/March 1988): 35–41; see also Wagner A. Kamakura and Jose Alfonso Mazzon, "Value Segmentation: A Model for the Measurement of Values and Value Systems," *Journal of Consumer Research* 18 (September 1991): 28; Jagdish N. Sheth, Bruce I. Newman, and Barbara L. Gross, *Consumption Values and Market Choices: Theory and Applications* (Cincinnati: South-Western Publishing Co., 1991).

42. Thomas J. Reynolds and Jonathan Gutman, "Laddering Theory, Method, Analysis, and Interpretation," *Journal of Advertising Research* 28 (February/March 1988): 11–34; Beth Walker, Richard Celsi, and Jerry Olson, "Exploring the Structural Characteristics of Consumers' Knowledge," in eds. Melanie Wallendorf and Paul Anderson, *Advances in Consumer Research* 14 (Provo, UT: Association for Consumer Research, 1986): 17–21.

43. Reynolds and Gutman, "Laddering Theory, Method, Analysis, and Interpretation."

44. Thomas J. Reynolds and Alyce Byrd Craddock, "The Application of the MECCAS Model to the Development and Assessment of Advertising Strategy: A Case Study," *Journal of Advertising Research* (April/May 1988): 43–54.

45. "25 Years of Attitude," *Marketing Tools* (November/December 1995): 38–9.

46. William O. Bearden, Richard G. Netemeyer, and Jesse E. Teel, "Measurement of Consumer Susceptibility to Interpersonal Influence," *Journal of Consumer Research* 9 (1989)3: 183–94; Lynn R. Kahle, "Observations: Role-Relaxed Consumers: A Trend of the Nineties," *Journal of Advertising Research* (March/April 1995): 66–71; Lynn R. Kahle and Aviv Shoham, "Observations: Role-Relaxed Consumers: Empirical Evidence,"

Journal of Advertising Research 35 (May/June 1995)3: 59–62.

47. Russell W. Belk, "Possessions and the Extended Self," *Journal of Consumer Research* 15 (September 1988): 139–68; Melanie Wallendorf and Eric J. Arnould, "'My Favorite Things': A Cross-Cultural Inquiry into Object Attachment, Possessiveness, and Social Linkage," *Journal of Consumer Research* 14 (March 1988): 531–47.

48. Güliz Ger and Russell W. Belk, "Cross-Cultural Differences in Materialism," *Journal of Economic Psychology* 17 (1996): 55–77.

49. Fabian Linden, "Who Has Buying Power?" *American Demographics* (August 1987): 4, 6.

50. Marsha L. Richins, "Special Possessions and the Expression of Material Values," *Journal of Consumer Research* 21 (December, 1994): 522–33.

51. Richins, "Special Possessions and the Expression of Material Values."

52. Paul H. Ray, "The Emerging Culture," *American Demographics* (February 1997): 29 (9 pp.).

53. Jan Larson, "Sweet Charity," *Marketing Tools* (May 1995): 69–72.

RHODA IS TRYING TO concentrate on the report her client is expecting by five o'clock. Rhoda has always worked hard to maintain this important account for the firm, but today she is distracted thinking about her date last night with Rob. Although things seemed to go okay, why couldn't she shake the feeling that Rob regarded her more as a friend than as a potential romantic partner?

Leafing through *Glamour* and *Cosmopolitan* during her lunch hour, Rhoda is struck by all of the articles about ways to become more attractive by dieting, exercise, and wearing sexy clothes. Rhoda begins to feel depressed as she looks at the models in the many advertisements for perfumes, apparel, and makeup. Each woman is more glamorous and beautiful than the next. She could swear that some of them must have had breast implants and other assorted "adjustments"—women just don't look that way in real life. Then again, it's unlikely that Rob could ever be mistaken for Fabio on the street.

In her down mood, though, Rhoda actually entertains the thought that maybe she should look into cosmetic surgery. Even though she's never considered herself unattractive, who knows—maybe a new nose or larger breasts are what it will take to turn Rob around. On second thought, though, is he even worth it? . . .

The Self

PERSPECTIVES ON THE SELF

Rhoda is not alone in feeling that her physical appearance and possessions affect her "value" as a person. Consumers' insecurities about their appearance are rampant: It has been estimated that 72 percent of men and 85 percent of women are unhappy with at least one aspect of their appearance.[1] Many products, from cars to cologne, are bought because the person is trying to highlight or hide some aspect of the self. In this chapter, we'll focus on how consumers' feelings about themselves shape their consumption practices, particularly as they strive to fulfill their society's expectations about how a male or female should look and act.

DOES THE SELF EXIST?

The 1980s were called the "Me Decade" because for many this time was marked by an absorption with the self. Although it seems natural to think about each consumer as having a self, this concept is actually a relatively new way of regarding individuals and their relationship to society.

The idea that each single human life is unique, rather than a part of a group, only developed in late medieval times (between the eleventh and fifteenth centuries). The notion that the self is an object to be pampered is even more recent. Furthermore, the emphasis on the unique nature of the self is much greater in Western societies.[2] Many Eastern cultures instead stress the importance of a collective self, where the person's identity is derived in large measure from his or her social group.

Both Eastern and Western cultures see the self as divided into an inner, private self and an outer, public self. But where they differ is in terms of which part is seen as the "real you"—the West tends to subscribe to an independent construal of the self, which emphasizes the inherent separateness of each individual. Non-Western cultures, in contrast, tend to focus on an interdependent self, where one's identity is largely defined by the relationships one has with others.[3]

For example, a Confucian perspective stresses the importance of "face"—others' perceptions of the self and maintaining one's desired status in their eyes. One dimension of face is *mien-tzu*—reputation achieved through success and ostentation. Some Asian cultures developed explicit rules about the specific garments and even colors that certain social classes and occupations were allowed to display, and these traditions live on today in Japanese style manuals that provide very detailed instructions for dressing and for addressing a particular individual.[4] That orientation is a bit at odds with such Western conventions as "casual Fridays," which encourage employees to express their unique selves.

SELF-CONCEPT

The **self-concept** refers to the beliefs a person holds about his or her own attributes, and how he or she evaluates these qualities. While one's overall self-concept may be positive, there certainly are parts of the self that are evaluated more positively than others. For example, Rhoda feels better about her professional identity than she does about her feminine identity.

COMPONENTS OF THE SELF-CONCEPT

The self-concept is a very complex structure. It is composed of many attributes, some of which are given greater emphasis when the overall self is being evaluated. Attributes of self-concept can be described along such dimensions as their content (e.g., facial attractiveness versus mental aptitude), positivity or negativity (i.e., self-esteem), intensity, stability over time, and accuracy (i.e., the degree to which one's self-assessment corresponds to reality).[5] As we'll see later in the chapter, consumers' self-assessments can be quite distorted, especially with regard to their physical appearance.

SELF-ESTEEM

Self-esteem refers to the positivity of a person's self-concept. People with low self-esteem expect that they will not perform very well, and they will try to avoid embarrassment, failure, or rejection. In developing a new line of snack cakes, for example, Sara Lee found that consumers low in self-esteem preferred portion-controlled snack items because they felt they lacked self-control.[6] In contrast, people with high self-esteem expect to be successful, will take more risks, and are more willing to be the center of attention.[7] Self-esteem is often related to acceptance by others. As you probably remember, high school students who hang out in high-status "crowds" seem to have higher self-esteem than their classmates (even though this may not be deserved!).[8]

Marketing communications can influence a consumer's level of self-esteem. Exposure to ads like the ones Rhoda was checking out can trigger a process of *social comparison,* where the person tries to evaluate his or her self by comparing it to the people depicted in these artificial images. This form of comparison appears to be a basic human motive, and many marketers have tapped into this need by supplying idealized images of happy, attractive people who just happen to be using their products.

A recent study illustrates the social comparison process: It showed that female college students tend to compare their physical appearance with models who appear in advertising. Furthermore, study participants who were exposed to beautiful women in advertisements afterwards expressed lowered satisfaction with their own appearance, as compared to other participants who did not view ads with attractive models.[9] Another study demonstrated that young women's perceptions of their own body shapes and sizes can be altered after being exposed to as little as 30 minutes of TV programming.[10]

Self-esteem advertising attempts to change product attitudes by stimulating positive feelings about the self. One strategy is to challenge the consumer's self-esteem and then show a linkage to a product that will provide a remedy. For example, the Marine Corps uses this strategy with its theme "If you have what it takes . . ." Another strategy is outright flattery, as when Virginia Slims cigarettes proclaims, "You've come a long way, baby."

Sometimes such compliments are derived by an implicit comparison of the consumer to others. For instance, many consumers are socialized to consider body odors repulsive and are motivated to protect their self-image by denying the existence of these odors in themselves. This attitude explains the success of the theme for Dial soap's advertising: "Aren't you glad you use Dial, don't you wish everyone did?"[11] Other examples of self-esteem appeals include "You're not getting older, you're getting better" by Clairol; "For all you do, this Bud's for you" by Budweiser; and "Perks, you've earned them" by Republic Airlines.[12]

REAL AND IDEAL SELVES

Self-esteem is influenced by a process in which the consumer compares his or her actual standing on some attribute to some ideal. A consumer might ask, "Am I as attractive as I would like to be?," "Do I make as much money as I should?," and so on. The **ideal self** is a person's conception of how he or she would like to be, whereas the **actual self** refers to our more realistic appraisal of the qualities we have and don't have.

The ideal self is partly molded by elements of the consumer's culture, such as heroes or people depicted in advertising, who serve as models of achievement or appearance.[13] We might purchase products because they are believed to be instrumental in helping us achieve these goals. Some products are chosen because they are perceived to be consistent with the consumer's actual self, whereas others are used to help in reaching the standard set by the ideal self.

FANTASY: BRIDGING THE GAP BETWEEN THE SELVES

Most people experience a discrepancy between their real and ideal selves, but for some consumers this gap is especially large. These people are especially good targets for marketing communications that employ *fantasy appeals*.[14] A **fantasy** or daydream is a self-induced shift in consciousness, which is sometimes a way of compensating for a lack of external stimulation or of escaping from problems in the real world.[15] Many products and services are successful because they appeal to consumers' fantasies. These marketing strategies allow us to extend our vision of ourselves by placing us in unfamiliar, exciting situations or by permitting us to "try on" interesting or provocative roles.

MULTIPLE SELVES

In a way, each of us really is a number of different people—your mother probably would not recognize the "you" that emerges on vacation with a group of friends! We have as many selves as we do different social roles. Depending on the situation, we act differently, use different products and services, and we even vary in terms of how much we like the "me" that is on display at various times. A person may require a different set of products to play a desired role: She may choose a sedate, understated perfume when she is being her professional self, but splash on something more provocative on Saturday night as she becomes her *femme fatale* self. As we saw in chapter 1, the dramaturgical perspective on consumer behavior views people as actors who play different roles. We each play many roles, and each has its own script, props, and costumes.[16]

The self can be thought of as having different components, or *role identities*, and only some of these are active at any given time. Some identities (e.g., husband, boss, student) are more central to the self than others, but other identities (e.g., stamp collector, dancer, or advocate for the homeless) may be dominant in specific situations. For example, in a survey done in the United States, the United Kingdom, and some Pacific Rim countries, executives said that different aspects of their personalities come into play depending on whether they are making purchase decisions

If I had a Nissan 240SX . . . it would be a red coupe.

Wait! A silver fastback. And I'd go for a spin up Route 7, the twisty part.

Just me and Astro . . .

no, Amy.

Heck, Christie Brinkley!

Wow! Yeah, me and Christie . . .

This storyboard for a Nissan 240SX ad illustrates the use of the fantasy theme, which allows consumers to try on new roles and extend their vision of the ideal self.

In my silver—no, red 240SX . . . driving into the sunset.

at home or at work. Not surprisingly, they report being less time conscious, more emotional, and less disciplined in their home roles.[17]

SYMBOLIC INTERACTIONISM

If each person potentially has many social selves, how does each develop and how do we decide which self to "activate" at any point in time? The sociological tradition of **symbolic interactionism** stresses that relationships with other people play a large part in forming the self.[18] This perspective maintains that people exist in a symbolic environment, and the meaning attached to any situation or object is determined by the interpretation of these symbols. As members of society, we learn to agree on shared meanings. Thus, we "know" that a red light means stop, the "golden arches" means fast food, and "blondes have more fun."

The meanings of consumers themselves, like other social objects, are defined by social consensus. The consumer interprets his or her own identity, and this assessment is continually evolving as he or she encounters new situations and people. In symbolic interactionist terms, we *negotiate* these meanings over time. Essentially the consumer poses the question, "Who am I in this situation?" The answer to this question is greatly influenced by those around us: "Who do *other people* think I am?" We tend to pattern our behavior on the perceived expectations of others in a form of *self-fulfilling prophecy*. By acting the way we assume others expect us to act, we often wind up confirming these perceptions.

THE LOOKING-GLASS SELF

This process of imagining the reactions of others toward us is known as "taking the role of the other," or the **looking-glass self**.[19] According to this view, our desire to define ourselves operates as a sort of psychological sonar: We take readings of our own identity by "bouncing" signals off of others and trying to project what impression they have of us. The looking-glass image we receive will differ depending on whose views we are considering.

Like the distorted mirrors in a funhouse, our appraisal of who we are can vary, depending on whose perspective we are taking and how accurately we are able to predict their evaluations of us. A confident career woman such as Rhoda may sit morosely at a nightclub, imagining that others see her as an unattractive, woman with little sex appeal (whether these perceptions are true or not). A *self-fulfilling prophecy* can operate here, since these "signals" can influence Rhoda's actual behavior. If she doesn't believe she's attractive, she may choose dowdy clothing that actually does make her less attractive. On the other hand, her confidence in herself in a professional setting may cause her to assume that others hold her "executive self" in even higher regard than they actually do (we've all known people like that!).

SELF-CONSCIOUSNESS

There are times when people seem to be painfully aware of themselves. If you have ever walked into a class in the middle of a lecture and noticed that all eyes were on you, you can understand this feeling of *self-consciousness*. In contrast, consumers sometimes behave with shockingly little self-consciousness. For example, people may do things in a stadium, a riot, or at a fraternity party that they would never do if they were highly conscious of their behavior.[20]

Some people seem to be more sensitive in general to the image they communicate to others. On the other hand, we all know people who act as if they're oblivious to the impression they are making! A heightened concern about the nature of one's public "image" also results in more concern about the social appropriateness of products and consumption activities.

Several techniques have been devised to measure this tendency. Consumers who score high on a scale of *public self-consciousness,* for example, are also more interested in clothing and are heavier users of cosmetics.[21] A similar measure is *self-monitoring.* High self-monitors are more attuned to how they present themselves in their social environments, and their product choices are influenced by their estimates of how these items will be perceived by others.[22] Self-monitoring is assessed by consumers' extent of agreement with statements such as "I guess I put on a show to impress or entertain others," or "I would probably make a good actor."[23] High self-monitors are more likely than low self-monitors to evaluate products consumed in public in terms of the impressions they make on others.[24] Similarly, some recent research has looked at aspects of *vanity,* such as a fixation on physical appearance or on the achievement of personal goals. Perhaps not surprisingly, groups such as college football players and fashion models tend to score higher on this dimension.[25]

CONSUMPTION AND SELF-CONCEPT

By extending the dramaturgical perspective a bit farther, it is easy to see how the consumption of products and services contributes to the definition of the self. For an actor to play a role convincingly, he or she needs the correct props, stage setting, and so on. Consumers learn that different roles are accompanied by *constellations* of products and activities that help to define these roles.[26] Some "props" are so important to the roles we play that they can be viewed as a part of the *extended self,* a concept to be discussed shortly.

PRODUCTS THAT SHAPE THE SELF: YOU ARE WHAT YOU CONSUME

Recall that the reflected self helps to shape self-concept, which implies that people see themselves as they imagine others see them. Because what others see includes a person's clothing, jewelry, furniture, car, and so on, it stands to reason that these products also help to determine the perceived self. A consumer's possessions place him or her into a social role, which helps to answer the question, "Who am I now?"

People use an individual's consumption behaviors to help them make judgments about that person's social identity. In addition to considering a person's clothes, grooming habits, and so on, we make inferences about personality based on a person's choice of leisure activities (e.g., squash versus bowling), food preferences (e.g., tofu and beans versus steak and potatoes), cars, home decorating choices, and so on. People who are shown pictures of someone's living room, for example, are able to make surprisingly accurate guesses about his or her personality.[27] In the same way that a consumer's use of products influences others' perceptions, the same products can help to determine his or her *own* self-concept and social identity.[28]

A consumer exhibits *attachment* to an object to the extent that it is used by that person to maintain his or her self-concept.[29] Objects can act as a sort of security blanket by reinforcing our identities, especially in unfamiliar situations. For example, students who decorate their dorm rooms with personal items are less likely to drop out of college. This coping process may protect the self from being diluted in a strange environment.[30]

The use of consumption information to define the self is especially important when an identity is yet to be adequately formed, as occurs when a consumer plays a new or unfamiliar role. **Symbolic self-completion theory** suggests that people who

In emphasizing the notion that looking the right way gives one confidence, this Yes Clothing ad relies on symbolic self-completion theory to appeal to consumers.

have an incomplete self-definition tend to complete this identity by acquiring and displaying symbols associated with it.[31] Adolescent boys, for example, may use "macho" products such as cars and cigarettes to bolster their developing masculinity; these items act as a "social crutch" during a period of uncertainty about identity.

LOSS OF SELF

The contribution of possessions to self-identity is perhaps most apparent when these treasured objects are lost or stolen. One of the first acts performed by institutions that want to repress individuality and encourage group identity, such as prisons or military forces, is to confiscate personal possessions.[32] Victims of burglaries and natural disasters commonly report feelings of alienation, depression, or of being "violated." One consumer's comment after being robbed is typical: "It's the next worse thing to being bereaved; it's like being raped."[33] Burglary victims exhibit a diminished sense of community, lowered feelings of privacy, and less pride in their houses' appearance than do their neighbors.[34]

The dramatic impact of product loss is highlighted by studying postdisaster conditions, in which consumers may have lost literally almost everything but the clothes on their backs following a fire, hurricane, flood, or earthquake. Some people are reluctant to undergo the process of recreating their identity by acquiring new possessions. Interviews with disaster victims reveal that some hesitate to invest the self in new possessions and so become more detached about what they buy. This comment from a woman in her fifties is representative of this attitude: "I had so much love tied up in my things. I can't go through that kind of loss again. What I'm buying now won't be as important to me."[35]

SELF/PRODUCT CONGRUENCE

Because many consumption activities are related to self-definition, it is not surprising to learn that consumers demonstrate consistency between their values (see chapter 4) and the things they buy.[36] **Self-image congruence models** suggest that products will be chosen when their attributes match some aspect of the self.[37] These models assume a process of cognitive matching between product attributes and the consumer's self-image.[38]

Although results are somewhat mixed, the ideal self appears to be more relevant than the actual self as a comparison standard for highly expressive social products such as perfume. In contrast, the actual self is more relevant for everyday, functional products. These standards are also likely to vary by usage situation. For example, a consumer might want a functional, reliable car to commute to work every day, but a flashier model with more "zing" when going out on a date in the evening.

Research tends to support the idea of congruence between product usage and self-image. One of the earliest studies to examine this process found that car owners' ratings of themselves tended to match their perceptions of their cars: Pontiac drivers saw themselves as more active and flashy than did Volkswagen drivers.[39] Congruity also has been found between consumers and their most-preferred brands of beer, soap, toothpaste, and cigarettes relative to their least-preferred brands, as well as between consumers' self-images and their favorite stores.[40] Some specific attributes that have been found to be useful in describing some of the matches between consumers and products include *rugged/delicate, excitable/calm, rational/emotional,* and *formal/informal.*[41]

Although these findings make some intuitive sense, we cannot blithely assume that consumers will always buy products whose characteristics match their own. It is not clear that consumers really see aspects of themselves in down-to-earth, functional products that don't have very complex or humanlike images. It is one thing to consider a brand personality for an expressive, image-oriented product such as perfume and quite another to impute human characteristics to a toaster.

Consumers often attempt to express their self-concepts through their choice of an automobile. These British ads take the process a step farther.

Another problem is the old "chicken-and-egg" question: Do people buy products because the products are seen as similar to the self, or do people *assume* that these products must be similar to themselves because they have bought them? The similarity between a person's self-image and the images of products purchased does tend to increase over the time the product is owned, so this explanation cannot be ruled out.

THE EXTENDED SELF

As noted earlier, many of the props and settings consumers use to define their social roles in a sense become parts of their selves. Those external objects that we consider a part of us comprise the **extended self.** In some cultures, people literally incorporate objects into the self—they lick new possessions, take the names of conquered enemies (or in some cases eat them), or bury the dead with their possessions.[42]

We don't usually go that far, but some people do cherish possessions as if they were a part of themselves. Many material objects, ranging from personal possessions and pets to national monuments or landmarks, help to form a consumer's identity. Just about everyone can name a valued possession that has a lot of the self "wrapped up" in it, whether it is a beloved photograph, a trophy, an old shirt, a car, or a cat. Indeed, it is often possible to construct a pretty accurate "biography" of someone just by cataloguing the items on display in his or her bedroom or office.

In one study on the extended self, people were given a list of items that ranged from electronic equipment, facial tissues, and television programs to parents, body parts, and favorite clothes. They were asked to rate each in terms of its closeness to the self. Objects were more likely to be considered a part of the extended self if "psychic energy" was invested in the effort to obtain them, or because they were personalized and kept for a long time.[43]

Four levels of the extended self have been described. These range from very personal objects to places and things that allow people to feel like they are rooted in their larger social environments:[44]

- *Individual level:* Consumers include many of their personal possessions in self-definition. These products can include jewelry, cars, clothing, and so on. The saying "You are what you wear" reflects the belief that one's things are a part of one's identity.
- *Family level:* This part of the extended self includes a consumer's residence and the furnishings in it. The house can be thought of as a symbolic body for the family, and often is a central aspect of identity.
- *Community level:* It is common for consumers to describe themselves in terms of the neighborhood or town from which they come. For farm families or other residents with close ties to a community, this sense of belonging is particularly important.
- *Group level:* Our attachments to certain social groups also can be considered a part of the self—we'll consider some of these *consumer subcultures* in later chapters. A consumer also may feel that landmarks, monuments, or sports teams are a part of the extended self.

SEX ROLES

Sexual identity is a very important component of a consumer's self-concept. People often conform to their culture's expectations about how those of their gender should act, dress, speak, and so on. Of course, these guidelines change over time, and they can differ radically across societies. It's unclear to what extent gender differences are innate versus culturally shaped—but they're certainly evident in many consumption decisions.

Consider the gender differences market researchers have observed when comparing the food preferences of men versus women. Women eat more fruit; men are more likely to eat meat. As one food writer put it, "Boy food doesn't grow. It is hunted or killed." Men are more likely to eat Frosted Flakes or Corn Pops, but women prefer multigrain cereals. Men are big root beer drinkers; women account for the bulk of sales of bottled water.

The sexes differ sharply in the quantities of food they eat: When researchers at Hershey's discovered that women eat smaller amounts of candy, the company created a white chocolate confection called Hugs, one of the most successful food introductions of all time. On the other hand, men are more likely to take their food and drink in larger servings. When Lipton advertised its iced tea during the Super Bowl, it told its (predominantly male) viewers, "This ain't no sippin' tea," and encouraged them to chug it down.

GENDER DIFFERENCES IN SOCIALIZATION

A society's assumptions about the proper roles of men and women is communicated in terms of the ideal behaviors that are stressed for each gender (in advertising, among other places). It's likely, for instance, that many women eat smaller quantities because they have been "trained" to be more delicate and dainty.

GENDER GOALS AND EXPECTATIONS

In many societies, males are controlled by **agentic goals,** which stress self-assertion and mastery. Females, on the other hand, are taught to value **communal goals,** such as affiliation and the fostering of harmonious relations.[45]

Each society creates a set of expectations regarding the behaviors appropriate for men and women and finds ways to communicate these priorities. This training begins very early; even children's birthday stories reinforce gender roles. A recent analysis showed that while stereotypical depictions have decreased over time, female characters in children's books are still far more likely to take on nurturant roles such as baking and gift-giving. The adult who prepares the birthday celebration is virtually always the mother—often no adult male is present at all. On the other hand, the male figure in these stories is often cast in the role of a miraculous provider of gifts.[46]

MACHO MARKETERS?

The field of marketing tends to be dominated by male values. Competition rather than cooperation is stressed, and the language of warfare and domination is often used. Strategists often use distinctly masculine concepts: "market penetration" or "competitive thrusts," for example. Academic marketing articles also emphasize agentic rather than communal goals. The most pervasive theme is power and control over others. Other themes include instrumentality (manipulating people for the good of an organization) and competition.[47] This bias may diminish in coming years, as more marketing researchers begin to stress such factors as emotions and aesthetics in purchase decisions—and as increasing numbers of women major in marketing!

GENDER VERSUS SEXUAL IDENTITY

Gender role identity is a state of mind as well as body. A person's biological gender (i.e., male or female) does not totally determine whether he or she will exhibit **sex-typed traits,** characteristics that are stereotypically associated with one gen-

This ad for Bijan illustrates how sex-role identities are culturally bound by contrasting the expectations of how women should appear in two different countries.

der or the other. A consumer's subjective feelings about his or her sexuality are crucial as well.[48]

Unlike maleness and femaleness, masculinity and femininity are *not* biological characteristics. A behavior considered masculine in one culture may not be viewed as such in another. For example, the norm in the United States is that males should be "strong" and repress tender feelings ("real men don't eat quiche"), and male friends avoid touching each other (except in "safe" situations such as on the football field). In some Latin and European cultures, however, it is common for men to hug and kiss one another. Each society determines what "real" men and women should and should not do.

SEX-TYPED PRODUCTS

Many products (in addition to quiche) also are *sex typed;* they take on masculine or feminine attributes, and consumers often associate them with one gender or another.[49] The sex typing of products is often created or perpetuated by marketers (e.g., Princess telephones, boys' and girls' toys, and Luvs color-coded diapers). Even brand names appear to be sex typed: Those containing *alphanumerics* (e.g., Formula 409, 10W40, Clorox 2) are assumed to be technical and hence masculine.[50] Some sex-typed products are listed in Table 5–1.

ANDROGYNY

Masculinity and femininity are not opposite ends of the same spectrum. **Androgyny** refers to the possession of both masculine and feminine traits.[51] Researchers make a distinction between *sex-typed people,* who are stereotypically masculine or feminine, and *androgynous people,* whose mixture of characteristics allows them to function well in a variety of social situations.

Differences in sex-role orientation can influence responses to marketing stimuli, at least under some circumstances.[52] For example, research indicates that females are more likely to undergo more elaborate processing of message content, so they tend to be more sensitive to specific pieces of information when forming a judgment, whereas males are more influenced by overall themes.[53] In addition, women with a relatively strong masculine component in their sex-role identity pre-

MASCULINE	FEMININE
Pocket knife	Scarf
Tool kit	Baby oil
Shaving cream	Bedroom slippers
Briefcase	Hand lotion
Camera (35 mm)	Clothes dryer
Stereo system	Food processor
Scotch	Wine
IRA account	Long-distance phone service
Wall paint	Facial tissue

Source: Adapted from Kathleen Debevec and Easwar Iyer, "Sex Roles and Consumer Perceptions of Promotions, Products, and Self: What Do We Know and Where Should We Be Headed," in *Advances in Consumer Research* 13, ed. Richard J. Lutz (Provo, UT: Association for Consumer Research, 1986): 210–4.

TABLE 5-1 ■ Sex-Typed Products

fer ad portrayals that include nontraditional women.[54] Some research indicates that sex-typed people are more sensitive to the sex-role depictions of characters in advertising, although women appear to be more sensitive generally to gender-role relationships than are men.

In one study, subjects read two versions of a beer advertisement, couched in either masculine or feminine terms. The masculine version contained phrases such as "X beer has the strong aggressive flavor that really asserts itself with good food and good company . . .," and the feminine version made claims such as "Brewed with tender care, X beer is a full-bodied beer that goes down smooth and gentle. . . ." People who rated themselves as highly masculine or highly feminine preferred the version that was described in (respectively) very masculine or feminine terms.[55] Sex-typed people in general are more concerned with ensuring that their behavior is consistent with their culture's definition of gender appropriateness.

FEMALE GENDER ROLES

Gender roles for women are changing rapidly. Social changes, such as the dramatic increase in the proportion of women working outside of the home, have led to an upheaval in the way women are regarded by men, the way they regard themselves, and in the products they choose to buy. Modern women now play a greater role in decisions regarding traditionally male purchases. For example, more than six in ten new car buyers under the age of 50 are female, and women even buy almost half of all condoms sold.[56]

THE FEMALE MARKET

In the 1949 movie *Adam's Rib*, Katharine Hepburn played a stylish and competent lawyer. This film was one of the first to show that a woman can have a successful career and still be happily married. The presence of women in positions of authority is a fairly recent phenomenon. The evolution of a new managerial class of women

MULTICULTURAL DIMENSIONS

One of the most marked changes in gender roles is occurring in Japan. Traditional Japanese wives stay home and care for children while their husbands work late and entertain clients. The good Japanese wife is expected to walk two paces behind her husband. However, these patterns are changing as women are less willing to live vicariously through their husbands. More than half of Japanese women aged 25 to 29 are either working or looking for a job.[57] Japanese marketers and advertisers are beginning to depict women in professional situations (though still usually in subservient roles), and even to develop female market segments for traditionally male products such as automobiles.

has forced marketers to change their traditional assumptions about women as they target this growing market.

Ironically, it seems that in some cases marketers have overcompensated for their former emphasis on women as homemakers. Many attempts to target the vast market of females employed outside the home tend to depict all these women in glamorous, executive positions. This portrayal ignores the facts that the majority of women do not hold such jobs, and that many work because they have to, rather than for self-fulfillment. This diversity means that not all women should be expected to respond to marketing campaigns that stress professional achievement or the glamour of the working life.

Whether or not they work outside of the home, many women have come to value greater independence and respond positively to marketing campaigns that stress the freedom to make their own lifestyle decisions. The American Express Company has been targeting women for a long time, but the company found that its "Do you know me?" campaign did not appeal to women as much as to men. A campaign aimed specifically at women instead featured confident women using their American Express cards. By depicting women in active situations, the company greatly increased its share of the woman's credit card market.[58]

CHEESECAKE: THE DEPICTION OF WOMEN IN ADVERTISING

As implied by the ads for Virginia Slims cigarettes—"You've come a long way, baby!"—attitudes about the female sex role have changed remarkably in this century. Still, women continue to be depicted by advertisers and the media in stereotypical ways. Analyses of ads in magazines such as *Time, Newsweek, Playboy,* and even *Ms.,* show that the large majority of women included were presented as sex objects (so-called "cheesecake" ads) or in traditional roles.[59] Similar findings have been obtained in the United Kingdom.[60] One of the biggest culprits may be rock videos, which tend to reinforce traditional women's roles.

Ads may also reinforce negative stereotypes. Women are often portrayed as stupid, submissive, temperamental, or as sexual objects who exist solely for the pleasure of men. An ad for Newport cigarettes illustrates how the theme of female submission can be subtly perpetuated. The copy "Alive with pleasure!" is accompanied by a photo of a woman in the woods, playfully hanging from a pole being carried by two men. The underlying message may be interpreted as two men bringing home their captured prey.[61]

Although women continue to be depicted in traditional roles, this situation is changing as advertisers scramble to catch up with reality. For example, Avon Products is trying to shed its old-fashioned image by focusing on the concerns of contemporary women. As one recent ad proclaims, "After all, you have more on

MARKETING PITFALL

Marketers continue to grapple with ways to entice female customers for traditionally male-oriented products, such as cars and computers, without offending them. One early effort by Tandy Corp. illustrates the potential for these efforts to backfire. When the company decided to market personal computers to women in 1990, it did so by packaging them with software for doing such "feminine" tasks as making Christmas lists, taking inventory of silverware and china, and generating recipes. Women were not amused by the homemaker stereotype, and the campaign flopped.[62]

your mind than what's on your lips. And Avon thinks that's beautiful."[63] Women are now as likely as men to be central characters in television commercials. Still, although males are increasingly depicted as spouses and parents, women are still more likely than men to be seen in domestic settings. Also, about 90 percent of all narrators in commercials are male. The deeper male voice is apparently perceived as more authoritative and credible.[64]

Some modern ads now feature *role reversal,* in which women occupy traditional men's roles. Ironically, current advertising is more free to emphasize traditional female traits now that sexual equality is becoming more of an accepted fact. This freedom is demonstrated in a German poster for a women's magazine. The caption reads "Today's women can sometimes show weakness, because they are strong."

MALE SEX ROLES

The traditional conception of the ideal male as a tough, aggressive, muscular man who enjoys "manly" sports and activities is not dead, but society's definition of the male role is evolving. Men in the late 1990s are "allowed" to be more compassionate and to have close friendships with other men. In contrast to the depiction of macho men who do not show feelings, some marketers are promoting men's "sensitive" side. An emphasis on male bonding has been the centerpiece of many ad campaigns, especially for beer companies.[65]

MARKETING OPPORTUNITY

As sex roles for males evolve, formerly "feminine products" such as fragrances and hair coloring have been successfully marketed to men in recent years. Cosmetics companies such as Aramis, Clinique, and Urban Decay are attempting to expand the male market even further. Even nail polish is slowly making its way onto men's shelves—the Hard Candy line offers its Candy Man collection that includes a metallic gold called Cowboy and a forest green shade named Oedipus.[66]

Ironically, these companies have gotten a boost by the recent trend toward corporate downsizing, which seems to have spurred men's interest in shortcuts to looking younger. To avoid being "outsourced" due to their age, American men are spending $9.5 billion a year on face-lifts, hairpieces, makeup, girdles, and other items in pursuit of The Fountain of Youth.[67] They are flocking to products like Rogaine to thicken hair, Bodyslimmers underwear that sucks in the waist, and Super Shaper Briefs that round out the buttocks (for an extra $5 the buyer can get an "endowment pad" that slips in the front). A corporate recruiter has nicknamed the customer for these products "The Bionic Executive."[68]

THE JOYS OF FATHERHOOD

Males' lifestyles are changing to allow greater freedom of expression in clothing choices, hobbies such as cooking, and so on. Men also are getting more involved in parenting, and advertising campaigns for companies such as Kodak, Omega watches, and Pioneer electronics stress the theme of fatherhood.[69] Still, this change is coming slowly. A commercial for 7-Eleven stores shows two men out for a walk, each pushing a stroller. As they near a 7-Eleven, they begin to push their strollers faster until they are racing. The campaign's creative director explained, "We showed them engaged in a competition to make it easier for men to accept the concept of taking care of children."[70]

BEEFCAKE: THE DEPICTION OF MEN IN ADVERTISING

Men as well as women are often depicted in a negative fashion in advertising. They frequently come across as helpless or bumbling. As one advertising executive put it, "The woman's movement raised consciousness in the ad business as to how women can be depicted. The thought now is, if we can't have women in these old-fashioned traditional roles, at least we can have men being dummies."[71]

Just as advertisers are often criticized for depicting women as sex objects, the same accusations can be made about how males are portrayed—a practice correspondingly known as "beefcake."[72] An ad campaign for Sansabelt trousers carried the copy, "What women look for in men's pants." Ads feature a woman who confides, "I always lower my eyes when a man passes [pause] to see if he's worth following." One female executive commented, ". . . turnabout is fair play. . . . If we can't put a stop to sexism in advertising . . . at least we can have some fun with it and do a little leering of our own."[73]

GAY AND LESBIAN CONSUMERS

The proportion of the population that is gay and lesbian is difficult to determine, and efforts to measure this group have been controversial.[74] However, the respected research company Yankelovich Partners Inc., which has tracked consumer values and attitudes since 1971 in its annual **Monitor™** survey, now includes a question

While you don't necessarily dress for men, it doesn't hurt, on occasion, to see one drool like the pathetic dog that he is.

This ad illustrates the "men-bashing" approach taken by some advertisers who are trying to appeal to women.

about sexual identity in its survey. This study was virtually the first to use a sample that reflects the population as a whole instead of polling only smaller or biased groups (such as readers of gay publications) whose responses may not be as representative of all consumers. About 6 percent of respondents identify themselves as gay/homosexual/lesbian.

These results help to paint a more accurate picture of the potential size and attractiveness of this segment. For example, contrary to earlier surveys that reported homosexuals to be far more affluent than the general population, this study found little difference in household income between the gay and "straight" populations. On the other hand, additional findings underscore the potential desirability of this segment for marketers: Homosexuals are twice as likely as heterosexuals to have attended graduate school, they are more concerned about physical fitness and self-improvement, they experience more stress in their daily lives, and they are much more likely to be self-employed. This means that they are an excellent market for cultural events, security systems and vacations, as well as fax machines, cellular phones, and other high-tech products.[75]

IKEA, a Swedish furniture retailer with stores in several major U.S. markets, broke new ground by running a TV spot featuring a gay couple who purchased a dining room table at the store.[76] Other major companies that now make an effort to market to homosexuals include AT&T, Anheuser-Busch, Apple Computer, Benetton, Philip Morris, Seagram, and Sony.[77] Gay consumers can even get their own credit card—a Rainbow Visa card issued by Travelers Bank USA. Using tennis star Martina Navratilova as its spokeswoman, users of the card benefit groups such as the National Center for Lesbian Rights. The card allows people who don't qualify based on income to apply with a same-sex partner.[78]

As civil rights gains are made by gay activists, the social climate is becoming more favorable for firms targeting this market segment.[79] At least in some parts of the country, homosexuality appears to be becoming a bit more mainstream and accepted. Mattel even sold an Earring Magic Ken doll, complete with *faux*-leather vest, lavender mesh shirt, and two-tone hairdo, though the company removed the product from its line following reports that it had become a favorite of gay men.[80]

Still, about 40 percent of **Monitor™** respondents said they would prefer not to have a homosexual as a friend. When comedienne Ellen deGeneres "came out" as a lesbian on prime-time TV in 1997, many advertisers chose not to place commercials on the show. On the other hand, the episode's Nielsen rating was 144 percent higher than average, so clearly someone was watching![81]

Benetton is one of numerous major companies attempting to target homosexuals. This intent is illustrated here.

MARKETING OPPORTUNITY

Lesbian consumers have recently been in the cultural spotlight, perhaps due in part to such high-profile cultural figures as tennis star Martina Navratilova, singers k.d. lang and Melissa Etheridge, and actress Ellen deGeneres. Whatever the reason, American Express, Stolichnaya vodka, Atlantic Records, and Naya bottled water are among those corporations now running ads in lesbian publications (an ad for American Express Travelers Cheques for Two shows two women's signatures on a check). Acting on research that showed lesbians are four times as likely to own one of their cars, Subaru of America recently began to target this market as well.[82]

Subaru decided to specifically target lesbian drivers after the company's research showed that its cars were well-regarded by this market segment.

BODY IMAGE

A person's physical appearance is a large part of his or her self-concept. **Body image** refers to a consumer's subjective evaluation of his or her physical self. As was the case with the overall self-concept, this image is not necessarily accurate. A man may think of himself as being more muscular than he really is, or a woman may feel she appears fatter than is the case. In fact, it is not uncommon to find marketing strategies that exploit consumers' tendencies to distort their body images by preying on insecurities about appearance, thereby creating a gap between the real and ideal physical self and, consequently, the desire to purchase products and services to narrow that gap. Indeed, the success of the photo chain Glamour Shots, which provides dramatic makeovers to customers (90 percent of them women) and then gives them a pictorial record of their pinup potential, can be traced to the fantasies of everyday people to be supermodels—at least for an hour or two.[83]

BODY CATHEXIS

A person's feelings about his or her body can be described in terms of **body cathexis.** *Cathexis* refers to the emotional significance of some object or idea to a person, and some parts of the body are more central to self-concept than are others. One study of young adults' feelings about their bodies found that the respondents were the most satisfied with their hair and eyes and had the least positive feelings about their waists. These feelings also were related to usage of grooming products. Consumers who were more satisfied with their bodies were more frequent users of such "preening" products as hair conditioner, blow dryers, cologne, facial bronzer, tooth polish, and pumice soap.[84]

IDEALS OF BEAUTY

A person's satisfaction with the physical image he or she presents to others is affected by how closely that image corresponds to the image valued by his or her culture. In fact, infants as young as two months show a preference for attractive faces.[85] An **ideal of beauty** is a particular model, or *exemplar,* of appearance. Ideals of beauty for both men and women may include physical features (e.g., big breasts or small, bulging muscles or not) as well as clothing styles, cosmetics, hairstyles, skin tone (pale versus tan), and body type (petite, athletic, voluptuous, etc.).

IS BEAUTY UNIVERSAL?

Recent research indicates that preferences for some physical features over others are "wired in" genetically, and that these reactions tend to be the same among people around the world. Specifically, people appear to favor features associated with good health and youth, attributes linked to reproductive ability and strength. These characteristics include large eyes, high cheekbones, and a narrow jaw. Another cue that apparently is used by people across ethnic and racial groups to signal sexual desirability is whether the person's features are balanced. In one study men and women with greater facial symmetry started having sex three to four years earlier than lopsided people!

Men also are more likely to use a woman's body shape as a sexual cue, and it has been theorized that this is because feminine curves provide evidence of reproductive potential. During puberty a typical female gains almost 35 pounds of "reproductive fat" around hips and thighs that supply the approximately 80,000 extra calories needed for pregnancy. Most fertile women have waist–hip ratios of 0.6 to 0.8, an hourglass shape that also happens to be the one men rank highest. Even

MARKETING OPPORTUNITY

An estimated 43 million Americans have a physical disability. The Americans with Disabilities Act, which prohibits employers from discriminating against the disabled, has created opportunities as many companies are investing in facilities that feature greater accessibility for the disabled. To recoup this investment, these companies are working hard to attract more disabled customers and employees.[86]

Although this group has long been ignored in the marketplace, recently major marketers such as Budweiser, Levi Strauss, McDonald's, and Reebok have employed disabled actors in their advertising, and major retailers such as Nordstrom, Target, Eddie Bauer, and KMart increasingly feature the disabled in their catalogs. With great fanfare, Mattel recently unveiled its new "Share a Smile Becky" doll, complete with her own wheelchair.[87]

Some research indicates that balanced or symmetrical facial features are a cue used by men and women to decide who is attractive. Country singer Lyle Lovett is an example of a man with asymmetrical features. The left picture is the real Lovett; the right is a computerized image that is really two left sides of his face.

though preferences for total weight change, waist–hip ratios tend to stay in this range—even the superthin model Twiggy (who pioneered the "waif look" decades before Kate Moss) had a ratio of 0.73.[88] Other positively valued female characteristics include a higher than average forehead, fuller lips, a shorter jaw, and a smaller chin and nose. Women, on the other hand, favor men with a heavy lower face (an indication of high concentration of androgens that create strength), those who are slightly above-average height, and those with a prominent brow.

Of course, the way these faces are "packaged" still varies enormously, and that's where marketers come in: Advertising and other forms of mass media play a significant role in determining which forms of beauty are considered desirable at any point in time. An ideal of beauty functions as a sort of cultural yardstick. Consumers compare themselves to some standard (often advocated by the fashion media) and are dissatisfied with their appearance to the extent that they don't match up to it.

These cultural ideals often are summed up in a sort of cultural shorthand. We may talk about a "bimbo," a "girl-next-door," or an "ice queen," or we may refer to specific women who have come to embody an ideal, such as Courtney Love, Gwenyth Paltrow, or the late Princess Diana.[89] Similar descriptions for men include "jock," "pretty boy," and "bookworm," or a "Brad Pitt type," a "Wesley Snipes type," and so on.

IDEALS OF BEAUTY OVER TIME
Although beauty may be only skin deep, throughout history women in particular have worked very hard to attain it. They have starved themselves, painfully bound their feet, inserted plates into their lips, spent countless hours under hair dryers, in front of mirrors, and beneath tanning lights, and have undergone breast reduction or enlargement operations to alter their appearance and meet their society's expectations of what a beautiful woman should look like.

In retrospect, periods of history tend to be characterized by a specific "look," or ideal of beauty. American history can be described in terms of a succession of

As suggested by this Benetton ad, a global perspective on ideals of beauty is resulting in more ways to be considered attractive.

dominant ideals. For example, in sharp contrast to today's emphasis on health and vigor, in the early 1800s, it was fashionable to appear delicate to the point of looking ill. The poet Keats described the ideal woman of that time as "a milk white lamb that bleats for man's protection." Other looks have included the voluptuous, lusty woman as epitomized by Lillian Russell, the athletic Gibson Girl of the 1890s, and the small, boyish flapper of the 1920s as exemplified by Clara Bow.[90]

In much of the nineteenth century, the desirable waistline for American women was 18 inches, a circumference that required the use of corsets pulled so tight that they routinely caused headaches, fainting spells, and possibly even the uterine and spinal disorders common among women of the time. While modern women are not quite as "straightlaced," many still endure such indignities as high heels, body waxing, eye-lifts, and liposuction. In addition to the millions spent on cosmetics, clothing, health clubs, and fashion magazines, these practices remind us that—rightly or wrongly—the desire to conform to current standards of beauty is alive and well.

The ideal body type of Western women has changed radically over time, and these changes have resulted in a realignment of *sexual dimorphic markers*—those aspects of the body that distinguish between the sexes. For example, analyses of the measurements of *Playboy* centerfolds over a 20-year period from 1958 to 1978 show that these ideals got thinner and more muscular. The average hip measurement went from 36 inches in 1958 to just over 34 inches in 1978. Average bust size shrunk from almost 37 inches in 1958 to about 35 inches in 1978.[91]

The first part of the 1990s saw the emergence of the controversial "waif" look, in which successful models (most notably Kate Moss) were likely to have bodies resembling those of young boys. More recently, the pendulum seems to be shifting back a bit, as the more buxom, "hourglass figure" popular in the 1950s (exemplified by the Marilyn Monroe ideal) has reappeared.[92] One factor leading to this change has been the opposition by feminist groups to the use of overly thin models. Such models, feminists and others charge, encourage starvation diets and eating disorders among women and girls who want to emulate the look. These groups have advocated boycotts against companies like Coca-Cola and Calvin Klein who have used wafer-thin models in their advertising. Some protesters have even taken to pasting stickers over these ads that read "Feed this woman," or "Give me a cheeseburger."[93]

We can also distinguish among ideals of beauty for men in terms of facial features, musculature, and facial hair—who could confuse Tom Cruise with George Clooney? In fact, one recent national survey that asked both men and women to comment on male aspects of appearance found that the dominant standard of beauty for men is a strongly masculine, muscled body—though women tend to prefer men with less muscle mass than men themselves strive to attain.[94] Advertisers appear to have the males' ideal in mind—a recent study of men appearing in advertisements found that most sport the strong and muscular physique of the male stereotype.[95]

WORKING ON THE BODY

Because many consumers are motivated to match some ideal of appearance, they often go to great lengths to change aspects of their physical selves. From cosmetics to plastic surgery, tanning salons to diet drinks, a multitude of products and services are directed toward altering or maintaining aspects of the physical self in order to present a desirable appearance. It is difficult to overstate the importance of the physical self-concept (and the desire by consumers to improve their appearance) to many marketing activities.

FATTISM

As reflected in the expression "you can never be too thin or too rich," our society has an obsession with weight. Even elementary school children perceive obesity as worse than disability.[96] The pressure to be slim is continually reinforced both by advertising and by peers. Americans in particular are preoccupied by what they weigh. We are continually bombarded by images of thin, happy people.

How realistic are these appearance standards? Fashion dolls, such as the ubiquitous Barbie, reinforce an unnatural ideal of thinness. The dimensions of these dolls, when extrapolated to average female body sizes, are unnaturally long and thin.[97] If the traditional Barbie doll were a real woman, her dimensions would be 38-18-34! In 1998, Mattel conducted "plastic surgery" on Barbie to give her a less pronounced bust and slimmer hips, but she is still not exactly dumpy.[98]

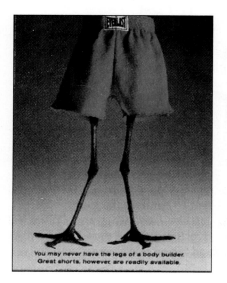

You may never have the legs of a body builder.
Great shorts, however, are readily available.

This Everlast apparel ad acknowledges the popularity of bodybuilding in a humorous way. As marketers know well, many kinds of athletic apparel, such as shoes and warmup suits, are purchased by "armchair athletes," who don't bother to play the sports for which these products were intended.

Still, many consumers focus on attaining an unrealistic ideal weight, sometimes by relying on height and weight charts compiled by the insurance industry that show what one *should* weigh. These charts are often outdated, because they don't take into account today's larger body frames or such factors as muscularity, age, or activity level.[100] Indeed, only 12 percent of blacks and 21 percent of whites (but 43 percent of Hispanics) weigh within the recommended range.[101] American women believe that the "ideal" body size is a 7, an unrealistic goal for most.[102] Even women who are at their best medical weight want on average to be eight pounds lighter.[103]

BODY IMAGE DISTORTIONS

Many people perceive a strong link between self-esteem and appearance, but some consumers unfortunately exaggerate this connection even more, and sacrifice greatly to attain what they consider to be a desirable body image. Women tend to

Society's emphasis on thinness and youth makes many consumers insecure about their body image. Numerous products, including diet drinks, appeal to the longing to conform to this ideal by touting their ability to help the consumer attain a desired weight. This South American ad promises, "You'll never have to go to the beach in a T-shirt again."

You'll never have to go to the beach in a T-shirt again.

pick up messages from the media more than men that the quality of their bodies reflects their self-worth, so it is not surprising that most major distortions of body image occur among females.

Men do not tend to differ in ratings of their current figure, their ideal figure, and the figure they think is most attractive to women. In contrast, women rate both the figure they think is most attractive to men and their ideal figure as much thinner than their actual figure.[104] In one survey, two-thirds of college women admitted resorting to unhealthy behavior to control weight. Advertising messages that convey an image of slimness help to reinforce these activities by arousing insecurities about weight.[105]

A distorted body image has been linked to the rise of eating disorders, which are particularly prevalent among young women. People with *anorexia* regard themselves as fat, and virtually starve themselves in the quest for thinness. This condition often results in *bulimia,* which involves two stages: First, binge eating occurs (usually in private), where more than 5,000 calories may be consumed at one time. The binge is then followed by induced vomiting, abuse of laxatives, fasting, and/or overly strenuous exercise—a "purging" process that reasserts the woman's sense of control.

Most eating disorders are found in white, upper-middle class teenage and college-age young women. Victims often have brothers or fathers who are hypercritical of their weight, and these disorders are also associated with a history of sexual abuse.[106] In addition, binge eating can be encouraged by one's peers. Groups such as athletic teams, cheerleading squads, and sororities may develop positive norms regarding binge eating. In one study of a college sorority, members' popularity within the group increased the more they binged.[107]

Eating disorders do affect some men as well. They are common among male athletes who must also conform to various weight requirements, such as jockeys, boxers, and male models.[108] In general, though, most men who have distorted body images consider themselves to be too light rather than too heavy: Society has taught them that they must be muscular to be masculine. Men are more likely than women are to express their insecurities about their bodies by becoming addicted to exercise. In fact, striking similarities have been found between male compulsive runners and female anorexics. These include a commitment to diet and exercise as a central part of one's identity and susceptibility to body-image distortions.[109]

COSMETIC SURGERY

Consumers are increasingly electing to have cosmetic surgery to change a poor body image.[110] More than half a million cosmetic surgeries are performed in the United States every year, and this number continues to grow.[111] There is no longer much (if any) social stigma associated with having this type of operation; it is commonplace and accepted among many segments of consumers.[112] In fact, men now account for as much as 20 percent of plastic surgery patients. Popular operations include the implantation of silicon pectoral muscles (for the chest) and even calf implants to fill out "chicken legs."[113]

Many women turn to surgery either to reduce weight or to increase sexual desirability. The use of the liposuction procedure, where fat is removed from the thighs with a vacuum-like device, has almost doubled since it was introduced in the United States in 1982.[114] Some women feel that larger breasts will increase their allure and undergo breast augmentation procedures.[115] Although some of these procedures have generated controversy due to possible negative side effects, it is unclear whether potential medical problems will deter large numbers of women from choosing surgical options to enhance their (perceived) femininity.

MULTICULTURAL DIMENSIONS

Bellybutton reconstruction is now a popular form of cosmetic surgery in Japan, as women strive for the perfect navel they can show off as they wear the midriff fashions now popular there. The navel is an important part of Japanese culture, and mothers often save a baby's umbilical cord in a wooden box. In Japanese, a "bent navel" is a grouch, and a phrase meaning "give me a break" translates as "yeah, and I brew tea in my bellybutton." A popular insult among children is "Your mother has an outie."[116]

The importance of breast size to self-concept resulted in an interesting and successful marketing strategy undertaken by an underwear company. While conducting focus groups on bras, an analyst noted that small-chested women typically reacted with hostility when discussing the subject. They would unconsciously cover their chests with their arms as they spoke and felt that their needs were ignored by the fashion industry. To meet this overlooked need, the company introduced a line of A-cup bras called "A-OK" and depicted wearers in a positive light. A new market segment was born.

If you've got it, flaunt it!
And if you don't...create it.

ATHENA
COLLECTION

The *"Bust Enhancer"* swimsuit by ATHENA COLLECTION ...
Create the illusion.

Hechts/Foleys/Filenes/Famous Barr •
Liberty House • Gaylers/Maison Blanche •
Lions/Bacons/McAlpins/Castner Knott •
McRae's • or call 1-800-766-8466

This "cleavage enhancement" product encourages women to "create the illusion" of a more buxom figure.

Other companies are going in the opposite direction by pushing bras that create the illusion of a larger cleavage. In Europe and the United States, both Gossard and Playtex are aggressively marketing specially designed bras offering "cleavage enhancement" that use a combination of wires and internal pads (called "cookies" in the industry) to create the desired effect. Despite some protests by feminists, sales are booming as consumers' preferences for the ideal body type shift once again.[117]

BODY DECORATION AND MUTILATION

The body is adorned or altered in some way in every culture. Decorating the self serves a number of purposes.[118]

- *To separate group members from nonmembers:* Chinook Indians of North America pressed the head of a newborn between two boards for a year, permanently altering its shape. In our society, teens go out of their way to adopt distinctive hair and clothing styles that will separate them from adults.

- *To place the individual in the social organization:* Many cultures engage in puberty rites, during which a boy symbolically becomes a man. Young men in Ghana paint their bodies with white stripes to resemble skeletons to symbolize the death of their child status. In Western culture, this rite may involve some form of mild self-mutilation or engaging in dangerous activities.

MULTICULTURAL DIMENSIONS

Cosmetic surgeons often try to mold their patients into a standard ideal of beauty, using the features of such Caucasian classic beauties as Grace Kelly or Katharine Hepburn as a guide. The aesthetic standard used by surgeons is called the *classic canon,* which spells out the ideal relationships among facial features. For example, it states that the width of the base of the nose should be the same as the distance between the eyes.

However, this standard applies to the Caucasian ideal, and it is being revised as people from other ethnic groups are demanding less rigidity in culture's definition of what is beautiful. Other cultures are rebelling against the need to conform to the Western ideal. For example, a rounded face is valued as a sign of beauty by many Asians, and thus giving cheek implants to an Asian patient would remove much of what makes her face attractive.

Some surgeons who work on African Americans are trying to change the guidelines they use when sculpting features. For example, they argue that an ideal African American nose is shorter and has a more rounded tip than does a Caucasian nose. Doctors are beginning to diversify their "product lines," offering consumers a broader assortment of features that better reflect the diversity of cultural ideals of beauty in a heterogeneous society.[119]

Racial differences in beauty ideals also surfaced in a recent study of teenagers. White girls who were asked to describe the "ideal" girl agreed she should be 5'7", weigh between 100 and 110 pounds, and have blue eyes and long flowing hair—in other words, she should look a lot like a Barbie doll. Almost 90 percent of the girls in this study said they were dissatisfied with their weight.

In contrast, 70 percent of the black girls in the study responded that they were *satisfied* with their weight. They were much less likely to use physical characteristics to describe the ideal girl, instead emphasizing someone who has a personal sense of style and who gets along with others. It was only when prodded that they named such features as fuller hips, large thighs, and a small waist, which the authors of the study say are attributes valued by black men.[120]

- *To place the person in a gender category:* The Tchikrin Indians of South America insert a string of beads in a boy's lip to enlarge it. Western women wear lipstick to enhance femininity. At the turn of the century, small lips were fashionable because they represented women's submissive role at that time.[121] Today, big, red lips are provocative and indicate an aggressive sexuality. Some women, including a number of famous actresses and models, receive collagen injections or lip inserts to create large, pouting lips (known in the modeling industry as "liver lips").[122]

- *To enhance sex-role identification:* The modern use of high heels, which podiatrists agree are a prime cause of knee and hip problems, backaches, and fatigue, can be compared with the traditional Oriental practice of foot-binding to enhance femininity. As one doctor observed, "When [women] get home, they can't get their high-heeled shoes off fast enough. But every doctor in the world could yell from now until Doomsday, and women would still wear them."[123]

- *To indicate desired social conduct:* The Suya of South America wear ear ornaments to emphasize the importance placed in their culture on listening and obedience. In Western society some gay men may wear an earring in the left or right ear to signal what role (submissive or dominant) they prefer in a relationship.

- *To indicate high status or rank:* The Hidates Indians of North America wear feather ornaments that indicate how many people they have killed. In our society, some people wear glasses with clear lenses, even though they do not have eye problems, to enhance their perceived status.

- *To provide a sense of security:* Consumers often wear lucky charms, amulets, rabbits' feet, and so on to protect them from the "evil eye." Some modern women wear a "mugger whistle" around their necks for a similar reason.

TATTOOS

Tattoos—both temporary and permanent—are a popular form of body adornment (and possibly mutilation). This body art can be used to communicate aspects of the self to onlookers and may serve some of the same functions that other kinds of body painting do in primitive cultures. Tattoos (from the Tahitian *ta-tu*) have deep roots in folk art. Until recently, the images were crude and were primarily either death symbols (e.g., a skull), animals (especially panthers, eagles, and snakes), pinup women, or military designs. More current influences include science fiction themes, Japanese symbolism, and tribal designs.

A tattoo may be viewed as a fairly risk-free way of expressing an adventurous side of the self. Tattoos have a long history of association with people who are social outcasts. For example, the faces and arms of criminals in sixth-century Japan were tattooed as a means to identify them, as were Massachusetts prison inmates in the nineteenth century and concentration camp internees in the twentieth century. These emblems are often used by marginal groups, such as bikers or Japanese *yakuze* (gang members), to express group identity and solidarity.

BODY PIERCING

Decorating the body with various kinds of metallic inserts also has evolved from a practice associated with some fringe groups to become a popular fashion statement. The initial impetus for the mainstreaming of what had been an underground

IT'S NOT NEARLY AS PAINFUL AS PUTTING ON A WEDDING RING.

Body piercing has practically become a mainstream fashion statement.

West Coast fad is credited to Aerosmith's 1993 video *Cryin'* in which Alicia Silverstone receives both a navel ring and a tattoo.[124] Piercings can range from a hoop protruding from a navel to scalp implants, where metal posts are inserted in the skull (do not try this at home!). Publications such as *Piercing Fans International Quarterly* are seeing their circulations soar, and Web sites such as http://www.xines.com/xines/bodyart/ are attracting numerous followers. This popularity is not pleasing to hard-core piercing fans, who view the practice as a sensual consciousness-raising ritual and are concerned that now people just do it because it's trendy. As one customer waiting for a nipple piercing remarked, "If your piercing doesn't mean anything, then it's just like buying a pair of platform shoes."[125]

CHAPTER SUMMARY

- Consumers' *self-concepts* are reflections of their attitudes toward themselves. Whether these attitudes are positive or negative, they will help to guide many purchase decisions; products can be used to bolster self-esteem or to "reward" the self.

- Many product choices are dictated by the consumer's perceived similarity between his or her personality and attributes of the product. The *symbolic interactionist perspective* on the self implies that each of us actually has many selves, and a different set of products is required as props to play each role. Many things other than the body can also be viewed as part of the self. Valued objects, cars, homes, and even attachments to sports teams or national monuments are used to define the self, when these are incorporated into the extended self.

- A person's *sex-role* identity is a major component of self-definition. Conceptions about masculinity and femininity, largely shaped by society, guide the acquisition of "sex-typed" products and services.

- Advertising and other media play an important role in socializing consumers to be male and female. Although traditional women's roles have often been perpetuated in advertising depictions, this situation is changing somewhat. The media do not always portray men accurately either.

- A person's conception of his or her body also provides feedback to self-image. A culture communicates certain ideals of beauty, and consumers go to great lengths to attain these. Many consumer activities involve manipulating the body, whether through dieting, cosmetic surgery, piercing, or tattooing.

- Sometimes these activities are carried to an extreme, as people try too hard to live up to cultural ideals. One common manifestation is eating disorders, where women in particular become obsessed with thinness.

- Body decoration and/or mutilation may serve such functions as separating group members from nonmembers, marking the individual's status or rank within a social organization or within a gender category (e.g., homosexual), or even to provide a sense of security or good luck.

KEY TERMS

Actual self p. 113
Agentic goals p. 140
Androgyny p. 141
Body cathexis p. 148
Body image p. 147
Communal goals p. 140
Extended self p. 139

Fantasy p. 133
Ideal of beauty p. 148
Ideal self p. 133
Looking-glass self p. 135
Self-concept p. 132
Self-image congruence
models p. 137

Sex-typed traits p. 140
Symbolic interactionism
p. 135
Symbolic self-completion
theory p. 136

CONSUMER BEHAVIOR CHALLENGE

1. How might the creation of a self-conscious state be related to consumers who are trying on clothing in dressing rooms? Does the act of preening in front of a mirror change the dynamics by which people evaluate their product choices? Why?

2. Is it ethical for marketers to encourage infatuation with the self?

3. List three dimensions by which the self-concept can be described.

4. Compare and contrast the real versus the ideal self. List three products for which each type of self is likely to be used as a reference point when a purchase is considered.

5. Watch a set of ads featuring men and women on television. Try to imagine the characters with reversed roles (i.e., the male parts played by women and vice versa). Can you see any differences in assumptions about sex-typed behavior?

6. To date, the bulk of advertising targeted to gay consumers has been placed in exclusively gay media. If it was your decision to make, would you consider using mainstream media as well to reach gays, who constitute a significant proportion of the general population? Or, remembering that members of some targeted segments have serious objections to this practice, especially when the product (e.g., liquor, cigarettes) may be viewed as harmful in some way, should gays should be singled out at all by marketers?

7. Do you agree that marketing strategies tend to have a male-oriented bias? If so, what are some possible consequences for specific marketing activities?

8. In the past, some marketers have been reluctant to use disabled people in advertising out of fear they would be seen as patronizing or that their ads would be depressing. Should the disabled be viewed as a distinct market segment, or should marketers continue to assume that their wants and needs are the same as the rest of the mainstream market?

9. Construct a "consumption biography" of a friend or family member. Make a list of and/or photograph his or her most favorite possessions, and see if you or others can describe this person's personality just from the information provided by this catalogue.

10. Some consumer advocates have protested the use of superthin models in advertising, claiming that these women encourage others to starve themselves in order to attain the "waif" look. Other critics respond that the media's power to shape behavior has been overestimated, and that it is insulting to people to assume that they are unable to separate fantasy from reality. What do you think?

11. Interview victims of burglaries, or people who have lost personal property in floods, hurricanes, or other natural disasters. How do they go about reconstructing their possessions, and what effect did the loss appear to have on them?

12. Locate additional examples of self-esteem advertising. Evaluate the probable effectiveness of these appeals—is it true that "flattery gets you everywhere?"

NOTES

1. Daniel Goleman, "When Ugliness is Only in Patient's Eye, Body Image Can Reflect Mental Disorder," *New York Times* (October 2, 1991): C13.

2. Harry C. Triandis, "The Self and Social Behavior in Differing Cultural Contexts," *Psychological Review* 96 (1989)3: 506–20; H. Markus and S. Kitayama, "Culture and the Self: Implications for Cognition, Emotion, and Motivation," *Psychological Review* 98 (1991): 224–53.

3. Markus and Kitayama, "Culture and the Self."

4. Nancy Wong and Aaron Ahuvia, "A Cross-Cultural Approach to Materialism and the Self," in ed. Dominique Bouchet, *Cultural Dimensions of International Marketing* (Denmark: Odense University, 1995): 68–89.

5. Morris Rosenberg, *Conceiving the Self* (New York: Basic Books, 1979); M. Joseph Sirgy, "Self-Concept in Consumer Behavior: A Critical Review," *Journal of Consumer Research* 9 (December 1982): 287–300.

6. Emily Yoffe, "You Are What You Buy," *Newsweek* (June 4, 1990): 59.

7. Roy F. Baumeister, Dianne M. Tice, and Debra G. Hutton, "Self-Presentational Motivations and Personality Differences in Self-Esteem," *Journal of Personality* 57 (September 1989): 547–75; Ronald J. Faber, "Are Self-Esteem Appeals Appealing?" in ed. Leonard N. Reid, *Proceedings of the 1992 Conference of the American Academy of Advertising* (1992): 230–35.

8. B. Bradford Brown and Mary Jane Lohr, "Peer-Group Affiliation and Adolescent Self-Esteem: An Integration of Ego-Identity and Symbolic-Interaction Theories," *Journal of Personality and Social Psychology* 52 (1987)1: 47–55.

9. Marsha L. Richins, "Social Comparison and the Idealized Images of Advertising," *Journal of Consumer Research* 18 (June 1991): 71–83; Mary C. Martin and Patricia F. Kennedy, "Advertising and Social Comparison: Consequences for Female Preadolescents and Adolescents," *Psychology & Marketing* 10 (November/December 1993)6: 513–30.

10. Philip N. Myers Jr. and Frank A. Biocca, "The Elastic Body Image: The Effect of Television Advertising and Programming on Body Image Distortions in Young Women," *Journal of Communication* 42 (Summer 1992): 108–33.

11. Ernest Dichter, *Handbook of Consumer Motivations* (New York: McGraw-Hill, 1964).

12. Jeffrey F. Durgee, "Self-Esteem Advertising," *Journal of Advertising* 14 (1986)4: 21.

13. Sigmund Freud, *New Introductory Lectures in Psychoanalysis* (New York: Norton, 1965).

14. Harrison G. Gough, Mario Fioravanti, and Renato Lazzari, "Some Implications of Self versus Ideal-Self Congruence on the Revised Adjective Check List," *Journal of Personality and Social Psychology* 44 (1983)6: 1214–20.

15. Steven Jay Lynn and Judith W. Rhue, "Daydream Believers," *Psychology Today* (September 1985): 14.

16. Erving Goffman, *The Presentation of Self in Everyday Life* (Garden City, NY: Doubleday, 1959); Michael R. Solomon, "The Role of Products as Social Stimuli: A Symbolic Interactionism Perspective," *Journal of Consumer Research* 10 (December 1983): 319–29.

17. Julie Skur Hill, "Purchasing Habits Shift for Execs," *Advertising Age* (April 27, 1992): I16.

18. George H. Mead, *Mind, Self and Society* (Chicago: University of Chicago Press, 1934).

19. Charles H. Cooley, *Human Nature and the Social Order* (New York: Scribner's, 1902).

20. J. G. Hull and A. S. Levy, "The Organizational Functions of the Self: An Alternative to the Duval and Wicklund Model of Self-Awareness," *Journal of Personality and Social Psychology* 37 (1979): 756–68; Jay G. Hull, Ronald R. Van Treuren, Susan J. Ashford, Pamela Propsom, and Bruce W. Andrus, "Self-Consciousness and the Processing of Self-Relevant Information," *Journal of Personality and Social Psychology* 54 (1988)3: 452–65.

21. Arnold W. Buss, *Self-Consciousness and Social Anxiety* (San Francisco: Freeman, 1980); Lynn Carol Miller and Cathryn Leigh Cox, "Public Self-Consciousness and Makeup Use," *Personality and Social Psychology Bulletin* 8 (1982)4: 748–51; Michael R. Solomon and John Schopler, "Self-Consciousness and Clothing," *Personality and Social Psychology Bulletin* 8 (1982)3: 508–14.

22. Morris B. Holbrook, Michael R. Solomon, and Stephen Bell, "A Re-Examination of Self-Monitoring and Judgments of Furniture Designs," *Home Economics Research Journal* 19 (September 1990): 6–16; Mark Snyder, "Self-Monitoring Processes," in *Advances in Experimental Social Psychology,* ed. Leonard Berkowitz (New York: Academic Press, 1979), 85–128.

23. Mark Snyder and Steve Gangestad, "On the Nature of Self-Monitoring: Matters of Assessment, Matters of Validity," *Journal of Personality and Social Psychology* 51 (1986): 125–39.

24. Timothy R. Graeff, "Image Congruence Effects on Product Evaluations: The Role of Self-Monitoring and Public/Private Consumption," *Psychology & Marketing* 13 (August 1996)5: 481–99.

25. Richard G. Netemeyer, Scot Burton, and Donald R. Lichtenstein, "Trait Aspects of Vanity: Measurement and Relevance to Consumer Behavior," *Journal of Consumer Research* 21 (March 1995): 612–26.

26. Michael R. Solomon and Henry Assael, "The Forest or the Trees?: A Gestalt Approach to Symbolic Consumption," in ed. Jean Umiker-Sebeok, *Marketing and Semiotics: New Directions in the Study of Signs for Sale* (Berlin: Mouton de Gruyter, 1987): 189–218.

27. Jack L. Nasar, "Symbolic Meanings of House Styles," *Environment and Behavior* 21 (May 1989): 235–57; E. K. Sadalla, B. Verschure, and J. Burroughs, "Identity Symbolism in Housing," *Environment and Behavior* 19 (1987): 599–87.

28. Michael R. Solomon,"The Role of Products as Social Stimuli: A Symbolic Interactionism Perspective," *Journal of Consumer Research* 10 (December 1983): 319–28; Robert E. Kleine III, Susan Schultz-Kleine, and Jerome B. Kernan, "Mundane Consumption and the Self: A Social-Identity Perspective," *Journal of Consumer Psychology* 2 (1993)3: 209–35; Newell D. Wright, C. B. Claiborne, and M. Joseph Sirgy, "The Effects of Product Symbolism on Consumer Self-Concept," in eds. John F. Sherry Jr. and Brian Sternthal, *Advances in Consumer Research* 19 (Provo, UT: Association for Consumer Research, 1992): 311–18; Susan Fournier, "A Person-Based Relationship Framework for Strategic Brand Management" (doctoral dissertation, University of Florida, 1994).

29. A. Dwayne Ball and Lori H. Tasaki, "The Role and Measurement of Attachment in Consumer Behavior," *Journal of Consumer Psychology* 1 (1992)2: 155–72.

30. William B. Hansen and Irwin Altman, "Decorating Personal Places: A Descriptive Analysis," *Environment and Behavior* 8 (December 1976): 491–504.

31. R. A. Wicklund and P. M. Gollwitzer, *Symbolic Self-Completion* (Hillsdale, NJ: Erlbaum, 1982).

32. Erving Goffman, *Asylums* (New York: Doubleday, 1961).

33. Quoted in Floyd Rudmin, "Property Crime Victimization Impact on Self, on Attachment, and on Territorial Dominance," *CPA Highlights,* Victims of Crime Supplement 9 (1987)2: 4–7.

34. Barbara B. Brown, "House and Block as Territory" (paper presented at the Conference of the Association for Consumer Research, San Francisco, 1982).

35. Quoted in Shay Sayre and David Horne, "I Shop, Therefore I Am: The Role of Possessions for Self Definition," in eds. Shay Sayre and David Horne, *Earth, Wind, and Fire and Water: Perspectives on Natural Disaster* (Pasadena CA: Open Door Publishers, 1996): 353–70.

36. Deborah A. Prentice, "Psychological Correspondence of Possessions, Attitudes, and Values," *Journal of Personality and Social Psychology* 53 (1987)6: 993–1002.

37. Sak Onkvisit and John Shaw, "Self-Concept and Image Congruence: Some Research and Managerial Implications," *Journal of Consumer Marketing* 4 (Winter 1987): 13–24. For a related treatment of congruence between advertising appeals and self-concept, see George M. Zinkhan and Jae W. Hong, "Self-Concept and Advertising Effectiveness: A Conceptual Model of Congruency, Conspicuousness, and Response Mode," in eds. Rebecca H. Holman and Michael R. Solomon, *Advances in Consumer Research* 18 (Provo, UT: Association for Consumer Research, 1991): 348–54.

38. C. B. Claiborne and M. Joseph Sirgy, "Self-Image Congruence as a Model of Consumer Attitude Formation and Behavior: A Conceptual Review and Guide for Further Research" (paper presented at the Academy of Marketing Science Conference, New Orleans, 1990).

39. Al E. Birdwell, "A Study of Influence of Image Congruence on Consumer Choice," *Journal of Business* 41 (January 1964): 76–88; Edward L. Grubb and Gregg Hupp, "Perception of Self, Generalized Stereotypes, and Brand Selection," *Journal of Marketing Research* 5 (February 1986): 58–63.

40. Ira J. Dolich, "Congruence Relationship between Self-Image and Product Brands," *Journal of Marketing Research* 6 (February 1969): 80–4; Danny N. Bellenger, Earle Steinberg, and Wilbur W. Stanton, "The Congruence of Store Image and Self Image as It Relates to Store Loyalty," *Journal of Retailing* 52 (1976)1: 17–32; Ronald J. Dornoff and Ronald L. Tatham, "Congruence between Personal Image and Store Image," *Journal of the Market Research Society* 14 (1972)1: 45–52.

41. Naresh K. Malhotra, "A Scale to Measure Self-Concepts, Person Concepts, and Product Concepts," *Journal of Marketing Research* 18 (November 1981): 456–64.

42. Ernest Beaglehole, Property: *A Study in Social Psychology* (New York: MacMillan, 1932).

43. M. Csikszentmihalyi and Eugene Rochberg-Halton, *The Meaning of Things: Domestic Symbols and the*

Self (Cambridge, UK: Cambridge University Press, 1981).

44. Russell W. Belk, "Possessions and the Extended Self," *Journal of Consumer Research* 15 (September 1988): 139–68.

45. Joan Meyers-Levy, "The Influence of Sex Roles on Judgment," *Journal of Consumer Research* 14 (March 1988): 522–30.

46. Kimberly J. Dodson and Russell W. Belk, "Gender in Children's Birthday Stories," in ed. Janeen Costa, *Gender, Marketing, and Consumer Behavior* (Salt Lake City: Association for Consumer Research, 1996): 96–108.

47. Elizabeth C. Hirschman, "A Feminist Critique of Marketing Theory: Toward Agentic-Communal Balance" (working paper, School of Business, Rutgers University, New Brunswick, NJ, l990).

48. Eileen Fischer and Stephen J. Arnold, "Sex, Gender Identity, Gender Role Attitudes, and Consumer Behavior," *Psychology & Marketing* 11 (March/April 1994)2: 163–182.

49. Kathleen Debevec and Easwar Iyer, "Sex Roles and Consumer Perceptions of Promotions, Products, and Self: What Do We Know and Where Should We Be Headed," in ed. Richard J. Lutz, *Advances in Consumer Research* 13 (Provo, UT: Association for Consumer Research, 1986): 210–14; Joseph A. Bellizzi and Laura Milner, "Gender Positioning of a Traditionally Male-Dominant Product," *Journal of Advertising Research* (June/July 1991): 72–9.

50. Janeen Arnold Costa and Teresa M. Pavia, "Alpha-Numeric Brand Names and Gender Stereotypes," *Research in Consumer Behavior* 6 (1993): 85–112.

51. Sandra L. Bem, "The Measurement of Psychological Androgyny," *Journal of Consulting and Clinical Psychology* 42 (1974): 155–62; Deborah E. S. Frable, "Sex Typing and Gender Ideology: Two Facets of the Individual's Gender Psychology That Go Together," *Journal of Personality and Social Psychology* 56 (1989)1: 95–108.

52. See D. Bruce Carter and Gary D. Levy, "Cognitive Aspects of Early Sex-Role Development: The Influence of Gender Schemas on Preschoolers' Memories and Prefer- ences for Sex-Typed Toys and Activities," *Child Development* 59 (1988): 782–92; Bernd H. Schmitt, France Le Clerc, and Laurette Dube-Rioux, "Sex Typing and Consumer Behavior: A Test of Gender Schema Theory," *Journal of Consumer Research* 15 (June 1988): 122–7.

53. Carol Gilligan, *In a Different Voice: Psychological Theory and Women's Development* (Cambridge, MA: Harvard University Press, 1982); Joan Meyers-Levy and Durairaj Maheswaran, "Exploring Differences in Males' and Females' Processing Strategies," *Journal of Consumer Research* 18 (June 1991): 63–70.

54. Lynn J. Jaffe and Paul D. Berger, "Impact on Purchase Intent of Sex-Role Identity and Product Positioning," *Psychology & Market- ing* (Fall 1988): 259–71; Lynn J. Jaffe, "The Unique Predictive Ability of Sex-Role Identity in Explaining Women's Response to Advertising," *Psychology & Marketing* 11 (September/October 1994)5: 467–82.

55. Leila T. Worth, Jeanne Smith, and Diane M. Mackie, "Gender Sche- maticity and Preference for Gender-Typed Products," *Psychology & Marketing* 9 (January 1992): 17–30.

56. Julie Candler, "Woman Car Buyer— Don't Call Her a Niche Anymore," *Advertising Age* (January 21, 1991): S8; see also Robin Widgery and Jack McGaugh, "Vehicle Message Appeals and the New Generation Woman," *Journal of Advertising Research* (September/October 1993): 36–42; Blayne Cutler, "Condom Mania," *American Demographics* (June 1989): 17.

57. Laurel Anderson and Marsha Wadkins, "The New Breed in Japan: Consumer Culture" (unpublished manuscript, Arizona State University, Tempe, 1990); Doris L. Walsh, "A Familiar Story," *American Demographics* (June 1987): 64.

58. B. Abrams, "American Express is Gearing New Ad Campaign to Women," *Wall Street Journal* (August 4, 1983): 23.

59. "Ads' Portrayal of Women Today is Hardly Innovative," *Marketing News* (November 6, 1989): 12; Jill Hicks Ferguson, Peggy J. Kreshel, and Spencer F. Tinkham, "In the Pages of *Ms.*: Sex Role Portrayals of Women in Advertising," *Journal of Advertising* 19 (1990)1: 40–51.

60. Sonia Livingstone and Gloria Greene, "Television Advertisements and the Portrayal of Gender," *British Journal of Social Psychology* 25 (1986): 149–54; for one of the origi- nal articles on this topics, see L. Z. McArthur and B. G. Resko, "The Portrayal of Men and Women in American Television Commercials," *Journal of Social Psychology* 97 (1975): 209–20.

61. Richard Edel, "American Dream Vendors," *Advertising Age* (November 9, 1988): 153.

62. Kyle Pope, "High-Tech Marketers Try to Attract Women without Causing Offense," *Wall Street Journal* (March 17, 1994): B1 (2 pp.).

63. Stuart Elliott, "Avon Products is Abandoning Its Old-Fashioned Image in an Appeal to Contemporary Women," *New York Times* (April 27, 1993): D21.

64. Daniel J. Brett and Joanne Cantor, "The Portrayal of Men and Women in U.S. Television Commercials: A Recent Content Analysis and Trends over 15 Years," *Sex Roles* 18 (1988): 595–609.

65. Gordon Sumner, "Tribal Rites of the American Male," *Marketing Insights* (Summer 1989): 13.

66. Cyndee Miller, "Cosmetics Makers to Men: Paint Those Nails," *Marketing News* (May 12, 1997): 14, 18.

67. Alan Farnham, "You're So Vain," *Fortune* (September 9, 1996): 66 (10 pp.).

68. Amy M. Spindler, "It's a Face-Lifted, Tummy-Tucked Jungle Out There," *New York Times* (June 9, 1996): Sec. 3, 1 (3 pp.).

69. "Changing Conceptions of Fatherhood," *USA Today* (May 1988): 10.

70. Quoted in Kim Foltz, "In Ads, Men's Image Becomes Softer," *New York Times* (March 26, 1990): D12.

71. Quoted in Jennifer Foote, "The Ad World's New Bimbos," *Newsweek* (January 25, 1988): 44.

72. Margaret G. Maples, "Beefcake Marketing: The Sexy Sell," *Marketing Communications* (April 1983): 21–5.

73. Quoted in Lynn G. Coleman, "What Do People Really Lust After in Ads?" *Marketing News* (November 6, 1989): 12.

74. Projections of the incidence of homosexuality in the general popu- lation often are influenced by assumptions of the researchers, as

well as the methodology they employ (e.g., self-report, behavioral measures, fantasy measures). For a discussion of these factors, see Edward O. Laumann, John H. Gagnon, Robert T. Michael, and Stuart Michaels, *The Social Organization of Homosexuality* (Chicago: University of Chicago Press, 1994).

75. Stuart Elliott, "A Sharper View of Gay Consumers," *New York Times* (June 9, 1994): D1 (2 pp.).

76. Kate Fitzgerald (1994), "Ikea Dares to Reveal Gays Buy Tables, Too," *Advertising Age*, March 28, 3 (2); Cyndee Miller, "Top Marketers Take Bolder Approach in Targeting Gays," *Marketing News* (July 4, 1994): 1(2); Michael Wilke, "Big Advertisers Join Move to Embrace Gay Market," *Advertising Age* (August 4, 197): 1(2).

77. Elliott, "A Sharper View of Gay Consumers"; Kate Fitzgerald, "AT&T Addresses Gay Market," *Advertising Age* (May 16, 1994): 8.

78. James S. Hirsch, "New Credit Cards Base Appeals on Sexual Orientation and Race," *Wall Street Journal*, (November 6, 1995): B1 (2 pp.).

79. Lisa Peñaloza, "We're Here, We're Queer, and We're Going Shopping!: A Critical Perspective on the Accommodation of Gays and Lesbians in the U.S. Marketplace," *Journal of Homosexuality*, 31 (summer 1996) 1/2: 9–41.

80. Joseph Pereira, "These Particular Buyers of Dolls Don't Say, 'Don't Ask, Don't Tell'," *Wall Street Journal* (August 30, 1993): B1.

81. Joe Mandese and Mark Weiner, "ABC Scores as 'Ellen' Comes Out," *Advertising Age* (May 5, 1997): 6.

82. Michael Wilke, "Subaru Adds Lesbians to Niche Marketing Drive," *Advertising Age* (March 4, 1996): 8.

83. Stephanie N. Mehta, "Photo Chain Ventures beyond Big Hair," *Wall Street Journal* (May 13, 1996): B1 (2 pp.).

84. Dennis W. Rook, "Body Cathexis and Market Segmentation," in ed. Michael R. Solomon, *The Psychology of Fashion*, (Lexington, MA: Lexington Books, 1985): 233–41.

85. Carrie Goerne, "Marketing to the Disabled: New Workplace Law Stirs Interest in Largely Untapped Market," *Marketing News* 3 (September 14, 1992): 1; "Retailers Find a Market, and Models, in Disabled," *New York Times* (August 6, 1992): D4.

86. "New Barbie Friend Uses a Wheelchair," *Montgomery Advertiser* (May 22, 1997): 1.

87. Jane E. Brody, "Notions of Beauty Transcend Culture, New Study Suggests," *New York Times* (March 21, 1994): A14.

88. Geoffrey Cowley, "The Biology of Beauty," *Newsweek* (June 3, 1996): 61–6.

89. Englis, Basil G., Michael R. Solomon, and Richard D. Ashmore, "Beauty *before* the Eyes of Beholders: The Cultural Encoding of Beauty Types in Magazine Advertising and Music Television," *Journal of Advertising* 23 (June 1994): 49–64; Michael R. Solomon, Richard Ashmore, and Laura Longo, "The Beauty Match-Up Hypothesis: Congruence between Types of Beauty and Product Images in Advertising," *Journal of Advertising* 21 (December 1992): 23–34.

90. Lois W. Banner, *American Beauty* (Chicago: University of Chicago Press, 1980); for a philosophical perspective, see Barry Vacker and Wayne R. Key, "Beauty and the Beholder: The Pursuit of Beauty through Commodities," *Psychology & Marketing* 10 (November/December 1993)6: 471–94.

91. David M. Garner, Paul E. Garfinkel, Donald Schwartz, and Michael Thompson, "Cultural Expectations of Thinness in Women," *Psychological Reports* 47 (1980): 483–91.

92. Kathleen Boyes, "The New Grip of Girdles is Lightened by Lycra," *USA Today* (April 25, 1991): 6D.

93. Stuart Elliott, "Ultrathin Models in Coca-Cola and Calvin Klein Campaigns Draw Fire and a Boycott Call," *New York Times* (April 26, 1994): D18; Cyndee Miller, " 'Give Them a Cheeseburger'," *Marketing News* (June 6, 1994): 1 (2 pp.).

94. Jill Neimark, "The Beefcaking of America," *Psychology Today* (November/December 1994): 32 (11 pp.).

95. Richard H. Kolbe and Paul J. Albanese, "Man to Man: A Content Analysis of Sole-Male Images in Male-Audience Magazines," *Journal of Advertising* 25 (Winter 1996)4: 1–20.

96. "Girls at 7 Think Thin, Study Finds," *New York Times* (February 11, 1988): B9.

97. Elaine L. Pedersen and Nancy L. Markee, "Fashion Dolls: Communicators of Ideals of Beauty and Fashion" (paper presented at the International Conference on Marketing Meaning, Indianapolis, IN, 1989); Dalma Heyn, "Body Hate," *Ms.* (August 1989): 34; Mary C. Martin and James W. Gentry, "Assessing the Internalization of Physical Attractiveness Norms," *Proceedings of the American Marketing Association Summer Educators' Conference* (Summer 1994): 59–65.

98. Lisa Bannon, "Barbie is Getting Body Work, and Mattel Says She'll be 'Rad,' " *The Wall Street Journal Interactive Edition* (November 17, 1997).

99. Robin Givhan, "Living Large," *The Washington Post* (March 2, 1997): F3.

100. "How Much is Too Fat?" *USA Today* (February 1989): 8.

101. *American Demographics* (May 1987): 56.

102. Deborah Marquardt, "A Thinly Disguised Message," *Ms.* 15 (May 1987): 33.

103. Vincent Bozzi, "The Body in Question," *Psychology Today* 22 (February 1988): 10.

104. Debra A. Zellner, Debra F. Harner, and Robbie I. Adler, "Effects of Eating Abnormalities and Gender on Perceptions of Desirable Body Shape," *Journal of Abnormal Psychology* 98 (February 1989): 93–6.

105. Robin T. Peterson, "Bulimia and Anorexia in an Advertising Context," *Journal of Business Ethics* 6 (1987): 495–504.

106. Jane E. Brody, "Personal Health," *New York Times* (February 22, 1990): B9.

107. Christian S. Crandall, "Social Contagion of Binge Eating," *Journal of Personality and Social Psychology* 55 (1988): 588–98.

108. Judy Folkenberg, "Bulimia: Not For Women Only," *Psychology Today* (March 1984): 10.

109. Eleanor Grant, "The Exercise Fix: What Happens When Fitness Fanatics Just Can't Say No?" *Psychology Today* 22 (February 1988): 24.

110. John W. Schouten, "Selves in Transition: Symbolic Consumption in Personal Rites of Passage and Identity Reconstruction," *Journal of Consumer Research* 17 (March 1991): 412–25.

111. Monica Gonzalez, "Want a Lift?" *American Demographics* (February 1988): 20.

112. Annette C. Hamburger and Holly Hall, "Beauty Quest," *Psychology Today* (May 1988): 28.

113. Emily Yoffe, "Valley of the Silicon Dolls," *Newsweek* (November 26, 1990): 72.

114. Keith Greenberg, "What's Hot: Cosmetic Surgery," *Public Relations Journal* (June 1988): 23.

115. Jerry Adler, "New Bodies For Sale," *Newsweek* (May 27, 1985): 64.

116. Norihiko Shirouzu, "Reconstruction Boom in Tokyo: Perfecting Imperfect Bellybuttons," *Wall Street Journal* (October 4, 1995): B1.

117. Joshua Levine, "Bra Wars," *Forbes* (April 25, 1994): 120; Cyndee Miller, "Bra Marketers' Cup Runneth over With, Um, Big Success," *Marketing News* (October 24, 1994): 2 (2 pp.).

118. Ruth P. Rubinstein, "Color, Circumcision, Tatoos, and Scars," in ed. Michael R. Solomon, *The Psychology of Fashion* (Lexington, MA: Lexington Books, 1985): 243–54; Peter H. Bloch and Marsha L. Richins, "You Look 'Mahvelous': The Pursuit of Beauty and Marketing Concept," *Psychology & Marketing* 9 (January 1992): 3–16.

119. Kathy H. Merrell, "Saving Faces," *Allure* (January 1994): 66 (2 pp.).

120. "White Weight," *Psychology Today* (September/October 1994): 9.

121. Sondra Farganis, "Lip Service: The Evolution of Pouting, Pursing, and Painting Lips Red," *Health* (November 1988): 48–51.

122. Michael Gross, "Those Lips, Those Eyebrows; New Face of 1989 (New Look of Fashion Models)," *New York Times Magazine* (February 13, 1989): 24.

123. Quoted in "High Heels: Ecstasy's Worth the Agony," *New York Post* (December 31, 1981).

124. Accessed via alt.culture on August 22, 1997: http://www.pathfinder.com:80/altculture/aentries/p/piercing.html

125. Quoted in Wendy Bounds, "Body-Piercing Gets under America's Skin," *Wall Street Journal* (April 4, 1994): B1 (2 pp.), quoted on p. B4.

LISA AND ANNA, EXECUTIVES in a high-powered L.A. advertising agency, are exchanging ideas about how they are going to spend the big bonus everyone in the firm has been promised for landing the Gauntlet body jewelry account. They can't help but snicker at their friend Margie in Accounting, who has been avidly surfing the net for information about a state-of-the-art home theater system she plans to put into her condo. What a couch potato! Lisa, who fancies herself a bit of a thrill seeker, plans to blow her bonus on a wild trip to Colorado where a week of outrageous Bungee jumping awaits her (assuming she lives to tell about it, but that uncertainty is half the fun). Anna replies, "Been there, done that. . . . Believe it or not, I'm staying put right here—heading over to Santa Monica to catch some waves." Seems that Anna's been bitten by the surfing bug since she started leafing through *Wahine,* a magazine targeted to the growing numbers of women taking up the sport.

Lisa and Anna are sometimes amazed at how different they are from Margie, who's content to spend her downtime watching sappy old movies or reading books. All three women make about the same salary, and Anna and Margie even went to the same college together. How can their tastes be so different? Oh well, they figure, that's why they make chocolate and vanilla. . . .

Personality and Lifestyles

PERSONALITY

Lisa and Anna are typical of many people who search for new (and even risky) ways to spend their leisure time. This desire has meant big business for the "adventure travel" industry, which specializes in providing white-knuckle experiences. Sports such as Bungee jumping, white-water rafting, sky diving, mountain biking, and other physically stimulating activities now account for about one-fifth of the U.S. leisure travel market.[1] The U.S. Bungee Association estimates there have been 7 million jumps since the late 1980s, and the U.S. Parachute Association reports a 10 percent increase in membership for each of the last two years.[2] And, where once the California beach culture used to relegate women to the status of land-locked "Gidgets" who sat on shore while their boyfriends rode the big one, now it's women who are fueling the sports' resurgence in popularity (check out www.surfboards.com). Quicksilver Inc., the largest maker of surf apparel, is reaping huge profits with its female surfing gear including a line of boardshorts called Roxy, and at least 20 other companies now offer their own women's lines. *Wahine* magazine debuted in 1995, and Motorola, Chevron, and Sun Microsystems began using women surfers in their promotions soon after.[3]

Just what does make Lisa and Anna so different from their more sedate friend Margie? One answer may lie in the concept of **personality,** which refers to a person's unique psychological makeup and how it consistently influences the way a person responds to his or her environment.

In recent years, the nature of the personality construct has been hotly debated. Many studies have found that people do not seem to exhibit stable personalities. In fact, some researchers feel that people do not exhibit consistent behavior across different situations—they argue that this is merely a convenient way to think about other people.

This argument is a bit hard to accept intuitively, possibly because we tend to see others in a limited range of situations, and so most people appear to act consistently. On the other hand, we each know that we are not all that consistent; we may be wild and crazy at times and the model of respectability at others. Although certainly not all psychologists have abandoned the idea of personality, many now recognize that a person's underlying characteristics are but one part of the puzzle and that situational factors often play a very large role in determining behavior.[4]

Still, some aspects of personality continue to be included in marketing strategies. These dimensions are usually employed in concert with a person's choices of leisure activities, political outlook, aesthetic tastes, and other individual factors to segment consumers in terms of *lifestyles*, a process we'll focus on more fully later in this chapter.

Many approaches to understanding the complex concept of personality can be traced to psychological theorists who began to develop these perspectives in the early part of the twentieth century. These perspectives were qualitative, in the sense that they were largely based on analysts' interpretations of patients' accounts of dreams, traumatic experiences, and encounters with others.

CONSUMER BEHAVIOR ON THE COUCH: FREUDIAN THEORY

Sigmund Freud developed the idea that much of one's adult personality stems from a fundamental conflict between a person's desire to gratify his or her physical needs and the necessity to function as a responsible member of society. This struggle is carried out in the mind among three systems. (Note: These systems do *not* refer to physical parts of the brain.)

FREUDIAN SYSTEMS

The **id** is entirely oriented toward immediate gratification—it is the "party animal" of the mind. It operates according to the **pleasure principle;** behavior is guided by the primary desire to maximize pleasure and avoid pain. The id is selfish and illogical. It directs a person's psychic energy toward pleasurable acts without regard for any consequences.

The **superego** is the counterweight to the id. This system is essentially the person's conscience. It internalizes society's rules (especially as communicated by parents) and works to prevent the id from seeking selfish gratification.

Finally, the **ego** is the system that mediates between the id and the superego. It is in a way a referee in the fight between temptation and virtue. The ego tries to balance these opposing forces according to the **reality principle,** whereby it finds ways to gratify the id that will be acceptable to the outside world. These conflicts occur on an unconscious level, so the person is not necessarily aware of the underlying reasons for behavior.

Some of Freud's ideas have also been adapted by consumer researchers. In particular, his work highlights the potential importance of unconscious motives underlying purchases. The implication is that consumers cannot necessarily tell us their true motivation for choosing a product, even if we can devise a sensitive way to ask them directly.

The Freudian perspective also hints at the possibility that the ego relies on the symbolism in products to compromise between the demands of the id and the prohibitions of the superego. The person channels his or her unacceptable desire into acceptable outlets by using products that signify these underlying desires. This is the connection between product symbolism and motivation: The product stands for, or represents, a consumer's true goal, which is socially unacceptable or unattainable. By acquiring the product, the person is able to vicariously experience the forbidden fruit.

SOMETIMES A CIGAR IS JUST A CIGAR

Most Freudian applications in marketing are related to the sexuality of products. For example, some analysts have speculated that a sports car is a substitute for sexual gratification for many men. Indeed, some men do seem inordinately attached to their cars and may spend many hours lovingly washing and polishing them. An Infiniti ad reinforces the belief that cars symbolically satisfy consumers' sexual needs in addition to their functional ones by describing the J30 model as ". . . what happens when you cross sheet metal and desire."

Others focus on male-oriented symbolism—so-called *phallic symbols*—that appeals to women. Although Freud himself joked that "sometimes a cigar is *just* a cigar," many popular applications of Freud's ideas revolve around the use of objects that resemble sex organs (e.g., cigars, trees, or swords for male sex organs; tunnels for female sex organs). This focus stems from Freud's analysis of dreams, which he interpreted as communicating repressed desires through symbols.

MOTIVATIONAL RESEARCH

The first attempts to apply Freudian ideas to understand the deeper meanings of products and advertisements were made in the 1950s when a perspective known as **motivational research** was developed. This approach was largely based on psycho-analytic (Freudian) interpretations, with a heavy emphasis on unconscious motives. A basic assumption is that socially unacceptable needs are channeled into acceptable outlets. Product use or avoidance is motivated by unconscious forces that are often determined in childhood.

This form of research relies on *depth interviews* with individual consumers. Instead of asking many consumers a few general questions about product usage and combining these responses with those of many other consumers in a representative statistical sample, this technique uses relatively few consumers but probes deeply into each person's purchase motivations. A depth interview might take several hours and is based on the assumption that the respondent cannot immediately articulate his or her latent, or underlying, motives. These can be derived only after extensive questioning and interpretation on the part of a carefully trained interviewer.

This work was pioneered by Ernest Dichter, a psychoanalyst who was trained in Vienna in the early part of the century. Dichter conducted in-depth interview studies on over 230 different products, and many of his findings have been incorporated into actual marketing campaigns.[5] For example, Esso (now Exxon) for many years reminded consumers to "Put a Tiger in Your Tank" after Dichter found that people responded well to this powerful animal symbolism containing vaguely sexual undertones. A summary of major consumption motivations identified using this approach appears in Table 6–1.

Motivational research has been attacked for two opposing reasons. Some feel it does not work, whereas others feel it works *too* well. On the one hand, social critics reacted much the same way they had to subliminal perception studies (see chapter 2). They attacked this school of thought for giving advertisers the power to manipulate consumers.[6] On the other hand, many consumer researchers felt the research lacked sufficient rigor and validity, as interpretations were subjective and indirect.[7] Because conclusions are based on the analyst's own judgment and are derived from discussions with a small number of people, some researchers are dubious as to the degree to which these results can be generalized to a large market. In addition, because the original motivational researchers were heavily influenced by orthodox Freudian theory, their interpretations usually involved sexual themes. This emphasis tends to overlook other plausible causes for behavior.

Still, motivational research had great appeal to at least some marketers for several reasons, some of which are detailed here.

- Motivational research tends to be less expensive than large-scale, quantitative survey data because interviewing and data-processing costs are relatively minimal.

TABLE 6–1 ■ **Major Motives for Consumption as Identified by Ernest Dichter**

MOTIVE	ASSOCIATED PRODUCTS
Power-masculinity-virility	Power: Sugary products and large breakfasts (to charge oneself up), bowling, electric trains, hot rods, power tools
	Masculinity-virility: Coffee, red meat, heavy shoes, toy guns, buying fur coats for women, shaving with a razor
Security	Ice cream (to feel like a loved child again), full drawer of neatly ironed shirts, real plaster walls (to feel sheltered), home baking, hospital care
Eroticism	Sweets (to lick), gloves (to be removed by woman as a form of undressing), a man lighting a woman's cigarette (to create a tension-filled moment culminating in pressure, then relaxation)
Moral purity-cleanliness	White bread, cotton fabrics (to connote chastity), harsh household cleaning chemicals (to make housewives feel moral after using), bathing (to be equated with Pontius Pilate, who washed blood from his hands), oatmeal (sacrifice, virtue)
Social acceptance	Companionship: Ice cream (to share fun), coffee
	Love and affection: Toys (to express love for children), sugar and honey (to express terms of affection)
	Acceptance: Soap, beauty products
Individuality	Gourmet foods, foreign cars, cigarette holders, vodka, perfume, fountain pens
Status	Scotch; ulcers, heart attacks, indigestion (to show one has a high-stress, important job!); carpets (to show one does not live on bare earth like peasants)
Femininity	Cakes and cookies, dolls, silk, tea, household curios
Reward	Cigarettes, candy, alcohol, ice cream, cookies
Master over environment	Kitchen appliances, boats, sporting goods, cigarette lighters
Disalienation (a desire to feel connectedness to things)	Home decorating, skiing, morning radio broadcasts (to feel "in touch" with the world)
Magic-mystery	Soups (having healing powers), paints (change the mood of a room), carbonated drinks (magical effervescent property), vodka (romantic history), unwrapping of gifts

Source: Adapted from Jeffrey F. Durgee, "Interpreting Dichter's Interpretations: An Analysis of Consumption Symbolism in *The Handbook of Consumer Motivations*," *Marketing and Semiotics: Selected Papers from the Copenhagen Symposium,* eds. Hanne Hartvig-Larsen, David Glen Mick, and Christian Alstead (Copenhagen, 1991).

- The knowledge derived from motivational research can possibly help develop marketing communications that appeal to deep-seated needs and thus provide a more powerful hook to reel in consumers. Even if not necessarily valid for all consumers in a target market, these insights can be valuable when used in an exploratory way. For example, the rich imagery that may be associated with a product can be used creatively when developing advertising copy.

- Some of the findings seem intuitively plausible after the fact. For example, motivational studies concluded that coffee is associated with companionship, that people avoid prunes because they remind them of old age, and that men fondly equate the first car they owned as an adolescent with the onset of their sexual freedom.

Other interpretations were hard for some researchers to swallow, such as the observation that to a woman baking a cake symbolizes giving birth, or that men are reluctant to give blood because they feel that their vital fluids are being drained. On the other hand, a pregnant woman is sometimes described as "having a bun in the oven," and Pillsbury claims that "nothing says lovin' like something from the oven." Motivational research for the American Red Cross did find that men (but not women) tend to drastically overestimate the amount of blood that is taken during a donation. The Red Cross counteracted the fear of loss of virility by symbolically equating the act of giving blood with fertilization: "Give the gift of life." Despite its drawbacks, motivational research continues to be employed as a useful diagnostic tool. Its validity is enhanced, however, when used in conjunction with the other research techniques available to the consumer researcher.

This ad for United Airlines focuses on the conflict between the desire for hedonic gratification (represented by the id) versus the need to engage in rational, task-oriented activities (represented by the superego).

NEO-FREUDIAN THEORIES

Freud's work had a huge influence on subsequent theories of personality. Although Freud opened the door to the realization that explanations for behavior may lurk beneath the surface, many of his colleagues and students felt that an individual's personality was more influenced by how he or she handled relationships with others than by unresolved sexual conflicts. These theorists are often called *neo-Freudian* (meaning following from or being influenced by Freud).

KAREN HORNEY

One of the most prominent neo-Freudians was a psychoanalyst named Karen Horney. She proposed that people can be described as moving toward others (*compliant*), away from others (*detached*), or against others (*aggressive*).[8] Indeed, one early study found that compliant people are more likely to gravitate toward name-brand products, detached types are more likely to be tea drinkers, and males classified as aggressive prefer brands with a strong masculine orientation (e.g., Old Spice deodorant).[9]

Other well-known neo-Freudians include Alfred Adler, who proposed that many actions are motivated by people's desire to overcome feelings of inferiority relative to others; and Harry Stack Sullivan, who focused on how personality evolves to reduce anxiety in social relationships.[10]

CARL JUNG

Carl Jung was also a disciple of Freud's (and was being groomed by Freud to be his successor). However, Jung was unable to accept Freud's emphasis on sexual aspects of personality, and this was a contributing factor in the eventual dissolution of their relationship. Jung went on to develop his own method of psychotherapy, which became known as *analytical psychology.*

Jung believed that people are shaped by the cumulative experiences of past generations. A central part of his perspective was an emphasis on what he called the *collective unconscious,* a storehouse of memories inherited from our ancestral past. For example, Jung would argue that many people are afraid of the dark because their distant ancestors had good reason to exhibit this fear. These shared memories create **archetypes,** or universally shared ideas and behavior patterns. Archetypes involve themes, such as birth, death, or the devil, that appear frequently in myths, stories, and dreams.

Jung's ideas may seem a bit farfetched, but (at least intuitively) advertising messages often invoke archetypes to link products with underlying meanings. For example, some of the archetypes identified by Jung and his followers include the "old wise man" and the "earth mother."[11] These images appear frequently in marketing messages that use characters such as wizards, revered teachers, or even Mother Nature to convince people of the merits of products.

TRAIT THEORY

One approach to personality is to focus on the quantitative measurement of **traits,** or identifiable characteristics that define a person. For example, people can be distinguished by the degree to which they are socially outgoing (the trait of *extroversion*)—Margie might be described as an *introvert* (quiet and reserved), whereas her co-worker Lisa is an *extrovert.*

Some specific traits that are relevant to consumer behavior include: *innovativeness* (the degree to which a person likes to try new things); *materialism* (amount of emphasis placed on acquiring and owning products); *self-consciousness* (the degree to which a person deliberately monitors and controls the image of the self that is projected to others), and *need for cognition* (the degree to which a person likes to think about things and by extension expend the necessary effort to process brand information).[12]

PROBLEMS WITH TRAIT THEORY IN CONSUMER RESEARCH

Because large numbers of consumers can be categorized according to whether they exhibit various traits, these approaches can, in theory, be used for segmentation purposes. If a car manufacturer, for example, could determine that drivers who fit a given trait profile are more likely to prefer a car with certain features, this match could be used to great advantage. The notion that consumers buy products that are extensions of their personalities makes intuitive sense. As we'll see shortly, this idea is endorsed by many marketing managers, who try to create *brand personalities* that will appeal to different types of consumers.

However, the use of standard personality trait measurements to predict product choices has met with mixed success at best. In general, marketing researchers simply have not been able to predict consumers' behaviors on the basis of measured personality traits. A number of explanations have been offered for these equivocal results.[13]

- Many of the scales are not sufficiently valid or reliable; they do not adequately measure what they are supposed to measure, and their results may not be stable over time.
- Personality tests are often developed for specific populations (e.g., mentally ill people); these tests are then "borrowed" and applied to the general population where their relevance is questionable.
- Often the tests are not administered under the appropriate conditions; they may be given in a classroom or over a kitchen table by people who are not properly trained.
- The researchers often make changes in the instruments to adapt them to their own situations, in the process deleting or adding items and renaming variables. These ad hoc changes dilute the validity of the measures and also reduce researchers' ability to compare results across consumer samples.
- Many trait scales are intended to measure gross, overall tendencies (e.g., emotional stability or introversion); these results are then used to make predictions about purchases of specific brands.
- In many cases, a number of scales are given with no advance thought about how these measures should be related to consumer behavior. The researchers then use a shotgun approach, following up on anything that happens to look interesting.

Although the use of personality measures by marketing researchers was largely abandoned after many studies failed to yield meaningful results, some researchers have not abandoned the early promise of this line of work. More recent efforts (mainly in Europe) have focused on benefiting from past mistakes. Researchers are using more specific measures of personality traits that they have reason to believe are relevant to economic behavior. They are trying to increase the validity of these measures, primarily by using multiple measures of behavior rather than relying on the common practice of trying to predict purchasing responses from a single item on a personality test. In addition, these researchers have toned down their expectations of what personality traits can tell them about consumers. They now recognize that traits are only part of the solution, and personality data must be incorporated with information about people's social and economic conditions in order to be useful.[14] As a result, some more recent research has had better success at relating personality traits to such consumer behaviors as alcohol consumption among young men or shoppers' willingness to try new, healthier food products.[15]

BRAND PERSONALITY

In 1886, a momentous event occurred—the Quaker Oats man first appeared on boxes of hot cereal. Quakers had a reputation in nineteenth-century America for being shrewd but fair, and peddlers sometimes dressed as Quakers for this reason. When the cereal company decided to "borrow" this imagery for its packaging, this signaled the recognition that purchasers might make the same associations with their product.[16]

These inferences about a product's "personality" are an important part of **brand equity,** which refers to the extent to which a consumer holds strong, favorable, and unique associations with a brand in memory.[17] Some personality dimensions that can be used to compare and contrast the perceived characteristics of brands in various product categories include:[18]

Old fashioned, wholesome, traditional
Surprising, lively, with it
Serious, intelligent, efficient
Glamorous, romantic, sexy
Rugged, outdoorsy, tough, athletic

The following memo was written to help an advertising agency figure out how a client should be portrayed in advertising. Based on this description of the "client," can you guess who he is? "He is creative . . . unpredictable . . . an imp. . . . He not only walks and talks, but has the ability to sing, blush, wink, and work with little devices like pointers. . . . He can also play musical instruments. . . . His walking motion is characterized as a 'swagger.' . . . He is made of dough and has mass."[19] Of course, we all know today that packaging and other physical cues create a "personality" for a product (in this case, the Pillsbury Doughboy!). The marketing activities undertaken on behalf of the product also can influence inferences about its "personality," and some of these actions are shown in Table 6–2.

Indeed, consumers appear to have little trouble assigning personality qualities to all sorts of inanimate products, from personal care products to more mundane, functional ones—even kitchen appliances. In research done by Whirlpool, its products were seen as more feminine than were competing brands. They were imagined as a modern, family-oriented woman living in the suburbs—attractive but not flashy. In contrast, the company's KitchenAid brand was envisioned as a modern professional woman who was glamorous, wealthy and who enjoyed classical music and the theater.[20]

The creation and communication of a distinctive *brand personality* is one of the primary ways marketers can make a product stand out from the competition and inspire years of loyalty to it. This process can be understood in terms of **animism,** the practice found in many cultures whereby inanimate objects are given qualities that make them somehow alive. Animism is in some cases a part of a religion: Sacred objects, animals, or places are believed to have magical qualities or to contain the spirits of ancestors. In our society, objects may be "worshiped" in the sense that they are believed to impart desirable qualities to the owner or they may in a sense become so important to a person that they can be viewed as a "friend."

Table 6–2 ■ Brand Behaviors and Possible Personality Trait Inferences

BRAND ACTION	TRAIT INFERENCE
Brand is repositioned several times or changes its slogan repeatedly	Flighty, schizophrenic
Brand uses continuing character in its advertising	Familiar, comfortable
Brand charges a high price and uses exclusive distribution	Snobbish, sophisticated
Brand frequently available on deal	Cheap, uncultured
Brand offers many line extensions	Versatile, adaptable
Brand sponsors show on PBS or uses recycled materials	Helpful, supportive
Brand features easy-to-use packaging or speaks at consumer's level in advertising	Warm, approachable
Brand offers seasonal clearance sale	Planful, practical
Brand offers five-year warranty or free customer hot line	Reliable, dependable

Source: Adapted from Susan Fournier, "A Consumer-Brand Relationship Framework for Strategic Brand Management," unpublished doctoral dissertation, University of Florida, 1994, Table 2.2, p. 24.

Two types of animism can be identified to describe the extent to which human qualities are attributed to the product:[21]

Level 1: In the highest order of animism, the object is believed to be possessed by the soul of a being—as is sometimes the case for spokespersons in advertising. This strategy allows the consumer to feel that the spirit of the celebrity is available through the brand. In other cases, a brand may be strongly associated with a loved one, alive or deceased ("My grandmother always served Knottsberry Farm jam.").

Level 2: Objects are *anthropomorphized*—given human characteristics. A cartoon character or mythical creation may be treated as if it were a person, and even assumed to have human feelings. Think about familiar *spokescharacters* such as Charlie the Tuna, the Keebler Elves, or the Michelin Man, or even the frustration some people feel when they come to believe their computer is smarter than they are or may even be "conspiring" to make them crazy!

In the case of anthropomorphism, the product is given selected humanlike qualities, but is not treated as human. For example, products often are regarded affectionately and may even be given nicknames, such as a "Beamer" (BMW). Grey Advertising, in research for its client Sprint Business Services, found that when customers were asked to imagine long-distance carriers as animals, they envisioned AT&T as a lion, MCI as a snake, and Sprint as a puma. Grey used these results to position Sprint as a company that could "help you do more business" rather than taking the more aggressive approach of its competitors.[22]

The Zaltman Metaphor Elicitation Technique (ZMET) is one tool used to assess the strategic aspects of brand personality and is based on the premise that brands are expressed in terms of *metaphors;* that is, a representation of one thing in terms of another. These associations often are nonverbal, so the ZMET approach is based on a nonverbal representation of brands. Participants collect a minimum of twelve images representing their thoughts and feelings about a topic, and are interviewed in depth about the images and their feelings. Eventually, digital imaging techniques are used to create a *collage* summarizing these thoughts and feelings, and the person tells a story about the image created. The example shown here belongs to Alice, who is representing her feelings about Tide detergent. She explains that the digital image "shows . . . how I feel about doing laundry . . . I don't like to do it! . . . The picture also shows a sunrise which means freshness to me—a new day. If you look in the tree, you'll see a teddy bear—he represents how my clothes feel after they are washed in Tide, soft and comfortable. The teddy bear is holding a rose to let you know my clothes smell good when washed with Tide."[1]

LIFESTYLES AND PSYCHOGRAPHICS

Lisa, Anna, and Margie strongly resemble one another demographically. They were all raised in middle-class households, have similar educational backgrounds, are about the same age, and they work for the same company. However, as their leisure choices show, it would be a big mistake to assume that their consumption choices are similar as well. Each woman chooses products, services, and activities that help her define a unique *lifestyle.* This section first explores how marketers approach the issue of lifestyle and then how they use information about these consumption choices to tailor products and communications to individual lifestyle segments.

LIFESTYLE: WHO WE ARE, WHAT WE DO

In traditional societies, one's consumption options are largely dictated by class, caste, village, or family. In a modern consumer society, however, people are more free to select the set of products, services, and activities that define themselves and, in turn, create a social identity that is communicated to others. One's choice of goods and services indeed makes a statement about who one is and about the types of people with which one desires to identify—and even those whom we wish to avoid.

Lifestyle refers to a pattern of consumption reflecting a person's choices of how he or she spends time and money. In an economic sense, one's lifestyle represents the way one has elected to allocate income, both in terms of relative allocations to different products and services, and to specific alternatives within these categories.[23] Other somewhat similar distinctions have been made to describe consumers in terms of their broad patterns of consumption, such as those differentiating consumers in terms of those who devote a high proportion of total expenditures to food, advanced technology, or to such information-intensive goods as entertainment and education.[24]

A *lifestyle marketing perspective* recognizes that people sort themselves into groups on the basis of the things they like to do, how they like to spend their leisure time, and how they choose to spend their disposable income.[25] These choices in turn create opportunities for market segmentation strategies that recognize the potency of a consumer's chosen lifestyle in determining both the types of products purchased and the specific brands most likely to appeal to a designated lifestyle segment.

LIFESTYLES AS GROUP IDENTITIES

Economic approaches are useful in tracking changes in broad societal priorities, but they do not begin to embrace the symbolic nuances that separate lifestyle groups. Lifestyle is more than the allocation of discretionary income. It is a statement about who one *is* in society and who one *is not*. Group identities, whether of hobbyists, athletes, or drug users, gel around forms of expressive symbolism. The self-definitions of group members are derived from the common symbol system to which the group is dedicated. Such self-definitions have been described by a number of terms, including *lifestyle, taste public, consumer group, symbolic community,* and *status culture.*[26]

This pattern of consumption often comprises many ingredients that are shared by others in similar social and economic circumstances. Still, each person also provides a unique "twist" to the pattern that allows him or her to inject some individuality into a chosen lifestyle. For example, a "typical" college student (if there is such a thing) may dress much like his or her friends, hang out in the same places, and like the same foods, yet still indulge a passion for marathon running, stamp collecting, or community activism, that makes him or her a unique person.

And, lifestyles are not set in stone—unlike the deep-seated values we discussed in chapter 4—people's tastes and preferences evolve over time, so that consumption patterns that were viewed favorably during one life phase may be laughed at (or sneered at) a few years later. If you don't believe that, simply think back to what you and your friends were wearing five or ten years ago—where *did* you find those clothes?

Because people's attitudes regarding physical fitness, social activism, sex roles for men and women, the importance of home life and family, and so on do change, it is vital for marketers to continually monitor the social landscape to try to anticipate where these changes will lead. Some of the most important lifestyle changes (known as *trends*) in the late 1990s and beyond will be discussed later in this chapter.

PRODUCTS ARE THE BUILDING BLOCKS OF LIFESTYLES

Consumers often choose products, services, and activities over others because they are associated with a certain lifestyle. For this reason, lifestyle marketing strategies attempt to position a product by fitting it into an existing pattern of consumption. As an example of the power of this approach, take the case of Subaru, an early adherent to lifestyle marketing. When this car manufacturer entered the U.S. market in the early 1970s, it had virtually no name recognition and struggled to compete with other, better-known imports. Subaru became the official car of the U.S. ski team and linked itself to the lifestyles of people who enjoy skiing. The company now has the highest market share for imports in several Snow Belt states.[27]

Because a goal of lifestyle marketing is to allow consumers to pursue their chosen ways to enjoy their lives and express their social identities, a key aspect of this strategy is to focus on product usage in desirable social settings. The goal of associating a product with a social situation is a long-standing one for advertisers, whether the product is included in a round of golf, a family barbecue, or a night at a glamorous club surrounded by "jet-setters."[28] Thus people, products, and settings are combined to express a certain consumption style, as diagramed in Figure 6–1.

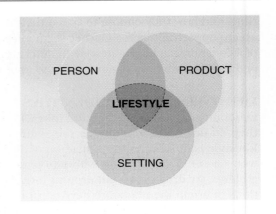

FIGURE 6–1 ■ Linking
Products to Lifestyles

The adoption of a lifestyle marketing perspective implies that we must look at *patterns of behavior* to understand consumers. We can get a clearer picture of how people use products to define lifestyles by examining how they make choices in a variety of product categories. As one study noted, ". . . all goods carry meaning, but none by itself. . . . The meaning is in the relations between all the goods, just as music is in the relations marked out by the sounds and not in any one note."[29]

Indeed, many products and services do seem to "go together," usually because they tend to be selected by the same types of people. In many cases, products do not seem to "make sense" if unaccompanied by companion products (e.g., fast food and paper plates, or a suit and tie) or are incongruous in the presence of others (e.g., a Chippendale chair in a high-tech office or Lucky Strike cigarettes with a solid gold

The recreational-vehicle ad shown here demonstrates how a market segment is defined by a particular allocation of time and money to a leisure activity. The ad's claim that the RV dealer has the product that ". . . says you're you!" implies that dedicated RVers derive a significant portion of their self-identities from the activities associated with this lifestyle.

Interior designers rely on consumption constellations when choosing items to furnish a room. A decorating style involves integrating products from many different categories—such as appliances, furnishings, knick-knacks, and even artwork—into a unified whole that conveys a certain "look."

lighter). Therefore, an important part of lifestyle marketing is to identify the set of products and services that seems to be linked in consumers' minds to a specific lifestyle. For example, one study found evidence that people in similar occupations share distinct preferences for certain living room furnishings as they make decorating decisions; their tastes set them apart from those in other walks of life.[30]

Product complementarity occurs when the symbolic meanings of different products are related to each other.[31] These sets of products, termed **consumption constellations,** are used by consumers to define, communicate, and perform social roles.[32] For example, the American "yuppie" of the 1980s was defined by such products as a Rolex watch, BMW automobile, Gucci briefcase, a squash racket, fresh pesto, white wine, and brie cheese. Somewhat similar constellations could be found for "Sloane Rangers" in the United Kingdom and "Bon Chic Bon Genres" in France. Although people today take pains to avoid being classified as yuppies, this social role had a major influence on defining cultural values and consumption priorities in the 1980s.[33] What consumption constellation might characterize you and your friends today?

PSYCHOGRAPHICS

Consider a marketer who wishes to target a student population. She identifies her ideal consumer as "a twenty-one-year-old senior business major living on a large university campus whose parents make between $30,000 and $60,000 per year." You may know a lot of people who fit this description. Do you think they are all the same? Would they all be likely to share common interests and buy the same products? Probably not, since their lifestyles are likely to differ considerably.

As Lisa, Anna, and Margie's choices demonstrated, consumers can share the same demographic characteristics and still be very different people. For this reason, marketers need a way to "breathe life" into demographic data to really identify, understand, and target consumer segments that will share a set of preferences for their products and services. This chapter earlier discussed some of the differences in consumers' personalities that play a role in determining product choices. When personality variables are combined with knowledge of lifestyle preferences, marketers have a powerful lens with which to focus on consumer segments.

This tool is known as **psychographics,** which involves the ". . . use of psychological, sociological, and anthropological factors . . . to determine how the market is segmented by the propensity of groups within the market—and their reasons—to make a particular decision about a product, person, ideology, or otherwise hold an attitude or use a medium."[34] Psychographics can help a marketer fine-tune its offerings to meet the needs of different segments. For example, the Discovery Channel surveyed those who watch at least one-half hour of its programming a week. It found that in fact there were eight distinct groups of watchers with different motivations and preferences—psychographic segments that were given descriptive names such as Entertain-Mes, Practicals, Scholars, and Escapists. Based on these results, Discovery was able to tailor its programming to different segments and increase its market share in the competitive cable television industry.[35]

THE ROOTS OF PSYCHOGRAPHICS

Psychographic research was first developed in the 1960s and 1970s to address the shortcomings of two other types of consumer research: motivational research and quantitative survey research. *Motivational research,* which involves intensive one-to-one interviews and projective tests, yields a lot of information about a few people. As we've seen though, this information is often idiosyncratic and may not be very reliable. At the other extreme, *quantitative survey research,* or large-scale demographic surveys, yields only a little information about a lot of people. As some researchers observed, "The marketing manager who wanted to know why people ate the competitor's cornflakes was told '32 percent of the respondents said taste, 21 percent said flavor, 15 percent said texture, 10 percent said price, and 22 percent said don't know or no answer.' "[36]

In many applications, the term psychographics is used interchangeably with lifestyle to denote the separation of consumers into categories based on differences in choices of consumption activities and product usage. There are many psychographic variables that can be used to segment consumers, but they all share the underlying principle of going beyond surface characteristics to understand consumers' motivations for purchasing and using products.

Demographics allow us to describe *who* buys, but psychographics allow us to understand *why* they do. To illustrate how this approach works, consider a very popular Canadian campaign for Molson Export beer that based its commercials on psychographic findings. Research showed that Molson's target customers tended to be like boys who never grew up, who were uncertain about the future, and who were intimidated by women's new-found freedoms. Accordingly, the ads featured a group of men, "Fred and the boys," whose get-togethers emphasize male companionship, protection against change, and that the beer "keeps on tasting great."[37]

CONDUCTING A PSYCHOGRAPHIC ANALYSIS

Some early attempts at lifestyle segmentation "borrowed" standard psychological scales (often used to measure pathology or personality disturbances) and tried to relate scores on these tests to product usage. As we saw earlier in the chapter, such efforts were largely disappointing. These tests were never intended to be related to everyday consumption activities and yielded little in the way of explanation for purchase behaviors. The technique is more effective when the variables included are more closely related to actual consumer behaviors. If you want to understand purchases of household cleaning products, you are better off asking people about their attitudes toward household cleanliness than testing for personality disorders!

Psychographic studies can take several different forms:

- A *lifestyle profile* that looks for items that differentiate between users and nonusers of a product
- A *product-specific profile* that identifies a target group and then profiles these consumers on product-relevant dimensions
- A *study that uses personality traits as descriptors,* in which some variable such as concern for the environment is analyzed to see which personality traits are most likely to be related to it
- A *general lifestyle segmentation* in which a large sample of respondents are placed into homogenous groups based on similarities of their overall preferences
- A *product-specific segmentation,* in which questions used in a general approach are tailored to a product category—for example, in a study done specifically for a stomach medicine, the item "I worry too much" might be rephrased as "I get stomach problems if I worry too much." This allows the researcher to more finely discriminate between users of competing brands.[38]

AIOs

Most contemporary psychographic research attempts to group consumers according to some combination of three categories of variables—activities, interests, and opinions—which are known as **AIOs.** Using data from large samples, marketers create profiles of customers who resemble each other in terms of their activities and patterns of product usage.[39] The dimensions used to assess lifestyle are listed in Table 6–3.

To group consumers into common AIO categories, respondents are given a long list of statements and are asked to indicate how much they agree with each one. Lifestyle is thus "boiled down" by discovering how people spend their time, what they find interesting and important, and how they view themselves and the world around them, as well as demographic information. By the way, the single most

TABLE 6-3 ■ **Lifestyle Dimensions**

ACTIVITIES	INTERESTS	OPINIONS	DEMOGRAPHICS
Work	Family	Themselves	Age
Hobbies	Home	Social issues	Education
Social events	Job	Politics	Income
Vacation	Community	Business	Occupation
Entertainment	Recreation	Economics	Family size
Club membership	Fashion	Education	Dwelling
Community	Food	Products	Geography
Shopping	Media	Future	City size
Sports	Achievements	Culture	Stage in life cycle

Source: William D. Wells and Douglas J. Tigert, "Activities, Interests, and Opinions," *Journal of Advertising Research* 11 (August 1971): 27–35. ©1971 by The Advertising Research Foundation.

common use of leisure time among Americans overall is—you guessed it—watching television![40]

Typically, the first step in conducting a psychographic analysis is to determine which lifestyle segments are producing the bulk of customers for a particular product. According to a very general rule of thumb frequently used in marketing research, the **80/20 principle,** only 20 percent of a product's users account for 80 percent of the volume of product sold. Researchers attempt to determine who uses the brand and try to isolate heavy, moderate, and light users. They also look for patterns of usage and attitudes toward the product. In many cases, just a few lifestyle segments account for the majority of brand users.[41] Marketers primarily target these heavy users, even though they may constitute a relatively small number of total users.

After the heavy users are identified and understood, the brand's relationship to them is considered. Heavy users may have quite different reasons for using the product; they can be further subdivided in terms of the *benefits* they derive from using the product or service. For instance, marketers at the beginning of the walking shoe craze assumed that purchasers were basically burned-out joggers. Subsequent psychographic research showed that there were actually several different groups of "walkers," ranging from those who walk to get to work to those who walk for fun. This realization resulted in shoes aimed at different segments, from Footjoy Joy-Walkers to Nike Healthwalkers.

USES OF PSYCHOGRAPHIC SEGMENTATION
Psychographic segmentation can be used in a variety of ways:

- *To define the target market:* This information allows the marketer to go beyond simple demographic or product usage descriptions (e.g., middle-aged men or frequent users).

- *To create a new view of the market:* Sometimes marketers create their strategies with a "typical" customer in mind. This stereotype may not be correct because the actual customer may not match these assumptions. For example, marketers of a facial cream for women were surprised to find their key market was composed of older, widowed women rather than the younger, more sociable women to whom they were pitching their appeals.

- *To position the product:* Psychographic information can allow the marketer to emphasize features of the product that fit in with a person's lifestyle. Products targeted to people whose lifestyle profiles show a high need to be around other people might focus on the product's ability to help meet this social need.

- *To better communicate product attributes:* Psychographic information can offer very useful input to advertising creatives who must communicate something about the product. The artist or writer obtains a much richer mental image of the target consumer than that obtained through dry statistics, and this insight improves his or her ability to "talk" to that consumer. For example, research conducted for Schlitz beer found that heavy beer drinkers tended to feel that life's pleasures were few and far between. Commercials were developed using the theme that told these drinkers, "You only go around once, so reach for all the gusto you can."[42]

- *To develop overall strategy:* Understanding how a product fits, or does not fit, into consumers' lifestyles allows the marketer to identify new product opportunities, chart media strategies, and create environments most consistent and harmonious with these consumption patterns.

- *To market social and political issues:* Psychographic segmentation can be an important tool in political campaigns and can also be employed to find commonalities among types of consumers who engage in destructive behaviors, such as drug use or excessive gambling. A psychographic study of men aged 18 to 24 who drink and drive highlights the potential for this perspective to help in the eradication of harmful behaviors. Researchers divided this segment into four groups: "good timers," "well adjusted," "nerds," and "problem kids." They found that one group in particular—"good timers"—is more likely to believe that it is fun to be drunk, that the chances of having an accident while driving drunk are low, and that drinking increases one's appeal to the opposite sex. Because the study showed that this group is also the most likely to drink at rock concerts and parties, is most likely to watch MTV, and tends to listen to album-oriented rock radio stations, reaching "good timers" with a prevention campaign was made easier because messages targeted to this segment could be placed where these drinkers are most likely to see and hear them.[43]

PSYCHOGRAPHIC SEGMENTATION TYPOLOGIES

Marketers are constantly on the prowl for new insights that will allow them to identify and reach groups of consumers that are united by a common lifestyle. To meet this need, many research companies and advertising agencies have developed their own *segmentation typologies.* Respondents answer a battery of questions that allow the researchers to cluster them into a set of distinct lifestyle groups. The questions usually include a mixture of AIOs, plus other items relating to their perceptions of specific brands, favorite celebrities, media preferences, and so on. These systems are usually sold to companies that want to learn more about their customers and potential customers.

At least at a superficial level, many of these typologies are fairly similar to one another, in that a typical typology breaks up the population into roughly five to eight segments. Each cluster is given a descriptive name and a profile of the "typical" member is provided to the client. Unfortunately, it is often difficult to compare or evaluate different typologies, as the methods and data used to devise these systems frequently are proprietary, that is, the information is developed and owned by the

MARKETING PITFALL

When the R.J. Reynolds Company made plans to introduce a new brand of cigarettes, called "Dakota," in several test markets, the tobacco company found out the hard way that a psychographic approach can be controversial. The marketing plan, submitted to the company by an outside consulting firm, specifically targeted the cigarette to 18- to 24-year-old women with a high school education or less who work in entry-level factory or service jobs. This segment is one of the few remaining consumer segments in the United States that exhibits an increase in smoking rates, so from a purely fiscal point of view it clearly has market potential.

The brand was developed to appeal to a lifestyle segment the company called the "Virile Female." This woman has the following psychographic characteristics: Her favorite pastimes are cruising, partying, and going to hot rod shows and tractor pulls with her boyfriend, and her favorite TV shows are *Roseanne* and evening soap operas. Her chief aspirations are to get married in her early twenties and to spend time with her boyfriend, doing whatever he does. Over 100 public health officials signed a resolution asking that Dakota be withdrawn from the market, but R.J. Reynolds claimed that the test brand was simply aimed at current Marlboro smokers. Regardless of the company's intentions, this attempt at lifestyle marketing resulted in a flood of unfavorable publicity as critics charged the company was trying to persuade more young women to take up the habit.[44]

company, and the company feels that it would not be desirable to release this information to outsiders.

VALS

One well-known segmentation system is **The Values and Lifestyles (VALS™) System,** developed at SRI International in California. The original VALS™ system was based on how consumers agreed or disagreed with various social issues, such as abortion rights.

After about ten years, SRI discovered that the social issues used to categorize consumers were not as predictive of consumer behavior as they once had been because greater number of people were in agreement with these ideas. SRI searched for a more powerful way to segment consumers, and discovered that certain lifestyle indicators such as "I like a lot of excitement in my life" were better predictors of purchase behavior than the degree to which a person agreed or disagreed with a social value.

The current VALS 2™ system uses a battery of 39 items (35 psychological and four demographic) to divide U.S. adults into groups, each with distinctive characteristics. As shown in Figure 6-2, groups are arranged vertically by their resources (including such factors as income, education, energy levels, and eagerness to buy), and horizontally by self orientation.

Key to the VALS 2™ system are three self-orientations which comprise the horizontal dimension. Consumers with a Principle orientation make purchase decisions guided by a belief system, and they are not concerned with the views of others. People with a Status orientation make decisions based on the perceived opinions of their peers. Action, or self oriented individuals, buy products to have an impact on the world around them.

The top VALS 2™ group is termed *Actualizers,* who are successful consumers with many resources. This group is concerned with social issues and is open to change. As one indication of this group's interest in cutting-edge technology, while only one in ten American adults is an Actualizer, half of all regular Internet users belong to this category.[45] The next three groups also have sufficient resources but differ in their outlooks on life:[46]

- *Fulfilleds* are satisfied, reflective, and comfortable. They tend to be practical and value functionality.
- *Achievers* are career-oriented and prefer predictability over risk or self-discovery.
- *Experiencers* are impulsive, young, and enjoy offbeat or risky experiences. The next four groups have fewer resources:
- *Believers* have strong principles, and favor proven brands.
- *Strivers* are like Achievers, but with fewer resources. They are very concerned about the approval of others.
- *Makers* are action-oriented and tend to focus their energies on self-sufficiency. They will often be found working on their cars, canning their own vegetables, or building their own houses.
- *Strugglers* are at the bottom of the economic ladder. They are most concerned with meeting the needs of the moment, and have limited ability to acquire anything beyond the basic goods needed for survival.

The VALS 2™ system has been a useful way to understand people like Lisa and Anna. SRI estimates that 12% of American adults are thrill seekers, who tend to fall into the system's Experiencer category and who are likely to agree with statements like "I like a lot of excitement in my life" and "I like to try new things." Experiencers like to break the rules, and are strongly attracted to extreme sports such as sky surf-

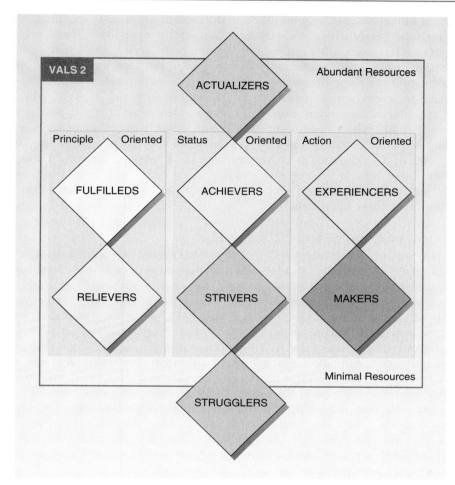

FIGURE 6–2 ■
VALS 2™
Segmentation System
Source: SRI International,
Menlo Park, CA.

ing or bungee jumping. Not too surprisingly, fully one-third of consumers aged 18–34 fall belong in this category, so it has attracted the interest of many marketers who are trying to appeal to younger people (more on this in chapter 15). For example, VALS 2™ helped Isuzu market its Rodeo sport utility vehicle by focusing on Experiencers, many of whom believe it is fun to break rules in ways that do not endanger others. The car was positioned as a vehicle that lets a driver break the rules. Advertising was created to support this idea by showing kids jumping in mud puddles, running with scissors, and coloring out of the lines.[47] Isuzu sales increased significantly after this campaign.

REGIONAL CONSUMPTION DIFFERENCES

If you have traveled to or lived in other parts of the country, you may have experienced the weird feeling of being slightly out of sync with your environment. The people may speak the same language, yet you may have difficulty understanding some things they say. Brands and store names may be confusing; some are familiar and some are not. Some familiar items may masquerade under different names. One person's "hero" is another's "grinder" is another person's "submarine sandwich" is another person's "hoagie."

Citizens of the United States share the same national identity, yet the consumption patterns of different regions have been shaped by unique climates, cultural influences, and resources. Such differences allow us to legitimately talk about "regional personalities" as well as a "national personality." These regional differences often exert a big impact on consumers' lifestyles, since many of our preferences in foods, entertainment, and so on are dictated by local customs and the availability of some diversions rather others: A resident of the Midwest would have to work hard to cultivate a "Florida beach bum" lifestyle, whereas a New Englander might be hard-pressed to find a rodeo show to attend on the weekend.

The lifestyles of people in each region differ in a variety of ways, some subtle and some noticeable, some easy to explain and some not so obvious. The fact that people in the Northeast are better customers for ski equipment than are those in the Southwest is fairly predictable. The reason that new mothers in the West are about 50 percent more likely to breast-feed their babies than their counterparts in the South is harder to fathom.[48]

FOOD PREFERENCES

Many national marketers regionalize their offerings to appeal to different tastes. Campbell's Soup puts a stronger dose of jalapeño pepper in its nacho cheese soup in the Southwest, and it sells "ranch-style" beans only in Texas.[49] Similarly, some leading brands do significantly better in some parts of the country than others: Kraft Miracle Whip is the nation's overall best-seller in the mayonnaise category, but it only turns in a third-place performance in the Northeast.[50]

Americans even differ in their preferences for "munchies." The average consumer eats 21 pounds of snack foods in a year (hopefully not all at one sitting), but people in the West Central part of the country consume the most (24 pounds per person) whereas those in the Pacific and Southeast regions eat "only" 19 pounds per person. Pretzels are the most popular snack in the Mid-Atlantic area, pork rinds are most likely to be eaten in the South, and multigrain chips turn up as a favorite in the West. Not surprisingly, the Hispanic influence in the Southwest has influenced snacking preferences—consumers in that part of the United States eat about 50 percent more tortilla chips than do people elsewhere.[51]

THE ARTS AND ENTERTAINMENT

The types of entertainment sought by consumers around the country differ markedly as well. Overall, country/western is the most popular form of music (though rock music leads in actual record sales). The blues, R&B, and soul category is rapidly gaining in popularity.[52]

Still, these preferences are by no means uniform across the country. A survey performed for the National Endowment for the Arts showed that jazz and classical music are the most popular in the West and Midwest, and that consumers in the West like museums and the theater more than other Americans.[53]

GEODEMOGRAPHY

Geodemography refers to analytical techniques that combine data on consumer expenditures and other socioeconomic factors with geographic information about the areas in which people live in order to identify consumers who share common consumption patterns. This approach is based on the assumption that "birds of a feather flock together"; people who have similar needs and tastes also tend to live near one another, so it should be possible to locate "pockets" of like-minded people who can then be reached more economically by direct mail and other methods. For example, a marketer who wants to reach white, single consumers who are college educated and tend to be fiscally conservative may find that it is more efficient to mail catalogs to zip codes 20770 (Greenbelt, MD) and 90277 (Redondo Beach, CA)

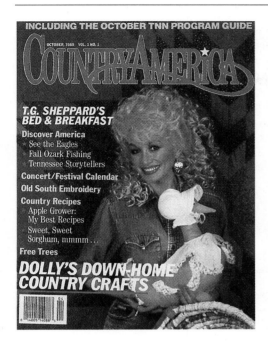

Country America is one of many media vehicles recently developed to appeal to readers' regional identifications.

than to adjoining areas in either Maryland or California where there are fewer consumers who exhibit these characteristics.

A statistical technique called *cluster analysis* allows marketers to identify groups of people who share important characteristics, even though they may live in different parts of the country. Geographic information is increasingly being combined with other data to paint an even more complete picture of the American consumer. Several marketing research ventures now employ **single-source data,** in which information about a person's actual purchasing history is combined with geodemographic data, thus allowing marketers to learn even more about the types of marketing strategies that motivate some people—but not others—to respond.

MARKETING OPPORTUNITY

With the aid of their trusty fax machines and computer modems that allow them to stay on-line even in remote places, growing numbers of "electronic pioneers" are forging a new lifestyle as they give up life in the big city to work in rural areas. Job growth in nonmetropolitan areas now exceeds that of metros, and counties in vacation or retirement areas or those that have a strong technology infrastructure are leading the way. In fact, farmers and mine workers now make up only 10 percent of the rural population.[54] About 25 million Americans operate a full- or part-time business from home, and another 8.4 million telecommute.[55]

And, whether they live in New York or New Mexico, growing numbers of middle-age and well-educated suburbanites are trying to regain a sense of mastery over their environment by rebuilding their own homes, running their own businesses, managing their own finances, and using their own labor to buy cheaper groceries at warehouse clubs. Aided by technology, they are banking by computer, using specialized software to select mutual funds instead of relying on a broker, and using on-line travel agents to book vacations. The value of time spent doing tasks ourselves that could have been done by someone else is estimated to be 40 percent of the gross domestic product. Recognizing this trend, Home Depot Inc. recently opened a new store called Crossroads, which offers do-it-yourself tools and other devices needed to keep these displaced urbanites humming along in their home offices.

Their idea of precise geocoding.

Ours.

Matchmaker/2000® for Windows™ is the only geocoding system that matches street address ranges to latitude and longitude coordinates. So you end up with a more precise and useful picture of where your customers and prospects are located. Matchmaker/2000 offers nationwide street coverage,

with more than 12 million address ranges. Other programs offer only half as many. Matchmaker/2000 is continuously updated. So your data is always current. And you'll achieve the highest match percentage available in the industry today. Matchmaker/2000 is an invaluable tool for market penetration studies. Point and cluster evaluations. Sales effectiveness analyses.

Scheduling and routing. And custom zone creation. You'll work smarter. And faster. The program is offered with a range of expandable and upgradable database options to meet your specific budget and application. Contact Geographic Data Technology, Inc., 13 Dartmouth College Highway, Lyme, NH 03768-9713. Or call 1-800-331-7881, x1101.

GEOGRAPHIC DATA TECHNOLOGY, INC.

1-800-331-7881 x1101

Reprinted from **American Demographics** magazine.

Modern geodemographic techniques allow companies to go well beyond broad regional differences. Many now segment markets down to the neighborhood block. The provision of this type of analysis to marketers has become a profitable niche for several market research companies.

This comprehensive strategy was first implemented in the BehaviorScan project, begun in 1980 by Information Resources, Inc. The system combined grocery store UPC scanners, household consumers panels, and responses to different television commercials that were transmitted to selected parts of a market area to track purchases. This type of total approach allows marketers to test the impact of changes in advertising, pricing, shelf placement, and promotions on consumer behavior patterns. Similar systems are now available or under development by other organizations, such as Nielsen and SAMI/Burke.[56]

Marketers have been successful at adapting sophisticated analytical techniques originally developed for other applications, such as the military and oil and gas exploration. These techniques, which can now employ data at the neighborhood or even household level, are being used in a variety of ways:

- A bank examined its penetration of accounts by customer zip codes.
- A utility company compared demographic data with billing patterns to fine-tune energy conservation campaigns.
- A chain of ice cream stores helped franchisees develop sales promotion programs for local markets by providing them with demographic profiles of actual users and information about the sales potential of untapped customer groups.
- The Western Union Company improved the cost-effectiveness of its network of offices by analyzing the number of Western Union agents needed in an area and determining where new agents would most profitably be located.[57]

One commercial system is ClusterPlus, distributed by Donnelly Marketing. This system assigns each of the country's census block groups into one of 47 clusters.

The groupings range in affluence from the "established wealthy" (e.g., Greenwich, Connecticut) to "lowest income black female-headed families" (e.g., the Watts section of Los Angeles). A manufacturer of baking goods used the ClusterPlus system to target consumers who bake from scratch. The top-ranking clusters for this activity were in older, rural, blue-collar areas in the South and Midwest. Commercials for this segment were placed on popular shows such as *Rescue: 911* and *America's Funniest Home Videos,* which are widely watched in these areas.[58]

Another clustering technique is the PRIZM system developed by Claritas, Inc. (PRIZM stands for Potential Rating Index by Zip Market). This system classifies every U.S. zip code into one of 62 categories, ranging from the most affluent "Blue-Blood Estates" to the least well-off "Public Assistance."[59] A resident of Southern California might be classified as "Money & Brains" if he or she lives in Encino (zip code 91316), whereas someone living in Sherman Oaks (zip code 91423) would be a "Young Influential."[60] The system was updated from its original set of 40 clusters to reflect the growing ethnic and economic diversity of the United States; some new clusters include "American Dreams," "Kids & Cul-de-Sacs," and "Young Literati".[61]

Residents of different clusters display marked differences in their consumption of products, from annuities to zip-lock bags. These groupings also are ranked in terms of income, home value, and occupation (i.e., a rough index of social class) on a ZQ (Zip Quality) scale. Table 6–4 provides an idea of how dramatically different the consumption patterns of two clusters can be. This table compares consumption data for "Furs & Station Wagons," the third highest ranking cluster, with "Tobacco Roads," the third lowest.

TABLE 6–4 ■ A Comparison of Two PRIZM Clusters

FURS & STATION WAGONS (ZQ3)		TOBACCO ROADS (ZQ38)	
New money, parents in 40s and 50s		Racially mixed farm towns in the South	
Newly built subdivisions with tennis courts, swimming pools, gardens		Small downtowns with thrift shops, diners, and laundromats; shanty-type homes without indoor plumbing	
Sample neighborhoods		**Sample neighborhoods**	
Plano, TX (75075)		Belzoni, MI (39038)	
Dunwoody, GA (30338)		Warrenton, NC (27589)	
Needham, MA (02192)		Gates, VA (27937)	
High Usage	**Low Usage**	**High Usage**	**Low Usage**
Country clubs	Motorcycles	Travel by bus	Knitting
Wine by the case	Laxatives	Asthma relief remedies	Live theater
Lawn furniture	Nonfilter cigarettes		Smoke detectors
Gourmet magazine		Malt liquors	*Ms.* magazine
BMW 5 Series	Chewing tobacco	*Grit* magazine	Ferraris
Rye bread	*Hunting* magazine	Pregnancy tests	Whole-wheat bread
Natural cold cereal	Chevrolet Chevettes	Pontiac Bonnevilles	Mexican foods
	Canned stews	Shortening	

Note: Usage rates as indexed to average consumption across all 40 clusters.

Source: "A Comparison of Two Prizm Clusters" from *The Clustering of America* by Michael J. Weiss. Copyright © 1988 by Michael J. Weiss. Reprinted by permission of HarperCollins Publishers, Inc.

The PRIZM system is used to guide media buying and for direct mail targeting. Both *Time* and *Newsweek* have sorted their mailing lists by cluster, sending special editions with ads for luxury products to residents of "Money & Brains" and "Blue-Blood Estates." Colgate-Palmolive sent samples of a new detergent developed for young families to occupants of "Blue-Collar Nursery" cluster, which is largely made up of new families. When Time Inc. Ventures launched *VIBE,* its urban-culture magazine, it needed to convince advertisers that the new outlet was not read solely by inner-city kids. A PRIZM analysis showed that *VIBE* also appealed to "Young Influentials" and even middle-age members of the "Money & Brains" cluster; evidence that led to advertising buys for liquor and electronics marketers.[62]

Although some products may be purchased at an equivalent rate by consumers in two very different clusters, these similarities end when other purchases are taken into account. These differences highlight the importance of going beyond simple product category purchase data and demographics to really understand a market (remember the earlier discussion of product complementarity). For example, high-quality binoculars are bought by people in "Urban Gold Coast," "Money & Brains," and "Blue-Blood Estates" communities, but also by consumers in the "Grain Belt," "New Homesteaders," and "Agri-Business" clusters. The difference is that the former groups use the binoculars to watch birds and other wildlife, but the latter use them to help line up the animals in their gun sights. Furthermore, whereas the bird watchers do a lot of foreign travel, listen to classical music, and host cocktail parties, the bird hunters travel by bus, like country music, and belong to veterans' clubs.

These two bowling centers, both located in a Kansas City suburb, are only six miles apart. However, they are light years apart in terms of the PRIZM clusters they draw upon as their clientele. The architectural firm that designed both centers found that the patrons at Olathe Lanes East came for relaxation and exercise, while those at the West Lanes were hard-core bowlers who came to compete. The customers at East came from 3 upscale clusters: Young Suburbia, Pools and Patios, and Furs and Station Wagons, and the firm selected an Art Deco motif and used soft lines to create a relaxing, upscale atmosphere. Bowlers at West came from the Blue Collar Nursery, Middle America, Blue Chip Blues, and Shotguns and Pickups clusters. The firm redid the bowling alley, using a Southwest theme with squares and energetic triangles to appeal to these groups.[1]
1. Barbara J. Eichhorn, "Selling by Design: Using Lifestyle Analysis to Revamp Retail Space," *American Demographics* (October 1996): 45–48.

INTERNATIONAL LIFESTYLE SEGMENTATION

Increasingly sophisticated efforts are being made to develop lifestyle typologies that transcend national borders. Many of these systems have been developed to better understand European buying habits, and in particular to determine if it is possible to identify "Euroconsumers," who share the same lifestyle orientations despite living in, say, Sweden versus Spain. These studies have had mixed success, with most researchers reporting that people in each nation still have a lot of idiosyncracies that make it difficult to lump them together.[63] Let's take a quick look at some of these attempts.

- McCann-Erickson London, a British advertising agency, segments male and female consumers separately. Lifestyle categories in this system include segments such as "Avant Guardians" (interested in change), "Pontificators" (traditionalists, very British), "Chameleons" (follow the crowd), and "Sleepwalkers" (contented underachievers). An ambitious project to develop a typology of consumers in the United Kingdom (England, Wales, and Scotland) by a company called Socioconsult is described in Figure 6–3.

- Japanese culture values conformity; one way to refer to the desire to fit in is *hitonami consciousness,* which translates as "aligning oneself with other people." Despite this overall emphasis on conformity, there is a growing segment of Japanese consumers fighting the tide. These people have been called "life designers" to reflect their interest in crafting their own unique lifestyle patterns. One Japanese segmentation scheme divides consumers into "tribes" and includes among others the "Crystal Tribe" (which prefers well-known brands), "My Home Tribe" (family oriented), and "Impulse Buyer Tribe."[64]

- As countries in Eastern Europe convert to free-market economies, many marketers are exploring ways to segment these increasingly consumption-oriented societies. Some Western products such as Marlboro cigarettes and McDonald's fast food are already firmly entrenched in Russia. The D'Arcy Masius Benton & Bowles Advertising Agency, which has offices in Moscow and St. Petersburg, conducted a psychographic study of Russian consumers, and proclaimed that the country's 150 million consumers can be divided into five segments, including "Cossacks" (status-seeking nationalists who drive BMWs, smoke Dunhill cigarettes, and drink Rémy Martin cognac), "Kuptsi" (or merchants who value practical products and tend to drive Volkswagens, smoke Chesterfields, and drink Stolichnaya vodka), and "Russian Souls" (passive consumers who drive Russian-made Lada cars, smoke Marlboros, and drink Smirnoff vodka).[65]

LIFESTYLE TRENDS: CONSUMER BEHAVIOR IN THE MILLENNIUM

Consumer lifestyles are a moving target. Society's priorities and preferences are constantly evolving, and it is essential for marketers to track these changes and more importantly, try to anticipate them. Of course, many lifestyle changes are rooted in economic and demographic patterns, so understanding these developments usually entails an appreciation of factors such as employment rates, educational attainment, and population growth.

For example, the "go-go" economic conditions of the 1980s fed a boom in self-interest and the belief in upward mobility. In contrast, the leaner years of the early

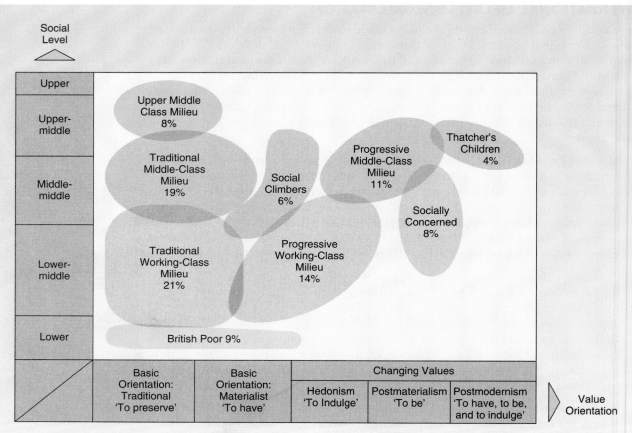

Socioconsult, based in Paris, attempts to identify segments of consumers in different countries who share common values and outlooks on life. Respondents answer a battery of questions that are designed to assess their outlook on life (including work, leisure, family, consumption, and aesthetics). Based on the responses received, consumers are grouped into what the company calls "social milieus." The nine social milieus obtained for Great Britain are shown here. These clusters are derived by using two types of information: (1) social level (i.e., income and social class) and (2) value orientation, which is related to attitudes toward change and outlook on life. Each of the nine clusters exhibits different attitudes and behaviors; this information is then provided to the company's clients, who select segments to target and who design product and promotional strategies calculated to appeal to members of that "social milieu."

FIGURE 6–3 ■ **Social Milieus: An Example of International Lifestyle Segmentation**
Source: Socioconsult, Paris, 1994.

1990s fed people's fears about their futures. As corporations continue to downsize, many consumers now face the grim prospect of downward mobility, and others reject the nine-to-five mold by starting their own businesses. Consumer confidence can turn into pessimism, which tends to make people more frugal, more conservative, and to some extent more distrustful of other types of people who are viewed as threats to the well-being of one's family or community.

As a result, in the 1990s we see such developments as *affinitization,* in which groups organize around special interests such as immigration policy, the environment, or religious education. We also witness a return to an emphasis on "value" in products, as advertisers redouble their efforts to emphasize the practical benefits of what they sell. As people age, they tend to become more concerned with preservation of assets, both financial and personal. This means a renewed interest in products that allow consumers to conserve money to ensure an easier retirement as well as those that slow the aging process.[66] In this section, we'll take a look at some of the important lifestyle issues currently shaping consumer behavior.

TREND FORECASTING: PEERING INTO THE CRYSTAL BALL OF CONSUMER BEHAVIOR

If a marketer could see into the future, he or she would obviously have an enormous advantage when developing products and services that will meet the needs of consumers next year, in five years, or in ten years. No one is able to do that yet, but a number of marketing research firms do try very hard to predict **social trends,** or broad changes in people's attitudes and behaviors. For example, the Lifestyle Monitor, now run by the firm Yankelovich Clancy Shulman, interviews 2,500 American adults annually. Advertising agency Backer Spielvogel Bates' Global Scan program divides markets in 18 countries into psychographic segments and charts changes in attitudes, and advertising agency Ogilvy & Mather scans consumer trends with its New Wave program.[67]

Since 1975, the DDB Needham Worldwide advertising agency has been conducting its Lifestyle Study, an ongoing study of changes in consumer behavior consisting of a sample of 4,000 Americans' answers to a battery of 1,000 questions. The 1996 report indicated that an earlier trend toward self-sacrifice appears to be eroding: Americans in the late 1990s want to eat what they want, dress for comfort, and embrace traditional values—as long as these beliefs don't interfere with convenience or individualism. People are paying less attention to nutrition and diet, exercise is declining as a regular activity, and fewer people believe that dressing well is important.

In addition, the study found a decrease in support for pollution standards or willingness to accept a lower standard of living to save energy. More than 85 percent of men and women say they have somewhat old-fashioned tastes and habits, yet the percentage of both sexes who say couples should live together before marriage is up, as is support for legalization of both abortion and marijuana.[68] Figure 6–4 highlights some of the long-term trends tracked by the Lifestyle Study.

MAJOR CONSUMER TRENDS

Of course, trend forecasting is a bit like reading one's horoscope in the paper. Sometimes forecasts are so general they can't help but come true, and only some proportion of more specific ones actually do. The problem is, we don't know until after the fact which ones will. The following sections discuss some recent predictions of trends we can expect in the last few years of the twentieth century (note that they sometimes contradict each other). Which will be accurate? Take your pick . . .

ENVIRONMENTALISM AND GREEN MARKETING
Concern for the environment, or the *green movement,* is a priority for many consumers around the world. With the introduction of its Origins line of cosmetics, the Estee Lauder Company was the first major U.S. beauty company to bring natural, non-animal-tested products in recyclable containers into department stores.[69]

Still, although many consumers give preference to products that help the environment, there are signs that interest in the green movement is waning. Membership in environmental groups like The Sierra Club is down sharply, and some marketers' abuse of the claim that their products are safe have led some con-

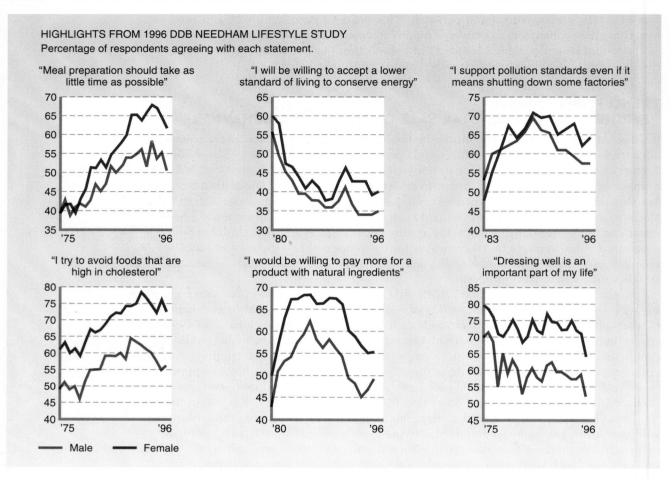

HIGHLIGHTS FROM 1996 DDB NEEDHAM LIFESTYLE STUDY
Percentage of respondents agreeing with each statement.

"Meal preparation should take as little time as possible"

"I will be willing to accept a lower standard of living to conserve energy"

"I support pollution standards even if it means shutting down some factories"

"I try to avoid foods that are high in cholesterol"

"I would be willing to pay more for a product with natural ingredients"

"Dressing well is an important part of my life"

—— Male   —— Female

FIGURE 6-4 ■ **DDB Needham Longitudinal Graphs** DDB Needham Worldwide's Lifestyle Study has been tracking American consumer trends for almost a quarter century. Some of the changes in people's priorities over time are shown here. Source: Bill McDowell, "New DDB Needham Report: Consumers Want It all," Advertising Age (November 18, 1996): 32–33.

sumers to discount these claims. To compound the problem, other worries about crime, the homeless, and so on, appear to have taken precedence for many people.[70]

A RETURN TO VALUE

Many consumers are no longer interested in the niceties of fancy stores, especially when the products for sale there are marked up too high. They are becoming what the Grey Advertising agency calls "precision shoppers." Picking and choosing carefully, they no longer shy away from lesser-known house brands and are flocking in droves to warehouse stores offering self-serve products by the case in drab surroundings.

Ironically, this emphasis on quality at a reasonable price has turned many people into more loyal shoppers—once they find a store that provides the value they seek, they reward it with consistent business. This type of ongoing relationship is also more efficient because consumers no longer have to spend so much time comparing prices in different stores. Retailers are responding by offering what they call

This Swedish ad for a manufacturer of ecologically friendly packaging materials reflects the desire of many marketers to participate in the green movement.

EDLP—everyday low prices—instead of making shoppers wait for periodic specials. This strategy adds value by making people's lives simpler.[71] Marketers of everything from autos to suits are scrambling to find ways to offer value and build bonds with customers who are weary of glitzy promotions and overpriced goodies.

TIME POVERTY

An increasing emphasis on the value of time as a commodity is motivating consumers to look for new ways to acquire experiences and products in more convenient and accessible forms. Advances in technology make possible more home-centered activities, whether for entertainment (e.g., the proliferation of cable stations) or for work (e.g., the trend toward "telecommuting" as more people use their personal computers and faxes to establish offices at home).

The increase in working couples leads to greater value placed on convenience products and services that minimize time and effort spent in purchasing. Although couples in which both partners work and couples in which only one works both average two weekly trips to the market and spend about the same ($57.00 per trip), working couples spend 15 percent less time in the market. To facilitate this "race" through the market, some chains now display floor plans at the entrance.[72] Home delivery of food is growing twice as fast as take-out or drive-through. In addition, look for increased reliance on catalogs, professional shoppers, and home automation to occur.[73]

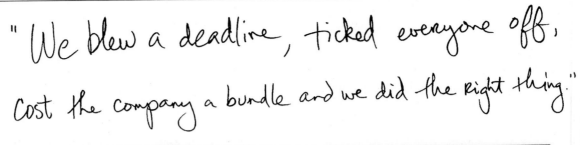

This ad for General Motors reflects the new spirit of quality and relationship building that many marketers espouse in the 1990s.

Reflecting the consumer trend toward self-fulfillment and away from materialism, this ad for *Harper's Magazine* describes people in a lifestyle segment it dubs IMPs (inner-motivated people).

MARKETING OPPORTUNITY

As one consequence of the time pressures facing many consumers, the car is becoming a popular dining room. The practice of eating on the run has become so widespread that one out of every ten meals bought in a restaurant is eaten in a car! That figure climbs even higher when convenience store snacks are included.

Some marketers are beginning to develop new food products that make it easier to eat with at least one hand on the steering wheel. Burger King Corp. is testing a new sandwich wrapper with a pocket that is easier to pick up and put down in traffic. Southland Corp., which operates 7-Eleven convenience stores, is developing healthier alternatives that also are road-friendly, such as a grilled chicken sandwich shaped like a hot dog, and a tray of bite-sized pieces of vegetables with a spill-proof receptacle for salad dressing. Still, some marketers are reluctant to push the idea of in-car dining too much further, citing the safety risks involved. Perhaps they are chastened by the multimillion dollar lawsuit brought against McDonald's by a woman who claimed that the coffee she bought in a drive-through line was too hot and caused her to burn herself.[74]

DISILLUSIONMENT OF WORKING WOMEN

Changes are taking place in the sex roles of men and women as ideas regarding marriages, homosexuality, child rearing, and career choices evolve. As uncertainty about the proper roles of men and women in our culture increases, consumers will continue to be influenced by how notions of masculinity and femininity are translated into product concepts and advertising practices by marketers.

Women will discover that working outside of the home is not as "liberating" as they thought. Look for a return to traditional husband/wife roles to occur, as women abandon careers and stay home with the children. Women are now more likely than men to say they "work very hard most of the time," and their use of pain relievers is growing dramatically. In surveys, the number of women who say they would prefer to stay home is steadily increasing. Many observers have noted a shift toward "neo-traditionalism," which includes a renewed commitment to the family. In the words of one observer, the 1990s have ushered in an emphasis on "romance, religion, and rattles."[75]

DECREASED EMPHASIS ON NUTRITION AND EXERCISE

Changing priorities regarding exercise, nutrition, and self-indulgence, coupled with a premium placed on "anti-stress" services ranging from aroma therapy to personal trainers, are being sought as people try to cope with the numerous demands of their roles as parents and workers. The personal demands placed on us by modern society also affect the "dark side" of consumer behavior, as we grapple with problems such as addiction, prostitution, compulsive shopping, theft, and vandalism.

While Americans still appear to be concerned about their health, the obsession of many with diet and exercise appears to be subsiding as people are adopting more of an "okay-in-moderation" outlook. A few years ago McDonald's introduced its McLean Deluxe reduced-fat beef patty with great fanfare, but now the chain is test-marketing the Mega Mac, a half-pound burger with cheese and sauce. An antidiet book, called "Stop the Insanity!" by Susan Powter, sold close to a million copies.[76] Words like "real" and "rich" are being used more frequently to describe full-flavored ice creams, peanut butter, and other "comfort foods" that make people feel better in anxious times.[77] Fewer consumers are avoiding salty products or foods with additives, and lower numbers of people report a willingness to pay more for "all-natural" foods.[78] Opposition to the consumption of red meat also appears to have peaked.[79]

THE MAIDENFORM WOMAN.
YOU NEVER KNOW WHERE SHE'LL TURN UP.

Sweet Nothings Demi-Bra by Maidenform

The increasing desire among women to return to domestic activities is reflected in new advertising for Maidenform. In the last two decades, the Maidenform woman was depicted (in her underwear!) in active, professional settings, such as an operating room or a stock exchange. In a recent execution created by Ogilvy & Mather, however, she turns up (fully clothed) at a PTA meeting. According to one executive who works on the account, "The PTA spot [has] been specifically created to talk to women who are blending motherhood with all the other facets of their lives, whatever they chose."

The shift toward indulgence has also moderated the fitness craze. Fewer Americans are taking exercise classes, jogging, or playing tennis.[80] Finding that 70 million people say they walk for exercise, Reebok is putting a much bigger emphasis on its walking shoes—a far cry from the "run 'til you drop" attitude of a few years ago. The fastest-growing sports are now low impact and home centered, such as in-line skating and stair-climbing machines.

"COCOONING"

Consumers will insulate themselves from world problems such as pollution and crime by staying home as much as possible: "They're going to go home and pull the covers over their heads, eat comfort food, watch VCRs, have babies, and stay married."[81] This emphasis on spending leisure time at home creates opportunities for businesses such as movie rentals, board games, and home spas.

Reflecting this trend, there is a growing market for big-ticket "home theaters," as furniture companies are teaming up with electronics marketers to offer sophisticated wide-screen TV and sound systems camouflaged in wall units. As one executive of the newly formed Home Theater Industry Association put it, "People are scared to go out of their homes. That is going to help drive home theater sales."[82]

NONCONSUMPTION

People will look for products and services that will help them to shed bad habits. In recent years, abstention from certain products and practices has become a way of life for many consumers who have adopted "non" as the code word for a lifestyle. Membership in support groups that help people to stop various forms of consumption, including alcohol, narcotics, gambling, food, and even sex, has doubled in the last decade. Some products have succeeded at positioning themselves in terms of attributes they do *not* possess. These include 7-UP ("The Un-Cola"), Club Med ("The antidote to civilization"), and even Max Factor's "No color mascara."[83]

INDIVIDUALIZATION AND MASS CUSTOMIZATION

Modern consumers have a strong sense of individualism, partly due to the dominance of the baby boomer generation that came of age in the late 1960s. Children raised during this time grew up in a period of affluence in which their wishes were indulged and they were encouraged to "think for themselves." For better or for worse, consumers now tend to put their personal needs ahead of their loyalties to groups or organizations.[84]

Technological and marketing developments have fanned the fires of individualism. Increasing numbers of people are going to work for themselves rather than for big companies. They are communicating with one another from the isolation of their homes via the Internet, and are tailoring their own entertainment options from hundreds of offerings. Advances in database marketing are allowing marketers to target very specific groups of people with well-defined interests, who receive specialized information about products where and when they want it. Advertisers are even talking about "ad-directed channels"—cable stations devoted to programming about specific subjects. For example, *Car & Driver* magazine recently spawned an automotive cable TV network, and its parent company is looking into creating other channels devoted to fashion or home decorating.[85]

Some forward-looking consumer-oriented companies are moving toward **mass customization,** in which a basic product or service is modified to meet the needs of an individual.[86] For example, Marriott's Honored Guest program tracks the preferences of repeat customers so that when they check in to one of the company's hotels they are assigned a room that best conforms to their individual preferences, such as smoking versus nonsmoking, low floor versus high floor, and so on.[87] Hallmark Cards allows card buyers to create their own greeting cards by adding personal information to a basic design. Levi Strauss introduced made-to-order jeans: For about $10 more than a mass-produced pair, a customer's actual measurements are transmitted to a Levi's factory, where denim is cut to exact specifications.[88]

A LAID-BACK LIFESTYLE

Americans are renewing their interest in living casually, and this informality is even extending to the workplace. Many companies are instituting a relaxed dress code, led by the "casual Friday" movement that allows employees to leave their ties and pantyhose at home one day a week. Not surprisingly, Levi Strauss has led the charge by promoting its casual clothing lines as an alternative to suits. As one company executive observed, "Casual office dressing is becoming mainstream."[89]

LIFE IN THE FAST LANE

Consumers continue their relentless search for thrills and chills, and fantasy entertainment is growing in popularity. New attractions in Las Vegas epitomize this trend. One company blew up a real hotel on New Year's Eve in 1997 in front of 200,000

Steven Spielberg's chain of arcades, Sega Gameworks, is positioned as "an alternative to discos for the young adult." Vertical Reality is an interactive game that is the centerpiece of these arcades. A player's chair rises with each skill level to a height of 24 feet, and then drops in free fall if the player loses.
Quoted in Jerry Adler, "Fast and Furious Fun," *Newsweek* (January 27, 1997): 68 (4), p. 73.

tourists. This was done to make way for a 4,000 room resort whose theme is an ancient forbidden city discovered on a tropical island. It will include a swim-up shark exhibit and scheduled rain showers. Other Vegas attractions include a sky-diving simulator with a 100-mile-an-hour updraft.

WHERE TO FROM HERE?

Of course, new lifestyle trends constantly are bubbling to the surface. As we'll see in chapters 15 and 17, many of these sea changes in consumer behavior are driven by young consumers who continually are redefining what's hot and what's not. These transformations may come from such growing movements as the new hip hop poets and performance artists who express their alienation from mainstream culture at open-mike nights in poets' cafes. Maybe the gamers who prowl the Internet playing Quake, Obsidian or Doom will lead the charge, or perhaps "technorganics" who believe in a minimalist lifestyle but who embrace new technologies and spend their time in chat rooms sharing their philosophy of the future will lead the way. Or, the freestylers who value spontaneity and freedom will rule the day (accompanied by the insistent beat of a techno soundtrack) and skateboarding brands like DC Droors, Menace and Girl, and Chocolate will hit the mainstream. On the other hand, perhaps adherents of "Barrier-Tec" (technology that protects us from pollutants like germs and acid rain) will prevail, and in a few years we will all be sheathed in clothes like those sold by W&LT (Wild and Lethal Trash), a line of street clothing from Europe that features gas masks and other protective gear.[90] Right now, it's anyone's bet: But savvy marketers understand that the only thing they can count on is that lifestyles will continue to change.

- The concept of *personality* refers to a person's unique psychological makeup and how it consistently influences the way a person responds to his or her environment. Marketing strategies based on personality differences have met with mixed success, partly because of the way these differences in *personality traits* have been measured and applied to consumption contexts. Some approaches have attempted to understand underlying differences in small samples of consumers by employing techniques based on Freudian psychology and variations of this perspective, whereas others have tried to assess these dimensions more objectively in large samples using sophisticated quantitative techniques.

- A consumer's *lifestyle* refers to the ways he or she chooses to spend time and money and how his or her values and tastes are reflected in consumption choices. Lifestyle research is useful to track societal consumption preferences and also to position specific products and services to different segments. Marketers segment by lifestyle differences, often by grouping consumers in terms of their AIOs (activities, interests, and opinions).

- *Psychographic* techniques attempt to classify consumers in terms of psychological, subjective variables in addition to observable characteristics (demographics). A variety of systems, such as VALS, have been developed to identify consumer "types" and to differentiate them in terms of their brand or product preferences, media usage, leisure time activities, and attitudes toward broad issues such as politics and religion.

- Interrelated sets of products and activities are associated with social roles to form *consumption constellations*. People often purchase a product or service because it is associated with a constellation that, in turn, is linked to a lifestyle they find desirable.

- Place of residence often is a significant determinant of lifestyle. Many marketers recognize regional differences in product preferences, and develop different versions of their products for different markets. A set of techniques called *geodemography* analyzes consumption patterns using geographical and demographic data, and identifies clusters of consumers who exhibit similar psychographic characteristics.

- Important changes are occurring in consumer priorities and practices in the late 1990s. Some major lifestyle trends include an emphasis on environmentalism, a resurgence of importance placed on value-oriented products and services, a decreased emphasis on nutrition and exercise, renewed interest in devoting more time to families versus careers, and more emphasis on individuality as consumers gravitate to marketers that practice *mass customization*, in which products and services can be tailored to the specific needs of individual consumers.

AIOs p. 179
Animism p. 172
Archetype p. 170
Brand equity p. 172
Consumption constellations
     p. 177
Ego p. 166
Geodemography p. 184
Id p. 166

Lifestyle p. 174
Mass customization p. 197
Motivational research
     p. 167
Personality p. 165
Pleasure principle p. 166
Product complementarity
     p. 177
Psychographics p. 178

Reality principle p. 166
Single-source data p. 185
Social trends p. 191
Superego p. 166
Traits p. 170
VALS (Values and
     Lifestyles) p. 182
80/20 principle p. 180

CONSUMER BEHAVIOR CHALLENGE

1. Construct a brand personality inventory for three different brands within a product category. Ask a small number of consumers to rate each brand on about 10 different personality dimensions. What differences can you locate? Do these "personalities" relate to the advertising and packaging strategies used to differentiate these products?

2. In what situations is demographic information likely to be more useful than psychographic data, and vice versa?

3. Alcohol drinkers vary sharply in terms of the number of drinks they may consume, from those who occasionally have one at a cocktail party to regular imbibers. Explain how the 80-20 principle applies to this product category.

4. Compile a set of recent ads that attempt to link consumption of a product with a specific lifestyle. How is this goal usually accomplished?

5. Psychographic analyses can be used to market politicians. Conduct research on the marketing strategies used in a recent, major election. How were voters segmented in terms of values? Can you find evidence that communications strategies were guided by this information?

6. Construct separate advertising executions for a cosmetics product targeted to the Belonger, Achiever, Experiencer, and Maker VALS types. How would the basic appeal differ for each group?

7. Using media targeted to the group, construct a consumption constellation for the social role of college students. What set of products, activities, and interests tend to appear in advertisements depicting "typical" college students? How realistic is this constellation?

8. Geodemographic techniques assume that people who live in the same neighborhood have other things in common as well. Why is this assumption made, and how accurate is it?

9. Single-source data systems give marketers access to a wide range of information about a consumer, just by knowing his or her address. Do you believe this "knowledge power" presents any ethical problems with regard to consumers' privacy? Should access to such information be regulated by the government or other bodies? Should consumers have the right to limit access to these data?

NOTES

1. For an interesting ethnographic account of sky diving as a voluntary high-risk consumption activity, see Richard L. Celsi, Randall L. Rose, and Thomas W. Leigh, "An Exploration of High-Risk Leisure Consumption through Skydiving," *Journal of Consumer Research* 20 (June 1993): 1–23. See also Jerry Adler, "Been There, Done That," *Newsweek* (July 19, 1993): 43 (7 pp.).

2. Rebecca Piirto Heath, "You Can Buy a Thrill: Chasing the Ultimate Rush," *American Demographics* (June 1997): 47–51.

3. Ann Marsh, "Surfer Girls," *Forbes* (August 11, 1997): 42 (2 pp.).

4. See J. Aronoff and J. P. Wilson, *Personality in the Social Process* (Hillsdale, NJ: Erlbaum, 1985);

Walter Mischel, *Personality and Assessment* (New York: Wiley, 1968).

5. Ernest Dichter, *A Strategy of Desire* (Garden City, NY: Doubleday, 1960); Ernest Dichter, *The Handbook of Consumer Motivations* (New York: McGraw-Hill, 1964); Jeffrey J. Durgee, "Interpreting Dichter's Interpretations: An Analysis of Consumption Symbolism in *The Handbook of Consumer Motivations*," unpublished manuscript, Rensselaer Polytechnic Institute, Troy, NY, 1989; Pierre Martineau, *Motivation in Advertising* (New York: McGraw-Hill, 1957).

6. Vance Packard, *The Hidden Persuaders* (New York: D. McKay, 1957).

7. Harold Kassarjian, "Personality and Consumer Behavior: A Review," *Journal of Marketing Research* 8 (November 1971): 409–18.

8. Karen Horney, *Neurosis and Human Growth* (New York: Norton, 1950).

9. Joel B. Cohen, "An Interpersonal Orientation to the Study of Consumer Behavior," *Journal of Marketing Research* 6 (August 1967): 270–8; Pradeep K. Tyagi, "Validation of the CAD Instrument: A Replication," in eds. Richard P. Bagozzi and Alice M. Tybout, *Advances in Consumer Research* 10 (Ann Arbor, MI: Association for Consumer Research, 1983): 112–14.

10. For a comprehensive review of classic perspectives on personality theory, see Calvin S. Hall and Gardner

Lindzey, *Theories of Personality*, 2nd ed. (New York: Wiley, 1970).

11. See Carl G. Jung, "The Archetypes and the Collective Unconscious," in eds. H. Read, M. Fordham, and G. Adler, *Collected Works* Vol. 9, Part I (Princeton: Princeton University Press, 1959).

12. Linda L. Price and Nancy Ridgway, "Development of a Scale to Measure Innovativeness," in eds. Richard P. Bagozzi and Alice M. Tybout, *Advances in Consumer Research* 10 (Ann Arbor, MI: Association for Consumer Research, 1983): 679–84; Russell W. Belk, "Three Scales to Measure Constructs Related to Materialism: Reliability, Validity, and Relationships to Measures of Happiness," in ed. Thomas C. Kinnear, *Advances in Consumer Research* 11 (Ann Arbor, MI: Association for Consumer Research, 1984): 291; Mark Snyder, "Self-Monitoring Processes," in ed. Leonard Berkowitz, *Advances in Experimental Social Psychology* (New York: Academic Press, 1979): 85–128; Gordon R. Foxall and Ronald E. Goldsmith, "Personality and Consumer Research: Another Look," *Journal of the Market Research Society* 30 (1988)2: 111–25; Ronald E. Goldsmith and Charles F. Hofacker, "Measuring Consumer Innovativeness," *Journal of the Academy of Marketing Science* 19 (1991)3: 209–21; Curtis P. Haugtvedt, Richard E. Petty, and John T. Cacioppo, "Need for Cognition and Advertising: Understanding the Role of Personality Variables in Consumer Behavior," *Journal of Consumer Psychology* 1 (1992)3: 239–60.

13. Jacob Jacoby, "Personality and Consumer Behavior: How Not to Find Relationships," in *Purdue Papers in Consumer Psychology,* No. 102 (Lafayette, IN: Purdue University, 1969); Harold H. Kassarjian and Mary Jane Sheffet, "Personality and Consumer Behavior: An Update," in eds. Harold H. Kassarjian and Thomas S. Robertson, *Perspectives in Consumer Behavior,* 4th ed. (Glenview, IL: Scott, Foresman, 1991): 291–353; John Lastovicka and Erich Joachimsthaler, "Improving the Detection of Personality Behavior Relationships in Consumer Research," *Journal of Consumer Research* 14 (March 1988): 583–7;

for an approach that ties the notion of personality more directly to marketing issues, see Jennifer L. Aaker, "Dimensions of Brand Personality," *Journal of Marketing Research* 34 (August 1997): 347–357.

14. See Girish N. Punj and David W. Stewart, "An Interaction Framework of Consumer Decision Making," *Journal of Consumer Research* 10 (September 1983): 181–96.

15. J. F. Allsopp, "The Distribution of On-Licence Beer and Cider Consumption and Its Personality Determinants among Young Men," *European Journal of Marketing* 20 (1986)3: 44–62; Gordon R. Foxall and Ronald E. Goldsmith, "Personality and Consumer Research: Another Look," *Journal of the Market Research Society* 30 (April 1988)2: 111–25.

16. Thomas Hine, "Why We Buy: The Silent Persuasion of Boxes, Bottles, Cans, and Tubes," *Worth* (May 1995): 78–83.

17. Kevin L. Keller, "Conceptualization, Measuring, and Managing Customer-based Brand Equity," *Journal of Marketing* 57 (January 1993): 1–22.

18. Aaker, "Dimensions of Brand Personality."

19. Quoted in Bradley Johnson, "They All Have Half-Baked Ideas," *Advertising Age* (May 12, 1997): 8.

20. Tim Triplett, "Brand Personality Must be Managed or It Will Assume a Life of Its Own," *Marketing News* (May 9, 1994): 9.

21. Susan Fournier, "Consumers and Their Brands: Developing Relationship Theory in Consumer Research," *Journal of Consumer Research* 24 (March 1998)4: 343–373.

22. Rebecca Piirto Heath, "The Frontiers of Psychographics," *American Demographics* (July 1996): 38–43.

23. Benjamin D. Zablocki and Rosabeth Moss Kanter, "The Differentiation of Life-Styles," *Annual Review of Sociology* (1976): 269–97.

24. Mary Twe Douglas and Baron C. Isherwood, *The World of Goods* (New York: Basic Books, 1979).

25. Zablocki and Kanter, "The Differentiation of Life-Styles."

26. Richard A. Peterson, "Revitalizing the Culture Concept," *Annual Review of Sociology* 5 (1979): 137–66.

27. Chester A. Swenson, "How to Sell to a Segmented Market," *Journal of Business Strategy* 9 (January–February 1988): 18.

28. William Leiss, Stephen Kline, and Sut Jhally, *Social Communication in Advertising* (Toronto: Methuen, 1986).

29. Douglas and Isherwood, *The World of Goods,* quoted on pp. 72–3.

30. Kathleen M. Rassuli and Gilbert D. Harrell, "Group Differences in the Construction of Consumption Sets," in eds. Kim P. Corfman and John G. Lynch Jr., *Advances in Consumer Research* 23 (Provo, UT: Association for Consumer Research, 1996): 446–53.

31. Michael R. Solomon, "The Role of Products as Social Stimuli: A Symbolic Interactionism Perspective," *Journal of Consumer Research* 10 (December 1983): 319–29.

32. Michael R. Solomon and Henry Assael, "The Forest or the Trees?: A Gestalt Approach to Symbolic Consumption," in ed. Jean Umiker-Sebeok, *Marketing and Semiotics: New Directions in the Study of Signs for Sale* (Berlin: Mouton de Gruyter, 1988): 189–218; Michael R. Solomon, "Mapping Product Constellations: A Social Categorization Approach to Symbolic Consumption," *Psychology & Marketing* 5 (1988)3: 233–58; see also Stephen C. Cosmas, "Life Styles and Consumption Patterns," *Journal of Consumer Research* 8 (March 1982)4: 453–5.

33. Russell W. Belk, "Yuppies as Arbiters of the Emerging Consumption Style," in ed. Richard J. Lutz, *Advances in Consumer Research* 13 (Provo, UT: Association for Consumer Research, 1986): 514–19.

34. See Lewis Alpert and Ronald Gatty, "Product Positioning by Behavioral Life Styles," *Journal of Marketing* 33 (April 1969): 65–9; Emanuel H. Demby, "Psychographics Revisited: The Birth of a Technique," *Marketing News* (January 2, 1989): 21; William D. Wells, "Backward Segmentation," in ed. Johan Arndt, *Insights into Consumer Behavior* (Boston: Allyn & Bacon, 1968): 85–100.

35. Rebecca Piirto Heath, "Psychographics: 'Q'est-ce que c'est'?" *Marketing Tools* (November/December 1995): 73 (6 pp.).

36. William D. Wells and Douglas J. Tigert, "Activities, Interests, and Opinions," *Journal of Advertising Research* 11 (August 1971): 27.

37. Ian Pearson, "Social Studies: Psychographics in Advertising,"

Canadian Business (December 1985): 67.

38. Piirto Heath, "Psychographics: 'Q'est-ce que c'est'?"

39. Alfred S. Boote, "Psychographics: Mind Over Matter," *American Demographics* (April 1980): 26–9; William D. Wells, "Psychographics: A Critical Review," *Journal of Marketing Research* 12 (May 1975): 196–213.

40. "At Leisure: Americans' Use of Down Time," *New York Times* (May 9, 1993): E2.

41. Joseph T. Plummer, "The Concept and Application of Life Style Segmentation," *Journal of Marketing* 38 (January 1974): 33–37.

42. Berkeley Rice, "The Selling of Lifestyles," *Psychology Today* (March 1988): 46.

43. John L. Lastovicka, John P. Murry, Erich A. Joachimsthaler, Gurav Bhalla, and Jim Scheurich, "A Lifestyle Typology to Model Young Male Drinking and Driving," *Journal of Consumer Research* 14 (September 1987): 257–63.

44. Anthony Ramirez, "New Cigarettes Raising Issue of Target Market," *New York Times* (February 18, 1990): 28.

45. Rebecca Piirto Heath, "The Frontiers of Psychographics," *American Demographics* (July 1996): 38–43.

46. Martha Farnsworth Riche, "VALS 2," *American Demographics* (July 1989): 25; additional information provided by William D. Guns, Director, Business Intelligence Center, SRI Consulting, Inc., personal communication, May 1997.

47. Rebecca Piirto Heath, "You Can Buy a Thrill: Chasing the Ultimate Rush," *American Demographics* (June 1997): 47–51.

48. "States of Stress," *American Demographics* (February 18, 1987).

49. Brad Edmondson, "From Dixie to Detroit," *American Demographics* (January 1987): 27.

50. Brad Edmondson, "America's Hot Spots," *American Demographics* (1988): 24–30.

51. Marcia Mogelonsky, "The Geography of Junk Food," *American Demographics* (July 1994): 13–14.

52. Nicholas Zill and John Robinson, "Name That Tune," *American Demographics* (August 1994): 22–7.

53. Edmondson, "From Dixie to Detroit."

54. David Greising, "The Boonies are Booming," *Business Week* (October 9,1995): 104 (6 pp.).

55. Ronald Henkoff, "Why Every Red-Blooded Consumer Owns a Truck, and a Five-Pound Jar of Peanut Butter, and a Personal Computer, and a Tool Belt, and a Case of Energy-Saving Light Bulbs, and Why it All Matters on a Nearly Cosmic Scale," *Fortune* (May 29, 1995): 86 (8 pp.).

56. Thomas W. Osborn, "Analytic Techniques for Opportunity Marketing," *Marketing Communications* (September 1987): 49–63.

57. Osborn, "Analytic Techniques for Opportunity Marketing."

58. Jonathan Marks, "Clusters Plus Nielsen Equals Efficient Marketing," *American Demographics* (September 1991): 16.

59. Michael J. Weiss, *The Clustering of America* (New York: Harper & Row, 1988).

60. Bob Minzesheimer, "You Are What You Zip," *Los Angeles* (November 1984): 175.

61. Christina Del Valle, "They Know Where You Live and How You Buy," *Business Week* (February 7, 1994): 89.

62. Del Valle, "They Know Where You Live and How You Buy."

63. Valerie Latham, "Do Euroconsumers Exist?" *Marketing* (June 24, 1993): 3.

64. Leiss et al., *Social Communication in Advertising*.

65. Stuart Elliott, "Sampling Tastes of a Changing Russia," *New York Times* (April 1, 1992)2: D1.

66. Peter Francese, "The Trend Evolution," *American Demographics* (October 1993): 3.

67. Roberta Piirto Heath, "Measuring Minds in the 1990s," *American Demographics* (December 1990)5: 31.

68. Bill McDowell,"New DDB Needham Report: Consumers Want It All," *Advertising Age* (November 18, 1996): 32–3.

69. Pat Sloan, "Cosmetics: Color it Green," *Advertising Age* (July 23, 1990): 1.

70. Timothy Aeppel, "Green Groups Enter a Dry Season as Movement Matures," *Wall Street Journal* (October 21, 1994): B1 (2 pp.).

71. Rahul Jacob, "Beyond Quality & Value," *Fortune* (Autumn/Winter 1993): 8 (3 pp.).

72. Ronald D. Michman, "New Directions for Life-Style Behavior Patterns," *Business Horizons* (July/August 1984): 60.

73. Timothy Harris, "Fast and Easy: US Supermarkets Market Convenience Foods as Lifestyles," *Marketing* (October 29, 1987): 17.

74. Kathleen Deveny, "Movable Feasts: More People Dine and Drive," *Wall Street Journal* (January 4, 1994): B1.

75. Sandra Pesmen, "Home Front," *Advertising Age* (September 19, 1994): 1 (2); Lenore Skenazy, "Welcome Home: Trend Experts Point to 'Neo-traditional'," *Advertising Age* (May 16, 1988): 38; Lynn R. Kahle, Basil Poulos, and Ajay Sukhdial, "Changes in Social Values in the United States During the Past Decade," *Journal of Advertising Research* 28 (February/March 1988): 35–41; DDB Needham Worldwide's Life Style Study, reported in *Advertising Age* (September 24, 1990): 25.

76. Molly O'Neill, " 'Eat, Drink and Be Merry' May Be the Next Trend," *New York Times* (January 4, 1994): 1 (2 pp.); Cyndee Miller, "The 'Real Food' Movement: Consumers Stay Health-Conscious, But Now They Splurge," *Marketing News* (June 7, 1993): 1 (2 pp.).

77. Sunita Wadekar Bhargava, "Gimme a Double Shake and a Lard on White," *Business Week* (March 1, 1993): 59.

78. *DDB Needham Worldwide's Life Style Study*, 25.

79. Burdette Breidenstein, "Changes in Consumers' Attitudes toward Red Meat and Their Effect on Marketing Strategy," *Food Technology* (January 1988): 112–16.

80. *DDB Needham Worldwide's Life Style Study*, 25; John P. Robinson and Geoffrey Godbey, "Has Fitness Peaked?" *American Demographics* (September 1993): 36 (5 pp.); Priscilla Painton, "Couch Potatoes, Arise!" *Time* (August 9, 1993): 55–6.

81. David Streitfeld, "What's Up, Trendwise?" *Washington Post* (November 28, 1988): D5.

82. Quoted in Liz Seymour, "Wall Unit? Big TV? No, 'an Experience'," *New York Times* (October 21, 1993): C2.

83. Molly O'Neill, "Words to Survive Life With: None of This, None of That," *New York Times* (May 27, 1990): 1.

84. Cheryl Russell, "The Master Trend," *American Demographics* (October 1993): 28 (6 pp.).

85. Lisa Schoenfein, "Ad-Directed Channels a Reality," *Advertising Age* (April 11, 1994): S6 (2 pp.).

86. See B. Joseph Pine II, Bart Victor, and Andrew C. Boynton, "Making Mass Customization Work," *Harvard Business Review* (September/October 1993): 108–19.

87. Philip Kotler, "From Mass Marketing to Mass Customization," *Planning Review* (September/October, 1989): 10–47.

88. Glenn Rifkin, "Digital Blue Jeans Pour Data and Legs into Customized Fit," *New York Times* (November 8, 1994): A1 (2 pp.).

89. Quoted in June Weir, "Casual Look 'Defining Character of the '90s'," *Advertising Age* (April 7, 1994): S2 (2 pp.); Jeanne Whalen, "Casual Dining, Not Fast Food, Challenges Mom's Meatloaf," *Advertising Age* (April 7, 1994): S6.

90. Janine Lopiano-Misdom and Joanne de Luca, *Street Trends,* New York: HarperBusiness, 1997.

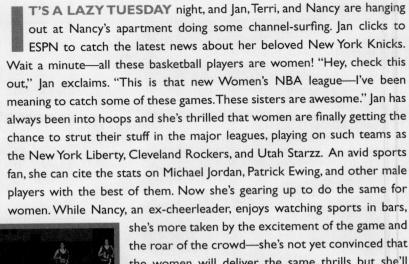

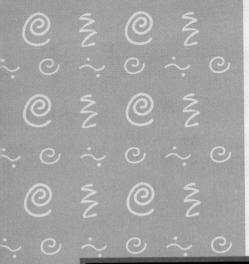

IT'S A LAZY TUESDAY night, and Jan, Terri, and Nancy are hanging out at Nancy's apartment doing some channel-surfing. Jan clicks to ESPN to catch the latest news about her beloved New York Knicks. Wait a minute—all these basketball players are women! "Hey, check this out," Jan exclaims. "This is that new Women's NBA league—I've been meaning to catch some of these games. These sisters are awesome." Jan has always been into hoops and she's thrilled that women are finally getting the chance to strut their stuff in the major leagues, playing on such teams as the New York Liberty, Cleveland Rockers, and Utah Starzz. An avid sports fan, she can cite the stats on Michael Jordan, Patrick Ewing, and other male players with the best of them. Now she's gearing up to do the same for women. While Nancy, an ex-cheerleader, enjoys watching sports in bars, she's more taken by the excitement of the game and the roar of the crowd—she's not yet convinced that the women will deliver the same thrills but she'll suspend judgment until she watches a few games. Terri, on the other hand, doesn't know a Phi Slamma Jamma from a technical foul. As long as she gets to hang out with her girlfriends, she doesn't really care what they do—if women's basketball is what it will take to get away from housework and nagging kids, so be it . . .

Attitudes

THE POWER OF ATTITUDES

Jan is just the kind of fan sponsoring companies like Lee Jeans, Champion, and Anheuser-Busch are counting on to make the WNBA a success. Still, the league has its job cut out for it. The WNBA, which began in 1997 and now consists of ten teams operated by the National Basketball Association, has to get viewers used to the idea that women's basketball is here to stay, and be sure that fans have positive attitudes toward the sport and toward women's athletics in general.[1] But, it seems as if these new attitudes are taking hold—four new magazines focusing on women's sports have recently been launched, and major athletic companies such as Nike are now turning their marketing clout to the creation of female fan-atics. Nike's "If You Let Me Play" campaign addressed the need to support women's athletics by featuring women in its ads saying "If you let me play, I will be more likely to leave a man who beats me. If you let me play, I will be less likely to get pregnant before I want to; I will learn what it means to be strong."[2] To score a slam dunk, it all comes down to a question of attitudes.

The term *attitude* is widely used in popular culture. You might be asked, "What is your attitude toward abortion?" A parent might scold, "Young man, I don't like your attitude." Some bars even euphemistically refer to Happy Hour as "an attitude adjustment period." For our purposes, though, an **attitude** is a lasting, general evaluation of people (including oneself), objects, advertisements, or issues.[3] Anything toward which one has an attitude is called an **attitude object** (A_o).

An attitude is *lasting* because it tends to endure over time. It is *general* because it applies to more than a momentary event such as hearing a loud noise, though you might over time develop a negative attitude toward all loud noises. Consumers have attitudes toward a wide range of attitude objects; from very product-specific behaviors (e.g., using Crest toothpaste rather than Colgate) to more general consumption-related behaviors (e.g., how often one should brush one's teeth). Attitudes help to determine whom a person chooses to date, what music he or she listens to, whether he or she will recycle or discard aluminum cans, or whether he or she chooses to become a consumer researcher for a living. This chapter will consider the contents of an attitude, how attitudes are formed, how they can be measured, and review some of the surprisingly complex relationships between attitudes and behavior. In the next chapter, we'll take a closer look at how attitudes can be changed—certainly an issue of prime importance to marketers.

THE FUNCTIONS OF ATTITUDES

The **functional theory of attitudes** was initially developed by psychologist Daniel Katz to explain how attitudes facilitate social behavior.[4] According to this pragmatic approach, attitudes exist *because* they serve some function for the person. That is,

This Norwegian ad addresses young people's smoking attitudes by arousing strong negative feelings. The ad reads (left panel): "Smokers are more sociable than others." (Right panel): "While it lasts."

they are determined by a person's motives. Consumers who expect that they will need to deal with similar situations at a future time will be more likely to start forming attitudes in anticipation of this event.[5]

Two people can each have an attitude toward some object for very different reasons. As a result it can be helpful for a marketer to know *why* an attitude is held before attempting to change it. The following are attitude functions as identified by Katz:

- *Utilitarian function:* The utilitarian function is related to the basic principles of reward and punishment. We develop some attitudes toward products simply on the basis of whether these products provide pleasure or pain. If a person likes

This company coaches students who are about to take standardized admissions tests. Its appeal is based on an instrumental attitude function: increasing one's chances of getting admitted to a good school.

the taste of a cheeseburger, that person will develop a positive attitude toward cheeseburgers. Ads that stress straightforward product benefits (e.g., you should drink Diet Coke "just for the taste of it") appeal to the utilitarian function.

- *Value-expressive function:* Attitudes that perform a value-expressive function express the consumer's central values or self-concept. A person forms a product attitude not because of its objective benefits, but because of what the product says about him or her as a person (e.g., "What sort of man reads Playboy?"). Value-expressive attitudes are highly relevant to lifestyle analyses, which look at how consumers cultivate a cluster of activities, interests, and opinions to express a particular social identity.

- *Ego-defensive function:* Attitudes that are formed to protect the person, either from external threats or internal feelings, perform an ego-defensive function. An early marketing study indicated that housewives in the 1950s resisted the use of instant coffee because it threatened their conception of themselves as capable homemakers.[6] Products that promise to help a man project a "macho" image (e.g., Marlboro cigarettes) may be appealing to his insecurities about his masculinity. Another example is deodorant campaigns that stress the dire, embarrassing consequences of being caught with underarm odor in public.

- *Knowledge function:* Some attitudes are formed as the result of a need for order, structure, or meaning. This need is often present when a person is in an ambiguous situation or is confronted with a new product (e.g., "Bayer wants you to know about pain relievers").

An attitude can serve more than one function, but in many cases a particular one will be dominant. By identifying the dominant function a product serves for consumers—what *benefits* it provides—marketers can emphasize these benefits in their communications and packaging. Ads relevant to the function prompt more favorable thoughts about what is being marketed and can result in a heightened preference for both the ad and the product.

One study determined that for most people coffee serves more of a utilitarian function than a value-expressive function. As a consequence, subjects responded more positively to copy for a (fictitious) coffee that read, "The delicious, hearty flavor and aroma of Sterling Blend coffee comes from a blend of the freshest coffee beans" (utilitarian appeal) than to, "The coffee you drink says something about the type of person you are. It can reveal your rare, discriminating taste" (value-expressive function).[7]

THE ABC MODEL OF ATTITUDES

Most researchers agree that an attitude has three components: affect, behavior, and cognition. **Affect** refers to the way a consumer *feels* about an attitude object. **Behavior** involves the person's intentions to *do* something with regard to an attitude object (but, as will be discussed at a later point, an intention does not always result in an actual behavior). **Cognition** refers to the *beliefs* a consumer has about an attitude object. These three components of an attitude can be remembered as the *ABC model of attitudes.*

This model emphasizes the interrelationships among knowing, feeling, and doing. Consumers' attitudes toward a product cannot be determined by simply identifying their beliefs about it. For example, a researcher may find that shoppers "know" a particular camcorder has an 8:1 power zoom lens, autofocus, and a flying erase head, but such findings do not indicate whether they feel these attributes are good, bad, or irrelevant or whether they would actually buy the camcorder.

MARKETING OPPORTUNITY

Social marketing involves the promotion of positive attitudes toward important issues such as responsible drinking, energy conservation, and population control.[8] According to a Roper Starch Worldwide survey, consumers expect business to be socially responsible and almost two-thirds say they factor this into their buying decisions. One in five say they frequently refuse to buy the best quality product because they don't like the company.[9]

A project conducted in Latin America by the Johns Hopkins Center for Communication Programs illustrates how marketing tools can be used to bring about changes in consumers' attitudes. To promote sexual responsibility among young people, the popular Latin pop duo Tatiana and Johnny sang a song promoting abstinence and protection. It was produced by health communication specialists and researchers and went on to become a Top 10 hit in Latin American countries. The record jacket folded out to become a poster with information about youth centers in Latin America.[10]

HIERARCHIES OF EFFECTS

All three components of an attitude are important, but their relative importance will vary depending on a consumer's level of motivation with regard to the attitude object. The differences in athletic interests among the three women in Nancy's apartment illustrate how these elements can be combined in different ways to create an attitude. Attitude researchers have developed the concept of a **hierarchy of effects** to explain the relative impact of the three components. Each hierarchy specifies that a fixed sequence of steps occurs en route to an attitude. Three different hierarchies are summarized in Figure 7–1.

The Standard Learning Hierarchy. Jan's positive attitude toward women's basketball closely resembles the process by which most attitudes have been assumed to be constructed. A consumer approaches a product decision as a problem-solving process. First, he or she forms beliefs about a product by accumulating knowledge (beliefs) regarding relevant attributes. Next, the consumer evaluates these beliefs and forms a feeling about the product (affect).[11] Over time, Jan assembled information about the sport, began to recognize the players, and learned which teams were superior to others.

Finally, based on this evaluation, the consumer engages in a relevant behavior, such as buying the product or supporting a particular team by wearing its jersey. This careful choice process often results in the type of loyalty displayed by Jan; the consumer "bonds" with the product over time and is not easily persuaded to experiment with other brands. The standard learning hierarchy assumes that a consumer is highly involved in making a purchase decision.[12] The person is motivated to seek out a lot of information, carefully weigh alternatives, and come to a thoughtful decision.

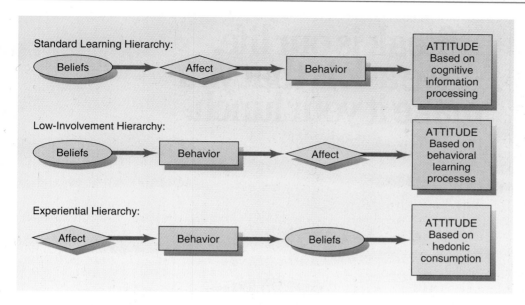

Standard Learning Hierarchy:

Beliefs → Affect → Behavior → ATTITUDE Based on cognitive information processing

Low-Involvement Hierarchy:

Beliefs → Behavior → Affect → ATTITUDE Based on behavioral learning processes

Experiential Hierarchy:

Affect → Behavior → Beliefs → ATTITUDE Based on hedonic consumption

FIGURE 7–1 ■ Three Hierarchies of Effects

The Low-Involvement Hierarchy. In contrast to Jan, Nancy's interest in the attitude object (the WNBA) is at best lukewarm. She is not particularly knowledgeable about the sport, and she may have an emotional response to an exciting game but not to a specific team. Nancy is typical of a consumer who forms an attitude via the *low-involvement hierarchy of effects*. In this sequence, the consumer does not initially have a strong preference for one brand over another, but instead acts on the basis of limited knowledge and then forms an evaluation only after the product has been purchased or used.[13] The attitude is likely to come about through behavioral learning, in which the consumer's choice is reinforced by good or bad experiences with the product after purchase—Nancy will probably be more likely to tune in to future games if this one is decided by a free throw in the last two seconds.

The possibility that consumers simply don't care enough about many decisions to carefully assemble a set of product beliefs and then evaluate them is important, because it implies that all of the concern about influencing beliefs and carefully communicating information about product attributes may be largely wasted. Consumers aren't necessarily going to pay attention anyway; they are more likely to respond to simple stimulus–response connections when making purchase decisions. For example, a consumer choosing among paper towels might remember that "Bounty is the quicker picker-upper" rather than bothering to systematically compare all of the brands on the shelf.

The notion of low involvement on the part of consumers is a bitter pill for some marketers to swallow. Who wants to admit that what they market is not very important or involving? A brand manager for, say, a brand of bubble gum or cat food may find it hard to believe that consumers don't put that much thought into purchasing her product because she herself spends many of her waking (and perhaps sleeping) hours thinking about it.

For marketers, the ironic silver lining to this low-involvement cloud is that under these conditions, consumers are not motivated to process a lot of complex brand-related information. Instead, they will be swayed by principles of behavioral learning, such as the simple responses caused by conditioned brand names, point-of-purchase displays, and so on. This results in what we might call the *involvement*

**Steak is our life.
All we ask is that you
make it your lunch.**

Smith & Wollensky.
The quintessential New York City steakhouse.
49th St. & 3rd Ave. (212) 753-1530.

Winner of The *Wine Spectator's* 1987 Grand Award.

This ad for New York's famous Smith & Wollensky restaurant emphasizes that marketers and others associated with a product or service are often more involved with it than are their consumers.

paradox: The *less* important the product is to consumers, the *more* important are many of the marketing stimuli (e.g., packages, jingles) that must be devised to sell it.

The Experiential Hierarchy. Researchers in recent years have begun to stress the significance of emotional response as a central aspect of an attitude. According to the *experiential hierarchy of effects,* consumers act on the basis of their emotional reactions—Terri just enjoys watching the tube with her friends, regardless of what is on.

This perspective highlights the idea that attitudes can be strongly influenced by intangible product attributes, such as package design, and by consumers' reactions toward accompanying stimuli, such as advertising, brand names, and the nature of the setting in which the experience occurs. As discussed in chapter 4, resulting attitudes will be affected by consumers' hedonic motivations, such as how the product makes them feel or the fun its use will provide.

One important debate about the experiential hierarchy concerns the *independence* of cognition and affect. On the one hand, the *cognitive–affective* model argues that an affective judgment is but the last step in a series of cognitive processes. Earlier steps include the sensory registration of stimuli and the retrieval of meaningful information from memory to categorize these stimuli.[14]

On the other hand, the *independence hypothesis* takes the position that affect and cognition involve two separate, partially independent systems; affective responses do not always require prior cognitions.[15] A number one song on the *Billboard* "Top 40" may possess the same attributes as many other songs (e.g., dominant bass guitar, raspy vocals, persistent downbeat), but beliefs about these attributes cannot explain why one song becomes a classic while another sharing the same characteristics winds up in the bargain bin at the local record store. The independence hypothesis does not eliminate the role of cognition in experience. It simply balances this traditional, rational emphasis on calculated decision making by pay-

It's cold. You're hurting.
And three rookies
will kill for your job.

How does it feel?

Sports Illustrated
Get the feeling.

This *Sports Illustrated* ad,
which emphasizes feelings,
underscores the importance
of affect in forming attitudes.

ing more attention to the impact of aesthetic, subjective experience. This type of
holistic processing is more likely to occur when the product is perceived as primarily expressive or delivers sensory pleasure rather than utilitarian benefits.[16]

PRODUCT ATTITUDES DON'T TELL THE WHOLE STORY

Marketers who are concerned with understanding consumers' attitudes have to contend with an even more complex issue: In decision-making situations, people form
attitudes toward objects other than the product itself that can influence their ultimate selections. One additional factor to consider is attitudes toward the act of buying in general—as we'll see later in the chapter, sometimes people simply are reluctant, embarrassed, or just plain too lazy to expend the effort to actually obtain a
desired product or service.

ATTITUDE TOWARD THE ADVERTISEMENT

Consumers' reactions to a product are also influenced by their evaluations of its
advertising, over and above their feelings about the product itself. Our evaluation of
a product can be determined solely by our appraisal of how it's depicted in marketing communications—we don't hesitate to form attitudes toward products we've
never even seen in person, much less used.

One special type of attitude object, then, is the marketing message itself. The
attitude toward the advertisement (A_{ad}) is defined as a predisposition to respond in
a favorable or unfavorable manner to a particular advertising stimulus during a particular exposure occasion. Determinants of A_{ad} include attitude toward the advertiser, evaluations of the ad execution itself, the mood evoked by the ad, and the
degree to which the ad affects viewers' arousal levels.[17] A viewer's feelings about the
context in which an ad appears can also influence brand attitudes. For example,
attitudes about an ad and the brand depicted will be influenced if the consumer sees
the ad while watching a favorite TV program.[18] The effects demonstrated by A_{ad}
emphasize the potential importance of an ad's entertainment value in the purchase
process.[19]

ADS HAVE FEELINGS, TOO . . .

The feelings generated by an ad have the capacity to directly affect brand attitudes. Commercials can evoke a wide range of emotional responses, from disgust to happiness. These feelings can be influenced both by the way the ad is done (i.e., the specific advertising *execution*) and by the consumer's reactions to the advertiser's motives. For example, many advertisers who are trying to craft messages for adolescents and young adults are encountering problems because this age group, having grown up in a "marketing society," tends to be skeptical about attempts to get them to buy things.[20] These reactions can in turn influence memory for advertising content.[21]

At least three emotional dimensions have been identified in commercials: pleasure, arousal, and intimidation.[22] Specific types of feelings that can be generated by an ad include the following:[23]

- *Upbeat feelings:* amused, delighted, playful
- *Warm feelings:* affectionate, contemplative, hopeful
- *Negative feelings:* critical, defiant, offended

FORMING ATTITUDES

We all have lots of attitudes, and we don't usually question how we got them. Certainly, a person isn't born with the conviction that, say, Pepsi is better than Coke, or that alternative music liberates the soul. Where do these attitudes come from?

An attitude can form in several different ways, depending on the particular hierarchy of effects in operation and how the attitude is learned (see chapter 3). It can occur because of classical conditioning, in which an attitude object such as the Pepsi name is repeatedly paired with a catchy jingle ("You're in the Pepsi Generation . . ."). Or, it can be formed through instrumental conditioning, in which consumption of the attitude object is reinforced (e.g., Pepsi quenches one's thirst). Or the learning of an attitude can be the outcome of a very complex cognitive process. For example, a teenager may come to model the behavior of friends and media figures who drink Pepsi because she believes that this act will allow her to fit in with the desirable images of the Pepsi Generation.

 MARKETING PITFALL

In a study of irritating advertising, researchers examined over 500 prime-time network commercials that had registered negative reactions by consumers. The most irritating commercials were for feminine hygiene products, hemorrhoid medication or laxatives, and women's underwear. The researchers identified the following factors as prime offenders:[24]

- A sensitive product is shown (e.g., hemorrhoid medicine), and its use or package is emphasized.
- The situation is contrived or overdramatized.

- A person is put down in terms of appearance, knowledge, or sophistication.
- An important relationship, such as a marriage, is threatened.
- There is a graphic demonstration of physical discomfort.
- Uncomfortable tension is created by an argument or by an antagonistic character.
- An unattractive or unsympathetic character is portrayed.
- A sexually suggestive scene is included.
- The commercial suffers from poor casting or execution.

NOT ALL ATTITUDES ARE CREATED EQUAL

It is thus important to distinguish among types of attitudes, because not all are formed the same way.[25] For example, a highly brand-loyal consumer like Jan, the Knicks fan, has an enduring, deeply held positive attitude toward an attitude object, and this involvement will be difficult to weaken. On the other hand, another consumer like Nancy, the ex-cheerleader, may be a more fickle consumer: She may have a mildly positive attitude toward a product but be quite willing to abandon it when something better comes along. This section will consider the differences between strongly and weakly held attitudes, and briefly review some of the major theoretical perspectives that have been developed to explain how attitudes form and relate to one another in the minds of consumers.

LEVELS OF COMMITMENT TO AN ATTITUDE

Consumers vary in their *commitment* to an attitude; the degree of commitment is related to their level of involvement with the attitude object.[26]

- *Compliance:* At the lowest level of involvement, *compliance,* an attitude is formed because it helps in gaining rewards or avoiding punishments from others. This attitude is very superficial; it is likely to change when the person's behavior is no longer monitored by others or when another option becomes available. A person may drink Pepsi because this brand is sold in the cafeteria, and it is too much trouble to go elsewhere for a Coca-Cola.

- *Identification:* A process of identification occurs when attitudes are formed in order to conform with another person or group. Advertising that depicts the social consequences of choosing some products over others is relying on the tendency of consumers to imitate the behavior of desirable models.

- *Internalization:* At a high level of involvement, deep-seated attitudes are internalized and become part of the person's value system. These attitudes are very difficult to change because they are so important to the individual. For example, many consumers had strong attitudes toward Coca-Cola and reacted quite negatively when the company attempted to switch to the New Coke formula. This allegiance to Coke was obviously more than a minor preference for these people; the brand had become intertwined with their social identities, taking on patriotic and nostalgic properties.

THE CONSISTENCY PRINCIPLE

Have you ever heard someone say, "Pepsi is my favorite soft drink. It tastes terrible," or "I love my husband. He's the biggest idiot I've ever met"? Probably not too often, because these beliefs or evaluations are not consistent with one another. According to the **principle of cognitive consistency,** consumers value harmony among their thoughts, feelings, and behaviors, and they are motivated to maintain uniformity among these elements. This desire means that, if necessary, consumers will change their thoughts, feelings, or behaviors to make them consistent with their other experiences. The consistency principle is an important reminder that attitudes are not formed in a vacuum. A significant determinant of the way an attitude object will be evaluated is how it fits with other, related attitudes already held by the consumer.

MARKETING OPPORTUNITY

As we saw in the experiences of the three women watching a basketball game, the importance of an attitude object may differ quite a bit for different people. Understanding the attitude's centrality to an individual and to others who share similar characteristics can be useful to marketers who are trying to devise strategies that will appeal to different customer segments. A recent study of football game attendance illustrates that varying levels of commitment result in different fan "profiles."[27] The study identified three distinct clusters of fans:[28]

- One cluster consisted of the real die-hard fans who were highly committed to their team and who displayed an enduring love of the game. To reach these fans, the researchers recommend that sports marketers should focus on providing them with greater sports knowledge and relate their attendance to their personal goals and values.

- Another cluster was looking for camaraderie above all—they attended games primarily to take part in small-group activities such as tailgating that accompanied the event. Marketers could appeal to this cluster by providing improved peripheral benefits, such as making it easier for groups to meet at the stadium, improving parking, and offering multiple-unit pricing.

- A third cluster's attitude was based on the unique, self-expressive experience provided by the game—these people enjoy the stimulation of cheering for a team and the drama of the competition itself. They are more likely to be "brand switchers" who are fair-weather fans, shifting allegiances when the home team no longer provides the thrills they need. This segment can be appealed to by publicizing aspects of the visiting teams, such as advertising the appearance of stars who are likely to give the fans a game they will remember.

COGNITIVE DISSONANCE AND HARMONY AMONG ATTITUDES

The **theory of cognitive dissonance** states that when a person is confronted with inconsistencies among attitudes or behaviors, he or she will take some action to resolve this "dissonance," perhaps by changing an attitude or modifying a behavior. The theory has important ramifications for attitudes, because people are often confronted with situations where there is some conflict between their attitudes and behaviors.[29]

According to the theory, people are motivated to reduce the negative feelings caused by dissonance by somehow making things fit with one another. The theory

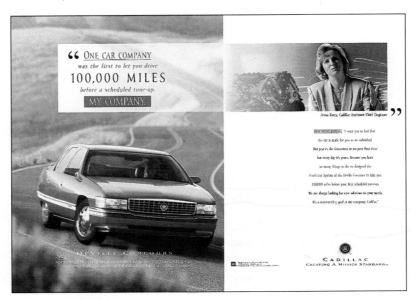

By describing Cadillac as "my company," the woman featured in this ad is exhibiting a high level of attitudinal commitment to her employer.

This ad for *Woman's Day* attempts to counter the role consistency plays in shaping attitudes: Consumers often distort information so that it fits with what they already know or believe.

focuses on situations in which two *cognitive elements* are inconsistent with one another. A cognitive element can be something a person believes about himself, a behavior he performs, or an observation about his surroundings. For example, the two cognitive elements, "I know smoking cigarettes causes cancer" and "I smoke cigarettes" are *dissonant* with one another. This psychological inconsistency creates a feeling of discomfort that the smoker is motivated to reduce. The magnitude of dissonance depends on both the importance and number of dissonant elements.[30] In other words, the pressure to reduce dissonance is more likely to be observed in high-involvement situations, in which the elements are more important to the individual.

Dissonance reduction can occur either by eliminating, adding, or changing elements. For example, the person could stop smoking (eliminating) or remember great aunt Sophie, who smoked until the day she died at age 90 (adding). Alternatively, he might question the research that links cancer and smoking (changing), perhaps by believing industry-sponsored studies that try to refute this connection.

Dissonance theory can help to explain why evaluations of a product tend to increase *after* it has been purchased. The cognitive element "I made a stupid decision" is dissonant with the element "I am not a stupid person" so people tend to find even more reasons to like something after it becomes theirs.

A field study performed at a horse race demonstrated postpurchase dissonance. Bettors evaluated their chosen horse more highly and were more confident of its success *after* they had placed a bet than before. Since the bettor is financially committed to the choice, he or she reduces dissonance by increasing the attractiveness of the chosen alternative relative to the unchosen ones.[31] One implication of this phenomenon is that consumers actively seek support for their purchase decisions, so marketers should supply them with additional reinforcement to build positive brand attitudes.

SELF-PERCEPTION THEORY

Do attitudes necessarily change following behavior because people are motivated to feel good about their decisions? **Self-perception theory** provides an alternative explanation of dissonance effects.[32] It assumes that people use observations of their own behavior to determine what their attitudes are, just as we assume that we know the attitudes of others by watching what they do. The theory states that we maintain consistency by inferring that we must have a positive attitude toward an object if we have bought or consumed it (assuming that we freely made this choice). Thus Jan might say to herself, "I guess I must be into sports pretty big time. I sure choose to watch it a lot."

Self-perception theory is relevant to the *low-involvement hierarchy*, because it involves situations in which behaviors are initially performed in the absence of a strong internal attitude. After the fact, the cognitive and affective components of attitude fall into line. Thus, buying a product out of habit may result in a positive attitude toward it after the fact—why would I buy it if I didn't like it?

Self-perception theory helps to explain the effectiveness of a sales strategy called the **foot-in-the-door technique,** which is based on the observation that a consumer is more likely to comply with a request if he or she has first agreed to comply with a smaller request.[33] The name for this technique comes from the practice of door-to-door selling, in which salespeople were taught to plant their foot in a door so the prospect could not slam it on them. A good salesperson knows that he or she is more likely to get an order if the customer can be persuaded to open the door and talk. By agreeing to do so, the customer has established that she or he is willing to listen to the salesperson. Placing an order is consistent with this self-perception. This technique is especially useful for inducing consumers to answer surveys or to donate money to charity. Such factors as the time lag between the first and second request, the similarity between the two requests, and whether the same person makes both requests have been found to influence its effectiveness.[34]

SOCIAL JUDGMENT THEORY

Social judgment theory also assumes that people assimilate new information about attitude objects in light of what they already know or feel.[35] The initial attitude acts as a frame of reference, and new information is categorized in terms of this existing standard. Just as our decision that a box is heavy depends in part on the weight of other boxes we have lifted, we develop a subjective standard when making judgments about attitude objects.

One important aspect of the theory is the notion that people differ in terms of the information they will find acceptable or unacceptable. They form **latitudes of acceptance and rejection** around an attitude standard. Ideas that fall within a latitude will be favorably received, but those falling outside of this zone will not. Because Jan already had a favorable attitude toward the concept of women playing professional basketball, she is likely to be receptive to ads such as Nike's that promote female athletic participation. If she were opposed to these activities, these messages would probably not be considered.

Messages that fall within the latitude of acceptance tend to be seen as more consistent with one's position than they actually are. This process is called an *assimilation effect.* On the other hand, messages falling in the latitude of rejection tend to be seen as even *farther* from one's position than they actually are, resulting in a *contrast effect.*[36]

As a person becomes more involved with an attitude object, his or her latitude of acceptance gets smaller. In other words, the consumer accepts fewer ideas that are removed from his or her own position and tends to oppose even mildly divergent positions. This tendency is evident in ads that appeal to discriminating buyers, which claim that knowledgeable people will reject anything but the very best (e.g., "choosy mothers choose Jif peanut butter"). On the other hand, relatively uninvolved consumers will consider a wider range of alternatives. They are less likely to be brand loyal and will be more likely to be brand switchers.[37]

BALANCE THEORY

Balance theory considers relations among elements a person might perceive as belonging together.[38] This perspective involves relations (always from the perceiver's subjective point of view) among three elements, so the resulting attitude structures are called *triads*. Each triad contains (1) a person and his or her perceptions of (2) an attitude object and (3) some other person or object.

These perceptions can be either positive or negative. More importantly, people *alter* these perceptions in order to make relations among them consistent. The theory specifies that people desire relations among elements in a triad to be harmonious, or *balanced*. If they are not, a state of tension will result until somehow perceptions are changed and balance is restored.

Elements can be perceived as going together in one of two ways: They can have either a *unit relation*, in which one element is seen as somehow belonging to or being a part of the other (something like a belief) or a *sentiment relation*, in which the two elements are linked because one has expressed a preference (or dislike) for the other. A dating couple might be seen as having a positive sentiment relation. On getting married, they will have a positive unit relation. The process of divorce is an attempt to sever a unit relation.

To see how balance theory might work, consider the following scenario:

- Alex would like to date Larry, who is in her consumer behavior class. In balance theory terms, Alex has a positive sentiment relation with Larry.
- One day, Larry shows up in class wearing an earring. Larry has a positive unit relation with the earring. It belongs to him and is literally a part of him.
- Alex does not like men who wear earrings. She has a negative sentiment relation with men's earrings.

According to balance theory, Alex faces an unbalanced triad, and she will experience pressure to restore balance by altering some aspect of the triad, as shown in Figure 7–2. She could, for example, decide that she does not like Larry after all. Or, her liking for Larry could prompt a change in her attitude toward earrings. She might even try to negate the unit relation between Larry and the earring by deciding that he must be wearing it as part of a fraternity initiation (thus reducing the free-choice element). Finally, she could choose to "leave the field" by not thinking any more about Larry and his controversial earring.

Note that while the theory does not specify which of these routes will be taken, it does predict that one or more of Alex's perceptions will probably change in order to achieve balance. Although this distortion is most likely an oversimplified representation of most attitude processes, it helps to explain a number of consumer behavior phenomena.

MARKETING APPLICATIONS OF BALANCE THEORY

Balance theory reminds us that when perceptions are balanced, attitudes are likely to be stable. On the other hand, when inconsistencies are observed, we are more likely to observe changes in attitudes. Balance theory also helps explain why consumers like to be associated with positively valued objects. Forming a unit relation with a popular product (e.g., buying and wearing fashionable clothing, driving a flashy car) may improve one's chances of being included as a positive sentiment relation in other people's triads.

Finally, balance theory is useful in accounting for the widespread use of celebrities to endorse products. When a triad is not fully formed (e.g., perceptions about a new product or one about which the consumer does not yet have a well-defined attitude), the marketer can create a positive sentiment relation between the consumer

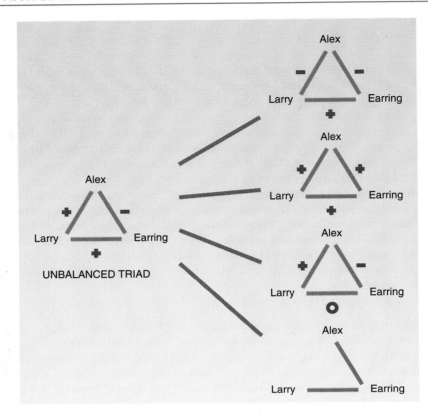

FIGURE 7–2 ■
Alternative Routes to Restoring Balance in a Triad

and the product by depicting a positive unit relation between the product and a well-known personality. In other cases, behaviors are discouraged when admired people argue against them, as is the goal when athletes appear in antidrug public service advertisements.

This "balancing act" is at the heart of celebrity endorsements, where it is hoped that the star's popularity will transfer to the product. This strategy will be considered at length in the next chapter. For now, it pays to remember that this creation of a unit relation between product and star can backfire if the public's opinion of the celebrity endorser shifts from positive to negative, as happened when Pepsi pulled an ad featuring Madonna after she was associated with a controversial music video involving religion and sex. The strategy can also cause trouble if the star–product unit relation is questioned, as happened when singer Michael Jackson, who also did promotions for Pepsi, subsequently confessed that he does not drink soda.

ATTITUDE MODELS

A consumer's overall evaluation of a product sometimes accounts for the bulk of his or her attitude. When market researchers want to assess attitudes, it can be sufficient for them to simply ask consumers, "How do you feel about Budweiser?" However, as we saw earlier, attitudes can be a lot more complex than that. One problem is that a product or service may be composed of many *attributes,* or qualities—some of these may be more important than others to particular people. Another problem is that a person's decision to act on his or her attitude is affected by other factors, such as whether it is felt that buying a product would be met with

MARKETING OPPORTUNITY

Consumers often like to publicize their connections with successful people or organizations (no matter how tenuous the connection) to enhance their own standing. In balance theory terms, they are attempting to create a unit relation with a positively valued attitude object. This tactic has been called "basking in reflected glory."[39]

For example, a series of studies performed at Arizona State University showed how students' desire to identify with a winning image—in this case, ASU's football team—influenced their consumption behaviors. After the team played a game each weekend, observers went around campus and recorded the incidence of school-related items displayed by students (e.g., ASU T-shirts, caps, etc.). The frequency of these behaviors was related to the team's performance. If the team had won, students were more likely to show off their school affiliation (basking in reflected glory) than if the team had lost. This relationship was affected by the magnitude of the win—the bigger the point spread, the more likely were observers to note a sea of ASU insignias the following Monday.

The desire to bask in reflected glory by purchasing products associated with a valued attitude object has created numerous marketing opportunities. College bookstores reap over $400 million a year by selling items bearing their school's name and logo, and the total market for collegiate licensing amounts to about $750 million annually. The UCLA bookstore alone sells $5 million worth of Bruin items a year. Many schools now license their names (usually for a 6.5 percent royalty) to get a stake in this market (see chapter 3). Because people tend to identify with successful teams, it is not surprising that the most successful licensing universities also happen to have renowned athletic programs, including Michigan, Ohio State, Florida, Penn State, Texas, Kentucky, Alabama, Florida State, Indiana, and Washington.[40]

approval by friends or family. As a result *attitude models* have been developed that try to specify the different elements that might work together to influence people's evaluations of attitude objects.

MULTIATTRIBUTE ATTITUDE MODELS

A simple response does not always tell us everything we need to know about either *why* the consumer feels a certain way toward a product, or about what marketers can do to change the consumer's attitude. For this reason, **multiattribute attitude models** have been extremely popular among marketing researchers. This type of model assumes that a consumer's attitude (evaluation) of an attitude object (A_o) will depend on the beliefs he or she has about several or many attributes of the object. The use of a multiattribute model implies that an attitude toward a product or brand can be predicted by identifying these specific beliefs and combining them to derive a measure of the consumer's overall attitude. We'll describe how these work, using the example of a consumer evaluating a complex attitude object that should be very familiar to you: a college.

Basic multiattribute models specify three elements.[41]

- *Attributes* are characteristics of the A_o. Most models assume that the relevant characteristics can be identified. That is, the researcher can include those attributes that consumers take into consideration when evaluating the A_o. For example, scholarly reputation is an attribute of a college.

- *Beliefs* are cognitions about the specific A_o (usually relative to others like it). A belief measure assesses the extent to which the consumer perceives that a brand possesses a particular attribute. For example, a student might have a belief that the University of North Carolina has a strong academic standing.

- *Importance weights* reflect the relative priority of an attribute to the consumer. Although an A_o can be considered on a number of attributes, some are likely to be more important than others (i.e., they will be given greater weight). Furthermore, these weights are likely to differ across consumers. In the case of colleges and universities, for example, one student might stress research opportunities, whereas another might assign greater weight to athletic programs.

THE FISHBEIN MODEL

The most influential multiattribute model is called the *Fishbein model,* named after its primary developer.[42] The model measures three components of attitude:

1. *Salient beliefs* people have about an A_o (i.e., those beliefs about the object that are considered during evaluation)
2. *Object–attribute linkages,* or the probability that a particular object has an important attribute
3. *Evaluation* of each of the important attributes

Note, however, that the model makes some assumptions that may not always be warranted. It assumes that we have been able to adequately specify all of the relevant attributes that, for example, a student will use in evaluating his or her choices about which college to attend. The model also assumes that he or she will go through the process (formally or informally) of identifying a set of relevant attributes, weighing them, and summing them. Although this particular decision is likely to be highly involving, it is still possible that his or her attitude will instead be formed by an overall affective response (a process known as *affect referral*).

By combining these three elements, a consumer's overall attitude toward an object can be computed (we'll see later how this basic equation has been modified to increase its accuracy). The basic formula is

$$A_{ijk} = \Sigma B_{ijk} I_{ik}$$

where

i = attribute
j = brand
k = consumer
I = the importance weight given attribute i by consumer k
B = consumer k's belief regarding the extent to which brand j possesses attribute i
A = a particular consumer's (k's) attitude score for brand j

The overall attitude score (A) is obtained by multiplying a consumer's rating of each attribute for all of the brands considered, by the importance rating for that attribute.

To see how this basic multiattribute model might work, let's suppose we want to predict which college a high school senior is likely to attend. After months of waiting, Saundra has been accepted to four schools. Because she must now decide among these, we would first like to know which attributes Saundra will consider in forming an attitude toward each school. We can then ask Saundra to assign a rating regarding how well each school performs on each attribute and also determine the relative importance of the attributes to her. An overall attitude score for each school can then be computed by summing scores on each attribute (after weighing each by its relative importance). These hypothetical ratings are shown in Table 7–1.

Based on this analysis, it seems that Saundra has the most favorable attitude toward Smith. She is clearly someone who would like to attend an all-woman's school with a solid academic reputation rather than a school that offers a strong athletic program or a party atmosphere.

STRATEGIC APPLICATIONS OF THE MULTIATTRIBUTE MODEL

Suppose you were the director of marketing for Northland College, another school Saundra was considering. How might you use the data from this analysis to improve your image?

Capitalize on Relative Advantage. If one's brand is viewed as being superior on a particular attribute, consumers like Saundra need to be convinced that this particular attribute is an important one. For example, although Saundra rates Northland's social atmosphere highly, she does not believe this attribute is a valued aspect for a college. As Northland's marketing director, you might emphasize the importance of an active social life, varied experiences, or even the development of future business contacts forged through strong college friendships.

Strengthen Perceived Product/Attribute Linkages. A marketer may discover that consumers do not equate his or her brand with a certain attribute. This problem is commonly addressed by campaigns that stress the product's qualities to consumers (e.g., "new and improved"). Saundra apparently does not think much of Northland's academic quality, athletic programs, or library facilities. You might develop an informational campaign to improve these perceptions (e.g., "little known facts about Northland").

TABLE 7–1 ■ The Basic Multiattribute Model: Saundra's College Decision

ATTRIBUTE (I)	Importance (I)	BELIEFS (B)			
		Smith	Princeton	Rutgers	Northland
Academic reputation	6	8	9	6	3
All women	7	9	3	3	3
Cost	4	2	2	6	9
Proximity to home	3	2	2	6	9
Athletics	1	1	2	5	1
Party atmosphere	2	1	3	7	9
Library facilities	5	7	9	7	2
Attitude score		163	142	153	131

Note: These hypothetical ratings are scored from 1 to 10, and higher numbers indicate "better" standing on an attribute. For a negative attribute (e.g., cost), higher scores indicate that the school is believed to have "less" of that attribute (i.e., to be cheaper).

Add a New Attribute. Product marketers frequently try to create a distinctive position from their competitors by adding a product feature. Northland College might try to emphasize some unique aspect, such as a hands-on internship program for business majors that takes advantage of ties to the local community.

Influence Competitors' Ratings. Finally, you might try to decrease the positivity of competitors. This type of action is the rationale for a strategy of *comparative advertising*. One tactic might be to publish an ad that lists the tuition rates of a number of area schools, as well as their attributes with which Northland can be favorably compared, as the basis for emphasizing the value obtained for the money at Northland.

USING ATTITUDES TO PREDICT BEHAVIOR

Although multiattribute models have been used by consumer researchers for many years, they have been plagued by a major problem: In many cases, knowledge of a person's attitude is *not* a very good predictor of behavior. In a classic demonstration of "do as I say, not as I do," many studies have obtained a very low correlation between a person's reported attitude toward something and his or her actual behavior toward it. Some researchers have been so discouraged that they have questioned whether attitudes are of any use at all in understanding behavior.[43]

This questionable linkage between attitudes and behavior can be a big headache for advertisers: Consumers can love a commercial, yet still not buy the product. For example, one of the most popular TV commercials in recent years featured basketball player Shaquille O'Neal for Pepsi. Although the company spent $67 million on this spot and other similar ones in a single year, sales of Pepsi-Cola fell by close to 2 percent, even as sales of archrival Coca-Cola increased by 8 percent in the same period.[44]

THE EXTENDED FISHBEIN MODEL

The original Fishbein model, which focused on measuring a consumer's attitude toward a product, has been extended in several ways to improve its predictive ability. The newer version is called the **theory of reasoned action.**[45] This model contains several important additions to the original, and although the model is still not perfect, its ability to predict relevant behavior has been improved.[46] Some of the modifications to this model are considered here.

INTENTIONS VERSUS BEHAVIOR

Like the motivations discussed in chapter 4, attitudes have both direction and strength. A person may like or dislike an attitude object with varying degrees of confidence or conviction. It is helpful to distinguish between firmly held attitudes and those that are more superficial, especially since an attitude held with greater conviction is more likely to be acted on.[47] One study on environmental issues and marketing activities found, for example, that people who express greater conviction in their feelings regarding environmentally responsible behaviors such as recycling show greater consistency between attitudes and behavioral intentions.[48]

However, as the old expression goes, "the road to Hell is paved with good intentions." Many factors might interfere with performance of actual behavior, even if the consumer has sincere intentions. He or she might save up with the intention of buying a stereo system. In the interim, though, any number of things could happen: losing a job, getting mugged on the way to the store, or arriving at the store to find that the desired model is out of stock. It is not surprising, then, that in some instances past purchase behavior has been found to be a better predictor of future behavior than is a consumer's behavioral intention.[49] The theory of reasoned action aims to measure behavioral intentions, recognizing that certain uncontrollable factors inhibit prediction of actual behavior.

SOCIAL PRESSURE

The theory acknowledges the power of other people in influencing behavior. Many of our behaviors are not determined in a vacuum. Much as we may hate to admit it, what we think others would *like* us to do may be more crucial than our own individual preferences.

In the case of Saundra's college choice, note that she was very positive about going to a predominantly female school. However, if she felt that this choice would be unpopular (perhaps her friends would think she was crazy), she might ignore or downgrade this preference when coming to a decision. A new element, the *subjective norm* (SN) was thus added to include the effects of what we believe other people think we should do. The value of SN is arrived at by including two other factors: (1) the intensity of a *normative belief* (NB) that others believe an action should be taken or not taken, and (2) the *motivation to comply* (MC) with that belief (i.e., the degree to which the consumer takes others' anticipated reactions into account when evaluating a course of action or a purchase).

ATTITUDE TOWARD BUYING

The model now measures **attitude toward the act of buying (A_{act})**, rather than only the attitude toward the product itself. In other words, it focuses on the perceived consequences of a purchase. Knowing how someone feels about buying or using an object turns out to be more valid than merely knowing the consumer's evaluation of the object itself.[50]

To understand this distinction, consider a problem that might arise when measuring attitudes toward condoms. Although a group of college students might have a positive attitude toward condoms, does this necessarily predict that they will buy and use them? Better prediction would be obtained by asking the students how likely they are to *buy* condoms. A person might have a positive A_o toward condoms, but A_{act} might be negative due to the embarrassment or the hassle involved.

OBSTACLES TO PREDICTING BEHAVIOR
IN THE THEORY OF REASONED ACTION

Despite improvements to the Fishbein model, problems arise when it is misapplied. In many cases, the model is used in ways for which it was not intended, or where certain assumptions about human behavior may not be warranted.[51] Other obstacles to predicting behavior include the following:

- The model was developed to deal with actual behavior (e.g., taking a diet pill), not with the *outcomes* of behavior that are instead assessed in some studies (e.g., losing weight).

- Some outcomes are beyond the consumer's control, such as when the purchase requires the cooperation of other people. For instance, a woman might *want* to get a mortgage, but this intention will be worthless if she cannot find a banker to give her one.

- The basic assumption that behavior is intentional may be invalid in a variety of cases, including impulsive acts, sudden changes in one's situation, novelty seeking, or even simple repeat buying. One study found that such unexpected events as having guests, changes in the weather, or reading articles about the healthfulness of certain foods exerted a significant effect on actual behaviors.[52]

● Measures of attitude often do not really correspond to the behavior they are supposed to predict, either in terms of the A_o or when the act will occur. One common problem is a difference in the level of *abstraction* employed. For example, knowing a person's attitude toward sports cars may not predict whether he or she will purchase a Nissan 300ZX. It is very important to match the level of specificity between the attitude and the behavioral intention.

● A similar problem relates to the *time frame* of the attitude measure. In general, the longer the time between the attitude measurement and the behavior it is supposed to assess, the weaker the relationship will be. For example, predictability would improve markedly by asking consumers the likelihood that they would buy a house in the next week as opposed to within the next five years.

● Attitudes formed by direct, personal experience with an A_o are stronger and more predictive of behavior than those formed indirectly, such as through advertising.[53] According to the *attitude accessibility perspective,* behavior is a function of the person's immediate perceptions of the A_o in the context of the situation in which it is encountered. An attitude will guide the evaluation of the object, but *only* if it is activated from memory when the object is observed. These findings underscore the importance of strategies that induce trial (e.g., by widespread product sampling to encourage the consumer to try the product at home, by taste tests, test drives, etc.) as well as those that maximize exposure to marketing communications.

TRYING TO CONSUME
Another perspective tries to address some of these problems by instead focusing on consumers' goals and what they believe is required to attain them. The *theory of trying* states that the criterion of *behavior* in the reasoned action model should be replaced with *trying* to reach a goal.[54] This perspective recognizes that additional factors might intervene between intent and performance—both personal and environmental barriers might prevent the individual from attaining the goal. For example, a person who intends to lose weight may have to deal with numerous issues: He may not believe he is capable of slimming down, he may have a roommate who loves to cook and who leaves tempting goodies lying around the apartment, his friends may be jealous of his attempts to diet and will encourage him to pig out, or he may be genetically predisposed to obesity and cutting down on calories simply will not produce the desired results.

The theory of trying includes several new components that attempt to account for the complex situations where many factors either help or hurt our changes of turning intentions into actions, as shown in Figure 7–3. These factors include the amount of control the person has over the situation, his or her expectations of success or failure in achieving the goal, social norms related to attaining the goal, and his or her attitude toward the process of trying (i.e., how the action required to attain the goal makes him or her feel, regardless of the outcome). Still other new variables are the frequency and recency of past trying of the behavior—for example, even if a person does not have specific plans to go on a diet in the next month, the frequency with which he or she has tried to do so in the recent past (and the success—however fleeting—he or she may have experienced) would be the best pre-

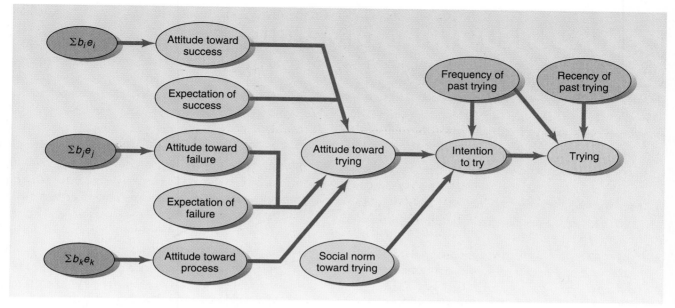

FIGURE 7–3 ■ **The Theory of Trying (TT)**
Note.—Regarding the Σbe terms, the bs are consequence likelihoods, the es are consequence evaluations; subscript i refers to consequences contingent on success, subscript j refers to consequences contingent on failure, and subscript k refers to consequences associated with the process of trying, independent of success or failure considerations. Richard P. Bagozzi and Paul R. Warshaw, "Trying to Consume," *Journal of Consumer Research* 17, 2 (September 1990): 127–140.

dictor of future attempts to shed some pounds. To predict whether someone would try to lose weight, here are a few sample issues that might be addressed:

- *Past frequency:* How many times in the past year did the person try to lose weight?
- *Recency:* Did he try to lose weight in the last week?
- *Beliefs:* Did he believe he would be healthier if he lost weight?
- *Evaluations of consequences:* Did he believe his girlfriend would be happier if he succeeded in losing weight? Did he believe his friends would make fun of him if he tried but failed to lose weight?
- *The process:* Would the diet make him uncomfortable or depressed?
- *Expectations of success and failure:* Did he believe it likely he would be able to lose weight if he tried?
- *Subjective norms toward trying:* Would the people who are important to him approve of his efforts to lose weight?

TRACKING ATTITUDES OVER TIME

An attitude survey is like a snapshot taken at a single point in time. It may tell us a lot about a brand's position at that moment, but it does not permit many inferences about progress the brand has made over time or any predictions about possible future changes in consumer attitudes. To accomplish that, it is necessary to develop an *attitude-tracking* program. This activity helps to increase the predictability of behavior by allowing researchers to analyze attitude trends over an extended period of time. It is more like a movie than a snapshot. For example, a longitudinal survey conducted by the Food Marketing Institute of consumers' attitudes toward food con-

MULTICULTURAL DIMENSIONS

The theory of reasoned action has primarily been applied in Western settings. Certain assumptions inherent in the model may not necessarily apply to consumers from other cultures. Several cultural roadblocks diminish the universality of the theory of reasoned action.

- The model was developed to predict the performance of any voluntary act. Across cultures, however, many consumer activities, ranging from taking exams and entering military service to receiving an inoculation or even choosing a marriage partner, are not necessarily voluntary.

- The relative impact of subjective norms may vary across cultures. For example, Asian cultures tend to value conformity and "face saving," so it is possible that subjective norms that involve the anticipated reactions of others to the choice will have an even greater impact on behavior for many Asian consumers. Indeed, a recent study conducted among voters in Singapore was able to predict voting for political candidates from their voting intentions, which in turn were influenced by such factors as voters' attitudes toward the candidate, attitudes toward the political party, and subjective norms—which in Singapore included an emphasis on harmonious and close ties among members of the society.[55]

- The model measures behavioral intentions, and thus presupposes that consumers are actively thinking ahead and planning future behaviors. The intention concept assumes that consumers have a linear time sense; they think in terms of past, present, and future. As will be discussed in chapter 10, this perspective on time is not held by all cultures.

- A consumer who forms an intention is (implicitly) claiming that he or she is in control of his or her actions. Some cultures (e.g., Muslim peoples) tend to be fatalistic and do not necessarily believe in the concept of free will. Indeed, one study comparing students from the United States, Jordan, and Thailand found evidence for cultural differences in assumptions about fatalism and control over the future.[56]

tent over the last decade illustrates how priorities can shift in a fairly short time.[57] Concerns about fat and cholesterol content rose dramatically during this period, while *nutritional issues* such as interest in sugar content decreased.

ONGOING TRACKING STUDIES

Attitude tracking involves the administration of an attitude survey at regular intervals. Preferably, the identical methodology is used each time so that results can be reliably compared. Several syndicated services, such as the Gallup Poll or the Yankelovich Monitor, track consumer attitudes over time (see chapter 6). Results from a tracking study of ecological attitudes among young people in a set of European countries is shown in Figure 7–4.

This activity can be extremely valuable for many strategic decisions. For example, one firm monitored changes in consumer attitudes toward one-stop financial centers. Although a large number of consumers were warm to the idea when it was first introduced, the number of people who liked the concept did not increase over time despite the millions of dollars invested in advertising to promote the centers. This finding indicated some problems with the way the concept was being presented to consumers, and the company decided to "go back to the drawing board," eventually coming up with a new way to communicate the advantages of this service.

CHANGES TO LOOK FOR OVER TIME

Some of the dimensions that can be included in attitude tracking include the following:

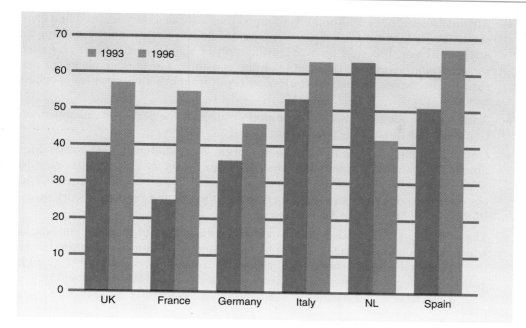

FIGURE 7–4 ■
Percentage of
16–24-Year-Olds Who
Agree "We Must Take
Radical Action to Cut
Down on How We Use
Our Cars."
Source: The Henley Centre,
Frontiers: Planning for
Consumer Change in Europe
1996/97.

- *Changes in different age groups:* Attitudes tend to change as people age (a *life-cycle effect*). In addition, *cohort effects* occur, whereby members of a particular generation tend to share certain outlooks (e.g., the yuppie). Also, *historical effects* can be observed as large groups of people are affected by profound cultural changes (such as the Great Depression or the democratization of Eastern Europe).

- *Scenarios about the future:* Consumers are frequently tracked in terms of their future plans, confidence in the economy, and so on. These measures can provide valuable data about future behavior and yield insights for public policy. For example, Americans tend to overestimate how much they will earn after retirement, which is a potentially dangerous miscalculation.

- *Identification of change agents:* Social phenomena can alter people's attitudes toward basic consumption activities over time, as when consumers' willingness to buy fur changes. Or, consumers' likelihood of desiring a divorce may be affected by such *facilitators* as changes in the legal system that make this action easier, or by *inhibitors,* such as the prevalence of AIDS and the value of two paychecks in today's economy.[58]

- An *attitude* is a predisposition to evaluate an object or product positively or negatively.
- *Social marketing* refers to attempts to change consumers' attitudes and behaviors in ways that are beneficial to the society as a whole.
- Attitudes are made up of three components: *beliefs, affect,* and *behavioral intentions.*

**CHAPTER
SUMMARY**

- Attitude researchers traditionally assumed that attitudes were learned in a fixed sequence, consisting first of the formation of beliefs (*cognitions*) regarding an attitude object, followed by some evaluation of that object (*affect*) and then some action (*behavior*). Depending on the consumer's level of involvement and the circumstances, though, attitudes can result from other hierarchies of effects as well.

- A key to attitude formation is the function the attitude plays for the consumer (e.g., is it utilitarian or ego defensive?).

- One organizing principle of attitude formation is the importance of consistency among attitudinal components—that is, some parts of an attitude may be altered to be in line with others. Such theoretical approaches to attitudes as *cognitive dissonance theory, self-perception theory,* and *balance theory* stress the vital role of the need for consistency.

- The complexity of attitudes is underscored by *multiattribute attitude models,* in which a set of beliefs and evaluations is identified and combined to predict an overall attitude. Factors such as subjective norms and the specificity of attitude scales have been integrated into attitude measures to improve predictability.

KEY TERMS

ABC model of attitudes p. 207
Affect p. 207
Attitude p. 205
Attitude object (A_o) p. 205
Attitude toward the act of buying (A_{act}) p. 223
Attitude toward the advertisement (A_{ad}) p. 211
Balance theory p. 217
Behavior p. 207

Cognition p. 207
Foot-in-the-door technique p. 216
Functional theory of attitudes p. 205
Hierarchy of effects p. 208
Latitudes of acceptance and rejection p. 216
Multiattribute attitude models p. 219

Principle of cognitive consistency p. 213
Self-perception theory p. 215
Social judgment theory p. 216
Social marketing p. 208
Theory of cognitive dissonance p. 214
Theory of reasoned action p. 222

CONSUMER BEHAVIOR CHALLENGE

1. Contrast the hierarchies of effects outlined in the chapter. How will strategic decisions related to the marketing mix be influenced by which hierarchy is operative among target consumers?

2. List three functions performed by attitudes, giving an example of how each function is employed in a marketing situation.

3. Think of a behavior someone does that is inconsistent with his or her attitudes (e.g., attitudes toward cholesterol, drug use, or even buying things to make him or her stand out or attain status). Ask the person to elaborate on why he or she does the behavior, and try to identify the way the person has resolved dissonant elements.

4. Devise an attitude survey for a set of competing automobiles. Identify areas of competitive advantage or disadvantage for each model you incorporate.

5. Construct a multiattribute model for a set of local restaurants. Based on your findings, suggest how restaurant managers can improve an establishment's image via the strategies described in the chapter.

NOTES

1. Margaret Littman, "Sponsors Take to the Court with New Women's NBA," *Marketing News* (March 3, 1997): 1 (2 pp.).

2. Chad Rubel, "Marketers Giving Better Treatment to Females," *Marketing News* (April 22, 1996): 10.

3. Robert A. Baron and Donn Byrne, *Social Psychology: Understanding Human Interaction,* 5th ed. (Boston: Allyn & Bacon, 1987).

4. Daniel Katz, "The Functional Approach to the Study of Attitudes," *Public Opinion Quarterly* 24 (Summer 1960): 163–204; Richard J. Lutz, "Changing Brand Attitudes through Modification of Cognitive Structure," *Journal of Consumer Research* 1 (March 1975): 49–59.

5. Russell H. Fazio, T. M. Lenn, and E. A. Effrein, "Spontaneous Attitude Formation," *Social Cognition* 2 (1984): 214–34.

6. Mason Haire, "Projective Techniques in Marketing Research," *Journal of Marketing* 14 (April 1950): 649–56.

7. Sharon Shavitt, "The Role of Attitude Objects in Attitude Functions," *Journal of Experimental Social Psychology* 26 (1990): 124–48; see also J. S. Johar and M. Joseph Sirgy, "Value-Expressive Versus Utilitarian Advertising Appeals: When and Why to Use Which Appeal," *Journal of Advertising* 20 (September 1991): 23–34.

8. Seymour H. Fine, *Social Marketing: Promoting the Causes of Public and Nonprofit Agencies* (Boston: Allyn & Bacon, 1990); Katryna Malafarina and Barbara Loken, "Progress and Limitations of Social Marketing: A Review of Empirical Literature on the Consumption of Social Ideas," in eds. Leigh McAllister and Michael Rothschild, *Advances in Consumer Research* 20, (Provo, UT: Association for Consumer Research, 1993): 397–404.

9. Carol Krol, "Consumers Note Marketers' Good Causes: Roper," *Advertising Age* (November 11, 1996): 51.

10. Patricia Braus, "Selling Good Behavior," *American Demographics* (November 1995): 60–4.

11. For a study that found evidence of simultaneous causation of beliefs and attitudes, see Gary M. Erickson, Johny K. Johansson, and Paul Chao, "Image Variables in Multi-Attribute Product Evaluations: Country-of-Origin Effects," *Journal of Consumer Research* 11 (September 1984): 694–9.

12. Michael Ray, "Marketing Communications and the Hierarchy-of-Effects," in ed. P. Clarke, *New Models for Mass Communications* (Beverly Hills, CA: Sage, 1973): 147–76.

13. Herbert Krugman, "The Impact of Television Advertising: Learning without Involvement," *Public Opinion Quarterly* 29 (Fall 1965): 349–56; Robert Lavidge and Gary Steiner, "A Model for Predictive Measurements of Advertising Effectiveness," *Journal of Marketing* 25 (October 1961): 59–62.

14. Punam Anand, Morris B. Holbrook, and Debra Stephens, "The Formation of Affective Judgments: The Cognitive–Affective Model versus the Independence Hypothesis," *Journal of Consumer Research* 15 (December 1988): 386–91; Richard S. Lazarus, "Thoughts on the Relations between Emotion and Cognition," *American Psychologist* 37 (1982)9: 1019–24.

15. Robert B. Zajonc, "Feeling and Thinking: Preferences Need No Inferences," *American Psychologist* 35 (1980)2: 151–75.

16. Banwari Mittal, "The Role of Affective Choice Mode in the Consumer Purchase of Expressive Products," *Journal of Economic Psychology* 4 (1988)9: 499–524.

17. Scot Burton and Donald R. Lichtenstein, "The Effect of Ad Claims and Ad Context on Attitude toward the Advertisement," *Journal of Advertising* 17 (1988)1: 3–11; Karen A. Machleit and R. Dale Wilson, "Emotional Feelings and Attitude toward the Advertisement: The Roles of Brand Familiarity and Repetition," *Journal of Advertising* 17 (1988)3: 27–35; Scott B. Mackenzie and Richard J. Lutz, "An Empirical Examination of the Structural Antecedents of Attitude toward the Ad in an Advertising Pretesting Context," *Journal of Marketing* 53 (April 1989): 48–65; Scott B. Mackenzie, Richard J. Lutz, and George E. Belch, "The Role of Attitude toward the Ad as a Mediator of Advertising Effectiveness: A Test of Competing Explanations," *Journal of Marketing Research* 23 (May 1986): 130–43; Darrel D. Muehling and Russell N. Laczniak, "Advertising's Immediate and Delayed Influence on Brand Attitudes: Considerations Across Message-Involvement Levels," *Journal of Advertising* 17 (1988)4: 23–34; Mark A. Pavelchak, Meryl P. Gardner, and V. Carter Broach, "Effect of Ad Pacing and Optimal Level of Arousal on Attitude toward the Ad," in eds. Rebecca H. Holman and Michael R. Solomon, *Advances in Consumer Research* 18 (Provo, UT: Association for Consumer Research, 1991): 94–99. Some research evidence indicates that a separate attitude is also formed regarding the brand name itself, see George M. Zinkhan and Claude R. Martin Jr., "New Brand Names and Inferential Beliefs: Some Insights on Naming New Products," *Journal of Business Research* 15 (1987): 157–72.

18. John P. Murry Jr., John L. Lastovicka, and Surendra N. Singh, "Feeling and Liking Responses to Television Programs: An Examination of Two Explanations for Media-Context Effects," *Journal of Consumer Research* 18 (March 1992): 441–51.

19. Barbara Stern and Judith Lynne Zaichkowsky, "The Impact of 'Entertaining' Advertising on Consumer Responses," *Australian Marketing Researcher* 14 (August 1991): 68–80.

20. For a recent study that examined the impact of skepticism on advertising issues, see David M. Boush, Marian Friestad, and Gregory M. Rose, "Adolescent Skepticism toward TV Advertising and Knowledge of Advertiser Tactics," *Journal of Consumer Research* 21 (June 1994): 167–75.

21. Basil G. Englis, "Consumer Emotional Reactions to Television Advertising and Their Effects on Message Recall," in eds. S. Agres, J. A. Edell, and T. M. Dubitsky, *Emotion in Advertising: Theoretical and Practical Explorations* (Westport, CT: Quorum Books, 1990): 231–54.

22. Morris B. Holbrook and Rajeev Batra, "Assessing the Role of

Emotions as Mediators of Consumer Responses to Advertising," *Journal of Consumer Research* 14 (December 1987): 404–20.

23. Marian Burke and Julie Edell, "Ad Reactions over Time: Capturing Changes in the Real World," *Journal of Consumer Research* 13 (June 1986): 114–18.

24. David A. Aaker and Donald E. Bruzzone, "Causes of Irritation in Advertising," *Journal of Marketing* 49 (Spring 1985): 47–57.

25. Herbert Kelman, "Compliance, Identification, and Internalization: Three Processes of Attitude Change," *Journal of Conflict Resolution* 2 (1958): 51–60.

26. See Sharon E. Beatty and Lynn R. Kahle, "Alternative Hierarchies of the Attitude-Behavior Relationship: The Impact of Brand Commitment and Habit," *Journal of the Academy of Marketing Science* 16 (Summer 1988): 1–10.

27. For the original work that focused on the issue of levels of attitudinal commitment, see H. C. Kelman, "Compliance, Identification, and Internalization: Three Processes of Attitude Change," *Journal of Conflict Resolution* 2 (1958): 51–60.

28. Lynn R. Kahle, Kenneth M. Kambara, and Gregory M. Rose, "A Functional Model of Fan Attendance Motivations for College Football," *Sports Marketing Quarterly V,* 4 (1996): 51–60.

29. Leon Festinger, *A Theory of Cognitive Dissonance* (Stanford, CA: Stanford University Press, 1957).

30. Chester A. Insko and John Schopler, *Experimental Social Psychology* (New York: Academic Press, 1972).

31. Robert E. Knox and James A. Inkster, "Postdecision Dissonance at Post Time," *Journal of Personality and Social Psychology* 8 (1968)4: 319–23.

32. Daryl J. Bem, "Self-Perception Theory," in ed. Leonard Berkowitz, *Advances in Experimental Social Psychology* (New York: Academic Press, 1972): 1–62.

33. Jonathan L. Freedman and Scott C. Fraser, "Compliance without Pressure: The Foot-in-the-Door Technique," *Journal of Personality and Social Psychology* 4 (August 1966): 195–202; for further consideration of possible explanations for this effect, see William DeJong, "An Examination of Self-Perception Mediation of the Foot-in-the-Door

Effect," *Journal of Personality and Social Psychology* 37 (December 1979): 221–31; Alice M. Tybout, Brian Sternthal, and Bobby J. Calder, "Information Availability as a Determinant of Multiple-Request Effectiveness," *Journal of Marketing Research* 20 (August 1988): 280–90.

34. David H. Furse, David W. Stewart, and David L. Rados, "Effects of Foot-in-the-Door, Cash Incentives and Follow-ups on Survey Response," *Journal of Marketing Research* 18 (November 1981): 473–8; Carol A. Scott, "The Effects of Trial and Incentives on Repeat Purchase Behavior," *Journal of Marketing Research* 13 (August 1976): 263–9.

35. Muzafer Sherif and Carl I. Hovland, *Social Judgment: Assimilation and Contrast Effects in Communication and Attitude Change* (New Haven, CT: Yale University Press, 1961).

36. See Joan Meyers-Levy and Brian Sternthal, "A Two-Factor Explanation of Assimilation and Contrast Effects," *Journal of Marketing Research* 30 (August 1993): 359–368.

37. Mark B. Traylor, "Product Involvement and Brand Commitment," *Journal of Advertising Research* (December 1981): 51–6.

38. Fritz Heider, *The Psychology of Interpersonal Relations* (New York: Wiley, 1958).

39. R. B. Cialdini, R. J. Borden, A. Thorne, M. R. Walker, S. Freeman, and L. R. Sloan, "Basking in Reflected Glory: Three (Football) Field Studies," *Journal of Personality and Social Psychology* 34 (1976): 366–75.

40. Howard G. Ruben, "College Stores Cash in on School Logos," *Daily News Record* (May 20, 1987): 1.

41. William L. Wilkie, *Consumer Behavior* (New York: Wiley, 1986).

42. M. Fishbein, "An Investigation of the Relationships between Beliefs about an Object and the Attitude toward that Object," *Human Relations* 16 (1983): 233–40.

43. Allan Wicker, "Attitudes versus Actions: The Relationship of Verbal and Overt Behavioral Responses to Attitude Objects," *Journal of Social Issues* 25 (Autumn 1969): 65.

44. Laura Bird, "Loved the Ad. May (or May Not) Buy the Product," *Wall Street Journal* (April 7, 1994): B1 (2 pp.).

45. Icek Ajzen and Martin Fishbein, "Attitude-Behavior Relations: A Theoretical Analysis and Review of

Empirical Research," *Psychological Bulletin* 84 (September 1977): 888–918.

46. Morris B. Holbrook and William J. Havlena, "Assessing the Real-to-Artificial Generalizability of Multi-Attribute Attitude Models in Tests of New Product Designs," *Journal of Marketing Research* 25 (February 1988): 25–35; Terence A. Shimp and Alican Kavas, "The Theory of Reasoned Action Applied to Coupon Usage," *Journal of Consumer Research* 11 (December 1984): 795–809.

47. R. P. Abelson, "Conviction," *American Psychologist*, 43 (1988): 267–75; R. E. Petty and J. A. Krosnick, *Attitude Strength: Antecedents and Consequences* (Mahwah, NJ: Erlbaum, 1995); Ida E. Berger and Linda F. Alwitt, "Attitude Conviction: A Self-Reflective Measure of Attitude Strength," *Journal of Social Behavior and Personality* 11 (1996)3: 557–72.

48. Berger and Alwitt, "Attitude Conviction."

49. Richard P. Bagozzi, Hans Baumgartner, and Youjae Yi, "Coupon Usage and the Theory of Reasoned Action," in eds. Rebecca H. Holman and Michael R. Solomon, *Advances in Consumer Research* 18 (Provo, UT: Association for Consumer Research, 1991): 24–7; Edward F. McQuarrie, "An Alternative to Purchase Intentions: The Role of Prior Behavior in Consumer Expenditure on Computers," *Journal of the Market Research Society* 30 (October 1988): 407–37; Arch G. Woodside and William O. Bearden, "Longitudinal Analysis of Consumer Attitude, Intention, and Behavior toward Beer Brand Choice," in ed. William D. Perrault Jr., *Advances in Consumer Research* 4 (Ann Arbor, MI: Association for Consumer Research, 1977): 349–56.

50. Michael J. Ryan and Edward H. Bonfield, "The Fishbein Extended Model and Consumer Behavior," *Journal of Consumer Research* 2 (1975): 118–36.

51. Blair H. Sheppard, Jon Hartwick, and Paul R. Warshaw, "The Theory of Reasoned Action: A Meta-Analysis of Past Research with Recommendations for Modifications and Future Research," *Journal of Consumer Research* 15 (December 1988): 325–43.

52. Joseph A. Cote, James McCullough, and Michael Reilly, "Effects of Unexpected Situations on Behavior-

Intention Differences: A Garbology Analysis," *Journal of Consumer Research* 12 (September 1985): 188–94.

53. Russell H. Fazio, Martha C. Powell, and Carol J. Williams, "The Role of Attitude Accessibility in the Attitude-to-Behavior Process," *Journal of Consumer Research* 16 (December 1989): 280–8; Robert E. Smith and William R. Swinyard, "Attitude-Behavior Consistency: The Impact of Product Trial versus Advertising," *Journal of Marketing Research* 20 (August 1983): 257–67.

54. Richard P. Bagozzi and Paul R. Warshaw, "Trying to Consume," *Journal of Consumer Research* 17 (September 1990)2: 127–40.

55. Kulwant Singh, Siew Meng Leong, Chin Tiong Tan, and Kwei Cheong Wong, "A Theory of Reasoned Action Perspective of Voting Behavior: Model and Empirical Test," *Psychology & Marketing* 12 (January 1995)1: 37–51.

56. Joseph A. Cote and Patriya S. Tansuhaj, "Culture Bound Assumptions in Behavior Intention Models," in ed. Thom Srull, *Advances in Consumer Research* 16 (Provo, UT: Association for Consumer Research, 1989): 105–9.

57. Barbara Presley Noble, "After Years of Deregulation, a New Push to Inform the Public," *New York Times* (October 27, 1991): F5.

58. Matthew Greenwald and John P. Katosh, "How to Track Changes in Attitudes," *American Demographics* (August 1987): 46.

FOR CELE, THE UNTHINKABLE was about to happen. Here she was, her mouth wrapped around a big stogie. A few short months ago, Cele believed that cigars were only smoked by large, foul-smelling men in loud plaid pants. Lately, though, her attitudes have started to change. First, her friend Mary Ann returned from a trip to Europe and reported that cigar smoking among women was definitely more commonplace there than in the United States. Then, she seemed to be reading more and more news stories about famous women lighting up. The clincher was coming across her heroine, supermodel Linda Evangelista, on the cover of *Cigar Aficionado*—somehow knowing that such an elegant woman as Linda was a cigar fan put to rest any anxieties Cele had about sacrificing her femininity if she took a puff now and then.

Apparently, many women have taken up cigars for as a way to navigate the "old boy network," and as a new form of rebellion. Cele didn't care too much about that, but she did find she actually liked to kick back after a good meal and savor the taste. Seemingly overnight, her beliefs about the un-savory characteristics of cigar smokers had changed—and several of her friends admired her brazenness for lighting up in public. She even went so far as to surf the net for more information about cigar products. She particularly liked the www.cigar.com site, through which she could link with several cigar retailers, read about people's experiences with different brands, and even access short stories about cigars. As Cele closed her eyes and exhaled a long plume of rich blue-gray smoke, fantasies of an illicit trip to Havana to acquire the real article began to fill her head. . . .

AUTUMN 1995   CANADA $5.95•U.K. £4 $4.95

CIGAR
Aficionado

LINDA EVANGELISTA

SUPER SUPERMODEL

RATING CHURCHILLS: OUR BIGGEST TASTING EVER

TRAVEL GUIDE TO CUBA

PLUS SCHLESINGER, STEREOS, BUTLERS, COFFEE AND MUCH MORE

8

Attitude Change and Interactive Communications

CHANGING ATTITUDES THROUGH COMMUNICATION

The signs are everywhere—women across the country are joining men in their scramble to spend time in smoke-filled cigar bars. Some restaurants like Morton's of Chicago steakhouse have sponsored women-only smokers to promote this trend. *Cigar Aficionado,* the bible of the craze, reached a circulation of more than 410,000 in 1997. The hip-hop set has even taken up the habit—cigars are showing up on videos and album covers, including Wu-Tang Clan's CD, *Wu-Tang Forever.* The industry estimates that by 1997 women constituted 1 to 5 percent of the market—not a huge proportion but certainly more significant than in the past. The Consolidated Cigar Corporation picked up early on this sea change and introduced its Cleopatra Collection, featuring cigars tapered at both ends to make it easier for women to light and hold in their mouths.[1]

Prominent women from Marlene Dietrich to Madonna have sported cigars for their shock value and to communicate an image of rebellion and political incorrectness. More recently, though, the cigar industry itself has climbed on the bandwagon as some savvy marketers realized the potential to nurture a new market by persuading "everyday" women such as Cele to light up. Of course, inspiring such a radical change in behavior first required an equally drastic change in the way women felt about the tobacco product and their beliefs about the type of people who indulged.

Consumers are constantly bombarded by messages inducing them to change their attitudes. These persuasion attempts can range from logical arguments to graphic pictures, and from intimidation by peers to exhortations by celebrity spokespeople. And, communications flow both ways—the consumer may seek out information sources in order to learn more about these options (as Cele did by surfing the net).

This chapter will review some of the factors that help to determine the effectiveness of such communication devices. Our focus will be on some basic aspects of communication that specifically help to determine how and if attitudes will be created or modified. This objective relates to **persuasion,** which refers to an active attempt to change attitudes. Persuasion is, of course, the central goal of many marketing communications.

Of course, persuasion attempts can work in negative ways, too. Due in part to the current cigar hoopla, more than a quarter of American teens have smoked a cigar in the past year, according to the Centers for Disease Control and Prevention. The Director of CDC's Office on Smoking and Health laments, "Everywhere you turn, there's a cigar bar or a cigar shop. Kids are very perceptive of what they think cool adults do."[2] The American Cancer Society is attempting some persuasion of its own by putting out an ad suggesting that the trendy cigar cutters many converts are buying to clip their stogies could also be used to excise lip tumors.[3] As with many other products, the battle for consumers' pocketbooks (and in this case, their lungs) will be largely fought on the media battleground by savvy communicators.

DECISIONS, DECISIONS: TACTICAL COMMUNICATIONS OPTIONS

Suppose that a cigar company wants to create an advertising campaign for a new product targeted to female smokers. As it plans this campaign, it must develop a message that will create desire for the cigar by potential customers—many of whom (like Cele) have been raised to believe that smelly, nasty cigars are about the last thing with which a woman would want to be caught dead. To craft persuasive messages that might change this attitude, a number of questions must be answered:

- Who will be featured smoking a cigar in an ad? Should it be linked to a glamorous celebrity? A career woman? A rock star? The source of a message helps to determine consumers' acceptance of it as well as their desire to try the product.

- How should the message be constructed? Should it emphasize the negative consequences of being left out when others are hanging out at the cigar bar? Should it directly compare the cigar with others already on the market, or maybe present a fantasy in which a tough-minded female executive meets a dashing stranger while ducking out of a board meeting to grab a smoke?

- What media should be used to transmit the message? Should it be depicted in a print ad? On television? Sold door to door? If a print ad is produced, should it be run in the pages of *Vogue*? *Good Housekeeping*? *Cigar Aficionado*? Sometimes *where* something is said can be as important as *what* is said. Ideally, the attributes of the product should be matched to those of the medium. For example, magazines with high prestige are more effective at communicating messages about overall product image and quality, whereas specialized, expert magazines do a better job at conveying factual information.[4]

- What characteristics of the target market might influence the ad's acceptance? If targeted users are frustrated in their daily lives, these women might be more receptive to a fantasy appeal. If they don't smoke cigars or don't know anyone who does, they may not pay any attention to a traditional cigar ad at all.

THE ELEMENTS OF COMMUNICATION

Marketers and advertisers have traditionally tried to understand how marketing messages can change consumers' attitudes by thinking in terms of the **communications model,** which specifies that a number of elements are necessary for communication to be achieved. In this model, a *source* must choose and encode a message (i.e., initiate the transfer of meaning by choosing appropriate symbolic images that represent that meaning). For example, the publishers of *Cigar Aficionado* magazine attempted to send the message that it's "cool" for women to light up by highlighting famous females who are cigar fans.

This meaning must be put in the form of a *message.* There are many ways to say something, and the structure of the message has a big effect on how it is perceived. In the example shown at the beginning of this chapter, a visual image of a well-known supermodel holding a cigar spoke a thousand words about the sexiness and trendiness of the habit.

The message must be transmitted via a *medium,* which could be television, radio, magazines, billboards, personal contact, or even a matchbook cover. In this case, the message appeared in a specialized magazine targeted to current—and prospective—cigar smokers. The message is then decoded by one or more *receivers,* Cele for instance, who interpret the symbols in light of their own experiences. Finally, *feedback* must be received by the source, who uses the reactions of receivers to modify aspects of the message. Favorable reactions by readers led *Cigar Aficionado* to continue to feature prominent women within its pages. The traditional communications process is depicted in Figure 8–1.

AN UPDATED VIEW: INTERACTIVE COMMUNICATIONS

Although the traditional communications model is not entirely wrong, it also doesn't tell the whole story—especially in today's dynamic world of interactivity, in which consumers have many more choices available to them and greater control over which messages they will choose to process.[5] The traditional model was developed to understand mass communications, in which information is transferred from a producer (source) to many consumers (receivers) at one time—typically via print, television, or radio. This perspective essentially views advertising as the process of transferring information to the buyer before a sale. A message is seen as perishable—it is repeated (perhaps frequently) for a fairly short period of time and then it "vanishes" as a new campaign eventually takes its place.

This model was strongly influenced by a group of theorists known as the *Frankfurt School,* which dominated mass communications research for most of this century. In this view, the media exert direct and powerful effects on individuals, and often are used by those in power to brainwash and exploit the population. The receiver is basically a passive being—a "couch potato" who simply is the receptacle for many messages—and who is often duped or persuaded to act based on the information he or she is "fed" by the media.

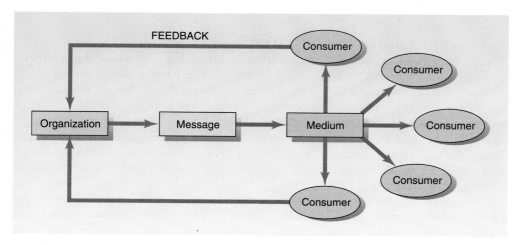

FIGURE 8–1 ■ The Traditional Communications Model

USES AND GRATIFICATIONS

Is this an accurate picture of the way we relate to marketing communications? Proponents of **uses and gratifications theory** argue instead that consumers constitute an active, goal-directed audience that draws on mass media as a resource to satisfy needs. Instead of asking what media do *for* or *to* people, they ask what people do *with* the media.[6]

The uses and gratifications approach emphasizes that media compete with other sources to satisfy needs, and that these needs include diversion and entertainment as well as information. This also means that the line between marketing information and entertainment is continuing to blur—especially as companies are being forced to design more attractive retail outlets, catalogs, and Web sites in order to attract consumers. For example, Toyota's Web site (www.toyota.com) provides a lot more than the latest specs about available engine horsepower options; it also addresses interests like gardening, travel, and sports.

In a twist on the traditional communications model, thanks to the World Wide Web consumers can now turn the tables and become publishers themselves. "Webzines," collections of articles, photos, and graphics typically created by amateurs, have blossomed on the Web. These creations have a small but fiercely loyal readership and began to attract corporate sponsors following the introduction of *HotWired,* the online sister of *Wired* magazine.[7] Since it costs no more to electronically distribute 30 million copies than it does one, there is plenty of room for small niche markets. Webzines cover everything from city nightlife (*Total New York*) to the punk rock scene (*Intrrr Nrrrd*) to extremely focused groups such as FaT GiRL, which is designed exclusively for overweight lesbians.

Research with young people in Great Britain finds that they rely on advertising for many gratifications including entertainment (some report that the "adverts" are better than the programs), escapism, play (some report singing along with jingles, others make posters out of magazine ads), and self-affirmation (ads can reinforce their own values or provide role models). It's important to note that this perspective is not arguing that media play a uniformly positive role in our lives, only that recipients are making use of the information in a number of ways. For example, marketing messages have the potential to undermine self-esteem as consumers use the media to establish unrealistic standards for behavior, attitudes, or even their own appearance. A comment by one study participant illustrates this negative impact. She observes that when she's watching TV with her boyfriend, ". . . really, it makes you think 'oh no, what must I be like?' I mean you're sitting with your boyfriend and he's saying 'oh, look at her. What a body!'"[8]

WHO'S IN CHARGE OF THE REMOTE?

Whether for good or bad, though, exciting technological and social developments certainly are forcing us to rethink the picture of the passive consumer, as people increasingly are playing a proactive role in communications. In other words, they are to a greater extent becoming partners—rather than potatoes—in the communications process. Their input is helping to shape the messages they and others like them receive, and furthermore they may seek out these messages rather than sit home and wait to see them on TV or in the paper (just as Cele surfed the net to get more information about cigars). This updated approach to interactive communications is illustrated in Figure 8–2.

Consider, for example, an interactive music sampling kiosk called the iStation. In 300 retail locations, the installation offers on-line information and sound bites from more than 37,000 recordings. Consumers can also listen to cuts from a CD sit-

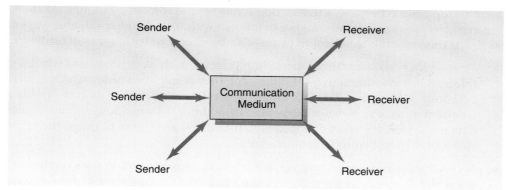

FIGURE 8–2 ■
**Interactive
Communication Model**
Adapted from Donna L.
Hoffman and Thomas P.
Novak, "Marketing in
Hypermedia Computer-
Mediated Environments:
Conceptual Foundations,"
Journal of Marketing 60,
(July 1996): 350–68, Fig. 4.

ting on a store shelf by passing a laser over its bar code—essentially choosing which products they wish to sample, rather than being spoon-fed the Top 40 of that week. Users must register with the company, giving information about their musical preferences, ethnic background, and electronics usage in the home. The company then uses the data it obtains to send targeted mailings informing subscribers of upcoming concerts and releases tailored to their musical preferences.[9]

One of the early signs of this communications revolution was the humble hand-held remote control device. As VCRs began to be commonplace in homes, suddenly consumers had more input into what they wanted to watch—and when. No longer were they at the mercy of the TV networks to decide when to see their favorite shows, and neither did they necessarily have to forsake a show because it conflicted with another's time slot.

Since that time, of course, our ability to control our media environment has mushroomed. Many people have access to video-on-demand or pay-per-view TV. Home-shopping networks encourage us to call in and discuss our passion for cubic zirconium jewelry live on the air. Caller ID devices and answering machines allow us to decide if we will accept a phone call during dinner, and to know the source of the message before picking up the phone. A bit of Web surfing allows us to identify kindred spirits around the globe, to request information about products, and even to provide suggestions to product designers and market researchers.

For example, a technology called the *radio data system* (R.D.S.) allows a radio station to transmit data on the unused portion of its frequency, known as a subcarrier. The system has been adopted in Europe by the British Broadcasting Corporation and is slowly coming to the United States. R.D.S. is the concept behind Coupon Radio, a car radio system now being tested that lets listeners "capture" information and give stations and advertisers feedback about their choices. A driver who hears a new song he or she likes could request more information about the musicians, or this person could also get the names and addresses of retailers that sell an advertised product.[10]

LEVELS OF INTERACTIVE RESPONSE

A key to understanding the dynamics of interactive marketing communications is to consider exactly what is meant by a response.[11] The early perspective on communications primarily regarded feedback in terms of behavior—did the recipient run out and buy the laundry detergent after being exposed to an ad for it?

However, a variety of other responses are possible as well, including building awareness of the brand, informing us about product features, reminding us to buy a new package when we've run out, and—perhaps most importantly—building a long-term relationship. Therefore a transaction is *one* type of response, but forward-thinking marketers realize that customers can interact with them in other valuable ways as well. For this reason it is helpful to distinguish between two basic types of feedback.

- *First-order response:* Direct marketing vehicles such as catalogs and television infomercials are interactive—if successful, they result in an order, which is most definitely a response! So, let's think of a product offer that directly yields a transaction as a *first-order response*. In addition to providing revenue, sales data are a valuable source of feedback that allow marketers to gauge the effectiveness of their communications efforts.

- *Second-order response:* However, a marketing communication does not have to immediately result in a purchase to be an important component of interactive marketing. Messages can prompt useful responses from customers, even though these recipients do not necessarily place an order immediately after being exposed to the communication. Customer feedback in response to a marketing message that is not in the form of a transaction is a *second-order response*.

A second-order response may take the form of a request for more information about a product, service, or organization, or perhaps receipt of a "wish list" from the customer that specifies the types of product information he or she would like to get in the future. This response may even be in the form of recommendations for other potential customers: MCI's Friends & Family program, for example, offers a 20 percent discount to customers who give them the names of people they call regularly. The phone company then targets these people with promotion messages to get *them* to switch to MCI.

A second-order response program called the Pepperidge Farm No Fuss Pastry Club illustrates how a firm communicates directly with users without trying to make an immediate sale. The club boasts more than 30,000 members that have been generated through a combination of promotion efforts, including a magazine mail-in offer, an offer on packages of Pepperidge Farm products, publicity created by news reports about the club, and a sign-up form available in grocery stores. Pepperidge Farm uses surveys to determine members' attitudes toward issues related to its business, and the company also collects valuable information on how these people actually use frozen puff pastry products.[12] Although the company's immediate goal is not to generate the first-order response of selling frozen pastry, it knows that the second-order responses received from club members will result in loyal customers over time—and many more first-order responses down the line as a result.

THE SOURCE

Regardless of whether a message is received by "snail mail" (net-heads' slang for the postal service) or e-mail, common sense tells us that the same words uttered or written by different people can have very different effects. Research on *source effects* has been carried out for over 30 years. By attributing the same message to different sources and measuring the degree of attitude change that occurs after listeners hear it, it is possible to determine which aspects of a communicator will induce attitude change.[13]

Under most conditions, the source of a message can have a big impact on the likelihood the message will be accepted. The choice of a source to maximize attitude change can tap into several dimensions. The source can be chosen because he or she is an expert, attractive, famous, or even a "typical" consumer who is both likable and trustworthy. Two particularly important source characteristics are *credibility* and *attractiveness*.[14]

SOURCE CREDIBILITY

Source credibility refers to a source's perceived expertise, objectivity, or trustworthiness. This dimension relates to consumers' beliefs that a communicator is competent, and he or she is willing to provide the necessary information to adequately evaluate competing products. A credible source can be particularly persuasive when the consumer has not yet learned much about a product or formed an opinion of it.[15] The decision to pay an expert or a celebrity to tout a product can be a very costly one, but researchers have concluded that on average the investment is worth it simply because the announcement of an endorsement contract is often used by market analysts to evaluate a firm's potential profitability, thereby affecting its expected return. On average, then, the impact of endorsements on stock returns appears to be so positive that it offsets the cost of hiring the spokesperson.[16]

BUILDING CREDIBILITY

Credibility can be enhanced if the souce's qualifications are perceived as somehow relevant to the product being endorsed. This linkage can overcome other objections people may have to the endorser or the product. When former baseball pitcher Jim Palmer endorsed Jockey International products, his athleticism was instrumental in reassuring men that it was acceptable for them to wear skimpy underwear in unusual colors.[17] Similarly, Ronald Biggs, whose claim to fame was his 1963 role in "The Great Train Robbery" in the United Kingdom, successfully served as a spokesman in Brazil for a company that makes door locks—a topic about which he is presumably knowledgeable![18]

SOURCE BIASES

A consumer's beliefs about a product's attributes can be weakened if the source is perceived to be the victim of bias in presenting information.[19] *Knowledge bias* implies that a source's knowledge about a topic is not accurate. *Reporting bias* occurs when

MARKETING PITFALL

TV programs such as news or talk shows are generally thought to have more credibility than a commercial because they are assumed to be impartial and thus low in reporting bias. The line between objective programming and commercials, however, has been blurring over the last decade with the proliferation of *infomercials* on cable and broadcast television. These are half-hour or hour commercials that may resemble a program, but in actuality are intended to sell products, like rock-and-roll collections or self-help courses. They often feature a celebrity such as singer Dionne Warwick's Psychic Friends Network, a very successful program that lets viewers call psychics on a 900 number.[20]

One of the hottest infomercials in 1997 was a half-hour spot for the Sobakawa pillow, which is filled with buckwheat husks—a material favored by the Japanese to relieve neck pain. When the American manufacturers brought the pillow to the United States, they produced a $250,000 infomercial that took no chances by featuring both a credible source and an attractive one—a doctor of Oriental medicine alongside Jennilee Harrison, who starred in the popular TV show *Three's Company.*[21]

The Federal Trade Commission has taken action against several infomercial producers when it decided their programs had the potential to be deceptive because viewers might believe the infomercial is a *bona fide* show. Some viewers have sued TV stations for losses when they were deceived by the advertisers. To avoid these problems, some infomercial producers and television stations voluntarily include a disclaimer to avoid lawsuits claiming deception or FTC actions. But because people tend to switch channels frequently, they still may not be aware of the show's bias if it resembles a talk show or a news feature and the label or disclaimer appears only at the start of the show.[22] That makes it more likely that a lot of attitudes about psychics, pillows, or painkillers will be influenced by this evolving communications format.

a source has the required knowledge, but his or her willingness to convey it accurately is compromised, as when a star tennis player is paid by a racket manufacturer to use its products exclusively. The source's credentials might be appropriate, but the fact that the expert is perceived as a "hired gun" compromises believability. In a controversial campaign for Maxwell House coffee, TV newscasters Linda Ellerbee and Willard Scott plugged the product in a setting resembling a news show and critics charged that this endorsement compromised their objectivity as journalists.[23]

SOURCE ATTRACTIVENESS

Source attractiveness refers to the source's perceived social value. This quality can emanate from the person's physical appearance, personality, social status, or his or her similarity to the receiver (we like to listen to people who are like us).

STAR POWER: CELEBRITIES AS COMMUNICATIONS SOURCES

The sight of a supermodel holding a cigar had a big impact on Cele's attitudes toward cigar smoking. The use of celebrity endorsers is an expensive but common strategy—as golfing sensation Tiger Woods discovered when Nike signed him as its premiere endorser in 1997. A celebrity endorsement strategy can pay off handsomely.[24]

To stimulate demand for milk, an industry trade group tapped a huge range of celebrities to show off their milk mustaches.

BETTER GET YOURS BEFORE SHAQ GETS IT ALL.

A celebrity endorsement strategy can be an effective way to differentiate among similar products; this is especially important when consumers do not perceive many actual differences among competitors, as often occurs when brands are in the mature stage of the product life cycle. That explains why Coca-Cola and Pepsi rely heavily upon celebrity endorsements as they battle each other for market share. Coca-Cola's stable of endorsers include hockey player Wayne Gretzky, singer George Michael, model Elle MacPherson, Roger Rabbit, and the rap group Run-DMC. In turn, Pepsi has enlisted the aide of hoopster Shaquille O'Neal, singer David Bowie, actor Michael J. Fox, pitcher Dwight Gooden, Madonna, and Tina Turner, among many others.

When Panasonic sponsored the R&B group Earth, Wind & Fire, for example, position the radio/cassette player market rose from last to first in a short time.[25]

When used properly, famous or expert spokespeople can be of great value in improving the fortunes of a product. Celebrities increase awareness of a firm's advertising and enhance both company image and brand attitudes.[26] One reason for this effectiveness is that consumers are better able to identify products that are associated with a spokesperson.[27]

More generally, star power works because celebrities embody *cultural meanings*—they symbolize important categories such as status and social class (a "working-class heroine," such as Roseanne), gender (a "manly man," such as Sylvester Stallone), age (the boyish Michael J. Fox), and even personality types (the eccentric Kramer on *Seinfeld*). Ideally, the advertiser decides what meanings the product should convey (that is, how it should be positioned in the marketplace), and then chooses a celebrity who has come to embody a similar meaning. The product's meaning thus moves from the manufacturer to the consumer, using the star as a vehicle.[28]

Famous people can be effective because they are credible, attractive, or both, depending on the reasons for their fame. Computer guru Bill Gates is unlikely to be

MULTICULTURAL DIMENSIONS

Some celebrities choose to maintain their credibility by endorsing products only in other countries, so these ads will not be seen by consumers in their own land. Many celebrities who do not do many American advertisements appear frequently in Japan. Mel Gibson endorses Asahi beer, Sly Stallone appears for Kirin beer, Sean Connery plugs Ito hams, and the singer Sheena Easton—dressed in a kimono and wig was featured in ads for Shochu liquor. Even the normally reclusive comedian and film director Woody Allen was featured in a campaign for a large Tokyo department store.[29]

a "sex symbol," but he may be quite effective at influencing people's attitudes toward unrestricted access to the Internet. On the other hand, game show star Vanna White may not be perceived as highly expert, but she might be a persuasive source for a message about perfume or clothing.

The effectiveness of celebrities as communications sources often depends on their perceived credibility. Consumers may not trust a celebrity's motives for endorsing a product, or they may question the star's competence to critically evaluate the product's claims. The lack of credibility is aggravated by incidences in which celebrities endorse products that they do not really believe in, or in some cases do not use. After Pepsi paid over $5 million to singer Michael Jackson in an endorsement deal, the company was not pleased by his later confession that he doesn't drink soda—and cola fans weren't too impressed either.[30]

Another potential problem is what to do about celebrity endorsers who "misbehave." Pepsi had to abandon its sponsorship of Michael Jackson after the singer was accused of child molestation, and the company had to drop boxer Mike Tyson following allegations of wife beating. Madonna met a similar fate following the release of her controversial *Like a Prayer* music video. Then, of course, there's O. J. Simpson. . . . To avoid some of these problems, most endorsement contracts now contain a morality clause that allows the company to release the celebrity if so warranted.[31] Still, some advertisers are looking a lot more favorably at animated spokescharacters such as Bugs Bunny, who tend to stay out of trouble!

"WHAT IS BEAUTIFUL IS GOOD"

Almost everywhere we turn, beautiful people are trying to persuade us to buy or do something. Our society places a very high premium on physical attractiveness, and we tend to assume that people who are good-looking are smarter, cooler, and happier. Such an assumption is called a *halo effect,* which occurs when persons who rank high on one dimension are assumed to excel on others as well. The effect can be explained in terms of the consistency principle discussed in chapter 7, which states that people are more comfortable when all of their judgments about a person go together. This notion has been termed the "what is beautiful is good" stereotype.[32]

MARKETING PITFALL

For celebrity campaigns to be effective, the endorser must have a clear and popular image. In addition, the celebrity's image and that of the product he or she endorses should be similar—this is known as the **match-up hypothesis.**[33] Many promotional strategies employing stars fail because the endorser has not been selected very carefully—some marketers just assume that because a person is "famous" he or she will serve as a successful spokesperson.

The images of celebrities can, however, be pretested to increase the probability of consumer acceptance. One widely used technique is the so-called *Q rating* (Q stands for quality) developed by a market research company. This rating considers two factors in surveys: consumers' level of familiarity with a name, and the number of respondents who indicate that a person, program, or character is a favorite. Although it yields a rather rough measure, the Q rating acknowledges that mere familiarity with a celebrity's name is not sufficient to gauge popularity, because some widely known people also are widely disliked. Celebrities with low Q ratings include athlete Bruce Jenner, Michael Jackson, Gene Simmons, Wayne Newton, Madonna, and Cyndi Lauper. Some with high ratings are Stevie Wonder, Billy Joel, Phil Collins, George Michael, Whitney Houston, Cher, and Dolly Parton.[34] However, even a high Q rating does not guarantee success if the celebrity's specific image doesn't match up with the featured product.

A physically attractive source tends to facilitate attitude change. His or her degree of attractiveness exerts at least modest effects on consumers' purchase intentions or product evaluation.[35] How does this happen?

One explanation is that physical attractiveness functions as a cue that facilitates or modifies information processing by directing consumers' attention to relevant marketing stimuli. Some evidence indicates that consumers pay more attention to ads that contain attractive models, though not necessarily to the ad copy.[36] In other words, an ad with a beautiful person may stand a better chance of getting noticed but not necessarily read. We may enjoy looking at a beautiful or handsome person, but these positive feelings do not necessarily affect product attitudes or purchase intentions.[37]

Beauty can also function as a source of information. The effectiveness of highly attractive spokespeople in ads appears to be largely limited to those situations in which the advertised product is overtly related to attractiveness or sexuality.[38] The *social adaptation perspective* assumes that information seen to be instrumental in forming an attitude will be more heavily weighted by the perceiver. We filter out irrelevant information to minimize cognitive effort.

Under the right circumstances, an endorser's level of attractiveness constitutes a source of information instrumental to the attitude change process and thus functions as a central, task-relevant cue.[39] An attractive spokesperson, for this reason, is more likely to be an effective source when the product is relevant to attractiveness. For example, attractiveness affects attitudes toward ads about perfume or cologne (where attractiveness is relevant) but not toward coffee ads, where attractiveness is not.

CREDIBILITY VERSUS ATTRACTIVENESS

How do marketing specialists decide whether to stress credibility or attractiveness when choosing a message source? There should be a match between the needs of the recipient and the potential rewards offered by the source. When this match occurs, the recipient is more motivated to process the message. People who tend to be sensitive about social acceptance and the opinions of others, for example, are more persuaded by an attractive source, whereas those who are more internally oriented are swayed by a credible, expert source.[40]

The choice may also depend on the type of product. A positive source can help to reduce risk and increase message acceptance overall, but particular types of sources are more effective at reducing different kinds of risk. Experts are effective at changing attitudes toward utilitarian products that have high *performance risk,* such as vacuums (i.e., they may be complex and not work as expected). Celebrities are more effective when they focus on products such as jewelry and furniture that have high *social risk;* the user of such products is aware of their effect on the impression others have of him or her. Finally, "typical" consumers, who are appealing sources because of their similarity to the recipient, tend to be most effective when providing real-life endorsements for everyday products that are low risk, such as cookies.[41]

THE SLEEPER EFFECT

Although in general more positive sources tend to increase attitude change, exceptions can occur. Sometimes a source can be obnoxious or disliked and still manage to be effective at getting the product's message across. A case in point is Mr. Whipple, the irritating but well-known television character who for many years scolded toilet paper shoppers, "Please don't squeeze the Charmin!"

In some instances the differences in attitude change between positive sources and less positive sources seem to get erased over time. After a while people appear to "forget" about the negative source and wind up changing their attitudes anyway. This process is known as the **sleeper effect.**[42]

The explanation for the sleeper effect is a subject of debate, as is the more basic question regarding whether and when it really exists. Initially, the *dissociative cue hypothesis* proposed that over time the message and the source become disassociated in the consumer's mind. The message remains on its own in memory, causing the delayed attitude change.[43]

A more recent explanation is the *availability-valence hypothesis,* which emphasizes the selectivity of memory owing to limited capacity.[44] If the associations linked to the negative source are less available than those linked to the message information, the residual impact of the message enhances persuasion. Consistent with this view, the sleeper effect has been obtained only when the message was encoded deeply; it had stronger associations in memory than did the source.[45]

THE MESSAGE

A major study of over 1,000 commercials identified factors that appear to determine whether or not a commercial message will be persuasive. The single most important feature was whether the communications contained a brand-differentiating message. In other words, did the communication stress a unique attribute or benefit of the product? Other good and bad elements are depicted in Table 8–1.[46]

Characteristics of the message itself help to determine its impact on attitudes. These variables include *how* the message is said as well as *what* is said. Some of the issues facing marketers include the following:

- Should the message be conveyed in words or pictures?
- How often should the message be repeated?
- Should a conclusion be drawn, or should this be left up to the listener?
- Should both sides of an argument be presented?
- Is it effective to explicitly compare one's product to competitors?
- Should a blatant sexual appeal be used?
- Should negative emotions, such as fear, ever be aroused?
- How concrete or vivid should the arguments and imagery be?
- Should the ad be funny?

SENDING THE MESSAGE

The saying "one picture is worth more than ten thousand words" captures the idea that visual stimuli can economically deliver big impact, especially when the communicator wants to influence receivers' emotional responses. For this reason, advertisers often place great emphasis on vivid and creative illustrations or photography.[47]

On the other hand, a picture is not always as effective at communicating factual information. Ads that contain the same information, presented in either visual or verbal form, have been found to elicit different reactions. The verbal version affects ratings on the utilitarian aspects of a product, whereas the visual version affects aesthetic evaluations.[48] Verbal elements are more effective when reinforced by an accompanying picture, especially if the illustration is *framed* (the message in the picture is strongly related to the copy).[49]

TABLE 8–1 ■ **Positive and Negative Effects of Elements in Television Commercials**

POSITIVE EFFECTS	NEGATIVE EFFECTS
Showing convenience of use	Extensive information on components, ingredients, or nutrition
Showing new product or improved features	
Casting background (i.e., people are incidental to message)	Outdoor setting (message gets lost)
	Large number of on-screen characters
Indirect comparison to other products	Graphic displays
Demonstration of the product in use	
Demonstration of tangible results (e.g., bouncy hair)	
An actor playing the role of an ordinary person	
No principal character (i.e., more time is devoted to the product)	

Source: Adapted from David W. Stewart and David H. Furse, "The Effects of Television Advertising Execution on Recall, Comprehension, and Persuasion," *Psychology & Marketing* 2 (Fall 1985): 135–60. Copyright © 1985 by John Wiley & Sons, Inc. Reprinted by permission.

Because it requires more effort to process, a verbal message is most appropriate for high-involvement situations, such as in print contexts in which the reader is motivated to really pay attention to the advertising. Because verbal material decays more rapidly in memory, more frequent exposures are needed to obtain the desired effect. Visual images, in contrast, allow the receiver to *chunk* information at the time of encoding (see chapter 3). Chunking results in a stronger memory trace that aids retrieval over time.[50]

Which one makes a
beer taste great?

☐ Blondes in bikinis
☐ Sports stars
☐ Catchy jingles
☐ Snow-capped mountains

Just being the best is enough.

This ad pokes fun at the typical elements one would expect to see in a persuasive communication targeted to beer drinkers.

Visual elements may affect brand attitudes in one of two ways. First, the consumer may form inferences about the brand and change his or her beliefs because of an illustration's imagery. For example, people in a study who saw an ad for a facial tissue accompanied by a photo of a sunset were more likely to believe that the brand came in attractive colors. Second, brand attitudes may be affected more directly; for example, a strong positive or negative reaction elicited by the visual elements will influence the consumer's attitude toward the ad (A_{ad}), which will then affect brand attitudes (A_b). This *dual component model* of brand attitudes is illustrated in Figure 8–3.[51]

VIVIDNESS
Both pictures and words can differ in *vividness.* Powerful descriptions or graphics command attention and are more strongly embedded in memory. The reason may be because they tend to activate mental imagery, whereas abstract stimuli inhibit this process.[52] Of course, this effect can cut both ways: Negative information presented in a vivid manner may result in more negative evaluations at a later time.[53]

The concrete discussion of a product attribute in ad copy also influences the importance of that attribute, because more attention is drawn to it. For example, the copy for a watch that read "According to industry sources, three out of every four watch breakdowns are due to water getting into the case" was more effective than this version: "According to industry sources, many watch breakdowns are due to water getting into the case."[54]

REPETITION
Repetition can be a two-edged sword for marketers. As noted in chapter 3, multiple exposures to a stimulus are usually required for learning (especially conditioning) to occur. Contrary to the saying "familiarity breeds contempt," people tend to like things that are more familiar to them, even if they were not that keen on them initially.[55] This is known as the *mere exposure* phenomenon. Positive effects for advertising repetition are found even in mature product categories—repeating product information has been shown to boost consumers' awareness of the brand, even though nothing new has been said.[56] On the other hand, as we saw in chapter 2 too much repetition creates *habituation,* whereby the consumer no longer pays attention to the stimulus because of fatigue or boredom. Excessive exposure can cause *advertising wear-out,* which can result in negative reactions to an ad after seeing it too much.[57]

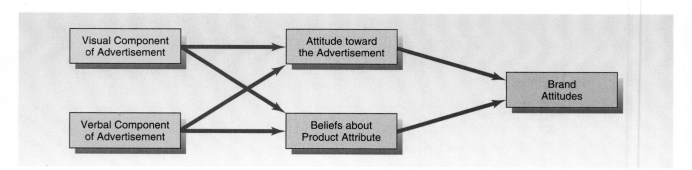

FIGURE 8–3 ■ **Effects of Visual and Verbal Components of Advertisements on Brand Attitudes**
Source: Andrew A. Mitchell, "The Effect of Verbal and Visual Components of Advertisements on Brand Attitudes and Attitude toward the Advertisement," *Journal of Consumer Research* 13 (June 1986): 21. Reprinted by permission of The University of Chicago Press.

The fine line between familiarity and boredom has been explained by the **two-factor theory**, which proposes that two separate psychological processes are operating when a person is repeatedly exposed to an ad. The positive side of repetition is that it increases familiarity and thus reduces uncertainty about the product. The negative side is that over time boredom increases with each exposure. At some point the amount of boredom incurred begins to exceed the amount of uncertainty reduced, resulting in wear-out. This pattern is depicted in Figure 8–4. Its effect is especially pronounced when each exposure is of a fairly long duration (such as a 60-second commercial).[58]

The theory implies that advertisers can overcome this problem by limiting the amount of exposure per repetition (such as using 15-second spots). They can also maintain familiarity but alleviate boredom by slightly varying the content of ads over time through campaigns that revolve around a common theme, although each spot may be different. Recipients who are exposed to varied ads about the product absorb more information about product attributes and experience more positive thoughts about the brand than do those exposed to the same information repeatedly. This additional information allows the person to resist attempts to change his or her attitude in the face of a counterattack by a competing brand.[59]

CONSTRUCTING THE ARGUMENT

Many marketing messages are similar to debates or trials, in which someone presents arguments and tries to convince the receiver to shift his or her opinion accordingly. The way the argument is presented can thus be very important.

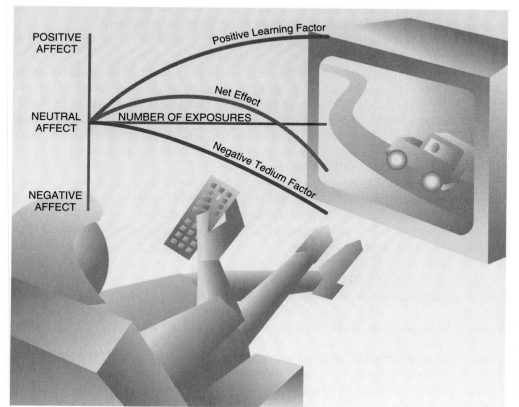

FIGURE 8–4 ■ Two-Factor Theory and Advertising Wear-out
Source: Adapted from Arno J. Rathans, John L. Swasy, and Lawrence Marks, "Effects of Television Commercial Repetition. Receiver Knowledge," *Journal of Marketing Research* 23 (February 1986): 50–61, Figure 1. By permission of American Marketing Association.

ONE- VERSUS TWO-SIDED ARGUMENTS

Most messages merely present one or more positive attributes about the product or reasons to buy it. These are known as *supportive arguments.* An alternative is to use a *two-sided message,* in which both positive and negative information is presented. Research has indicated that two-sided ads can be quite effective, yet they are not widely used.[60]

Why would a marketer want to devote advertising space to publicizing a product's negative attributes? Under the right circumstances, the use of *refutational arguments,* in which a negative issue is raised and then dismissed, can be quite effective. This approach can increase source credibility by reducing reporting bias. Also, people who are skeptical about the product may be more receptive to a balanced argument instead of a "whitewash."[61] In one novel application, a Chateau Potelle winery ad included both positive and negative reviews of a wine by two experts. The ad suggested that consumers develop their own taste rather than relying on reviews in wine magazines.[62]

This is not to say that the marketer should go overboard in presenting major problems with the product. In the typical refutational strategy, relatively minor attributes are discussed that may present a problem or fall short when compared with competitors. These drawbacks are then refuted by emphasizing positive, important attributes. For example, Avis got a lot of mileage out of claiming to be only the "No. 2" car rental company, whereas an ad for Volkswagen woefully described one of its cars as a "lemon" because there was a scratch on the glove compartment chrome strip.[63]

A two-sided strategy appears to be the most effective when the audience is well educated (and presumably more impressed by a balanced argument).[64] It is also best to use when receivers are not already loyal to the product; "preaching to the converted" about possible drawbacks may raise doubts unnecessarily.

DRAWING CONCLUSIONS

A related factor is the issue of whether the argument should draw conclusions, or whether the points should merely be presented, permitting the consumer to arrive at his or her own. Should the message only say "Our brand is superior," or should it add "You should buy our brand"? On the one hand, consumers who make their own inferences instead of having them spoon-fed will form stronger, more accessible attitudes. On the other, leaving the conclusion ambiguous increases the chance that the desired attitude will not be formed.

The response to this issue depends on the consumers' motivation to process the ad and the complexity of the arguments. If the message is personally relevant, people will pay attention to it and spontaneously form inferences. However, if the arguments are hard to follow or consumers' motivation to follow them is lacking, it is safer for the ad to draw conclusions.[65]

COMPARATIVE ADVERTISING

In 1971, the FTC issued guidelines that encouraged advertisers to name competing brands in their ads. This action was taken to improve the information available to consumers in ads, and indeed recent evidence indicates that at least under some conditions this type of presentation does result in more informed decision making.[66] **Comparative advertising** refers to a strategy in which a message compares two or more specifically named or recognizably presented brands and makes a comparison of them in terms of one or more specific attributes.[67] For example, Schering-Plough claimed that "New OcuClear relieves three times longer than Visine," and Bristol-

Myers stated that "New Liquid Vanish really does clean tough rust stains below the water line better than Lysol." This strategy can cut both ways, especially if the sponsor depicts the competition in a nasty or negative way. Although some comparative ads result in desired attitude change or positive A_{ad}, they have also been found to be lower in believability and may result in more source derogation (i.e., the consumer may doubt the credibility of a biased presentation).[68] Indeed, in some cultures (such as Asia) comparative advertising is rare because people find such a confrontational approach offensive.

Comparative ads do appear to be effective in the case of new products. Here, they are superior in anchoring a new brand closer to a dominant one and in building a clear brand image. However, if the aim is to compare the new brand with the market leader in terms of specific product attributes, merely saying it is as good or better than the leader is not sufficient. For example, the use of the claim "Spring has the same fluoride as Crest" in a study resulted in attitude change for the fictitious product, but the more global statement "Preferred by Europeans in comparison with Crest" did not.[69]

TYPES OF MESSAGE APPEALS

The *way* something is said can be as significant as *what* is said—the same idea can be encoded in many different ways. It can tug at the heartstrings or scare you, make you laugh, make you cry, or leave you wanting to learn more. In this section, we'll review the major alternatives available to communicators who wish to *appeal* to a message recipient.

EMOTIONAL VERSUS RATIONAL APPEALS

A few years ago, both Toyota and Nissan introduced a large luxury car that sold for over $40,000. The two companies chose very different ways to communicate their product's attributes, as seen in the ads shown here. Toyota's advertising for its Lexus model used a rational appeal, with ads concentrating on the large number of technical advancements incorporated in the car's design. Print ads were dominated by copy describing these engineering features.

MARKETING PITFALL

Many consumers are skeptical about claims made or implied in advertising, and some ads are challenged after being aired, either by the government, by concerned citizens, or by a competitor. About half of those challenged are either modified or taken off the air completely. In some cases, the company makes an attempt to correct the misinformation. An example is a recent Volvo ad that was challenged by the Texas attorney general's office. In an ad showing a row of cars being crushed by a pickup truck, only the Volvo was unharmed; but the investigation revealed that the Volvo used in the ad had been specially reinforced for the shoot. The company later ran ads acknowledging that the dramatization had been faked.

When a marketer makes a specific comparative claim relative to a competing product, he or she must be prepared for the possibility that the rival company will respond with a lawsuit. Many companies have gotten involved in complex lawsuits after using the comparative approach, and the costs of such litigation are high for both parties. As one judge who was involved in a 10-year court battle being fought between two makers of rival analgesics noted, "Small nations have fought for their very survival with less resources."

As a result of these and other incidents, marketers are learning to exercise extra care when making product claims, and some are beginning to supply disclaimers to protect themselves against lawsuits.[70]

These ads demonstrate rational versus emotional message appeals. At the time of the initial ad campaign for the new Infiniti automobiles, the ads for rival Lexus (top) emphasized design and engineering, while the ads for Infiniti (bottom) did not even show the car.

In sharp contrast, Nissan's controversial campaign for its Infiniti used an emotional appeal. The new model was introduced with a series of print and television ads that did not even discuss the car at all. The ads instead focused on the Zen-like experience of driving and featured long shots of serene landscapes. As one executive involved with the campaign explained, "We're not selling the skin of the car; we're selling the spirit."[71] Although these ads were innovative, most American consumers had trouble grasping the Japanese conception of luxury, which diverged sharply from U.S. associations with sleekly dressed, high-powered executives surrounded by creature comforts. Later ads for the Infiniti emphasized functional features of the car to compensate for this initial confusion.

The goal of an emotional appeal is to establish a connection between the product and the consumer, a strategy known as *bonding*.[72] Emotional appeals have the potential to increase the chance the message will be perceived, they may be more likely to be retained in memory, and they can also increase the consumer's involvement with the product. Although Nissan's gamble on emphasizing the aesthetic aspects of its product did not pay off in this case, other emotional appeals are quite effective—indeed, a later Nissan campaign revolves around a mysterious, impish man in a baseball cap who appears at the end of offbeat vignettes that have little to do with the company's actual cars.

Many companies turned to an emotional strategy after realizing that consumers do not find many differences among brands, especially those in well-established, mature categories. Ads for products ranging from cars (Lincoln Mercury) to cards (Hallmark) focus instead on emotional aspects. Mercury's capitalization on emotional attachments to old rock songs succeeded in lowering the median age of their consumers for some models by 10 years.[73]

The precise effects of rational versus emotional appeals are hard to gauge. Although recall of ad contents tends to be better for "thinking" ads than for "feeling" ads, conventional measures of advertising effectiveness (e.g., day-after recall) may not be adequate to assess cumulative effects of emotional ads. These open-ended measures are oriented toward cognitive responses, and feeling ads may be penalized because the reactions are not as easy to articulate.[74]

Emotional appeals can make a strong impression, but they also run the risk of not getting across an adequate amount of product-related information. This potential problem is reminding some advertisers that the arousal of emotions is functional only to the extent that it sells the product. Procter & Gamble's original ads for Bounce fabric softener showed a happy young couple dancing to the Van Halen song "Jump," with the message that Bounce is for clothes "you can't wait to jump into." In later spots, a woman discusses why the product makes her clothes feel and smell better. It is still somewhat emotional and experiential, but the main selling point of "softness without static cling" is driven home.[75]

SEX APPEALS

Under the assumption that "sex sells," many marketing communications for everything from perfumes to autos feature heavy doses of erotic suggestions that range from subtle hints to blatant displays of skin. Of course, the prevalence of sex appeals varies from country to country (see chapter 17). Bare flesh is so much a part of French advertising that a minor backlash is brewing as some critics complain the advertising industry is making sex boring![76] Perhaps not surprisingly, female nudity in print ads generates negative feelings and tension among female consumers, whereas men's reactions are more positive.[77] In a case of turnabout being fair play, another study found that males dislike nude males in ads, whereas females responded well to undressed males—but not totally nude ones.[78]

Does sex work? Although the use of sex does appear to draw attention to an ad, its use may actually be counterproductive to the marketer. Ironically, a provocative picture can be *too* effective; it attracts so much attention that it hinders processing and recall of the ad's contents. Sexual appeals appear to be ineffective when used merely as a "trick" to grab attention. They do, however, appear to work when the product is *itself* related to sex. Overall, though, use of a strong sexual appeal is not very well received.[79]

 # MULTICULTURAL DIMENSIONS

Nike is the master craftsman of "in your face" emotional messages about sports that barely acknowledge the shoes they are trying to sell. These appeals have played very well in the United States, but now the company has hit some bumps in the road as it tries to export this attitude overseas. As the company searches for new markets, it is trying to conquer soccer the way it did basketball. An ad in *Soccer America* magazine announced the impending invasion: "Europe, Asia, and Latin America: Barricade your stadiums. Hide your trophies. Invest in some deodorant." This message was not very well received in some soccer quarters, and similarly a successful American TV commercial featuring Satan and his demons playing soccer against Nike endorsers was banned by some European stations on the grounds that it was too scary for children to see and offensive to boot. A British TV ad featuring a French soccer player saying how his spitting at a fan and insulting his coach won him a Nike contract resulted in a scathing editorial against Nike in the sport's international federation newsletter. Nike has a tough task ahead of it: to win over European soccer fans where rival Adidas is king—in a game that traditionally doesn't have the glitz and packaging of basketball. Now a bit chastized, Nike is modifying its "question authority" approach as it tries to win over the sports organizations in countries that don't appreciate its violent messages and antiestablishment themes. Only time will tell if the athletic giant will get "red-carded" by European fans and game officials.[80]

HUMOROUS APPEALS

The use of humor can be tricky, particularly since what is funny to one person may be offensive or incomprehensible to another. Specific cultures may have different senses of humor and use funny material in diverse ways. For example, commercials in the United Kingdom are more likely to use puns and satire than they are in the United States.[81]

Does humor work? Overall, humorous advertisements do get attention. One study found that recognition scores for humorous liquor ads were better than average. However, the verdict is mixed as to whether humor affects recall or product attitudes in a significant way.[82] One function it may play is to provide a source of *distraction*. A funny ad inhibits the consumer from counterarguing, thereby increasing the likelihood of message acceptance.[83]

Humor is more likely to be effective when the brand is clearly identified and the funny material does not "swamp" the message. This danger is similar to that of beautiful models diverting attention from copy points. Subtle humor is usually better, as is humor that does not make fun of the potential consumer. Finally, humor should be appropriate to the product's image. An undertaker or a bank might want to avoid humor, but other products adapt to it quite well. Sales of Sunsweet pitted prunes improved dramatically based on the claim, "Today the pits, tomorrow the wrinkles."[84]

An antismoking public service campaign recently sponsored by the State of Arizona illustrates how humor can be used to transmit a serious message to an audience that may not be otherwise receptive to it. In a television commercial, a teenager

This Dutch economy hotel relies on a bit of earthy humor to poke fun at the basic services it provides to guests.

sitting in a movie theater with his date spits gooey chewed tobacco in a cup. His date, who doesn't realize this, reaches over and takes a drink. The caption says, "Tobacco: a tumor-causing, teeth-staining, smelly, puking habit." The campaign is also selling merchandise with the slogan through its Smelly, Puking Habit Merchandise Center.[85]

FEAR APPEALS

Fear appeals emphasize the negative consequences that can occur unless the consumer changes a behavior or an attitude. In 1997, Schering-Plough placed ads that read, "A government panel has determined some laxatives may cause cancer." The ads implicated Ex-Lax, a rival brand, even though the Food and Drug Administration hadn't made a final determination regarding this issue (Ex-Lax eventually did withdraw the product to reformulate it after the FDA decided to ban its active ingredient).[86] Recently, Advil used the same tactic by suggesting Tylenol can damage the livers of heavy drinkers.[87] A fear strategy is widely used in marketing communications, though more commonly in social marketing contexts in which organizations are encouraging people to convert to a healthier lifestyle by quitting smoking, using contraception, relying on a designated driver, and so on.

In addition to preying on anxieties about physical risk, some fear appeals are directed toward social risk—this tactic has half-jokingly been called the "slice-of-death" approach to communications. For example, an advertisement might address people's concerns about losing their jobs in bad economic times. A spot for Contact cold medicine depicted a construction worker laboring in a rainstorm despite having a bad cold because he wanted to keep his job; the spot was developed after interviews with about 800 consumers revealed widespread anxieties about unemployment.[88]

Does fear work? Most research on this topic indicates that these negative appeals are usually most effective when only a moderate threat is used, and when a solution to the problem is presented (otherwise, consumers will tune out the ad since they can do nothing to solve the problem).[89] This approach also works better when source credibility is high.[90]

When a weak threat is ineffective, this may be because there is insufficient elaboration of the harmful consequences of engaging in the behavior. When a strong threat doesn't work, it may be because *too much* elaboration interferes with the processing of the recommended change in behavior—the receiver is too busy thinking of reasons why the message doesn't apply to him or her to pay attention to the offered solution.[91]

A study that manipulated subjects' degree of anxiety about AIDS, for example, found that condom ads were evaluated most positively when a moderate threat was used. In this context, copy that promoted the use of the condom because "Sex is a risky business" (moderate threat) resulted in more attitude change than either a weaker threat that instead emphasized the product's sensitivity, or a strong threat that discussed the certainty of death from AIDS.[92] Similarly, scare tactics have not been as effective as hoped in getting teen-agers to decrease their use of alcohol or drugs. Teens simply tune out the message or deny its relevance to them.[93] On the other hand, a study of adolescent responses to social versus physical threat appeals in drug prevention messages found that social threat is a more effective strategy.[94]

Some of the research on fear appeals may be confusing a threat (the literal content of a message, such as saying "engage in safe sex or die") with fear (an emotional response to the message). According to this argument, greater fear does result in greater persuasion—but not all threats are equally effective because different people will respond differently to the same threat. Therefore, the strongest threats are not always the most persuasive because they may not have the desired impact on the perceiver. For example, raising the specter of AIDS is about the strongest threat that can be delivered to sexually active kids—but this tactic is only effective if the kids believe they will get the disease. Since many young people (especially those who live in fairly affluent suburban or rural areas) don't believe that "people like them" will be exposed to the AIDS virus, this strong threat may not actually result in a high level of fear.[98] The bottom line is that more precise measures of actual fear responses are needed before definitive conclusions can be drawn about the impact of fear appeals on consumption decisions.

THE MESSAGE AS ART FORM: METAPHORS BE WITH YOU

Marketers may be thought of as storytellers who supply visions of reality similar to those provided by authors, poets, and artists. These communications take the form of stories because the product benefits they describe are intangible and must be given tangible meaning by expressing them in a form that is concrete and visible. Advertising creatives rely (consciously or not) on various literary devices to communicate these meanings. For example, a product or service might be personified by a character such as Mr. Goodwrench, the Jolly Green Giant, or the California Raisins. Many ads take the form of an *allegory,* a story told about an abstract trait or concept that has been personified as a person, animal, or vegetable.

This Australian toothpaste ad uses a mild fear appeal to make its point about the consequences of not brushing one's teeth after every meal.

A **metaphor** involves placing two dissimilar objects into a close relationship such that "A is B" whereas a simile compares two objects, "A is like B." This is accomplished because A and B, however seemingly dissimilar, share some quality that is, in turn, highlighted by the metaphor. Metaphors allow the marketer to activate meaningful images and apply them to everyday events. In the stock market, "white knights" battle "hostile raiders" using "poison pills," Tony the Tiger allows us to equate cereal with strength, and the Merrill Lynch bull sends the message that the company is "a breed apart."[99]

Resonance is another type of literary device that is frequently used in advertising. It is a form of presentation that combines a play on words with a relevant picture. Table 8–2 gives some examples of actual ads that rely on the principle of resonance. Whereas metaphor substitutes one meaning for another by connecting two things that are in some way similar, resonance uses an element that has a double meaning, such as a pun where there is a similarity in the sound of a word but a difference in meaning. For example, an ad for a diet strawberry shortcake dessert might bear the copy "berried treasure" so that qualities associated with buried treasure—being rich, hidden, and associated with adventurous pirates—are conveyed for the brand. Because the text departs from expectations, it creates a state of tension or uncertainty on the part of the viewer until he or she figures out the word play. Once the consumer "gets it," he or she may prefer the ad over a more straightforward message.[100]

FORMS OF STORY PRESENTATION

Just as a story can be told in words or pictures, the way the audience is addressed can also differ. Commercials are structured similarly to other art forms, borrowing conventions from literature and art as they communicate their messages.[101]

One important distinction is between a *drama* and a *lecture*.[102] A lecture is like a speech in which the source speaks directly to the audience in an attempt to inform them about a product or persuade them to buy it. Because a lecture clearly implies an attempt at persuasion, the audience will regard it as such. Assuming listeners are motivated to do so, the merits of the message will be weighed, along with the credibility of the source. Cognitive responses, such as counterargumentation, will occur. The appeal will be accepted to the extent that it overcomes objections and is congruent with a person's beliefs.

TABLE 8–2 ■ Some Examples of Advertising Resonance

PRODUCT/HEADLINE	VISUAL
Embassy Suites: "This Year, We're Unwrapping Suites by the Dozen"	Chocolate kisses with hotel names underneath each
Toyota auto parts: "Our Lifetime Guarantee May Come as a Shock"	Man holding a shock absorber
Bucks filter cigarettes: "Herd of These?"	Cigarette pack with a picture of a stag
Bounce fabric softener: "Is There Something Creeping up behind You?"	Woman's dress bunched up on her back due to static
Pepsi: "This Year, Hit the Beach Topless"	Pepsi bottle cap lying on the sand
ASICS athletic shoes: "We Believe Women Should Be Running the Country"	Woman jogging in a rural setting

Source: Adapted from Edward F. McQuarrie and David Glen Mick, "On Resonance: A Critical Pluralistic Inquiry into Advertising Rhetoric," *Journal of Consumer Research* 19 (September 1992): 182, Table 1. Reprinted with permission of The University of Chicago Press.

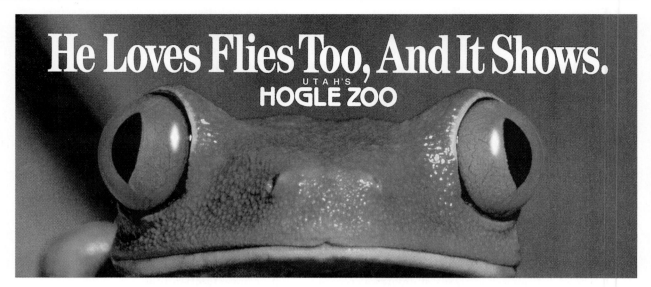

Some messages "work" by playing off of others. For such a message to be effective, however, the perceiver must be aware of the original meaning and make the connection. This ad assumes the viewer is familiar with Delta Airlines' long-running slogan, "We love to fly, and it shows."

In contrast, a drama is similar to a play or movie. Whereas an argument holds the viewer at arm's length, a drama draws the viewer into the action. The characters only indirectly address the audience; they interact with each other about a product or service in an imaginary setting. Dramas attempt to be experiential—to involve the audience emotionally. In *transformational advertising,* the consumer associates the experience of product usage with some subjective sensation. Thus, ads for the Infiniti attempted to transform the "driving experience" into a mystical, spiritual event.

THE SOURCE VERSUS THE MESSAGE: SELL THE STEAK OR THE SIZZLE?

Two major components of the communications model, the source and the message, have been reviewed. Which aspect has the most impact on persuading consumers to change their attitudes? Should marketers worry more about *what* is said, or *how* it's said and *who* says it?

The answer is, it depends. Variations in a consumer's level of involvement, as discussed in chapter 4, result in the activation of very different cognitive processes when a message is received. Research indicates that this level of involvement will determine which aspects of a communication are processed. The situation appears to resemble a traveler who comes to a fork in the road: One or the other path is chosen, and this choice has a big impact on the factors that will make a difference in persuasion attempts.

THE ELABORATION LIKELIHOOD MODEL

The **elaboration likelihood model (ELM)** assumes that once a consumer receives a message he or she begins to process it.[103] Depending on the personal relevance of this information, the receiver will follow one of two routes to persuasion. Under conditions of high involvement, the consumer takes the *central route to persuasion.* Under conditions of low involvement, a *peripheral route* is taken instead. This model is diagrammed in Figure 8–5.

THE CENTRAL ROUTE TO PERSUASION

When the consumer finds the information in a persuasive message to be relevant or somehow interesting, he or she will carefully attend to the message content. The person is likely to actively think about the arguments presented and generate *cognitive responses* to these arguments. On hearing a radio message warning about drinking while pregnant, an expectant mother might say to herself, "She's right. I really should stop drinking alcohol now that I'm pregnant." Or, she might offer counterarguments, such as "That's a bunch of baloney. My mother had a cocktail every night when she was pregnant with me, and I turned out fine." If a person generates counterarguments in response to a message, it is less likely that he or she will yield to the message, whereas the generation of further supporting arguments by the consumer increases the probability of compliance.[104]

The central route to persuasion is likely to involve the traditional hierarchy of effects, as discussed in chapter 7. Beliefs are carefully formed and evaluated, and strong attitudes that result will be likely to guide behavior. The implication is that message factors, such as the quality of arguments presented, will be important in determining attitude change. Prior knowledge about a topic results in more thoughts about the message and also increases the number of counterarguments.[105]

THE PERIPHERAL ROUTE TO PERSUASION

In contrast, the peripheral route is taken when the person is not motivated to really think about the arguments presented. Instead, the consumer is likely to use other cues in deciding on the suitability of the message. These cues might include the product's package, the attractiveness of the source, or the context in which the message is presented. Sources of information extraneous to the actual message content are called *peripheral cues* because they surround the actual message.

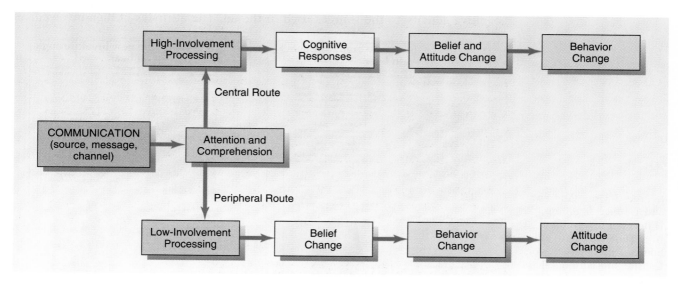

FIGURE 8-5 ■ The Elaboration Likelihood Model of Persuasion
Reprinted with the permission of Macmillan Publishing Company from *Consumer Behavior,* 2d. ed., by John C. Mowen. Copyright © 1990 by Macmillan Publishing Company.

The peripheral route to persuasion highlights the paradox of low involvement discussed in chapter 4: When consumers do not care about a product, the stimuli associated with it *increase* in importance. The implication here is that low-involvement products may be purchased chiefly because the marketer has done a good job in designing a "sexy" package, choosing a popular spokesperson, or perhaps just creating a pleasant shopping environment.

SUPPORT FOR THE ELM MODEL

The ELM model has received a lot of research support.[106] In a typical study, undergraduates were exposed to one of several mock advertisements for Break, a new brand of low-alcohol beer. Using the technique of *thought listing,* they were asked to provide their thoughts about the ads, which were later analyzed by the researchers. Two versions of the ads are shown here.[107] Three independent variables crucial to the ELM model were manipulated.

1. *Message-processing involvement:* Some subjects were motivated to be highly involved with the ads. They were promised a gift of low-alcohol beer for participating in the study and were told that the brand would soon be available in their area. Low-involvement subjects, who were not promised a gift, were told that the brand would be introduced in a distant area.

2. *Argument strength:* One version of the ad used strong, compelling arguments to drink Break (e.g., "Break contains one-half of the amount of alcohol of regular beers and, therefore, has less calories than regular beer. . . ."), whereas the other listed only weak arguments (e.g., "Break is just as good as any other regular beer").

3. *Source characteristics:* Both ads contained a photo of a couple drinking the beer, but their relative social attractiveness was varied by their dress, their posture and nonverbal expressions, and the background information given about their educational achievements and occupations.

Consistent with the ELM model, high-involvement subjects had more thoughts related to the ad messages than did low-involvement subjects, who devoted more cognitive activity to the sources used in the ad. The attitudes of high-involvement

Source: J. Craig Andrews and Terence A. Shimp, "Effects of Involvement, Argument, Strength, and Source Characteristics on Central and Peripheral Processing in Advertising," *Psychology & Marketing* 7 (Fall 1990): 195–214.

subjects were more likely to be swayed by powerful arguments, whereas the attitudes of low-involvement subjects were more likely to be influenced by the ad version using attractive sources. The results of this study, paired with numerous others, indicate that the relative effectiveness of a strong message and a favorable source depends on consumers' level of involvement with the product being advertised.

These results underscore the basic idea that highly involved consumers look for the "steak" (e.g., strong, rational arguments). Those who are less involved are more affected by the "sizzle" (e.g., the colors and images used in packaging or endorsements by famous people). It is important to remember, however, that the *same* communications variable can be both a central and a peripheral cue, depending on its relation to the attitude object. The physical attractiveness of a model might serve as a peripheral cue in a car commercial, but her beauty might be a central cue for a product such as shampoo, as the product's benefits are directly tied to enhancing attractiveness.[108]

CHAPTER SUMMARY

- *Persuasion* refers to an attempt to change consumers' attitudes.

- The *communications model* specifies the elements needed to transmit meaning. These include a source, message, medium, receiver, and feedback.

- The traditional view of communications tends to regard the perceiver as a passive element in the process. Proponents of the *uses and gratifications approach* instead regard the consumer as an active participant who uses media for a variety of reasons.

- New developments in interactive communications highlight the need to consider the active roles a consumer might play in obtaining product information and building a relationship with a company. A product-related communication that directly yields a transaction is a *first-order response.* Customer feedback in response to a marketing message that is not in the form of a transaction is a *second-order response.* This may take the form of a request for more information about a good, service, or organization, or perhaps receipt of a "wish list" from the customer that specifies the types of product information he or she would like to get in the future.

- Two important characteristics that determine the effectiveness of a source are its *attractiveness* and *credibility.* Although celebrities often serve this purpose, their credibility is not always as strong as marketers hope.

- Some elements of a message that help to determine its effectiveness are whether it is conveyed in words or pictures, whether an emotional or a rational appeal is employed, the frequency with which it is repeated, whether a conclusion is drawn, whether both sides of the argument are presented, and whether the message includes fear, humor, or sexual references.

- Advertising messages often incorporate elements from art or literature such as dramas, lectures, metaphors, allegories, and resonance.

- The relative influence of the source versus the message depends on the receiver's level of involvement with the communication. The *elaboration likelihood model* specifies that a less-involved consumer will more likely be swayed by source effects, whereas a more-involved consumer will more likely attend to and process components of the actual message.

KEY TERMS

Communications model p. 234
Comparative advertising p. 248
Elaboration likelihood model (ELM) p. 256

Fear appeals p. 253
Match-up hypothesis p. 255
Metaphor p. 255
Persuasion p. 233
Resonance p. 255
Sleeper effect p. 244

Source attractiveness p. 240
Source credibility p. 239
Two-factor theory p. 247
Uses and gratifications theory p. 236

CONSUMER BEHAVIOR CHALLENGE

1. A government agency wants to encourage the use of designated drivers by people who have been drinking. What advice could you give the organization about constructing persuasive communications? Discuss some factors that might be important, including the structure of the communications, where they should appear, and who should deliver them. Should fear appeals be used, and if so, how?

2. Are infomercials ethical? Should marketers be allowed to use any format they want to present product-related information?

3. Discuss some conditions in which it would be advisable to use a comparative advertising strategy.

4. Why would a marketer consider saying negative things about his or her product? When is this strategy feasible? Can you find examples of it?

5. A marketer must decide whether to incorporate rational or emotional appeals in its communications strategy. Describe conditions that are more favorable to using one or the other.

6. Collect ads that rely on sex appeal to sell products. How often are benefits of the actual product communicated to the reader?

7. To observe the process of counterargumentation, ask a friend to talk out loud while watching a commercial. Ask him or her to respond to each point in the ad or to write down reactions to the claims made. How much skepticism regarding the claims can you detect?

8. Make a log of all the commercials shown on one network television channel over a two-hour period. Categorize each according to product category, and whether they are presented as drama or argument. Describe the types of messages used (e.g., two-sided arguments), and keep track of the types of spokespeople (e.g., TV actors, famous people, animated characters). What can you conclude about the dominant forms of persuasive tactics currently employed by marketers?

9. Collect examples of ads that rely on the use of metaphors or resonance. Do you feel these ads are effective? If you were working with the products, would you feel more comfortable with ads that use a more straightforward, "hard-sell" approach? Why or why not?

10. Create a list of current celebrities whom you feel typify cultural categories (e.g., clown, mother figure, etc.). What specific brands do you feel each could effectively endorse?

11. Locate current advertisements featuring models that correspond to each of the "looks" described in the chapter. Are these models correctly matched vis à vis the brand personalities with which they are linked?

12. Recently the American Medical Association encountered a firestorm of controversy when it agreed to sponsor a line of health care products manufactured by Sunbeam (a decision it later revised). Should trade or professional organizations, journalists, professors, and others who are entrusted to objectively evaluate information be permitted to endorse products?

NOTES

1. Tim Triplett, "Women and Cigars: Puffery or Promise?" *Marketing News* (December 4, 1995):1 (3 pp.).

2. Quoted in "Cigars Attracting Teen-Age Smokers," *Montgomery Advertiser* (May 23, 1997): 8A.

3. Kendall Hamilton, "Blowing Smoke," *Newsweek* (July 21,1997): 54 (7 pp.).

4. Gert Assmus, "An Empirical Investigation into the Perception of Vehicle Source Effects," *Journal of Advertising* 7 (Winter 1978): 4–10; for a more thorough discussion of the pros and cons of different media, see Stephen Baker, *Systematic Approach to Advertising Creativity* (New York: McGraw-Hill, 1979).

5. Alladi Venkatesh, Ruby Roy Dholakia, and Nikhilesh Dholakia, "New Visions of Information Technology and Postmodernism: Implications for Advertising and Marketing Communications," in eds. Walter Brenner and Lutz Kolbe, *The Information Superhighway and Private Households: Case Studies of Business Impacts* (Heidelberg: Physical-Verlag, 1996): 319–37; Donna L. Hoffman and Thomas P. Novak, "Marketing in Hypermedia Computer-Mediated Environments: Conceptual Foundations," *Journal of Marketing* 60 (July 1996)3: 50–68; for an early theoretical discussion of interactivity in communications paradigms, see R., Aubrey Fisher, *Perspectives on Human Communication* (New York: Macmillan, 1978).

6. First proposed by Elihu Katz, "Mass Communication Research and the Study of Popular Culture: An Editorial Note on a Possible Future for this Journal," *Studies in Public Communication, 2* (1959): 1–6. For a recent discussion of this approach, see Stephanie O'Donohoe, "Advertising Uses and Gratifications," *European Journal of Marketing* 28 (1994)8/9: 52–75.

7. Joshua Quittner, "Hot 'Zines on the Web," *Time* (September 4, 1995): 64.

8. Quoted in O'Donohoe, "Advertising Uses and Gratifications," p. 66.

9. Alice Z. Cuneo, "With an 'i' toward Music Lovers," *Advertising Age* (August 29, 1994): 18.

10. Michael Wilke, "A Radio Entrepreneur Reaches for the Interactive Age," *New York Times* (September 4, 1994): F7.

11. This section is adapted from a discussion in Michael R. Solomon and Elnora W. Stuart, *Marketing: Real People, Real Choices* (Upper Saddle River, NJ: Prentice Hall, 1997.)

12. Thomas L. Harris, "PR Gets Personal," *Direct Marketing* (April 1994): 29–32.

13. Carl I. Hovland and W. Weiss, "The Influence of Source Credibility on Communication Effectiveness," *Public Opinion Quarterly* 15 (1952): 635–50.

14. Herbert Kelman, "Processes of Opinion Change," *Public Opinion Quarterly* 25 (Spring 1961): 57–78; Susan M. Petroshuis and Kenneth E. Crocker, "An Empirical Analysis of Spokesperson Characteristics on Advertisement and Product Evaluations," *Journal of the Academy of Marketing Science* 17 (Summer 1989): 217–26.

15. S. Ratneshwar and Shelly Chaiken, "Comprehension's Role in Persuasion: The Case of Its Moderating Effect on the Persuasive Impact of Source Cues," *Journal of Consumer Research* 18 (June 1991): 52–62.

16. Jagdish Agrawal and Wagner A. Kamakura, "The Economic Worth of Celebrity Endorsers: An Event Study Analysis," *Journal of Marketing* 59 (July 1995): 56–62.

17. "Jim Palmer Pitches 'Style' for Jockey," *New York Times* (August 29, 1982).

18. "Robber Makes It Biggs in Ad," *Advertising Age* (May 29, 1989): 26.

19. Alice H. Eagly, Andy Wood, and Shelly Chaiken, "Causal Inferences about Communicators and Their Effect in Opinion Change," *Journal of Personality and Social Psychology* 36 (1978)4: 424–35.

20. Rick Marin, "The Stepford Channel," *New York Times* (October 4, 1992)2: 1v.

21. Lisa Brownlee, "Sobakawa Pillow Wakes up Sleepy Infomercial World," *Wall Street Journal Interactive Edition* (May 27, 1997).

22. Prof. Herbert Rotfeld, Auburn University, personal communication, May 1997.

23. James Cox, "Star-Struck Advertisers Lean on Celebs," *USA Today* (June 20, 1990): 80.

24. Judith Graham, "Sponsors Line Up for Rockin' Role," *Advertising Age* (December 11, 1989): 50.

25. Pamela Hollie, "A Rush for Singers to Promote Goods," *New York Times* (May 14, 1984): D1.

26. Michael A. Kamins, "Celebrity and Noncelebrity Advertising in a Two-Sided Context," *Journal of Advertising Research* 29 (June–July 1989): 34; Joseph M. Kamen, A. C. Azhari, and J. R. Kragh, "What a Spokesman Does for a Sponsor," *Journal of Advertising Research* 15 (1975)2: 17–24; Lynn Langmeyer and Mary Walker, "A First Step to Identify the Meaning in Celebrity Endorsers," in eds. Rebecca H. Holman and Michael R. Solomon, *Advances in Consumer Research* 18 (Provo, UT: Association for Consumer Research, 1991): 364–71.

27. Jeffrey Burroughs and Richard A. Feinberg, "Using Response Latency to Assess Spokesperson Effectiveness," *Journal of Consumer Research* 14 (September 1987): 295–9.

28. Grant McCracken, "Who is the Celebrity Endorser? Cultural Foundations of the Endorsement Process," *Journal of Consumer Research* 16 (December 1989)3: 310–21.

29. Marie Okabe, "Fading Yen for Foreign Stars in Ads," *Singapore Straits-Times* (1986).

30. Pamela G. Hollie, "A Rush for Singers to Promote Goods," *New York Times* (May 14, 1984): D1

31. Larry Armstrong, "Still Starstruck," *Business Week* (July 4, 1994): 38; Jeff Giles, "The Risks of Wishing upon a Star," *Newsweek* (September 6, 1993): 38.

32. Karen K. Dion, "What is Beautiful is Good," *Journal of Personality and Social Psychology* 24 (December 1972): 285–90.

33. Michael A. Kamins, "An Investigation into the 'Match-Up' Hypothesis in Celebrity Advertising: When Beauty May Be Only Skin Deep," *Journal of Advertising* 19 (1990)1: 4–13; Lynn R. Kahle and Pamela M. Homer, "Physical

Attractiveness of the Celebrity Endorser: A Social Adaptation Perspective," *Journal of Consumer Research* 11 (March 1985): 954–61.

34. Bruce Haring, "Company Totes up Popularity Quotients," *Billboard* (1989): 12.

35. Michael J. Baker and Gilbert A. Churchill Jr., "The Impact of Physically Attractive Models on Advertising Evaluations," *Journal of Marketing Research* 14 (November 1977): 538–55; Marjorie J. Caballero and William M. Pride, "Selected Effects of Salesperson Sex and Attractiveness in Direct Mail Advertisements," *Journal of Marketing* 48 (January 1984): 94–100; W. Benoy Joseph, "The Credibility of Physically Attractive Communicators: A Review," *Journal of Advertising* 11 (1982)3: 15–24; Kahle and Homer, "Physical Attractiveness of the Celebrity Endorser; Judson Mills and Eliot Aronson, "Opinion Change as a Function of Communicator's Attractiveness and Desire to Influence," *Journal of Personality and Social Psychology* 1 (1965): 173–7.

36. Leonard N. Reid and Lawrence C. Soley, "Decorative Models and the Readership of Magazine Ads," *Journal of Advertising Research* 23 (1983)2: 27–32.

37. Marjorie J. Caballero, James R. Lumpkin, and Charles S. Madden, "Using Physical Attractiveness as an Advertising Tool: An Empirical Test of the Attraction Phenomenon," *Journal of Advertising Research* (August/September 1989): 16–22.

38. Baker and Churchill Jr., "The Impact of Physically Attractive Models on Advertising Evaluations"; George E. Belch, Michael A. Belch, and Angelina Villareal, "Effects of Advertising Communications: Review of Research," in *Research in Marketing* (Greenwich, CT: JAI Press, 1987)9: 59–117; A. E. Courtney and T. W. Whipple, *Sex Stereotyping in Advertising* (Lexington, MA: Lexington Books, 1983).

39. Kahle and Homer, "Physical Attractiveness of the Celebrity Endorser."

40. Kenneth G. DeBono and Richard J. Harnish, "Source Expertise, Source Attractiveness, and the Processing of

Persuasive Information: A Functional Approach," *Journal of Personality and Social Psychology* 55 (1988)4: 541–6.

41. Hershey H. Friedman and Linda Friedman, "Endorser Effectiveness by Product Type," *Journal of Advertising Research* 19 (1979)5: 63–71.

42. Anthony R. Pratkanis, Anthony G. Greenwald, Michael R. Leippe, and Michael H. Baumgardner, "In Search of Reliable Persuasion Effects: III. The Sleeper Effect Is Dead, Long Live the Sleeper Effect," *Journal of Personality and Social Psychology* 54 (1988): 203–18.

43. Herbert C. Kelman and Carl I. Hovland, "Reinstatement of the Communication in Delayed Measurement of Opinion Change," *Journal of Abnormal Psychology* 4, 48 (1953)3: 327–35.

44. Darlene Hannah and Brian Sternthal, "Detecting and Explaining the Sleeper Effect," *Journal of Consumer Research* (September 1984)11: 632–42.

45. David Mazursky and Yaacov Schul, "The Effects of Advertisment Encoding on the Failure to Discount Information: Implications for the Sleeper Effect," *Journal of Consumer Research* 15 (June 1988): 24–36.

46. David W. Stewart and David H. Furse, "The Effects of Television Advertising Execution on Recall, Comprehension, and Persuasion," *Psychology & Marketing* 2 (Fall 1985): 135–60.

47. R. C. Grass and W. H. Wallace, "Advertising Communication: Print Vs. TV," *Journal of Advertising Research* 14 (1974): 19–23.

48. Elizabeth C. Hirschman and Michael R. Solomon, "Utilitarian, Aesthetic, and Familiarity Responses to Verbal versus Visual Advertisements," in ed. Thomas C. Kinnear, *Advances in Consumer Research* 11 (Provo, UT: Association for Consumer Research, 1984): 426–31.

49. Andrew A. Mitchell and Jerry C. Olson, "Are Product Attribute Beliefs the Only Mediator of Advertising Effects on Brand Attitude?" *Journal of Marketing Research* 18 (1981)3: 318–32.

50. Terry L. Childers and Michael J. Houston, "Conditions for a Picture-Superiority Effect on Consumer

Memory," *Journal of Consumer Research* 11 (September 1984): 643–54.

51. Andrew A. Mitchell, "The Effect of Verbal and Visual Components of Advertisements on Brand Attitudes and Attitude toward the Advertisement," *Journal of Consumer Research* 13 (June 1986): 12–24.

52. John R. Rossiter and Larry Percy, "Attitude Change through Visual Imagery in Advertising," *Journal of Advertising Research* 9 (1980)2: 10–16.

53. Jolita Kiselius and Brian Sternthal, "Examining the Vividness Controversy: An Availability-Valence Interpretation," *Journal of Consumer Research* 12 (March 1986): 418–31.

54. Scott B. Mackenzie, "The Role of Attention in Mediating the Effect of Advertising on Attribute Importance," *Journal of Consumer Research* 13 (September 1986): 174–95.

55. Robert B. Zajonc, "Attitudinal Effects of Mere Exposure," Monograph, *Journal of Personality and Social Psychology* 8 (1968): 1–29.

56. Giles D'Souza and Ram C. Rao, "Can Repeating an Advertisement More Frequently Than the Competition Affect Brand Preference in a Mature Market?" *Journal of Marketing* 59 (April 1995): 32–42.

57. George E. Belch, "The Effects of Television Commercial Repetition on Cognitive Response and Message Acceptance," *Journal of Consumer Research* 9 (June 1982): 56–65; Marian Burke and Julie Edell, "Ad Reactions over Time: Capturing Changes in the Real World," *Journal of Consumer Research* 13 (June 1986): 114–18; Herbert Krugman, "Why Three Exposures May Be Enough," *Journal of Advertising Research* 12 (December 1972): 11–14.

58. Robert F. Bornstein, "Exposure and Affect: Overview and Meta-Analysis of Research, 1968–1987," *Psychological Bulletin* 106 (1989)2: 265–89; Arno Rethans, John Swasy, and Lawrence Marks, "Effects of Television Commercial Repetition, Receiver Knowledge, and Commercial Length: A Test of the Two-Factor Model," *Journal of Marketing Research* 23 (February 1986): 50–61.

59. Curtis P. Haugtvedt, David W. Schumann, Wendy L. Schneier, and Wendy L. Warren, "Advertising Repetition and Variation Strategies: Implications for Understanding Attitude Strength," *Journal of Consumer Research* 21 (June 1994): 176–89.

60. Linda L. Golden and Mark I. Alpert, "Comparative Analysis of the Relative Effectiveness of One- and Two-Sided Communication for Contrasting Products," *Journal of Advertising* 16 (1987): 18–25; Kamins, "Celebrity and Noncelebrity Advertising in a Two-Sided Context"; Robert B. Settle and Linda L. Golden, "Attribution Theory and Advertiser Credibility," *Journal of Marketing Research* 11 (May 1974): 181–5.

61. See Alan G. Sawyer, "The Effects of Repetition of Refutational and Supportive Advertising Appeals," *Journal of Marketing Research* 10 (February 1973): 23–33; George J. Szybillo and Richard Heslin, "Resistance to Persuasion: Inoculation Theory in a Marketing Context," *Journal of Marketing Research* 10 (November 1973): 396–403.

62. Lawrence M. Fisher, "Winery's Answer to Critics: Print Good and Bad Reviews," *New York Times* (January 9, 1991): D5.

63. Golden and Alpert, "Comparative Analysis of the Relative Effectiveness of One- and Two-Sided Communication for Contrasting Products."

64. Belch et al., "Effects of Advertising Communications."

65. Frank R. Kardes, "Spontaneous Inference Processes in Advertising: The Effects of Conclusion Omission and Involvement on Persuasion," *Journal of Consumer Research* 15 (September 1988): 225–33.

66. Belch et al., "Effects of Advertising Communications"; Cornelia Pechmann and Gabriel Esteban, "Persuasion Processes Associated with Direct Comparative and Noncomparative Advertising and Implications for Advertising Effectiveness," *Journal of Consumer Psychology* 2 (1994)4: 403–32.

67. Cornelia Dröge and Rene Y. Darmon, "Associative Positioning Strategies through Comparative Advertising: Attribute vs. Overall Similarity Approaches," *Journal of Marketing Research* 24 (1987): 377–89; D. Muehling and N. Kangun, "The Multidimensionality of Comparative Advertising: Implications for the FTC," *Journal of Public Policy and Marketing* (1985): 112–28; Beth A. Walker and Helen H. Anderson, "Reconceptualizing Comparative Advertising: A Framework and Theory of Effects," in eds. Rebecca H. Holman and Michael R. Solomon, *Advances in Consumer Research* 18 (Provo, UT: Association for Consumer Research, 1991): 342–47; William L. Wilkie and Paul W. Farris, "Comparison Advertising: Problems and Potential," *Journal of Marketing* 39 (October 1975): 7–15; R. G. Wyckham, "Implied Superiority Claims," *Journal of Advertising Research* (February/March 1987): 54–63.

68. Stephen A. Goodwin and Michael Etgar, "An Experimental Investigation of Comparative Advertising: Impact of Message Appeal, Information Load, and Utility of Product Class," *Journal of Marketing Research* 17 (May 1980): 187–202; Gerald J. Gorn and Charles B. Weinberg, "The Impact of Comparative Advertising on Perception and Attitude: Some Positive Findings," *Journal of Consumer Research* 11 (September 1984): 719–27; Terence A. Shimp and David C. Dyer, "The Effects of Comparative Advertising Mediated by Market Position of Sponsoring Brand," *Journal of Advertising* 3 (Summer 1978): 13–19; R. Dale Wilson, "An Empirical Evaluation of Comparative Advertising Messages: Subjects' Responses to Perceptual Dimensions," in ed. B.B. Anderson, *Advances in Consumer Research* 3 (Ann Arbor, MI: Association for Consumer Research, 1976): 53–57.

69. Dröge and Darmon, "Associative Positioning Strategies through Comparative Advertising: Attribute vs. Overall Similarity Approaches."

70. Dottie Enrico, "Guaranteed! Greatest Advertising Story Ever Told!" *Newsday* (October 16, 1991): 43; Bruce Buchanan and Doron Goldman, "Us vs. Them: The Minefield of Comparative Ads," *Harvard Business Review* 38 (May–June 1989)7: 50.

71. Michael Lev, "For Car Buyers, Technology or Zen," *New York Times* (May 22, 1989): D1.

72. "Connecting Consumer and Product," *New York Times* (January 18, 1990): D19.

73. Edward F. Cone, "Image and Reality," *Forbes* (December 14, 1987): 226.

74. H. Zielske, "Does Day-after Recall Penalize 'Feeling' Ads?" *Journal of Advertising Research* 22 (1982): 19–22.

75. Cone, "Image and Reality."

76. John Lichfield, "French Get Bored with Sex," *The Independent,* London, accessed via ssnewslink.com, July 30, 1997.

77. Belch et al., "Effects of Advertising Communications"; Courtney and Whipple, "Sex Stereotyping in Advertising"; Michael S. LaTour, "Female Nudity in Print Advertising: An Analysis of Gender Differences in Arousal and Ad Response," *Psychology & Marketing* 7 (1990)1: 65–81; B.G. Yovovich, "Sex in Advertising—The Power and the Perils," *Advertising Age* (May 2, 1983): M4–M5; for an interesting interpretive analysis, cf. Richard Elliott and Mark Ritson, "Practicing Existential Consumption: The Lived Meaning of Sexuality in Advertising," in eds. Frank R. Kardes and Mita Sujan, *Advances in Consumer Behavior* 22 (1995): 740–745.

78. Penny M. Simpson, Steve Horton, and Gene Brown, "Male Nudity in Advertisements: A Modified Replication and Extension of Gender and Product Effects," *Journal of the Academy of Marketing Science* 24 (1996)3: 257–62.

79. Michael S. LaTour and Tony L. Henthorne, "Ethical Judgments of Sexual Appeals in Print Advertising," *Journal of Advertising* 23 (September 1994)3: 81–90.

80. Roger Thurow, "As In-Your-Face Ads Backfire, Nike Finds a New Global Tack," *Wall Street Journal Interactive Edition* (May 5, 1997).

81. Marc G. Weinberger and Harlan E. Spotts, "Humor in U.S. versus U.K. TV Commercials: A Comparison," *Journal of Advertising* 18 (1989)2: 39–44.

82. Thomas J. Madden, "Humor in Advertising: An Experimental Analysis" (working paper no. 83-27, University of Massachusetts, 1984);

Thomas J. Madden and Marc G. Weinberger, "The Effects of Humor on Attention in Magazine Advertising," *Journal of Advertising* 11 (1982)3: 8–14; Weinberger and Spotts, "Humor in U.S. Versus U.K. TV Commercials."

83. David Gardner, "The Distraction Hypothesis in Marketing," *Journal of Advertising Research* 10 (1970): 25–30.

84. "Funny Ads Provide Welcome Relief during These Gloom and Doom Days," *Marketing News* (April 17, 1981): 3.

85. Barbara Martinez, "Advertising: Antismoking Ads Attempt to Gross out Arizona Teens," *Wall Street Journal Interactive Edition* (March 31, 1997).

86. "Ex-Lax Taken off Shelves for Now," *Montgomery Advertiser* (August 30, 1997): 1A.

87. Sally Goll Beatty and Bruce Ingersoll, "Drug Companies Attempt New Tactic: Spreading Fear," *Wall Street Journal Interactive Edition* (June 12, 1997), accessed 6/18/97.

88. Kevin Goldman, "Everybody's Afraid of the Big Bad Boss," *New York Times* (January 12, 1994): B1 (2 pp.).

89. Michael L. Ray and William L. Wilkie, "Fear: The Potential of an Appeal Neglected by Marketing," *Journal of Marketing* 34 (1970)1: 54–62.

90. Brian Sternthal and C. Samuel Craig, "Fear Appeals: Revisited and Revised," *Journal of Consumer Research* 1 (December 1974): 22–34.

91. Punam Anand Keller and Lauren Goldberg Block, "Increasing the Effectiveness of Fear Appeals: The Effect of Arousal and Elaboration," *Journal of Consumer Research* 22 (March 1996); 448–459.

92. Ronald Paul Hill, "An Exploration of the Relationship Between AIDS-Related Anxiety and the Evaluation of Condom Advertisements," *Journal of Advertising* 17 (1988)4: 35–42.

93. Randall Rothenberg, "Talking Too Tough on Life's Risks?" *New York Times* (February 16, 1990): D1.

94. Denise D. Schoenbachler and Tommy E. Whittler, "Adolescent Processing of Social and Physical Threat Communications," *Journal of Advertising* XXV, 4 (Winter 1996): 37–54.

95. "A Drive to Woo Women—And Invigorate Sales," *New York Times* (April 2, 1989).

96. Carrie Goerne, "Gun Companies Target Women: Foes Call it 'Marketing to Fear'," *Marketing News* (August 31, 1992)2: 1.

97. Kelly Shermach, "Scared Consumers Shop for Personal Safety," *Marketing News* (January 16, 1995): 1 (2 pp.).

98. Prof. Herbert J. Rotfeld, Auburn University, personal communication, December 9, 1997; Herbert J. Rotfeld, "Fear Appeals and Persuasion: Assumptions and Errors in Advertising Research," *Current Issues & Research in Advertising* 11 (1988)1: 21–40; Michael S. LaTour and Herbert J. Rotfeld, "There are Threats and (Maybe) Fear-Caused Arousal: Theory & Confusions of Appeals to Fear and Fear Arousal Itself," *Journal of Advertising* 26 (Fall 1997)3: 45–59.

99. Barbara Stern, "Medieval Allegory: Roots of Advertising Strategy for the Mass Market," *Journal of Marketing* 52 (July 1988): 84–94.

100. Edward F. McQuarrie and David Glen Mick, "On Resonance: A Critical Pluralistic Inquiry into Advertising Rhetoric," *Journal of Consumer Research* 19 (September 1992): 180–97.

101. See Linda M. Scott, "The Troupe: Celebrities as Dramatis Personae in Advertisements," in eds. Rebecca H. Holman and Michael R. Solomon, *Advances in Consumer Research* 18 (Provo, UT: Association for Consumer Research, 1991): 355–63; Barbara Stern, "Literary Criticism and Consumer Research: Overview and Illustrative Analysis," *Journal of Consumer Research* 16 (1989): 322–34; Judith Williamson, *Decoding Advertisements* (Boston: Marion Boyars, 1978).

102. John Deighton, Daniel Romer, and Josh McQueen, "Using Drama to Persuade," *Journal of Consumer Research* 16 (December 1989): 335–43.

103. Richard E. Petty, John T. Cacioppo, and David Schumann, "Central and Peripheral Routes to Advertising Effectiveness: The Moderating Role of Involvement," *Journal of Consumer Research* 10 (1983)2: 135–46.

104. Jerry C. Olson, Daniel R. Toy, and Philip A. Dover, "Do Cognitive Responses Mediate the Effects of Advertising Content on Cognitive Structure?" *Journal of Consumer Research* 9 (1982)3: 245–62.

105. Julie A. Edell and Andrew A. Mitchell, "An Information Processing Approach to Cognitive Responses," in ed. S.C. Jain, *Research Frontiers in Marketing: Dialogues and Directions,* (Chicago: American Marketing Association, 1978).

106. See Mary Jo Bitner and Carl Obermiller, "The Elaboration Likelihood Model: Limitations and Extensions in Marketing," in eds. Elizabeth C. Hirschman, and Morris B. Holbrook, *Advances in Consumer Research* 12 (Provo, UT: Association for Consumer Research, 1985): 420–5; Meryl P. Gardner, "Does Attitude toward the Ad Affect Brand Attitude under a Brand Evaluation Set?" *Journal of Marketing Research* 22 (1985): 192–8; C. W. Park and S. M. Young, "Consumer Response to Television Commercials: The Impact of Involvement and Background Music on Brand Attitude Formation," *Journal of Marketing Research* 23 (1986): 11–24; Petty, Cacioppo, and Schumann, "Central and Peripheral Routes to Advertising Effectiveness"; for a discussion of how different kinds of involvement interact with the ELM, see Robin A. Higie, Lawrence F. Feick, and Linda L. Price, "The Importance of Peripheral Cues in Attitude Formation for Enduring and Task-Involved Individuals," in eds. Rebecca H. Holman and Michael R. Solomon, *Advances in Consumer Research* 18 (Provo, UT: Association for Consumer Research, 1991): 187–93.

107. J. Craig Andrews and Terence A. Shimp, "Effects of Involvement, Argument Strength, and Source Characteristics on Central and Peripheral Processing in Advertising," *Psychology & Marketing* 7 (Fall 1990): 195–214.

108. Richard E. Petty, John T. Cacioppo, Constantine Sedikides, and Alan J. Strathman, "Affect and Persuasion: A Contemporary Perspective," *American Behavioral Scientist* 31 (1988)3: 355–71.

CONSUMERS AS DECISION MAKERS

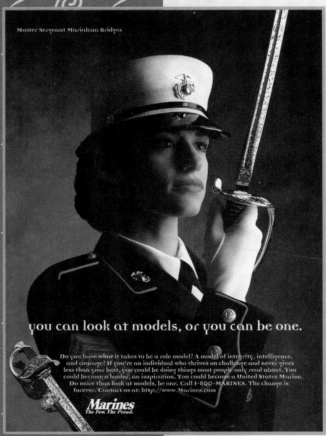

Master Sergeant Marialean Bridges

you can look at models, or you can be one.

Do you have what it takes to be a role model? A model of integrity, intelligence, and courage. If you're an individual who thrives on challenge and never gives less than your best, you could be doing things most people only read about. You could become a leader, an inspiration. You could become a United States Marine. Do more than look at models, be one. Call 1-800-MARINES. The change is forever. Contact us at: http://www.Marines.com

Marines
The Few. The Proud.

This section explores how we make consumption decisions and discusses the many influences exerted by others during this process. Chapter 9 focuses on the basic sequence of steps we undergo when making a decision. Chapter 10 considers how the particular situation in which we find ourselves affects these decisions and how we go about evaluating the results of our choices. Chapter 11 provides an overview of group processes and discusses the reasons we are motivated to conform to the expectations of others when we choose and display our purchases. Chapter 12 goes on to consider the many instances in which our purchase decisions are made in conjunction with others, especially co-workers or family members.

BILLY HAS HAD IT. There's only so much longer he can go on watching TV on his tiny, antiquated black-and-white set. It was bad enough trying to listen to the scratchy music in MTV videos and squinting through *The Simpsons* and *Friends*. The final straw was when he couldn't tell the Cowboys from the Raiders during NFL football. When he went next door to watch the second half on Mark's home theater setup, he really realized what he had been missing. Budget or not, it was time to act: A man has to have his priorities.

Billy figures he'll probably get a decent selection (and an affordable price) at one of those huge new warehouse stores. Arriving at Zany Zack's Appliance Emporium, Billy heads straight for the Video Zone in the back—barely noticing the rows of toasters, microwave ovens, and stereos on his way. Within minutes, he's accosted by a smiling salesman in a cheap suit. Even though he could use some help, Billy tells the salesman he's just browsing—he figures these guys don't know what they're talking about, and they're just out to make a sale no matter what.

Billy starts to examine some of the features on the 52-inch color sets. He knew his friend Carol had a set by Prime Wave that she really liked, and his sister Diane had warned him to stay away from the Kamashita. Although Billy finds a Prime Wave model loaded to the max with features such as a sleep timer, on-screen programming menu, cable compatible tuner, and remote control, he chooses the less-expensive Precision 2000X because it has one feature that really catches his fancy: stereo broadcast reception.

Later that day, Billy is a happy man as he sits in his easy chair, watching Puff Daddy do his thing on MTV. If he's going to be a couch potato, he's going in style. . . .

9

Individual Decision Making

CONSUMERS AS PROBLEM SOLVERS

A consumer purchase is a response to a problem, which in Billy's case is the perceived need for a new TV. His situation is similar to that encountered by consumers virtually every day of their lives. He realizes that he wants to make a purchase, and he goes through a series of steps in order to make it. These steps can be described as (1) problem recognition, (2) information search, (3) evaluation of alternatives, and (4) product choice. Of course, after the decision is made, the quality of that decision affects the final step in the process, in which learning occurs based on how well the choice worked out. This learning process, of course, influences the likelihood that the same choice will be made the next time the need for a similar decision occurs.

An overview of this decision-making process appears in Figure 9–1. This chapter begins by considering various approaches consumers use when faced with a purchase decision. It then focuses on three of the steps in the decision process: how consumers recognize the problem, or need for a product; their search for information about product choices; and the ways in which they evaluate alternatives to arrive at a decision. Chapter 10 considers influences in the actual purchase situation, as well as the person's satisfaction with the decision.

This print ad, part of the "Smart Solutions" advertising campaign by the U.S. Postal Service, presents a problem, illustrates the decision-making process, and highlights a solution.

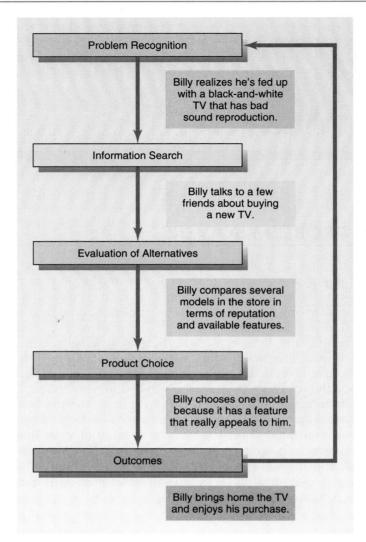

FIGURE 9–1 ■ **Stages in Consumer Decision Making**

Because some purchase decisions are more important than others, the amount of effort we put into each one differs. Sometimes the decision-making process is almost automatic; we seem to make snap judgments based on very little information. At other times, coming to a purchase decision begins to resemble a full-time job. A person may literally spend days or weeks thinking about an important purchase such as a new home, even to the point of obsession.

PERSPECTIVES ON DECISION MAKING

Traditionally, consumer researchers have approached decision makers from a **rational perspective.** In this view, people calmly and carefully integrate as much information as possible with what they already know about a product, painstakingly weigh the pluses and minuses of each alternative, and arrive at a satisfactory decision. This process implies that steps in decision making should be carefully studied by marketing managers to understand how information is obtained, how beliefs are formed, and what product choice criteria are specified by consumers. Products then can be developed that emphasize appropriate attributes, and promotional strategies can be tailored to deliver the types of information most likely to be desired in the most effective formats.[1]

The steps in decision making are followed by consumers for some purchases, but such a process is not an accurate portrayal of many purchase decisions.[2] Consumers simply do not go through this elaborate sequence for every decision. If they did, their entire lives would be spent making such decisions, leaving them very little time to enjoy the things they eventually decide to buy.

Researchers are now beginning to realize that decision makers actually possess a repertoire of strategies. A consumer evaluates the effort required to make a particular choice, and then he or she chooses a strategy best suited to the level of effort required. This sequence of events is known as *constructive processing.* Rather than using a big club to kill an ant, consumers tailor their degree of cognitive "effort" to the task at hand.[3]

Some decisions are made under conditions of low involvement, as discussed in chapter 4. In many of these situations, the consumer's decision is a learned response to environmental cues (see chapter 3), as when he or she decides to buy something on impulse that is promoted as a "surprise special" in a store. A concentration on these types of decisions can be described as the **behavioral influence perspective.** Under these circumstances, managers must concentrate on assessing the characteristics of the environment, such as the design of a retail outlet or whether a package is enticing, that influence members of a target market.[4]

In other cases, consumers are highly involved in a decision, but still the selections made cannot wholly be explained rationally. For example, the traditional approach is hard pressed to explain a person's choice of art, music, or even a spouse. In these cases, no single quality may be the determining factor. Instead, the **experiential perspective** stresses the *Gestalt,* or totality, of the product or service. Marketers in these areas focus on measuring consumers' affective responses to products or services, and develop offerings that elicit appropriate subjective reactions.

TYPES OF CONSUMER DECISIONS

One helpful way to characterize the decision-making process is to consider the amount of effort that goes into the decision each time it must be made. Consumer researchers have found it convenient to think in terms of a continuum, which is anchored on one end by **habitual decision making** and at the other extreme by **extended problem solving.** Many decisions fall somewhere in the middle and are characterized by **limited problem solving.** This continuum is presented in Figure 9–2.

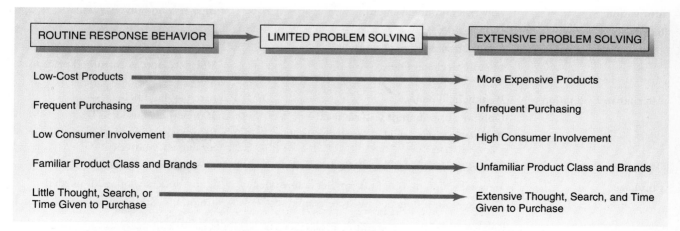

FIGURE 9–2 ■ **A Continuum of Buying Decision Behavior**

EXTENDED PROBLEM SOLVING

Decisions involving extended problem solving correspond most closely to the traditional decision-making perspective. As indicated in Table 9–1, the extended problem-solving process is usually initiated by a motive that is fairly central to the self-concept (see chapter 5), and the eventual decision is perceived to carry a fair degree of risk. The consumer tries to collect as much information as possible, both from memory (internal search) and from outside sources (external search). Based on the importance of the decision, each product alternative is carefully evaluated. The evaluation is often made by considering the attributes of one brand at a time and seeing how each brand's attributes shape up to some set of desired characteristics.

LIMITED PROBLEM SOLVING

Limited problem solving is usually more straightforward and simple. Buyers are not as motivated to search for information or to evaluate each alternative rigorously. People instead use simple *decision rules* to choose among alternatives. These cognitive shortcuts (more about these later) enable them to fall back on general guidelines, instead of having to start from scratch every time a decision is to be made.

HABITUAL DECISION MAKING

Both extended and limited problem-solving modes involve some degree of information search and deliberation, though they vary in the degree to which these activities are undertaken. At the other end of the choice continuum, however, are decisions that are made with little to no conscious effort. Many purchase decisions are so routinized that we may not realize we've made them until we look in our shopping carts. Choices characterized by *automaticity* are performed with minimal effort and without conscious control.[5] Although this kind of thoughtless activity may seem dangerous or at best stupid, it is actually quite efficient in many cases. The development of habitual, repetitive behavior allows consumers to minimize the time and energy spent on mundane purchase decisions.

TABLE 9–1 ■ **Characteristics of Limited versus Extended Problem Solving**

	LIMITED PROBLEM SOLVING	EXTENDED PROBLEM SOLVING
Motivation	Low risk and involvement	High risk and involvement
Information Search	Little search	Extensive search
	Information processed passively	Information processed actively
	In-store decision likely	Multiple sources consulted prior to store visits
Alternative Evaluation	Weakly held beliefs	Strongly held beliefs
	Only most prominent criteria used	Many criteria used
	Alternatives perceived as basically similar	Significant differences perceived among alternatives
	Noncompensatory strategy used	Compensatory strategy used
Purchase	Limited shopping time; may prefer self-service	Many outlets shopped if needed
	Choice often influenced by store displays	Communication with store personnel often desirable

PROBLEM RECOGNITION

Problem recognition occurs whenever the consumer sees a significant difference between his or her current state of affairs and some desired or ideal state. The consumer perceives there is a problem to be solved, which may be small or large, simple or complex. A person who unexpectedly runs out of gas on the highway has a problem, as does the person who becomes dissatisfied with the image of his or her car, even though there is nothing mechanically wrong with it. Although the quality of Billy's TV had not changed, for example, his *standard of comparison* was altered, and he was confronted with a desire he did not have prior to watching his friend's TV.

Figure 9–3 shows that a problem can arise in one of two ways. As in the case of the person running out of gas, the quality of the consumer's *actual state* can move downward (*need recognition*). On the other hand, as in the case of the person who craves a newer, flashier car, the consumer's *ideal state* can move upward (*opportunity recognition*). Either way, a gulf occurs between the actual state and the ideal state.[6] In Billy's case, a problem was perceived as a result of opportunity recognition; his ideal state in terms of television reception quality was altered.

Need recognition can occur in several ways. The quality of the person's actual state can be diminished simply by running out of a product, by buying a product that turns out not to adequately satisfy needs, or by creating new needs (e.g., buying a house can set off an avalanche of other choices, because many new things are needed to fill the house). Opportunity recognition often occurs when a consumer is exposed to different or better-quality products. This shift often occurs because the person's circumstances have somehow changed, as when an individual goes to college or gets a new job. As the person's frame of reference shifts, purchases are made to adapt to the new environment.

While problem recognition can and does occur naturally, this process is often spurred by marketing efforts. In some cases, marketers attempt to create *primary demand,* where consumers are encouraged to use a product or service regardless of the brand they choose. Such needs are often encouraged in the early stages of a product's life cycle, as, for example, when microwave ovens were first introduced. *Secondary demand,* where consumers are prompted to prefer a specific brand over others, can occur only if primary demand already exists. At this point, marketers must convince consumers that a problem can best be solved by choosing their brand over others in a category.

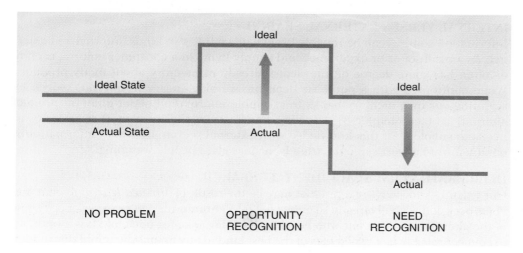

FIGURE 9–3 ■ Problem Recognition: Shifts in Actual or Ideal States

MARKETING PITFALL

A common structure for advertisements has been to present a person who has a physical or social problem, and then show how the product will "miraculously" resolve it. Some marketers have gone so far as to *invent* a problem and then offer a remedy for it. In the 1940s, for example, the Talon zipper was touted as a cure for *gaposis,* the horrifying condition that develops when puckers appear around the buttons on a woman's skirt. Listerine, which was originally sold to fight dandruff, carried warnings about "bottle bacillus," which caused "infectious dandruff." Geritol gave us a remedy for "tired blood," and Wisk detergent drew our attention to the shame of "ring around the collar."[7]

Even when real problems are depicted in ads, the solutions offered are sometimes overly simplistic, implying that the problem will disappear if the product is used. One analysis of over 1,000 television ads found that about eight in ten suggest that the problem will be resolved within seconds or minutes after using the product. In addition, 75 percent of the ads make definite claims that the product will solve the problem, and over 75 percent imply that this solution is a one-step process—all the consumer needs to do is buy the product, and the problem will go away.[8] Consumers, however, are becoming more cynical and less susceptible to such claims. As many marketers are discovering, modern consumers are more receptive to realistic ads that provide solid information about the product. In addition, both the government and consumer groups are now taking a more active interest in product claims, and marketers are being more cautious about the content of their ads.

INFORMATION SEARCH

Once a problem has been recognized, consumers need adequate information to resolve it. **Information search** is the process by which the consumer surveys his or her environment for appropriate data to make a reasonable decision. This section will review some of the factors involved in this search.

TYPES OF INFORMATION SEARCH

A consumer may explicitly search the marketplace for specific information after a need has been recognized (a process called *prepurchase search*.) On the other hand, many consumers, especially veteran shoppers, enjoy browsing just for the fun of it, or because they like to stay up-to-date on what's happening in the marketplace. They are engaging in *ongoing search.*[9] Some differences between these two search modes are described in Table 9–2.

INTERNAL VERSUS EXTERNAL SEARCH

Information sources can be roughly broken down into two kinds: internal and external. As a result of prior experience and simply living in a consumer culture, each of us often has some degree of knowledge already in memory about many products. When confronted with a purchase decision, we may engage in *internal search* by scanning our own memory banks to assemble information about different product alternatives (see chapter 3). Usually, though, even the most market savvy of us needs to supplement this knowledge with external search, by which information is obtained from advertisements, friends, or just plain people watching.

DELIBERATE VERSUS "ACCIDENTAL" SEARCH

Our existing knowledge of a product may be the result of *directed learning:* on a previous occasion we had already searched for relevant information or experienced some of the alternatives. A parent who bought a birthday cake for one child last month, for example, probably has a good idea of the best kind to buy for another child this month.

TABLE 9–2 ■ **A Framework for Consumer Information Search**

PREPURCHASE SEARCH	ONGOING SEARCH
Determinants	
Involvement in the purchase	Involvement with the product
Market environment	Market environment
Situational factors	Situational factors
Motives	
Making better purchase decisions	Building a bank of information for future use
	Experiencing fun and pleasure
Outcomes	
Increased product and market knowledge	Increased product and market knowledge leading to
Better purchase decisions	• future buying efficiencies
Increased satisfaction with the purchase outcome	• personal influence
	Increased impulse buying
	Increased satisfaction from search and other outcomes

Source: Peter H. Bloch, Daniel L. Sherrell, and Nancy M. Ridgway, "Consumer Search: An Extended Framework," *Journal of Consumer Research* 13 (June 1986): 120. Reprinted with permission by The University of Chicago Press.

Alternatively, we might have acquired information in a more passive manner. Even though a product may not be of interest, exposure to advertising, packaging, and sales promotion activities may result in *incidental learning*. Mere exposure over time to conditioned stimuli and observations of others results in the learning of much material that may not be needed for some time after the fact, if ever. For marketers, this result is a benefit of steady, "low-dose" advertising, as product associations are established and maintained until the time they are needed.[10]

In some cases, we may be so expert about a product category (or at least believe we are) that no additional search is undertaken. Frequently, however, our own existing state of knowledge is not satisfactory to make an adequate decision, and we must look elsewhere for more information. The sources we consult for advice vary: They may be impersonal and marketer-dominated sources, such as retailers and catalogs; they may be friends and family members; or they may be unbiased third parties such as *Consumer Reports*.[11]

MARKETING PITFALL

Consumers are very skeptical about the nutrition information they receive from marketers. According to a Food Marketing Institute study, only 4 percent of American shoppers feel that food advertising that promotes health benefits is very believable, and 41 percent say they've been misled by advertising that supposedly touts these benefits. The United States recently tried to make grocery decision making easier and healthier by mandating that foods present Nutrition Facts in a standardized format. Those that do take the time to read the label often act on what they see: A third of consumers decided to stop buying a regularly purchased item because of something they read on this revised label.[12]

MARKETING OPPORTUNITY

Advances in technology are helping to feed consumers' growing appetites for information about products and services. One in three American households has a computer, one in seven has a modem, and 3 million households have accessed the Internet. A survey by the research firm Find/SVP shows that Americans spend almost $500 per year on "pure" information—papers, magazines, reference books, nonentertainment videos, and on-line services.[13] Ironically, the problem for many is too much information rather than too little. The World Wide Web is a victim of its own success—the volume of available information is staggering, and noise and congestion makes it hard to attract visitors and keep them coming back.

Now, the ability to *narrowcast* is promising to turn the Web into a personalized broadcast system, whereby the user can obtain only the information he or she requests and not have to sift through all the rest. Programs called "tuners" organize information into "channels" and "push delivery" gets it out to viewers who have filled out a profile specifying what they want. Providers are gambling that viewers will be willing to pay extra for this customized service. Retailers such as Lands' End are already experimenting with direct marketing on the Web, notifying subscribers of promotions and sending them order forms. By the year 2000 Webcasting is projected to generate a third of the $14 billion spent on net advertising, subscriptions, and retail revenues. Major players developing push technology include America Online, Marimba (which can send programs and applets along with content), Microsoft, Netscape Constellation, and Pointcast.[14] Firefly (www.firefly.com), a company started by former graduate students at MIT, learns consumers' tastes over time and makes recommendations about new music and entertainment based on the user's prior preferences.[15] Users also can post their own reviews for others to read and react to.[16]

The Adfinity software package illustrates one way push technology can simplify decision making. When a surfer first visits a Web site, he or she is asked for some basic facts in exchange for access to the site's content. Adfinity will connect with files on that user from participating company databases, and send ads fine-tuned to his or her interests. For example, someone who has purchased golf vacation packages in the past might be offered a discount at a golf course as an incentive to fly a participating airline. Of course, a strategy that requires several corporations to pool their knowledge about customers can backfire, if consumers get scared away by the specter of Big Brother and issues of privacy are not respected.[17] Push technology can be a two-edged sword that can cut the wrong way if it falls into the wrong hands.

THE ECONOMICS OF INFORMATION

The traditional decision-making perspective incorporates the *economics-of-information* approach to the search process; it assumes that consumers will gather as much data as needed to make an informed decision. Consumers form expectations of the value of additional information and continue to search to the extent that the rewards of doing so (what economists call the *utility*) exceed the costs. This utilitarian assumption also implies that the most valuable units of information will be collected first. Additional pieces will be absorbed only to the extent that they are seen to augment to what is already known.[18] In other words, people will put themselves out to collect as much information as possible, as long as the process of gathering it is not too onerous or time consuming.[19]

DO CONSUMERS ALWAYS SEARCH RATIONALLY?

This assumption of rational search is not always supported. The amount of external search for most products is surprisingly small, even when additional information would most likely benefit the consumer. For example, lower-income shoppers, who have more to lose by making a bad purchase, actually search *less* prior to buying than do more affluent people.[20]

Like our friend Billy, some consumers typically visit only one or two stores and rarely seek out unbiased information sources prior to making a purchase decision, especially when little time is available to do so.[21] This pattern is especially prevalent for decisions regarding durable goods such as appliances or autos, even when these products represent significant investments. One study of Australian car buyers found that more than a third had made only two or fewer trips to inspect cars prior to buying one.[22]

This tendency to avoid external search is less prevalent when consumers consider the purchase of symbolic items, such as clothing. In those cases, not surprisingly, people tend to do a fair amount of external search, although most of it involves seeking the opinions of peers.[23] Although the stakes may be lower financially, these self-expressive decisions may be seen as having dire social consequences if the wrong choice is made. The level of perceived risk, a concept to be discussed shortly, is high.

In addition, consumers often are observed to engage in *brand switching*, even if their current brand satisfies their needs. For example, researchers for British brewer Bass Export who were studying the American beer market discovered a consumer trend toward having a repertoire of two to six favorite brands, rather than sticking to only one. This preference for brand switching led the firm to begin

May cause
drowsiness, dizzy spells,
and vomiting.
If affected, carry on.
It's normal.

La Guillotine Beer 9·1% Proof. Have a nice coma.

This Singaporean beer ad reminds us that not all product decisions are made rationally.

exporting their Tennent's 1885 lager to the United States, positioning the brew as an alternative to young drinkers' usual favorite brands.[24]

Sometimes, it seems that people just plain like to try new things—they are interested in *variety seeking,* in which the priority is to vary one's product experiences, perhaps as a form of stimulation or to reduce boredom. Variety seeking is especially likely to occur when people are in a good mood, or when there is relatively little stimulation elsewhere in their environment.[25]

On the other hand, when the decision situation is ambiguous or when there is little information about competing brands, consumers tend to opt for the safe choice by selecting familiar brands and maintaining the status quo. The need for certainty appears to be growing; a declining percentage of consumers tell survey takers they are "always looking for something new" in products and services. For example, in 1996, 25 percent of vacationers said they were always on the lookout for new places to go, down from 37 percent who said this in 1988.[26]

BIASES IN THE DECISION-MAKING PROCESS

Consider the following scenario: You've been given a free ticket to an important football game. At the last minute, though, a sudden snowstorm makes getting to the stadium somewhat dangerous. Would you still go? Now, assume the same game and snowstorm, except this time you paid handsomely for the ticket. Would you head out in the storm in this case?

Analyses of people's responses to this situation and to other similar puzzles illustrates principles of *mental accounting,* in which decisions are influenced by the way a problem is posed (called *framing*), and by whether it is put in terms of gains or losses.[27] In this case, researchers find that people are more likely to risk their personal safety in the storm *if* they paid for the football ticket. Only the most die-hard fan would fail to recognize that this is an irrational choice, as the risk to the person is the same regardless of whether he or she got a great deal on the ticket. This decision making bias is called the *sunk-cost fallacy*—having paid for something makes us reluctant to waste it.

Another bias is known as *loss aversion.* People place much more emphasis on loss than they do on gain. For example, for most people losing money is more unpleasant than gaining money is pleasant. *Prospect theory,* a descriptive model of choice, finds that utility is a function of gains and losses, and risk differs when the consumer faces options involving gains versus those involving losses.[28]

To illustrate this bias, consider the following choices. For each, would you take the safe bet or choose to gamble?

Option #1. You're given $30 and then offered a chance to flip a coin: Heads you win $9; tails you lose $9.
Option #2. You're given a choice of getting $30 outright, or accepting a coin flip that will win you either $39 or $21.

In one study, 70 percent of those given option #1 chose to gamble, compared to just 43 percent of those offered option #2. Yet, the odds are the same for both options! The difference is that people prefer "playing with the house money"; they are more willing to take risks when they perceive they're using someone else's resources. So, contrary to a rational decision-making perspective, we value money differently depending on where it comes from. This explains, for example, why someone might choose to blow a big bonus on some frivolous purchase, but they would never consider taking that same amount out of their savings account for this purpose.

Finally, research in mental accounting demonstrates that extraneous characteristics of the choice situation can influence our selections, even though they wouldn't if we were totally rational decision makers. As one example, participants in a survey were provided with one of two versions of this scenario:

> You are lying on the beach on a hot day. All you have to drink is ice water. For the last hour you have been thinking about how much you would enjoy a nice cold bottle of your favorite brand of beer. A companion gets up to go make a phone call and offers to bring back a beer from the only nearby place where beer is sold (either a fancy resort hotel or a small, run-down grocery store, depending on the version you're given). He says that the beer might be expensive and so asks how much you are willing to pay for it. . . . What price do you tell him?

In this survey, the median price given by participants who were in the fancy resort version was $2.65, but those given the grocery store version were only willing to pay $1.50! In both versions the consumption act is the same, the beer is the same, and no "atmosphere" is consumed because the beer is being brought back to the beach.[29] So much for rational decision making!

HOW MUCH SEARCH OCCURS?

As a general rule, search activity is greater when the purchase is important, when there is a need to learn more about the purchase, and/or when the relevant information is easily obtained and utilized.[30] Consumers differ in the amount of search they tend to undertake, regardless of the product category in question. All things being equal, younger, better-educated people who enjoy the shopping/fact-finding process tend to conduct more information search. Women are more inclined to search than men are, as are those who place greater value on style and the image they present.[31]

THE CONSUMER'S PRIOR EXPERTISE

Should prior product knowledge make it more or less likely that consumers will engage in search? Products experts and novices use very different procedures during decision making. Novices, who know little about a product, should be the most motivated to find out more about it. However, experts are more familiar with the product category, so they should be able to better understand the meaning of any new product information they might acquire.

So, who searches more? The answer is neither: Search tends to be greatest among those consumers who are *moderately* knowledgeable about the product. There is an inverted-U relationship between knowledge and external search effort, as shown in Figure 9–4. People with very limited expertise may not feel they are capable of searching extensively. In fact, they may not even know where to start. Billy, who did not spend a lot of time researching his purchase, is representative of this situation. He visited one store, and he only looked at brands with which he was already familiar. In addition, he focused on only a small number of product features.[32]

The *type* of search undertaken by people with varying levels of expertise differs as well. Because experts have a better sense of what information is relevant to the decision, they tend to engage in *selective search,* which means their efforts are more focused and efficient. In contrast, novices are more likely to rely on the opinions of others and to rely on "nonfunctional" attributes, such as brand name and price, to distinguish among alternatives. They may also process information in a

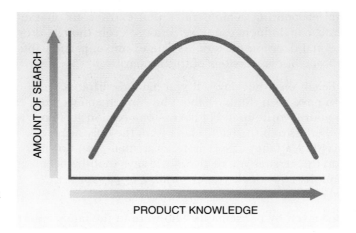

FIGURE 9–4 ■ **The Relationship between Amount of Information Search and Product Knowledge**

"top-down" rather than a "bottom-up" manner, focusing less on details than on the big picture. For instance, they may be more impressed by the sheer amount of technical information presented in an ad than by the actual significance of the claims made.[33]

PERCEIVED RISK

As a rule, purchase decisions that involve extensive search also entail some kind of **perceived risk,** or the belief that the product has potentially negative consequences. Perceived risk may be present if the product is expensive or is complex and hard to understand. Alternatively, perceived risk can be a factor when a product choice is visible to others, and we run the risk of embarrassment if the wrong choice is made.

Figure 9–5 lists five kinds of risk—including both objective (e.g., physical danger) and subjective factors (e.g., social embarrassment)—as well as the products that tend to be affected by each type. As this figure notes, consumers with greater "risk capital" are less affected by perceived risks associated with the products. For

Minolta features a No-Risk Guarantee as a way to reduce the perceived risk in buying an office copier.

	BUYERS MOST SENSITIVE TO RISK	PURCHASES MOST SUBJECT TO RISK
MONETARY RISK	Risk capital consists of money and property. Those with relatively little income and wealth are most vulnerable.	High-ticket items that require substantial expenditures are most subject to this form of risk.
FUNCTIONAL RISK	Risk capital consists of alternative means of performing the function or meeting the need. Practical consumers are most sensitive.	Products or services whose purchase and use requires the buyer's exclusive commitment and precludes redundancy are most sensitive.
PHYSICAL RISK	Risk capital consists of physical vigor, health, and vitality. Those who are elderly, frail, or in ill health are most vulnerable.	Mechanical or electrical goods (such as vehicles or flammables), drugs and medical treatment, and food and beverages are most sensitive.
SOCIAL RISK	Risk capital consists of self-esteem and self-confidence. Those who are insecure and uncertain are most sensitive.	Socially visible or symbolic goods, such as clothes, jewelry, cars, homes, or sports equipment are most subject to it.
PSYCHO-LOGICAL RISK	Risk capital consists of affiliations and status. Those lacking self-respect or attractiveness to peers are most sensitive.	Expensive personal luxuries that may engender guilt; durables; and services whose use demands self-discipline or sacrifice are most sensitive.

FIGURE 9–5 ■ Five Types of Perceived Risk

example, a highly self-confident person would be less worried about the social risk inherent in a product, whereas a more vulnerable, insecure consumer might be reluctant to take a chance on a product that might not be accepted by peers.

MARKETING OPPORTUNITY

The spread of the HIV virus has created a boom in home-testing kits that encourage people to determine if they have been infected with AIDS in a less-threatening environment than a clinic or a doctor's office. The typical kit allows the consumer to send a blood sample to a testing lab, and results are returned in three to seven days. Although high-risk groups such as adolescents and gay men need the kits most, some speculate that sales will instead come primarily from the "worried well"—those who are less likely to be infected in the first place. Companies are taking different approaches, ranging from humorous to provocative to serious, as they try to find the best way to reach people who are unlikely to go to a clinic to be tested. In one ad for Home Access, the copy (targeted to young straight males) says "nothing arouses a woman like knowing you're responsible."[34]

EVALUATION OF ALTERNATIVES

Much of the effort that goes into a purchase decision occurs at the stage in which a choice must be made from the available alternatives. After all, modern consumer society abounds with choices. In some cases, there may literally be hundreds of different brands (as in cigarettes) or different variations of the same brand (as in shades of lipstick), each screaming for our attention.

Just for fun, ask a friend to name all of the brands of perfume she can think of. The odds are she will reel off three to five names rather quickly, then stop and think awhile before coming up with a few more. It is likely that the first set of brands are those with which she is highly familiar, and she probably wears one or more of these. The list may also contain one or two brands that she does not like and would perhaps like to forget. Note also that there are many, many more brands on the market she did not name at all.

If your friend were to go to the store to buy perfume, it is likely that she would consider buying some or most of the brands she listed initially. She might also consider a few more possibilities if these were forcefully brought to her attention while at the store—for example, if she is "ambushed" by a representative who is spraying scent samples on shoppers, which is a common occurrence in some department stores.

IDENTIFYING ALTERNATIVES

How do we decide which criteria are important, and how do we narrow down product alternatives to an acceptable number and eventually choose one over the others? The answer varies depending on the decision-making process used. A consumer engaged in extended problem solving may carefully evaluate several brands, whereas someone making a habitual decision may not consider any alternatives to their normal brand. Furthermore, some evidence indicates that more extended processing occurs in situations in which negative emotions are aroused due to conflicts among the choices available. This is most likely to occur where difficult tradeoffs are involved, as when a person must choose between the risk involved in undergoing a bypass operation versus the potential improvement in his or her life if the operation is successful.[35]

 The alternatives actively considered during a consumer's choice process are his or her **evoked set.** The evoked set comprises those products already in memory (the retrieval set), plus those prominent in the retail environment. For example, recall that Billy did not know much about the technical aspects of television sets, and he had only a few major brands in memory. Of these, two were acceptable possibilities and one was not. The alternatives that the consumer is aware of but would not consider buying are his or her **inept set,** whereas those not entering the game at all comprise the **inert set.** You can easily guess in which set a marketer wants its brand to appear! These categories are depicted in Figure 9–6.

Consumers often include a surprisingly small number of alternatives in their evoked set. One study combined results from several large-scale investigations of consumers' evoked sets and found that the number of products included in these sets is limited, although there are some marked variations by product category and across countries. For example, the average evoked set size for American beer consumers was fewer than three, whereas Canadian consumers typically considered seven brands. In contrast, whereas auto buyers in Norway studied two alternatives, American consumers on average looked at more than eight models before making a decision.[36]

For obvious reasons, a marketer who finds that her or his brand is not in the evoked set of target market has cause to worry. A product is not likely to be placed

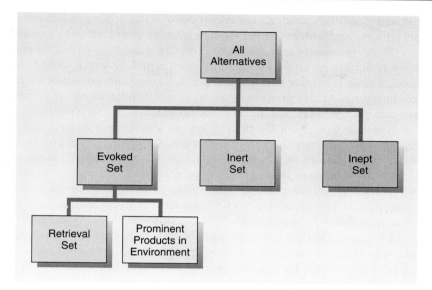

FIGURE 9–6 ■
Identifying
Alternatives: Getting in
the Game

in the evoked set after it has previously been considered and rejected. Indeed, a new brand is more likely to be added to the evoked set than is an existing brand that was previously considered but passed over, even after additional positive information has been provided for that brand.[37] For marketers, consumers' unwillingness to give a rejected product a second chance underscores the importance of ensuring that it performs well from the time it is introduced.

PRODUCT CATEGORIZATION

Remember that when consumers process product information, they do not do so in a vacuum. Instead, a product stimulus is evaluated in terms of what people already know about a product or things to which it is similar. A person evaluating a particular 35 mm camera will most likely compare it to other 35 mm cameras rather than to a Polaroid camera, and the consumer would certainly not compare it to a slide projector or VCR. Because the category in which a product is placed determines the other products it will be compared to, *categorization* is a crucial determinant of how a product is evaluated.

The products in a consumer's evoked set are likely to be those that share some similar features. It is important to understand how this knowledge is represented in a consumer's **cognitive structure,** which refers to a set of factual knowledge about products (i.e., beliefs) and the way these beliefs are organized in people's minds.[38] These knowledge structures were discussed in chapter 4. One reason is that marketers want to ensure that their products are correctly grouped. For example, General Foods brought out a new line of Jell-O flavors, such as Cranberry Orange, that it called Jell-O Gelatin Flavors for Salads. Unfortunately, the company discovered that people would use it only for salad, because the name encouraged them to put the product in their "salad" structure rather than in their "dessert" structure. The product line was dropped.[39]

LEVELS OF CATEGORIZATION

People not only group things into categories, but these groupings occur at different levels of specificity. Typically, a product is represented in a cognitive structure at one of three levels. To understand this idea, consider how someone might respond to these questions about an ice cream cone: What other products share similar characteristics, and which would be considered as alternatives to eating a cone?

These questions may be more complex than they first appear. At one level, a cone is similar to an apple, because both could be eaten as a dessert. At another level, a cone is similar to a piece of pie, because both are eaten for dessert and both are fattening. At still another level, a cone is similar to an ice cream sundae—both are eaten for dessert, are made of ice cream, and are fattening.

It is easy to see that the items a person associates with, say, the category "fattening dessert" influence the choices he or she will make for what to eat after dinner. The middle level, known as a *basic level category*, is typically the most useful in classifying products, because items grouped together tend to have a lot in common with each other but still permit a range of alternatives to be considered. The broader *superordinate category* is more abstract, whereas the more specific *subordinate category* often includes individual brands.[40] These three levels are depicted in Figure 9–7.

Of course, not all items fit equally well into a category. Apple pie is a better example of the subordinate category "pie" than is rhubarb pie, even though both are types of pies. Apple pie is more *prototypical,* and would tend to be considered first, especially by category novices. In contrast, pie experts will tend to have knowledge about both typical and atypical category examples.[41]

STRATEGIC IMPLICATIONS OF PRODUCT CATEGORIZATION

Product categorization has many strategic implications. The way a product is grouped with others has very important ramifications for determining both its competitors for adoption and what criteria will be used to make this choice.

Product Positioning. The success of a *positioning strategy* often hinges on the marketer's ability to convince the consumer that his or her product should be considered within a given category. For example, the orange juice industry tried to reposition orange juice as a drink that could be enjoyed all day long ("It's not just for breakfast anymore"). On the other hand, soft drink companies are now attempting the opposite by portraying sodas as suitable for breakfast consumption. They are trying to make their way into consumers' "breakfast drink" category, along with orange juice, grapefruit juice, and coffee (and indeed, this categorization already exists for many consumers in the southern United States, who, based on the author's personal experience, routinely guzzle a soft drink with their breakfast meal!). Of course, this strategy can backfire, as Pepsi-Cola discovered when it introduced Pepsi A.M. and positioned it as a coffee substitute. The company did such a good job of categorizing the drink as a morning beverage that customers wouldn't drink it at any other time and the product failed.[42]

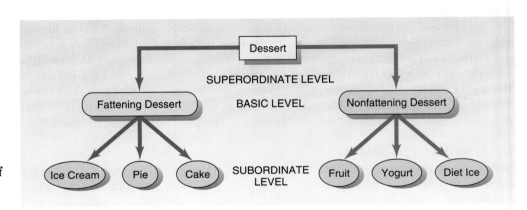

FIGURE 9–7 ■ **Levels of Abstraction in Dessert Categories**

S'alternative.

This ad for Sunkist lemon juice attempts to establish a new category for the product by repositioning it as a salt substitute.

Identifying Competitors. At the abstract, superordinate level, many different product forms compete for membership. The category "entertainment" might comprise both bowling and the ballet, but not many people would consider the substitution of one of these activities for the other. Products and services that on the surface are quite different, however, actually compete with each other at a broad level for consumers' discretionary dollars. While bowling or ballet may not be a likely trade-off for many people, it is feasible, for example, that a symphony might try to lure away season ticket holders to the ballet by positioning itself as an equivalent member of the category "cultural event."[43]

Consumers are often faced with choices between noncomparable categories, in which a number of attributes exist that cannot be directly related to one another (the old problem of comparing apples and oranges). The comparison process is easier when consumers can derive an overlapping category that encompasses both items (e.g., entertainment, value, usefulness) and then rate each alternative in terms of that superordinate category.[44]

Exemplar Products. As we saw with the case of apple pie versus rhubarb, if a product is a really good example of a category it is more familiar to consumers and is more easily recognized and recalled.[45] Judgments about category attributes tend to be disproportionately influenced by the characteristics of category exemplars.[46] In a sense, brands that are strongly associated with a category get to "call the shots" by defining the criteria that should be used to evaluate all category members.

Being a bit less than prototypical is not necessarily a bad thing, however. Products that are moderately unusual within their product category may stimulate more information processing and positive evaluations, because they are neither so familiar that they will be taken for granted nor so discrepant that they will be dismissed.[47] A brand that is strongly discrepant (like Zima, a clear malt beverage) may occupy a unique niche position, whereas those that are moderately discrepant (like local microbrews) remain in a distinct position within the general category.[48]

Locating products. Product categorization also can affect consumers' expectations regarding the places they can locate a desired product. If products do not clearly fit into categories (e.g., is a rug furniture?), consumers' ability to find them or make

MARKETING OPPORTUNITY

Changes in consumers' entertainment priorities are prompting some bowling alley owners to rethink their marketing strategies and target new customers by competing with other forms of entertainment. League bowling dropped by 40 percent between 1980 and 1993, forcing owners to focus on less-frequent bowlers.[49] Enter *cosmic bowling*—a cross between regular bowling and a night out at a club. To capture younger people, alleys are adding fog machines, laser light shows, and glow-in-the-dark bowling shoes.[50] Proprietors hope these innovations will open up a new market, as a more "hip" atmosphere puts this entertainment alternative in an evoked set along with nightclubs and restaurants.

sense of them may be diminished. For instance, a frozen dog food that had to be thawed and cooked failed in the market, partly because people could not adapt to the idea of buying dog food in the "frozen foods for people" section of their grocery stores.

PRODUCT CHOICE: SELECTING AMONG ALTERNATIVES

Once the relevant options from a category have been assembled and evaluated, a choice must be made among them.[51] Recall that the decision rules guiding choice can range from very simple and quick strategies to complicated processes requiring a lot of attention and cognitive processing. The choice can be influenced by integrating information from sources such as prior experience with the product or a similar one, information present at the time of purchase, and beliefs about the brands that have been created by advertising.[52]

EVALUATIVE CRITERIA

When Billy was looking at different television sets, he focused on one or two product features and completely ignored several others. He narrowed down his choices by only considering two specific brand names, and from the Prime Wave and Precision models, he chose one that featured stereo capability.

Evaluative criteria are the dimensions used to judge the merits of competing options. In comparing alternative products, Billy could have chosen from among any number of criteria, ranging from very functional attributes ("does this TV come with remote control?") to experiential ones ("does this TV's sound reproduction make me imagine I'm in a concert hall?").

Another important point is that criteria on which products *differ* from one another carry more weight in the decision process than do those where the alternatives are *similar*. If all brands being considered rate equally well on one attribute (e.g., if all TVs come with remote control), consumers will have to find other reasons to choose one over another. The attributes actually used to differentiate among choices are *determinant attributes*.

Marketers can play a role in educating consumers about which criteria should be used as determinant attributes. For example, consumer research by Church & Dwight indicated that many consumers view the use of natural ingredients as a determinant attribute. The result was promotion of a toothpaste made from baking soda, which the company already manufactured for Church & Dwight's Arm & Hammer brand.[53] And sometimes, the company can even invent a determinant attribute: Pepsi-Cola accomplished this by stamping freshness dates on soda cans. The company spent about $25 million on an advertising and promotional campaign to convince consumers that ther's nothing quite as horrible as a stale can of soda—even though it has been estimated that 98% of all cans are consumed well before this could be a problem. Six months after introducing the campaign, an independent survey found that 61% of respondents felt that freshness dating is an important attribute for a soft drink![54]

The decision about which attributes to use is the result of *procedural learning*, where a person undergoes a series of cognitive steps before making a choice. These steps include identifying important attributes, remembering whether competing brands differ on those attributes, and so on. In order for a marketer to effectively recommend a new decision criterion, its communication should convey three pieces of information:[55]

1. It should point out that there are significant differences among brands on the attribute.
2. It should supply the consumer with a decision-making rule, such as *if* (deciding among competing brands), *then* . . . (use the attribute as a criterion).
3. It should convey a rule that can be easily integrated with how the person has made this decision in the past. Otherwise, the recommendation is likely to be ignored because it requires too much mental work.

HEURISTICS: MENTAL SHORTCUTS

Do we actually perform complex mental calculations every time we make a purchase decision? Get a life! To simplify decisions, consumers often employ decision rules that allow them to use some dimensions as substitutes for others. For example, Billy relied on certain assumptions as substitutes for prolonged information search. In particular, he assumed the selection at Zany Zack's would be more than sufficient, so he did not bother to shop any of Zack's competitors. This assumption served as a shortcut to more extended information processing.[56]

Especially when limited problem solving occurs prior to making a choice, consumers often fall back on **heuristics,** or mental rules-of-thumb that lead to a speedy decision. These rules range from the very general (e.g., "Higher-priced products are higher-quality products" or "Buy the same brand I bought last time") to the very specific (e.g., "Buy Domino, the brand of sugar my mother always bought").[57]

Sometimes these shortcuts may not be in consumers' best interests. A consumer who personally knows one or two people who have had problems with a particular make of car, for example, might assume he or she would have similar trouble with it and thus overlook the model's overall excellent repair record.[58] The influence of such assumptions may be enhanced if the product has an unusual name, which makes it *and* the experiences with it more distinctive.[59]

RELYING ON A PRODUCT SIGNAL

One frequently used shortcut is the tendency to infer hidden dimensions of products from observable attributes. The aspect of the product that is visible acts as a *signal* of some underlying quality. Such inferences explain why someone trying to sell a used car takes great pains to be sure the car's exterior is clean and shiny: Potential buyers often judge the vehicle's mechanical condition by its appearance, even though this means they may drive away in a shiny, clean clunker.[60]

When product information is incomplete, judgments are often derived from beliefs about *covariation,* or perceived associations among events that may or may not actually influence one another.[61] For example, a consumer may form an association between product quality and the length of time a manufacturer has been in business. Other signals or attributes believed to coexist with good or bad products include well-known brand names, country of origin, price, and the retail outlets that carry the product.

Unfortunately, consumers tend to be poor estimators of covariation. Their beliefs persist despite evidence to the contrary. In a process similar to the consistency principle discussed in chapter 7, people tend to see what they are looking for. They will look for product information that confirms their guesses. In one experiment, consumers sampled four sets of products to determine if price and quality were related. Those who believed in this relationship prior to the study elected to sample higher-priced products, thus creating a sort of self-fulfilling prophecy.[62]

MARKET BELIEFS: IS IT BETTER IF I PAY MORE FOR IT?

Consumers often form assumptions about companies, products, and stores. These **market beliefs** then become the shortcuts that guide their decisions—whether or not they are accurate.[63] Recall, for instance, that Billy chose to shop at a large "electronics supermarket" because he *assumed* the selection would be better there than at a specialty store. A large number of market beliefs have been identified. Some of these are listed in Table 9–3. How many do you share?

Do higher prices mean higher quality? The assumption of a *price–quality relationship* is one of the most pervasive market beliefs.[64] Novice consumers may in fact consider price as the only relevant product attribute. Experts also consider this information, although in these cases price tends to be used for its informational value, especially for products (e.g., virgin wool) that are known to have wide quality variations in the marketplace. When this quality level is more standard or strictly regulated (e.g., Harris Tweed sport coats), experts do not weigh price in their decisions. For the most part, this belief is justified; you do tend to get what you pay for. However, let the buyer beware: The price–quality relationship is not always justified.[65]

COUNTRY-OF-ORIGIN AS A PRODUCT SIGNAL

Modern consumers choose among products made in many countries. Americans may buy Brazilian shoes, Japanese cars, clothing imported from Taiwan, or microwave ovens built in South Korea. Consumers' reactions to these imports are mixed. In some cases, people have come to assume that a product made overseas is of better quality (e.g., cameras, cars), whereas in other cases the knowledge that a

TABLE 9–3 ■ Common Market Beliefs

Brand	All brands are basically the same.
	Generic products are just name brands sold under a different label at a lower price.
	The best brands are the ones that are purchased the most.
	When in doubt, a national brand is always a safe bet.
Store	Specialty stores are great places to familiarize yourself with the best brands; but once you figure out what you want, it's cheaper to buy it at a discount outlet.
	A store's character is reflected in its window displays.
	Salespeople in specialty stores are more knowledgeable than other sales personnel.
	Larger stores offer better prices than small stores.
	Locally owned stores give the best service.
	A store that offers a good value on one of its products probably offers good values on all of its items.
	Credit and return policies are most lenient at large department stores.
	Stores that have just opened usually charge attractive prices.
Prices/Discounts/Sales	Sales are typically run to get rid of slow-moving merchandise.
	Stores that are constantly having sales don't really save you money.
	Within a given store, higher prices generally indicate higher quality.
Advertising and Sales Promotion	"Hard-sell" advertising is associated with low-quality products.
	Items tied to "giveaways" are not a good value (even with the freebee).
	Coupons represent real savings for customers because they are not offered by the store.
	When you buy heavily advertised products, you are paying for the label, not for higher quality.
Product/Packaging	Largest-sized containers are almost always cheaper per unit than smaller sizes.
	New products are more expensive when they're first introduced; prices tend to settle down as time goes by.
	When you are not sure what you need in a product, it's a good idea to invest in the extra features, because you'll probably wish you had them later.
	In general, synthetic goods are lower in quality than goods made of natural materials.
	It's advisable to stay away from products when they are new to the market; it usually takes the manufacturer a little time to work the bugs out.

Source: Adapted from Calvin P. Duncan, "Consumer Market Beliefs: A Review of the Literature and an Agenda for Future Research," in eds. Marvin E. Goldberg, Gerald Gorn, and Richard W. Pollay, *Advances in Consumer Research* 17 (Provo, UT: Association for Consumer Resaerch, 1990): 729–35.

product has been imported tends to lower perceptions of product quality (e.g., apparel).[66] In general, people tend to rate their own country's products more favorably than do people who live elsewhere, and products from industrialized countries are rated better than are those from developing countries.

A product's *country-of-origin* in some cases is an important piece of information in the decision-making process.[67] Of course, the extent to which this is a factor depends on the product category: In a recent Gallup Poll of American consumers, only 3 percent of respondents felt that this information is important when they buy shoes and only 7 percent relied on it for toy purchases, but 51 percent said country-of-origin is a key factor when they buy clothing, and 54 percent agreed that a car's nationality is important.[68] The importance attached to a car's origin can be problematic, however. In recent years an auto's heritage has become hard to figure out, as automakers diversify their manufacturing operations around the world. A Chevrolet Camaro ad, for example, trades on its American image by asking. "What else would you expect from the country that invented rock-and-roll?" One minor detail: Camaro is made in Canada! The American Automobile Labeling Act of 1992 was intended to create uniform standards in calculating the domestic content of cars. Still, confusion abounds: The Dodge Stealth is built by Mitsubishi in Japan, but the Mitsubishi Eclipse has a Chrysler engine and is built in Normal, Illinois.[69]

Nonetheless, a product's origin often is used as a signal of quality. Certain items are strongly associated with specific countries, and products from those countries often attempt to benefit from these linkages. Country-of-origin can function as a *stereotype*—a knowledge structure based on inferences across products. These stereotypes are often biased or inaccurate, but they do play a constructive role in simplifying complex choice situations.[70] For example, a Brazilian soft drink company is now trying to market a beverage it is calling Samba in the United States. Samba is made from the guaraná berry; this sweet, flowery-tasting soda is extremely popular in Brazil. The company is capitalizing on the care-free, partying image that many Americans have of Brazilians to get them to try the soda. In its commercials, a scantily clad woman says, "In Brazil we do things a little different. We laugh a little more, wear a little less, and dance the samba. Dance the dance. Drink the drink."[71]

Recent evidence indicates that learning of a product's country-of-origin is not necessarily good or bad. Instead, it has the effect of stimulating the consumer's interest in the product to a greater degree. The purchaser thinks more extensively about the product and evaluates it more carefully.[72] The origin of the product thus can act as a product attribute that combines with others attributes to influence evaluations.[73] In addition, the consumer's own expertise with the product category moderates the effects of this attribute. When other information is available, experts tend

The growing popularity of *faux* Irish pubs around the world attests to the power of country stereotypes to influence consumers' preferences. About 800 Irish-themed pubs have been opened in countries including South Africa, Italy, Hong Kong, and Russia. The Irish brewer Guinness Plc encourages the establishment of these outputs, since an Irish pub is mere blarney without Guinness on tap. The company helps owners design the pub and even assists in locating Irish bar staff to dispense its thick brew. As one Guinness executive explained, "We've created a mythology of an Irish ambience."
Quoted in Howard Banks, "We'll Provide the Shillelaghs," *Forbes* (April 8, 1996): 68 (2), p. 72.

Too bad you're so addicted to import cars.

Demand Better. Eighty Eight LSS By Oldsmobile

Oldsmobile is appealing to Americans who are looking for a reason to buy domestically manufactured cars.

to ignore country-of-origin information whereas novices continue to rely on it. However, when other information is unavailable or ambiguous, both experts and novices will rely on this attribute to make a decision.[74]

The tendency to prefer products or people of one's own culture over those from other countries is called **ethnocentrism.** Ethnocentric consumers are likely to feel it is wrong to buy products from other countries, particularly because of the negative effect this may have on the domestic economy. Marketing campaigns stressing the desirability of "buying American" are more likely to appeal to this consumer segment. This trait has been measured on The Consumer Ethnocentrism Scale (CETSCALE) that was devised for this purpose: The scale identifies ethnocentric consumers by their extent of agreement with items such as:

- purchasing foreign-made products is un-American,
- curbs should be put on all imports,
- American consumers who purchase products made in other countries are responsible for putting their fellow Americans out of work.[75]

MULTICULTURAL DIMENSIONS

The French tend to be a bit finicky about their food, and products from other countries are evaluated critically. However, despite the particularly unappealing reputation of British cuisine in France, the upscale department store Marks & Spencer is slowly making inroads by selling "produce of England" and ethnic dishes such as chicken tikka masala that are not widely found in France. The French are buying $60,000 a week of English-style sandwiches such as egg and watercress on whole-wheat bread. Positioned primarily as convenience foods for young office workers, these choices have less calories and are less expensive than the traditional French loaf split down the middle and lathered with butter and ham or Camembert cheese. This modest British invasion began 20 years ago when Marks & Spencer began to sell tea and biscuits to curious shoppers. At that time, British managers were so naive it took them awhile to realize how closely the word "preserves," which they used to refer to the jams they sold, was to the French term for condom![76] Nowadays they market with a bit more *savoir-faire.*

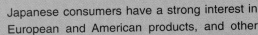

MULTICULTURAL DIMENSIONS

Japanese consumers have a strong interest in European and American products, and other countries work hard to cultivate a favorable image in the discriminating Japanese market. Dentsu, the largest Japanese advertising agency, has conducted several studies for The Commission of the European Communities to determine how Japanese consumers perceive European countries, the United States, and some Asian countries, and how they evaluate products from those countries.

The study involved personal interviews with 1,600 consumers ranging in age from 15 to 59. Respondents rated countries on such overall dimensions as "rich in history/tradition," "abundant natural scenery," and "would like to visit," as well as on product-related characteristics, such as "high-quality, performance products" and "well-designed, stylish products."

The results showed that the Japanese public associates Europe with history, tradition, and well-designed products, whereas American advanced technology and agriculture are highly rated (products from South Korea and Taiwan tended to be rated lower than those from the United States or Europe).

Overall, respondents told the researchers that foreign products (i.e., non-Japanese) are well regarded in terms of style, but are assumed to be lower in technological sophistication than most Japanese products. There was also widespread sentiment that many non-Japanese products are not well suited to Japanese needs. These consumers felt that many foreign goods are too expensive and are in need of more thorough after-sales service.

A perceptual map (these were described in chapter 2) that summarizes Japanese consumers' images of European countries and the United States is shown in Figure 9–8. The five countries in Group 1 have the most "image wealth"; they are strong in both overall appeal and in ratings of product quality. Germany is the sole country in Group 2, indicating that its products are better regarded than is the country as a whole. The countries in Group 3 have positive images, but these good feelings have yet to transfer to their products. Finally, the countries in Group 4 appear to have their work cut out for them if they hope to win over the hearts and wallets of Japanese consumers.[77]

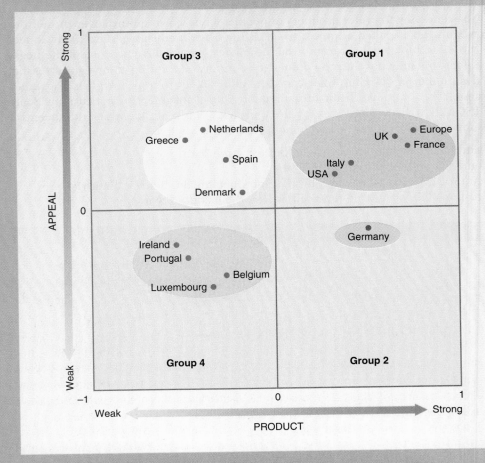

FIGURE 9–8 ■
Perceptual Positioning by Country of Origin among Japanese Consumers
Source: *Images of Europe: A Survey of Japanese Attitudes toward European Products* (report prepared by Dentsu Inc. for the Commission of the European Communities, Brussels, 1994): 5.

CHOOSING FAMILIAR BRAND NAMES: LOYALTY OR HABIT?

Branding is a marketing strategy that often functions as a heuristic. People form preferences for a favorite brand, and then they literally may never change their minds in the course of a lifetime. In a study by the Boston Consulting Group of the market leaders in 30 product categories, it was found that 27 of the brands that were number one in 1930 remain at the top today. These include such perennial favorites as Ivory Soap, Campbell's Soup, and Gold Medal Flour.[78]

A brand that exhibits that kind of staying power is treasured by marketers, and for good reason. Brands that dominate their markets are as much as 50 percent more profitable than their nearest competitors.[79] A survey of 3,000 consumers on brand power in Japan, Europe, and the United States combined awareness and esteem scores to produce the following list of the most positively regarded brand names around the world.[80]

1. Coca-Cola
2. IBM
3. Sony
4. Porsche
5. McDonald's
6. Disney
7. Honda
8. Toyota
9. Seiko
10. BMW

Consumers' attachments to certain brands, such as Marlboro, Coca-Cola, Gerber, and Levi's, are so powerful that this loyalty is often considered as a positive product attribute in and of itself. Recently, the British company Grand Metropolitan actually decided to record brand names it had acquired on its balance sheets, including these intangible assets in its financial reports to shareholders.[81] Marlboro is the most valuable brand name in the world. It was recently valued at $31.2 billion.[82]

INERTIA: THE LAZY CUSTOMER

Many people tend to buy the same brand just about every time they go to the store. This consistent pattern is often due to **inertia**—a brand is bought out of habit merely because less effort is required. If another product comes along that is for some reason easier to buy (e.g., it is cheaper or the original product is out of stock), the consumer will not hesitate to do so. A competitor who is trying to change a buying pattern based on inertia often can do so rather easily, because little resistance to brand switching will be encountered if the right incentive is offered. When there is little to no underlying commitment to a particular brand, promotional tools such as point-of-purchase displays, extensive couponing, or noticeable price reductions may be sufficient to "unfreeze" a consumer's habitual pattern.

BRAND LOYALTY: A "FRIEND," TRIED-AND-TRUE

This kind of fickleness will not occur if true **brand loyalty** exists. In contrast to inertia, brand loyalty is a form of repeat purchasing behavior reflecting a conscious decision to continue buying the same brand.[83] For brand loyalty to exist, a pattern of repeat purchase must be accompanied by an underlying positive attitude toward the brand. Brand loyalty may be initiated by customer preference based on objective reasons, but after the brand has been around for a long time and is heavily advertised it can also engender an emotional attachment, either by being incorporated into the consumer's self-image or because it is associated with prior experiences.[84] Purchase decisions based on brand loyalty also become habitual over time, though in these cases the underlying commitment to the product is much firmer.

Compared to an inertia situation in which the consumer passively accepts a brand, a brand-loyal consumer is actively (sometimes passionately) involved with

his or her favorite. Because of the emotional bonds that can come about between brand-loyal consumers and products, "true-blue" users react more vehemently when these products are altered, redesigned, or eliminated.[85] For example, when Coca-Cola replaced its tried-and-true formula with New Coke in the 1980s, a firestorm of national call-in campaigns, boycotts, and other protests occurred.

In recent years, marketers have struggled with the problem of *brand parity,* which refers to consumers' beliefs that there are no significant differences among brands. For example, one survey found that more than 70 percent of consumers worldwide believe that all paper towels, soaps, and snack chips are alike.[86] Some analysts even proclaimed that brand names are dead, killed off by private label or generic products that offer the same value for less money.

However, the reports of this death appear to be premature—major brands are making a comeback. This renaissance is attributed to information overload—with too many alternatives (many of them unfamiliar names) to choose from, people are looking for a few clear signals of quality. Following a period in the late 1980s and early 1990s when people had strong doubts about the ability of large companies to produce quality products, more recent surveys indicate consumers slowly are beginning to trust major manufacturers again.[87] Brand names are very much alive in the millennium.

DECISION RULES

Consumers consider sets of product attributes by using different rules, depending on the complexity of the decision and the importance of the decision to them. As we have seen, in some cases these rules are quite simple: People simply rely on a "shortcut" to make a choice. In other cases, though, more effort and thought is put into carefully weighing alternatives before coming to a decision.

One way to differentiate among decision rules is to divide them into those that are *compensatory* versus those that are *noncompensatory.* To aid the discussion of some of these rules, the attributes of TV sets considered by Billy are summarized in Table 9–4. Now, let's see how some of these rules result in different brand choices.

NONCOMPENSATORY DECISION RULES

Simple decision rules are **noncompensatory,** meaning that a product with a low standing on one attribute cannot make up for this position by being better on another attribute. In other words, people simply eliminate all options that do not meet some basic standards. A consumer like Billy who uses the decision rule, "Only buy well-known brand names," would not consider a new brand, even if it was equal

TABLE 9–4 ■ **Hypothetical Alternatives for a TV Set**

ATTRIBUTE	IMPORTANCE RANKING	BRAND RATINGS		
		PRIME WAVE	PRECISION	KAMASHITA
Size of screen	1	Excellent	Excellent	Excellent
Stereo broadcast capability	2	Poor	Excellent	Good
Brand reputation	3	Excellent	Excellent	Poor
Onscreen programming	4	Excellent	Poor	Poor
Cable-ready capability	5	Good	Good	Good
Sleep timer	6	Excellent	Poor	Good

or superior to existing ones. When people are less familiar with a product category or are not very motivated to process complex information, they tend to use simple, noncompensatory rules, which are summarized below.[88]

The Lexicographic Rule. When the *lexicographic rule* is used, the brand that is the best on the most important attribute is selected. If two or more brands are seen as being equally good on that attribute, the consumer then compares them on the second most important attribute. This selection process goes on until the tie is broken. In Billy's case, since both the Prime Wave and Precision models were tied on his most important attribute (a 52-inch screen), the Precision was chosen because of its rating on this second most important attribute—its stereo capability.

The Elimination-by-Aspects Rule. Using the *elimination-by-aspects rule,* brands are also evaluated on the most important attribute. In this case, though, specific cutoffs are imposed. For example, if Billy had been more interested in having a sleep timer on his TV (i.e., if it had a higher importance ranking), he might have stipulated that his choice "must have a sleep timer." Because the Prime Wave model had one and the Precision did not, the Prime Wave would have been chosen.

The Conjunctive Rule. Whereas the two former rules involve processing by attribute, the *conjunctive rule* entails processing by brand. As with the elimination-by-aspects procedure, cutoffs are established for each attribute. A brand is chosen if it meets all of the cutoffs, but failure to meet any one cutoff means it will be rejected. If none of the brands meet all of the cutoffs, the choice may be delayed, the decision rule may be changed, or the cutoffs may be modified.

If Billy had stipulated that all attributes had to be rated "good" or better, he would not have been able to choose any of the options. He might then have modified his decision rule, conceding that it was not possible to attain these high standards in the price range he was considering. In this case, perhaps Billy could decide that he could live without on-screen programming, so the Precision model could again be considered.

COMPENSATORY DECISION RULES

Unlike noncompensatory decision rules, **compensatory decision rules** give a product a chance to make up for its shortcomings. Consumers who employ these rules tend to be more involved in the purchase and thus are willing to exert the effort to consider the entire picture in a more exacting way. The willingness to let good and bad product qualities balance out can result in quite different choices. For example, if Billy were not concerned about having stereo reception, he might have chosen the Prime Wave model. But because this brand doesn't feature this highly ranked attribute, it doesn't stand a chance when he uses a noncompensatory rule.

Two basic types of compensatory rules have been identified. When using the *simple additive rule,* the consumer merely chooses the alternative that has the largest number of positive attributes. This choice is most likely to occur when his or her ability or motivation to process information is limited. One drawback to this approach for the consumer is that some of these attributes may not be very meaningful or important. An ad containing a long list of product benefits may be persuasive, despite the fact that many of the benefits included are actually standard within the product class and aren't determinant attributes at all.

The more complex version is known as the *weighted additive rule.*[89] When using this rule, the consumer also takes into account the relative importance of positively rated attributes, essentially multiplying brand ratings by importance weights. If this process sounds familiar, it should. The calculation process strongly resembles the multiattribute attitude model described in chapter 7.

CHAPTER SUMMARY

- Consumers are faced with the need to make decisions about products all of the time. Some of these decisions are very important and entail great effort, whereas others are made on a virtually automatic basis.

- Perspectives on decision making range from a focus on habits that people develop over time to novel situations involving a great deal of risk, in which consumers must carefully collect and analyze information prior to making a choice.

- A typical decision process involves several steps. The first is *problem recognition,* in which the consumer first realizes that some action must be taken. This realization may be prompted in a variety of ways, ranging from the actual malfunction of a current purchase to a desire for new things based on exposure to different circumstances or advertising that provides a glimpse into what is needed to "live the good life."

- Once a problem has been recognized and is seen as sufficiently important to warrant some action, *information search* begins. This search may range from simply scanning memory to determine what has been done to resolve the problem in the past to extensive fieldwork in which the consumer consults a variety of sources to amass as much information as possible. In many cases, people engage in surprisingly little search. Instead, they rely on various mental shortcuts, such as brand names or price, or they may simply imitate others.

- In the *evaluation of alternatives* stage, the product alternatives that are considered comprise the individual's *evoked set.* Members of the evoked set usually share some characteristics; they are categorized similarly. The way products are mentally grouped influences which alternatives will be considered, and some brands are more strongly associated with these categories than are others (i.e., they are more prototypical).

- Research in the field of *behavioral economics* illustrates that decision making is not always strictly rational. Principles of *mental accounting* demonstrate that decisions can be influenced by the way a problem is posed (called *framing*), and by whether it is put in terms of gains or losses.

- When the consumer eventually must make a product choice from among alternatives, a number of decision rules may be used. *Noncompensatory rules* eliminate alternatives that are deficient on any of the criteria the consumer has chosen to use. *Compensatory rules,* which are more likely to be applied in high-involvement situations, allow the decision maker to consider each alternative's good and bad points more carefully to arrive at the overall best choice.

- Very often, *heuristics,* or mental rules-of-thumb, are used to simplify decision making. In particular, people develop many market beliefs over time. One of the most common beliefs is that price is positively related to quality. Other heuristics rely on well-known brand names or a product's country of origin as signals of product quality. When a brand is consistently purchased over time, this pattern may be due to true *brand loyalty,* or simply to *inertia* because it's the easiest thing to do.

CONSUMER BEHAVIOR CHALLENGE

1. If people are not always rational decision makers, is it worth the effort to study how purchasing decisions are made? What techniques might be employed to understand experiential consumption and to translate this knowledge into marketing strategy?

2. List three product attributes that can be used as quality signals and provide an example of each.

3. Why is it difficult to place a product in a consumer's evoked set after it has already been rejected? What strategies might a marketer use in an attempt to accomplish this goal?

4. Define the three levels of product categorization described in the chapter. Diagram these levels for a health club.

5. Discuss two different noncompensatory decision rules and highlight the difference(s) between them. How might the use of one rule versus another result in a different product choice?

6. Choose a friend or parent who grocery shops on a regular basis and keep a log of their purchases of common consumer products over the semester. Can you detect any evidence of brand loyalty in any categories based on consistency of purchases? If so, talk to the person about these purchases. Try to determine if his or her choices are based on true brand loyalty or on inertia. What techniques might you use to differentiate between the two?

7. Form a group of three. Pick a product and develop a marketing plan based on each of the three approaches to consumer decision making: rational, experiential, and behavioral influence. What are the major differences in emphasis among the three perspectives? Which is the most likely type of problem-solving activity for the product you have selected? What characteristics of the product make this so?

8. Locate a person who is about to make a major purchase. Ask that person to make a chronological list of all the information sources consulted prior to making a decision. How would you characterize the types of sources used (i.e., internal versus external, media versus personal, etc.)? Which sources appeared to have the most impact on the person's decision?

9. Perform a survey of country-of-origin stereotypes. Compile a list of five countries and ask people what products they associate with each. What are their evaluations of the products and likely attributes of these different products? The power of a country stereotype can also be demonstrated in another way. Prepare a brief description of a product, including a list of features, and ask people to rate it in terms of quality, likelihood of purchase, and so on. Make several versions of the description, varying only the country from which it comes. Do ratings change as a function of the country-of-origin?

10. Ask a friend to "talk through" the process he or she used to choose one brand over others during a recent purchase. Based on this description, can you identify the decision rule that was most likely employed?

11. Push technologies have the potential to make our lives easier by reducing the amount of clutter we need to work through in order to access the information on the Internet that really interests us. On the other hand, critics point to a host of privacy issues that are raised when companies begin to learn more about our tastes and preferences. Are the positive aspects of these software agents worth the negative ones? How can or should push technologies be designed and regulated to insure consumers' privacy while still meeting their information search needs?

12. Give one of the scenarios described in the section on biases in decision making to 10 to 20 people. How do the results you obtain compare with those reported in the chapter?

NOTES

1. John C. Mowen, "Beyond Consumer Decision Making," *Journal of Consumer Marketing* 5 (1988)1: 15–25.

2. Richard W. Olshavsky and Donald H. Granbois, "Consumer Decision Making—Fact or Fiction," *Journal of Consumer Research* 6 (September 1989): 93–100.

3. James R. Bettman, "The Decision Maker Who Came in from the Cold" (presidential address), in eds. Leigh McAllister and Michael Rothschild, *Advances in Consumer Research* 20 (Provo, UT: Association for Consumer Research, (1993)); 7–11. John W. Payne, James R. Bettman, and Eric J. Johnson, "Behavioral Decision Research: A Constructive Processing Perspective," *Annual Review of Psychology* 4 (1992): 87–131; for an overview of recent developments in individual choice models, see Robert J. Meyer and Barbara E. Kahn, "Probabilistic Models of Consumer Choice Behavior," in eds. Thomas S. Robertson and Harold H. Kassarjian, *Handbook of Consumer Behavior* (Upper Saddle River, NJ: Prentice Hall, 1991): 85–123.

4. Mowen, "Beyond Consumer Decision Making."

5. Joseph W. Alba and J. Wesley Hutchinson, "Dimensions of Consumer Expertise," *Journal of Consumer Research* 13 (March 1988): 411–54.

6. Gordon C. Bruner III and Richard J. Pomazal, "Problem Recognition: The Crucial First Stage of the Consumer Decision Process," *Journal of Consumer Marketing* 5 (1988)1: 53–63.

7. Ross K. Baker, "Textually Transmitted Diseases," *American Demographics* (December 1987): 64.

8. Julia Marlowe, Gary Selnow, and Lois Blosser, "A Content Analysis of Problem-Resolution Appeals in Television Commercials," *The Journal of Consumer Affairs* 23 (1989)1: 175–94.

9. Peter H. Bloch, Daniel L. Sherrell, and Nancy M. Ridgway, "Consumer Search: An Extended Framework," *Journal of Consumer Research* 13 (June 1986): 119–26.

10. Girish Punj, "Presearch Decision Making in Consumer Durable Purchases," *Journal of Consumer Marketing* 4 (Winter 1987): 71–82.

11. H. Beales, M. B. Jagis, S. C. Salop, and R. Staelin, "Consumer Search and Public Policy," *Journal of Consumer Research* 8 (June 1981): 11–22.

12. Adrienne Ward Fawcett, "Look for the Label—and Shoppers Really Are Listening," *Advertising Age* (May 8, 1995): S10.

13. Thomas E. Miller, "New Markets for Information," *American Demographics* (April 1995): 46–50.

14. Amy Cortese, "A Way Out of the Web Maze," *Business Week* (February 24, 1997): 93 (8 pp.).

15. Daniel Lyons, "Firefly: Software That Can Be a Personal Shopper . . . or a Spy," *New York Times Magazine,* accessed via ssnewslink.com, August 25, 1997.

16. Paul C. Judge, "Why Firefly Has Mad Ave. Buzzing," *Business Week* (October 7, 1996): 100 (2 pp.).

17. Thomas E. Weber, "Advertising: New Software Lets Marketers Target Their Ads on Internet," *Wall Street Journal Interactive Edition* (April 21, 1997).

18. Itamar Simonson, Joel Huber, and John Payne, "The Relationship between Prior Brand Knowledge and Information Acquisition Order," *Journal of Consumer Research* 14 (March 1988): 566–78.

19. John R. Hauser, Glen L. Urban, and Bruce D. Weinberg, "How Consumers Allocate Their Time When Searching for Information," *Journal of Marketing Research* 30 (November 1993): 452–66; George J. Stigler, "The Economics of Information," *Journal of Political Economy* 69 (June 1961): 213–25.

20. Cathy J. Cobb and Wayne D. Hoyer, "Direct Observation of Search Behavior," *Psychology & Marketing* 2 (Fall 1985): 161–79.

21. Sharon E. Beatty and Scott M. Smith, "External Search Effort: An Investigation across Several Product Categories," *Journal of Consumer Research* 14 (June 1987): 83–95; William L. Moore and Donald R. Lehmann, "Individual Differences in Search Behavior for a Nondurable," *Journal of Consumer Research* 7 (December 1980): 296–307.

22. Geoffrey C. Kiel and Roger A. Layton, "Dimensions of Consumer Information Seeking Behavior," *Journal of Marketing Research* 28 (May 1981): 233–9; see also Narasimhan Srinivasan and Brian T. Ratchford, "An Empirical Test of a Model of External Search for Automobiles," *Journal of Consumer Research* 18 (September 1991): 233–42.

23. David F. Midgley, "Patterns of Interpersonal Information Seeking for the Purchase of a Symbolic Product," *Journal of Marketing Research* 20 (February 1983): 74–83.

24. Cyndee Miller, "Scotland to U.S.: 'This Tennent's for You'," *Marketing News* (August 29, 1994): 26.

25. Satya Menon and Barbara E. Kahn, "The Impact of Context on Variety Seeking in Product Choices," *Journal of Consumer Research* 22 (December 1995): 285–95; Barbara E. Kahn and Alice M. Isen, "The Influence of Positive Affect on Variety Seeking among Safe, Enjoyable Products," *Journal of Consumer Research* 20 (September 1993): 257–70

26. "Known Quantities," *American Demographics* (June 1997): 37.

27. Gary Belsky, "Why Smart People Make Major Money Mistakes," *Money* (July 1995): 76 (10 pp.); Richard Thaler and Eric J. Johnson, "Gambling with the House Money or Trying to Break Even: The Effects of Prior Outcomes on Risky Choice," *Management Science* 36 (June 1990): 643–60; Richard Thaler, "Mental Accounting and Consumer Choice," *Marketing Science* 4 (Summer 1985): 199–214.

28. Daniel Kahneman and Amos Tversky, "Prospect Theory: An Analysis of Decision under Risk," *Econometrica* 47 (March 1979): 263–91; Timothy B. Heath, Subimal Chatterjee, and Karen Russo France, "Mental Accounting and Changes in Price: The Frame Dependence of Reference Dependence," *Journal of Consumer Research* 22 (June 1995)1: 90–7.

29. Quoted in Richard Thaler, "Mental Accounting and Consumer Choice," *Marketing Science* 4 (Summer 1985): 199–214, quoted on p. 206

30. Girish N. Punj and Richard Staelin, "A Model of Consumer Search Behavior for New Automobiles," *Journal of Consumer Research* 9 (March 1983): 366–80.

31. Cobb and Hoyer, "Direct Observation of Search Behavior"; Moore and Lehmann, "Individual Differences in Search Behavior for a Nondurable"; Punj and Staelin, "A Model of Consumer Search Behavior for New Automobiles."

32. James R. Bettman and C. Whan Park, "Effects of Prior Knowledge and Experience and Phase of the Choice Process on Consumer Decision Processes: A Protocol Analysis," *Journal of Consumer Research* 7 (December 1980): 234–48.

33. Alba and Hutchinson, "Dimensions of Consumer Expertise"; Bettman and Park, "Effects of Prior Knowledge and Experience and Phase of the Choice Process on Consumer Decision Processes"; Merrie Brucks, "The Effects of Product Class Knowledge on Information Search Behavior," *Journal of Consumer Research* 12 (June l985): 1–16; Joel E. Urbany, Peter R. Dickson, and William L. Wilkie, "Buyer Uncertainty and Information Search," *Journal of Consumer Research* 16 (September 1989): 208–15.

34. Cyndee Miller, "HIV Kits Target Untested Market," *Marketing News* (January 20, 1997): 1, 11.

35. Mary Frances Luce, James R. Bettman, and John W. Payne, "Choice Processing in Emotionally Difficult Decisions," *Journal of Experimental Psychology: Learning, Memory, and Cognition* 23 (March 1997): 384–405; example provided by Prof. James Bettman, personal communication, December 17, 1997.

36. John R. Hauser and Birger Wernerfelt, "An Evaluation Cost Model of Consideration Sets," *Journal of Consumer Research* 16 (March 1990): 393–408.

37. Robert J. Sutton, "Using Empirical Data to Investigate the Likelihood of Brands Being Admitted or Readmitted into an Established Evoked Set," *Journal of the Academy of Marketing Science* 15 (Fall 1987): 82.

38. Alba and Hutchison, "Dimensions of Consumer Expertise"; Joel B. Cohen and Kunal Basu, "Alternative Models of Categorization: Toward a Contingent Processing Framework," *Journal of Consumer Research* 13 (March 1987): 455–72.

39. Robert M. McMath, "The Perils of Typecasting," *American Demographics* (February 1997): 60.

40. Eleanor Rosch, "Principles of Categorization," in eds. E. Rosch and B.B. Lloyd, *Recognition and Categorization* (Hillsdale, NJ: Erlbaum, 1978).

41. Michael R. Solomon, "Mapping Product Constellations: A Social Categorization Approach to Symbolic Consumption," *Psychology & Marketing* 5 (1988)3: 233–58.

42. Robert M. McMath, "The Perils of Typecasting," *American Demographics* (February 1997): 60.

43. Elizabeth C. Hirschman and Michael R. Solomon, "Competition and Cooperation among Culture Production Systems," in eds. Ronald F. Bush and Shelby D. Hunt, *Marketing Theory: Philosophy of Science Perspectives* (Chicago: American Marketing Association, 1982): 269–72.

44. Michael D. Johnson, "The Differential Processing of Product Category and Noncomparable Choice Alternatives," *Journal of Consumer Research* 16 (December 1989): 300–9.

45. Mita Sujan, "Consumer Knowledge: Effects on Evaluation Strategies Mediating Consumer Judgments," *Journal of Consumer Research* 12 (June 1985): 31–46.

46. Rosch, "Principles of Categorization."

47. Joan Meyers-Levy and Alice M. Tybout, "Schema Congruity as a Basis for Product Evaluation," *Journal of Consumer Research* 16 (June 1989): 39–55.

48. Mita Sujan and James R. Bettman, "The Effects of Brand Positioning Strategies on Consumers' Brand and Category Perceptions: Some Insights from Schema Research," *Journal of Marketing Research* 26 (November 1989): 454–67.

49. Kendall Hamilton, "Step into a Dark Alley," *Newsweek* (March 25, 1996): 67.

50. Cathy Hainer, "Putting a Cosmic Spin on Bowling," *USA Today* (November 13, 1996): 9A.

51. See William P. Putsis Jr. and Narasimhan Srinivasan, "Buying or Just Browsing? The Duration of Purchase Deliberation," *Journal of Marketing Research* 31 (August 1994): 393–402.

52. Robert E. Smith, "Integrating Information from Advertising and Trial: Processes and Effects on Consumer Response to Product Information," *Journal of Marketing Research* 30 (May 1993): 204–19.

53. Jack Trout, "Marketing in Tough Times," *Boardroom Reports* (October 1992)2: 8.

54. Stuart Elliott, "Pepsi-Cola to Stamp Dates for Freshness on Soda Cans,"

New York Times (March 31, 1994): Emily DeNitto, D1 (2; "Pepsi's Gamble Hits Freshness Dating Jackpot," *Advertising Age* (September 19, 1994): 50.

55. Amna Kirmani and Peter Wright, "Procedural Learning, Consumer Decision Making and Marketing Communication," *Marketing Letters* 4, 1(1993): 39–48.

56. Robert A. Baron, *Psychology: The Essential Science* (Boston: Allyn & Bacon, 1989); Valerie S. Folkes, "The Availability Heuristic and Perceived Risk," *Journal of Consumer Research* 15 (June 1989): 13–23; Daniel Kahneman and Amos Tversky, "Prospect Theory: An Analysis of Decision Under Risk," *Econometrica* 47 (1979): 263–91.

57. Wayne D. Hoyer, "An Examination of Consumer Decision Making for a Common Repeat Purchase Product," *Journal of Consumer Research* 11 (December 1984): 822–9; Calvin P. Duncan, "Consumer Market Beliefs: A Review of the Literature and an Agenda for Future Research," in eds. Marvin E. Goldberg, Gerald Gorn, and Richard W. Pollay, *Advances in Consumer Research* 17 (Provo, UT: Association for Consumer Research, 1990): 729–35; Frank Alpert, "Consumer Market Beliefs and Their Managerial Implications: An Empirical Examination," *Journal of Consumer Marketing* 10 (1993)2: 56–70.

58. Michael R. Solomon, Sarah Drenan, and Chester A. Insko, "Popular Induction: When is Consensus Information Informative?" *Journal of Personality* 49 (1981)2: 212–24.

59. Folkes, "The Availability Heuristic and Perceived Risk."

60. Beales et al., "Consumer Search and Public Policy."

61. Gary T. Ford and Ruth Ann Smith, "Inferential Beliefs in Consumer Evaluations: An Assessment of Alternative Processing Strategies," *Journal of Consumer Research* 14 (December 1987): 363–71; Deborah Roedder John, Carol A. Scott, and James R. Bettman, "Sampling Data for Covariation Assessment: The Effects of Prior Beliefs on Search Patterns," *Journal of Consumer Research* 13 (June 1986): 38–47; Gary L. Sullivan and Kenneth J. Berger, "An Investigation of the Determinants of Cue Utilization," *Psychology & Marketing* 4 (Spring 1987): 63–74.

62. John et al., "Sampling Data for Covariation Assessment."

63. Duncan, "Consumer Market Beliefs."

64. Chr. Hjorth-Andersen, "Price as a Risk Indicator," *Journal of Consumer Policy* 10 (1987): 267–81.

65. David M. Gardner, "Is There a Generalized Price-Quality Relationship?" *Journal of Marketing Research* 8 (May 1971): 241–3; Kent B. Monroe, "Buyers' Subjective Perceptions of Price," *Journal of Marketing Research* 10 (1973): 70–80.

66. Durairaj Maheswaran, "Country of Origin as a Stereotype: Effects of Consumer Expertise and Attribute Strength on Product Evaluations," *Journal of Consumer Research* 21 (September 1994): 354–65; Ingrid M. Martin and Sevgin Eroglu, "Measuring a Multi-Dimensional Construct: Country Image," *Journal of Business Research* 28 (1993): 191–210; Richard Ettenson, Janet Wagner, and Gary Gaeth, "Evaluating the Effect of Country of Origin and the 'Made in the U.S.A.' Campaign: A Conjoint Approach," *Journal of Retailing* 64 (Spring 1988): 85–100; C. Min Han and Vern Terpstra, "Country-of-Origin Effects for Uni-National & Bi-National Products," *Journal of International Business* 19 (Summer 1988): 235–55; Michelle A. Morganosky and Michelle M. Lazarde, "Foreign-Made Apparel: Influences on Consumers' Perceptions of Brand and Store Quality," *International Journal of Advertising* 6 (Fall 1987): 339–48.

67. See Richard Jackson Harris, Bettina Garner-Earl, Sara J. Sprick, and Collette Carroll, "Effects of Foreign Product Names and Country-of-Origin Attributions on Advertisement Evaluations," *Psychology & Marketing* 11 (March/April 1994)2: 129–45; Terence A. Shimp, Saeed Samiee, and Thomas J. Madden, "Countries and Their Products: A Cognitive Structure Perspective," *Journal of the Academy of Marketing Science* 21 (Fall 1993)4: 323–30.

68. "American Pie," *Business Week* (June 27, 1994): 6.

69. James Bennet, "Want a U.S. Car? Read the Label," *New York Times* (September 18, 1994): E6.

70. Durairaj Maheswaran, "Country of Origin as a Stereotype: Effects of Consumer Expertise and Attribute Strength on Product Evaluations,"

Journal of Consumer Research 21 (September 1994): 354–65.

71. Joshua Levine, "The Dance Drink," *Forbes* (September 12, 1994): 232.

72. Sung-Tai Hong and Robert S. Wyer Jr., "Effects of Country-of-Origin and Product-Attribute Information on Product Evaluation: An Information Processing Perspective," *Journal of Consumer Research* 16 (September 1989): 175–87; Marjorie Wall, John Liefield, and Louise A. Heslop, "Impact of Country-of-Origin Cues on Consumer Judgments in Multi-Cue Situations: A Covariance Analysis," *Journal of the Academy of Marketing Science* 19 (1991)2: 105–13.

73. Wai-Kwan Li and Robert S. Wyer Jr., "The Role of Country of Origin in Product Evaluations: Informational and Standard-of-Comparison Effects," *Journal of Consumer Psychology* 3 (1994)2: 187–212.

74. Maheswaran, "Country of Origin as a Stereotype."

75. Items excerpted from Terence A. Shimp and Subhash Sharma, "Consumer Ethnocentrism: Construction and Validation of the CETSCALE," *Journal of Marketing Research* 24 (August 1987): 282.

76. Craig R. Whitney, "Seducing France with Watercress Sandwiches," *New York Times* (May 19, 1995): A4.

77. *Images of Europe: A Survey of Japanese Attitudes toward European Products* (report prepared by Dentsu Inc. for the Commission of the European Communities, Brussels, 1994).

78. Richard W. Stevenson, "The Brands with Billion-Dollar Names," *New York Times* (October 28, 1988): A1.

79. Ronald Alsop, "Enduring Brands Hold Their Allure by Sticking Close to Their Roots," *Wall Street Journal,* centennial ed. (1989): B4.

80. Laura Clark, "Porsche Top Auto Brand Name; Honda, Toyota, BMW Follow in U.S., Japan, Europe Survey," *Automotive News* (December 12, 1988): 62.

81. "What's in a Name?" *The Economist* (August 27, 1988): 62.

82. Stuart Elliott, "What's in a Name? Perhaps Billions," *New York Times* (August 12, 1992): D6.

83. Jacob Jacoby and Robert Chestnut, *Brand Loyalty: Measurement and Management* (New York: Wiley, 1978).

84. Anne B. Fisher, "Coke's Brand Loyalty Lesson," *Fortune* (August 5, 1985): 44.

85. Jacoby and Chestnut, *Brand Loyalty.*

86. Ronald Alsop, "Brand Loyalty is Rarely Blind Loyalty," *Wall Street Journal* (October 19, 1989): B1.

87. Betsy Morris, "The Brand's the Thing," *Fortune* (March 4, 1996): 72 (8 pp.).

88. C. Whan Park, "The Effect of Individual and Situation-related Factors on Consumer Selection of Judgmental Models," *Journal of Marketing Research* 13 (May 1976): 144–51.

89. Joseph W. Alba and Howard Marmorstein, "The Effects of Frequency Knowledge on Consumer Decision Making," *Journal of Consumer Research* 14 (June 1987): 14–25.

MARK IS REALLY PSYCHED. The big day has actually arrived: He's going to buy a car! He hasn't had time to shop around, but he's had his eye on that silver 1987 Camaro parked in the lot of Russ's Auto-Rama. Although the sticker says $2,999, Mark figures he can probably get this baby for a cool $2,000—Russ's looks like just the kind of place where they're hungry to move some cars. Unlike some of the newer, flashy car showrooms he's been in lately, this place is a real nuts-and-bolts operation—it's so dingy and depressing he can't wait to get out of there and take a shower. Mark dreads the prospect of haggling over the price, but he hopes to convince the salesman to take his offer, especially because he can write a check for the full amount today. He's been working two jobs to save up for that car, and a little more suffering in the showroom will be worth it.

At the Auto-Rama lot, big signs on all the cars proclaim that today is Russ's Auto-Rama Rip Us Off Day! Things look better than Mark expected—maybe he can get the Camaro for even less than he had planned. He heads for the Camaro and is a bit surprised when a salesperson who introduces herself as Melanie comes over to him. He had expected to be dealing with a middle-aged man in a loud sport coat (a stereotype he has about used-car salespeople), but this is more good luck: He figures he won't have to be so tough when dealing with a woman who looks to be about his age.

Melanie laughs when he offers her $1,800 for the Camaro, pointing out that she can't take such a low bid for such a sweet car to her boss or she'll lose her job. Melanie's enthusiasm for the car convinces him all the more that he has to have it. When he finally writes a check for $2,700, he's exhausted from all the haggling. What an ordeal! In any case, Mark figures he'll get his money back when he sells the car in a few years, and he did manage to convince Melanie to sell him the car for less than the sticker price.

Actually, he's not only pleased with the car, but with himself—he's a tougher negotiator than he thought. . . .

The Purchase Situation, Postpurchase Evaluation, and Product Disposal

INTRODUCTION

Many consumers dread the act of buying a car. In fact, a survey by Yankelovich Partners, Inc. found that buying a car is the most anxiety-provoking and least-satisfying of any retail experience.[1] But, change is in the wind as the car showroom is being transformed. Car shoppers are logging onto Internet buying services, calling auto brokers who negotiate for them, buying cars at warehouse clubs, and visiting giant auto malls where they can comparison shop.

In addition, although the ritual of haggling over price is a time-honored one in the automobile industry, alternatives to this bazaar mentality are appearing. A growing number of dealerships (about 2 percent of the total) are responding to consumers' reluctance to enter into battle by introducing a "no-dicker" policy—the sticker price is the price people actually pay. The Saturn division of General Motors encourages this policy, as does Ford for sales of its Escort model. Although the profit per car tends to be smaller, dealers who have gone this route report they more than make up for this loss due to increased sales volume. Industry research indicates that these dealers are both better liked and busier than are traditional dealers. The new approach seems especially likely to benefit women and minority buyers, who (research indicates) are less likely to negotiate than are white males.[2]

Car dealers are working hard to find ways to make car shopping a more pleasurable experience. Ford recently sent out a list of guidelines on how to treat shoppers, which included directions such as "customers courteously acknowledged within two minutes of arrival" and "advisory relationship established by knowledgeable sales consultant who listens to customers, identifies needs and ensures needs are met."[3] These efforts highlight the importance of the purchase situation for marketers: You can have the best car in the world, but people have to be willing to do what it takes to obtain it.

Mark's experience in buying a car illustrates some of the concepts to be discussed in this chapter. Making a purchase is often not a simple, routine matter of going to a store and quickly picking out something. As illustrated in Figure 10–1, a consumer's choices are affected by many personal factors, such as his or her mood,

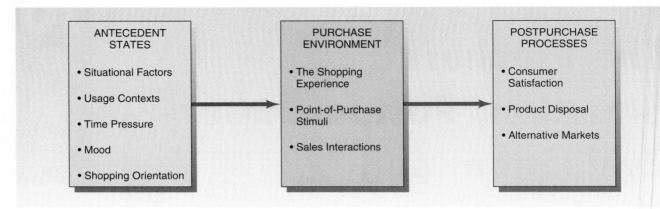

FIGURE 10–1 ■ Issues Related to Purchase and Postpurchase Activities

whether there is time pressure to make the purchase, and the particular situation or context for which the product is needed. In some situations, such as the purchase of a car or a home, the salesperson or realtor plays a pivotal role in the final selection.

The store environment also exerts a big influence: Shopping is like a performance of a play, in which the customer is involved as either an audience member or an active participant. The quality of this performance is affected by the other *cast members* (e.g., salespeople or other shoppers), as well as by the *setting* of the play (e.g., the image of a particular store and the "feeling" it imparts to the shopper) and *props* (e.g., store decorations and promotional materials that try to influence the shopper's decisions).

In addition, a lot of important consumer activity occurs *after* a product has been purchased and brought home. After using a product, the consumer must decide whether he or she is satisfied with it. The satisfaction process is especially important to savvy marketers who realize that the key to success is not selling a product one time, but rather forging a relationship with the consumer so that he or she will continue to buy one's products in the future. Finally, just as Mark thought about the resale value of his car, we must also consider how consumers go about disposing of products and how secondary markets (e.g., used-car dealers) often play a pivotal role in product acquisition. This chapter considers many issues related to purchase and postpurchase phenomena.

SITUATIONAL EFFECTS ON CONSUMER BEHAVIOR

A *consumption situation* is defined by factors beyond characteristics of the person and of the product that influence the buying and/or using of products and services. Situational effects can be behavioral (e.g., entertaining friends) or perceptual (e.g., being depressed or feeling pressed for time).[4] Common sense tells us that people tailor their purchases to specific occasions, and that the way we feel at a specific point in time affects what we feel like buying or doing.

Smart marketers understand these patterns, and tailor their efforts to coincide with situations in which people are most prone to buy. For example, book clubs tend to invest heavily in promotional campaigns in June, since many people are looking to stock up on "beach books" to read during the summer.[5]

When the advertising agency Goodby, Silverstein was hired to reverse a steady decline in milk sales, it found that although milk had been depicted as a beverage that was consumed alone, in "the real world" it is consumed primarily with foods. The agency paid people not to drink any milk for a week before a focus group meeting, and it was only then that they discovered how hard it is to go without cereal in the morning. Knowledge of this situational factor formed the basis for a successful advertising campaign that used the "Got Milk?" tag line. For example, one spot featuring a man taking milk from his baby's bowl was based on a focus group participant's comment that he was so desperate he'd even steal milk from his child.[6]

In addition to the functional relationships between products and usage situation, though, another reason to take environmental circumstances seriously is that the role a person plays at any one time is partly determined by his or her *situational self-image*—he or she basically asks: "Who am I *right now*?" (see chapter 5).[7] Someone trying to impress his date by playing the role of "man-about-town" may spend more lavishly, ordering champagne instead of beer and buying flowers—purchases he would never consider when he is hanging out with his friends, slurping beer, and playing the role of "one of the boys."

As this example demonstrates, knowledge of what consumers are doing at the time a product is consumed, and the role they are playing at that time, can improve predictions of product and brand choice.[8] One aspect of situational role is the degree to which a consumer's ethnic identity, or *felt ethnicity,* is activated during a purchase situation. When people are reminded of this connection, they are more likely to buy products specifically targeted to their ethnic group.[9]

SITUATIONAL SEGMENTATION

By systematically identifying important usage situations, market segmentation strategies can be developed to position products that will meet the specific needs arising from these situations. Many product categories are amenable to this form of segmentation. For example, consumers' furniture choices are often tailored to specific settings. We prefer different styles for a city apartment, beach house, or an executive suite. Similarly, motorcycles can be distinguished in terms of what riders use them for, including commuting, riding them as dirt bikes, using them on a farm versus highway travel, and so on.[10]

Table 10–1 gives one example of how situations can be used to fine-tune a segmentation strategy. By listing the major contexts in which a product is used (e.g., snow skiing and sunbathing for a suntan lotion) and the different users of the product, a matrix can be constructed that identifies specific product features that should

MARKETING PITFALL

Sometimes a marketing strategy can work *too* well. This is the case with Nabisco's Grey Poupon mustard brand, which the company has successfully positioned as a premium product. The problem is that consumers tend to save the brand for special occasions rather than slathering the mustard on just any old sandwich.

Grey Poupon's "special" cachet is due to its long-running ad campaign, in which stuffy aristocrats pass the mustard through the windows of their limousines. The campaign is so well known that the familiar tag line, "Pardon me, would you have any Grey Poupon?" was even repeated in the movie *Wayne's World*.

To dig themselves out of this situational hole, the brand's advertising agency developed new magazine ads that feature simpler occasions, such as a picnic. In one ad, readers are reminded to "Poupon the potato salad" or "class up the cold cuts."[11]

TABLE 10–1 ■ A Person-Situation-Segmentation Matrix for Suntan Lotion

SITUATION	YOUNG CHILDREN		TEENAGERS		ADULT WOMEN	
	FAIR SKIN	DARK SKIN	FAIR SKIN	DARK SKIN	FAIR SKIN	DARK SKIN
Beach/boat sunbathing	Combined insect repellent				Summer perfume	
Home-poolside sunbathing					Combined moisterizer	
Sunlamp bathing					Combined moisterizer and massage oil	
Snow skiing					Winter perfume	
Person benefit/ features	Special protection a. Protection is critical b. Formula is non-poisonous		Special protection a. Product fits in jean pocket b. Product used by opinion leaders		Special protection Female perfume	

Source: Adapted from Peter R. Dickson, "Person-Situation: Segmentation's Missing Link," *Journal of Marketing* 46 (fall 1982): 62. By permission of American Marketing Association.

be emphasized for each situation. For example, during the summer a lotion manufacturer might promote the fact that the bottle floats and is hard to lose, but tout its nonfreeze formula during the winter season.

SOCIAL AND PHYSICAL SURROUNDINGS

A consumer's physical and social environment can make a big difference in motives for product usage and also affect how the product is evaluated. Important cues include the person's physical surroundings, as well as the amount and type of other consumers also present in that situation. Dimensions of the physical environment, such as decor, smells, and even temperature, can significantly influence consumption. One study even found that pumping in certain odors in a Las Vegas casino actually increased the amount of money patrons fed into slot machines![12] We'll take a closer look at some of these factors a bit later in the chapter when considering strategic issues related to store design.

In addition to physical cues, though, many of a consumer's purchase decisions are significantly affected by groups or social settings. In some cases, the sheer presence or absence of other patrons ("*co-consumers*") in a setting actually can function as a product attribute, as when an exclusive resort or boutique promises to provide privacy to privileged customers. At other times, the presence of others can

ADULT MEN		
FAIR SKIN	DARK SKIN	BENEFITS/FEATURES
		a. Product serves as windburn protection
		b. Formula and container can stand heat
		c. Container floats and is distinctive (not easily lost)
		a. Product has large pump dispenser
		b. Product won't stain wood, concrete, furnishings
		a. Product is designed specifically for type of lamp
		b. Product has an artificial tanning ingredient
		a. Product provides special protection from special light rays and weather
		b. Product has antifreeze formula
Special protection		
Male perfume		

have positive value. A sparsely attended ball game or an empty bar can be depressing sights.

The presence of large numbers of people in a consumer environment increases arousal levels, so a consumer's subjective experience of a setting tends to be more intense. This polarization, however, can be both positive and negative. While the presence of other people creates a state of arousal, the consumer's actual experience depends on his or her *interpretation* of this arousal. It is important to distinguish between *density* and *crowding* for this reason. The former term refers to the actual number of people occupying a space, while the psychological state of crowding exists only if a negative affective state occurs as a result of this density.[13] For example, 100 students packed into a classroom designed for 75 may result in an unpleasant situation for all concerned, but the same number of people jammed together at a party occupying a room of the same size might just make for a great bash.

In addition, the *type* of consumers who patronize a store or service or who use a product can influence evaluations. We often infer something about a store by examining its customers. For this reason, some restaurants require men to wear a jacket for dinner (and supply a rather tacky one if they don't), and bouncers at some "hot" nightspots handpick people waiting on line based on whether they have the right "look" for the club. To paraphrase the comedian Groucho Marx, "I would never join a club that would have me for a member!"

TEMPORAL FACTORS

Time is one of consumers' most precious resources. We talk about "making time" or "spending time," and we frequently are reminded that "time is money." Our perspectives on time can affect many stages of decision making and consumption, such as needs that are stimulated, the amount of information search we undertake, and so on. Common sense tells us that more careful information search and deliberation occurs when we have the luxury of taking our time. A meticulous shopper who would normally price an item at three different stores before buying might be found sprinting through the mall at 9 PM on Christmas Eve, furiously scooping up anything left on the shelves that might serve as a last-minute gift.

ECONOMIC TIME

Time is an economic variable; it is a resource that must be divided among activities.[14] Consumers try to maximize satisfaction by allocating time to the appropriate combination of tasks. Of course, people's allocation decisions differ; we all know people who seem to play all of the time, and others who are workaholics. An individual's priorities determine his or her *timestyle.*[15]

Many consumers believe they are more pressed for time than ever before. This feeling may, however, be due more to perception than to fact. People may just have more options for spending their time and feel pressured by the weight of all of these choices. The average working day at the turn of the century was 10 hours (6 days per week), and women did 27 hours of housework per week, compared to under 5 hours weekly now. Of course, in some cases husbands are sharing these burdens more, and in some families maintaining an absolutely spotless home may not be as important as it used to be.[16] Still, about a third of Americans report always feeling rushed—up from 25 percent of the population in 1964.[17]

This sense of time poverty has made consumers very responsive to marketing innovations that allow them to save time. As an executive at Campbell's Soup observed, "Time [is] . . . the currency of the 1990s."[18] This priority has created new opportunities for services as diverse as photograph processing, optometrists, and car repair, for which speed of delivery has become an important attribute.[19] To cater to this need, a Chicago funeral home even offers drive-through service, whereby viewers can see a loved one on a screen without taking the time to leave their cars. The owner notes, "The working person doesn't have time to come in. They want to see the body but they don't want to wait."[20]

With the increase in time poverty, researchers also are noting a rise in *polychronic activity,* by which consumers do more than one thing at a time.[21] This type of activity is especially prevalent in eating. Consumers often do not allocate a specific time to dining, but instead eat on the run. In a recent poll, 64 percent of respondents said they usually do something else while eating. As one food industry executive commented, "We've moved beyond grazing and into gulping."[22]

PSYCHOLOGICAL TIME

The psychological dimension of time, or how it is experienced, is an important factor in *queuing theory,* the mathematical study of waiting lines. A consumer's experience of waiting can radically influence his or her perceptions of service quality. Although we assume that something must be pretty good if we have to wait for it, the negative feelings aroused by long waits can quickly turn off customers.[23]

Some products and services are believed to be appropriate for certain times and not for others. One study of fast-food preferences found that consumers were more likely to choose Wendy's over other fast-food outlets for an evening meal when they

MULTICULTURAL DIMENSIONS

To most Western consumers, time is a neatly compartmentalized thing: We wake up in the morning, go to school or work, come home, eat dinner, go out, go to sleep . . . wake up and do it all over again. This perspective is called *linear separable time;* events proceed in an orderly sequence and different times are well defined: "There's a time and a place for everything." There is a clear sense of past, present, and future. Many activities are performed as the means to some end that will occur later, as when people "save for a rainy day."

This conception of time is not universal. Large cultural differences exist in terms of people's time perspectives.[24] Some cultures run on *procedural time* and ignore the clock completely—people simply decide to do something "when the time is right." Much of the world appears to live on "event time"; for example, in Burundi people might arrange to meet when the cows return from the watering hole, whereas in Madagascar the response if someone asks how long it takes to get to the market might be, "the time it takes to cook rice."[25]

Alternatively, in *circular* or *cyclic* time, people are governed by natural cycles, such as the regular occurrence of the seasons (a perspective found in many Hispanic cultures). To these consumers, the notion of the future does not make sense, because that time will be much like the present. Because the concept of future value does not exist, these consumers often prefer to buy an inferior product that is available now to waiting for a better one that may be available later. Also, it is hard to convince people who function on circular time to buy insurance or save for a rainy day when they do not think in terms of a linear future.

A social scientist recently compared the pace of life in 31 cities around the world as part of a study on timestyles. He and his assistants timed how long it takes pedestrians to walk 60 feet and postal clerks to sell a stamp.[26] Based on these responses, he claims that the fastest and slowest countries are:

Fastest Countries: (1) Switzerland, (2) Ireland, (3) Germany, (4) Japan, (5) Italy

Slowest Countries: (31) Mexico, (30) Indonesia, (29) Brazil, (28) El Salvador, (27) Syria

When groups of college students were asked to draw a picture of time, the resulting sketches in Figure 10–2 illustrate some of these different temporal perspectives.[27] The drawing at the top left represents procedural time; there is lack of direction from left to right and little sense of past, present, and future. The three drawings in the middle denote cyclical time, with regular cycles designated by markers. The bottom drawing represents linear time, with a segmented time line moving from left to right in a well-defined sequence.

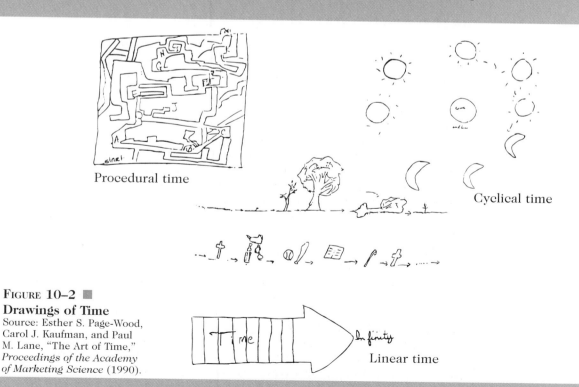

Procedural time

Cyclical time

Linear time

FIGURE 10–2 ■

Drawings of Time
Source: Esther S. Page-Wood, Carol J. Kaufman, and Paul M. Lane, "The Art of Time," *Proceedings of the Academy of Marketing Science* (1990).

were not rushed than when they were pressed for time.[28] Also, we may be more receptive to advertising messages at certain times (other than a few party animals, who wants to hear a beer commercial at 7 in the morning?). There is some evidence that consumers' arousal levels are lower in the morning than in the evening, which affects their style and quality of information processing.[29]

Marketers have adopted a variety of "tricks" to minimize psychological waiting time. These techniques range from altering customers' perceptions of a line's length to providing distractions that divert attention away from waiting.[30]

- One hotel chain, after receiving excessive complaints about the wait for elevators, installed mirrors near the elevator banks. People's natural tendency to check their appearance reduced complaints, even though the actual waiting time was unchanged.

- Airline passengers often complain of the time they must wait to claim their baggage. In one airport, they would walk one minute from the plane to the baggage carousel and then wait seven minutes for their luggage. By changing the layout so that the walk to the carousel took six minutes and bags arrived two minutes after that, complaints were almost entirely eliminated.

- McDonald's uses a multiple-line system, in which each server deals with a separate line of people. Wendy's uses a multistage system, in which the first server takes orders, the second prepares burgers, the third pours drinks, and so on. Wendy's lines are longer, but customers move continuously through stages, so signs of progress can be seen and psychological time is shortened. Similarly, Disneyland often disguises the length of its lines by bending them around corners so that customers are prevented from judging the actual length of the line and anticipated waiting time.

ANTECEDENT STATES: IF IT FEELS GOOD, BUY IT . . .

A person's mood or physiological condition active at the time of purchase can have a big impact on what is bought and can also affect how products are evaluated.[31] One reason is that behavior is directed toward certain goal states, as was discussed in chapter 3. People spend more money in the grocery store if they have not eaten for awhile, because food is a priority at that time.

A consumer's mood can have a big impact on purchase decisions. For example, stress can impair information-processing and problem-solving abilities.[32] Two dimensions, *pleasure* and *arousal*, determine if a shopper will react positively or negatively to a consumption environment. A person can enjoy or not enjoy a situation, and he or she can feel stimulated or not. As Figure 10–3 indicates, different combinations of pleasure and arousal levels result in a variety of emotional states.

MARKETING PITFALL

An emphasis on speed resulted in some serious public relations problems for Domino's Pizza, which guarantees delivery within 30 minutes. Critics claimed that this policy encouraged reckless driving and backed up this charge with some damaging statistics. In 1989, more than a dozen lawsuits, stemming from death or serious injuries caused by delivery people rushing to make the half-hour deadline, were filed against the company. The employee death rate was 50 per 100,000, equal to that suffered in the mining industry.[33] Domino's no longer offers the guarantee.

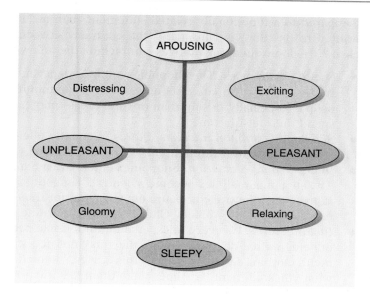

FIGURE 10–3 ■
Dimensions of Emotional States
Source: James Russell and Geraldine Pratt, "A Description of the Affective Quality Attributed to Environment," *Journal of Personality and Social Psychology* 38 (August 1980): 311–22. © Copyright 1980 by the American Psychological Association. Adapted by permission.

For example, an arousing situation can be either distressing or exciting, depending on whether the context is positive or negative (e.g., a street riot versus a street festival). Maintaining an "up" feeling in a pleasant context is one factor behind the success of theme parks such as Disney World, which try to provide consistent doses of carefully calculated stimulation to patrons.[34]

A specific mood is some combination of pleasure and arousal. For example, the state of happiness is high in pleasantness and moderate in arousal, whereas elation is high on both dimensions.[35] In general, a mood state (either positive or negative) biases judgments of products and service in that direction.[36] Put simply, consumers like things better when they are in a good mood (this explains the popularity of the business lunch!).

Moods can be affected by store design, the weather, or other factors specific to the consumer. In addition, music and television programming can affect mood, which has important consequences for commercials.[37] When consumers hear happy music or watch happy programs, they have more positive reactions to commercials and products, especially when the marketing appeals are aimed at arousing emotional reactions.[38] When in positive moods, consumers process ads with less elaboration. They pay less attention to specifics of the message and rely more on heuristic processing (see chapter 9).[39]

SHOPPING: A JOB OR AN ADVENTURE?

Some people shop even though they do not necessarily intend to buy anything at all, whereas others have to be dragged to a mall. Shopping is a way to acquire needed products and services, but social motives for shopping also are important. Thus, shopping is an activity that can be performed for either utilitarian (functional or tangible) or hedonic (pleasurable or intangible) reasons.[40]

REASONS FOR SHOPPING

These different motives are illustrated by scale items used by researchers to assess people's underlying reasons for shopping. One item that measures hedonic value is "During the trip, I felt the excitement of the hunt." When that type of sentiment is compared to a functionally related statement such as "I accomplished just what I wanted to on this shopping trip," the contrast between these two dimensions is clear.[41] Hedonic shopping motives can include the following.[42]

- *Social experiences:* The shopping center or department store has replaced the traditional town square or county fair as a community gathering place. Many people (especially in suburban or rural areas) may have no place else to go to spend their leisure time.
- *Sharing of common interests:* Stores frequently offer specialized goods that allow people with shared interests to communicate.
- *Interpersonal attraction:* Shopping centers are a natural place to congregate. The shopping mall has become a central "hangout" for teenagers. It also represents a controlled, secure environment for the elderly, and many malls now feature "Mall Walkers' Clubs" for early morning workouts.
- *Instant status:* As every salesperson knows, some people savor the experience of being waited on, even though they may not necessarily buy anything. One men's clothing salesman offered this advice, "Remember their size, remember what you sold them last time. Make them feel important! If you can make people feel important, they are going to come back. Everybody likes to feel important!"[43]
- *"The thrill of the chase":* Some people pride themselves on their knowledge of the marketplace. Unlike Mark, they may relish the process of haggling and bargaining, viewing it almost as a sport.

SHOPPING ORIENTATION

Which way is it? Do people hate to shop or love it? It depends. Consumers can be segmented in terms of their **shopping orientation**, or general attitudes about shopping. These orientations may vary depending on the particular product categories and store types considered. Mark hates to shop for a car, but he may love to browse in record stores. Several shopping types have been identified:[44]

- *The economic shopper:* a rational, goal-oriented shopper who is primarily interested in maximizing the value of his or her money.

MARKETING OPPORTUNITY

As electronic commerce mushrooms in popularity, marketers are working hard to better understand who is most likely to make purchases on the Web instead of in a store, and how they should be reached. As of now, the "typical" electronic shopper is 32 years old, male, and well educated, though many firms are optimistic that with time other segments will increase their involvement with the Web.

One source of information is the New Media Pathfinder Study conducted by Arbitron, which identified several segments of interactive shoppers.[45] Not surprisingly, younger consumers tended to be most receptive to new shopping technologies. A segment the company labeled "Fast Laners" (about 14 percent of the study population) was the most open to Web buying. This group was primarily made up of teens and people in their twenties. In contrast, another segment called "Bystanders" (about 16 percent of the population) was older, the least-confident about these possibilities, and not willing to experiment. Still, even the most die-hard traditional shopper might be persuaded to try electronic shopping if the virtual environment is made sufficiently user-friendly. It's up to the next generation of marketers to figure out how to do this. Good luck!

- *The personalized shopper:* a shopper who tends to form strong attachments to store personnel ("I shop where they know my name").
- *The ethical shopper:* a shopper who likes to help out the underdog and will support locally owned stores rather than big chains.
- *The apathetic shopper:* one who does not like to shop and sees it as a necessary but unpleasant chore.
- *The recreational shopper:* a person who views shopping as a fun, social activity—a preferred way to spend leisure time.

THE PURCHASE ENVIRONMENT

We see bumper stickers and T-shirts everywhere: "Shop 'til you drop," "When the going gets tough, the tough go shopping," "Born to shop." On the average, American consumers spend about 6 percent of their waking hours shopping.[46] According to data reported by Nielsen North America's 40,000 household consumer panel, consumers on average make almost 90 trips a year to the grocery store alone.[47]

However, the competition for shoppers continues to escalate. About 200 million square feet of shopping mall space is added every year, but population growth is not sufficient to absorb this supply.[48] The competition for customers is becoming even more intense as nonstore alternatives that bring retail services to the home continue to multiply. Popular nonstore alternatives include mail-order catalogs, electronic Web sites, TV shopping networks, and home shopping parties (e.g., Tupperware).

MARKETING OPPORTUNITY

Some marketers are choosing to follow people to work in order to boost sales. After realizing that many of its female customers are no longer home during the day, even Avon has expanded its distribution network to the office, where representatives make presentations during lunch and coffee breaks. Similarly, Tupperware features "rush-hour parties" at the end of the work day and now finds that about 20 percent of its sales are made outside of homes. An employee of Mary Kay cosmetics, another company adapting this strategy, offered another explanation for its success: "Working women buy more in the office because they are not looking at the wallpaper that needs replacing. They feel richer away from home."[49]

Recognizing that modern women have many time pressures, Spiegel brings retailing to the office.

RETAILING AS THEATER

With all of these shopping alternatives available, how can a traditional store compete? Shopping malls have tried to gain the loyalty of shoppers by appealing to their social motives as well as providing access to desired goods. The mall is often a focal point in a community. In the United States, 94 percent of adults visit a mall at least once a month. More than half of all retail purchases (excluding autos and gasoline) are made in a mall.[50]

Malls are becoming giant entertainment centers, almost to the point where their traditional retail occupants seem like an afterthought. It is now typical to find such features as carousels, miniature golf, or batting cages in a suburban mall. As one retailing executive put it, "Malls are becoming the new mini-amusement parks."[51] The importance of creating a positive, vibrant, and interesting image has led innovative marketers to blur the line between shopping and theater. Both shopping malls and individual stores must create environments that stimulate people and allow them to shop and be simultaneously entertained.[52]

One new illustration of this philosophy is the Circle Center mall in Indianapolis, an experimental mall featuring a Starport entertainment center developed by United Artists Theater Circuit, Inc. The center offers shoppers virtual reality games such as virtual hang gliding, or a death-race through mining tunnels on Mars. As one mall executive observed, "People don't have to go to Orlando to be entertained. Companies are figuring out ways to make it portable. And what better place to locate than in a mall?" The downside? There is some concern that these virtual reality high-tech options are primarily attracting the group mall operators want least: packs of teenage boys that intimidate shoppers.[53]

Other retailers are seeking to combine two favorite consumer activities, shopping and eating, by developing elaborate *themed environments*. According to a recent Roper Starch survey, eating out is the top form of out-of-home-entertain-

The Hard Rock Café, now a familiar tourist attraction in cities around the world, combines entertainment with retailing by creating a themed environment built around rock-and-roll music and culture.

ment, and innovative firms are scrambling to offer customers a chance to eat, buy, and be entertained all at once. The Hard Rock Cafe, first established in London over 25 years ago, now has over 45 restaurants around the world. Planet Hollywood, which first opened in New York in 1991, is crammed full of costumes and props, and the chain now grosses over $200 million a year. Motown Cafe opened in New York, with part ownership by Diana Ross and Boyz II Men. The Harley-Davidson Cafe features the roar of a "Hog" engine. With profit margins on the merchandise sold at these restaurants as high as 60 percent, it's not surprising that as much as 50 percent of a theme chain's revenues come from T-shirts and other goods rather than T-bones and other foods![54]

STORE IMAGE

With so many stores competing for customers, how do consumers pick one over another? Like products (see chapter 6), stores may be thought of as having "personalities." Some stores have very clearly defined images (either good or bad). Others tend to blend into the crowd. They may not have anything distinctive about them and may be overlooked for this reason. This personality, or **store image**, comprises many different factors. Store features, coupled with such consumer characteristics as shopping orientation, help to predict which shopping outlets people will prefer.[55] Some of the important dimensions of a store's profile are location, merchandise suitability, and the knowledge and congeniality of the sales staff.[56]

These features typically work together to create an overall impression. When shoppers think about stores, they may not say, "Well, that place is fairly good in terms of convenience, the salespeople are acceptable, and services are good." They are more likely to say, "That place gives me the creeps," or "I always enjoy shopping there." Consumers often evaluate stores using a general evaluation, and this overall feeling may have more to do with intangibles such as interior design and the types of people one finds in the store than with aspects such as return policies or credit availability. As a result, some stores are likely to consistently be in consumers' evoked sets (see chapter 9), whereas others will never be considered.[57]

ATMOSPHERICS

Because a store's image is now recognized as a very important aspect of the retailing mix, attention is increasingly paid to **atmospherics,** or the "conscious designing of space and its various dimensions to evoke certain effects in buyers."[58] These dimensions include colors, scents, and sounds. For example, stores done in red tend to make people tense, whereas a blue decor imparts a calmer feeling.[59] As was

MULTICULTURAL DIMENSIONS

American retailers including Blockbuster Video, Original Levi's stores, Foot Locker, Toys "Я" Us, and The Gap are exporting their version of dynamic retail environments to Europe—with some adaptations. These overseas "invasions" often begin in Britain, since bureaucratic hurdles tend to be lower, and weaker unions yield reduced personnel costs. Malls are still rare in most of the European Union, so these chains must usually bid for high-rent sites on city streets. The Gap found that it needed to stock smaller sizes than in the United States, and that many of its European customers prefer darker colors. Also, some retailers have done away with "greeters" who now stand at the entrance in many American stores—Europeans tend to find them intimidating.[60]

noted in chapter 2, some preliminary evidence indicates that smells (olfactory cues) also can influence evaluations of a store's environment.[61] A store's atmosphere in turn affects purchasing behavior—one recent study reported that the extent of pleasure reported by shoppers five minutes after entering a store was predictive of the amount of time spent in the store as well as the level of spending there.[62]

Many elements of store design can be cleverly controlled to attract customers and produce desired effects on consumers. Light colors impart a feeling of spaciousness and serenity, and signs in bright colors create excitement. In one subtle but effective application, fashion designer Norma Kamali replaced fluorescent lights with pink ones in department store dressing rooms. The light had the effect of flattering the face and banishing wrinkles, making female customers more willing to try on (and buy) the company's bathing suits.[63] Wal-Mart found that sales were higher in areas of a prototype store lit in natural daylight compared to the more typical artificial light.[64] One study found that brighter in-store lighting influenced people to examine and handle more merchandise.[65]

In addition to visual stimuli, all sorts of cues can influence behaviors.[66] For example, patrons of country-and-western bars drink more when the jukebox music is slower. According to a researcher, "Hard drinkers prefer listening to slower paced, wailing, lonesome, self-pitying music. . . ."[67] Similarly, music can affect eating habits. Another study found that diners who listened to loud, fast music ate more food. In contrast, those who listened to Mozart or Brahms ate less and more slowly. The researchers concluded that diners who choose soothing music at mealtimes can increase weight loss by at least five pounds a month![68]

IN-STORE DECISION MAKING

Despite all their efforts to "presell" consumers through advertising, marketers increasingly are recognizing the significant degree to which many purchases are influenced by the store environment. It has been estimated that about two out of every three supermarket purchases are decided in the aisles. The proportion of unplanned purchases is even higher for some product categories. It is estimated that 85 percent of candy and gum, almost 70 percent of cosmetics, and 75 percent of oral hygiene purchases are unplanned.[69]

MARKETING OPPORTUNITY

Shop the store, buy the soundtrack: Growing recognition of the important role played by a store or restaurant's audio environment has created a new niche, as some companies now are selling musical collections tailored to different activities. These include RCA Victor's "Classical Music for Home Improvements" and Sony Classics' "Cyber Classics" that is billed as music specifically for computer hackers to listen to while programming! In contrast, Sony's "Extreme Classics," packaged for Bungee jumpers, claims to be the "loudest and most dangerous music ever written." Whereas a standard hit classical CD might sell 25,000 copies, PolyGram's Philips label has sold more than 500,000 units of its "Set Your Life to Music" series including "Mozart in the Morning," and "Baroque at Bathtime," and Rising Star Records shipped 10,000 copies of "Classical Erotica" in three months. Both Ralph Lauren and Victoria's Secret are packaging the music played in store outlets, and the bakery chain Au Bon Pain started selling its background music on a CD.[70] Similar spin-offs are in the works by Pottery Barn and Starbucks, which licensed the Blue Note label from Capitol Records for this purpose.[71]

Smart retailers recognize that many purchase decisions are made at the time the shopper is in the store. That's one reason why grocery carts sometimes resemble billboards on wheels.

SPONTANEOUS SHOPPING

When a shopper is prompted to buy something in the store, one of two different processes may be at work: *Unplanned buying* may occur when a person is unfamiliar with a store's layout or perhaps when under some time pressure; or, a person may be reminded to buy something by seeing it on a store shelf. About one-third of unplanned buying has been attributed to the recognition of new needs while within the store.[72]

IMPULSE BUYING

In contrast, **impulse buying** occurs when the person experiences a sudden urge that he or she cannot resist. The tendency to buy spontaneously is most likely to result in a purchase when the consumers believe acting on impulse is appropriate, such as purchasing a gift for a sick friend or picking up the tab for a meal.[73] To cater to these urges, so-called *impulse items* such as candy and gum are conveniently placed near the checkout. Similarly, many supermarkets have installed wider aisles to encourage browsing, and the widest tend to contain products with the highest profit margins. In contrast, low markup items that are purchased regularly tend to be stacked high in narrower aisles, to allow shopping carts to speed through.[74] A more recent high-tech tool has been added to encourage impulse buying: A device called The Portable Shopper is a personal scanning gun that allows customers to ring up their own purchases as they shop. The gun was initially developed for Albert Hejin, the Netherlands' largest grocery chain, to move customers through the store more quickly. It's now in use in over 150 groceries worldwide.[75]

Shoppers can be categorized in terms of how much advance planning they do. *Planners* tend to know what products and specific brands they will buy beforehand; *partial planners* know they need certain products, but do not decide on specific brands until they are in the store; and *impulse purchasers* do no advance planning whatsoever.[76] Figure 10–4 was drawn by a consumer, participating in a study on consumers' shopping experiences, who was asked to sketch a typical impulse purchaser.

POINT-OF-PURCHASE STIMULI

Because so much decision making apparently occurs while the shopper is in the purchasing environment, retailers are beginning to pay more attention to the amount of information in their stores, as well as to the way it is presented. It has been estimated that impulse purchases increase by 10 percent when appropriate displays are used. Each year, U.S. companies spend more than $13 billion on **point-of-purchase stimuli (POP)**. A point-of-purchase stimulus can be an elaborate product display or demonstration, a coupon-dispensing machine, or even someone giving out free samples of a new cookie in the grocery aisle.

In-store advertising is becoming very sophisticated, as marketers come to appreciate the influence of the shopping environment in steering consumers toward

DRAW-A-PICTURE

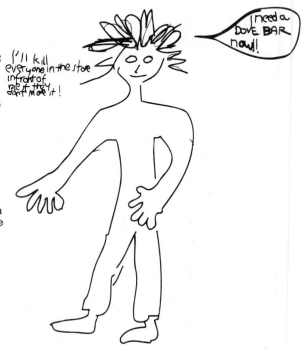

1. Think about your image of what kind of person an impulse buyer is. In the space provided below, draw a picture of your image of a typical impulse buyer who is about to make an impulse purchase. Be creative and don't worry about your artistic skills! If you feel that some features of your drawing are unclear, don't hesitate to identify them with a written label.

2. After you have completed your drawing, imagine what is going through your character's mind as he or she is about to make his or her impulse purchase. Then write down your shopper's thoughts in a speech balloon (like you might see in a cartoon strip) that connects to your character's head.

FIGURE 10–4 ■ One Consumer's Image of an Impulse Buyer
Source: Dennis Rook, "Is Impulse Buying (Yet) a Useful Marketing Concept?" (unpublished manuscript, University of Southern California, Los Angeles, 1990): Fig. 7–A.

promoted items. Even Muzak, the company that provides bland background music to stores (see chapter 2), is getting in on the act. Muzak is now using the receivers it has already placed in about 200,000 U.S. stores to broadcast advertising pitches that can be tailored to a store's location and needs. The company claims that its audio ads have resulted in sales increases of almost 30 percent in some product categories, such as toothpaste and cold medicines.[78]

In-store displays are yet another commonly used device to attract attention in the store environment. Most displays consist of simple racks that dispense the product and/or related coupons, but some highlight the value of regarding retailing as theater by supplying the "audience" with elaborate performances and scenery. Some of the more dramatic POP displays have included the following:[79]

Music samplers that allow shoppers to check out the latest tunes before buying have become a fixture in many stores.

- *Timex:* A ticking watch sits in the bottom of a filled aquarium.
- *Kellogg's Corn Flakes:* A button with a picture of Cornelius the Rooster is placed within the reach of children near Corn Flakes. When a child presses the button, he hears the rooster cock-a-doodle-doo.
- *Elizabeth Arden:* The company introduced "Elizabeth," a computer and video makeover system that allows customers to test out their images with different shades of makeup, without having to actually apply the products first.
- *Tower Records:* A music sampler allows customers to hear records before buying them and to custom-design their own recordings by mixing and matching singles from assorted artists.
- *Trifari:* This company offered paper punch-out versions of its jewelry so that customers can "try on" the pieces at home.
- *Charmin:* Building on the familiar "Please don't squeeze the Charmin" theme, the company deployed the Charmin Squeeze Squad. Employees hid behind stacks of the toilet tissue and jumped out and blew horns at any "squeezers" they caught in the aisles.
- *The Farnam Company:* As somber music plays in the background, a huge plastic rat draped in a black shroud lay next to a tombstone to promote the company's Just One Bite rat poison.

Advertisers are also being more aggressive about hitting consumers with their messages, wherever they may be. *Place-based media* is a growing specialized medium that targets consumers based on locations in which the message is delivered. These places can be anything from airports, doctors' offices, college campuses, or health clubs. Turner Broadcasting System has begun such ventures as Checkout Channel for grocery stores and Airport Channel, and it has even tested McDTV for McDonald's restaurants.[80] Even MTV is getting into the act: Its new Music Report, to be shown in record stores, is a two-hour "video capsule" featuring video spots and ads for music retailers and corporate sponsors. An MTV executive observed, "They're already out there at the retail environment. They're ready to spend money."[81]

Much of the growth in point-of-purchase activity has been in new electronic technologies.[82] Some stores feature talking posters that contain a human body sensor that speaks up when a shopper approaches. The Point-of-Purchase Radio Corporation offers in-store radio networks that are now used by about 60 grocery chains.[83] Some new shopping carts have a small screen that displays advertising, which is keyed to the specific areas of the store through which the cart is wheeled.[84] In-store video displays allow advertisers to reinforce major media campaigns at the point of purchase.[85]

Some of the most interesting innovations can be found in state-of-the-art vending machines, which now dispense everything from Hormel's microwaveable chili and beef stew and Ore-Ida french fries to software. French consumers can purchase

MARKETING PITFALL

You can run, but you can't hide: A company called Privy Promotions sells ad space on restroom walls in stadiums. For $2,000, the company will mount a framed ad for a year in a restroom stall, above a sink, or ". . . wherever it looks nice and appropriate," according to Privy's president. He claims ". . . it's a decided opportunity for an advertiser to reach a captive audience."[86]

Levi's jeans from a machine called "Libre Service," which offers the pants in 10 different sizes. The customer uses a seatbelt to find his or her size, and the jeans sell for about $10 less than the same versions sold in more conventional stores. Due to their frenetic lifestyles, the Japanese are particularly avid users of vending machines. These machines dispense virtually all of life's necessities, plus many luxuries people in other countries would not consider obtaining from a machine. The list includes jewelry, fresh flowers, frozen beef, pornography, business cards, underwear and even the names of possible dates.[87]

THE SALESPERSON

One of the most important in-store factors is the salesperson, who attempts to influence the buying behavior of the customer.[88] This influence can be understood in terms of **exchange theory,** which stresses that every interaction involves an exchange of value. Each participant gives something to the other and hopes to receive something in return.[89]

RESOURCE EXCHANGE

What "value" does the customer look for in a sales interaction? There are a variety of resources a salesperson might offer. He or she, for example, might offer expertise about the product to make the shopper's choice easier. Alternatively, the customer may be reassured because the salesperson is a likable person whose tastes are similar and is seen as someone who can be trusted.[90] Mark's car purchase, for example, was strongly influenced by the age and sex of Melanie, the salesperson with whom he negotiated. In fact, a long stream of research attests to the impact of a salesperson's appearance on sales effectiveness. In sales, as in much of life, attractive people appear to hold the upper hand.[91]

THE SALES INTERACTION

A buyer/seller situation is like many other dyadic encounters (two-person groups); it is a relationship in which some agreement must be reached about the roles of each participant: A process of *identity negotiation* occurs.[92] For example, if Melanie immediately establishes herself as an expert (and Mark accepts this position), she is likely to have more influence over him through the course of the relationship. Some of the factors that help to determine a salesperson's role (and relative effectiveness) are his or her age, appearance, educational level, and motivation to sell.[93]

In addition, more effective salespersons usually know their customers' traits and preferences better than do ineffective salespersons, because this knowledge allows them to adapt their approach to meet the needs of the specific customer.[94] The ability to be adaptable is especially vital when customers and salespeople differ in terms of their *interaction styles.*[95] Consumers, for example, vary in the degree of assertiveness they bring to interactions. At one extreme, nonassertive people believe that complaining is not socially acceptable and may be intimidated in sales situations. Assertive people are more likely to stand up for themselves in a firm but nonthreatening way. Aggressives may resort to rudeness and threats if they do not get their way.[96]

POSTPURCHASE SATISFACTION

Consumer satisfaction/dissatisfaction (CS/D) is determined by the overall feelings, or attitude, a person has about a product after it has been purchased. Consumers are engaged in a constant process of evaluating the things they buy as these prod-

MARKETING PITFALL

Not exactly an ideal test drive: A woman recently sued a car dealer in Iowa, claiming that a salesperson persuaded her to climb into the trunk of a Chrysler Concorde to check out its spaciousness. He then slammed the trunk shut and bounced the car several times, apparently to the delight of his coworkers. This bizarre act apparently came about because the manager offered a prize of $100 to the salesperson who could get a customer to climb in. At last report, this persuasive salesperson is selling vacuum cleaners door to door.[97]

ucts are integrated into their daily consumption activities.[98] And, customer satisfaction has a real impact on the bottom line: A recent study conducted among a large sample of Swedish consumers found that product quality affects customer satisfaction, which in turn results in increased profitability among firms who provide quality products.[99] Quality is more than a marketing "buzzword."

PERCEPTIONS OF PRODUCT QUALITY

Just what do consumers look for in products? That's easy: They want quality and value. Especially because of foreign competition, claims of product quality have become strategically crucial to maintaining a competitive advantage.[100] Consumers use a number of cues to infer quality, including brand name, price, and even their own estimates of how much money has been put into a new product's advertising campaign.[101] These cues, as well as others such as product warranties and follow-up letters from the company, are often used by consumers to relieve perceived risk and assure themselves that they have made smart purchase decisions.[102]

However, the weighting assigned to different cues has changed as consumers' priorities have evolved in the 1990s. Many people are part of a trend that the Grey Advertising agency has called "downshifting." They are reigning in spending, and trying to maximize the value of every dollar. The net result is that price has become a bigger concern; consumers are no longer willing to pay a premium for brand names if they don't see a tangible difference between these well-known items and other product alternatives.

A study done by Grey Advertising found that Americans' definition of value has changed from "best in class" to "best in budget range." Two factors are most likely at the heart of this trend: (1) A sluggish economy in the early 1990s dampened people's expectations that their financial well-being will continue to improve, and (2) Consumers view many products, such as cereal, diapers, or cigarettes, as commodities with very few differences among brands.[103]

Although everyone wants quality, it is not clear exactly what it means. Certainly, many manufacturers claim to provide it. The Ford Motor Company emphasizes that *"Quality* is Job 1." Similar claims that have been made at one time or another by car manufacturers include the following:[104]

Lincoln-Mercury: ". . . the highest quality cars of any major American car company"
Chrysler: ". . . quality engineered to be the best"
GMC Trucks: ". . . quality built yet economical"
Oldsmobile: ". . . fulfilling the quality needs of American drivers"
Audi: ". . . quality backed by our outstanding new warranty"

This ad for Ford relies on a common claim about "quality."

QUALITY IS WHAT WE EXPECT IT TO BE

In the book *Zen and the Art of Motorcycle Maintenance*, a cult hero of college students in an earlier generation literally went crazy trying to figure out the meaning of quality.[105] Marketers appear to use the word quality as a catch-all term for "good." Because of its wide and imprecise usage, the attribute of "quality" threatens to become a meaningless claim. If everyone has it, what good is it?

To muddy the waters a bit more, satisfaction or dissatisfaction is more than a reaction to the actual performance quality of a product or service. It is influenced by prior expectations regarding the level of quality. According to the **expectancy disconfirmation model,** consumers form beliefs about product performance based on prior experience with the product and/or communications about the product that imply a certain level of quality.[106] When something performs the way we thought it would, we may not think much about it. If, on the other hand, it fails to live to expectations, negative affect may result. Furthermore, if performance happens to exceed our expectations, we are satisfied and pleased.

To understand this perspective, think about different types of restaurants. People expect to be provided with sparkling clear glassware at fancy restaurants, and they might become upset if they discover a grimy glass. On the other hand, they may not be surprised to find fingerprints on a beer mug at a local greasy spoon; they may even shrug it off because it contributes to the place's "charm." An important lesson emerges for marketers from this perspective: Don't overpromise.[107]

This perspective underscores the importance of *managing expectations*—customer dissatisfaction is usually due to expectations exceeding the company's ability to deliver. Figure 10–5 illustrates the alternative strategies a firm can choose in these situations. When confronted with unrealistic expectations about what it can do, the firm can either accommodate these demands by improving the range or quality of products it offers, alter the expectations, or perhaps even choose to abandon the customer if it is not feasible to meet his or her needs.[108] Expectations are altered, for example, when waiters tell patrons in advance that the portion size they have ordered will not be very big, or when new car buyers are warned of strange

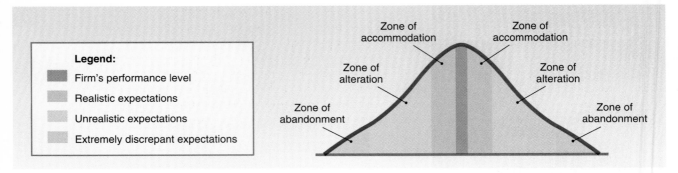

FIGURE 10–5 ■ Zones

Source: Adapted from Jagdish N. Sheth and Banwari Mittal, "A Framework for Managing Customer Expectations," *Journal of Market Focused Management* 1 (1996): 137–158. Fig. 2., p.140

smells they will experience during the break-in period. A firm also can *under-promise*, as when Xerox inflates the time it will take for a service rep to visit. When the rep arrives a day earlier, the customer is impressed.

The power of quality claims is most evident when a company's product fails. Here, consumers' expectations are dashed and dissatisfaction results. In these situations, marketers must immediately take steps to reassure customers. When the company confronts the problem truthfully, consumers are often willing to forgive and forget, as was the case for Tylenol (product tampering), Chrysler (disconnecting odometers on executives' cars and reselling them as new), or Perrier (traces of benzene found in the water). When the company appears to be dragging its heels or covering up, on the other hand, consumer resentment will grow, as occurred during Union Carbide's chemical disaster in India and Exxon's massive Alaskan oil spill caused by the tanker, the *Exxon Valdez*.

ACTING ON DISSATISFACTION

If a person is not happy with a product or service, what can be done? A consumer has three possible courses of action (more than one can be taken):[109]

1. *Voice response:* The consumer can appeal directly to the retailer for redress (e.g., a refund).
2. *Private response:* Express dissatisfaction about the store or product to friends and/or boycott the store. As will be discussed in chapter 11, negative word of mouth (WOM) can be very damaging to a store's reputation.
3. *Third-party response:* The consumer can take legal action against the merchant, register a complaint with the Better Business Bureau, or perhaps write a letter to the newspaper.

In one study, business majors wrote complaint letters to companies. Those who were sent a free sample in response indicated their image of the company significantly improved, but those who received only a letter of apology did not change their evaluations of the company. However, students who got no response reported an even more negative image than before, indicating that some form of response is better than none.[110]

A number of factors influence which route is eventually taken. The consumer may be a generally assertive or meek person. Action is more likely to be taken for expensive products such as household durables, cars, and clothing than for inexpensive products.[111] In addition, consumers who are satisfied with a store are *more* likely to complain; they take the time to complain because they feel connected to the store. Older people are more likely to complain, and are much more likely to believe the store will actually resolve the problem. Shoppers who get their problems resolved feel even *better* about the store than if nothing went wrong.[112] On the other hand, if the consumer does not believe that the store will respond well to a complaint, the person will be more likely to simply switch than fight.[113] Ironically, marketers should actually *encourage* consumers to complain to them: People are more likely to spread the word about unresolved negative experiences to their friends than they are to boast about positive occurrences.[114]

PRODUCT DISPOSAL

Because people often do form strong attachments to products, the decision to dispose of something may be a painful one. One function performed by possessions is to serve as anchors for our identities: Our past lives on in our things.[115] This attachment is exemplified by the Japanese, who ritually "retire" worn-out sewing needles, chopsticks, and even computer chips by burning them as thanks for good service.[116]

Although some people have more trouble than others in discarding things, even a "pack rat" does not keep everything. Consumers must often dispose of things, either because they have fulfilled their designated functions, or possibly because they no longer fit with consumers' view of themselves. Concern about the environment coupled with a need for convenience has made ease of product disposal a key attribute in categories from razors to diapers.

DISPOSAL OPTIONS

When a consumer decides that a product is no longer of use, several choices are available. The person can either (1) keep the item, (2) temporarily dispose of it, or (3) permanently dispose of it. In many cases, a new product is acquired even though the old one still functions. Some reasons for this replacement include a desire for new features, a change in the person's environment (e.g., a refrigerator is the wrong color for a freshly painted kitchen), or a change in the person's role or self-image.[117] Figure 10–6 provides an overview of consumers' disposal options.

The issue of product disposition is doubly vital because of its enormous public policy implications. We live in a throwaway society, which creates problems for the environment and also results in a great deal of unfortunate waste. Training consumers to recycle has become a priority in many countries. Japan recycles about 40 percent of its garbage, and this relatively high rate of compliance is partly due to the social value the Japanese place on recycling: Citizens are encouraged by garbage trucks that periodically rumble through the streets playing classical music or children's songs.[118] Companies continue to search for ways to use resources more efficiently, often at the prompting of activist consumer groups. For example, McDonald's restaurants bowed to pressure by eliminating the use of styrofoam packages, and its outlets in Europe are experimenting with edible breakfast platters made of maize.[119]

A recent study examined the relevant goals consumers have in recycling. It used a means–end chain analysis of the type described in chapter 4 to identify how specific instrumental goals are linked to more abstract terminal values. The most important lower-order goals identified were "avoid filling up landfills," "reduce waste," "reuse materials," and "save the environment." These were linked to the terminal values of "promote health/avoid sickness," "achieve life-sustaining ends," and "provide for future generations."

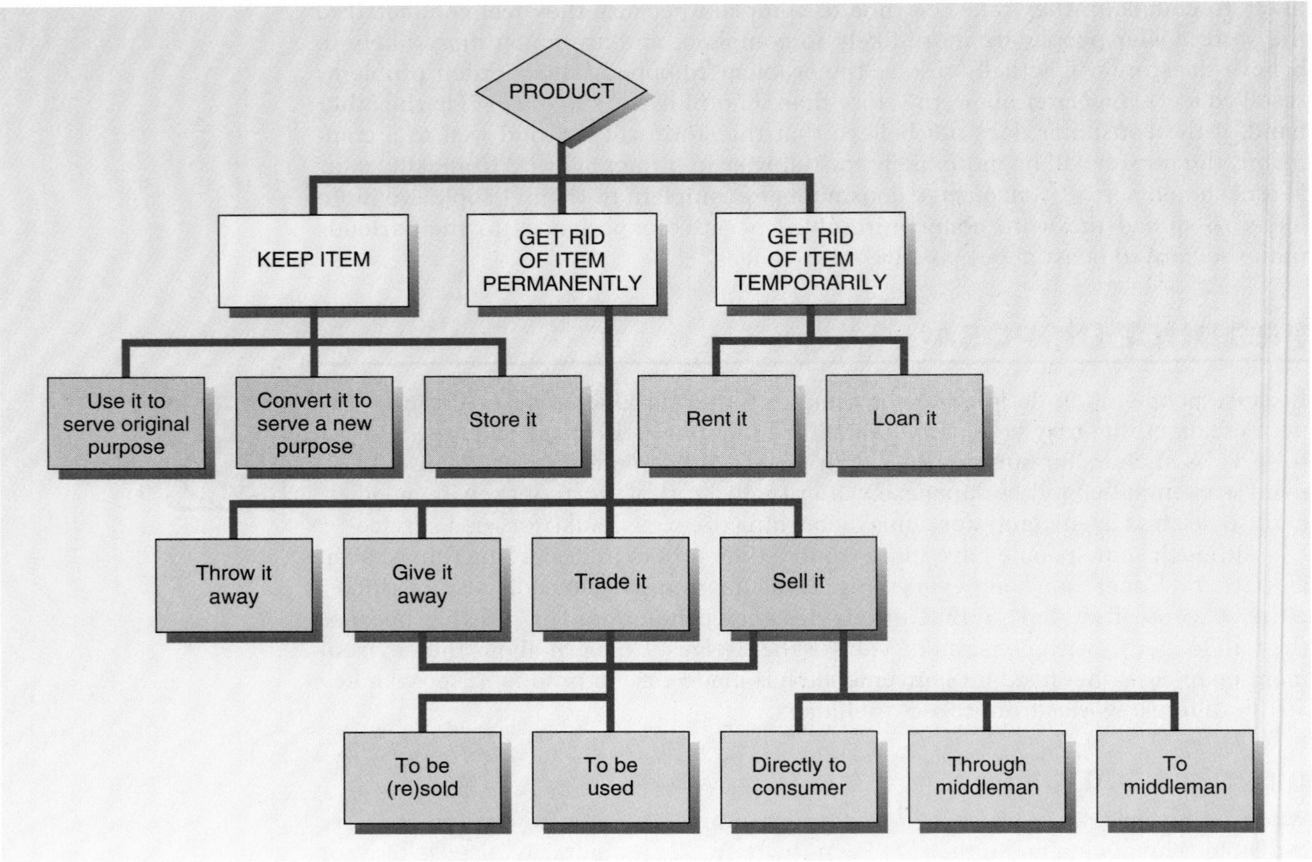

FIGURE 10–6 ■ Consumers' Disposal Options
Source: Jacob Jacoby, Carol K. Berning, and Thomas F. Dietvorst. "What About Disposition?" *Journal of Marketing* 41 (April 1977): 23. By permission of American Marketing Association.

Another study reported that the perceived effort involved in recycling was the best predictor of whether people would go to the trouble—this pragmatic dimension outweighed general attitudes toward recycling and the environment in predicting intention to recycle.[120] By applying such techniques to study recycling and other product disposal behaviors, it will be easier for social marketers to design advertising copy and other messages that tap into the underlying values that will motivate people to increase environmentally responsible behavior.[121]

MARKETING OPPORTUNITY

Some enterprising entrepreneurs have found profitable ways to encourage recycling by creating fashion items out of recycled materials. Two young jewelry designers in New York created a fad by making necklaces out of old bottle caps. They even pay homeless people to collect the caps. A Pittsburgh-based company called Little Earth Productions, Inc. makes all of its products from recycled materials. They sell backpacks decorated with old license plates, a shoulder bag made from rubber and hubcaps, and even purses crafted from discarded tuna cans.[122]

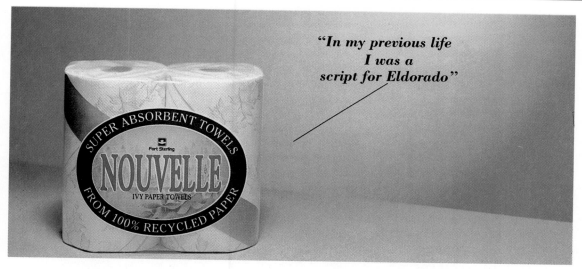

*"In my previous life
I was a
script for Eldorado"*

This British ad for paper towels takes a humorous route to emphasize that the paper towels are made from recycled paper.

LATERAL CYCLING: JUNK VERSUS "JUNQUE"

Interesting consumer processes occur during **lateral cycling,** in which already-purchased objects are sold to others or exchanged for still other things. Many purchases are made secondhand, rather than new. The reuse of other people's things is especially important in our throwaway society because, as one researcher put it, ". . . there is no longer an 'away' to throw things to."[123]

Flea markets, garage sales, classified advertisements, bartering for services, hand-me-downs, and the black market all represent important alternative marketing systems that operate alongside the formal marketplace. For example, the

This Dutch Volkswagen ad focuses on recycling. The copy says, "And when you've had enough of it, we'll clear it away nicely."

Flea markets are an important form of lateral cycling.

number of used-merchandise retail establishments has grown at about 10 times the rate of other stores.[124] Although traditional marketers have not paid much attention to used-product sellers, factors such as concern about the environment, demands for quality, and cost and fashion consciousness are conspiring to make these "secondary" markets more important.[125]

Interest in antiques, period accessories, and specialty magazines catering to this niche is increasing. Other growth areas include student markets for used computers and textbooks, as well as ski swaps, at which millions of dollars worth of used ski equipment is exchanged. A new generation of secondhand store owners is developing markets for everything from used office equipment to cast-off kitchen sinks. Many are nonprofit ventures started with government funding, and their efforts are encouraged by a trade association called the Reuse Development Organization (or ReDO). These efforts remind us that recycling is actually the last step in the familiar mantra of the environmental movement: Reduce, reuse, recycle: Only if no use is found for an item should it be shredded and made into something else.[126]

CHAPTER SUMMARY

- The *act of purchase* can be affected by many factors. These include the consumer's antecedent state (e.g., his/her mood, time pressure, or disposition toward shopping). Time is an important resource that often determines how much effort and search will go into a decision. Mood can be affected by the degree of pleasure and arousal present in a store environment.

- The *usage context* of a product can be a basis for segmentation; consumers look for different product attributes depending on the use to which they intend to put their purchase. The presence or absence of other people—and the types of people they are—can also affect a consumer's decisions.

- The *shopping experience* is a pivotal part of the purchase decision. In many cases, retailing is like theater—the consumer's evaluation of stores and products may depend on the type of "performance" he or she witnesses. This evaluation can be influenced by the actors (e.g., salespeople), the setting (the store environment), and props (e.g., store displays). A *store image*, like a brand personality, is determined by a number of factors, such as perceived convenience, sophistication, expertise of salespeople, and so on. With increasing competition from nonstore alternatives, the creation of a positive shopping experience has never been more important.

- Because many purchase decisions are not made until the time the consumer is actually in the store, *point-of-purchase (POP) stimuli* are very important sales tools. These include product samples, elaborate package displays, place-based media, and in-store promotional materials such as "shelf talkers." POP stimuli are particularly useful in stimulating impulse buying, in which a consumer yields to a sudden urge for a product.

- The consumer's encounter with a salesperson is a complex and important process. The outcome can be affected by such factors as the salesperson's similarity to the customer and his or her perceived credibility.

- *Consumer satisfaction* is determined by the person's overall feeling toward the product after purchase. Many factors influence perceptions of product quality, including price, brand name, and product performance. Satisfaction is often determined by the degree to which a product's performance is consistent with the consumer's prior expectations of how well it will function.

- *Product disposal* is an increasingly important problem. Recycling is one option that will continue to be stressed as consumers' environmental awareness grows. Products may also be introduced by consumers into secondary markets during a process of *lateral cycling*, which occurs when objects are bought and sold secondhand, fenced, or bartered.

KEY TERMS

CONSUMER BEHAVIOR CHALLENGE

1. Discuss some of the motivations for shopping as described in the chapter. How might a retailer adjust his or her strategy to accommodate these motivations?

2. A number of court cases in recent years have attempted to prohibit special interest groups from distributing literature in shopping malls. Mall management claims that these centers are private property. On the other hand, these groups argue that the mall is the modern-day version of the town square and as such is a public forum. Find some recent court cases involving this free-speech issue, and examine the arguments pro and con. What is the current status of the mall as a public forum? Do you agree with this concept?

3. What are some positive and negative aspects of requiring employees who interact with customers to wear some kind of uniform or of mandating a dress code in the office?

4. Think about exceptionally good and bad salespeople you have encountered in the past. What qualities seem to differentiate them?

5. Discuss the concept of "timestyle." Based on your own experiences, how might consumers be segmented in terms of their timestyles?

6. Compare and contrast different cultures' conceptions of time. What are some implications for marketing strategy within each of these frameworks?

7. The movement away from a "disposable consumer society" toward one that emphasizes creative recycling creates many opportunities for marketers. Can you identify some?

8. Conduct naturalistic observation at a local mall. Sit in a central location and observe the activities of mall employees and patrons. Keep a log of the nonretailing activity you observe (e.g., special performances, exhibits, socializing, etc.). Does this activity enhance or detract from business conducted at the mall? As malls become more like high-tech game rooms, how valid is the criticism raised that shopping areas are only encouraging more loitering by teenage boys, who don't spend a lot in stores and simply scare away other customers?

9. Select three competing clothing stores in your area and conduct a store image study for them. Ask a group of consumers to rate each store on a set of attributes and plot these ratings on the same graph. Based on your findings, are there any areas of competitive advantage or disadvantage you could bring to the attention of store management?

10. Using Table 10–1 as a model, construct a person/situation segmentation matrix for a brand of perfume.

11. What applications of queuing theory can you find employed among local services? Interview consumers who are waiting in lines to determine how (if at all) this experience affects their satisfaction with the service.

12. The store environment is heating up as more and more companies put their promotional dollars into point-of-purchase efforts. Shoppers are now confronted by videos at the checkout counter, computer monitors attached to their shopping carts, and so on. Place-based media even expose us to ads in nonshopping environments. Recently, a health club in New York was forced to remove TV monitors that showed advertising on the Health Club Media Networks, claiming that they interfered with workouts. Do you feel that these innovations are overly intrusive? At what point might shoppers "rebel" and demand some peace and quiet while shopping? Do you see any market potential in the future for stores that "countermarket" by promising a "hands-off" shopping environment?

NOTES

1. Keith Naughton, "Revolution in the Showroom," *Business Week* (February 19, 1996): 70 (8 pp.).
2. Michelle Krebs, "Moving out the Cars with a 'No-Dicker Sticker'," *New York Times* (October 11, 1992): F12; "No-Dicker Car Dealers Gaining Popularity," *Marketing News* (September 28, 1992): 19.
3. Paul Gray, "Nice Guys Finish First?" *Time* (July 25, 1994): 48–9.
4. Pradeep Kakkar and Richard J. Lutz, "Situational Influence on Consumer Behavior: A Review," in eds. Harold H. Kassarjian and Thomas S. Robertson, *Perspectives in Consumer Behavior,* 3rd ed. (Glenview, IL: Scott, Foresman, 1981): 204–14.
5. Shelly Reese, "Every Product Has a Season," *American Demographics* (December 1995): 17–18.

6. Paula Mergenhagen, "How 'got milk?' Got Sales," *Marketing Tools* (September 1996): 4 (3 pp.).
7. Carolyn Turner Schenk and Rebecca H. Holman, "A Sociological Approach to Brand Choice: The Concept of Situational Self-Image," in ed. Jerry C. Olson, *Advances in Consumer Research* 7, (Ann Arbor, MI: Association for Consumer Research, 1980): 610–14.
8. Russell W. Belk, "An Exploratory Assessment of Situational Effects in Buyer Behavior," *Journal of Marketing Research* 11 (May 1974): 156–63; U. N. Umesh and Joseph A. Cote, "Influence of Situational Variables on Brand-Choice Models," *Journal of Business Research* 16 (1988)2: 91–9; see also J. Wesley Hutchinson and Joseph W. Alba, "Ignoring Irrelevant Information:

Situational Determinants of Consumer Learning," *Journal of Consumer Research* 18 (December 1991): 325–45.
9. Peter J. Burke and Stephen L. Franzoi, "Studying Situations and Identities Using Experimental Sampling Methodology," *American Sociological Review* 53 (August 1988): 559–68; Douglas M. Stayman and Rohit Deshpande, "Situational Ethnicity and Consumer Behavior," *Journal of Consumer Research* 16 (December 1989): 361–71.
10. Peter R. Dickson, "Person-Situation: Segmentation's Missing Link," *Journal of Marketing* 46 (Fall 1982): 56–64.
11. Laura Bird, "Grey Poupon Tones Down Tony Image," *Wall Street Journal* (July 22, 1994): B2.

12. Alan R. Hirsch, "Effects of Ambient Odors on Slot-Machine Usage in a Las Vegas Casino," *Psychology & Marketing* 12 (October 1995)7: 585–94.

13. Daniel Stokols, "On the Distinction between Density and Crowding: Some Implications for Future Research," *Psychological Review* 79 (1972): 275–7.

14. Carol Felker Kaufman, Paul M. Lane, and Jay D. Lindquist, "Exploring More Than 24 Hours a Day: A Preliminary Investigation of Polychronic Time Use," *Journal of Consumer Research* 18 (December 1991): 392–401.

15. Laurence P. Feldman and Jacob Hornik, "The Use of Time: An Integrated Conceptual Model," *Journal of Consumer Research* 7 (March 1981): 407–19; see also Michelle M. Bergadaa, "The Role of Time in the Action of the Consumer," *Journal of Consumer Research* 17 (December 1990): 289–302.

16. Robert J. Samuelson, "Rediscovering the Rat Race," *Newsweek* (May 15, 1989): 57.

17. John P. Robinson, "Time Squeeze," *Advertising Age* (February 1990): 30–3.

18. Quoted in Judann Dagnoli, "Time—The Currency of the 90's," *Advertising Age* (November 13, 1989): S2.

19. Leonard L. Berry, "Market to the Perception," *American Demographics* (February 1990): 32.

20. Quoted in Isabel Wilkerson, "New Funeral Options for Those in a Rush," *New York Times* (February 25, 1989): A16.

21. Lane, Kaufman, and Lindquist, "Exploring More Than 24 Hours a Day."

22. Quoted in Dena Kleiman, "Fast Food? It Just Isn't Fast Enough Anymore," *New York Times* (December 6, 1989): C12.

23. See Shirley Taylor, "Waiting for Service: The Relationship between Delays and Evaluations of Service," *Journal of Marketing* 58 (April 1994): 56–69.

24. Robert J. Graham, "The Role of Perception of Time in Consumer Research," *Journal of Consumer Research* 7 (March 1981): 335–42.

25. Alan Zarembo, "What If There Weren't Any Clocks to Watch,?" *Newsweek* (June 30, 1997): 14; based on research reported in Robert Levine, *A Geography of Time: The Temporal Misadventures of a Social Psychologist, or How Every Culture Keeps Time Just a Little Bit Differently* (New York: Basic Books, 1997).

26. Zarembo, "What If There Weren't Any Clocks to Watch,?"

27. Esther S. Page-Wood, Carol J. Kaufman, and Paul M. Lane, "The Art of Time," in *Proceedings of the Academy of Marketing Science* (1990).

28. Kenneth E. Miller and James L. Ginter, "An Investigation of Situational Variation in Brand Choice Behavior and Attitude," *Journal of Marketing Research* 16 (February 1979): 111–23.

29. Jacob Hornik, "Diurnal Variation in Consumer Response," *Journal of Consumer Research* 14 (March 1988): 588–91.

30. David H. Maister, "The Psychology of Waiting Lines," in eds. John A. Czepiel, Michael R. Solomon, and Carol F. Surprenant, *The Service Encounter: Managing Employee/Customer Interaction in Service Businesses* (Lexington, MA: Lexington Books, 1985): 113–24.

31. Laurette Dube and Bernd H. Schmitt, "The Processing of Emotional and Cognitive Aspects of Product Usage in Satisfaction Judgments," in eds. Rebecca H. Holman and Michael R. Solomon, *Advances in Consumer Research* 18 (Provo, UT: Association for Consumer Research, 1991): 52–6; Lalita A. Manrai and Meryl P. Gardner, "The Influence of Affect on Attributions for Product Failure," in eds. Rebecca H. Holman and Michael R. Solomon, *Advances in Consumer Research* 18 (Provo, UT: Association for Consumer Research, 1991), 249–54.

32. Kevin G. Celuch and Linda S. Showers, "It's Time to Stress Stress : The Stress-Purchase/Consumption Relationship," in eds. Rebecca H. Holman and Michael R. Solomon, *Advances in Consumer Research* 18 (Provo, UT: Association for Consumer Research, 1991): 284–9; Lawrence R. Lepisto, J. Kathleen Stuenkel, and Linda K. Anglin, "Stress: An Ignored Situational Influence," in eds. Rebecca H. Holman and Michael R. Solomon, *Advances in Consumer Research* 18 (Provo, UT: Association for Consumer Research, 1991): 296–302.

33. Eric N. Berg, "Fight on Quick Pizza Delivery Grows," *New York Times* (August 29, 1989): D6.

34. See Eben Shapiro, "Need a Little Fantasy? A Bevy of New Companies Can Help," *New York Times* (March 10, 1991): F4.

35. John D. Mayer and Yvonne N. Gaschke, "The Experience and Meta-Experience of Mood," *Journal of Personality and Social Psychology* 55 (July 1988): 102–11.

36. Meryl Paula Gardner, "Mood States and Consumer Behavior: A Critical Review," *Journal of Consumer Research* 12 (December 1985): 281–300; Scott Dawson, Peter H. Bloch, and Nancy M. Ridgway, "Shopping Motives, Emotional States, and Retail Outcomes," *Journal of Retailing* 66 (Winter 1990): 408–27; Patricia A. Knowles, Stephen J. Grove, and W. Jeffrey Burroughs (1993), "An Experimental Examination of Mood States on Retrieval and Evaluation of Advertisement and Brand Information," *Journal of the Academy of Marketing Science* 21 (April 1993); Paul W. Miniard, Sunil Bhatla, and Deepak Sirdeskmuhk, "Mood as a Determinant of Postconsumption Product Evaluations: Mood Effects and Their Dependency on the Affective Intensity of the Consumption Experience," *Journal of Consumer Psychology* 1 (1992)2: 173–95; Mary T. Curren and Katrin R. Harich, "Consumers' Mood States: The Mitigating Influence of Personal Relevance on Product Evaluations," *Psychology & Marketing* 11 (March/April 1994)2: 91–107; Gerald J. Gorn, Marvin E. Rosenberg, and Kunal Basu, "Mood, Awareness, and Product Evaluation," *Journal of Consumer Psychology* 2 (1993)3: 237–56.

37. Gordon C. Bruner, "Music, Mood, and Marketing," *Journal of Marketing* 54 (October 1990): 94–104; Basil G. Englis, "Music Television and Its Influences on Consumers, Consumer Culture, and the Transmission of Consumption Messages," in eds. Rebecca H. Holman and Michael R. Solomon, *Advances in Consumer Research* 18 (Provo, UT: Association for Consumer Research, 1991): 111–114.

38. Marvin E. Goldberg and Gerald J. Gorn, "Happy and Sad TV Programs: How They Affect Reactions to Commercials," *Journal of Consu-*

mer Research 14 (December 1987): 387–403; Gorn, Goldberg, and Basu, "Mood, Awareness, and Product Evaluation"; Curren and Harich, "Consumers' Mood States."

39. Rajeev Batra and Douglas M. Stayman, "The Role of Mood in Advertising Effectiveness," *Journal of Consumer Research* 17 (September 1990): 203; John P. Murry Jr. and Peter A. Dacin, "Cognitive Moderators of Negative-Emotion Effects: Implications for Understanding Media Context," *Journal of Consumer Research* 22 (March 1996): 439–47; see also Curren and Harich, "Consumers' Mood States"; Gorn, Goldberg, and Basu, "Mood, Awareness, and Product Evaluation."

40. For a scale that was devised to assess these dimensions of the shopping experience, see Barry J. Babin, William R. Darden, and Mitch Griffin, "Work and/or Fun: Measuring Hedonic and Utilitarian Shopping Value," *Journal of Consumer Research* 20 (March 1994): 644–56.

41. Babin, Darden, and Griffin, "Work and/or Fun."

42. Edward M. Tauber, "Why Do People Shop?" *Journal of Marketing* 36 (October 1972): 47–8.

43. Quoted in Robert C. Prus, *Making Sales: Influence as Interpersonal Accomplishment* (Newbury Park, CA: Sage Library of Social Research, Sage Publications, Inc., 1989): 225.

44. Gregory P. Stone, "City Shoppers and Urban Identification: Observations on the Social Psychology of City Life," *American Journal of Sociology* 60 (1954): 36–45; Danny Bellenger and Pradeep K. Korgaonkar, "Profiling the Recreational Shopper," *Journal of Retailing* 56 (1980)3: 77–92.

45. Kelly Shermach, "Study Identifies Types of Interactive Shoppers," *Marketing News* (September 25, 195): 22.

46. John P. Robinson, "When the Going Gets Tough," *Advertising Age* (February 1989): 50.

47. "Shop, Shop, Shop," *Advertising Age* (August 22, 1994): 3.

48. Isabel Wilkerson, "Megamall, A New Fix for Future Shopping Addicts," *New York Times* (June 9, 1989): A14.

49. Quoted in Kate Ballen, "Get Ready for Shopping at Work," *Fortune* (February 15, 1988): 95.

50. For a recent study of consumer shopping patterns that views the mall as an ecological habitat, see Peter N. Bloch, Nancy M. Ridgway, and Scott A. Dawson, "The Shopping Mall as Consumer Habitat," *Journal of Retailing* 70 (1994)1: 23–42.

51. Quoted in Jacquelyn Bivins, "Fun and Mall Games," *Stores* (August 1989): 35.

52. Sallie Hook, "All the Retail World's a Stage: Consumers Conditioned to Entertainment in Shopping Environment," *Marketing News* 21 (July 31, 1987): 16.

53. Quoted in Mitchell Pacelle, "Malls Add Fun and Games to Attract Shoppers," *Wall Street Journal* (January 23, 1996): B1 (2 pp.), quoted on p. B1.

54. Joshua Levine, "Hamburgers and Tennis Socks," *Forbes* (November 20, 1995): 184–5; Iris Cohen Selinger, "Lights! Camera! But Can We Get a Table?" *Advertising Age* (April 17, 1995): 48.

55. Susan Spiggle and Murphy A. Sewall, "A Choice Sets Model of Retail Selection," *Journal of Marketing* 51 (April 1987): 97–111; William R. Darden and Barry J. Babin, "The Role of Emotions in Expanding the Concept of Retail Personality," *Stores* 76 (April 1994)4: RR7–RR8.

56. Most measures of store image are quite similar to other attitude measures, as discussed in chapter 5. For an excellent bibliography of store image studies, see Mary R. Zimmer and Linda L. Golden, "Impressions of Retail Stores: A Content Analysis of Consumer Images," *Journal of Retailing* 64 (Fall 1988): 265–93.

57. Spiggle and Sewall, "A Choice Sets Model of Retail Selection."

58. Philip Kotler, "Atmospherics as a Marketing Tool," *Journal of Retailing* (Winter 1973–74): 10–43, 48–64, 50; for a review of some recent research, see J. Duncan Herrington, "An Integrative Path Model of the Effects of Retail Environments on Shopper Behavior," ed. Robert L. King, *Marketing: Toward the Twenty-First Century* (Richmond, VA: Southern Marketing Association, 1991): 58–62.

59. Joseph A. Bellizzi and Robert E. Hite, "Environmental Color, Consumer Feelings, and Purchase Likelihood," *Psychology & Marketing* 9 (September/October 1992) 5: 347–63.

60. John Tagliabue, "Enticing Europe's Shoppers: U.S. Way of Dressing and of Retailing Spreading Fast," *New York Times* (April 24, 1996): D1 (2 pp.).

61. See Eric R. Spangenberg, Ayn E. Crowley, and Pamela W. Henderson, "Improving the Store Environment: Do Olfactory Cues Affect Evaluations and Behaviors?" *Journal of Marketing* 60 (April 1996): 67–80 for a study that assessed olfaction in a controlled, simulated store environment.

62. Robert J. Donovan, John R. Rossiter, Gilian Marcoolyn, and Andrew Nesdale, "Store Atmosphere and Purchasing Behavior," *Journal of Retailing* 70 (1994)3: 283–94.

63. Deborah Blumenthal, "Scenic Design for In-Store Try-ons," *New York Times* (April 9, 1988).

64. John Pierson, "If Sun Shines in, Workers Work Better, Buyers Buy More," *Wall Street Journal* (November 20, 1995): B1 (2 pp.).

65. Charles S. Areni and David Kim, "The Influence of In-Store Lighting on Consumers' Examination of Merchandise in a Wine Store," *International Journal of Research in Marketing* 11 (March 1994)2: 117–25.

66. Judy I. Alpert and Mark I. Alpert, "Music Influences on Mood and Purchase Intentions," *Psychology & Marketing* 7 (Summer 1990): 109–34.

67. Quoted in "Slow Music Makes Fast Drinkers," *Psychology Today* (March 1989): 18.

68. Brad Edmondson, "Pass the Meat Loaf," *American Demographics* (January 1989): 19.

69. Marianne Meyer, "Attention Shoppers!" *Marketing and Media Decisions* 23 (May 1988): 67.

70. Robert La Franco, "Wallpaper Sonatas," *Forbes* (March 25, 1996): 114.

71. Louise Lee, "Background Music Becomes Hoity-Toity," *Wall Street Journal* (December 22, 1995): B1 (2 pp.).

72. Easwar S. Iyer, "Unplanned Purchasing: Knowledge of Shopping Environment and Time Pressure," *Journal of Retailing* 65 (Spring 1989): 40–57; C. Whan Park, Easwar S. Iyer, and Daniel C. Smith, "The Effects of Situational Factors on In-Store Grocery Shopping," *Journal of Consumer Research* 15 (March 1989): 422–33.

73. Dennis W. Rook and Robert J. Fisher, "Normative Influences on Impulsive Buying Behavior," *Journal of Consumer Research* 22 (December 1995): 305–13; Francis Piron, "Defining Impulse Purchasing," in eds. Rebecca H. Holman and Michael R. Solomon, *Advances in Consumer Research* 18 (Provo, UT: Association for Consumer Research, 1991): 509–14; Dennis W. Rook, "The Buying Impulse," *Journal of Consumer Research* 14 (September 1987): 189–99.

74. Michael Wahl, "Eye POPping Persuasion," *Marketing Insights* (June 1989): 130.

75. "Zipping Down the Aisles," *New York Times Magazine* (April 6, 1997): 30

76. Cathy J. Cobb and Wayne D. Hoyer, "Planned versus Impulse Purchase Behavior," *Journal of Retailing* 62 (Winter 1986): 384–409; Easwar S. Iyer and Sucheta S. Ahlawat, "Deviations from a Shopping Plan: When and Why Do Consumers Not Buy as Planned," in eds. Melanie Wallendorf and Paul Anderson, *Advances in Consumer Research* 14 (Provo, UT: Association for Consumer Research, 1987): 246–9.

77. See Aradhna Krishna, Imran S. Currim, and Robert W. Shoemaker, "Consumer Perceptions of Promotional Activity," *Journal of Marketing* 55 (April 1991): 4–16; see also H. Bruce Lammers, "The Effect of Free Samples on Immediate Consumer Purchase," *Journal of Consumer Marketing* 8 (Spring 1991): 31–7; Kapil Bawa and Robert W. Shoemaker, "The Effects of a Direct Mail Coupon on Brand Choice Behavior," *Journal of Marketing Research* 24 (November 1987): 370–6.

78. Dori Jones Yang, "Hear the Muzak, Buy the Ketchup," *Business Week* (June 28, 1993): 70 (2 pp.).

79. Bernice Kanner, "Trolling in the Aisles," *New York* (January 16, 1989): 12; Michael Janofsky, "Using Crowing Roosters and Ringing Business Cards to Tap a Boom in Point-of-Purchase Displays," *New York Times* (March 21, 1994): D9.

80. John P. Cortez, "Media Pioneers Try to Corral On-the-Go Consumers," *Advertising Age* (August 17, 1992): 25.

81. Cyndee Miller, "MTV 'Video Capsule' Features Sports for Music Retailers, Corporate Sponsors," *Marketing News* (February 3, 1992): 5.

82. William Keenan Jr., "Point-of-Purchase: From Clutter to Techno-clutter," *Sales and Marketing Management* 141 (April 1989): 96.

83. Meyer, "Attention Shoppers!"

84. Cyndee Miller, "Videocart Spruces up for New Tests," *Marketing News* (February 19, 1990): 19; William E. Sheeline, "User-Friendly Shopping Carts," *Fortune* (December 5, 1988): 9.

85. Paco Underhill, "In-Store Video Ads Can Reinforce Media Campaigns," *Marketing News* (May 1989): 5.

86. Quoted in John P. Cortez, "Ads Head for Bathroom," *Advertising Age* (May 18, 1992): 24.

87. James Sterngold, "Why Japanese Adore Vending Machines," *New York Times* (January 5, 1992)2: A1.

88. See Robert B. Cialdini, *Influence: Science and Practice,* 2nd. ed. (Glenview, IL: Scott, Foresman, 1988).

89. Richard P. Bagozzi, "Marketing as Exchange," *Journal of Marketing* 39 (October 1975): 32–9; Peter M. Blau, *Exchange and Power in Social Life* (New York: Wiley, 1964); Marjorie Caballero and Alan J. Resnik, "The Attraction Paradigm in Dyadic Exchange," *Psychology & Marketing* 3 (1986)1: 17–34; George C. Homans, "Social Behavior as Exchange," *American Journal of Sociology* 63 (1958): 597–606; Paul H. Schurr and Julie L. Ozanne, "Influences on Exchange Processes: Buyers' Preconceptions of a Seller's Trustworthiness and Bargaining Toughness," *Journal of Consumer Research* 11 (March 1985): 939–53; Arch G. Woodside and J. W. Davenport, "The Effect of Salesman Similarity and Expertise on Consumer Purchasing Behavior," *Journal of Marketing Research* 8 (1974): 433–6.

90. Paul Busch and David T. Wilson, "An Experimental Analysis of a Salesman's Expert and Referent Bases of Social Power in the Buyer-Seller Dyad," *Journal of Marketing Research* 13 (February 1976): 3–11; John E. Swan, Fred Trawick Jr., David R. Rink, and Jenny J. Roberts, "Measuring Dimensions of Purchaser Trust of Industrial Salespeople," *Journal of Personal Selling and Sales Management* 8 (May 1988): 1.

91. For a recent study in this area, see Peter H. Reingen and Jerome B. Kernan, "Social Perception and Interpersonal Influence: Some

Consequences of the Physical Attractiveness Stereotype in a Personal Selling Setting," *Journal of Consumer Psychology* (2 (1993) 1: 25–38.

92. Mary Jo Bitner, Bernard H. Booms, and Mary Stansfield Tetreault, "The Service Encounter: Diagnosing Favorable and Unfavorable Incidents," *Journal of Marketing* 54 (January 1990): 7–84; Robert C. Prus, *Making Sales* (Newbury Park, CA: Sage Publications, Inc., 1989); Arch G. Woodside and James L. Taylor, "Identity Negotiations in Buyer-Seller Interactions," in eds. Elizabeth C. Hirschman and Morris B. Holbrook, *Advances in Consumer Research* 12 (Provo, UT: Association for Consumer Research, 1985): 443–9.

93. Barry J. Babin, James S. Boles, and William R. Darden, "Salesperson Stereotypes, Consumer Emotions, and Their Impact on Information Processing," *Journal of the Academy of Marketing Science* 23 (1995)2: 94–105; Gilbert A. Churchill Jr., Neil M. Ford, Steven W. Hartley, and Orville C. Walker Jr., "The Determinants of Salesperson Performance: A Meta-Analysis," *Journal of Marketing Research* 22 (May 1985): 103–18.

94. Siew Meng Leong, Paul S. Busch, and Deborah Roedder John, "Knowledge Bases and Salesperson Effectiveness: A Script-Theoretic Analysis," *Journal of Marketing Research* 26 (May 1989): 164; Harish Sujan, Mita Sujan, and James R. Bettman, "Knowledge Structure Differences between More Effective and Less Effective Salespeople," *Journal of Marketing Research* 25 (February 1988): 81–6; Robert Saxe and Barton Weitz, "The SOCCO Scale: A Measure of the Customer Orientation of Salespeople," *Journal of Marketing Research* 19 (August 1982): 343–51; David M. Szymanski, "Determinants of Selling Effectiveness: The Importance of Declarative Knowledge to the Personal Selling Concept," *Journal of Marketing* 52 (January 1988): 64–77; Barton A. Weitz, "Effectiveness in Sales Interactions: A Contingency Framework," *Journal of Marketing* 45 (Winter 1981): 85–103.

95. Jagdish M. Sheth, "Buyer-Seller Interaction: A Conceptual Framework," in *Advances in Consumer Research* (Cincinnati, OH: Associa-

tion for Consumer Research, 1976): 382–6; Kaylene C. Williams and Rosann L. Spiro, "Communication Style in the Salesperson-Customer Dyad," *Journal of Marketing Research* 22 (November 1985): 434–42.

96. Marsha L. Richins, "An Analysis of Consumer Interaction Styles in the Marketplace," *Journal of Consumer Research* 10 (June 1983): 73–82.

97. Calmetta Y. Coleman, "A Car Salesman's Bizarre Prank May End up Backfiring in Court," *Wall Street Journal* (May 2, 1995): B1.

98. Rama Jayanti and Anita Jackson, "Service Satisfaction: Investigation of Three Models," in eds. Rebecca H. Holman and Michael R. Solomon, *Advances in Consumer Research* 18 (Provo, UT: Association for Consumer Research, 1991): 603–10; David K. Tse, Franco M. Nicosia, and Peter C. Wilton, "Consumer Satisfaction as a Process," *Psychology & Marketing* 7 (Fall 1990): 177–93.

99. Eugene W. Anderson, Claes Fornell, and Donald R. Lehmann, "Customer Satisfaction, Market Share, and Profitability: Findings from Sweden," *Journal of Marketing* 58 (July 1994)3: 53–66.

100. Robert Jacobson and David A. Aaker, "The Strategic Role of Product Quality," *Journal of Marketing* 51 (October 1987): 31–44; for a review of issues regarding the measurement of service quality, see J. Joseph Cronin Jr. and Steven A. Taylor, "Measuring Service Quality: A Reexamination and Extension," *Journal of Marketing* 56 (July 1992): 55–68.

101. Anna Kirmani and Peter Wright, "Money Talks: Perceived Advertising Expense and Expected Product Quality," *Journal of Consumer Research* 16 (December 1989): 344–53; Donald R. Lichtenstein and Scot Burton, "The Relationship between Perceived and Objective Price-Quality," *Journal of Marketing Research* 26 (November 1989): 429–43; Akshay R. Rao and Kent B. Monroe, "The Effect of Price, Brand Name, and Store Name on Buyers' Perceptions of Product Quality: An Integrative Review," *Journal of Marketing Research* 26 (August 1989): 351–7.

102. Shelby Hunt, "Post-Transactional Communication and Dissonance Reduction," *Journal of Marketing* 34 (January 1970): 46–51; Daniel E. Innis and H. Rao Unnava, "The Usefulness of Product Warranties for Reputable and New Brands," in eds. Rebecca H. Holman and Michael R. Solomon, *Advances in Consumer Research* 18 (Provo, UT: Association for Consumer Research, 1991): 317–22; Terence A. Shimp and William O. Bearden, "Warranty and Other Extrinsic Cue Effects on Consumers' Risk Perceptions," *Journal of Consumer Research* 9 (June 1982): 38–46.

103. Faye Rice, "What Intelligent Consumers Want," *Marketing Executive Report!* 3 (January 1993)1: 1 (5 pp.).

104. Morris B. Holbrook and Kim P. Corfman, "Quality and Value in the Consumption Experience: Phaedrus Rides Again," in eds. Jacob Jacoby and Jerry C. Olson, *Perceived Quality: How Consumers View Stores and Merchandise* (Lexington, MA: Lexington Books, 1985): 31–58.

105. Holbrook and Corfman, "Quality and Value in the Consumption Experience"; Robert M. Pirsig, *Zen and the Art of Motorcycle Maintenance: An Inquiry into Values* (New York: Bantam Books, 1974).

106. Gilbert A. Churchill Jr. and Carol F. Surprenant, "An Investigation into the Determinants of Customer Satisfaction," *Journal of Marketing Research* 19 (November 1983): 491–504; John E. Swan and I. Frederick Trawick, "Disconfirmation of Expectations and Satisfaction with a Retail Service," *Journal of Retailing* 57 (Fall 1981): 49–67; Peter C. Wilton and David K. Tse, "Models of Consumer Satisfaction Formation: An Extension," *Journal of Marketing Research* 25 (May 1988): 204–12; for a discussion of what may occur when customers evaluate a new service for which comparison standards do not yet exist, see Ann L. McGill and Dawn Iacobucci, "The Role of Post-Experience Comparison Standards in the Evaluation of Unfamiliar Services," in eds. John F. Sherry Jr. and Brian Sternthal, *Advances in Consumer Research* 19 (Provo, UT: Association for Consumer Research, 1992): 570–8; William Boulding, Ajay Kalra, Richard Staelin, and Valarie A. Zeithaml, "A Dynamic Process Model of Service Quality: From Expectations to Behavioral Intentions," *Journal of Marketing*

Research 30 (February 1993): 7–27.

107. John W. Gamble, "The Expectations Paradox: The More You Offer Customer, Closer You Are to Failure," *Marketing News* (March 14, 1988): 38.

108. Jagdish N. Sheth and Banwari Mittal, "A Framework for Managing Customer Expectations," *Journal of Market Focused Management* 1 (1996): 137–58.

109. Mary C. Gilly and Betsy D. Gelb, "Post-Purchase Consumer Processes and the Complaining Consumer," *Journal of Consumer Research* 9 (December 1982): 323–8; Diane Halstead and Cornelia Droge, "Consumer Attitudes toward Complaining and the Prediction of Multiple Complaint Responses," in eds. Rebecca H. Holman and Michael R. Solomon, *Advances in Consumer Research* 18 (Provo, UT: Association for Consumer Research, 1991): 210–16; Jagdip Singh, "Consumer Complaint Intentions and Behavior: Definitional and Taxonomical Issues," *Journal of Marketing* 52 (January 1988): 93–107.

110. Gary L. Clark, Peter F. Kaminski, and David R. Rink, "Consumer Complaints: Advice on How Companies Should Respond Based on an Empirical Study," *Journal of Services Marketing*, 6 (Winter 1992)1: 41–50.

111. Alan Andreasen and Arthur Best, "Consumers Complain—Does Business Respond?" *Harvard Business Review* 55 (July–August 1977): 93–101.

112. Tibbett L. Speer, "They Complain Because They Care," *American Demographics* (May 1996): 13–14.

113. Ingrid Martin, "Expert-Novice Differences in Complaint Scripts," in eds. Rebecca H. Holman and Michael R. Solomon, *Advances in Consumer Research* 18 (Provo, UT: Association for Consumer Research, 1991): 225–31; Marsha L. Richins, "A Multivariate Analysis of Responses to Dissatisfaction," *Journal of the Academy of Marketing Science* 15 (Fall 1987): 24–31.

114. John A. Schibrowsky and Richard S. Lapidus, "Gaining a Competitive Advantage by Analyzing Aggregate Complaints," *Journal of Consumer Marketing* 11 (1994)1: 15–26.

115. Russell W. Belk, "The Role of Possessions in Constructing and Maintaining a Sense of Past," in eds.

Marvin E. Goldberg, Gerald Gorn, and Richard W. Pollay, *Advances in Consumer Research* 17 (Provo, UT: Association for Consumer Research, 1989): 669–76.

116. David E. Sanger, "For a Job Well Done, Japanese Enshrine the Chip," *New York Times* (December 11, 1990): A4.

117. Jacob Jacoby, Carol K. Berning, and Thomas F. Dietvorst, "What About Disposition?" *Journal of Marketing* 41 (April 1977): 22–8.

118. Mike Tharp, "Tchaikovsky and Toilet Paper," *U.S. News and World Report* (December 1987): 62; B. Van Voorst, "The Recycling Bottleneck," *Time* (September 14, 1992) 52–4; Richard P. Bagozzi and Pratibha A. Dabholkar, "Consumer Recycling Goals and Their Effect on Decisions to Recycle: A Means-End Chain Analysis," *Psychology & Marketing* 11 (July/August 1994)4: 313–40.

119. "Finally, Something at McDonald's You Can Actually Eat," *Utne Reader* (May–June 1997): 12.

120. Debra J. Dahab, James W. Gentry, and Wanru Su, "New Ways to Reach Non-Recyclers: An Extension of the Model of Reasoned Action to Recycling Behaviors" (paper presented at the meetings of the Association for Consumer Research, 1994).

121. Bagozzi and Dabholkar, "Consumer Recycling Goals and Their Effect on Decisions to Recycle"; see also L. J. Shrum, Tina M. Lowrey, and John A. McCarty, "Recycling as a Marketing Problem: A Framework for Strategy Development," *Psychology & Marketing* 11 (July/August 1994): 393–416; Dahab, Gentry, and Su, "New Ways to Reach Non-Recyclers."

122. Timothy Aeppel, "From License Plates to Fashion Plates," *Wall Street Journal* (September 21, 1994): B1 (2 pp.).

123. John F. Sherry Jr., "A Sociocultural Analysis of a Midwestern American Flea Market," *Journal of Consumer Research* 17 (June 1990): 13–30.

124. Diane Crispell, "Collecting Memories," *American Demographics* (November 1988): 38–42.

125. Allan J. Magrath, "If Used Product Sellers Ever Get Organized, Watch Out," *Marketing News* (June 25, 1990): 9; Kevin McCrohan and James D. Smith, "Consumer Participation in the Informal Economy," *Journal of the Academy of Marketing Science* 15 (Winter 1990): 62.

126. "New Kind of Store Getting More Use Out of Used Goods," *Montgomery Advertiser* (December 12, 1996): 7A.

ZACHARY LEADS A SECRET life. During the week, he is a straight-laced stock analyst for a major investment firm. The weekend is another story. Come Friday evening, it's off with the Brooks Brothers suit and on with the black leather, as he trades in his BMW for his treasured Harley-Davidson motorcycle. A dedicated member of HOG (Harley Owners Group), Zachary belongs to the faction of Harley riders known as "RUBs" (rich urban bikers). Everyone in his group wears expensive leather vests with Harley insignias and owns customized "Low Riders." Just this week, Zack finally got his new Harley belt buckle that his fellow riders had pointed out to him in *Hog Tails* magazine—now he won't have to take any more ribbing from them about his old "wimpy" belt.

Zack has spent a lot of money on his bike and on outfitting himself to be like the rest of the group. But it's worth it. Zachary feels a real sense of brotherhood with his fellow RUBs. The group rides together in two-column formation to bike rallies that sometimes attract up to 300,000 cycle enthusiasts. What a sense of power he feels when they're all cruising together—it's them against the world!

Of course, an added benefit is the business networking he's been able to accomplish during his weekend jaunts with his fellow professionals who also wait for the weekend to "ride on the wild side."[1] Sometimes sharing a secret can pay off in more ways than one. . . .

11

Group Influence and Opinion Leadership

REFERENCE GROUPS

Humans are social animals. We all belong to groups, try to please others, and take cues about how to behave by observing the actions of those around us. In fact, our desire to "fit in" or to identify with desirable individuals or groups is the primary motivation for many of our purchases and activities. We will often go to great lengths to please the members of a group whose acceptance we covet.[2]

Zachary's biker group is an important part of his identity, and this membership influences many of his buying decisions. He has spent many thousands of dollars on parts and accessories since acquiring his identity as a RUB. His fellow riders are united by their consumption choices, so that total strangers feel an immediate bond with each other when they meet. The publisher of *American Iron,* an industry magazine, observed, "You don't buy a Harley because it's a superior bike, you buy a Harley to be a part of a family."[3]

Zachary doesn't model himself after just *any* biker—only the people with whom he really identifies can exert that kind of influence on him. For example, Zachary's group doesn't have much to do with outlaw clubs, which are primarily composed of blue-collar riders sporting Harley tattoos. The members of his group also have only polite contact with "Ma and Pa" bikers, whose bikes are the epitome of comfort, featuring such niceties as radios, heated handgrips, and floorboards. Essentially, only the RUBs comprise Zachary's *reference group.*

A **reference group** is ". . . an actual or imaginary individual or group conceived of having significant relevance upon an individual's evaluations, aspirations, or behavior."[4] Reference groups influence consumers in three ways. These influences, *informational, utilitarian,* and *value-expressive,* are described in Table 11–1. The chapter focuses on how other people, whether fellow bikers, coworkers, friends, and family, or just casual acquaintances influence our purchase decisions. It considers how our preferences are shaped by our group memberships, by our desire to please or be accepted by others, or even by the actions of famous people whom we've never even met. Finally, it explores why some people are more influential than others in affecting consumer's product preferences, and how marketers go about finding those people and enlisting their support in the persuasion process.

TABLE 11–1 ■ Three Forms of Reference Group Influence
_____

Informational Influence	● The individual seeks information about various brands from an association of professionals or independent group of experts. ● The individual seeks information from those who work with the product as a profession. ● The individual seeks brand-related knowledge and experience (such as how Brand A's performance compares to Brand B's) from those friends, neighbors, relatives, or work associates who have reliable information about the brands. ● The brand the individual selects is influenced by observing a seal of approval of an independent testing agency (such as *Good Housekeeping*). ● The individual's observation of what experts do (such as observing the type of car that police drive or the brand of television that repairmen buy) influences his or her choice of a brand.
Utilitarian Influence	● So that he or she satisfies the expectations of fellow work associates, the individual's decision to purchase a particular brand is influenced by their preferences. ● The individual's decision to purchase a particular brand is influenced by the preferences of people with whom he or she has social interaction. ● The individual's decision to purchase a particular brand is influenced by the preferences of family members. ● The desire to satisfy the expectations that others have of him or her has an impact on the individual's brand choice.
Value-Expressive Influence	● The individual feels that the purchase or use of a particular brand will enhance the image others have of him or her. ● The individual feels that those who purchase or use a particular brand possess the characteristics that he or she would like to have. ● The individual sometimes feels that it would be nice to be like the type of person that advertisements show using a particular brand. ● The individual feels that the people who purchase a particular brand are admired or respected by others. ● The individual feels that the purchase of a particular brand would help show others what he or she is or would like to be (such as an athlete, successful business person, good parent, etc.).

Source: Adapted from C. Whan Park and V. Parker Lessig, "Students and Housewives: Differences in Susceptibility to Reference Group Influence," *Journal of Consumer Research* 4 (September 1977): 102. Reprinted with permission by The University of Chicago Press.

TYPES OF REFERENCE GROUPS

Although two or more people are normally required to form a group, the term *reference group* is often used a bit more loosely to describe *any* external influence that provides social cues.[5] The referent may be a cultural figure and have an impact on many people (e.g., Louis Farrakhan) or a person or group whose influence is confined to the consumer's immediate environment (e.g., Zachary's biker club). Reference groups that affect consumption can include parents, fellow motorcycle enthusiasts, the Democratic party, or even the Chicago Bears, the Red Hot Chili Peppers, or Spike Lee.

Obviously, some groups and individuals exert a greater influence than others, and affect a broader range of consumption decisions. For example, our parents may play a pivotal role in forming our values toward many important issues, such as attitudes about marriage or where to go to college. This type of influence is **normative influence**—that is, the reference group helps to set and enforce fundamental standards of conduct. In contrast, a Harley-Davidson club might exert **comparative influence**, whereby decisions about specific brands or activities are affected.[6]

FORMAL VERSUS INFORMAL GROUPS

A reference group can take the form of a large, formal organization that has a recognized structure, complete with a charter, regular meeting times, and officers. Or it can be small and informal, such as a group of friends or students living in a dormitory. Marketers tend to be more successful at influencing formal groups because they are more easily identifiable and accessible. However, as a rule it is small, informal groups that exert a more powerful influence on individual consumers. For example, in a recent Roper Starch Worldwide survey, 34 percent of teens said that their friends' ideas had the greatest influence on how they spend their money, but only 25 percent said that advertising had the same impact.[7] Small, informal groups tend to be more a part of our day-to-day lives and to be more important to us, because they are high in normative influence. Larger, formal groups tend to be more product- or activity-specific and thus are high in comparative influence.

MEMBERSHIP VERSUS ASPIRATIONAL REFERENCE GROUPS

Some reference groups consist of people the consumer actually knows; others comprise either people the consumer can identify with or admire. Not surprisingly, many marketing efforts that specifically adopt a reference group appeal concentrate on highly visible, widely admired figures (such as well-known athletes or performers).

Because people tend to compare themselves to others who are similar, they are often swayed by knowing how people like them conduct their lives. For this reason, many promotional strategies include "ordinary" people whose consumption activities provide informational social influence. For example, MasterCard shifted the focus of its advertising away from glamorous, affluent lifestyles of professionals to relatively ordinary activities such as those of a young man furnishing his first apartment (and, of course, using his MasterCard to pay for it). The campaign's slogan: "For the Way We Really Live."[8]

The likelihood that people will become part of a consumer's identificational reference group is affected by several factors, including the following.

MULTICULTURAL DIMENSIONS

"Common man" or "slice-of-life" depictions, which highlight "real" people, are more realistic and thus more credible than those featuring celebrities or superstars. Although we admire perfect people, it can be frustrating to compare ourselves to them. By including people who are successful but not perfect in ad compaigns, marketers can enhance consumers' identification with the spokespeople. This strategy has been successfully employed in the classic "Dewar's Profiles," a series of ads describing the lifestyles of noncelebrity high achievers who happen to drink Dewar's Scotch. Since the strategy entails the use of real people from many different walks of life, the company has expanded its ad executions to focus on accomplished people in different countries. For example, a Thai ad highlights a successful architect who lives in Bangkok, whereas a Spanish campaign features a 29-year-old flight instructor.[9]

- *Propinquity:* As physical distance between people decreases and opportunities for interaction increase, relationships are more likely to form. Physical nearness is called *propinquity.* An early study on friendship patterns in a housing complex showed this factor's strong effects: Residents were much more likely to be friends with the people next door than with those who lived only two doors away. Furthermore, people who lived next to a staircase had more friends than those at the ends of a hall (presumably, they were more likely to "bump into" people using the stairs).[10] Physical structure has a lot to do with whom we get to know and how popular we are.

- *Mere exposure:* We come to like persons or things simply as a result of seeing them more often, which is known as the *mere exposure phenomenon.*[11] Greater frequency of contact, even if unintentional, may help to determine one's set of local referents. The same effect holds when evaluating works of art, or even political candidates.[12] One study predicted 83 percent of the winners of political primaries solely by the amount of media exposure given to candidates.[13]

- *Group cohesiveness:* **Cohesiveness** refers to the degree that members of a group are attracted to each other and value their group membership. As the value of the group to the individual increases, so too does the likelihood that the group will guide consumption decisions. Smaller groups tend to be more cohesive, because in larger groups the contributions of each member are usually less important or noticeable. By the same token, groups often try to restrict membership to a select few, which increases the value of membership to those who are admitted. Exclusivity of membership is a benefit often touted by credit card companies, book clubs, and so on, even though the actual membership base might be fairly large.

The consumer may have no direct contact with reference groups, but they can have powerful influences on his or her tastes and preferences because they provide guidance as to the types of products used by admired people.[14] The MasterCard campaign noted previously is taking a bit of a risk, because most credit card advertising is "aspirational." As one executive noted, "In this industry, you market to who you want to be, rather than who you are."[15] *Aspirational reference groups* comprise idealized figures such as successful business people, athletes, or performers. For example, one study that included business students who aspired to the "executive" role found a strong relationship between products they associated with their *ideal selves* (see chapter 5) and those they assumed would be owned or used by executives.[16]

POSITIVE VERSUS NEGATIVE REFERENCE GROUPS

Reference groups may exert *either* a positive or a negative influence on consumption behaviors. In most cases, consumers model their behavior to be consistent with what they think the group expects of them. In some cases, though, a consumer may try to distance him- or herself from other people or groups that function as *avoidance groups.* He or she may carefully study the dress or mannerisms of a disliked group (e.g., "nerds," "druggies," or "preppies") and scrupulously avoid buying anything that might identify him or her with that group. For example, rebellious adolescents often resent parental influence and may deliberately do the opposite of what their parents would like as a way of making a statement about their independence. As Romeo and Juliet discovered, nothing makes a dating partner more attractive than a little parental opposition.

Many products, especially those targeted to young people, are often touted as a way to take the inside track to popularity. This Brazilian shoe ad proclaims, "Anyone who doesn't like them is a nerd."

WHEN REFERENCE GROUPS ARE IMPORTANT

Reference group influences are not equally powerful for all types of products and consumption activities. For example, products that are not very complex, that are low in perceived risk, and that can be tried prior to purchase are less susceptible to personal influence.[17] In addition, the specific impact of reference groups may vary. At times it may determine the use of certain products rather than others (e.g., owning or not owning a computer, eating junk food versus health food), whereas at other times it may have specific effects on brand decisions within a product category (e.g., wearing Levi's jeans versus Calvin Klein jeans, or smoking Marlboro cigarettes rather than Virginia Slims).

Two dimensions that influence the degree to which reference groups are important are whether the purchase is to be consumed publicly or privately and whether it is a luxury or a necessity. As a rule, reference group effects are more robust for purchases that are (1) luxuries rather than necessities (e.g., sailboats), because products that are purchased with discretionary income are subject to individual tastes and preferences, whereas necessities do not offer this range of choices; and (2) socially

MARKETING OPPORTUNITY

Group membership has entered cyberspace, as "netizens" around the world rapidly are forming virtual communities. Members are linked to one another only via their computer modems, and all of their interactions are digital.[18] This electronic anonymity opens exciting new vistas for many, especially those who have difficulty interacting in face-to-face settings (e.g., the Net has made a dramatic difference in the lives of many disabled people who can now interact with others around the globe without having to leave home). New technologies allow people to chat about their mutual interests, to help one another with inquiries and suggestions, and to get suggestions for new products and services. Some of the most popular virtual communities to date include:

- Tripod (www.tripod.com): A big hit with Web surfers in their twenties, about 270,000 people have signed up to pose questions to one another or just to sound off on issues.

- Parent Soup (www.parentsoup.com): More than 200,000 parents chat about the trials and tribulations of being—what else—parents.
- Geocities (www.geocities.com): "Homesteaders" get free home pages and access to one of 37 themed communities, from Arts or Autos to Sports and Recreation or Travel.
- Utne Online (www.utne.com): Members log onto the Utne Cafe and discuss New Age issues and current affairs.
- The Well (www.com): At least 260 active discussion groups for the *digerati*.

conspicuous or visible to others (e.g., living room furniture or clothing) because consumers do not tend to be swayed as much by the opinions of others if their purchases will never be observed by anyone but themselves.[19] The relative effects of reference group influences on some specific product classes are shown in Figure 11–1.

THE POWER OF REFERENCE GROUPS

Social Power. Social power refers to ". . . the capacity to alter the actions of others."[20] To the degree that you are able to make someone else do something, whether they do it willingly or not, you have power over that person. The following classification of *power bases* can help us to distinguish among the reasons a person can exert power over another, the degree to which the influence is allowed voluntarily, and whether this influence will continue to have an effect in the absence of the power source.[21]

Referent Power. If a person admires the qualities of a person or a group, he or she will try to imitate those qualities by copying the referent's behaviors (e.g., choice of clothing, cars, leisure activities) as a guide to forming consumption preferences, just as Zack's preferences were affected by his fellow bikers. Prominent people in all walks of life can affect people's consumption behaviors by virtue of product endorsements (e.g., Michael Jordan for Air Nike), distinctive fashion statements (e.g., Madonna's use of lingerie as outerwear), or championing causes (e.g., Jerry Lewis' work for muscular dystrophy). **Referent power** is important to many marketing strategies because consumers voluntarily change behaviors to please or identify with a referent.

Information Power. A person can have power simply because he or she knows something others would like to know. Editors of trade publications such as *Women's Wear Daily* often possess power due to their ability to compile and disseminate information that can make or break individual designers or companies. People with **infor-**

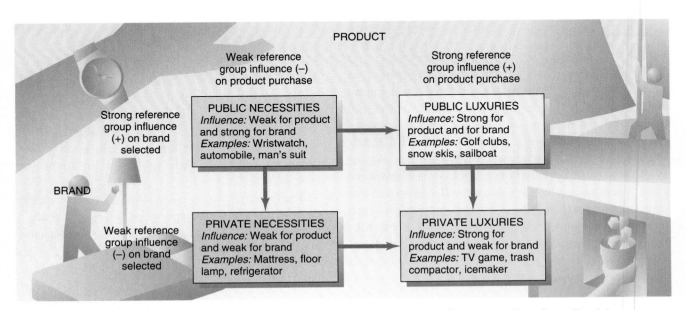

FIGURE 11–1 ■ **Relative Reference Group Influence on Purchase Decisions**
Adapted from William O. Bearden and Michael J. Etzel, "Reference Group Influence on Product and Brand Purchase Decisions," *Journal of Consumer Research* (September 1982): 185. Reprinted with permission by The University of Chicago Press.

Master Sergeant Marialena Bridges

you can look at models, or you can be one.

Do you have what it takes to be a role model? A model of integrity, intelligence, and courage? If you're an individual who thrives on challenge and never gives less than your best, you could be doing things most people only read about. You could become a leader, an inspiration. You could become a United States Marine. Do more than look at models, be one. Call 1-800-MARINES. The change is forever. Contact us at: http://www.Marines.com

Marines
The Few. The Proud.

This recruiting ad presents a compelling role model for young women contemplating a career in the armed forces.

mation power are able to influence consumer opinion by virtue of their (assumed) access to the "truth."

Legitimate Power. Sometimes people are granted power by virtue of social agreements, such as the power given to policemen and professors. The **legitimate power** conferred by a uniform is recognized in many consumer contexts, including teaching hospitals, in which medical students don white coats to enhance their aura of authority with patients, and banks, in which tellers' uniforms communicate trustworthiness.[22] This form of power may be "borrowed" by marketers

MARKETING OPPORTUNITY

One of the most recent and widespread applications of reference group influences to consumer behavior is **affinity marketing**. This strategy allows consumers to underscore their identification with some organization by attaching the group's identification to aspects of their personal life.

In the most common form of affinity marketing, banks promote special credit cards known as *affinity cards,* which can be tied to a membership group, such as a church or college alumni organization, or to a symbolic group, such as an NFL team or a rock group.[23] Priests and nuns have been targeted to adopt the Caritas card, issued by Catholic Charities,[24] and even Elvis has appeared on an affinity card. Use of these cards has surged since 1985, when rules regarding what could be pictured on a credit card were relaxed.

to influence consumers. For example, an ad featuring a model wearing a white doctor's coat can add an aura of legitimacy or authority to the presentation of the product.

Expert Power. To attract the casual Internet user, U.S. Robotics signed up British physicist Stephen Hawking to endorse its modems. A company executive commented, "We wanted to generate trust. So we found visionaries who use U.S. Robotics technology, and we let them tell the consumer how it makes their lives more productive." Hawking, who has Lou Gehrig's disease and speaks via a synthesizer, says in one TV spot, "My body may be stuck in this chair, but with the Internet my mind can go to the end of the universe."[25] **Expert power** such as that possessed by Hawking is derived from possessing a specific knowledge or skill.

Consumers are often influenced by experts who are assumed to be able to evaluate products in an objective, informed way. Occasionally, this trust is exploited— for example, Upjohn Company settled a lawsuit after it was discovered that the company was paying pharmacists $8 every time they induced their patients to switch to a diabetes drug made by the firm.[26]

Reward Power. When a person or group has the means to provide positive reinforcement (see chapter 3), that entity will have power over a consumer to the extent that this reinforcement is valued or desired. The reward may be tangible, as occurs when an employee is given a raise. Or, the reward may be intangible: Social approval or acceptance is often what is exchanged in return for molding one's behavior to a group or buying the products expected of group members.

Coercive Power. Coercive power refers to influencing a person by social or physical intimidation. A threat is often effective in the short-term, but it does not tend to produce permanent attitudinal or behavioral change. Fortunately, coercive power is rarely employed in marketing situations. However, elements of this power base are evident in fear appeals, intimidation in personal selling, and some campaigns that emphasize the negative consequences that might occur if people do not use a product.

MARKETING OPPORTUNITY

The power of celebrity experts can be measured by their visibility on talk shows, lecture circuits, and so on. Prominent economists, for example, can receive between $5,000 and $20,000 for a speech, depending on their level of perceived expertise. One analysis of economist superstars noted these requirements for success:[27]

- Affiliation with an elite university, think tank, or investment house
- Authorship of a slim, easy-reading book that yields a vision of the future
- An advisory relationship with at least one presidential candidate

The need to provide evidence of expert power creates other marketing opportunities, ranging from the provision of certificates and diplomas to coaching for licensing exams. A number of industries in which the criteria for expertise are poorly defined are grappling with the need for *credentialing,* or defining what knowledge and experience is necessary to make a person an expert and providing a mechanism to weed out people who do not meet these criteria. Hitting close to home, the American Marketing Association periodically debates the need for licensing of its members as a way to boost the perceived professionalism of marketing research as a discipline.

CONFORMITY

Conformity refers to a change in beliefs or actions as a reaction to real or imagined group pressure. In order for a society to function, its members develop **norms,** or informal rules that govern behavior. If such a system of agreements did not evolve, social chaos would result. Imagine the confusion if a simple norm such as stopping for a red traffic light did not exist.

Norms change slowly over time, but there is general agreement within a society about which ones should be obeyed, and we adjust our way of thinking to conform to these norms. A powerful example is the change in American society's attitude toward smoking since this practice was first linked with health concerns such as cancer and emphysema in the 1960s. By the mid-1990s some communities even had tried to outlaw smoking in public places. Although tobacco sales to minors are illegal, most smokers begin puffing before the age of 18. Much of the motivation to begin smoking at an early age is due to peer pressure; the alluring advertising images of smokers as cool, sexy, or mature help to convince many young people that beginning the habit is a path to social acceptance.

Because the power of advertising to influence attitudes is widely recognized, some groups have tried to fight fire with fire by creating antismoking ads that depict smoking as an ugly habit that turns people off. Are these ads effective? One recent study of nonsmoking seventh graders by a pair of consumer researchers examined the kids' perceptions of smokers after being exposed to both cigarette ads and antismoking ads. Results were promising: The researchers found that kids who saw the antismoking ads were more likely to rate smokers lower in terms of both personal appeal and common sense. These findings imply that it is possible to use advertising to debunk myths about the glamour of smoking, especially if used in tandem with other health-education efforts.[28]

Unspoken rules govern many aspects of consumption. In addition to norms regarding appropriate use of clothing and other personal items, we conform to rules that include gift giving (we expect birthday presents from loved ones and get upset if they do not materialize), sex roles (men often are expected to pick up the check on a first date), and personal hygiene (we are expected to shower regularly to avoid offending others).

TYPES OF SOCIAL INFLUENCE

Just as the bases for social power can vary, the process of social influence operates in several ways.[29] Sometimes a person is motivated to mimic the behavior of others because this behavior is believed to yield rewards such as social approval or money. At other times, the social influence process occurs simply because the person honestly does not *know* the correct way to respond and is using the behavior of the other person or group as a cue to ensure that he or she is responding correctly.[30] **Normative social influence** occurs when a person conforms to meet the expectations of a person or group.

In contrast, **informational social influence** refers to conformity that occurs because the group's behavior is taken as evidence about reality: If other people respond in a certain way in an ambiguous situation, we may mimic their behavior because this appears to be the correct thing to do.[31]

Conformity is not an automatic process, and many factors contribute to the likelihood that consumers will pattern their behavior after others.[32] Among the factors that affect the likelihood of conformity are the following:

An example of an antismoking ad targeted to youth.

- *Cultural pressures:* Different cultures encourage conformity to a greater or lesser degree. The American slogan "Do your own thing" in the 1960s reflected a movement away from conformity and toward individualism. In contrast, Japanese society is characterized by the dominance of collective well-being and group loyalty over individuals' needs.

- *Fear of deviance:* The individual may have reason to believe that the group will apply *sanctions* to punish behavior that differs from the group's. It is not unusual to observe adolescents shunning a peer who is "different" or a corporation passing over a person for promotion because he or she is not a "team player."

- *Commitment:* The more a person is dedicated to a group and values membership in it, the more motivated he or she will be to follow the dictates of the group. Rock groupies and followers of TV evangelists may do anything that is asked of them, and terrorists may be willing to die for the good of their cause. According to *the principle of least interest,* the person or group that is least committed to staying in a relationship has the most power, because that party won't be susceptible to threatened rejection.[33]

- *Group unanimity, size, and expertise:* As groups gain in power, compliance increases. It is often harder to resist the demands of a large number of people than just a few, and this difficulty is compounded when the group members are perceived to know what they are talking about.

- *Sex differences:* It has often been assumed that women are more susceptible than men to interpersonal influence, because they are more sensitive to social cues and tend to be more group-oriented and cooperative in nature. However, recent indications show this reasoning is flawed: Both men and women who possess feminine personality traits tend to conform more (see chapter 5).[34]

- *Susceptibility to interpersonal influence:* This trait refers to an individual's need to identify or enhance his or her image in the opinion of significant others. This enhancement process is often accompanied by the acquisition of products the person believes will impress his or her audience, and by the tendency to learn about products by observing how others use them.[35] Consumers who are low on this trait have been called *role relaxed;* they tend to be older, affluent, and to have high self-confidence. Based on research identifying role-relaxed consumers, Subaru created a communications strategy to reach these people. In one commercial, a man is heard saying, "I want a car.... Don't tell me about wood paneling, about winning the respect of my neighbors. They're my neighbors. They're not my heroes...."

SOCIAL COMPARISON: "HOW'M I DOING?"

Informational social influence implies that sometimes we look to the behavior of others to provide a yardstick about reality. **Social comparison theory** asserts that this process occurs as a way to increase the stability of one's self-evaluation, especially when physical evidence is unavailable.[36] Social comparison even applies to choices for which there is no objectively correct answer. Stylistic decisions such as tastes in music and art are assumed to be a matter of individual choice, yet people often assume that some choices are "better" or more "correct" than others.[37] If you have ever been responsible for choosing the music to play at a party, you can probably appreciate the social pressure involved in choosing the right "mix."

Although people often like to compare their judgments and actions to those of others, they tend to be selective about precisely whom they will use as benchmarks. Similarity between the consumer and others used for social comparison boosts confidence that the information is accurate and relevant (though we may find it more threatening to be outperformed by someone similar to ourselves).[38] We tend to value the views of obviously dissimilar others only when we are reasonably certain of our own.[39]

In general people tend to choose a *co-oriented peer,* or a person of equivalent standing, when performing social comparison. For example, a study of adult cosmetics users found that women were more likely to seek information about product choices from similar friends to reduce uncertainty and to trust the judgments of similar others.[40] The same effects have been found for evaluations of products as diverse as men's suits and coffee.[41]

COMPLIANCE AND OBEDIENCE

The discussion of persuasive communications in chapter 8 indicated that source and message characteristics have a big impact on the likelihood of influence. Influencers have been found to be more successful at gaining compliance if they are perceived to be confident or expert.[42] In addition, the way a request is phrased can influence the likelihood of compliance.

TACTICAL REQUESTS

The way a request for compliance is phrased or structured can make a difference. One well-known sales tactic is known as the *foot-in-the-door technique,* in which the consumer is first asked a small request and then is hit up for something bigger.[43] This term is adapted from door-to-door selling. Experienced salespeople know that they are much more likely to make a sale if they first convince a customer to let them in the house to deliver a sales pitch. Once the person has agreed to this small request, it is more difficult to refuse a larger one, because the consumer has legitimized the salesperson's presence by entering into a dialogue. He or she is no longer a threatening stranger at the door.

Other variations on this strategy include the *low-ball technique,* in which a person is asked for a small favor and is informed after agreeing to it that it will be very costly; or the *door-in-the-face technique,* in which a person is first asked to do something extreme (a request that is usually refused) and then is asked to do something smaller. In each of these cases, people tend to go along with the smaller request, possibly because they feel guilty about denying the larger one.[44]

GROUP EFFECTS ON INDIVIDUAL BEHAVIOR

With more people in a group, it becomes less likely any one member will be singled out for attention. People in larger groups or those in situations in which they are likely to be unidentified tend to focus less attention on themselves, so normal restraints on behavior are reduced. You may have observed that people sometimes behave more wildly at costume parties or on Hallowe'en than they do normally. This phenomenon is known as **deindividuation,** in which individual identities get submerged within a group.

Social loafing refers to the fact that people do not devote as much to a task when their contribution is part of a larger group effort.[45] Waitresses are painfully aware of social loafing: People who eat in groups tend to tip less per person than when they are eating alone.[46] For this reason, many restaurants automatically tack on a fixed gratuity for groups of six or more.

There is some evidence that decisions made by groups differ from those that would be made by each individual. In many cases, group members show a greater willingness to consider riskier alternatives following group discussion than they would if each member made his or her own decision with no discussion. This change is known as the *risky shift.*[47]

Several explanations have been advanced to explain this increased riskiness. One possibility is that something similar to social loafing occurs. As more people are involved in a decision, each individual is less accountable for the outcome, so *diffusion of responsibility* occurs.[48] The practice of placing blanks in at least one of the rifles used by a firing squad is one way of diffusing each soldier's responsibility for the death of a prisoner. Another explanation is termed the *value hypothesis.* In this case, riskiness is a culturally valued characteristic, and social pressures operate on individuals to conform to attributes valued by society.[49]

Evidence for the risky shift is mixed. A more general effect appears to be that group discussion tends to increase **decision polarization.** Whichever direction the group members were leaning before discussion began, toward a risky choice or toward a conservative choice, becomes even more extreme in that direction after discussion. Group discussions regarding product purchases tend to create a risky shift for low-risk items, but they yield even more conservative group decisions for high-risk products.[50]

MARKETING PITFALL

A downside to deindividuation can be observed at many college parties, where students are encouraged by their peers to consume almost superhuman volumes of alcohol. It's been estimated that 4.5 million young people are alcohol dependent or are problem drinkers. Binge drinking among college students is reaching epidemic proportions. In a two-week period, 42 percent of all college students engage in binge drinking (more than five drinks at a time) versus 33 percent of their noncollege counterparts. One in three students drinks primarily to get drunk, including 35 percent of college women.[51]

Even shopping behavior changes when people do it in groups. For example, people who shop with at least one other person tend to make more unplanned purchases, buy more, and cover more areas of a store than those who go alone.[52] These effects are due to both normative and informational social influence. Group members may be convinced to buy something to gain the approval of the others, or they may simply be exposed to more products and stores by pooling information with the group. For these reasons, retailers are well advised to encourage group shopping activities.

Home shopping parties, as epitomized by the Tupperware Party, capitalize on group pressures to boost sales.[53] A company representative makes a sales presentation to a group of people who have gathered in the home of a friend or acquaintance. This format is effective because of informational social influence: Participants model the behavior of others who can provide them with information about how to use certain products, especially because the home party is likely to be attended by a relatively homogenous group (e.g., neighborhood homemakers) that serves as a valuable benchmark. Normative social influence also operates because actions are publicly observed. Pressures to conform may be particularly intense and may escalate as more and more group members begin to "cave in" (this process is sometimes termed the *bandwagon effect*). In addition, deindividuation and/or the risky shift may be activated: As consumers get caught up in the group, they may find themselves willing to try new products they would not normally consider.

RESISTANCE TO INFLUENCE

Many people pride themselves on their independence, unique style, or ability to resist the best efforts of salespeople and advertisers to buy products.[54] Indeed, individuality should be encouraged by the marketing system: Innovation creates change and demand for new products and styles.

ANTICONFORMITY VERSUS INDEPENDENCE

It is important to distinguish between *independence* and *anticonformity*; in anticonformity, defiance of the group is the actual object of behavior.[55] Some people will go out of their way *not* to buy whatever happens to be in at the moment. Indeed, they may spend a lot of time and effort to ensure that they will not be caught "in style." This behavior is a bit of a paradox, because in order to be vigilant about not doing what is expected, one must always be aware of what is expected. In contrast, truly independent people are oblivious to what is expected; they "march to their own drummers."

REACTANCE AND NEED FOR UNIQUENESS

People have a deep-seated need to preserve freedom of choice. When they are threatened with a loss of this freedom, they try to overcome this loss. This negative emotional state is termed **reactance.**[56] For example, efforts to censor books, television shows, or rock music because some people find the content objectionable may result in an *increased* desire for these products by the public.[57] Similarly, extremely overbearing promotions that tell consumers they must or should use a product may wind up losing more customers in the long run, even those who were already loyal to the advertised brand! Reactance is more likely to occur when the perceived threat to one's freedom increases and as the threatened behavior's importance to the consumer also increases.

If you have ever shown up at a party wearing the same outfit as someone else, you know how upsetting the discovery can be. Some psychologists believe this reaction is a result of a *need for uniqueness*.[58] Consumers who have been led to believe they are not unique are more likely to try to compensate by increasing their creativity, or even to engage in unusual experiences. In fact, this need could be one explanation for the purchase of relatively obscure brands. People may try to establish a unique identity by deliberately *not* buying market leaders. This desire to carve out a unique identity was the rationale behind Saab's recent shift from stressing engineering and safety in its marketing messages to appealing to people to "find your own road." According to a Saab executive, "Research companies tell us we're moving into a period where people feel good about their choices because it fits [sic] their own self-concept rather than social conventions."[59]

WORD-OF-MOUTH COMMUNICATION

Despite the abundance of formal means of communication (such as newspapers, magazines, and television), much information about the world actually is conveyed by individuals on an informal basis. If you think carefully about the content of your own conversations in the course of a normal day, you will probably agree that much of what you discuss with friends, family members, or coworkers is product-related: Whether you compliment someone on her dress and ask her where she bought it, recommend a new restaurant to a friend, or complain to your neighbor about the shoddy treatment you got at the bank, you are engaging in **word-of-mouth communication (WOM)**. Recall, for example, that many of Zachary's biker purchases were directly initiated by comments and suggestions from his fellow RUBs. The power of this process was recognized by Make-up Art Cosmetics, Ltd. This company is an anomaly in the $6 billion cosmetics industry, because it doesn't advertise. Instead, the firm built WOM by offering discounts to professional makeup artists to encourage them to use the line.[60] By cultivating an image as the choice of beauty professionals, this company has become a huge success.

Not every firm can do without advertising (fortunately for our friends in the ad business!), but information obtained from those we know or talk with directly tends to be more reliable and trustworthy than that received through more formal marketing channels. Unlike advertising, WOM often is backed up by social pressure to conform with these recommendations.[61] The importance of personal, informal product communication to marketers is underscored by one advertising executive who stated, "Today, 80 percent of all buying decisions are influenced by someone's direct recommendations."[62]

Sometimes these recommendations are obtained by giving out samples of the product and hoping people will talk about it. When RJR Nabisco revived a 60-year-old brand called Red Kamel, the company tried to woo young smokers by handing out samples at hip bars. The company hopes to create a "cool" cachet for the brand by only giving it out to people "in the know" (following the death of Joe Camel, cigarette marketers need to work harder to do this . . .). As a marketing research executive observed about this strategy, "You're letting them discover you—that's a very powerful tool."[63]

THE DOMINANCE OF WOM

As far back as the Stone Age (well, the 1950s, anyway), communications theorists began to challenge the assumption that advertising is the primary determinant of purchases. It is now generally accepted that advertising is more effective at reinforcing existing product preferences than at creating new ones.[64] Studies in both industrial and consumer purchase settings underscore the idea that although information from impersonal sources is important for creating brand awareness, word-of-mouth is relied on in the later stages of evaluation and adoption.[65] The more positive information a consumer gets about a product from peers, the more likely he or she will be to adopt the product.[66] The influence of others' opinions is at times even more powerful than one's own perceptions. In one study of furniture choices, consumers' estimates of how much their friends would like the furniture was a better predictor of purchase than their *own* evaluations.[67]

FACTORS ENCOURAGING WOM

Most WOM campaigns happen spontaneously, as a product begins to develop a regional following, as was the case with Ben & Jerry's ice cream. Occasionally, a "buzz" is intentionally created. For example, Henry Weinhards' Private Reserve, a superpremium beer in the Pacific Northwest, was first introduced at selected bars after bartenders had been briefed on the brand's unusual brewing process. The beer was introduced to stores only when demand from bar patrons mounted.[68]

Product-related conversations can be motivated by a number of factors:[69]

- A person might be highly involved with a type of product or activity and get pleasure in talking about it. Computer hackers, avid bird-watchers, and "fashion plates" seem to share the ability to steer a conversation toward their particular interests.
- A person might be knowledgeable about a product and use conversations as a way to let others know it. Thus, word-of-mouth communication sometimes enhances the ego of the individual who wants to impress others with his or her expertise.
- A person might initiate such a discussion out of genuine concern for someone else. We are often motivated to ensure that people we care about buy what is good for them, do not waste their money, and so on.
- One way to reduce uncertainty about the wisdom of a purchase is to talk about it. Talking gives the consumer an opportunity to generate more supporting arguments for the purchase and to garner support for this decision from others.

THE EFFICIENCY OF WOM

Interpersonal transmissions can be quite rapid. The producers of the movie *Batman* showed a trailer to 300 Batman fans months before its release to counteract widespread anger about the casting of Michael Keaton as the star. The film makers

MARKETING PITFALL

A 30-second commercial on *The Today Show* costs more than $25,000. To avoid paying this fee, several companies have tried to drum up word of mouth by getting free exposure on *Today's* live cameras, which periodically pan over the crowd gathered outside the studio window at Rockefeller Center in Manhattan. Companies including The Gap, General Mills, Avon, Oscar Mayer, and BMW have all tried to entice the cameras by dressing employees in outlandish costumes or performing attention-grabbing stunts. The Gap's Old Navy division dressed five people as Old Navy candy bars to mingle with tourists and pass out samples.[70] When Philip Morris introduced Red Dog beer in 1995, the company hired people to put on Red Dog masks and elbow their way to the front of the waving crowd.[71] The *Today* show staff is not amused.

attribute the film's eventual huge success to the positive word-of-mouth that quickly spread following the screening.[72]

The current revival of an obscure, 200 year-old breath mint called Altoids can be directly attributed to the WOM boost the product received from members of the "grunge" subculture. This process began when the mint began to attract a devoted following among smokers and coffee drinkers who hung out in the blossoming Seattle club scene during the 1980s. Until 1993, when manufacturer Callard & Bowers was bought by Kraft, the product was only bought by those "in the know." At that point, the brand's marketing manager persuaded this bigger company to hire advertising agency Leo Burnett to develop a modest promotional effort. The agency decided to publicize the candy by using subway posters containing retro imagery and other "low-tech" media to avoid making the product seem mainstream and as a result turn off the original audience.[73]

WOM is especially powerful in cases in which the consumer is relatively unfamiliar with the product category. Such a situation would be expected in the case of new products (e.g., medications to prevent hair loss) or those that are technologically complex (e.g., CD players). As one example, the strongest predictor of a person's intention to buy a residential solar water-heating system was found to be the number of solar-heating users the person knows.[74]

NEGATIVE WOM

Word-of-mouth is a two-edged sword that can cut both ways for marketers. Informal discussions among consumers can make or break a product or store. Furthermore, negative word-of-mouth is weighted *more* heavily by consumers than are positive comments. According to a study by the White House Office of Consumer Affairs, 90 percent of unhappy customers will not do business with a company again. Each of these people is likely to share their grievance with at least 9 other people, and 13 percent of these disgruntled customers will go on to tell more than *30 people* of their negative experience.[75] Especially when making a decision about trying a product innovation, the consumer is more likely to pay more attention to negative information than positive information and to relate news of this experience to others.[76] Negative WOM has been shown to reduce the credibility of a firm's advertising and to influence consumers' attitudes toward a product as well as their intention to buy it.[77]

RUMORS: DISTORTION IN THE WORD-OF-MOUTH PROCESS

In the 1930s, "professional rumor mongers" were hired to organize word-of-mouth campaigns to promote clients' products and criticize those of competitors.[78] A rumor, even if it has no basis in fact, can be a very dangerous thing. As information is transmitted among consumers, it tends to change. The resulting message usually does not at all resemble the original.

Social scientists who study rumors have examined the process by which information gets distorted. The British psychologist Frederic Bartlett used the method of *serial reproduction* to examine this phenomenon. As in the game of "Telephone," a subject is asked to reproduce a stimulus, such as a drawing or a story. Another subject is given this reproduction and asked to copy that, and so on. This technique is shown in Figure 11–2. Bartlett found that distortions almost inevitably follow a pattern: They tend to change from ambiguous forms to more conventional ones as subjects try to make them consistent with preexisting schemas. This process, known as *assimilation,* is characterized by *leveling,* in which details are omitted to simplify the structure, or *sharpening,* in which prominent details are accentuated.

Original Drawing

Reproduction 2

Reproduction 3 *Reproduction 4* *Reproduction 5* *Reproduction 6*

Reproduction 7 *Reproduction 8* *Reproduction 9* *Reproduction 10*

FIGURE 11–2 ■ **The Transmission of Misinformation:** These drawings provide a classic example of the distortions that can occur as information is transmitted from person to person. As each participant reproduces the figure, it gradually changes from an owl to a cat.
Source: Kenneth J. Gergen and Mary Gergen, *Social Psychology* (New York: Harcourt Brace Jovanovich, 1981): 365, Fig. 10–3; adapted from F. C. Bartlett, *Remembering* (Cambridge, UK: Cambridge University Press, 1932).

In general, people have been shown to prefer transmitting good news rather than bad, perhaps because they like to avoid unpleasantness or dislike arousing hostility.[79] However, this reluctance does not appear to occur when companies are the topic of conversation. Corporations such as Procter & Gamble and McDonald's have been the subjects of rumors about their products, sometimes with noticeable effects on sales.

Rumors are thought to reveal the underlying fears of a society. For example, one rumor regarding snakes coming out of teddy bears imported from the Orient was interpreted to signify Western consumers' apprehensions about Asian influences. The Disney organization recently came under attack from conservative religious groups after a rumor spread among members that the company was sending subversive subliminal messages in its videotapes. They insisted, for example, that in the movie Aladdin, a character says, "All good teenagers take off your clothes." Disney countered that the real line is, "Scat, good tiger, take off and go."[80]

CONSUMER BOYCOTTS

Sometimes a negative experience can trigger an organized and devastating response, as when a consumer group organizes a *boycott* of a company's products. These efforts can include protests against everything from the use of products from a politically undesirable country (as when Proctor & Gamble used Salvadoran beans for its Folgers coffee), the inclusion of obscene or inflammatory song lyrics (as when law enforcement organizations threatened to boycott Time Warner after it distributed a

MULTICULTURAL DIMENSIONS

Multinational firms are especially prone to damage from rumors, because they have less control over product quality, content, or word-of-mouth. Several marketers in Indonesia, including Nestlé, were hurt by rumors that their foods contain pork, which is prohibited to the 160 million Muslim consumers in that country. Islamic preachers, or mullahs, responded to these rumors by warning consumers not to buy products that might be tainted with pork fat. Nestlé spent more than $250,000 on an ad campaign to counteract the rumors.[81] Pabst Blue Ribbon beer was hit by a product-tampering scare in China. Rumors about poisoned bottles spread quickly, apparently following an incident in which home-brewed beer was poured into empty Pabst bottles and resold.[82]

rap song by Ice-T entitled "Cop Killer"), or even objections to an organization's management practices (as when the Southern Baptist Convention voted to boycott Disney products in 1997 due to its conviction that the company's policies were inappropriately pro-gay and lesbian).

Boycotts are not always effective—studies show that only 18 percent of Americans participate in them. However, those who do are disproportionately upscale and well educated, so they are a group companies especially don't want to alienate. One increasingly popular solution used by marketers is setting up a joint task force with the boycotting organization to try to iron out the problem. McDonald's recently used this approach with the Environmental Defense Fund, which was concerned about its use of polystyrene containers and bleached paper. The company agreed to test a composting program and to switch to plain brown bags.[83]

OPINION LEADERSHIP

Although consumers get information from personal sources, they do not tend to ask just *anyone* for advice about purchases. If you decide to buy a new stereo, you will most likely seek advice from a friend who knows a lot about sound systems. This friend may own a sophisticated system, or she may subscribe to specialized magazines such as *Stereo Review* and spend free time browsing through electronics stores. On the other hand, you may have another friend who has a reputation for being stylish and who spends *his* free time reading *Gentlemen's Quarterly* and shopping at trendy boutiques. You might not bring up your stereo problem with him, but you may take him with you to shop for a new fall wardrobe.

THE NATURE OF OPINION LEADERSHIP

Everyone knows people who are knowledgeable about products and whose advice is taken seriously by others. These individuals are **opinion leaders.** An opinion leader is a person who is frequently able to influence others' attitudes or behaviors.[84] Opinion leaders are extremely valuable information sources for a number of reasons.

1. They are technically competent and thus convincing because they possess expert power.[85]

2. They have prescreened, evaluated, and synthesized product information in an unbiased way, so they possess knowledge power.[86] Unlike commercial endorsers, opinion leaders do not actually represent the interests of one company. Thus, they are more credible because they have no "axe to grind."

3. They tend to be socially active and highly interconnected in their community.[87] They are likely to hold office in community groups and clubs and to be active outside of the home. As a result, opinion leaders often have legitimate power by virtue of their social standing.

4. They tend to be similar to the consumer in terms of their values and beliefs, so they possess referent power. Note that although opinion leaders are set apart by their interest or expertise in a product category, they are more convincing to the extent that they are *homophilous* rather than *heterophilous*. *Homophily* refers to the degree that a pair of individuals is similar in terms of education, social status, and beliefs.[88] Effective opinion leaders tend to be slightly higher in terms of status and educational attainment than those they influence but not so high as to be in a different social class.

5. Opinion leaders are often among the first to buy new products, so they absorb much of the risk. This experience reduces uncertainty for others who are not as courageous. Furthermore, whereas company-sponsored communications tend to focus exclusively on the positive aspects of a product, the hands-on experience of opinion leaders makes them more likely to impart *both* positive and negative information about product performance.

THE EXTENT OF AN OPINION LEADER'S INFLUENCE

When marketers and social scientists initially developed the concept of the opinion leader, it was assumed that certain influential people in a community would exert an overall impact on group members' attitudes. Later work, however, began to question the assumption that there is such a thing as a *generalized opinion leader,* somebody whose recommendations are sought for all types of purchases. Very few people are capable of being expert in a number of fields. Sociologists distinguish between those who are *monomorphic,* or expert in a limited field, and those who are *polymorphic,* or expert in several fields.[89] Even opinion leaders who are polymorphic, however, tend to concentrate on one broad domain, such as electronics or fashion.

Research on opinion leadership generally indicates that although opinion leaders do exist for multiple product categories, expertise tends to overlap across similar categories. It is rare to find a generalized opinion leader. An opinion leader for home appliances is likely to serve a similar function for home cleaners but not for cosmetics. In contrast, a fashion opinion leader whose primary influence is on clothing choices may also be consulted for recommendations on cosmetics purchases but not necessarily on microwave ovens.[90]

OPINION LEADERS VERSUS OTHER CONSUMER TYPES

Early conceptions of the opinion leader role also assumed a static process: The opinion leader absorbs information from the mass media and in turn transmits data to opinion receivers. This view has turned out to be overly simplified; it confuses the functions of several different types of consumers.

Opinion leaders may or may not be purchasers of the products they recommend. As we will see in chapter 17, early purchasers are known as *innovators.* Opinion leaders who also are early purchasers have been termed *innovative communicators.* One study identified a number of characteristics of college men who were innovative communicators for fashion products. These men were among the first to buy new fashions, and their fashion opinions were incorporated by other students in their own clothing decisions. Other characteristics of the men included the following:[91]

- They were socially active.
- They were appearance-conscious and narcissistic (i.e., they were quite fond of themselves and self-centered).
- They were involved in rock culture.
- They were heavy magazine readers, including *Playboy* and *Sports Illustrated.*
- They were likely to own more clothing, and a broader range of styles, than other students.

Opinion leaders also are likely to be *opinion seekers.* They are generally more involved in a product category and actively search for information. As a result, they are more likely to talk about products with others and to solicit others' opinions as well.[92] Contrary to the static view of opinion leadership, most product-related conversation does not take place in a "lecture" format, in which one person does all of the talking. A lot of product-related conversation is prompted by the situation and occurs in the context of a casual interaction rather than as formal instruction.[93] One study, which found that opinion seeking is especially high for food products, revealed that two-thirds of opinion seekers also view themselves as opinion leaders.[94] This updated view of interpersonal product communication is contrasted with the traditional view in Figure 11–3.

Consumers who are expert in a product category may not actively communicate with others, whereas other consumers may have a more general interest in being involved in product discussions. A consumer category called the **market maven** has been proposed to describe people who are actively involved in transmitting marketplace information of all types. Market mavens are not necessarily interested in certain products and may not necessarily be early purchasers of products. They come closer to the function of a generalized opinion leader because they tend to have a solid overall knowledge of how and where to procure products. The following scale items, to which respondents indicate how much they agree or disagree, have been used to identify market mavens:[95]

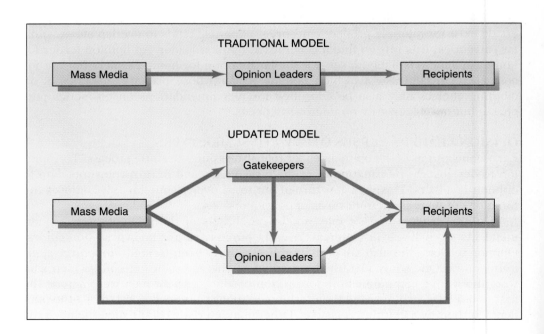

FIGURE 11–3 ■
Perspectives on the Communications Process

1. I like introducing new brands and products to my friends.
2. I like helping people by providing them with information about many kinds of products.
3. People ask me for information about products, places to shop, or sales.
4. If someone asked me where to get the best buy on several types of products, I could tell him or her where to shop.
5. My friends think of me as a good source of information when it comes to new products or sales.
6. Think about a person who has information about a variety of products and likes to share this information with others. This person knows about new products, sales, stores, and so on, but does not necessarily feel he or she is an expert on one particular product. How well would you say this description fits you?

In addition to everyday consumers who are influential in influencing others' purchase decisions, a class of marketing intermediary called the **surrogate consumer** is an active player in many categories. A surrogate consumer is a person who is hired to provide input into purchase decisions. Unlike the opinion leader or market maven, the surrogate is usually compensated for this involvement.

Opinion leadership is heavily emphasized in athletic shoe marketing. Athletic shoes are very much a fashion statement and a phenomenon largely fueled by inner city kids, despite price tags of $120 and more. Many of the sneaker styles originate in the inner city and then spread outward by word-of-mouth.

Interior decorators, stockbrokers, professional shoppers, or college consultants can all be thought of as surrogate consumers. Whether or not they actually make the purchase on behalf of the consumer, surrogates' recommendations can be enormously influential. The consumer in essence relinquishes control over several or all decision-making functions, such as information search, evaluation of alternatives, or the actual purchase. For example, a client may commission an interior decorator to redo her house, and a broker may be entrusted to make crucial buy/sell decisions on behalf of investors. The involvement of surrogates in a wide range of purchase decisions tends to be overlooked by many marketers, who may be mistargeting their communications to end consumers instead of to the surrogates who are actually sifting through product information.[96]

IDENTIFYING OPINION LEADERS

Because opinion leaders are so central to consumer decision making, marketers are quite interested in identifying influential people for a product category. In fact, many ads are intended to reach these influentials rather than the average consumer, especially if the ads contain a lot of technical information. For example, CBS recently sent a CD-ROM to 10,000 critics, affiliates, advertising agencies, and others it had identified as "influencers" in order to plug the network's prime-time shows.[97]

Unfortunately, because most opinion leaders are everyday consumers and are not formally included in marketing efforts, they are harder to find. A celebrity or an influential industry executive is by definition easy to locate. He or she has national or at least regional visibility or may be listed in published directories. In contrast, opinion leaders tend to operate at the local level and may influence five to ten consumers rather than an entire market segment. In some cases, companies have been known to identify influentials and involve them directly in their marketing efforts, hoping to create a "ripple effect" as these consumers sing the company's praises to their friends. Many department stores, for example, have fashion panels, usually composed of adolescent girls, who provide input into fashion trends, participate in fashion shows, and so on.

Because of the difficulties involved in identifying specific opinion leaders in a large market, most attempts to do so instead focus on exploratory studies through which the characteristics of representative opinion leaders can be identified and then generalized to the larger market. This knowledge helps marketers target their product-related information to appropriate settings and media. For example, one attempt to identify financial opinion leaders found that these consumers were more likely to be involved in managing their own finances and tended to use a computer to do so. They also were more likely to follow their investments on a daily basis and to read books and watch television shows devoted to financial issues.[98]

THE SELF-DESIGNATING METHOD

The most commonly used technique to identify opinion leaders is simply to ask individual consumers whether they consider themselves to be opinion leaders. Although respondents who report a greater degree of interest in a product category are more likely to be opinion leaders, the results of surveys intended to identify self-designated opinion leaders must be viewed with some skepticism. Some people have a tendency to inflate their own importance and influence, whereas others who really are influential might not admit to this quality or be conscious of it.[99] Just because we transmit advice about products does not mean other people *take* that advice. For someone to be considered a *bona fide* opinion leader, his or her advice must actually be heard and heeded by opinion seekers. An alternative is to select certain group members (*key informants*) who in turn are asked to identify opinion leaders. The success of this approach hinges on locating those who have accurate knowledge of the group and on minimizing their response biases (e.g., the tendency to inflate one's own influence on the choices of others).

The self-designating method is not as reliable as a more systematic analysis (in which individual claims of influence can be verified by asking others whether the person is really influential), but it does have the advantage of being easy to apply to a large group of potential opinion leaders. In some cases not all members of a community are surveyed. One of the measurement scales developed for self-designation of opinion leaders is shown in Figure 11–4.

SOCIOMETRY

A web-based service has been created that is based on the popular play "Six Degrees of Separation." The basic premise of the plot is that everyone on the planet indirectly knows everyone else—if they go through a process of identifying "mutual friends" about six times eventually they will link up with every other person. While it's doubtful that this process will literally work in many cases, the website allows a person to register and provide names and e-mail addresses of other people, so that when the user needs to network a connection can be made with others in the database.[100] Its slogan "You'd be surprised who you know."

This site is a digital version of more conventional **sociometric methods**, which trace communication patterns among members of a group. These techniques allow researchers to systematically map out the interactions that take place among group members. By interviewing participants and asking them to whom they go for prod-

Please rate yourself on the following scales relating to your interactions with friends and neighbors regarding ________.

1. In general, do you talk to your friends and neighbors about ________:

very often				never
5	4	3	2	1

2. When you talk to your friends and neighbors about ________ do you:

give a great deal of information			give very little information	
5	4	3	2	1

3. During the past six months, how many people have you told about a new ________?

told a number of people				told no one
5	4	3	2	1

4. Compared with your circle of friends, how likely are you to be asked about new ________?

very likely to be asked			not at all likely to be asked	
5	4	3	2	1

5. In discussion of new ________, which of the following happens most?

you tell your friends about ________			your friends tell you about ________	
5	4	3	2	1

6. Overall in all of your discussions with friends and neighbors are you:

often used as a source of advice			not used as a source of advice	
5	4	3	2	1

FIGURE 11–4 ■ A Revised and Updated Version of the Opinion Leadership Scale
Source: Adapted from Terry L. Childers, "Assessment of the Psychometric Properties of an Opinion Leadership Scale," *Journal of Marketing Research* 23 (May 1986): 184–8; and Leisa Reinecke Flynn, Ronald E. Goldsmith, and Jacqueline K. Eastman, "The King and Summers Opinion Leadership Scale: Revision and Refinement," *Journal of Business Research* 31 (1994): 55–64.

uct information, those who tend to be sources of product-related information can be identified. This method is the most precise, but it is very hard and expensive to implement because it involves very close study of interaction patterns in small groups. For this reason, sociometric techniques are best applied in a closed, self-contained social setting, such as in hospitals, prisons, and army bases, in which members are largely isolated from other social networks.

Many professionals and services marketers depend primarily on word-of-mouth to generate business. In many cases consumers recommend a service provider to a friend or coworker, and in other cases business people will make recommendations to their customers. For example, only 0.2 percent of respondents in one study reported choosing a physician based on advertising. Advice from family and friends was the most widely used criterion.[101]

Sociometric analyses can be used to better understand *referral behavior* and to locate strengths and weaknesses in terms of how one's reputation is communicated through a community.[102] *Network analysis* focuses on communication in social systems, considers the relations among people in a *referral network* and measures the *tie strength* among them. Tie strength refers to the nature of the bond between people. It can range from strong primary (e.g., one's spouse) to weak secondary (e.g., an acquaintance that one rarely sees). A strong tie relationship may be thought of as a primary reference group; interactions are frequent and important to the individual.

Although strong ties are important, weak ties can perform a *bridging function*. This type of connection allows a consumer access between subgroups. For example, you might have a regular group of friends who serve as a primary reference group (strong ties). If you have an interest in tennis, say, one of these friends might introduce you to a group of people in her dorm who play on the tennis team. As a result, you gain access to their valuable expertise through this bridging function. This referral process demonstrates the strength of weak ties. One study using this method examined similarities in brand choice among members of a college sorority. The researchers found evidence that subgroups, or *cliques,* within the sorority were likely to share preferences for various products. In some cases, even choices of "private" (i.e., socially inconspicuous products) were shared, possibly because of structural variables such as shared bathrooms in the sorority house.[103]

CHAPTER SUMMARY

- Consumers belong to or admire many different groups and are often influenced in their purchase decisions by a desire to be accepted by others.

- Individuals have influence in a group to the extent that they possess *social power;* types of social power include information power, referent power, legitimate power, expert power, reward power, and coercive power.

- We conform to the desires of others for one of two basic reasons. (1) People who model their behavior after others because they take others' behavior as evidence of the correct way to act are conforming because of *informational social influence.* (2) Those who conform to satisfy the expectations of others and/or to be accepted by the group are affected by *normative social influence.*

- Group members often do things they would not do as individuals because their identities become merged with the group; they become *deindividuated.*

- Individuals or groups whose opinions or behavior are particularly important to consumers are *reference groups.* Both formal and informal groups influence the individual's purchase decisions, although the impact of reference group influence is affected by such factors as the conspicuousness of the product and the relevance of the reference group for a particular purchase.

- *Opinion leaders* who are knowledgeable about a product and whose opinions are highly regarded tend to influence others' choices. Specific opinion leaders are somewhat hard to identify, but marketers who know their general characteristics can try to target them in their media and promotional strategies.

- Other influencers include *market mavens,* who have a general interest in marketplace activities, and *surrogate consumers,* who are compensated for their advice about purchases.

- Much of what we know about products comes about through *word-of-mouth communication* (WOM) rather than formal advertising. Product-related information tends to be exchanged in casual conversations.

- Although word-of-mouth often is helpful for making consumers aware of products, it can also hurt companies when damaging product rumors or negative word-of-mouth occurs.

- *Sociometric methods* are used to trace referral patterns. This information can be used to identify opinion leaders and other influential consumers.

KEY TERMS

Affinity marketing p. 343
Comparative influence
   p. 339
Conformity p. 345
Decision polarization p. 348
Deindividuation p. 348
Expert power p. 344
Information power p. 342
Informational social
   influence p. 345

Legitimate power p. 343
Market maven p. 356
Normative influence p. 339
Normative social influence
   p. 345
Norms p. 345
Opinion leaders p. 354
Reactance p. 349
Reference group p. 337
Referent power p. 342

Social comparison theory
   p. 347
Social power p. 342
Sociometric methods
   p. 359
Surrogate consumer p. 357
Word-of-mouth communi-
   cation (WOM) p. 350

CONSUMER BEHAVIOR CHALLENGE

1. Compare and contrast the five bases of power described in the text. Which are most likely to be relevant for marketing efforts?

2. Why is referent power an especially potent force for marketing appeals? What factors help to predict whether reference groups will or will not be a powerful influence on a person's purchase decisions?

3. Evaluate the strategic soundness of the concept of affinity marketing. For what type of linkages is this strategy most likely to be a success?

4. Discuss some factors that determine the amount of conformity likely to be observed among consumers.

5. Under what conditions are we more likely to engage in social comparison with dissimilar others versus similar others? How might this dimension be used in the design of marketing appeals?

6. Discuss some reasons for the effectiveness of home shopping parties as a selling tool. What other products might be sold this way?

7. Discuss some factors that influence whether membership groups will have a significant influence on a person's behavior.

8. Why is word-of-mouth communication often more persuasive than advertising?

9. Is there such a thing as a generalized opinion leader? What is likely to determine if an opinion leader will be influential with regard to a specific product category?

10. The adoption of a certain brand of shoe or apparel by athletes can be a powerful influence on students and other fans. Should high school and college coaches be paid to determine what brand of athletic equipment their players will wear?

11. The power of unspoken social norms often becomes obvious only when these norms are violated. To witness this result first hand, try one of the following: stand facing the back wall in an elevator; serve dessert before the main course; offer to pay cash for dinner at a friend's home; wear pajamas to class; or tell someone not to have a nice day.

12. Identify a set of avoidance groups for your peers. Can you identify any consumption decisions that are made with these groups in mind?

13. Identify fashion opinion leaders on your campus. Do they fit the profile discussed in the chapter?

14. Conduct a sociometric analysis within your dormitory or neighborhood. For a product category such as music or cars, ask each individual to identify other individuals with whom they share information. Systematically trace all of these avenues of communication, and identify opinion leaders by locating individuals who are repeatedly named as providing helpful information.

NOTES

1. Details adapted from John W. Schouten and James H. McAlexander, "Market Impact of a Consumption Subculture: The Harley-Davidson Mystique," in eds. Fred van Raaij and Gary Bamossy, *Proceedings of the 1992 European Conference of the Association for Consumer Research* (Amsterdam, 1992); John W. Schouten and James H. McAlexander, "Subcultures of Consumption: An Ethnography of the New Bikers," *Journal of Consumer Research* 22 (June 1995): 43–61.

2. Joel B. Cohen and Ellen Golden, "Informational Social Influence and Product Evaluation," *Journal of Applied Psychology* 56 (February 1972): 54–9; Robert E. Burnkrant and Alain Cousineau, "Informational and Normative Social Influence in Buyer Behavior," *Journal of Consumer Research* 2 (December 1975): 206–15; Peter H. Reingen, "Test of a List Procedure for Inducing Compliance with a Request to Donate Money," *Journal of Applied Psychology* 67 (1982): 110–18.

3. Quoted in Dyan Machan, "Is the Hog Going Soft?" *Forbes* (March 10, 1997): 114–19, quoted on p. 117.

4. C. Whan Park and V. Parker Lessig, "Students and Housewives: Differences in Susceptibility to Reference Group Influence," *Journal of Consumer Research* 4 (September 1977): 102–10.

5. Kenneth J. Gergen and Mary Gergen, *Social Psychology* (New York: Harcourt Brace Jovanovich, 1981).

6. Harold H. Kelley, "Two Functions of Reference Groups," in eds. Harold Proshansky and Bernard Siedenberg, *Basic Studies in Social Psychology* (New York: Holt, Rinehart and Winston, 1965): 210–14.

7. Carol Krol, "Survey: Friends Lead Pack in Kids' Spending Decisions," *Advertising Age* (March 10, 1997): 16.

8. Anthony Ramirez, "Mastercard's Shift from Glamour," *New York Times* (April 9, 1990): D1.

9. David Murrow, "Dewar's Profiles Travel Well," *Advertising Age* (August 14, 1989): 28.

10. L. Festinger, S. Schachter, and K. Back, *Social Pressures in Informal Groups: A Study of Human Factors in Housing* (New York: Harper, 1950).

11. R. B. Zajonc, H. M. Markus, and W. Wilson, "Exposure Effects and Associative Learning," *Journal of Experimental Social Psychology* 10 (1974): 248–63.

12. D. J. Stang, "Methodological Factors in Mere Exposure Research," *Psychological Bulletin* 81 (1974): 1014–25; R. B. Zajonc, P. Shaver, C. Tavris, and D. Van Kreveid, "Exposure, Satiation and Stimulus Discriminability," *Journal of Personality and Social Psychology* 21 (1972): 270–80.

13. J. E. Grush, K. L. McKeogh, and R. F. Ahlering, "Extrapolating Laboratory Exposure Research to Actual Political Elections," *Journal of Personality and Social Psychology* 36 (1978): 257–70.

14. A. Benton Cocanougher and Grady D. Bruce, "Socially Distant Reference Groups and Consumer Aspirations," *Journal of Marketing Research* 8 (August 1971): 79–81; James E. Stafford, "Effects of Group Influences on Consumer Brand Preferences," *Journal of Marketing Research* 3 (February 1966): 68–75.

15. Ramirez, "Mastercard's Shift from Glamour."

16. Cocanougher and Bruce, "Socially Distant Reference Groups and Consumer Aspirations."

17. Jeffrey D. Ford and Elwood A. Ellis, "A Re-examination of Group Influence on Member Brand Preference," *Journal of Marketing Research* 17 (February 1980): 125–32; Thomas S. Robertson, *Innovative Behavior and Communication* (New York: Holt, Rinehart and Winston, 1980): chapter 8.

18. Robert D. Hof, "Special Report: Internet Communities," *Business Week* (May 5,1997): 63 (8 pp.).

19. William O. Bearden and Michael J. Etzel, "Reference Group Influence on Product and Brand Purchase Decisions," *Journal of Consumer Research* 9 (1982)2: 183–94.

20. Gergen and Gergen, *Social Psychology*: 312.

21. J. R. P. French Jr. and B. Raven, "The Bases of Social Power," in ed. D. Cartwright, *Studies in Social Power* (Ann Arbor, MI: Institute for Social Research, 1959): 150–67.

22. Michael R. Solomon, "Packaging the Service Provider," *The Service Industries Journal* 5 (March 1985): 64–72.

23. Judith Waldrop, "Plastic Wars," *American Demographics* (November 1988): 6.

24. Elaine Santoro, "Catholic Charities Credit Card Unveiled," *Fund Raising Management* 20 (April 1989): 10.

25. Quoted in Tamar Charry, "Advertising: Hawking, Wozniak Pitch Modems for U.S. Robotics," *New York Times News Service* 1997, accessed 2/5/97.

26. Gina Kolata, "Upjohn Will Repay 8 States over Drug Marketing Plan," *Wall Street Journal* (August 2, 1994): D1.

27. Augustin Hedberg, "Lights! Camera! Economists!" (celebrity economists), *Money* (October 1987): 118.

28. Cornelia Pechmann and S. Ratneshwar, "The Effects of Antismoking and Cigarette Advertising on Young Adolescents' Perceptions of Peers Who Smoke," *Journal of Consumer Research* 21, (September 1994): 2 236–51.

29. See Robert B. Cialdini, *Influence: Science and Practice,* 2nd ed. (New York: Scott, Foresman, 1988) for an excellent and entertaining treatment of this process.

30. For the seminal work on conformity and social influence, see Solomon E. Asch, "Effects of Group Pressure upon the Modification and Distortion of Judgments," in eds. D. Cartwright and A. Zander, *Group Dynamics* (New York: Harper and Row, 1953); Richard S. Crutchfield, "Conformity and Character," *American Psychologist* 10 (1955): 191–8; Muzafer Sherif, "A Study of Some Social Factors in Perception," *Archives of Psychology* 27 (1935): 187.

31. Burnkrant and Cousineau, "Informational and Normative Social Influence in Buyer Behavior."

32. For a study attempting to measure individual differences in proclivity to conformity, see William O. Bearden, Richard G. Netemeyer, and Jesse E. Teel, "Measurement of Consumer Susceptibility to Interpersonal Influence," *Journal of Consumer Research* 15 (March 1989): 473–81.

33. John W. Thibaut and Harold H. Kelley, *The Social Psychology of Groups* (New York: Wiley, 1959); W. W. Waller and R. Hill, *The Family, a Dynamic Interpretation* (New York: Dryden, 1951).

34. Sandra L. Bem, "Sex Role Adaptability: One Consequence of Psychological Androgyny," *Journal of Personality and Social Psychology* 31 (1975): 634–43.

35. William O. Bearden, Richard G. Netemeyer, and Jesse E. Teel, "Measurement of Consumer Susceptibility to Interpersonal Influence," *Journal of Consumer Research* 9 (1989)3: 183–94; Lynn R. Kahle, "Observations: Role-Relaxed Consumers: A Trend of the Nineties," *Journal of Advertising Research* (March/April 1995): 66–71; Lynn R. Kahle and Aviv Shoham, "Observations: Role-Relaxed Consumers: Empirical Evidence," *Journal of Advertising Research* 35 (May/June 1995)3: 59–62.

36. Leon Festinger, "A Theory of Social Comparison Processes," *Human Relations* 7 (May 1954): 117–40.

37. Chester A. Insko, Sarah Drenan, Michael R. Solomon, Richard Smith, and Terry J. Wade, "Conformity as a Function of the Consistency of Positive Self-Evaluation with Being Liked and Being Right," *Journal of Experimental Social Psychology* 19 (1983): 341–58.

38. Abraham Tesser, Murray Millar, and Janet Moore, "Some Affective Consequences of Social Comparison and Reflection Processes: The Pain and Pleasure of Being Close," *Journal of Personality and Social Psychology* 54 (1988)1: 49–61.

39. L. Wheeler, K. G. Shaver, R. A. Jones, G. R. Goethals, J. Cooper, J. E. Robinson, C. L. Gruder, and K. W. Butzine, "Factors Determining the Choice of a Comparison Other," *Journal of Experimental Social Psychology* 5 (1969): 219–32.

40. George P. Moschis, "Social Comparison and Informal Group Influence," *Journal of Marketing Research* 13 (August 1976): 237–44.

41. Burnkrant and Cousineau, "Informational and Normative Social Influence in Buyer Behavior"; M. Venkatesan, "Experimental Study of Consumer Behavior Conformity and Independence," *Journal of Marketing Research* 3 (November 1966): 384–7.

42. Harvey London, *Psychology of the Persuader* (Morristown, NJ: Silver Burdett/General Learning Press, 1973); William J. McGuire, "The Nature of Attitudes and Attitude Change," in eds. G. Lindzey and E. Aronson, *The Handbook of Social Psychology* (Reading, MA: Addison-Wesley, 1968): 3; N. Miller, G. Naruyama, R. J. Baebert, and K. Valone, "Speed of Speech and Persuasion," *Journal of Personality and Social Psychology* 34 (1976): 615–24.

43. J. L. Freedman and S. Fraser, "Compliance without Pressure: The Foot-in-the-Door Technique," *Journal of Personality and Social Psychology* 4 (1966): 195–202.

44. R. B. Cialdini, J. E. Vincent, S. K. Lewis, J. Catalan, D. Wheeler, and B. L. Darby, "Reciprocal Concessions Procedure for Inducing Compliance: The Door-in-the-Face Effect," *Journal of Personality and Social Psychology* 31 (1975): 200–15.

45. B. Latane, K. Williams, and S. Harkins, "Many Hands Make Light the Work: The Causes and Consequences of Social Loafing," *Journal of Personality and Social Psychology* 37 (1979): 822–32.

46. S. Freeman, M. Walker, R. Borden, and B. Latane, "Diffusion of Responsibility and Restaurant Tipping: Cheaper by the Bunch," *Personality and Social Psychology Bulletin* 1 (1978): 584–7.

47. Nathan Kogan and Michael A. Wallach, "Risky Shift Phenomenon in Small Decision-Making Groups: A Test of the Information Exchange Hypothesis," *Journal of Experimental Social Psychology* 3 (January 1967): 75–84; Nathan Kogan and Michael A. Wallach, *Risk Taking* (New York: Holt, Rinehart and Winston, 1964); Arch G. Woodside and M. Wayne DeLozier, "Effects of Word-of-Mouth Advertising on Consumer Risk Taking," *Journal of Advertising* (Fall 1976): 12–19.

48. Kogan and Wallach, *Risk Taking*.

49. Roger Brown, *Social Psychology* (New York: The Free Press, 1965).

50. David L. Johnson and I. R. Andrews, "Risky Shift Phenomenon Tested with Consumer Product Stimuli," *Journal of Personality and Social Psychology* 20 (1971): 382–5; see

also Vithala R. Rao and Joel H. Steckel, "A Polarization Model for Describing Group Preferences," *Journal of Consumer Research* 18 (June 1991): 108–118.

51. J. Craig Andrews and Richard G. Netemeyer, "Alcohol Warning Label Effects: Socialization, Addiction, and Public Policy Issues," in ed. Ronald P. Hill, *Marketing and Consumer Research in the Public Interest* (Thousand Oaks, CA: Sage, 1996): 153–75.

52. Donald H. Granbois, "Improving the Study of Customer In-Store Behavior," *Journal of Marketing* 32 (October 1968): 28–32.

53. Len Strazewski, "Tupperware Locks in New Strategy," *Advertising Age* (February 8, 1988): 30.

54. Gergen and Gergen, *Social Psychology*.

55. L. J. Strickland, S. Messick, and D. N. Jackson, "Conformity, Anticonformity and Independence: Their Dimensionality and Generality," *Journal of Personality and Social Psychology* 16 (1970): 494–507.

56. Jack W. Brehm, *A Theory of Psychological Reactance* (New York: Academic Press, 1966).

57. R. D. Ashmore, V. Ramchandra, and R. Jones, "Censorship as an Attitude Change Induction" (paper presented at meeting of Eastern Psychological Association, New York, 1971); R. A. Wicklund and J. Brehm, *Perspectives on Cognitive Dissonance* (Hillsdale, NJ: Erlbaum, 1976).

58. C. R. Snyder and H. L. Fromkin, *Uniqueness: The Human Pursuit of Difference* (New York: Plenum Press, 1980).

59. Quoted in Raymond Serafin, "Non-Conformity Sparks Saab," *Advertising Age* (April 3, 1995): 27.

60. Yumiko Ono, "Earth Tones and Attitude Make a Tiny Cosmetics Company Hot," *Wall Street Journal* (February 23, 1995): B1 (2 pp.).

61. Johan Arndt, "Role of Product-Related Conversations in the Diffusion of a New Product," *Journal of Marketing Research* 4 (August 1967): 291–5.

62. Quoted in Barbara B. Stern and Stephen J. Gould, "The Consumer as Financial Opinion Leader," *Journal of Retail Banking* 10 (Summer 1988): 43–52.

63. Quoted in Yumiko Ono, "RJR's New Ad Campaign: It's Hip to Smoke," *New York Times* (April 16, 1996): B1 (2 pp.), quoted on p. B2.

64. Elihu Katz and Paul F. Lazarsfeld, *Personal Influence* (Glencoe, IL: The Free Press, 1955).

65. John A. Martilla, "Word-of-Mouth Communication in the Industrial Adoption Process," *Journal of Marketing Research* 8 (March 1971): 173–8; see also Marsha L. Richins, "Negative Word-of-Mouth by Dissatisfied Consumers: A Pilot Study," *Journal of Marketing* 47 (Winter 1983): 68–78.

66. Arndt, "Role of Product-Related Conversations in the Diffusion of a New Product."

67. James H. Myers and Thomas S. Robertson, "Dimensions of Opinion Leadership," *Journal of Marketing Research* 9 (February 1972): 41–6.

68. Barnaby J. Feder, "Those with Things to Sell Love Word-of-Mouth Ads," *New York Times* (June 23, 1992): D18.

69. James F. Engel, Robert J. Kegerreis, and Roger D. Blackwell, "Word of Mouth Communication by the Innovator," *Journal of Marketing* 33 (July 1969): 15–19.

70. David Kirkpatrick, "Advertisers Crash Crowd Outside 'Today'," *Wall Street Journal* (April 24, 1996): B1 (2 pp.).

71. Suein L. Hwang, "Philip Morris Makes Dave's—but Sh! Don't Tell," *Wall Street Journal* (March 22, 1995): B1 (2 pp.).

72. Bill Barol, "Batmania," *Newsweek* (June 26, 1989): 70.

73. Pat Wechsler, "A Curiously Strong Campaign," *Business Week* (April 21, 1997): 134.

74. Dorothy Leonard-Barton, "Experts as Negative Opinion Leaders in the Diffusion of a Technological Innovation," *Journal of Consumer Research* 11 (March 1985): 914–26.

75. Chip Walker, "Word of Mouth," *American Demographics* (July 1995): 38–44.

76. Richard J. Lutz, "Changing Brand Attitudes through Modification of Cognitive Structure," *Journal of Consumer Research* 1 (March 1975): 49–59; for some suggested remedies to bad publicity, see Mitch Griffin, Barry J. Babin, and Jill S. Attaway, "An Empirical Investigation of the Impact of Negative Public Publicity on Consumer Attitudes and Intentions," in eds. Rebecca H. Holman and Michael R. Solomon, *Advances in Consumer Research* 18 (Provo, UT: Association for Consumer

Research, 1991): 334–41; Alice M. Tybout, Bobby J. Calder, and Brian Sternthal, "Using Information Processing Theory to Design Marketing Strategies," *Journal of Marketing Research* 18 (1981): 73–9.

77. Robert E. Smith and Christine A. Vogt, "The Effects of Integrating Advertising and Negative Word-of-Mouth Communications on Message Processing and Response," *Journal of Consumer Psychology* 4 (1995)2: 133–51; Paula Fitzgerald Bone, "Word-of-Mouth Effects on Short-Term and Long-Term Product Judgments," *Journal of Business Research* 32 (1995): 213–23.

78. Charles W. King and John O. Summers, "Overlap of Opinion Leadership across Consumer Product Categories," *Journal of Marketing Research* 7 (February 1970): 43–50.

79. A. Tesser and S. Rosen, "The Reluctance to Transmit Bad News," in ed. L. Berkowitz, *Advances in Experimental Social Psychology* (New York: Academic Press, 1975): 8.

80. Lisa Bannon, "How a Rumor Spread about Subliminal Sex in Disney's 'Aladdin'," *Wall Street Journal* (October 24, 1995): B1 (2 pp.).

81. Sid Astbury, "Pork Rumors Vex Indonesia," *Advertising Age* (February 16, 1989): 36.

82. Craig S. Smith, "A Beer Tampering Scare in China Shows a Peril of Global Marketing," *Wall Street Journal* (November 3, 1995): B1.

83. Marcus Mabry, "Do Boycotts Work?" *Newsweek* (July 6, 1992)3: 35.

84. Everett M. Rogers, *Diffusion of Innovations*, 3rd ed. (New York: The Free Press, 1983).

85. Leonard-Barton, "Experts as Negative Opinion Leaders in the Diffusion of a Technological Innovation"; Rogers, *Diffusion of Innovations*.

86. Herbert Menzel, "Interpersonal and Unplanned Communications: Indispensable or Obsolete?" in *Biomedical Innovation* (Cambridge, MA: MIT Press, 1981): 155–63.

87. Meera P. Venkatraman, "Opinion Leaders, Adopters, and Communicative Adopters: A Role Analysis," *Psychology & Marketing* 6 (Spring 1989): 51–68.

88. Rogers, *Diffusion of Innovations*.

89. Robert Merton, *Social Theory and Social Structure*, (Glencoe, IL: The Free Press, 1957).

90. King and Summers, "Overlap of Opinion Leadership across Consumer Product Categories"; see also Ronald E. Goldsmith, Jeanne R. Heitmeyer, and Jon B. Freiden, "Social Values and Fashion Leadership," *Clothing and Textiles Research Journal* 10 (Fall 1991): 37–45; J. O. Summers, "Identity of Women's Clothing Fashion Opinion Leaders," *Journal of Marketing Research* 7 (1970): 178–85.

91. Steven A. Baumgarten, "The Innovative Communicator in the Diffusion Process," *Journal of Marketing Research* 12 (February 1975): 12–18.

92. Laura J. Yale and Mary C. Gilly, "Dyadic Perceptions in Personal Source Information Search," *Journal of Business Research* 32 (1995): 225–37.

93. Russell W. Belk, "Occurrence of Word-of-Mouth Buyer Behavior as a Function of Situation and Advertising Stimuli," in ed. Fred C. Allvine, *Combined Proceedings of the American Marketing Association,* series no. 33, (Chicago: American Marketing Association, 1971): 419–22.

94. Lawrence F. Feick, Linda L. Price, and Robin A. Higie, "People Who Use People: The Other Side of Opinion Leadership," in ed. Richard J. Lutz, *Advances in Consumer Research* 13 (Provo, UT: Association for Consumer Research, 1986): 301–5.

95. For discussion of the market maven construct, see Lawrence F. Feick and Linda L. Price, "The Market Maven," *Managing* (July 1985): 10; scale items adapted from Lawrence Feick and Linda Price, "The Market Maven: A Diffuser of Marketplace Information," *Journal of Marketing* 51 (January 1987): 83–7.

96. Michael R. Solomon, "The Missing Link: Surrogate Consumers in the Marketing Chain," *Journal of Marketing* 50 (October 1986): 208–18.

97. "CBS Extends its High-Tech Reach: CD-ROM Goes to 'Influencers'," *PROMO: The International Magazine for Promotion Marketing* (October 1994): 59.

98. Stern and Gould, "The Consumer as Financial Opinion Leader."

99. William R. Darden and Fred D. Reynolds, "Predicting Opinion Leadership for Men's Apparel Fashions," *Journal of Marketing Research* 1 (August 1972): 324–8. A modified version of the opinion leadership scale with improved reliability and validity can be found in Terry L. Childers, "Assessment of the Psychometric Properties of an Opinion Leadership Scale," *Journal of Marketing Research* 23 (May l986): 184–8.

100. "Connect," *Newsweek* (May 5, 1997): 11.

101. "Referrals Top Ads as Influence on Patients' Doctor Selections," *Marketing News* (January 30, 1987): 22.

102. Peter H. Reingen and Jerome B. Kernan, "Analysis of Referral Networks in Marketing: Methods and Illustration," *Journal of Marketing Research* 23 (November 1986): 370–8.

103. Peter H. Reingen, Brian L. Foster, Jacqueline Johnson Brown, and Stephen B. Seidman, "Brand Congruence in Interpersonal Relations: A Social Network Analysis," *Journal of Consumer Research* 11 (December 1984): 771–83; see also James C. Ward and Peter H. Reingen, "Sociocognitive Analysis of Group Decision Making among Consumers," *Journal of Consumer Research* 17 (December 1990): 245–62.

SHEILA IS ABOUT AS NERVOUS as she can be. Tonight is the first party she and her partner are throwing in their new apartment, and it's really coming down to the wire. Some of her friends and family who were skeptical about Sheila's plan to move out of her parents' house and to "shack up" with a man will have the chance to say "I told you so" if this debut of her new living arrangement self-destructs.

Life hasn't exactly been a bed of roses since she and John moved in together. It's a bit of a mystery—although his desk is tidy and organized at the publishing company where they both work, his personal habits are another story. John's really been making an effort to clean up his act, but

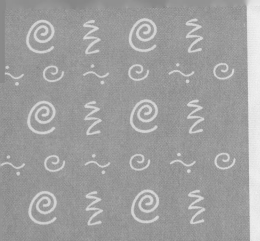

still Sheila's been forced to take on more than her share of cleaning duties—partly out of self-defense because they have to share a bathroom! And, she's learned the hard way not to trust John to do the grocery shopping—he goes to the store with a big list of staples and returns with beer and junk food. You would think that a man who is responsible for buying the firm's multimillion dollar computer network would have a bit more sense when it comes to sticking to a budget and picking out the right household supplies. What's even more frustrating is that although John can easily spend a week digging up information about the new big-screen TV they're buying (with her bonus!), she has to virtually drag him by the ear to look at dining room furniture. Then to add insult to injury, he's quick to criticize her choices—especially if they cost too much.

So, how likely is it that while she's at work John has been home cleaning up the apartment and making some *hors d'oeuvres* like he promised? This *soiree* could turn out to be a real proving ground for their relationship. Sheila sighs as she walks into an editors' meeting—seems like the old adage is true: "No man is a gentleman to his valet." She sure has learned a lot about relationships since setting up a new household . . . married life is going to be a lot bumpier than it's made out to be in some of those romance novels she likes so much.

Organizational and Household Decision Making

12

INTRODUCTION

Sheila's trials and tribulations with John illustrate that many consumer decisions are made jointly. The individual decision-making process described in detail in chapter 9 is, in many cases, overly simplistic, because more than one person may be involved in any stage of the problem-solving sequence, from initial problem recognition and information search to evaluation of alternatives and product choice. To complicate matters further, these decisions often involve two or more people who may not have the same level of investment in the outcome, the same tastes and preferences, or the same consumption priorities.

This chapter examines issues related to *collective decision making*, in which more than one person is involved in the purchasing process for products or services that may be used by multiple consumers. The first part of the chapter looks at organizational decision making, in which purchases are made on behalf of a larger group. We then move on to focus more specifically on one of the most important organizations to which most of us claim membership—the family unit. We'll consider how members of a family negotiate among themselves, and how important changes in modern family structure are affecting this process. The chapter concludes by focusing on how "new employees"—children—learn how to be consumers. First, though, let's focus on decision making that occurs when people leave their families at home and go to work.

ORGANIZATIONAL DECISION MAKING

Many employees of corporations or other organizations make purchase decisions on a daily basis. **Organizational buyers** are people, such as John, who purchase goods and services on behalf of companies for use in the process of manufacturing, distribution, or resale. These individuals buy from **business-to-business marketers,** who specialize in meeting the needs of organizations such as corporations, government agencies, hospitals, and retailers. In terms of sheer volume, business-to-business marketing is where the action is: Roughly $2 trillion worth of products and services change hands among organizations, which is actually *more* than is purchased by end consumers.

Organizational buyers have a lot of responsibility. They must decide on the vendors with whom they want to do business, and what specific items they require from these suppliers. The items considered can range in price and significance from paper clips to a multimillion dollar computer system. Obviously there is a lot at stake in understanding how these special and important decisions are made.

The organizational buyer's perception of the purchase situation is influenced by a number of factors. These include his/her *expectations* of the supplier (e.g., product quality, the competence and behavior of the firm's employees, and prior experiences in dealing with that supplier), the *organizational climate* of his/her own company (i.e., perceptions regarding how the company rewards performance and what it values), and the buyer's *assessment* of his/her own performance (e.g., whether he/she believes in taking risks).[1]

Like other consumers, organizational buyers engage in a learning process, in which members of the firm share information with one another, and develop an "organizational memory" consisting of shared beliefs and assumptions about the proper course of action.[2] Just as a buyer is influenced by "market beliefs" when he or she goes shopping with the family on the weekend (see chapter 9), the same person is also an information processor at the office. He or she (perhaps with fellow employees) attempts to solve problems by searching for information, evaluating alternatives, and making decisions.[3] There are, of course, some important differences between the two situations.

ORGANIZATIONAL DECISION MAKING VERSUS CONSUMER DECISION MAKING

Many factors have been identified to distinguish organizational and industrial purchase decisions from individual consumer decisions. Some of these differences are as follows:[4]

In the Information Age, organizational decision makers must work hard to stay on top of clients' complex needs. Many business-to-business marketers, such as UNISYS, prosper by helping organizations harness information in order to effectively navigate in today's turbulent marketplace. Reprinted with permission of Unisys Corporation.

- Purchase decisions made by companies frequently involve many people, including those who do the actual buying, those who directly or indirectly influence this decision, and the employees who will actually use the product or service.
- Organizational and industrial products are often bought according to precise, technical specifications, requiring rational criteria and knowledge about the product category.
- Impulse buying is rare (industrial buyers do not suddenly get an "urge to splurge" on lead pipe or silicon chips). Because buyers are professionals, their decisions are based on past experience and a careful weighing of alternatives.
- Decisions often are high risk, especially in the sense that a buyer's career may be riding on his/her demonstration of good judgment.
- Companies are usually part of a narrow customer base, and the dollar volume of purchases is often substantial, dwarfing most individual consumer grocery bills or even mortgage payments. One hundred to 250 organizational customers often account for more than half of a supplier's sales volume, which gives the buyers a fairly high degree of influence over the supplier.
- Business-to-business marketing often involves more of an emphasis on personal selling than on advertising or other forms of promotion, because dealing with organizational buyers typically requires more face-to-face contact than is necessary in the case of end consumers.

These important features must be considered when one tries to understand the purchasing decisions made by organizations. Still, there are actually more similarities between organizational buyers and ordinary consumers than many people seem to believe. Organizational purchase decisions do tend to have a higher economic or functional component compared to individual consumer choices, but the issue is one of degree more than kind. For example, although organizational buyers may appear to the outsider to be models of rationality, their decisions are sometimes guided by brand loyalty, by long-term relationships they have established with particular suppliers or salespeople, or even by aesthetic concerns.

These important differences must be considered when one tries to understand the purchasing decisions made by organizations. Still, there are actually more similarities between organizational buyers and ordinary consumers than many people seem to believe. Organizational purchase decisions do tend to have a higher economic or functional component relative to individual consumer choices, but the issue is one of degree more than an absolute difference. For example, while organizational buyers may appear to the outsider to be models of rationality, their decisions are sometimes guided by brand loyalty, by long-term relationships they have established with particular suppliers, or even by aesthetic concerns.

Intel's development of the hugely successful "Intel Inside" campaign illustrates how important issues like branding and product image can be in industrial contexts. Competitors had been using Intel's numerical sequencing to label their computer chips since the company had introduced its 286 model. These labels did not, however, guarantee that the rival versions possessed the same architecture as Intel's version, so this created confusion in the marketplace. After trying unsuccessfully to trademark the "386" name, the firm developed the "Intel Inside" logo and persuaded 240 other manufacturers to include the new logo in their packaging. In a three year period, Intel invested over $500 million in promotional programs and advertising to build recognition of the Intel brand name.[5]

THE ORGANIZATIONAL BUYER BEHAVIOR PROCESS

Like end consumers, organizational buyers are influenced by both internal and external stimuli. Internal stimuli include the buyer's unique psychological characteristics, such as willingness to take risky decisions, his or her job experience, and so on. External stimuli include the nature of the organization for which the buyer works, as well as the overall economic and technological environment in which the industry is operating. Another set of factors are cultural; vastly different norms for doing business can be found in different countries. For example, Americans tend to be less formal in their interactions than do many of their European or Asian counterparts.

TYPE OF PURCHASE

The nature of the item to be purchased is one of the biggest influences on the organizational buyer's decision-making process. As with consumer purchases, the more complex, novel, or risky the decision, the greater the amount of information search and effort will be devoted to evaluating alternatives. On the other hand, reliance on a fixed set of suppliers for routine purchases is one strategy that greatly reduces the information search and effort in evaluating competing alternatives that would otherwise be required.[6]

Typically, more complex organizational decisions also tend to be made by a group of people (members of a **buying center**) who play different roles in the decision. As we will see later on, this joint involvement is somewhat similar to family decision making, in which more family members are likely to be involved in more important purchases.

THE BUYCLASS FRAMEWORK

Organizational buying decisions can be divided into three types, which range from the most to the least complex. This classification scheme is called the **buyclass theory of purchasing,** and it uses three decision-making dimensions to describe the purchasing strategies of an organizational buyer:[7]

1. The level of information that must be gathered prior to making a decision
2. The seriousness with which all possible alternatives must be considered
3. The degree to which the buyer is familiar with the purchase

In practice, these three dimensions relate to how much cognitive effort will be expended in making a purchase decision. Three types of "buyclasses," strategies, based on these dimensions, encompass most organizational decision situations.[8] Each type of purchase corresponds to one of the three types of decisions discussed in chapter 9: habitual decision making, limited problem solving, and extensive problem solving. These strategies are summarized in Table 12–1.

TABLE 12–1 ■ **Types of Organizational Buying Decisions**

BUYING SITUATION	EXTENT OF EFFORT	RISK	BUYERS INVOLVED
Straight rebuy	Habitual decision making	Low	Automatic reorder
Modified rebuy	Limited problem solving	Low to moderate	One or a few
New task	Extensive problem solving	High	Many

Source: Adapted from Patrick J. Robinson, Charles W. Faris, and Yoram Wind, *Industrial Buying and Creative Marketing* (Boston: Allyn & Bacon, 1967).

A **straight rebuy** is like a habitual decision. This entails an automatic decision, as when an inventory level reaches a preestablished reorder point. Most organizations maintain an *approved vendor list,* and as long as experience with the vendor is satisfactory there is little or no ongoing information search or evaluation.

A **modified rebuy** situation involves limited decision making. It occurs when an organization wants to repurchase a product or service, but with some minor modifications. This decision might involve a limited search for information, most likely by speaking to a few vendors. The decision will probably be made by one or a few people.

A **new task** involves extensive problem solving. Because the decision has not been made before, there is often a serious risk that the product won't perform as it should or that it will be too costly. The organization designates a buying center with assorted specialists to evaluate the purchase, and they typically gather a lot of information before coming to a decision.

DECISION ROLES

A number of specific roles are played when a collective decision must be made, either by members of a household or by individuals in an organizational buying center.[9] Depending on the decision, some or all of the group members may be involved, and one person may play any number (or even all) of these roles. These roles include:

- *Initiator:* the person who brings up the idea or need.
- *Gatekeeper:* the person who conducts the information search and controls the flow of information available to the group. In organizational contexts the gatekeeper identifies possible vendors and products for the rest of the group to consider.
- *Influencer:* the person who tries to sway the outcome of the decision. Some people may be more motivated than others to get involved, and participants also differ in terms of the amount of power they have to convince others of their choice. In organizations, engineers are often influencers for product information, whereas purchasing agents play a similar role when the group evaluates the vendors that supply these items.
- *Buyer:* the person who actually makes the purchase. The buyer may or may not actually use the product. This person may pay for the item, actually procure it, or both.
- *User:* the person who winds up using the product or service.

TRENDS IN ORGANIZATIONAL BUYING BEHAVIOR

The emphasis in the mid-1990s on building strong, lasting bonds with customers has influenced marketing strategies related to organizations as well as to end consumers. Significant changes are occurring in the ways that business-to-business marketers interact with organizational buyers.[10] Customer relationships are now being viewed as a key strategic resource.[11] That helps to explain why loyalty programs that reward consistent customers are increasingly popular in business-to-business as well as in end consumer settings. For example, collection agents are some of Western Union's key customers. To cement relationships with them, the company initiated Quick Collect, a money transfer service through which a debtor can pay cash to a collection agent in any of Western Union's 180,000 agent locations. To accompany this service, Western Union introduced "The Winning Ticket"; a promotion whereby collectors are rewarded by getting to play a scratch-and-win

game. Each time a debtor uses the system, the agent gets a chance to win. AT&T's Global Contacts loyalty program rewards small business customers who spend more than $200 a month on long-distance service with discounts from AT&T and program partners such as Sheraton and UPS.[12]

As buyers and vendors begin to develop more cooperative relationships, this change in thinking has already resulted in these trends:

● *Consolidating vendors:* Just as many consumers are looking for ways to simplify their shopping by buying a broader range of items from fewer suppliers (e.g., at mammoth warehouse stores), organizational buyers are trying to simplify the ordering process by choosing a smaller number of suppliers and giving these valued partners more of their business.

● *Shifting attention to the user instead of the buyer:* Companies are putting more effort into studying the needs of the actual user of industrial supplies and equipment. These individuals often use different criteria when evaluating alternatives than do purchasing agents.

● *Changing from a technology orientation to a marketing orientation:* Industrial firms have been relatively slow to move to a marketing orientation that emphasizes the importance of designing products to meet customers' needs rather than trying to shape these needs to whatever products or technology is available. For example, it is not unusual for different divisions in a company to independently develop products targeted to the same buyers. Some of these firms are now devoting more effort to integrating their products to simplify the buyer's decision task.

THE FAMILY

It is not unusual to read in newspapers and magazines about the "death of the family unit." Although it is true that the proportion of people living in a traditional family structure, consisting of a married couple with children living at home, has declined (from 41 percent in 1970 to 27 percent in 1990), many other types of families are growing rapidly. Indeed, some experts have argued that as traditional family living arrangements have waned, people are placing even greater emphasis on siblings, close friends, and other relatives in providing companionship and social support.[13] Some people are even joining "intentional families"; groups of unrelated people who meet regularly for meals and who spend holidays together. By the mid-1990s, over 500 of these communities were operating in the United States.[14]

Many marketers have focused on the renewed interest in family life brought about by the more flexible definitions of what constitutes a family.[15] Although families were indeed "out of fashion" in the 1960s and 1970s, being seen by some as an infringement on personal freedom, 90 percent of the respondents in a survey confirmed that family life was one of the most important things to them.[16] In a radical departure from its old, "swinging singles" days, Club Med reports that half of the vacationers who stay at the resorts now bring their families along.[17]

DEFINING THE MODERN FAMILY

The **extended family** was once the most common family unit. It consisted of three generations living together and often included not only the grandparents, but aunts, uncles, and cousins. As evidenced by the Cleavers of *Leave It To Beaver* and other

TV families of the 1950s, the **nuclear family**—a mother and a father and one or more children (perhaps with a sheepdog thrown in for good measure)—became the model family unit over time. However, many changes have occurred since the days of Beaver Cleaver. Although people may continue to conjure up an image of the typical American family based on old shows like *Leave it to Beaver, Father Knows Best,* and *Ozzie and Harriet,* demographic data shows that this ideal image of the family is no longer a realistic or typical picture.

JUST WHAT IS A HOUSEHOLD?

In taking the national census every 10 years, the U.S. Census Bureau regards any occupied housing unit as a household, regardless of the relationships among people living there. A **family household,** as defined by the Census Bureau, contains at least two people who are related by blood or marriage. The Census Bureau and other survey firms compile a massive amount of data on family households, but certain categories are of particular interest to marketers. In addition, changes in consumers' family structures, such as the upheaval caused by divorce, often represent opportunities for marketers as normal purchasing patterns become unfrozen and people make new choices about products and brands.[18]

AGE OF THE FAMILY

Since 1980, the under-25, married couple age group declined by one-third, whereas the 65+ couples group increased by about 15 percent.[19] Overall, consumers between 35 and 44 were responsible for the largest increase in the number of households, growing by almost 40 percent since 1980.[20] Half of all family householders will fall into this age group by the year 2000. One reason for this shift is that people are waiting longer to get married: According to the U.S. Census Bureau, the average age of marriage is 24 for women and 26 for men. This trend has implications for businesses

 # MARKETING PITFALL

Although families are "in" now, some media critics worry that many advertisements teach undesirable lessons about what family life should be like during a time when many people are trying to juggle their desires to have successful careers *and* to be good parents. For example, a recent ad for Depo-Provera, a contraception injection, depicts a "Power Mom" in front of her word processor, engrossed in work with a phone in her ear. Sitting on her lap is her daughter, with a phone receiver glued to her ear as well. The caption reads, "Is it any wonder I sometimes forget my birth control pills?" What kind of message does this ad send? Other popular themes include the following:[21]

- *The solitary life:* Many contemporary ads depict a kid or a parent in solitary settings, perhaps reflecting the increasing proportion of unmarried people. In one ad for Whooz Blooz jeans, Miss Teen USA states, "Some of the best times are spent alone."

- *Materialism:* Some ads, it is argued, try to substitute products for family and friends. An ad for a backpack claims, "If only boyfriends came with the same guarantee we do." A record ad reads, "Prom Hints from Sony 550 Music: If the chaperones are like totally not cool, if your date has nothing interesting to say . . . , just turn your Walkman on high and listen to the best new music."

- *Narcissism:* In the past, many ads promised popularity if consumers shared the product depicted. Now, they are encouraged to grab it all for themselves. One example is the popular campaign for waffles in which actors protest, "Leggo my Eggo!"

Industry executives argue that critics overestimate advertising's influence; these messages merely reflect the dominant themes in society. What do you think?

ranging from catering to cutlery. For example, because couples tend to marry later and many have already acquired basic household items, the trend is toward giving nontraditional wedding gifts such as home electronics and PCs.[22] The retailer Marshall Field's even encourages couples to roam through the store and register their desired gifts with an electronic scanner. Then, its 1 800 I DO I DO line lets guests buy these goodies over the phone. Since the average wedding guest spends $70–$100 on the new couple, it's easy to understand why stores want to make it easier for these purchases to be made.

FAMILY SIZE

Worldwide, surveys show that almost all women want smaller families than they did even in the 1980s. In 1960, the average American household contained 3.3 people, but today that number has slipped to 2.6 people.[23] The number of U.S. households is projected to grow at an annual rate of about 1 percent over the next 10 to 15 years, slightly faster than the projected total population growth. This suggests an additional decline in average household size to about 2.5 members by the year 2010.[24]

Family size is dependent on such factors as educational level, the availability of birth control, and religion.[25] The **fertility rate** is determined by the number of births per year per 1,000 women of child-bearing age. The U.S. fertility rate increased dramatically in the late 1950s and early 1960s, when the so-called baby boomer began to reach child-rearing age. It declined in the 1970s and began to climb again in the 1980s as baby boomers began to have their own children in a new "baby boomlet."

Marketers keep a close eye on the population's birth rate to gauge how the pattern of births will affect demand for products in the future. Even when a married couple does have children at home, families are shrinking. The number of U.S. families with three or more children under age 18 living at home has fallen to 20 percent of all families. Still, large families are good marketing prospects. They use a lot of cleaning products, are more likely to have pets, and typically spend more than average on games, toys, and garments.[26]

The current fertility rate is about 66 babies born annually for every 1,000 women between the ages of 15 and 44, a rate almost half that during the baby boom period. Demographers predict that the fertility rate will continue to decline, even though the number of fertile women between 15 and 44 will grow.[27] Despite the fact that half of American women between the ages of 18 and 34 expect to have children, births will fall because most women are on the older edge of this age group.[28]

MARKETING OPPORTUNITY

Millions of American preschoolers are involved in child care programs. However, the number of families using day care has been projected to be only half of what the market can bear.[29]

Since the 1970s, large numbers of women have entered, or reentered, the workforce (even among married couples, about 50 percent of mothers work outside of the home).[30] Due to this trend and other changes in the family, fewer adult caregivers are available to supervise school-age children. These factors have created a generation of "latchkey children," who come home to a locked, empty home after school. It is estimated that almost 10 percent of American kids aged 5 to 13 qualify as latchkey kids.[31] Together with their parents, they represent a sizable segment for marketers of products ranging from convenience foods to security systems.

THE HEAD OF THE FAMILY

The number of family households headed by a single person grew by over 25 percent in the 1980s.[32] Well over 1 million couples divorce in a typical year. About one in every five families is headed by a woman.[33] Reflecting the prevalence of divorce situations, a Canadian entrepreneur has even come up with a way for disgruntled marriage partners to rewrite history: He is selling DivorceX, a digital imaging service that removes ex-spouses from family pictures![34]

The number of unmarried adults is steadily rising. By the mid-1990s, singles accounted for 39 percent of the U.S. adult population, and more than half the adult population will be single by the year 2005. Some marketers are beginning to address the fact that this group is underrepresented in advertising.[35] Taster's Choice coffee, for example, built a very popular campaign around a romance between two single neighbors, and Procter & Gamble introduced Folger's Singles—single-serve coffee bags for people who live alone and don't need a full pot.[36] On the other hand, many singles report that they avoid buying single-size food portions or eating alone in restaurants because both remind them of their unattached status—they prefer restaurant take-out food.[37]

Single men and women are quite different markets. More than half of single men are under the age of 35, whereas more than half of single women are over 65. Despite single males' greater incomes, single women dominate many markets because of their spending patterns. Single women are more likely to own a home, and they spend more on housing-related items and furniture. Single men, in contrast, spend more overall in restaurants and on cars. However, these spending patterns are also significantly affected by age: Middle-aged single women, for example, actually spend more than their male counterparts on cars.[38]

WHO'S LIVING AT HOME?

In many cases the nuclear family is being transformed to resemble the old-fashioned extended family. Many adults are being forced to care for parents as well as children. In fact, Americans on average spend 17 years caring for children, but 18 years

Folger's Coffee has addressed on important need by allowing single people to brew one cup of coffee at a time.

assisting aged parents.[39] Middle-aged people have been termed "the sandwich generation," because they must attend to those above and below them in age.

The problem of caring for aging parents became so acute in Singapore that the government established a Tribunal for the Maintenance of Parents in 1996. A new law now requires grown children to take care of their parents, a practice which traditionally is a priority in Asian cultures. Two hundred cases involving neglected parents were heard by the Tribunal in its first six months of operation.[40] As the population ages and life expectancies continue to climb in developed countries, the problem of allocating resources to the support of parents will only get worse.

In addition to dealing with live-in parents, many adults are surprised to find that their children are living with them longer or are moving back in, well after their "lease" has expired.[41] As a recent Argentinian jeans ad proclaimed, "If you are over 20 and still live with your parents, this is wrong. Isn't it high time you started looking for an apartment for them?"

These returnees have been termed **boomerang kids** by demographers. The number of children between 18 and 34 living at home is growing dramatically, and today more than one-fifth of 25-year-old Americans still live with their parents. The average non-Hispanic white child leaves home at age 19 and 1 month, three months later than in 1966–79 (but 17 months earlier than in the 1930s!). Young adults who do leave the nest to live by themselves are relatively unlikely to return, whereas those who move in with roommates are more likely to come back. And, young people who move in with a romantic partner are more likely than average to end up back home if the relationship fails![42] If this trend continues, it will affect a variety of markets as boomerang kids spend less on housing and staples and more on discretionary purchases like entertainment.

NONTRADITIONAL FAMILY STRUCTURES

As noted earlier, the U.S. Census Bureau regards any occupied housing unit as a household, regardless of the relationships among people living there. Thus, one person living alone, three roommates, or two lovers, all constitute households. The lat-

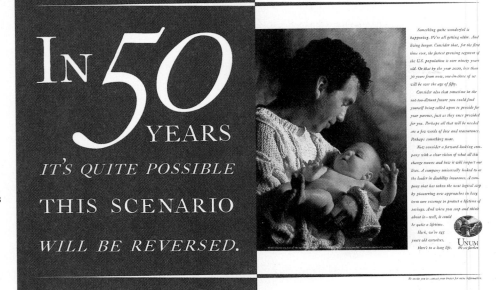

This insurance ad reminds us that children, especially those who belong to "the sandwich generation," are often eventually put in the position of caring for their parents.

ter arrangement is somewhat euphemistically referred to as *POSSLQ*, which stands for Persons of Opposite Sex Sharing Living Quarters.

Less-traditional households will rapidly increase in this decade if trends persist. For example, nonmarried households headed by men with children under the age of 18 increased by a third between 1981 and 1990.[44] Almost 10 million American children live in homes with a stepparent or with other kids who not full brothers or sisters, and 24 percent of all children live in one-parent families.[45]

Families worldwide are becoming smaller and less traditional. Although Scandinavian countries are pacesetters in developing nontraditional forms of family living, the United States has the highest incidence of divorce and single-parent households of any country.[46] To account for the rapid changes in the way families are structured, the U.S. Census included three new categories of family members for its most recent survey: (1) natural-born or adopted child, (2) foster child, and (3) unmarried partners. The first two classifications are intended to distinguish stepchildren from other children, and the latter category identifies cohabiting couples such as unmarried heterosexuals and homosexual or lesbian couples.[47]

Motorola recognizes the new, mobile lifestyles of many modern families. The company has positioned its paging products to meet the needs of on-the-go parents.

This ad for *Family Circle* magazine humorously emphasizes that some traditional family values persist among young people today.

MARKETING OPPORTUNITY

Many people are extremely attached to pets, to the point that companion animals are often treated as family members. Pets are seen by many as therapeutic, and are often assumed to share our emotions—perhaps that helps to explain why more than three-quarters of domestic cats and dogs receive presents on holidays and birthdays![48] Forty-two percent of American households own at least one pet. Americans spend $20 billion a year on their pets (more than they spend on movies and home videos combined).[49] This passion for pets is not confined to the United States: In France, there are twice as many dogs and cats as children.[50]

The inclusion of pets as family members creates many marketing opportunities, ranging from bejeweled leashes to professional dog-walkers. Listed below are samples of some recent attempts to cater to people's pet attachments.[51]

- Macy's department store opened a Petigree shop for dogs and cats. Says one employee, "You can put your dog in a pink satin party dress or a 1920s flapper dress with fringe." Other items include a wedding dress for dogs (for $100, and the veil is extra), a $48 black dinner jacket, and a $30 trench coat. Of course, the real hardcore pet lover can always purchase the $9,400 pet castle featured in the Neiman Marcus catalog.

- A veterinarian in Maryland offers holistic medicine for pets. He features natural foods, acupuncture, and chiropractic massages. The doctor also sells the Rodeo Drive Fragrance Collection, a set of spray colognes for dogs.

- Kennelwood Village, a day care center for dogs in St. Louis, features a swimming pool (with a lifeguard on duty), tetherball tournaments, and whirlpool therapy for arthritic canines.

- In Britain, pet insurance is a $150 million industry. In a pet-crazed country where some restaurants admit animals but not children, more than a million pets are covered. Similarly, about 85 percent of Swedish dogs carry health and life insurance.

- Some bakeries now feature fresh-baked dog treats, such as Snickerpoodles. The pet supply chain Petsmart is planning to add bakeshops to most of its 300 stores.

- A Columbus, Ohio company has even introduced hair care products for mules (with a scent of spring rain). The company advertises in *Mules and More,* a monthly magazine.

MARKETING OPPORTUNITY

Many women who work outside of the home are victims of what has been termed the "juggling lifestyle"; a frenzied, guilt-ridden compromise between conflicting cultural ideals of motherhood and professionalism.[52] Some marketers are picking up on one response to this conflict—they are beginning to target what they are calling "work-pausals," or women who are taking time off from careers to stay home with their children. As one advertising executive observed, "Women have stopped apologizing for staying home. Now it's a badge." Advertisers are seeking neutral territory when they design their messages, trying to avoid traditional home settings or office settings so their campaigns can be targeted both to women who work inside and outside of the home. For example, a Levi's Jeans for Women commercial depicts an animated figure trading in her dress for jeans and breaking out of the "prison" that held her.[53]

EFFECTS OF FAMILY STRUCTURE ON CONSUMPTION

A family's needs and expenditures are affected by factors such as the number of people (children and adults) in the family, their ages, and whether one, two, or more adults are employed outside of the home.

Two important factors that determine how a couple spends time and money are whether they have children and whether the woman works. Couples with children generally have higher expenses, such as for food and utility bills.[54] In addition, a recently married couple makes very different expenditures than do people with young children, who in turn are quite different from a couple with children in college, and so on. Families with working mothers also must often make allowances for such expenses as day care and a work wardrobe for the woman. In addition, about 11 percent of dual-income families pay for a home cleaning service.[55]

Choices of living environments provide a useful reflection of changing patterns and preferences in everyday life. The average new single family home in the U.S. grew from 1,645 sq. ft. in 1975 to 2,095 sq. ft. in 1995. Americans increasingly prefer homes with privacy, but common living space in the home is growing in popularity. People do more of their living in the kitchen, and formal areas are losing ground. These are being replaced by great rooms that accommodate multiple family activities in one location.[1] When people are asked to design their dream home, common responses include a state-of-the-art kitchen, fireplace, in-ground pool, and Jacuzzi. Women want walk-in closets; men name a game/billiard room, a workshop, or a high-tech entertainment center.[2]

1. Marcia Mogelonsky, "Reconfiguring the American Dream (House)" *American Demographics* (January 1997): 31–35.
2. Alison M. Torrillo, "Dens are Men's Territory," *American Demographics* (January 1995): 11 (2).

THE FAMILY LIFE CYCLE

Recognizing that family needs and expenditures change over time, the concept of the **family life cycle (FLC)** has been widely used by marketers. The FLC combines trends in income and family composition with the changes in demands placed upon this income. As we age, our preferences (and needs) for products and activities tend to change. In many cases, our income levels tend to rise (at least until retirement), so that we can afford more as well. In addition, many purchases that must be made at an early age do not have to be repeated very often. For example, we tend to accumulate durable goods, such as large appliances, and only replace them as necessary.

A life-cycle approach to the study of the family assumes that pivotal events alter role relationships and trigger new stages of life that alter our priorities. These events include couples like Sheila and John moving in together, the birth of a first child, the departure of the last child from the house, the death of a spouse, retirement of the principal wage earner, and divorce.[56] Movement through these life stages is indeed accompanied by significant changes in expenditures in leisure, food, durables, and services, even after the figures have been adjusted to reflect changes in income.[57]

This focus on longitudinal changes in priorities is particularly valuable in predicting demand for specific product categories over time. For example, the money spent by a couple with no children on dinners out and vacations will probably be diverted for quite different purchases after the birth of a child. A number of models have been proposed to describe family life cycle stages, but their usefulness has been limited because in many cases they have failed to take into account such important social trends as the changing role of women, the acceleration of alternative lifestyles, childless and delayed-child marriages, and single-parent households.

Four variables are necessary to adequately describe these changes: age, marital status, the presence or absence of children in the home, and how old they are if present. In addition, our definition of marital status (at least for analysis purposes) must be relaxed to include any couple living together who are in a long-term rela-

This furniture store claims to serve the needs of consumers across the family life cycle, from "full house" to "empty nest."

IKEA recently made history by daring to create what is believed to be the first mainstream TV ad to feature a gay relationship.

tionship. Thus, although roommates might not be considered "married," a man and woman who have established a household would be, as would two homosexual men who have a similar understanding.

When these changes are considered, this approach allows us to identify a set of categories that include many more types of family situations.[58] These categories, which are listed in Table 12–2, are derived by dividing consumers into groups in terms of age, whether there is more than one adult present, and whether there are children. For example, a distinction is made between the consumption needs of people in the Full Nest I category (in which the youngest child is less than six), the Full Nest II category (in which the youngest child is older than six), the Full Nest III category (in which the youngest child is older than six and the parents are middle-aged), and the Delayed Full Nest (in which the parents are middle-aged but the youngest child is younger than six).

LIFE-CYCLE EFFECTS ON BUYING

As might be expected, consumers classified into these categories show marked differences in consumption patterns. Young bachelors and newlyweds have the most "modern" sex-role attitudes; are the most likely to engage in exercise; to go out to

TABLE 12–2 ■ The Family Life Cycle: An Updated View

	AGE OF HEAD OF HOUSEHOLD		
	UNDER 35	35–64	OVER 64
One adult in household	Bachelor I	Bachelor II	Bachelor III
Two adults in household	Young couple	Childless couple	Older couple
Two adults plus children in household	Full nest I	Delayed full nest	
	Full nest II	Full nest III	

Source: Adapted from Mary C. Gilly and Ben M. Enis. "Recycling the Family Life Cycle: A Proposal for Redefinition," in ed. Andrew A. Mitchell, *Advances in Consumer Research* 9 (Ann Arbor, MI: Association for Consumer Research, 1982): 274, Fig. 1.

bars, concerts, movies, and restaurants; to go out dancing; and they consume more alcohol. Families with young children are more likely to consume health foods such as fruit, juice, and yogurt; and those made up of single parents and older children buy more junk foods. The dollar value of homes, cars, and other durables is lowest for bachelors and single parents, but increases as people go through the Full nest and Childless couple stages. Perhaps reflecting the bounty of wedding gifts, newlyweds are the most likely to own appliances such as toaster ovens and electric coffee grinders. Babysitter and day care usage is, of course, highest among single-parent and Full nest households, whereas home maintenance services (e.g., lawn-mowing) are most likely to be employed by older couples and bachelors.

The growth of these additional categories creates many opportunities for enterprising marketers. For example, divorced people undergo a process of transition to a new social role. This change is often accompanied by the disposition of possessions linked to the former role and the need to acquire a set of possessions that help express the person's new identity as he or she experiments with new lifestyles.[59] In another instance, couples in their fifties are flocking to urban areas to enjoy city amenities, such as access to theater and dining, that they gave up when they moved to the suburbs to raise families. This return to downtown is creating a boom in the urban housing market.[60]

THE INTIMATE CORPORATION: FAMILY DECISION MAKING

The decision process within a household unit in some ways resembles a business conference. Certain matters are put on the table for discussion, different members may have different priorities and agendas, and there may be power struggles to rival any tale of corporate intrigue. In just about every living situation, whether a conventional family, students sharing a sorority house or apartment, or some other nontraditional arrangement, group members seem to take on different roles just as purchasing agents, engineers, account executives, and others do within a company.

HOUSEHOLD DECISIONS

Two basic types of decisions are made by families.[61] In a **consensual purchase decision,** the group agrees on the desired purchase, differing only in terms of how it will be achieved. In these circumstances, the family will most likely engage in problem solving and consider alternatives until the means for satisfying the group's goal is found. For example, a household considering adding a dog to the family but concerned about who will take care of it might draw up a chart assigning individuals to specific duties.

Unfortunately, life is not always so easy. In an **accommodative purchase decision,** group members have different preferences or priorities and cannot agree on a purchase that will satisfy the minimum expectations of all involved. It is here that bargaining, coercion, compromise, and the wielding of power are all likely be used to achieve agreement on what to buy or who gets to use it. Family decisions often are characterized by an accommodative rather than a consensual decision. For example, about 27 million Americans use computers for work they bring home, and about a third of these people report they must fight other family members for time on the home PC or for access to a phone line. The computer industry is gearing up to sell us multiple computers to solve these problems, but for many of us less-expensive forms of diplomacy are required.[62]

Conflict occurs when there is not complete correspondence in family members' needs and preferences. Although money is the most common source of conflict between marriage partners, TV-viewing choices come in a close second![63] Some specific factors determining the degree of family decision conflict include the following:[64]

- *Interpersonal need* (a person's level of investment in the group): A child in a family situation may care more about what his or her family buys for the house than will a college student who is temporarily living in a dorm.

- *Product involvement and utility* (the degree to which the product in question will be used or will satisfy a need): A family member who is an avid coffee drinker will obviously be more interested in the purchase of a new coffee maker than a similar expenditure for some other item.

- *Responsibility* (for procurement, maintenance, payment, and so on): People are more likely to have disagreements about a decision if it entails long-term consequences and commitments. For example, a family decision about getting a dog may involve conflict regarding who will be responsible for walking it and feeding it.

- *Power* (or the degree to which one family member exerts influence over the others in making decisions): In traditional families, the husband tends to have more power than the wife, who in turn has more than the oldest child, and so on. In family decisions, conflict can arise when one person continually uses the power he or she has within the group to satisfy his or her priorities. For example, if a child believed that his life would end if he did not receive a Sega Game Gear for his birthday, he might be more willing to resort to extreme tactics to influence his parents, perhaps by throwing a tantrum or refusing to participate in family chores.

In general, decisions will involve conflict among family members to the extent that they are somehow important or novel and/or if individuals have strong opinions about good and bad alternatives. The degree to which these factors generate conflict determines the type of decision the family will make.[65]

SEX ROLES AND DECISION-MAKING RESPONSIBILITIES

Traditionally, some buying decisions, termed **autocratic decisions,** were usually made by one or the other spouse. Men, for instance, often had sole responsibility for selecting a car, whereas most decorating choices fell to women. Other decisions, such as vacation destinations, were made jointly; these are known as **syncratic decisions.** According to a study conducted by Roper Starch Worldwide, wives still tend to have the most say when buying groceries, children's toys, clothes, and medicines. Syncratic decisions are common for cars, vacations, homes, appliances, furniture, home electronics, interior design, and long-distance phone services. As the couple's education increases, more decisions are likely to be made together.[66]

IDENTIFYING THE DECISION MAKER
The nature of consumer decision making within a particular product category is an important issue for marketers, so that they know whom to target and whether they need to reach both spouses to influence a decision. For example, when market research in the 1950s indicated that women were playing a larger role in household purchasing decisions, lawn-mower manufacturers began to emphasize the rotary mower over other power mowers. Rotary mowers, which conceal the cutting blades and engine, were often depicted being used by young women and smiling grandmothers to downplay fears of injuries.[67]

Although many men still wear the pants in the family, it's women who buy them. Haggar is redirecting $8 million worth of advertising to target women who shop for and with men. The apparel manufacturer is placing menswear ads in about a dozen women's magazines after its research found that women exert tremendous influence over men's clothing choices. In a survey, nearly half of the females polled had purchased men's pants without the man present, and 41 percent said they accompanied the man when he bought pants. Female influence is strongest for decisions involving the matching of colors and the mixing/matching of separates.[1]

1. Robert Lohrer, "Haggar Targets Women with $8M Media Campaign," *Daily News Record* (January 8, 1997): 1 (3).

Researchers have paid special attention to which spouse plays the role of what has been called the **family financial officer (FFO)**, who keeps track of the family's bills and decides how any surplus funds will be spent. Among newlyweds, this role tends to be played jointly, and then over time one spouse or the other tends to take over these responsibilities.[68]

Spouses usually exert significant influence on decision making—even after one of them has died. An Irish study found that many widows claim to sense the continued presence of their dead husbands, and to conduct "conversations" with them about household matters![69]

In traditional families (and especially those with low educational levels), women are primarily responsible for family financial management—the man makes it, and the woman spends it.[70] Each spouse "specializes" in certain activities.[71] The pattern is different among families in which spouses adhere to more modern sex-role norms. These couples believe that there should be more shared participation in family maintenance activities. In these cases, husbands assume more responsibility for laundering, housecleaning, grocery shopping, and so on, in addition to such traditionally "male" tasks as home maintenance and garbage removal.[72] Of course, cultural background is an important determinant of the dominance of the husband or wife. For example, husbands tend to be more dominant in decision making among couples with a strong Hispanic ethnic identification.[73] Vietnamese Americans also are more likely to adhere to the traditional model: The man makes the decision for any large purchase, whereas the woman is given a budget to manage the home.[74] In a study comparing marital decision making in the United States versus China, American women reported more "wife decides" situations than did the Chinese.[75]

Four factors appear to determine the degree to which decisions will be made jointly or by one or the other spouse.[76]

1. *Sex-role stereotypes:* Couples who believe in traditional sex-role stereotypes tend to make individual decisions for sex-typed products (i.e., those considered to be "masculine" or "feminine").

2. *Spousal resources:* The spouse who contributes more resources to the family has the greater influence.

3. *Experience:* Individual decisions are made more frequently when the couple has gained experience as a decision-making unit.

4. *Socioeconomic status:* Joint decisions are made more by middle-class families than in either higher- or lower-class families.

With many women now working outside of the home, men are participating more in housekeeping activities. In one-fifth of American homes, men do most of the shopping, and nearly one-fifth of men do at least seven loads of laundry a week.[77] Still, as Sheila discovered to her chagrin, women continue to do the lion's share of household chores. Ironically, this even appears to be true when the woman's outside income actually exceeds that of her husband's![78] As shown in Table 12–3, a similar situation exists in other western countries like the U.K. Overall, the degree to which a couple adheres to traditional sex-role norms determines how much their allocation of responsibilities, including consumer decision making will fall along traditional lines.

Despite recent changes in decision-making responsibilities, women are still primarily responsible for the continuation of the family's **kin-network system:** They perform the rituals intended to maintain ties among family members, both immediate and extended. This function includes activities such as coordinating visits among relatives, calling and writing family members, sending greeting cards, making social engagements, and so on.[79] This organizing role means that women often

MULTICULTURAL DIMENSIONS

Traditional sex roles are quite prevalent in Japan, where women have less power than in any other industrialized country. The birth control pill is banned, and a wife is legally prohibited from using a different surname than her husband. Fewer than one in ten Japanese managers are women, which is one of the lowest ratios in the world (women are twice as likely to be managers in Mexico or Zimbabwe).

However, something of a quiet revolution is happening in Japanese homes as some obedient spouses have had enough. Recently women have started to rebel against the inevitability of getting married young and staying home with babies. The number of unmarried people older than 30 has doubled in the last 20 years.

For those that do marry, things are changing as well. Traditionally, a wife would wait up all night for a drunken husband to come home so she could kneel down with her forehead touching the floor and proclaim, "Welcome home, honorable sir." Now she is more likely to lock him out of the house until he sobers up. Most Japanese men are given a budget by their wives for lunch, cigarettes, and girlie magazines. One housewife noted, "Your home is managed very well if you make your men feel that they're in control when they are in front of others, while in reality you're in control."[80]

Men's attitudes toward family life also are changing. Japanese fathers spend so much time working that more than a quarter of children surveyed said their Dads never take them for a walk or play games with them. Due to long work hours, a typical Japanese father has only 36 minutes a day available to spend with his kids. About 60 percent of Japanese men typically do not eat breakfast at home, and about 30 percent regularly miss dinner. Now, balancing work and family is becoming a hot topic, especially as recession weakens the guarantee of lifetime employment and men are reexamining their own priorities.[81] This change was reflected in some recent McDonald's advertising, which showed doting fathers helping kids with their bikes. This would not be noteworthy in the United States, but it got a lot of attention in a country where fathers are typically shown as corporate warriors or even as superheroes (for example, a popular advertising character called PepsiMan sports a cape and bulging muscles!).

TABLE 12–3 ■ Division of Household Tasks in the U.K.

DIVISIONS OF HOUSEHOLD TASKS, 1994	ALWAYS THE WOMAN	USUALLY THE WOMAN	ABOUT EQUAL, OR BOTH TOGETHER	USUALLY THE MAN	ALWAYS THE MAN	ALL COUPLES
Washing and Ironing	47	32	18	1	1	100
Deciding what to have for dinner	27	32	35	3	1	100
Looking after sick family members	22	26	45	—	—	100
Shopping for groceries	20	21	52	4	1	100
Small repairs around the house	2	3	18	49	25	100

Source: Nicholas Timmins, "New Man Fails to Survive into the Nineties," *The Independent,* January 25, 1996.

make important decisions about the family's leisure activities, and they are more likely to decide with whom the family will socialize.

HEURISTICS IN JOINT DECISION MAKING

The **synoptic ideal** calls for the husband and wife to take a common view and act as joint decision makers. According to this ideal, they would very thoughtfully weigh alternatives, assign one another well-defined roles, and calmly make mutually beneficial consumer decisions. The couple would act rationally, analytically, and use as much information as possible to maximize joint utility. In reality, however, spousal decision making is often characterized by the use of influence or methods that are likely to reduce conflict. A couple "reaches" rather than "makes" a decision. This process has been described as "muddling through."[82]

One common technique for simplifying the decision-making process is the use of *heuristics* (see chapter 9). Some decision-making patterns frequently observed when a couple makes decisions in buying a new house illustrate the use of heuristics:

MULTICULTURAL DIMENSIONS

The Coca-Cola Co. developed a campaign to appeal to Latin American women based on an $800,000 research project the company conducted in Brazil. A motherly female kangaroo was found most likely to appeal to women shopping for their families—and who happen to account for 80 percent of Coke's $3.5 billion Brazilian sales. The ads are themed "Mom knows everything," after women in focus groups said they felt the media neglected them even though they were responsible for purchasing all the products in their households.[83]

- The couple's areas of common preference are based on salient, objective dimensions rather than more subtle, hard-to-define cues. For example, a couple may easily agree on the number of bedrooms they need in the new home, but will have more difficulty achieving a common view of how the home should look.

- The couple agrees on a system of *task specialization,* in which each is responsible for certain duties or decision areas and does not interfere on the other's "turf." For many couples, these assignments are likely to be influenced by their perceived sex roles. For example, the wife may scout out houses in advance that meet their requirements, and the husband determines whether the couple can obtain a mortgage.

- Concessions are based on the intensity of each spouse's preferences. One spouse will yield to the influence of the other in many cases simply because his or her level of preference for a certain attribute is not particularly intense, whereas in other situations he or she will be willing to exert effort to obtain a favorable decision.[84] In cases where intense preferences for different attributes exist, rather than attempt to influence each other, spouses will "trade off" a less-intense preference for a more strongly felt one. For example, a husband who is somewhat indifferent about kitchen design may give in to his wife, but expect that in turn he will be allowed to design his own garage workshop. It is interesting to note that many men apparently want to be very involved in making some decorating decisions and setting budgets—more than women want them to be. According to one survey, 70 percent of male respondents felt the husband should be involved in decorating the den, whereas only 51 percent of wives wanted them to be.[85]

CHILDREN AS DECISION MAKERS: CONSUMERS-IN-TRAINING

Anyone who has had the "delightful" experience of grocery shopping with one or more children in tow knows that kids often have a say in what their parents buy, especially with products such as cereal.[86] It has been estimated that children between the ages of 4 and 12 spend or influence their parents to spend about $140 billion a year.[87] Some Web sites that have been put up to cater to this attractive market include:

- www.nabiscokids.com—features an Oreo shooting game and a Chips Ahoy screen saver.
- www.oscar-mayer.com—Kids learn to surf the Web by logging onto a World Wide Weener tutorial.
- www.frito-lay.com—Kids can download wallpaper of Chester Cheetah to adorn their computer work space.[88]

In addition, children are increasingly being recognized as a potential market for traditionally adult products. General Motors recently placed a two-page spread for its Chevy Venture minivan in the 1997 issue of *Sports Illustrated for Kids,* and displayed the vans in malls with the movie *Hercules* running on a VCR inside to tempt kids to take a look. Kodak is working hard to encourage kids to become photographers. Currently, only 20 percent of children aged 5 to 12 own cameras, and they shoot an average of just one roll of film a year. In a new effort called "Big Shots," ads portray photography as a cool pursuit and as a form of rebellion. Cameras are packaged with an envelope to mail the film directly back so parents can't see the photos.[89] Table 12–4 documents kids' influence in ten different product categories.

TABLE 12–4 ■ Kids' Influence on Household Purchases

TOP 10 SELECTED PRODUCTS	INDUSTRY SALES ($ BILLIONS)	INFLUENCE FACTOR (%)	SALES INFLUENCE ($ BILLIONS)
Fruit snacks	0.30	80	0.24
Frozen novelties	1.40	75	1.05
Kids' beauty aids	1.20	70	0.84
Kids' fragrances	0.30	70	0.21
Toys	13.40	70	9.38
Canned pasta	0.57	60	0.34
Kids' clothing	18.40	60	11.04
Video games	3.50	60	2.10
Hot cereals	0.74	50	0.37
Kids' shoes	2.00	50	1.00

Source: "Charting the Children's Market," *Adweek* (February 10, 1992): 42. Reprinted with permission of James J. McNeal, Texas A&M University, College Station, Texas.

Parental yielding occurs when a parental decision maker is influenced by a child's request and "surrenders." The likelihood of this occurring is partly dependent on the dynamics within a particular family—as we all know, parental styles range from permissive to strict, and they also vary in terms of the amount of responsibility children are given to make decisions.[90] One study documented the strategies kids use to request purchases. Although most children simply asked for things, some other common tactics included saying they had seen it on TV, saying that a sibling or friend has it, or bargaining by offering to do chores. Other actions were less innocuous; they included directly placing the object in the cart and continuous pleading—often a "persuasive" behavior![91]

MULTICULTURAL DIMENSIONS

In a controversial effort to control the size of its population, The People's Republic of China offers many incentives for parents to have only one child. One by-product of this campaign is that some claim the country is producing a pampered generation of spoiled only children, who are called "little emperors." Parents are trying to give these kids a rich childhood that they themselves didn't experience during the dark days of the Cultural Revolution. They are spending a very large portion of family income on toys, books, and computers. Baby food, which didn't exist in China decade ago, is now a major budget item.[92]

Of course, the Chinese are not alone in viewing the child as a status symbol. In the West, as one marketing executive put it, "Babies are the BMWs of the Nineties." Infant wear and other items for toddlers has become a $23 billion business. Dual-career couples are waiting longer to have kids and thus are able to spend more on them—the number of women 30 or older when the first child is born has quadrupled since 1970, and the number of first children born to women over 40 has more than doubled. As a result, children's designer clothing is booming—Versace sells a $250 black motorcycle jacket for that junior James Dean, and Nicole Miller offers a $150 cocktail dress for that petite *femme fatale*.[93] Infants are not being left out: Ralph Lauren sells a cashmere receiving blanket for $350, L.L. Bean has added toddler snow suits to its catalogs, and Nike is marketing a line of toddler athletic wear.[94]

Children often play important roles in family consumer decision making, and they are gaining responsibility as consumers in their own right. They continue to support the toy and candy industries, of course, but now they also buy and/or influence the purchase of many other products as well. For better or for worse, the new generation is, as the bumper sticker proclaims, "Born to Shop." Shopping now ranks among the top seven interests and activities of America's children.[95] Over 80 percent of young respondents in one survey said their primary wish was to have more money to buy things.[96] In this section, we'll consider how kids learn to make these choices.

CONSUMER SOCIALIZATION

Children do not spring from the womb with consumer skills already in memory. **Consumer socialization** has been defined as the process "by which young people acquire skills, knowledge, and attitudes relevant to their functioning in the marketplace."[97] Where does this knowledge come from? Friends and teachers certainly participate in this process. For instance, children talk to one another about consumer products, and this tendency increases with age.[98] Especially for young children, though, the two primary socialization sources are the family and the media.

INFLUENCE OF PARENTS

Parents' influences in consumer socialization are both direct and indirect. They deliberately try to instill their own values about consumption in their children ("You're going to learn the value of a dollar"). Parents also determine the degree to which their children will be exposed to other information sources, such as television, salespeople, and peers.[99] And, grownups serve as significant models for observational learning (see chapter 3). Children learn about consumption by watching their parents' behavior and imitating it. This modeling is facilitated by marketers who package adult products in child versions.

The process of consumer socialization begins with infants, who accompany their parents to stores where they are initially exposed to marketing stimuli. Within the first two years, children begin to make requests for desired objects. As kids learn to walk, they also begin to make their own selections when they are in stores. By around the age of five, most kids are making purchases with the help of parents and grandparents, and by eight most are making independent purchases and have become full-fledged consumers.[100] The sequence of steps involved in turning kids into consumers is summarized in Figure 12–1.

Three dimensions combine to produce different "segments" of parental styles. Parents characterized by certain styles have been found to socialize their children differently.[101] For example, "authoritarian parents," who are hostile, restrictive, and emotionally uninvolved, do not have warm relationships with their children, are active in filtering the types of media to which their children are exposed, and tend to have negative views about advertising. "Neglecting parents" also do not have warm relationships, but they are more detached from their children and do not exercise much control over what their children do. In contrast, "indulgent parents" communicate more with their children about consumption-related matters and are less restrictive. They believe that children should be allowed to learn about the marketplace without much interference.

INFLUENCE OF TELEVISION: "THE ELECTRIC BABYSITTER"

It's no secret that kids watch a lot of television. As a result, they are constantly bombarded with messages about consumption, both contained in commercials and in the shows themselves. The media teaches people about a culture's values and myths. The

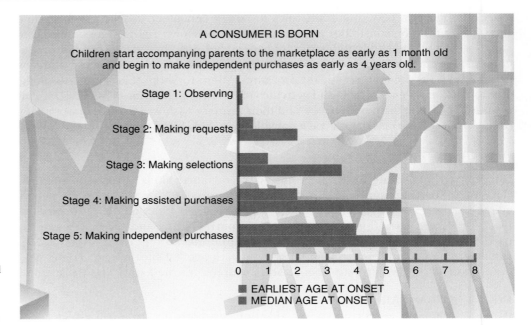

FIGURE 12–1 ■ **Five Stages of Consumer Development by Earliest Age at Onset and Median Age at Onset**
Source: Adapted from McNeal and Yeh, *American Demographics* (June 1993): 36. Reprinted by permission of American Demographics, Inc.

more a child is exposed to television, whether the show is *N.Y.P.D. Blue* or *Rugrats*, the more he or she will accept the images depicted there as real.[102] A TV show called *Teletubbies* that recently debuted in the United Kingdom goes a step further—it targets viewers from three months to two years old. The show has become a national obsession, attracting more than 2 million viewers every weekday morning.[103]

In addition to the large volume of programming targeted directly to children, kids are also exposed to idealized images of what it is like to be an adult. Because children over the age of six do about a quarter of their television viewing during prime time, they are affected by programs and commercials targeted to adults. For example, young girls exposed to adult lipstick commercials learn to associate lipstick with beauty.[104]

SEX-ROLE SOCIALIZATION

Children pick up on the concept of gender identity (see chapter 5) at an earlier age than was previously believed—perhaps as young as age one or two. By the age of three, most children categorize driving a truck as masculine and cooking and cleaning as feminine.[105] Even cartoon characters who are portrayed as helpless are more likely to wear frilly or ruffled dresses.[106] Toy companies perpetuate these stereotypes by promoting gender-linked toys with commercials that reinforce sex-role expectations through their casting, emotional tone, and copy.[107]

One function of child's play is to rehearse for adulthood. Children "act out" different roles they might assume later in life and learn about the expectations others have of them. The toy industry provides the props children use to perform these roles.[108] Depending on which side of the debate you're on, these toys either reflect or teach children about what society expects of males versus females. Preschool boys and girls do not exhibit many differences in toy preferences, but after the age of five they part company: Girls tend to stick with dolls, while boys gravitate toward "action figures" and high-tech diversions. Industry critics charge that this is because the toy industry is dominated by males, but toy company executives counter that they are simply responding to kids' natural preferences.[109]

Often "traditional" sex roles are stressed in children's products; the same item may be designed and positioned differently for boys and girls. Huffy, for example, manufactures bicycles for both boys and girls. The boys' versions have names like "Sigma" and "Vortex," and they are described as having ". . . maxed-out features that'll pump your pulse." The girls' version is more sedate. It is called "Sweet Style," and it comes in pink or purple. As a company executive described it in contrast to the boys' bikes, the girls' model ". . . is a fashion bike. It's not built for racing or jumping—just the look."[110]

COGNITIVE DEVELOPMENT

The ability of children to make mature, "adult" consumer decisions obviously increases with age (not that grown-ups always make mature decisions). Kids can be segmented by age in terms of their **stage of cognitive development,** or ability to comprehend concepts of increasing complexity. Some recent evidence indicates that young children are able to learn consumption-related information surprisingly well, depending on the format in which the information is presented (e.g., learning is enhanced if a videotaped vignette is presented to small children repeatedly).[111]

The foremost proponent of the idea that children pass through distinct stages of cognitive development was the Swiss psychologist Jean Piaget, who believed that each stage is characterized by a certain cognitive structure the child uses to handle information.[112] In one classic demonstration of cognitive development, Piaget poured the contents of a short, squat glass of lemonade into a taller, thinner glass. Five-year-olds, who still believed that the shape of the glass determined its contents, thought this glass held more liquid than the first glass. They are in what Piaget termed a *preoperational stage of development.* In contrast, six-year-olds tended to be unsure, but seven-year-olds knew the amount of lemonade had not changed.

Some companies have tried to level the playing field by doing research to understand differences in how boys and girls play. Lego Systems sells about 90% of its construction kits to boys, but the company would love to increase its sales by selling more sets to girls as well. When Lego introduced a special Lego set with parts that would allow girls to make jewelry, the product bombed. Still, there is hope: When Lego executives watched boys and girls play with Lego bricks in focus groups, they noticed that boys tend to build cars while girls are likely to build living areas. This observation led to the introduction in 1992 of Paradisa, a Lego set in colors like lavender and pink that is designed for building "socially oriented structures," such as homes, swimming pools, and stables. Sales to girls have picked up, although the company's sales to boys are still nine times larger than its sales to girls.[1]

1. Joseph Pereira, "Girls Favorite Playthings: Dolls, Dolls, and Dolls," *The Wall Street Journal* (September 23, 1994): B1 (2).

Many developmental specialists no longer believe that children necessarily pass through these fixed stages at the same time. An alternative approach regards children as differing in information-processing capability, or ability to store and retrieve information from memory (see chapter 3). The following three segments have been identified by this approach:[113]

1. *Limited:* Below the age of six, children do not employ storage and retrieval strategies.
2. *Cued:* Children between the ages of 6 and 12 employ these strategies, but only when prompted.
3. *Strategic:* Children 12 and older spontaneously employ storage and retrieval strategies.

This sequence of development underscores the notion that children do not think in the same way as adults do, and they cannot be expected to use information the same way. It also reminds us that they do not necessarily form the same conclusions as adults do when presented with product information. For example, kids are not as likely to realize that something they see on TV is not "real," and as a result they are more vulnerable to persuasive messages.

MARKETING RESEARCH AND CHILDREN

Despite children's buying power, relatively little real data on their preferences or influences on spending patterns is available. Compared to adults, kids are difficult subjects for market researchers. They tend to be undependable reporters of their own behavior, they have poor recall, and they often do not understand abstract questions.[114] This problem is compounded in Europe, where some countries restrict marketers' ability to interview children.

Still, market research can pay off, and many companies, as well as a number of specialized firms, have been successful researching some aspects of this segment.[115] After interviewing elementary school kids, Campbell's Soup discovered that kids like soup, but are afraid to admit it, because they associate it with "nerds." The company decided to reintroduce the Campbell Kids in its advertising after a prolonged absence, but they are now slimmed down and more athletic to reflect an updated, "un-nerdy" image.[116]

PRODUCT TESTING

A particularly helpful type of research with children is product testing. Young subjects can provide a valuable perspective on what products will succeed with other kids. One candy company has a Candy Tasters Club, composed of 1,200 kids aged 6 to 16, that evaluates its product ideas. For example, the group nixed the idea of a Batman lollipop, claiming that the superhero was too macho to be a sucker.[117] The Fisher-Price Company maintains a nursery known as the Playlab. Children are chosen from a waiting list of 4,000 to play with new toys, while staff members watch from behind a one-way mirror.[118] H.J. Heinz recently held a nationwide contest for kids to create new ketchup bottle labels and got about 60,000 entries, and Binney & Smith is asking kids to rename its Crayola crayons after personal heroes.[119]

Other techniques include ethnographic research, in which researchers hang out with kids or videotape them as they shop. The most successful interviewers are those who try not to be "adultcentric" (i.e., as an adult authority figure who assumes that children's beliefs are just unreal fantasies); they act as a friend to the children and are willing to use a variety of projective techniques and props to get children to express themselves in their own terms.[120]

MESSAGE COMPREHENSION

Because children differ in their abilities to process product-related information, many serious ethical issues are raised when advertisers try to appeal directly to them.[121] Kids tend to accept what they see on TV as real, and they do not necessarily understand the persuasive intent of commercials—that they are paid advertisements. Preschool children may not have the ability to make any distinctions between programming and commercials.

Kids' cognitive defenses are not yet sufficiently developed to filter out commercial appeals, so in a sense altering their brand preferences may be likened to "shooting fish in a barrel," as one critic put it.[122] Although some ads include a disclaimer, which is a disclosure intended to clarify a potentially misleading or deceptive statement, the evidence suggests that young children do not adequately understand these either.[123] The Children's Advertising Review Unit (CARU) recently unveiled guidelines for child-oriented Web sites after receiving complaints that kids had trouble distinguishing ads from content. These include clear identification of the sponsor and the right to cancel purchases made on-line.[124]

Assessing the comprehension of young children is especially hard, because preschoolers are not very good at verbal responses. One way around this problem is to show children pictures of kids in different scenarios, and ask them to point to which sketch corresponds to what a commercial is trying to get them to do (see Figure 12–2). The problem with children's processing of commercials has been exacerbated by TV programming that essentially showcases toys (e.g., Jem, G.I. Joe, Transformers). This format has been the target of a lot of criticism because it blurs the line between programming and commercials (much like "infomercials" for adults, as described in chapter 8).[125] Parents' groups object to such shows because, as one mother put it, the "... whole show is one big commercial."[126]

FIGURE 12–2 ■ Sketches used to Measure Children's Perception of the Intent of Commercials: In the example shown here, a child who points to sketch 1 after seeing a cereal commercial as opposed to, say, sketches 2 or 3 would be said to understand the underlying intent of the commercial. Sketch 1 was in fact selected by only 7.5 percent of four-year-olds but 20 percent of five-year-olds. *Source:* M. Carole Macklin, "Preschoolers' Understanding of the Informational Function of Television Advertising," *Journal of Consumer Research* 14 (September 1987): 234. Reprinted by permission of The University of Chicago Press.

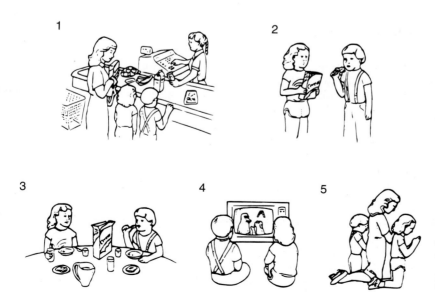

CHAPTER SUMMARY

- Many purchasing decisions are made by more than one person. *Collective decision making* occurs whenever two or more people are involved in evaluating, selecting, or using a product or service.

- *Organizational buyers* are people who make purchasing decisions on behalf of a company or other group. Although these buyers are influenced by many of the same factors that affect how they make decisions in their personal lives, organizational buying decisions tend to be more rationally based. They are also likely to involve more financial risk, and as they become more complex it is probable that a greater number of people will be involved in making the decision.

- The amount of cognitive effort that goes into organizational decisions is influenced by internal factors, such as the individuals' psychological characteristics, and by external factors, such as the company's willingness to tolerate risk. One of the most important determinants is the type of purchase being considered: The extent of problem solving required depends on whether the product or service to be procured is simply to be reordered (a *straight rebuy*), ordered with minor modifications (*modified rebuy*), or if it has never been purchased before or is complex and risky (*new task*).

- In organizations and in families, several different roles must be played during the decision-making process. These roles include the *gatekeeper, influencers, buyers,* and *users.*

- *Demographics* are statistics that measure a population's characteristics. Some of the most important of these relate to family structure (e.g., the birth rate, the marriage rate, and the divorce rate).

- A *household* is an occupied housing unit. The number and type of U.S. households is changing in many ways, including delays in getting married and having children, and in the composition of family households, which are increasingly headed by a single parent. New perspectives on the *family life cycle,* which focuses on how people's needs change as they move through different stages in their lives, are forcing marketers to more seriously consider consumer segments such as homosexuals, divorced persons, and childless couples when they develop targeting strategies.

- Families must be understood in terms of their decision-making dynamics. Spouses in particular have different priorities and exert varying amounts of influence in terms of effort and power. Children are also increasingly influential during a widening range of purchase decisions.

- Children undergo a process of *socialization,* whereby they learn how to be consumers. Some of this knowledge is instilled by parents and friends, but a lot of it comes from exposure to mass media and advertising. Because children are in some cases so easily persuaded, the ethical aspects of marketing to them are hotly debated among consumers, academics, and marketing practitioners.

KEY TERMS

Accommodative purchase decision p. 382
Autocratic decisions p. 383
Boomerang kids p. 376
Business-to-business marketers p. 367

Buyclass theory of purchasing p. 370
Buying center p. 370
Consensual purchase decision p. 382
Consumer socialization p. 389

Extended family p. 372
Family financial officer (FFO) p. 384
Family household p. 373
Family life-cycle (FLC) p. 380

1. Do you think market research should be performed on children? Give the reasons for your answer.

2. What do you think of the practice of companies and survey firms collecting public data (e.g., from marriage licenses, birth records, or even death announcements) to compile targeted mailing lists? State your opinion from both a consumer's and marketer's perspective.

3. Marketers have been criticized for donating products and services to educational institutions in exchange for free promotion. Is this a fair exchange, in your opinion, or should corporations be prohibited from attempting to influence youngsters in school?

4. For each of the following five product categories—groceries, automobiles, vacations, furniture, and appliances—describe the ways in which you believe a married couple's choices would be affected if they had children.

5. In identifying and targeting newly divorced couples, do you think marketers are exploiting these couples' situations? Are there instances in which you think marketers may actually be helpful to them? Support your answers with examples.

6. Arrange to interview two married couples, one younger and one older. Prepare a response form listing five product categories—groceries, furniture, appliances, vacations, and automobiles—and ask each spouse to indicate, without consulting the other, whether purchases in each category are made by joint or unilateral decisions and to indicate whether the unilateral decisions are made by the husband or the wife. Compare each couples' responses for agreement between husbands and wives relative to who makes the decisions and compare both couples' overall responses for differences relative to the number of joint versus unilateral decisions. Report your findings and conclusions.

7. Collect ads for three different product categories in which the family is targeted. Find another set of ads for different brands of the same items in which the family is not featured. Prepare a report comparing the probable effectiveness of the two approaches. Which specific categories would most likely benefit from a family emphasis?

8. Observe the interactions between parents and children in the cereal section of a local grocery store. Prepare a report on the number of children who expressed preferences, how they expressed their preferences, and how parents responded, including the number who purchased the child's choice.

9. Watch three hours of children's programming on commercial television stations and evaluate the marketing techniques used in the commercials in terms of the ethical issues raised in the final section of this chapter. Report your findings and conclusions.

10. Select a product category, and using the life-cycle stages given in the chapter, list the variables that will affect a purchase decision for the product by consumers in each stage of the cycle.

11. Consider three important changes in modern family structure. For each, find an example of a marketer who has attempted to be conscious of this change as reflected in product communications, retailing innovations, or other aspects of the marketing mix. If possible, also try to find examples of marketers who have failed to keep up with these developments.

12. Industrial purchase decisions are totally rational. Aesthetic or subjective factors don't— and shouldn't—play a role in this process. Do you agree?

NOTES

1. See J. Joseph Cronin Jr. and Michael H. Morris, "Satisfying Customer Expectations; the Effect on Conflict and Repurchase Intentions in Industrial Marketing Channels," *Journal of the Academy of Marketing Science* 17 (Winter 1989): 41–9; Thomas W. Leigh, and Patrick F. McGraw, "Mapping the Procedural Knowledge of Industrial Sales Personnel: A Script-Theoretic Investigation," *Journal of Marketing* 53 (January 1989): 16–34; William J. Qualls and Christopher P. Puto, "Organizational Climate and Decision Framing: An Integrated Approach to Analyzing Industrial Buying," *Journal of Marketing Research* 26 (May 1989): 179–92.

2. James M. Sinkula, "Market Information Processing and Organizational Learning," *Journal of Marketing* 58 (January 1994): 35–45.

3. Allen M. Weiss and Jan B. Heide, "The Nature of Organizational Search in High Technology Markets," *Journal of Marketing Research* 30 (May 1993): 220–33; Jennifer K. Glazing and Paul N. Bloom, "Buying Group Information Source Reliance," *Proceedings of the American Marketing Association Educators' Conference* (Summer 1994): 454.

4. B. Charles Ames and James D. Hlaracek, *Managerial Marketing for Industrial Firms* (New York: Random House Business Division, 1984); Edward F. Fern and James R. Brown, "The Industrial/Consumer Marketing Dichotomy: A Case of Insufficient Justification," *Journal of Marketing* 48 (Spring 1984): 68–77.

5. Kevin Keller, *Strategic Marketing Management* (Upper Saddle River, NJ: Prentice Hall 1998); Michael R. Solomon and Elnora W. Stuart, *Marketing: Real People, Real Choices* (Upper Saddle River, NJ: Prentice Hall, 1997).

6. Daniel H. McQuiston "Novelty, Complexity, and Importance as Causal Determinants of Industrial Buyer Behavior," *Journal of Marketing* 53 (April 1989): 66–79.

7. Patrick J. Robinson, Charles W. Faris, and Yoram Wind, *Industrial Buying and Creative Marketing* (Boston: Allyn & Bacon, 1967).

8. Erin Anderson, Wujin Chu, and Barton Weitz, "Industrial Purchasing: An Empirical Examination of the Buyclass Framework," *Journal of Marketing* 51 (July 1987): 71–86.

9. Fred E. Webster and Yoram Wind, *Organizational Buying Behavior* (Upper Saddle River, NJ: Prentice Hall, 1972).

10. B. G. Yovovich, "Revolutionary Marketing: Industrial Firms Reform Selling Practices to Focus on Customers," *Business Marketing* (March 1993): 34 (3 pp.).

11. See Frederick E. Webster Jr., "The Changing Role of Marketing in the Corporation," *Journal of Marketing* 56 (October 1992): 1–17; Judith M. Schmitz, "Central Versus Peripheral Routes of Persuasion in the Industrial Buying Center," *Proceedings of the American Marketing Association Educators' Conference* (Summer 1994): 461.

12. Ginger Conlon, "True Romance," *Sales & Marketing Management* (May 1996): 85–90.

13. Robert Boutilier, "Diversity in Family Structures," *American Demographics Marketing Tools* (1993): 4–6; W. Bradford Fay, "Families in the 1990s: Universal Values, Uncommon Experiences," *Marketing Research: A Magazine of Management & Applications* 5 (Winter 1993)1: 47.

14. Ellen Graham, "Craving Closer Ties, Strangers Come Together as Family," *Wall Street Journal* (March 4, 1996): B1 (2 pp.).

15. David Cheal, "The Ritualization of Family Ties," *American Behavioral Scientist* 31 (July/August 1988): 632.

16. "Families Come First," *Psychology Today* (September 1988): 11.

17. Christy Fisher, "Kidding Around Making Sense," *Advertising Age* (June 27, 1994): 34.

18. Alan R. Andreasen, "Life Status Changes and Changes in Consumer Preferences and Satisfaction," *Journal of Consumer Research* 11 (December 1984): 784–94; James H. McAlexander, John W. Schouten, and Scott D. Roberts, "Consumer Behavior and Divorce," *Research in Consumer Behavior* 6(1993): 153–84.

19. Judith Waldrop, "The Fashionable Family," *American Demographics* (March 1988): 22.

20. "The Big Picture," *American Demographics* (March 1989): 22–7; Thomas G. Exter, "Middle-Aging Households," *American Demographics* (July 1992): 63.

21. Laura Sessions Stepp, "Where Have All the Families Gone?" *The Washington Post* (March 1, 1994): C5.

22. Cyndee Miller, " 'Til Death Do They Part," *Marketing News* (March 27, 1995): 1–2.

23. Diane Crispell, "How Small a Household?" *American Demographics* (August 1994): 59.

24. Diane Crispell, "Family Futures," *American Demographics* (August 1996): 13–14.

25. Karen Hardee-Cleaveland, "Is Eight Enough?" *American Demographics* (June 1989): 60.

26. Diane Crispell, "Three's a Crowd," *American Demographics* (January 1989): 34.

27. Thomas Exter, "Peak-a-boo (Recent Baby Boomlet)," *American Demographics* (December 1988): 63.

28. Cheryl Russell, "Is Big Back?" *American Demographics* (May 1988): 15.

29. Blayne Cutler, "McChild Care," *American Demographics* (September 1989): 20.

30. Judith Waldrop, "A Lesson in Home Economics," *American Demographics* (August 1989): 26.

31. Mary Lou Padilla and Garry L. Landreth, "Latchkey Children: A Review of the Literature," *Child Welfare* 68 (July/August 1989): 445.

32. Judith Waldrop and Thomas Exter, "Lone Lifestyle," *American Demographics* (January 1990): 27.

33. Joe Schwartz, "After School," *American Demographics* (June 1987): 60.

34. Wendy Bounds, "An Easy Way to Get an Ex out of the Picture—and No Lawyer!" *Wall Street Journal* (June 16, 1994): B1.

35. Peg Masterson, "Agency Notes Rise of Singles Market," *Advertising Age* (August 9, 1993): 17.

36. Christy Fisher, "Census Data May Make Ads More Single-Minded," *Advertising Age* (July 20, 1992): 2.

37. Calmetta Y. Coleman, "The Unseemly Secrets of Eating Alone," *Wall Street Journal* (July 6, 1995): B1 (2 pp.).

38. Stephanie Shipp, "How Singles Spend," *American Demographics* (April 1988): 22–7; Patricia Braus, "Sex and the Single Spender," *American Demographics* (November 1993): 28–34.

39. "Mothers Bearing a Second Burden," *New York Times* (May 14, 1989): 26.

40. Seth Mydans, "A Tribunal to Get Neglected Parents Smiling Again," *New York Times* (December 27, 1996): A4.

41. Thomas Exter, "Disappearing Act," *American Demographics* (January 1989): 78; see also KerenAmi Johnson and Scott D. Roberts, "Incompletely-Launched and Returning Young Adults: Social Change, Consumption, and Family Environment," in eds. Robert P. Leone and V. Kumar, *Enhancing Knowledge Development in Marketing* (Chicago: American Marketing Association): 249–54; John Burnett and Denise Smart, "Returning Young Adults: Implications for Marketers," *Psychology & Marketing* 11 (May/June 1994)3: 253–69.

42. Marcia Mogelonsky, "The Rocky Road to Adulthood," *American Demographics* (May 1996): 26 (10 pp.).

43. Gary Levin, "A Moving Target for Mailers," *Advertising Age* (October 10, 1994): S6 (2 pp.).

44. "The Big Picture," *American Demographics*.

45. "Census Paints a New Picture of Family Life," *New York Times* (August 30, 1994): 22.

46. Constance Sorrentino, "The Changing Family in International Perspective," *Monthly Labor Review* (March 1990): 41.

47. Martha Farnsworth Riche, "Somebody's Baby," *American Demographics* (February 1988): 10.

48. For a review, see Russell W. Belk, "Metaphoric Relationships with Pets," *Society and Animals* 4 (1996)2: 121–46.

49. Diane Crispell, "Pet Projections," *American Demographics* (September 1994): 59; Howard G. Chua-Eoan, "Reigning Cats and Dogs," *Time* (August 16, 1993): 50 (2 pp.); Patricia Braus, "Cat Beats Dog, Wins Spot in House," *American Demographics* (September 1993): 24 (2 pp.).

50. Quoted in Youssef M. Ibrahim, "French Love for Animals: Too Fervent?" *New York Times* (February 2, 1990): A5.

51. Ian P. Murphy, "A Dog's Life: Products Go Upscale as Owners Pamper Four-Legged Friends," *Marketing News* (August 4, 1997): 1 (3 pp.). Woody Hochswender, "The Cat's Meow," *New York Times* (May 16, 1989): B7; Judann Dagnoli, "Toothcare for Terriers," *Advertising Age* (November 20, 1989): 8; "For Fido, Broccoli and Yogurt," *New York Times* (April 16, 1989); Chua-Eoan, "Reigning Cats and Dogs" William E. Schmidt, "Right, Then: Your Policy Covers Fido for Therapy," *New York Times* (May 15, 1994): 4; Patricia Davis, "New Shampoo for Hoofed Set Has the Mulish Looking Marvelous," *Wall Street Journal* (August 22, 1995): B1.

52. Craig J. Thompson, "Caring Consumers: Gendered Consumption Meanings and the Juggling Lifestyle," *Journal of Consumer Research* 22 (March 1996): 388–407.

53. Quoted in Bernice Kanner, "Advertisers Take Aim at Women at Home," *New York Times* (January 2, 1995): 42.

54. Waldrop, "A Lesson in Home Economics."

55. Shannon Dortch, "Maids Clean Up," *American Demographics* (November 1996): 4 (5 pp.).

56. Mary C. Gilly and Ben M. Enis, "Recycling the Family Life Cycle: A Proposal for Redefinition," in ed. Andrew A. Mitchell, *Advances in Consumer Research* 9 (Ann Arbor, MI: Association for Consumer Research, 1982): 271–6.

57. Charles M. Schaninger and William D. Danko, "A Conceptual and Empirical Comparison of Alternative Household Life Cycle Models," *Journal of Consumer Research* 19 (March 1993): 580–94; Robert E. Wilkes, "Household Life-Cycle Stages, Transitions, and Product Expenditures," *Journal of Consumer Research* 22 (June 1995)1: 27–42.

58. These categories are an adapted version of an FLC model proposed by Gilly and Enis (1982). Based on a recent empirical comparison of several competing models, Schaninger and Danko (1993) found that this framework outperformed others, especially in terms of its treatment of nonconventional households, though they recommend several improvements to this model as well. See Gilly and Enis, "Recycling the Family Life Cycle"; Schaninger and Danko, "A Conceptual and Empirical Comparison of Alternate Household Life Cycle Markets"; Scott D. Roberts, Patricia K. Voli, and KerenAmi Johnson, "Beyond the Family Life Cycle: An Inventory of Variables for Defining the Family as a Consumption Unit," in ed. Victoria L. Crittenden, *Developments in Marketing Science* 15 (Coral Gables, FL: Academy of Marketing Science, 1992): 71–5.

59. James H. McAlexander, John W. Schouten, and Scott D. Roberts, "Consumer Behavior and Divorce," in *Research in Consumer Behavior* (Greenwich, CT: JAI Press, 1992); Michael R. Solomon, "The Role of Products as Social Stimuli: A Symbolic Interactionism Perspective," *Journal of Consumer Research* 10 (December 1983): 319–29; Melissa Martin Young, "Disposition of Possession During Role Transitions," in eds. Rebecca H. Holman and Michael R. Solomon, *Advances in Consumer Research* 18 (Provo, UT: Association for Consumer Research, 1991): 33–9.

60. Haya El Nasser, "As Suburban Nests Empty, Couples Flocking to the City," *USA Today/International Edition* (November 6, 1996): 2A.

61. Harry L. Davis, "Decision Making within the Household," *Journal of Consumer Research* 2 (March 1972): 241–60; Michael B. Menasco and David J. Curry, "Utility and Choice: An Empirical Study of Wife/Husband Decision Making," *Journal of Consumer Research* 16 (June 1989): 87–97; Conway Lackman and John M. Lanasa, "Family Decision-Making Theory: An Overview and Assessment," *Psychology & Marketing* 10 (March/April 1993)2: 81–94.

62. Neal Templin, "The PC Wars: Who Gets to Use the Family Computer?" *Wall Street Journal* (October 5, 1995): B1 (2 pp.).

63. Shannon Dortch, "Money and Marital Discord," *American Demographics* (October 1994): 11 (3 pp.).

64. Daniel Seymour and Greg Lessne, "Spousal Conflict Arousal: Scale Development," *Journal of Consumer Research* 11 (December 1984): 810–21.

65. For research on factors influencing how much influence adolescents exert in family decision making, see Ellen Foxman, Patriya Tansuhaj, and Karin M. Ekstrom, "Family Members' Perceptions of Adolescents' Influence in Family Decision Making," *Journal of Consumer Research* 15 (March 1989)4: 482–91; Sharon E. Beatty and Salil Talpade, "Adolescent Influence in Family Decision Making: A Replication with Extension," *Journal of Consumer Research* 21 (September 1994)2: 332–41.

66. Diane Crispell, "Dual-Earner Diversity," *American Demographics* (July 1995): 32–7.

67. Thomas Hine, *Populuxe* (New York: Knopf, 1986).

68. Robert Boutilier, *Targeting Families: Marketing to and through the New Family*, (1993), *American Demographics Marketing Tools* (Ithaca, NY: 1993).

69. Darach Turley, "Dialogue with the Departed," *European Advances in Consumer Research* 2 (1995): 10–13.

70. Dennis L. Rosen and Donald H. Granbois, "Determinants of Role Structure in Family Financial Management," *Journal of Consumer Research* 10 (September 1983): 253–8.

71. Robert F. Bales, *Interaction Process Analysis: A Method for the Study of Small Groups* (Reading, MA: Addison-Wesley, 1950); for a cross-gender comparison of food-shopping strategies, see Rosemary Polegato and Judith L. Zaichkowsky, "Family Food Shopping: Strategies Used by Husbands and Wives," *The Journal of Consumer Affairs* 28 (1994)2: 278–99.

72. Alma S. Baron, "Working Parents: Shifting Traditional Roles," *Business* 37 (January/March 1987): 36; William J. Qualls, "Household Decision Behavior: The Impact of Husbands' and Wives' Sex Role Orientation," *Journal of Consumer Research* 14 (September 1987): 264–79; Charles M. Schaninger and W. Christian Buss, "The Relationship of Sex-Role Norms to Household Task Allocation," *Psychology & Marketing* 2 (Summer 1985): 93–104.

73. Cynthia Webster, "Effects of Hispanic Ethnic Identification on Marital Roles in the Purchase Decision Process," *Journal of Consumer Research* 21 (September 1994)2: 319–31; for a recent study that examined the effects of family depictions in advertising among Hispanic consumers, see Gary D. Gregory and James M. Munch, "Cultural Values in International Advertising: An Examination of Familial Norms and Roles in Mexico," *Psychology & Marketing* 14 (March 1997)2: 99–120.

74. John Steere, "How Asian-Americans Make Purchase Decisions," *Marketing News* (March 13, 1995): 9.

75. John B. Ford, Michael S. LaTour, and Tony L. Henthorne, "Perception of Marital Roles in Purchase Decision Processes: A Cross-Cultural Study," *Journal of the Academy of Marketing Science* 23 (Spring 1995)2: 120–31; for a recent study of husband–wife dyad decision making for home purchase decisions, see Chankon Kim and Hanjoon Lee, "A Taxonomy of Couples Based on Influence Strategies: The Case of Home Purchase," *Journal of Business Research* 36 (June 1996)2: 157–68.

76. Gary L. Sullivan and P. J. O'Connor, "The Family Purchase Decision Process: A Cross-Cultural Review and Framework for Research," *Southwest Journal of Business & Economics* (Fall 1988): 43; Marilyn Lavin, "Husband-Dominant, Wife-Dominant, Joint," *Journal of Consumer Marketing* 10 (1993)3: 33–42.

77. Diane Crispell, "Mr. Mom Goes Mainstream," *American Demographics* (March 1994): 59 (2 pp.); Gabrielle Sándor, "Attention Advertisers: Real Men Do Laundry," *American Demographics* (March 1994): 13 (2 pp.).

78. Tony Bizjak, "Chore Wars Rage On—Even When Wife Earns the Most," *The Sacramento Bee* (April 1, 1993): A1 (3 pp.).

79. Micaela DiLeonardo, "The Female World of Cards and Holidays: Women, Families, and the Work of Kinship," *Signs* 12 (Spring 1942): 440–53.

80. Quoted in Nicholas D. Kristof, "Japan is a Woman's World Once the Front Door is Shut," *New York Times* (June 19, 1996): A1 (2 pp.), quoted on p. A8.

81. Yumiko Ono, "McDonald's Doting Dads Strike a Chord in Japan," *Wall Street Journal Interactive Edition* (May 8, 1997).

82. C. Whan Park, "Joint Decisions in Home Purchasing: A Muddling-Through Process," *Journal of Consumer Research* 9 (September 1982): 151–62; see also William J. Qualls and Francoise Jaffe, "Measuring Conflict in Household Decision Behavior: Read My Lips and Read My Mind," in eds. John F. Sherry Jr. and Brian Sternthal, *Advances in Consumer Research* 19 (Provo, UT: Association for Consumer Research, 1992): 522–31.

83. Claudia Penteado, "Coke Taps Maternal Instinct with New Latin American Ads," *Advertising Age International* (January 1997): 15.

84. Kim P. Corfman and Donald R. Lehmann, "Models of Cooperative Group Decision-Making and Relative Influence: An Experimental Investigation of Family Purchase Decisions," *Journal of Consumer Research* 14 (June 1987): 1–13.

85. Alison M. Torrillo, "Dens are Men's Territory," *American Demographics* (January 1995): 11 (2 pp.).

86. Charles Atkin, "Observation of Parent-Child Interaction in Supermarket Decision-Making," *Journal of Marketing* 42 (October 1978): 41–5

87. Sharen Kindel, "They May be Small, But They Spend Big," *Adweek* (February 10, 1992)2: 38.

88. David Leonhardt, "Hey Kids, Buy This!" *Business Week* (June 30, 1997): 61 (6 pp.).

89. Emily Nelson, "Kodak Aims to Put Kids behind Its Cameras," *Wall Street Journal Interactive Edition* (May 6, 1997).

90. Les Carlson, Ann Walsh, Russell N. Laczniak, and Sanford Grossbart, "Family Communication Patterns and Marketplace Motivations, Attitudes, and Behaviors of Children and Mothers," *The Journal of Consumer Affairs* 28 (Summer 1994)1: 25–53; see also Roy L. Moore and George P. Moschis, "The Role of Family Communication in Consumer Learning," *Journal of Communication* 31 (Autumn 1981): 42–51.

91. Leslie Isler, Edward T. Popper, and Scott Ward, "Children's Purchase Requests and Parental Responses: Results from a Diary Study," *Journal of Advertising Research* 27 (October/November 1987): 28–39.

92. Patrick E. Tyler, "As a Pampered Generation Grows Up, Chinese Worry," *New York Times* (June 25, 1996): A1, A6.

93. Robert Berner, "Toddlers Dress to the Nines and Designers Rake it In," *Wall Street Journal Interactive Edition* (May 27, 1997).

94. Quoted in Lisa Gubernick and Marla Matzer, "Babies as Dolls," *Forbes* (February 27, 1995): 78–82, quoted on p. 79.

95. Horst H. Stipp, "Children as Consumers," *American Demographics* (February 1988): 27.

96. Melissa Turner, "Kids' Marketing Clout Man-Sized," *Atlanta Journal* (February 18, 1988): E10.

97. Scott Ward, "Consumer Socialization," in ed. Harold H. Kassarjian and Thomas S. Robertson, *Perspectives in Consumer Behavior* (Glenville, IL: Scott, Foresman, 1980): 380.

98. Thomas Lipscomb, "Indicators of Materialism in Children's Free Speech: Age and Gender Comparisons," *Journal of Consumer Marketing* (Fall 1988): 41–6.

99. George P. Moschis, "The Role of Family Communication in Consumer Socialization of Children and Adolescents," *Journal of Consumer Research* 11 (March 1985): 898–913.

100. James U. McNeal and Chyon-Hwa Yeh, "Born to Shop," *American Demographics* (June 1993): 34–9.

101. See Les Carlson, Sanford Grossbart, and J. Kathleen Stuenkel, "The Role of Parental Socialization Types on Differential Family Communication Patterns Regarding Consumption," *Journal of Consumer Psychology* 1 (1992)1: 31–52.

102. See Patricia M. Greenfield, Emily Yut, Mabel Chung, Deborah Land, Holly Kreider, Maurice Pantoja, and Kris Horsley, "The Program-Length Commercial: A Study of the Effects of Television/Toy Tie-Ins on Imaginative Play," *Psychology & Marketing* 7 (Winter 1990): 237–56 for a study on the effects of commercial programming on creative play.

103. Jill Goldsmith, "Ga, Ga, Goo, Goo, Where's the Remote? TV Show Targets Tots," *Dow Jones Business News* (February 5, 1997), accessed via *Wall Street Journal Interactive Edition* (February 6, 1997); Robert Frank, "Toddler Set Loves Teletubbies, But Parents Question Value," *Wall Street Journal Interactive Edition* (August 21, 1997).

104. Gerald J. Gorn and Renee Florsheim, "The Effects of Commercials for Adult Products on Children," *Journal of Consumer Research* 11 (March 1985): 962–7; for a recent study that assessed the impact of violent commercials on children, see V. Kanti Prasad and Lois J. Smith, "Television Commercials in Violent Programming: An Experimental Evaluation of Their Effects on Children," *Journal of the Academy of Marketing Science* 22 (1994)4: 340–51.

105. Glenn Collins, "New Studies on 'Girl Toys' and 'Boy Toys'," *New York Times* (February 13, 1984): D1.

106. Susan B. Kaiser, "Clothing and the Social Organization of Gender Perception: A Developmental Approach," *Clothing and Textiles Research Journal* 7 (Winter 1989): 46–56.

107. D. W. Rajecki, Jill Ann Dame, Kelly Jo Creek, P. J. Barrickman, Catherine A. Reid, and Drew C. Appleby, "Gender Casting in Television Toy Advertisements: Distributions, Message Content Analysis, and Evaluations," *Journal of Consumer Psychology* 2 (1993)3: 307–27.

108. Lori Schwartz and William Markham, "Sex Stereotyping in Children's Toy Advertisements," *Sex Roles* 12 (January 1985): 157–70.

109. Joseph Pereira, "Oh Boy! In Toyland, You Get More if You're Male," *Wall Street Journal* (September 23, 1994): B1 (2 pp.); Joseph Pereira, "Girls Favorite Playthings: Dolls, Dolls, and Dolls," *Wall Street Journal* (September 23, 1994): B1 (2 pp.).

110. Brad Edmondson, "Snakes, Snails, and Puppy Dogs' Tails," *American Demographics* (October 1987): 18.

111. Laura A. Peracchio, "How Do Young Children Learn to be Consumers? A Script-Processing Approach," *Journal of Consumer Research* 18 (March 1992): 425–40; Laura A. Peracchio, "Young Children's Processing of a Televised Narrative: Is a Picture Really Worth a Thousand Words?" *Journal of Consumer Research* 20 (September 1993)2: 281–93; see also M. Carole Macklin, "The Effects of an Advertising Retrieval Cue on Young Children's Memory and Brand Evaluations," *Psychology & Marketing* 11 (May/June 1994)3: 291–311.

112. Jean Piaget, "The Child and Modern Physics," *Scientific American* 196 (1957)3: 46–51; see also Kenneth D. Bahn, "How and When Do Brand Perceptions and Preferences First Form? A Cognitive Developmental Investigation," *Journal of Consumer Research* 13 (December 1986): 382–93.

113. Deborah L. Roedder, "Age Differences in Children's Responses to Television Advertising: An Information-Processing Approach," *Journal of Consumer Research* 8 (September 1981): 144–53; see also Deborah Roedder John and Ramnath Lakshmi-Ratan, "Age Differences in Children's Choice Behavior: The Impact of Available Alternatives," *Journal of Marketing Research* 29 (May 1992): 216–26; Jennifer Gregan-Paxton and Deborah Roedder John, "Are Young Children Adaptive Decision Makers? A Study of Age Differences in Information Search Behavior," *Journal of Consumer Research* 21, 4(1995): 567–80.

114. Janet Simons, "Youth Marketing: Children's Clothes Follow the Latest Fashion," *Advertising Age* (February 14, 1985): 16.

115. Stipp, "Children as Consumers"; see Laura A. Peracchio, "Designing Research to Reveal the Young Child's Emerging Competence," *Psychology & Marketing* 7 (Winter 1990): 257–76 for details regarding the design of research on children.

116. "Kid Power," *Forbes* (March 30, 1987): 9–10.

117. Dena Kleiman, "Candy to Frighten Your Parents With," *New York Times* (August 23, 1989): C1.

118. Laura Shapiro, "Where Little Boys Can Play with Nail Polish," *Newsweek* (May 28, 1990): 62.

119. Matt Murray, "Marketers Want Kids' Help and Their Parents' Loyalty," *Wall Street Journal Interactive Edition* (May 6, 1997).

120. Cindy Clark, "Putting Aside Adultcentrism: Child-Centered Ethnographic Research" (unpublished manuscript, C.D. Clark Limited, 1991); Cindy Clark, "Some Practical In's and Out's of Studying Children as Consumers" (paper presented at the AMA Research Roundtable, March 1986).

121. Gary Armstrong and Merrie Brucks, "Dealing with Children's Advertising: Public Policy Issues and Alternatives," *Journal of Public Policy and Marketing* 7 (1988): 98–113.

122. Bonnie Reece, "Children and Shopping: Some Public Policy Questions," *Journal of Public Policy and Marketing* (1986): 185–94.

123. Mary Ann Stutts and Garland G. Hunnicutt, "Can Young Children Understand Disclaimers in Television Commercials," *Journal of Advertising* 16 (Winter 1987): 41–6.

124. Ira Teinowitz, "CARU to Unveil Guidelines for Kid-Focused Web Sites," *Advertising Age* (April 21, 1997): 8.

125. Steve Weinstein, "Fight Heats up Against Kids' TV 'Commershows'," *Marketing News* (October 9, 1989): 2.

126. Alan Bunce, "Are TV Ads Turning Kids Into Consumers?" *Christian Science Monitor* (August 11, 1988): 1.

CONSUMERS AND SUBCULTURES

Tracy in NYC. She said if she spits her gum out from up here and it hit someone below, the force would totally split them in half.

The chapters in this section consider some of the social influences that help to determine who we are, with an emphasis on the subcultures that help to determine each of our unique identities. Chapter 13 focuses on factors that define social class, and how membership in a social class exerts a strong pull on what we want to buy with the money we make. Chapter 14 discusses the ways that our ethnic, racial, and religious identifications help to stamp our social identities. Chapter 15 considers how the bonds we share with others who were born at roughly the same time unite us.

SECTION OUTLINE

FINALLY, THE BIG DAY HAS COME! Phil is going home with Marilyn to meet her parents. Phil had been doing some contracting work at the securities firm where Marilyn works, and it was love at first sight. Even though Phil had attended "The School of Hard Knocks" on the streets of Brooklyn and Marilyn was fresh out of Princeton, somehow they knew they could work things out despite their vastly different backgrounds. Marilyn's been hinting that the Caldwells have money, but Phil doesn't feel intimidated. After all, he knows plenty of guys from his old neighborhood who have wheeled-and-dealed their way into six figures; he guesses he can handle one more big shot in a silk suit, flashing a roll of bills and showing off his expensive modern furniture with mirrors and gadgets everywhere you look.

When they arrive at the family estate in Connecticut, Phil looks for a Rolls-Royce parked in the circular driveway, but he sees only a Jeep Cherokee—which, he decides, must belong to one of the servants. Once inside, Phil is surprised by how simply the house is decorated and by how shabby everything seems. The hall entryway is covered with a faded Oriental rug, and all of the furniture looks really old—in fact, there doesn't seem to be a new stick of furniture anywhere, just a lot of antiques.

Phil is even more surprised when he meets Mr. Caldwell. He had half expected Marilyn's father to be wearing a tuxedo and holding a large glass of cognac like the people on *Lifestyles of the Rich and Famous*. In fact, Phil had put on his best black Italian suit in anticipation, and he wore his large cubic zirconium pinky ring so this guy would know that he had some money too.

When Marilyn's father emerges from his study wearing an old rumpled cardigan sweater and tennis sneakers, Phil realizes he's definitely not in the old neighborhood anymore. . . .

Income and Social Class

CONSUMER SPENDING AND ECONOMIC BEHAVIOR

As Phil's eye-opening experience at the Caldwells suggests, there are many ways to spend money, and a wide gulf exists between those who have it and those who don't. Perhaps an equally wide one exists between those who have had it for a long time and those who "made it the hard way—by earning it!" This chapter begins by briefly considering how general economic conditions affect the way consumers allocate their money. Then, reflecting the adage that says "The rich are different," it will explore how people who occupy different positions in society consume in very different ways.

Whether a skilled worker like Phil or a child of privilege like Marilyn, a person's social class has a profound impact on what he or she does with money and on how consumption choices reflect his or her "place" in society. As this chapter illustrates, these choices play another purpose as well. The specific products and services we buy are often intended to make sure *other* people know what our social standing is—or what we would like it to be. Products are frequently bought and displayed as markers of social class; they are valued as *status symbols*.

INCOME PATTERNS

Many Americans would probably say that they don't make enough money, but in reality the average American's standard of living continues to improve. These income shifts are linked to two key factors: a shift in women's roles and increases in educational attainment.[1]

WOMAN'S WORK

One reason for this increase in income is that there has also been a larger proportion of people of working age participating in the labor force. During the period from 1960 to 1990, the number of working adults rose from less than two-thirds to more than three-fourths.

More than 60 percent of this growth is due to women surging into jobs in record numbers. Furthermore, many of these jobs are in high-paying occupations that used to be dominated by men. For example, the proportion of female physicians has tripled, and the number of female architects went up sixfold during this time. Although women are still a minority in most professional occupations, their ranks continue to swell. The steady increase in the numbers of working women is a primary cause of the rapid growth of middle- and upper-income families. There are now more than 18 million married couples making more than $50,000 a year—but in almost two-thirds of these families, it is the wife's paycheck that is propelling the couple up the income ladder.

YES, IT PAYS TO GO TO SCHOOL!

Another factor that determines who gets a bigger piece of the pie is education. Although paying for college often entails great sacrifice, it still pays off in the long run. College graduates earn about 50 percent more than those who have only gone through high school during the course of their lives. Close to half of the increase in consumer spending power during the 1990s came from college grads. So, hang in there!

TO SPEND OR NOT TO SPEND, THAT IS THE QUESTION

Consumer demand for goods and services depends both on ability to buy and willingness to buy. Whereas demand for necessities tends to be stable over time, other expenditures can be postponed or eliminated if people don't feel that now is a good time to spend money.[2] For example, a person may decide to "make do" with his current clunker for another year rather than buying a new car right away.

DISCRETIONARY SPENDING

Discretionary income is the money available to a household over and above that required for a comfortable standard of living. American consumers are estimated to wield about $400 billion a year in discretionary spending power. People aged 35 to 55, whose incomes are at a peak, account for about half of this amount. As might be expected, discretionary income increases as overall income goes up: Although households earning more than $100,000 account for less than 5 percent of all families, they have more than half of the nation's discretionary income at their disposal.[3]

As the population ages and income levels rise, the typical U.S. household is changing the way it spends its money. The most noticeable change is that a much larger share of the budget is spent on shelter and transportation, and less on food and apparel. These shifts are due to factors such as an increase in the prevalence of home ownership (the number of home owners rose by over 80 percent in the last three decades) and in the need for working wives to pay commuting costs. On a more cheerful note, households are spending more now on entertainment, reading, and education than in the past. These changes are summarized in Figure 13–1.

INDIVIDUAL ATTITUDES TOWARD MONEY

Many consumers are experiencing doubts about their individual and collective futures, and they are anxious about holding on to what they have. Although half of the respondents in a recent American survey conducted by Roper/Starch Worldwide said they don't believe money can buy happiness, nearly 70 percent still report that if their earnings doubled they would be happier than they are now![4]

A consumer's anxieties about money are not necessarily related to how much he or she actually has: Acquiring and managing money is more a state of mind than of wallet. Money can have a variety of complex psychological meanings; it can be equated with success or failure, social acceptability, security, love, or freedom.[5] Some clinical psychologists even specialize in treating money-related disorders, and report that some people even feel guilty about their success and deliberately make bad investments to reduce this feeling! Some other clinical conditions include *atephobia* (fear of being ruined), *harpaxophiba* (fear of becoming a victim of robbers), *peniaphobia* (fear of poverty), and *aurophobia* (fear of gold).[6]

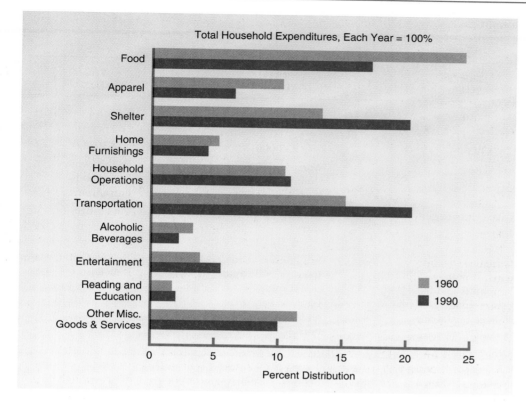

Total Household Expenditures, Each Year = 100%

FIGURE 13–1 ■ The Changing Household Budget
Source: Fabian Linden, *"Consumer Affluence: The Next Wave"* (The Conference Board, Inc., 1994).

The Roper/Starch survey found that by far security was the attribute most closely linked to the meaning of money. Other significant associations included comfort, being able to help one's children, freedom, and pleasure. The researchers identified seven distinct types of money personalities; these are summarized in Table 13–1.

CONSUMER CONFIDENCE

The field of **behavioral economics,** or economic psychology, is concerned with the "human" side of economic decisions (including the biases in decision making we examined in chapter 9). Beginning with the pioneering work of psychologist George Katona, this discipline studies how consumers' motives and their expectations about the future affect their current spending, and how these individual decisions add up to affect a society's economic well-being.[7]

Consumers' beliefs about what the future holds is an indicator of **consumer confidence,** which reflects the extent to which people are optimistic or pessimistic about the future health of the economy and how they will fare down the road. These beliefs influence how much money they will pump into the economy when making discretionary purchases.

Many businesses take forecasts about anticipated spending very seriously, and periodic surveys attempt to "take the pulse" of the American consumer. The Conference Board conducts a survey of consumer confidence, as does the Survey Research Center at The University of Michigan. The following are the types of questions posed to consumers in these surveys:[8]

TABLE 13–1 ■ **Money Personalities**

	TYPES		
	THE HUNTER	THE GATHERER	THE PROTECTOR
Percent of population	13	19	16
Mean income	$44,000	$35,000	$36,000
Exemplar	Bill Gates (CEO, Microsoft)	Warren Buffet (Nebraska-based investor)	Paul Newman (actor and entrepreneur)
Profile	Takes risks to get ahead	Is better safe than sorry	Puts others first
Characteristics	Is aggressive and equates money with happiness and achievement; is likely to have unstable personal life	Is a conservative investor with traditional values; tends to be thrifty and tries to minimize borrowing	Believes money is a means of protecting loved ones; tends to be predominantly women; is most likely married

Source: Adapted from Robert Sullivan, "Americans and Their Money," *Worth* (June 1994): 60 (8 pp.), based on a survey of approximately 2,000 American consumers conducted by Roper/Starch Worldwide. Reprinted by permission of *Worth* magazine.

- Would you say that you and your family are better off or worse off financially than a year ago?
- Will you be better off or worse off a year from now?
- Is now a good time or a bad time for people to buy major household items, such as furniture or a refrigerator?
- Do you plan to buy a car in the next year?

When people are pessimistic about their prospects and about the state of the economy, they tend to cut back their spending and take on less debt. On the other hand, when they are optimistic about the future, they tend to reduce the amount they save, take on more debt, and buy discretionary items. Thus the overall **savings rate** is influenced by individual consumers' pessimism or optimism about their personal circumstances (e.g., a fear of being laid off versus a sudden increase in personal wealth due to an inheritance), as well as by world events (e.g., the election of a new president or an international crisis such as the Gulf War in 1991) and cultural

MARKETING PITFALL

Anxieties about one's ability to procure popular items for one's kids are familiar to many parents. Publicity about toy shortages sent consumers scrambling for Tyco's Tickle Me Elmo doll and Nintendo 64 games during the 1996 Christmas season, and buying fever ran high among moms and dads. Tyco pulled its TV spots in early December after skirmishes erupted among some customers fighting over the last doll in stock.[9]

	TYPES		
THE SPLURGER	THE STRIVER	THE NESTER	THE IDEALIST
14	13	14	10
$33,000	$29,000	$31,000	$30,000
Elizabeth Taylor (movie star)	Tonya Harding disgraced figure skater)	Roseanne (comedienne/ actress)	Allen Ginsberg (deceased poet)
Travels first class or not at all	Is controlled by money	Needs just enough to take care of self	Believe there's more to life than money
Is self-indulgent; prefers to buy luxury items rather than practical items; is self-centered and not a good planner	Believes money makes the world go round; equates money with power; tends not to be well educated and most likely is divorced	Is not very interested in money; is mostly concerned about meeting immediate needs	Mostly believes that money is the root of all evil; is not very interested in material things

differences in attitudes toward saving (e.g., the Japanese have a much higher savings rate than do Americans).[10]

In an era of diminished resources, Americans are redefining traditional relationships among price, value, and quality. In the past (most notably in the "go-go" 1980s), people seemed to be willing to pay almost anything for products and services. Consumers still claim to want quality—but at the right price. Reflecting this new, more sober, state of mind, consider a survey conducted by Grey Advertising of 725 U.S. households to determine their priorities and values. Some of the findings are as follows:[11]

- The majority of respondents believe they have little control over economic and political events that affect them.
- Three out of four wonder if their hopes and dreams will ever come true.
- The majority are resigned to the fact that they cannot afford the lifestyles they thought they would have.
- Only 52 percent were optimistic about the future—a drop of 17 points from a similar survey conducted one year previously.
- Respondents reported a more down-to-earth attitude about spending. They are more cautious when making decisions, and they hold marketers accountable for the products they buy and the claims made about these products.

SOCIAL CLASS

All societies can be roughly divided into the "haves" and the "have-nots" (though sometimes having is a question of degree). The United States is a place where ". . . all men are created equal," but even so some people seem to be "more equal than

This Volkswagen ad reflects a shift in priorities today. The headline implies that consumers are moving from "nouveau riche" to "nouveau smart."

others." As Phil's encounter with the Caldwells suggests, a consumer's standing in society, or **social class,** is determined by a complex set of variables, including income, family background, and occupation.

The place one occupies in the social structure is an important determinant not only of *how much* money is spent, it also influences *how* it is spent. Phil was surprised that the Caldwells, who clearly had a lot of money, did not seem to flaunt it.

Consumers in their twenties are particularly skeptical about the economy and their place in it. Many younger people feel cheated because they are not advancing as previous generations have and they cannot aspire to the same quality of life (or better) that their parents enjoyed. Having grown up with MTV and other new forms of marketing, the "twentysomethings" tend to be more sophisticated when they respond to marketing efforts. *Generation X,* a book published in 1991, was one of the first to chronicle the disillusionment of this generation. It contains chapters such as "I am not a target market," "Our parents had more," and "Purchased experiences don't count." Some marketers have tried to foster identification with this group by producing ads that make fun of empty claims. For example, the copy for a tongue-in-cheek Priviet vodka ad reads, "Amazing Russian vodka . . . changes color when mixed with fruit juices!" [Rahul Jacob, "The Big Rise," *Fortune* (May 30, 1994): 74 (7 pp.).]

This understated way of living is a hallmark of so-called "old money"; people who have had it for a long time don't need to prove they've got it. In contrast, consumers who are relative newcomers to affluence might allocate the same amount of money very differently.

A UNIVERSAL PECKING ORDER

In many animal species, a social organization is developed whereby the most assertive or aggressive animals exert control over the others and have the first pick of food, living space, and even mating partners. Chickens, for example, develop a clearly defined dominance–submission hierarchy. Within this hierarchy, each hen has a position in which she is submissive to all of the hens above her and dominates all of the ones below her (hence, the origin of the term *pecking order*).[12]

People are not much different. They also develop a pecking order in which they are ranked in terms of their relative standing in society. This standing determines their access to such resources as education, housing, and consumer goods. People try to improve their ranking by moving up in the social order whenever possible. This desire to improve one's lot in life, and often to let others know that one has done so, is at the core of many marketing strategies.

Every culture has its social hierarchies, but variations in terms of how explicit these distinctions are can be observed. Stratification of one sort or another is universal, even in societies that officially disdain such a process. For example, in China, a supposedly classless society, many Chinese are irritated by the children of top party officials, who are called *gaoganzidi*. These offspring have a reputation for laziness, enjoying material pleasures, and getting the best jobs by virtue of their family connections. They are thus a privileged class in a classless society.[13]

SOCIAL CLASS AFFECTS ACCESS TO RESOURCES

Just as marketers try to carve society into groups for segmentation purposes, sociologists have developed ways to describe meaningful divisions of society in terms of people's relative social and economic resources. Some of these divisions involve political power, whereas others revolve around purely economic distinctions. Karl Marx, the nineteenth-century economic theorist, felt that position in a society was determined by one's relationship to the *means of production*. Some people (the

MARKETING OPPORTUNITY

As the old saying asserts, "The rich get richer, and the poor get poorer." Both the top and bottom ends of American income levels are swelling. Since 1980 the wealthiest fifth of the population has increased income by 21 percent, while wages for the bottom 60 percent have stagnated or dipped. America's most powerful brands, from Levi's jeans to Ivory soap, were built on a mass marketing premise but now that's changing. Stores such as Wal-Mart and Tiffany are reporting big earnings, whereas middle-class outlets like J.C. Penney have weak sales. This trend has led some companies to try to have their cake and eat it too by developing a *two-tiered marketing strategy*, in which separate plans are crafted for upscale and downscale consumers. For example, Walt Disney's Winnie the Pooh can be purchased as an original line-drawn figure on fine china or on pewter spoons in upscale specialty and department stores, while a plump cartoonlike Pooh is available on plastic key chains and polyester bed sheets at Wal-Mart. The Gap is remodeling its Banana Republic stores to make them more upscale, and simultaneously developing its Old Navy stores for the low end.[14]

haves) control resources, and they use the labor of others to preserve their privileged positions. The have-nots lack control and depend on their own labor for survival, so these people have the most to gain by changing the system. Distinctions among people that entitle some to more than others are perpetuated by those who will benefit by doing so.[15]

The German sociologist Max Weber (1864–1920) showed that the rankings people develop are not one-dimensional. Some involve prestige or "social honor" (he called these *status groups*), some rankings focus on power (or *party*), and some revolve around wealth and property (*class*).[16]

SOCIAL CLASS AFFECTS TASTE AND LIFESTYLES

The term social class is now used more generally to describe the overall rank of people in a society. People who are grouped within the same social class are approximately equal in terms of their social standing in the community. They work in roughly similar occupations, and they tend to have similar lifestyles by virtue of their income levels and common tastes. These people tend to socialize with one another and share many ideas and values regarding the way life should be lived.[17]

Social class is as much a state of being as it is of having: As Phil saw, class is also a matter of what one *does* with one's money and how one defines his or her role in society. Although people may not like the idea that some members of society are better off or "different" from others, most consumers do acknowledge the existence of different classes and the effect of class membership on consumption. As one wealthy woman observed when asked to define social class,

> I would suppose social class means where you went to school and how far. Your intelligence. Where you live. . . . Where you send your children to school. The hobbies you have. Skiing, for example, is higher than the snowmobile. . . . It can't be [just] money, because nobody ever knows that about you for sure.[18]

SOCIAL STRATIFICATION

In school, it always seems that some kids get all the breaks. They have access to many resources, such as special privileges, fancy cars, large allowances, or dates with other popular classmates. At work, some people are put on the fast track and are promoted to high-prestige jobs, given higher salaries, and perhaps perks such as a parking space, a large office, or the keys to the executive washroom.

In virtually every context, some people seem to be ranked higher than others. Patterns of social arrangements evolve whereby some members get more resources than others by virtue of their relative standing, power, and/or control in the group.[19] The phenomenon of **social stratification** refers to this creation of artificial divisions in a society: ". . . those processes in a social system by which scarce and valuable resources are distributed unequally to status positions that become more or less permanently ranked in terms of the share of valuable resources each receives."[20]

ACHIEVED VERSUS ASCRIBED STATUS

If you think back to groups you've belonged to, both large and small, you'll probably agree that in many instances some members seem to get more than their fair share of goodies, while other individuals are not so lucky. Some of these resources may have gone to people who earned them through hard work or diligent study. This allocation is due to *achieved status*. Other rewards may have been obtained because the person was lucky enough to be born rich or beautiful. Such good fortune reflects *ascribed status*.

Whether rewards go to the "best and the brightest" or to someone who happens to be related to the boss, allocations are rarely equal within a social group. Most groups exhibit a structure, or **status hierarchy,** in which some members are somehow better off than others. They may have more authority or power, or they are simply better liked or respected.

CLASS STRUCTURE IN THE UNITED STATES

The United States supposedly does not have a rigid, objectively defined class system. Nevertheless, America has tended to maintain a stable class structure in terms of income distribution. Unlike other countries, however, what *does* change are the groups (ethnic, racial, and religious) that have occupied different positions within this structure at different times.[21] The most influential and earliest attempt to describe American class structure was proposed by W. Lloyd Warner in 1941. Warner identified six social classes:[22]

1. Upper Upper
2. Lower Upper
3. Upper Middle
4. Lower Middle
5. Upper Lower
6. Lower Lower

Note that these classifications imply (in ascending order) some judgment of desirability in terms of access to resources such as money, education, and luxury goods. Variations on this system have been proposed over the years, but these six levels summarize fairly well the way social scientists think about class. A more current view of the American status structure is provided in Figure 13–2.

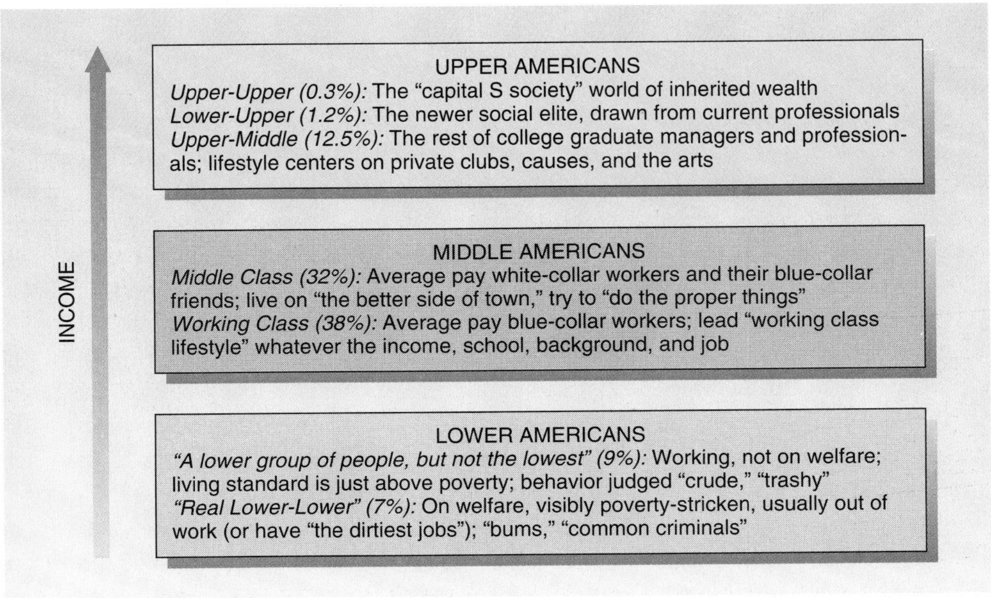

INCOME

UPPER AMERICANS
Upper-Upper (0.3%): The "capital S society" world of inherited wealth
Lower-Upper (1.2%): The newer social elite, drawn from current professionals
Upper-Middle (12.5%): The rest of college graduate managers and professionals; lifestyle centers on private clubs, causes, and the arts

MIDDLE AMERICANS
Middle Class (32%): Average pay white-collar workers and their blue-collar friends; live on "the better side of town," try to "do the proper things"
Working Class (38%): Average pay blue-collar workers; lead "working class lifestyle" whatever the income, school, background, and job

LOWER AMERICANS
"A lower group of people, but not the lowest" (9%): Working, not on welfare; living standard is just above poverty; behavior judged "crude," "trashy"
"Real Lower-Lower" (7%): On welfare, visibly poverty-stricken, usually out of work (or have "the dirtiest jobs"); "bums," "common criminals"

FIGURE 13–2 ■ A Contemporary View of the American Class Structure
Source: Richard P. Coleman, "The Continuing Significance of Social Class to Marketing," *Journal of Consumer Research* 10 (December 1983): 265–80. Reprinted with permission of The University of Chicago Press.

CLASS STRUCTURE AROUND THE WORLD

Every society has some type of hierarchical class structure, which determines people's access to products and services. Of course, the specific "markers" of success depend on what is valued in each culture. For the Chinese, who are just beginning to experience the bounties of capitalism, for example, one marker of success is hiring a bodyguard to protect oneself and one's newly acquired possessions![23]

Japan is a highly status-conscious society, in which upscale, designer labels are quite popular, and new forms of status are always being sought. To the Japanese, a traditional rock garden, formerly a vehicle for leisure and tranquillity, has become a sought-after item. Possession of a rock garden implies inherited wealth, because traditionally aristocrats were patrons of the arts. In addition, considerable assets are needed to afford the required land in a country in which real estate is extraordinarily costly. The scarcity of land also helps to explain why the Japanese are fanatic golfers: Because a golf course takes up so much space, membership in a golf club is extremely expensive.[24]

On the other side of the world, there is always Britain: Britain is also an extremely class-conscious country, and at least until recently, consumption patterns were preordained in terms of one's inherited position and family background. Members of the upper class were educated at schools such as Eton and Oxford and spoke like Henry Higgins in *My Fair Lady.* Remnants of this rigid class structure can still be found. "Hooray Henrys" (wealthy young men) play polo at Windsor and hereditary peers still dominate the House of Lords.

The dominance of inherited wealth appears to be fading in Britain's traditionally aristocratic society. According to a recent survey, 86 of the 200 wealthiest people in England made their money the old-fashioned way: They earned it. Even the

MULTICULTURAL DIMENSIONS

The relatively healthy state of the global economy is creating new pockets of wealth in developing countries. Now, makers of luxury products are going after this new money. The French conglomerate, LVMH-Moët Hennessy Louis Vuitton, which is a major player in categories from liqueur to leather, believes its future is in Asia rather than Europe. In 1996, Asian consumers bought 35 percent of the high-end luxury products exported from France. Vuitton is going into a new market each year; its latest conquest is Vietnam.[25]

However, not all of these ambitious plans to capture the pocketbooks of the rest of the world are working out that well. Many firms, for example, flocked to India when they realized that this huge country's emerging middle class was equal in size to the population of the entire United States. Now, many of these multinational companies are finding that "middle class" means something quite different in India. As the chairman of Hindustan Lever, the Indian subsidiary of Unilever

PLC, observed, ". . . middle class is a family that can afford to eat a balanced diet, send the children well clothed to school and buy a black-and-white television." According to a 1996 Gallup poll, the average Indian household earns $780 a year, and half that income goes to food and clothing. As manufacturers of cars, appliances, and other big-ticket consumer items scramble to move merchandise, some are resorting to drastic price cuts or outrageous promotions to stimulate interest. General Electric took rival Whirlpool to court in 1997 to force it to stop offering appliance buyers the chance to win such prizes as an apartment in New Delhi. The court agreed with GE's contention that Whirlpool was "luring gullible consumers" to buy a refrigerator or washer. Still, most firms are hanging in there and continue to have faith that Indian incomes will keep rising. As the director of Reebok's India unit puts it, "Nobody doubts that India will be one of the world's biggest markets. The question is how long will it take to get there."[26]

sanctity of the Royal Family, which epitomizes the aristocracy, has been diluted through tabloid exposure and the antics of younger family members who have been transformed into celebrities more like rock stars than royalty. As one observer put it, "... the royal family has gone down-market ... to the point that it sometimes resembles soap opera as much as grand opera."[27] In the wake of the return to power of the Labour Party, with Tony Blair as prime minister, and following the harsh criticism of the royal family following Princess Diana's death, there are changes afoot. Whether the changes heralding a "New Britain" will be more substance than form remains to be seen.

SOCIAL MOBILITY

To what degree do people tend to change their social classes? In some societies, such as India, one's social class is very difficult to change, but America is reported to be a country in which "any man (or woman?) can grow up to be president." **Social mobility** refers to the "passage of individuals from one social class to another."[28]

This passage can be upward, downward, or even horizontal. *Horizontal mobility* refers to movement from one position to another roughly equivalent in social status, for instance becoming a nurse instead of an elementary school teacher. *Downward mobility* is, of course, not very desirable, but this pattern is unfortunately quite evident in recent years as farmers and other displaced workers have been forced to go on welfare rolls or have joined the ranks of the homeless. A conservative estimate is that two million Americans are homeless on any given day.[29]

Despite that discouraging trend, demographics in fact decree that there must be *upward mobility* in our society. The middle and upper classes reproduce less (i.e., have fewer children per family) than the lower classes (an effect known as *differential fertility*), and they tend to restrict family size below replacement level (i.e., often having only one child). Therefore, so the reasoning goes, positions of higher status over time must be filled by those of lower status.[30] Overall, though, the offspring of blue-collar consumers tend also to be blue-collar, whereas the offspring of white-collar consumers also tend to wind up as white-collars.[31] People tend to improve their positions over time, but these increases are not usually dramatic enough to catapult them from one social class to another.

COMPONENTS OF SOCIAL CLASS

When we think about a person's social class, there are a number of pieces of information we may consider. Two major ones are occupation and income. A third important factor is educational attainment, which is strongly related to income and occupation.

OCCUPATIONAL PRESTIGE

In a system in which (like it or not) a consumer is defined to a great extent by what he or she does for a living, *occupational prestige* is one way to evaluate the "worth" of people. Hierarchies of occupational prestige tend to be quite stable over time, and they also tend to be similar across different societies. Similarities in occupational prestige have been found in countries as diverse as Brazil, Ghana, Guam, Japan, and Turkey.[32]

A typical ranking includes a variety of professional and business occupations at the top (e.g., CEO of a large corporation, physician, and college professor), whereas jobs hovering near the bottom include shoe shiner, ditch digger, and garbage collector. Because a person's occupation tends to be strongly linked to his or her use of leisure time, allocation of family resources, political orientation, and so on, this variable is often considered to be the single best indicator of social class.

INCOME

The distribution of wealth is of great interest to social scientists and to marketers, because it determines which groups have the greatest buying power and market potential. Wealth is by no means distributed evenly across the classes. The top fifth of the population controls about 75 percent of all assets.[33] As we have seen, income per se is not often a very good indicator of social class, because the way money is spent is more telling. Still, people need money to obtain the goods and services that they need to express their tastes, so obviously income is still very important. As Figure 13–3 shows, American consumers are getting both wealthier and older, and these changes will continue to influence consumption preferences.

THE RELATIONSHIP BETWEEN INCOME AND SOCIAL CLASS

Although consumers tend to equate money with class, the precise relationship between other aspects of social class and income is not clear and has been the subject of debate among social scientists.[34] The two are by no means synonymous, which is why many people with a lot of money try to use it to upgrade their social class.

One problem is that even if a family increases household income by adding wage earners, each additional job is likely to be of lower status. For example, a homemaker who gets a part-time job is not as likely to get one that is of equal or greater status than the primary wage earner's full-time job. In addition, the extra money earned is often not pooled toward the common good of the family. It is instead used by the indi-

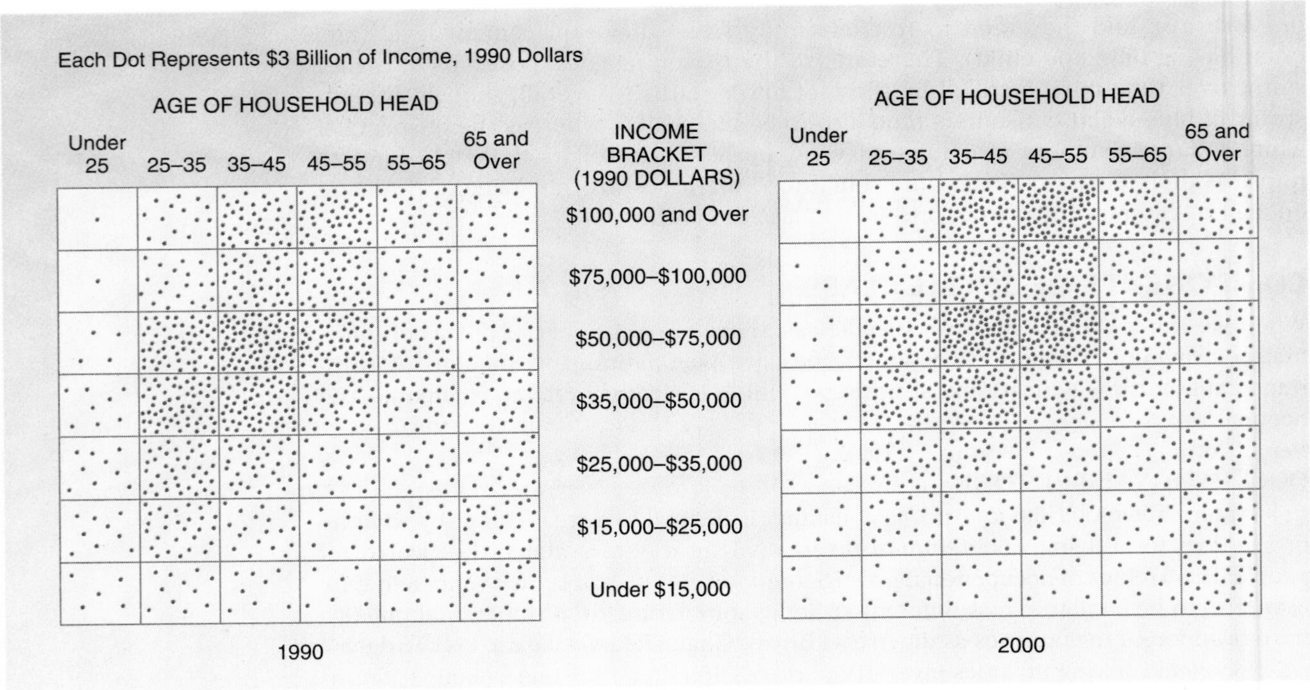

Each Dot Represents $3 Billion of Income, 1990 Dollars

| AGE OF HOUSEHOLD HEAD | | | | | | INCOME BRACKET (1990 DOLLARS) | AGE OF HOUSEHOLD HEAD | | | | | |
| Under 25 | 25–35 | 35–45 | 45–55 | 55–65 | 65 and Over | | Under 25 | 25–35 | 35–45 | 45–55 | 55–65 | 65 and Over |

$100,000 and Over

$75,000–$100,000

$50,000–$75,000

$35,000–$50,000

$25,000–$35,000

$15,000–$25,000

Under $15,000

1990   2000

FIGURE 13–3 ■ Income Changes by the Year 2000
Source: Fabian Linden, *Consumer Affluence: The Next Wave* (New York: The Conference Board, Inc., 1994).

vidual for his or her own personal spending. More money does not then result in increased status or changes in consumption patterns, because it tends to be devoted to buying more of the usual rather than upgrading to higher-status products.[35]

The following general conclusions can be made regarding the relative value of social class (i.e., place of residence, occupation, cultural interests, etc.) versus income in predicting consumers choices of products that are bought for functional reasons versus those bought primarily for symbolic reasons (e.g., to convey a desired impression to others).

- Social class appears to be a better predictor of purchases that have symbolic aspects, but low to moderate prices (e.g., cosmetics, liquor).
- Income is a better predictor of major expenditures that do not have status or symbolic aspects (e.g., major appliances).
- Both social class and income data are needed to predict purchases of expensive, symbolic products (e.g., cars, homes).

MEASUREMENT OF SOCIAL CLASS

Because social class is a complex concept that depends on a number of factors, so it is not surprisingly that it has proven difficult to measure. Early measures included the Index of Status Characteristics developed in the 1940s and the Index of Social Position developed by August Hollingshead in the 1950s.[36] These indices used various combinations of individual characteristics (e.g., income, type of housing) to arrive at a label of class standing. The accuracy of these composites is still a subject of debate among researchers; one recent study claimed that for segmentation purposes, raw education and income measures work as well as composite status measures.[37] One measurement instrument is shown in Figure 13–4.

American consumers generally have little difficulty placing themselves in either the working class (lower middle class) or middle class. Also, the number who reject the idea that such categories exist is rather small.[38] The proportion of consumers identifying themselves as working class tended to rise until about 1960, but it has been declining since.

Blue-collar workers with relatively high-prestige jobs still tend to view themselves as working class, even though their income levels may be equivalent to many white-collar workers.[39] This fact reinforces the idea that the labels of "working class" or "middle class" are very subjective. Their meanings say at least as much about self-identity as they do about economic well-being.

PROBLEMS WITH MEASURES OF SOCIAL CLASS

Market researchers were among the first to propose that people from different social classes can be distinguished from each other in important ways. Some of these class distinctions still exist, but others have changed.[40] Unfortunately, many of these measures are badly dated and are not as valid today for a variety of reasons, four of which are discussed here.[41]

Most measures of social class were designed to accommodate the traditional nuclear family, with a male wage earner in the middle of his career and a female full-time homemaker. Such measures have trouble accounting for two-income families, young singles living alone, or households headed by women that are so prevalent in today's society (see chapter 12).

Another problem with measuring social class is attributable to the increasing anonymity of our society. Earlier studies relied on the *reputational method,* in which extensive interviewing was done within a community to determine the reputations

Interviewer circles code numbers (for the computer) that in his/her judgment best fit the respondent and family. Interviewer asks for detail on occupation, then makes rating. Interviewer often asks the respondent to describe neighborhood in own words. Interviewer asks respondent to specify income—a card is presented to the respondent showing the eight brackets—and records R's response. If interviewer feels this is overstatement or understatement, a "better judgment" estimate should be given, along with an explanation.

EDUCATION:	Respondent	Respondent's Spouse
Grammar school (8 yrs or less)	−1	−1
Some high school (9 to 11 yrs)	−2 R's Age	−2 Spouse's Age
Graduated high school (12 yrs)	−3	−3
Some post high school (business, nursing, technical, 1 yr college)	−4	−4
Two, three years of college—possibly Associate of Arts degree	−5	−5
Graduated four-year college (B.A./B.S.)	−7	−7
Master's or five-year professional degree	−8	−8
Ph.D. or six/seven-year professional degree	−9	−9

OCCUPATION PRESTIGE LEVEL OF HOUSEHOLD HEAD: Interviewer's judgement of how head of household rates in occupational status.

(Respondent's description—asks for previous occupation if retired, or if R. is widow, asks husband's: _____)

Chronically unemployed—"day" laborers, unskilled; on welfare	−0
Steadily employed but in marginal semiskilled jobs; custodians, minimum pay factory help, service workers (gas attendants, etc.)	−1
Average-skill assembly-line workers, bus and truck drivers, police and firefighters, route deliverymen, carpenters, brickmasons	−2
Skilled craftsmen (electricians), small contractors, factory foremen, low-pay salesclerks, office workers, postal employees	−3
Owners of very small firms (2–4 employees), technicians, salespeople, office workers, civil servants with average-level salaries	−4
Middle management, teachers, social workers, lesser professionals	−5
Lesser corporate officials, owners of middle-sized businesses (10–20 employees), moderate-success professionals (dentists, engineers, etc.)	−7
Top corporate executives, "big successes" in the professional world (leading doctors and lawyers), "rich" business owners	−9

AREA OF RESIDENCE: Interviewer's impressions of the immediate neighborhood in terms of its reputation in the eyes of the community.

Slum area: people on relief, common laborers	−1
Strictly working class: not slummy but some very poor housing	−2
Predominantly blue-collar with some office workers	−3
Predominantly white-collar with some well-paid blue-collar	−4
Better white-collar area: not many executives, but hardly any blue-collar either	−5
Excellent area: professionals and well-paid managers	−7
"Wealthy" or "society"-type neighborhood	−9

TOTAL SCORE _____

TOTAL FAMILY INCOME PER YEAR:

Under $5,000	−1	$20,000 to $24,999	−5
$5,000 to $9,999	−2	$25,000 to $34,999	−6
$10,000 to $14,999	−3	$35,000 to $49,999	−7
$15,000 to $19,999	−4	$50,000 and over	−8

Estimated Status _____

(Interviewer's estimate: _____ and explanation _____)

R's MARITAL STATUS: Married ____ Divorced/Separated ____ Widowed ____ Single ____ (CODE: ____)

FIGURE 13–4 ■ **Example of a Computerized Status Index**
Source: Richard P. Coleman, "The Continuing Significance of Social Class to Marketing," *Journal of Consumer Research* 10 (December 1983): 265–80. Reprinted with permission of The University of Chicago Press.

and backgrounds of individuals (see the discussion of sociometry in chapter 11). This information, coupled with the tracing of interaction patterns among people, provided a very comprehensive view of social standing within a community. However, this approach is virtually impossible to implement in most communities today. One compromise is to interview individuals to obtain demographic data and to combine these data with the subjective impressions of the interviewer regarding the person's possessions and standard of living. An example of this approach appears in Figure 13–4. Note that the accuracy of this questionnaire relies largely on the interviewer's judgment, especially regarding the quality of the respondent's neighborhood. These impressions are in danger of being biased by the interviewer's own circumstances, which may affect his or her standard of comparison. Furthermore, the characteristics are described by highly subjective and relative terms: "slummy" and "excellent" are not objective measures. These potential problems highlight the need for adequate training of interviewers, as well as for some attempt to cross-validate such data, possibly by employing multiple judges to rate the same area.

One problem with assigning any group of people to a social class is that they may not be equal in their standing on all of the relevant dimensions. A person might come from a low-status ethnic group but have a high-status job, whereas another may live in a fancy part of town but did not finish high school. The concept of **status crystallization** was developed to assess the impact of inconsistency on the self and social behavior.[42] It was thought that since the rewards from each part of such an "unbalanced" person's life would be variable and unpredictable, stress would result. People who exhibit such inconsistencies tend to be more receptive to social change than are those whose identities are more firmly rooted.

A related problem occurs when a person's social class standing creates expectations that are not met. Some people find themselves in the not-unhappy position of making more money than is expected of those in their social class. This situation is known as an *overprivileged* condition and is usually defined as an income that is at least 25 to 30 percent over the median for one's class.[43] In contrast, *underprivileged* consumers, who earn at least 15 percent less than the median, must often allocate a big chunk of their income toward maintaining the impression that they occupy a certain status.

Lottery winners are examples of consumers who become overprivileged virtually overnight. As attractive as winning is to many people, it has its problems. Consumers with a certain standard of living and level of expectations may have trouble adapting to sudden affluence and engage in flamboyant and irresponsible displays of wealth. Ironically, it is not unusual for lottery winners to report feelings of depression in the months after cashing in. They may have trouble adjusting to an unfamiliar world, and they frequently experience pressure from friends, relatives, and business people to "share the wealth."

One New York winner who was prominently featured in the media is a case in point. He was employed as a mail porter until winning $5 million. After winning the lottery, he divorced his wife and married his girlfriend. She wore a $13,000 gown to the ceremony and the couple arrived in a horse-drawn carriage. Other purchases included a Cadillac with a Rolls-Royce grill and a $5,000 car phone. This individual later denied rumors that he was heavily in debt due to his extravagant spending.[44]

The traditional assumption is that husbands define a family's social class, whereas wives must live it. Women achieve their social status through their husbands.[45] Indeed, the evidence indicates that physically attractive women tend to "marry up" (*hierogamy*) in social class to a greater extent than attractive men do. Women trade the resource of sexual appeal, which historically has been one of the few assets they were allowed to possess, for the economic resources of men.[46]

The accuracy of this assumption in today's world must be questioned. Many women now contribute equally to the family's well-being, and they work in positions of comparable or even greater status than their spouses. *Cosmopolitan* magazine offered this revelation:

> Women who've become liberated enough to marry any man they please, regardless of his social position, report how much more fun and spontaneous their relationships with men have become now that they no longer view men only in terms of their power symbols.[47]

Employed women tend to average both their own and their husband's positions when estimating their own subjective status.[48] Nevertheless, a prospective spouse's social class is often an important "product attribute" when evaluating alternatives in the interpersonal marketplace (as Phil and Marilyn were to find out). *Cosmopolitan* also discussed this dilemma, implying that social class differences are still an issue in the dating game:

> You've met the (almost) perfect man. You both adore Dashiell Hammett thrillers, Mozart, and *Doonesbury*. He taught you to jet ski; you taught him the virtues of tofu. . . . The glitch? You're an executive earning 90-thousand dollars a year. He's a taxi driver. . . .[49]

PROBLEMS WITH SOCIAL CLASS SEGMENTATION: A SUMMARY

Social class remains an important way to categorize consumers. Many marketing strategies do target different social classes. However, marketers have failed to use social class information as effectively as they could for the following reasons:

- They have ignored status inconsistency.
- They have ignored intergenerational mobility.
- They have ignored subjective social class (i.e., the class a consumer identifies with rather than the one he or she objectively belongs to).
- They have ignored consumers' aspirations to change their class standing.
- They have ignored the social status of working wives.

HOW SOCIAL CLASS AFFECTS PURCHASE DECISIONS

Different products and stores are perceived by consumers to be appropriate for certain social classes.[50] Working-class consumers tend to evaluate products in more utilitarian terms such as sturdiness or comfort rather than style or fashionability. They are less likely to experiment with new products or styles, such as modern furniture or colored appliances.[51] In contrast, more affluent people living in the suburbs tend to be concerned about appearance and body image, so they are more avid consumers of diet foods and drinks compared to people in more downscale small towns. These differences mean that the cola market, for example, can be segmented by social class.[52]

CLASS DIFFERENCES IN WORLDVIEW

A major social class difference involves the *worldview* of consumers. The world of the working class (i.e., the lower middle class) is more intimate and constricted. For example, working-class men are likely to name local sports figures as heroes and are less likely to take long vacation trips to out-of-the-way places.[53] Immediate needs,

This ad for Libbey Glass implies that there are social class differences in leisure activities and preferred beverages.

such as a new refrigerator or TV, tend to dictate buying behavior for these consumers, whereas the higher classes tend to focus on more long-term goals, such as saving for college tuition or retirement.[54] Working-class consumers depend heavily on relatives for emotional support and tend to orient themselves in terms of the community rather than the world at large. They are more likely to be conservative and family oriented. Maintaining the appearance of one's home and property is a priority, regardless of the size of the house.

Although they would like to have more in the way of material goods, working-class people do not necessarily envy those who rank above them in social standing.[55] The maintenance of a high-status lifestyle is sometimes not seen as worth the effort. As one blue-collar consumer commented, "Life is very hectic for those people. There are more breakdowns and alcoholism. It must be very hard to sustain the status, the clothes, the parties that are expected. I don't think I'd want to take their place."[56]

The blue-collar consumer quoted here may be right. Although good things appear to go hand in hand with higher status and wealth, the picture is not that clear. The social scientist Émile Durkheim observed that suicide rates are much higher among the wealthy; he wrote in 1897, ". . . the possessors of most comfort suffer most."[57] The quest for riches has the potential to result in depression, deviant behavior, and ruin. In fact, a survey of affluent consumers (making an average of $176,000 a year) supports this notion. Although these people are in the top 2.5 percent income bracket in America, only 14 percent said they are very well off.[58]

The concept of a **taste culture,** which differentiates people in terms of their aesthetic and intellectual preferences, is helpful in understanding the important yet subtle distinctions in consumption choices among the social classes. Taste cultures largely reflect education (and also income).[59]

This ad for *US Magazine* uses a strategy that relies on cultural tastes of consumers in different social classes.

Although such perspectives have met with criticism due to the implicit value judgments involved, they are valuable because they recognize the existence of groupings based on shared tastes in literature, art, home decoration, and so on. In one of the classic studies of social differences in taste, researchers cataloged home owners' possessions while asking more typical questions about income and occupation. Clusters of furnishings and decorative items that seemed to appear together with some regularity were identified, and different clusters were found depending on the consumer's social status (see Figure 13–5). For example, religious objects, artificial flowers, and still-life portraits tended to be found together in relatively lower-status living rooms, whereas a cluster containing abstract paintings, sculptures, and modern furniture was more likely to appear in a higher-status home.[60]

Another approach to social class focuses on differences in the types of *codes* (the ways meanings are expressed and interpreted by consumers) used within different social strata. Discovery of these codes is valuable to marketers, because this knowledge allows them to communicate to markets using concepts and terms most likely to be understood and appreciated by specific consumers.

The nature of these codes varies among social classes. **Restricted codes** are dominant among the working class, whereas **elaborated codes** tend to be used by the middle and upper classes. Restricted codes focus on the content of objects, not on relationships among objects. Elaborated codes, in contrast, are more complex and depend on a more sophisticated worldview. Some differences between these two general types of codes are provided in Table 13–2. As this table indicates, these code

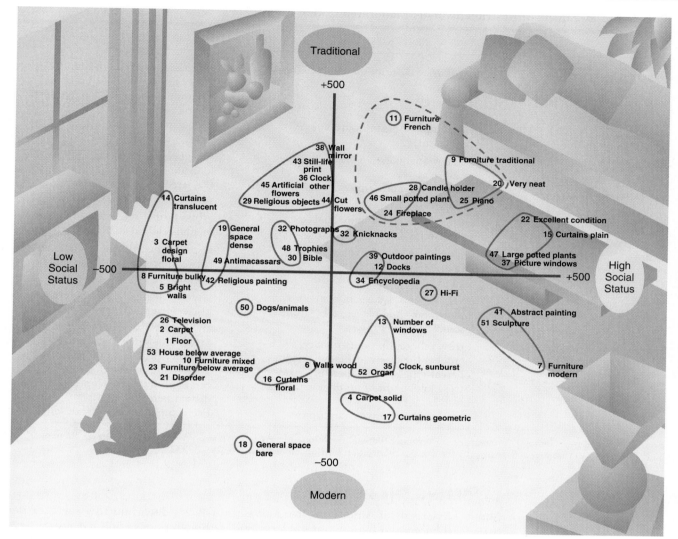

FIGURE 13–5 ■ Living Room Clusters and Social Class
Source: Edward O. Laumann and James S. House, "Living Room Styles and Social Attributes: The Patterning of Material Artifacts in a Modern Urban Community," *Sociology and Social Research* 54 (April 1970): 321–42.

differences extend to the way consumers approach basic concepts such as time, social relationships, and objects.

Marketing appeals that are constructed with these differences in mind will result in quite different messages. For example, a life insurance ad targeted to a lower-class person might depict in simple, straightforward terms a hard-working family man who feels good immediately after purchasing a policy. A more upscale appeal might depict a more affluent older couple surrounded by photos of their children and grandchildren and contain extensive copy emphasizing the satisfaction that comes from planning for the future and highlighting the benefits of a whole-life insurance policy.

TABLE 13–2 ■ **Effects of Restricted versus Elaborated Codes**

	RESTRICTED CODES	ELABORATED CODES
General characteristics	Emphasize description and contents of objects	Emphasize analysis and interrelationships between objects; i.e., hierarchical organization and instrumental connections
	Have implicit meanings (context dependent)	Have explicit meanings
Language	Use few qualifiers, i.e., few adjectives or adverbs	Have language rich in personal, individual qualifiers
	Use concrete, descriptive, tangible symbolism	Use large vocabulary, complex conceptual hierarchy
Social relationships	Stress attributes of individuals over formal roles	Stress formal role structure, instrumental relationships
Time	Focus on present; have only general notion of future	Focus on instrumental relationship between present activities and future rewards
Physical space	Locate rooms, spaces in context of other rooms and places: e.g., "front room," "corner store"	Identify rooms, spaces in terms of usage; formal ordering of spaces; e.g., "dining room," "financial district"
Implications for marketers	Stress inherent product quality, contents (or trustworthiness, goodness of "real-type"), spokesperson	Stress differences, advantages vis-à-vis other products in terms of some autonomous evaluation criteria
	Stress implicit fit of product with total lifestyle	Stress product's instrumental ties to distant benefits
	Use simple adjectives, descriptors	Use complex adjectives, descriptors

Source: Adapted from Jeffrey F. Durgee, "How Consumer Sub-Cultures Code Reality: A Look at Some Code Types," in ed. Richard J. Lutz, *Advances in Consumer Research* 13 (Provo, UT: Association for Consumer Research, 1986): 332.

TARGETING THE POOR

About 14 percent of Americans live below the poverty line, and this segment has been largely ignored by most marketers. Still, although poor people obviously have less to spend than do rich ones, they have the same basic needs as everyone else. Low-income families purchase staples such as milk, orange juice, and tea at the same rates as average-income families. Minimum wage-level households spend a greater than average share on out-of-pocket health care costs, rent, and food eaten at home.[61]

The unemployed do feel alienated in a consumer society, because they are unable to obtain many of the items that our culture tells us we "need" to be successful. However, idealized advertising portrayals don't appear to bother low-end consumers who have been interviewed by researchers. Apparently, one way to preserve self-esteem is by placing themselves outside of the culture of consumption and emphasizing the value of a simple way of life with less emphasis on materialism. In some cases, they enjoy the advertising as entertainment without actually yearning for the products; a comment by one 32-year-old British woman is typical, "They're not aimed at me, definitely not. It's fine to look at them, but they're not aimed at me so in the main I just pass over them."[62]

Some marketers are developing products and services especially for low-income consumers. These strategies may in some cases be in poor taste, as when S.C.

This group of magazines distributed by The Paisano Group targets young lower-class males by appealing to their interests in cars, motorcycles, and tattoos.

Johnson & Son, manufacturers of Raid insect spray, regularly hosts "roach evictions" at inner-city housing developments. Still other strategies raise important ethical issues, especially when marketers of so-called "sin products" such as alcohol and tobacco single out what many feel is a vulnerable audience. For example, manufacturers of malt liquors and fortified wines concentrate their efforts in poor areas where they know their products sell best.

Other marketers are trying to tap into poor families' needs to stretch their dollars and make efficient use of product information. *City Family* is a magazine targeted to poor women in New York. This target audience is concentrated in specific geographic areas, which makes readers relatively easy to reach. The magazine offers articles that help readers get the most out of city and health services. It also emphasizes

MARKETING PITFALL

Approximately 3.3 million Americans are institutionalized in nursing homes, correctional institutions, and rehabilitation centers. These residents require products that provide escape from boredom, can be traded, and can convey status.[63] Institutionalized consumers are vulnerable in that they face physical constraints on consumption activity, they are stigmatized by society, and they come disproportionately from lower social classes. They often try to rebuild their identities using goods they obtain from the outside, that they make themselves, or that they receive in trades with other inmates or residents. These disadvantaged consumers typically face more limited choices, pay more for comparable goods and services, and have less information on which to make decisions. They often must resort to an underground economy, bartering goods such as cigarettes for sex or drugs.[64]

the importance of home furnishings, particularly important items to consumers who cannot afford to leave on vacations and who often live in unsafe neighborhoods.[65]

Residents of poor neighborhoods must travel on average more than 2 miles to have the same access to supermarkets, large drug stores, and banks as do residents of nonpoor areas.[66] Some businesses that have prospered by locating branches in more accessible areas for this large market include the following:

- Banks are trying to improve relationships with the poor by opening mobile banking centers in different neighborhoods "underserved" by financial institutions. For example, the Mobile Banking Center, a division of the Huntington National Bank in Cincinnati, works through churches to offer banking services.[67]
- Vons Companies, California's largest supermarket operator, is investing $100 million in new stores that will be located in low-income urban areas.
- Fingerhut sells pots and pans, toys, and many other products, but its real business is extending credit to moderate- and low-income households that allows these consumers to purchase its inventory (at rates of about 24 percent a year). Even a pair of $40 sneakers can be bought on credit for 13 months at $7.49 a month. The $2 billion retailer has built a database that stores more than 500 pieces of information on each of more than 50 million active and potential customers, including their hobbies, birthdays, and payment histories.[68]

TARGETING THE RICH

We live in a time in which Bloomingdale's sells Donna Karan and Calvin Klein Barbies, and Mattel's Pink Splendor Barbie comes complete with crystal jewelry and a bouffant gown sewn with 24-karat threads.[69] To dress a "living doll," Victoria's Secret offers its Million Dollar Miracle Bra, with over 100 carats of real diamonds.[70] *Somebody* is buying this stuff. . . .

Many marketers try to target affluent, upscale markets. This practice often makes sense, because these consumers obviously have the resources to expend on costly products (often with higher profit margins). *The Robb Report,* a magazine targeted to the affluent (average reader income is $755,000) in 1996 estimated that 4.8 million American households had a net worth of at least $1 million, up 118 percent from 1992. The magazine segments the wealthy into three markets: the marginally rich (household income $70,000 to 99,999), the comfortably rich (income of $100,00 to $249,000), and the super rich ($250,000 and up).[71]

However, it is a mistake to assume that everyone with a high income should be placed into the same market segment. As noted earlier, social class involves more than absolute income; it is also a way of life, and affluent consumers' interests and spending priorities are significantly affected by factors such as where they got their money, how they got it, and how long they have had it.[72] For example, the marginally rich tend to prefer sporting events to cultural activities, and are only half as likely as the super rich to frequent art galleries or the opera.[73]

A recent survey of readers of *Town & Country,* another magazine that is targeted to the affluent, sheds some light on wealth in America today. Very few respondents equate wealth with success; they are more likely to say that success is related to high self-esteem, being a good parent, having a happy marriage, and having a strong sense of ethics (on the other hand, they can afford the luxury of not worrying as much about money!).

Luxury products are important to this group, but the highest-ranked symbol of achievement is being in charge of a cultural or educational institution and/or

Credit Lyonnais, France's biggest commercial bank, is targeting the wealthy by opening new upscale branches and offering special services for rich customers. In an unusual move, Credit Lyonnais hopes to accomplish its objectives by opening new branches in locations with heavy concentrations of wealthy people—for example, in one Paris neighborhood, four branches are clustered within a few hundred meters. At "Club Tourny," the nickname of one branch, customers do their banking in an elegant townhouse, where they sit at polished tables and discuss their financial needs over refreshments with bank staff. (Nicholas Bray, "Credit Lyonnais Targets Wealthy Clients," *Wall Street Journal* (June 24, 1993): B7A.)

one's own business. Affluent consumers want to be seen as smart, sophisticated shoppers, and they claim they don't want to flaunt what they own. These respondents are very socially active and enjoy socializing, particularly at country clubs. They report that the top reasons to buy a product are value, durability, and past experience.[74]

OLD MONEY

The "top-out-of-sight class" (e.g., the Rockefellers, Du Ponts, Fords, etc.) live primarily on inherited money, or "old money." People who have made vast amounts of money from their own labor do not tend to be included in this select group, though their flamboyant consumption patterns may represent an attempt to prove their wealth.[75] Thus, the mere presence of wealth is not sufficient to achieve social prominence. It must be accompanied by a family history of public service and philanthropy, which is often manifested in tangible markers that enable these donors to achieve a kind of immortality (e.g., Rockefeller University or the Whitney Museum).[76] "Old money" consumers tend to make distinctions among themselves in terms of ancestry and lineage rather than wealth.[77]

"Old money" consumers are often hard to identify. One commentator has called this group "... the class in hiding."[78] Following the Great Depression of the 1930s, monied families became more discreet about exhibiting their wealth, fleeing from mansions such as those found in Manhattan to hideaways in Virginia, Connecticut, and New Jersey. Old money people (like the Caldwells) are secure in their status. In a sense, they have been trained their whole lives to be rich.

THE *NOUVEAU RICHES*

Ironically, many other wealthy people do not know how to be rich. The Horatio Alger myth, in which a person goes from "rags to riches" through hard work and a bit of luck, is still a powerful force in American society. Although many people do in fact become "self-made millionaires," they often encounter a problem (although not the worst problem one could think of!) after they have become wealthy and have changed their social status: Consumers who have achieved extreme wealth and have relatively recently become members of upper social classes are known as the *nouveau riches,* a term that is usually used in a derogatory manner to describe new-comers to the world of wealth.

The *nouveau riche* phenomenon is also widespread in Russia and other Eastern European countries, where the transition to capitalism has paved the way for a new class of wealthy consumers who are spending lavishly on luxury items. One study of wealthy Russians identified a group of "super spenders," who earn about $1,000 a month and spend as much on discretionary items as they do on rent. They would like to spend more money, but are frustrated by the lack of quality products and services available to them![79]

Alas, many *nouveau riches* are plagued by *status anxiety*. They monitor the cultural environment to ensure that they are doing the "right" thing, wearing the "right clothes," being seen at the "right" places, using the "right" caterer, and so on.[80] Flamboyant consumption can thus be viewed as a form of symbolic self-completion, whereby the excessive display of symbols thought to denote "class" is used to make up for an internal lack of assurance about the "correct" way to behave.[81]

Advertising directed to this group often plays on these insecurities by emphasizing the importance of "looking the part." Clever merchandising supplies these consumers with the props necessary to masquerade by playing the role of old money people. For example, ads for *Colonial Homes* magazine feature consumers who ". . . have worked very hard to make it look like they never had to."

THE "GET SET"

Although the possession of wealth is clearly an important dimension of affluence, this quality may be as much determined by attitudes toward consumption as it is by level of income. Some marketers have identified a consumer segment comprising well-off, but not rich, people who desire the best products and services, even though they may have to be more selective about which items they are able to buy. These consumers are realistic about what they can afford and prefer to sacrifice in some areas so that they can have the best in others. Various advertising and marketing research agencies have labeled this segment with such terms as "Influentials," the "New Grown-Ups," and the "Get Set." This group has been estimated to represent up to almost 70 percent of U.S. buying power.

Many upper-class brands tried in the past to downscale themselves to attract the mass market, but there are some indications that this strategy is reversing. Because of the Get Set's emphasis on quality, one scenario is that marketers will encourage the masses to "buy up" into products associated with the upper classes, even if they are forced to buy less. A print campaign for Waterford Crystal exemplifies this approach. The theme line, "Steadfast in a world of wavering standards," is calculated to appeal to consumers who desire authenticity and lasting value.[82]

STATUS SYMBOLS

People have a deep-seated tendency to evaluate themselves, their professional accomplishments, their material well-being, and so on, relative to others. The popular phrase "keeping up with the Joneses" (in Japan it's "keeping up with the Satos") refers to the comparison between one's standard of living and that of one's neighbors.

Whether it's a swift horse, a smart hound or an agile car, the English have long known the importance of good breeding.

JAGUAR

This Jaguar ad uses a blatant appeal to status by playing on people's desires to show their old friends how well they've done in life.

Satisfaction is a relative concept, however. We hold ourselves to a standard defined by others that is constantly changing. Unfortunately, a major motivation for the purchase and display of products is not to enjoy them, but rather to let others know that we can afford them. In other words, these products function as **status symbols**. The desire to accumulate these "badges of achievement" is summarized by the popular bumper sticker slogan, "He who dies with the most toys, wins." Status-seeking is a significant source of motivation to procure appropriate products and services that the user hopes will let others know that he or she has "made it."

CONSPICUOUS CONSUMPTION

The motivation to consume for the sake of consuming was first discussed by the social analyst Thorstein Veblen at the turn of the century. Veblen felt that a major role of products was for **invidious distinction**—they are used to inspire envy in others through display of wealth or power.

Veblen coined the term **conspicuous consumption** to refer to people's desire to provide prominent visible evidence of their ability to afford luxury goods. Veblen's work was motivated by the excesses of his time. He wrote in the era of the robber barons, where the likes of J. P. Morgan, Henry Clay Frick, William Vanderbilt, and others were building massive financial empires and flaunting their wealth by throwing lavish parties. Some of these events of excess became legendary, as described in this account:

. . . there were tales, repeated in the newspapers, of dinners on horse-back; of banquets for pet dogs; of hundred-dollar bills folded into guests' dinner napkins; of a hostess who attracted attention by seating a chimpanzee at her table; of centerpieces in which lightly clad living maidens swam in glass tanks, or emerged from huge pies; of parties at which cigars were ceremoniously lighted with flaming banknotes of large denominations.[83]

THE BILLBOARD WIFE

This flaunting of one's possessions even extended to wives: Veblen criticized the "decorative" role women were often forced to play as they were bestowed with expensive clothes, pretentious homes, and a life of leisure as a way to advertise the wealth of their husbands—a sort of "walking billboard." Fashions such as high-heeled shoes, tight corsets, billowing trains on dresses, and elaborate hairstyles all conspired to ensure that wealthy women could barely move without assistance, much less perform manual labor. Similarly, the Chinese practice of foot-binding turned women into cripples who had to be carried from place to place.

THE MODERN POTLATCH

Veblen was inspired by anthropological studies of the Kwakiutl Indians, who lived in the Pacific Northwest. These Indians had a ceremony called a *potlatch,* a feast at which the host showed off his wealth and gave extravagant presents to the guests. The more one gave away, the better one looked to the others. Sometimes, the host would use an even more radical strategy to flaunt his wealth. He would publicly destroy some of his property to demonstrate how much he had.

This ritual was also used as a social weapon: Because guests were expected to reciprocate, a poorer rival could be humiliated by inviting him to a lavish potlatch. The need to give away as much as the host, even though he could not afford it, would essentially force the hapless guest into bankruptcy. If this practice sounds "primitive," think for a moment about many modern weddings. Parents commonly invest huge sums of money to throw a lavish party and compete with others for the distinction of giving their daughter the "best" or most extravagant wedding, even if they have to save for 20 years to do it.

THE LEISURE CLASS

This phenomenon of conspicuous consumption was, for Veblen, most evident among what he termed the *leisure class,* people for whom productive work is taboo. In Marxist terms, such an attitude reflects a desire to link oneself to ownership or control of the means of production, rather than to the production itself. Any evidence that one actually has to labor for a living is to be shunned, as suggested by the term the "idle rich."

Like the potlatch ritual, the desire to convince others that one has a surplus of resources creates the need for evidence of this abundance. Accordingly, priority is given to consumption activities that use up as many resources as possible in non-constructive pursuits. This *conspicuous waste* in turn shows others that one has the assets to spare. Veblen noted that ". . . we are told of certain Polynesian chiefs, who, under the stress of good form, preferred to starve rather than carry their food to their mouths with their own hands."[84]

THE DEATH—AND REBIRTH—OF STATUS SYMBOLS

While ostentatious products fell out of favor in the early part of the decade, the late 1990s are witnessing a resurgence of interest in luxury goods. Companies such as Hermes International, LVMH Hennessy Louis Vuitton, and Baccarat are enjoying sales gains of between 13 to 16 percent, as affluent consumers are once again indulging their desires for the finer things in life. Some of this resurgence can be attributed to the stock market boom of the late 1990s—in 1997, the securities industry earned nearly $12 billion, which is twice the profit realized during the best parts of the "go-go" 1980s. This prosperity has benefitted the Wall Street moguls, but it has also trickled down to many middle-class workers, some of whom are also reaping riches from the company stock options they receive. Maybe that's why Hermès is selling out if its handbags that cost up to $14,000, or why Gulfstream reports that it has back orders for about 100 luxury jets.[85]

One market researcher has termed this trend "the pleasure revenge"—people are just tired of buying moderately, eating low fat foods, and so on, and as a result sales are booming for self-indulgent products from fur coats to premium ice creams and caviar. As the Chairman of LVMH put it, "The appetite for luxury is as strong as ever. The only difference is that in the 1980s, people would put a luxury trademark on anything. Today only the best sells."[86]

While consumers appear to be displaying a renewed appetite for extravagance, many are trying to account for their lavish spending by rationalizing that these purchases merely represent good investments. An ad for an $8,000 Patek Philippe watch tells readers to "Begin your own tradition." A handmade cableknit sweater for $225 in a Lands' End catalog suggests, "could become an heirloom." Buying a pricey Land Rover is justified because it can be used for embarking on an adventure; showrooms now feature travel trunks, telescopes, and antique maps plus an off-road test track. The company's strategy is to offer drivers the cachet of a pricey car that is built for rugged performance without the stigma that is sometimes attached to a BMW or a Mercedes. One researcher terms this trend "conditional hedonism," explaining that "They [affluent consumers] want a rationale to have a blast."[87]

MARKETING OPPORTUNITY

Because the products and activities that connote high status are always changing, a significant amount of marketing effort goes into educating consumers as to what specific symbols they should be displaying and to ensuring that a product is accepted in the pantheon of status symbols.

The need to display the "right" symbols has been a boon to the publishing industry, where a variety of "how-to" books, magazines, and videos are available to school willing students of status. The concept of "dressing for success," in which detailed instructions are provided to allow people to dress as if they are members of the upper middle class (at least the authors' versions of this) was one popular example.[88] This guidance has now spread to other areas of consumption, including "power lunching," (e.g., order "steak tartare" to intimidate your partner, because raw meat is a power food), office furnishings, and home decoration.

Ripped jeans (especially the pricey kind that come that way when you buy them) are an example of parody display.

PARODY DISPLAY

As the competition to accumulate status symbols escalates, sometimes the best tactic is to switch gears and go in reverse. One way to do this is to deliberately *avoid* status symbols—that is, to seek status by mocking it. This sophisticated form of conspicuous consumption has been termed **parody display**.[89] A good example of parody display is the home furnishing style known as High Tech, which was in vogue a few years ago. This motif incorporated the use of industrial equipment (e.g., floors were covered with plates used on the decks of destroyers), and pipes and support beams were deliberately exposed.[90] This decorating strategy is intended to show that one is so witty and "in the know" that status symbols aren't necessary. Hence, the popularity of old, ripped blue jeans, and "utility" vehicles such as Jeeps among the upper classes (like the Caldwells). Thus, "true" status is shown by the adoption of product symbolism that is deliberately not fashionable.

- The field of behavioral economics considers how consumers decide what to do with their money. In particular, *discretionary expenditures* are made only when people are able and willing to spend money on items above and beyond their basic needs. *Consumer confidence*—the state of mind consumers have about their own personal situation, as well as their feelings about their overall economic prospects—helps to determine whether they will purchase goods and services, take on debt, or save their money.

- In the 1990s, consumers overall have been relatively pessimistic about their future prospects. A lower level of resources has caused a shift toward an emphasis on quality products that are reasonably priced. Consumers are less tolerant of exaggerated or vague product claims, and they are more skeptical about marketing activities. Consumers in their twenties are particularly skeptical about the economy and marketing targeted to their age group.

- A consumer's *social class* refers to his or her standing in society. It is determined by a number of factors, including education, occupation, and income.

- Virtually all groups make distinctions among members in terms of relative superiority, power, and access to valued resources. This *social stratification* creates a *status hierarchy*, in which some goods are preferred over others and are used to categorize their owners' social class.

- Although income is an important indicator of social class, the relationship is far from perfect. Social class is also determined by factors such as place of residence, cultural interests, and *worldview*.

- Purchase decisions are sometimes influenced by the desire to "buy up" to a higher social class or to engage in the process of *conspicuous consumption*, through which one's status is flaunted by the deliberate and nonconstructive use of valuable resources. This spending pattern is a characteristic of the *nouveau riches*, whose relatively recent acquisition of income, rather than ancestry or breeding, is responsible for their increased *social mobility*.

- Products often are used as status symbols to communicate real or desired social class. *Parody display* occurs when consumers seek status by deliberately avoiding fashionable products.

CONSUMER BEHAVIOR CHALLENGE

1. Sears, J.C. Penney, and, to a lesser degree, KMart, have made concerted efforts in recent years to upgrade their images and appeal to higher-class consumers. How successful have these efforts been? Do you believe this strategy is wise?

2. What are some of the obstacles to measuring social class in today's society? Discuss some ways to get around these obstacles.

3. What consumption differences might you expect to observe between a family characterized as underprivileged versus one whose income is average for its social class?

4. When is social class likely to be a better predictor of consumer behavior than mere knowledge of a person's income?

5. How do you assign people to social classes, or do you at all? What consumption cues do you use (e.g., clothing, speech, cars, etc.) to determine social standing?

6. Thorstein Veblen argued that women were often used as a vehicle to display their husbands' wealth. Is this argument still valid today?

7. Given present environmental conditions and dwindling resources, what is the future of "conspicuous waste?" Can the desire to impress others with affluence ever be eliminated? If not, can it take on a less dangerous form?

8. Some people argue that status symbols are dead. Do you agree?

9. Using the Status Index presented in Figure 13–4, compute a social class score for people you know, including their parents if possible. Ask several friends (preferably from different places) to compile similar information for people they know. How closely do your answers compare? If you find differences, how can you explain them?

10. Compile a list of occupations and ask a sample of students in a variety of majors (both business and nonbusiness) to rank the prestige of these jobs. Can you detect any differences in these rankings as a function of students' majors?

11. Compile a collection of ads that depict consumers of different social classes. What generalizations can you make about the reality of these ads and about the media in which they appear?

12. The chapter observes that some marketers are finding "greener pastures" by targeting low-income people. How ethical is it to single out consumers who cannot afford to waste their precious resources on discretionary items? Under what circumstances should this segmentation strategy be encouraged or discouraged?

NOTES

1. Data in this section adapted from Fabian Linden, *Consumer Affluence: The Next Wave* (New York: The Conference Board, Inc., 1994).
2. Christopher D. Carroll, "How Does Future Income Affect Current Consumption?" *Quarterly Journal of Economics* 109 (February 1994)1: 111–47.
3. Fabian Linden, *Consumer Affluence: The Next Wave* (New York: The Conference Board, Inc., 1994).
4. Robert Sullivan, "Americans and Their Money," *Worth* (June 1994): 60 (8 pp.).
5. José F. Medina, Joel Saegert, and Alicia Gresham, "Comparison of Mexican-American and Anglo-American Attitudes toward Money," *The Journal of Consumer Affairs* 30 (1996)1: 124–45.
6. Kirk Johnson, "Sit Down. Breathe Deeply. This is *Really* Scary Stuff," *New York Times* (April 16, 1995): F5.
7. Fred van Raaij, "Economic Psychology," *Journal of Economic Psychology* 1 (1981): 1–24.
8. Richard T. Curtin, "Indicators of Consumer Behavior: The University of Michigan Surveys of Consumers," *Public Opinion Quarterly* (1982): 340–52.
9. Kate Fitzgerald, "Publicity about Toy Shortages Feeds the Frenzy," *Advertising Age* (December 16, 1996): 12.
10. George Katona, "Consumer Saving Patterns," *Journal of Consumer Research* 1 (June 1974): 1–12.
11. Joe Schwartz, "Hard Times Harden Consumers," *American Demographics* (May 1992): 10; "Today's Americans, in Tough Times and Beyond," in *Grey Matter Alert* (New York: Grey Advertising, Inc., 1991).
12. Floyd L. Ruch and Philip G. Zimbardo, *Psychology and Life*, 8th ed. (Glenview, IL: Scott Foresman, 1971).
13. Louise Do Rosario, "Privilege in China's Classless Society," *World Press Review* 33 (December 1986): 58.
14. David Leonhardt, "Two-Tier Marketing," *Business Week* (March 17, 1997): 82 (7 pp.).
15. Jonathan H. Turner, *Sociology: Studying the Human System,* 2nd

ed. (Santa Monica, CA: Goodyear, 1981).
16. Turner, *Sociology.*
17. Richard P. Coleman, "The Continuing Significance of Social Class to Marketing," *Journal of Consumer Research* 10 (December 1983): 265–80; Turner, *Sociology.*
18. Quoted by Richard P. Coleman and Lee Rainwater, *Standing in America: New Dimensions of Class* (New York: Basic Books, 1978): 89.
19. Coleman and Rainwater, *Standing in America.*
20. Turner, *Sociology.*
21. James Fallows, "A Talent for Disorder (Class Structure)," *U.S. News & World Report* (February 1, 1988): 83.
22. Coleman, "The Continuing Significance of Social Class to Marketing"; W. Lloyd Warner with Paul S. Lunt, *The Social Life of a Modern Community* (New Haven, CT: Yale University Press, 1941).
23. Nicholas D. Kristof, "Women as Bodyguards: In China, It's All the Rage," *New York Times* (July 1, 1993): A4.
24. James Sterngold, "How Do You Define Status? A New BMW in the Drive. An Old Rock in the Garden," *New York Times* (December 28, 1989): C1.
25. Joshua Levine, "Liberté, Fraternité—But to Hell with Égalité!" *Forbes* (June 2, 1997): 80 (6 pp.).
26. Miriam Jordan, "Firms Discover Limits of India's Middle Class," 1997 *International Herald Tribune,* accessed via ssnewslink (June 27, 1997).
27. Robin Knight, "Just You Move Over, 'Enry 'Iggins; A New Regard for Profits and Talent Cracks Britain's Old Class System," *U.S. News & World Report* 106 (April 24, 1989): 40.
28. Turner, *Sociology:* 260.
29. See Ronald Paul Hill and Mark Stamey, "The Homeless in America: An Examination of Possessions and Consumption Behaviors," *Journal of Consumer Research* 17 (December 1990): 303–21; estimate provided by Dr. Ronald Hill, personal communication, December 1997.
30. Joseph Kahl, *The American Class Structure* (New York: Holt, Rinehart and Winston, 1961).

31. Leonard Beeghley, *Social Stratification in America: A Critical Analysis of Theory and Research* (Santa Monica, CA: Goodyear, 1978).
32. Coleman and Rainwater, *Standing in America:* 220.
33. Turner, *Sociology.*
34. See Coleman "The Continuing Significance of Social Class to Marketing"; Charles M. Schaninger, "Social Class versus Income Revisited: An Empirical Investigation," *Journal of Marketing Research* 18 (May 1981): 192–208.
35. Coleman, "The Continuing Significance of Social Class to Marketing."
36. August B. Hollingshead and Fredrick C. Redlich, *Social Class and Mental Illness: A Community Study* (New York: Wiley, 1958).
37. John Mager and Lynn R. Kahle, "Is the Whole More Than the Sum of the Parts? Re-evaluating Social Status in Marketing," *Journal of Business Psychology,* 10 (Fall 1995): 3–18.
38. Beeghley, *Social Stratification in America.*
39. R. Vanneman and F. C. Pampel, "The American Perception of Class and Status," *American Sociological Review* 42 (June 1977): 422–37.
40. Donald W. Hendon, Emelda L. Williams, and Douglas E. Huffman, "Social Class System Revisited," *Journal of Business Research* 17 (November 1988): 259.
41. Coleman, "The Continuing Significance of Social Class to Marketing."
42. Gerhard E. Lenski, "Status Crystallization: A Non-Vertical Dimension of Social Status," *American Sociological Review* 19 (August 1954): 405–12.
43. Richard P. Coleman, "The Significance of Social Stratification in Selling," in ed. Martin L. Bell, *Marketing: A Maturing Discipline, Proceedings of the American Marketing Association 43rd National Conference* (Chicago: American Marketing Association, 1960): 171–84.
44. Melinda Beck and Richard Sandza, "The Lottery Craze: Multimillion-Dollar Prizes Raise New Concerns That the Games Prey on the Poor," *Newsweek* (September 2, 1985): 16;

Rhoda E. McKinney, "Has Money Spoiled the Lottery Millionaires," *Ebony* (December 1988): 150.

45. E. Barth and W. Watson, "Questionable Assumptions in the Theory of Social Stratification," *Pacific Sociological Review* 7 (Spring 1964): 10–16.

46. Zick Rubin, "Do American Women Marry Up?" *American Sociological Review* 33 (1968): 750–60.

47. Sue Browder, "Don't be Afraid to Marry Down," *Cosmopolitan* (June 1987): 236.

48. K. U. Ritter and L. L. Hargens, "Occupational Positions and Class Identifications of Married Working Women: A Test of the Asymmetry Hypothesis," *American Journal of Sociology* 80 (January 1975): 934–48.

49. Browder, "Don't Be Afraid to Marry Down": 236.

50. J. Michael Munson and W. Austin Spivey, "Product and Brand-User Stereotypes among Social Classes: Implications for Advertising Strategy," *Journal of Advertising Research* 21 (August 1981): 37–45.

51. Stuart U. Rich and Subhash C. Jain, "Social Class and Life Cycle as Predictors of Shopping Behavior," *Journal of Marketing Research* 5 (February 1968): 41–9.

52. Thomas W. Osborn, "Analytic Techniques for Opportunity Marketing," *Marketing Communications* (September 1987): 49–63.

53. Coleman, "The Continuing Significance of Social Class to Marketing."

54. Jeffrey F. Durgee, "How Consumer Sub-Cultures Code Reality: A Look at Some Code Types," in ed. Richard J. Lutz, *Advances in Consumer Research* 13 (Provo, UT: Association for Consumer Research, 1986): 332–7.

55. David Halle, *America's Working Man: Work, Home, and Politics among Blue-Collar Owners* (Chicago: The University of Chicago Press, 1984); David Montgomery, "America's Working Man," *Monthly Review* (1985): 1.

56. Quoted in Coleman and Rainwater, *Standing in America:* 139.

57. Quoted in Roger Brown, *Social Psychology* (New York: The Free Press, 1965).

58. Lenore Skenazy, "Affluent, Like Masses, Are Flush with Worries," *Advertising Age* (July 10, 1989): 55.

59. Herbert J. Gans, "Popular Culture in America: Social Problem in a Mass Society or Social Asset in a Pluralist Society?" in ed. Howard S. Becker, *Social Problems: A Modern Approach* (New York: Wiley, 1966).

60. Edward O. Laumann and James S. House, "Living Room Styles and Social Attributes: The Patterning of Material Artifacts in a Modern Urban Community," *Sociology and Social Research* 54 (April 1970): 321–42; see also Stephen S. Bell, Morris B. Holbrook, and Michael R. Solomon, "Combining Esthetic and Social Value to Explain Preferences for Product Styles with the Incorporation of Personality and Ensemble Effects," *Journal of Social Behavior and Personality* (1991) 6: 243–74.

61. Paula Mergenhagen, "What Can Minimum Wage Buy?" *American Demographics* (January 1996): 32–6.

62. Quoted in Richard Elliott, "How Do the Unemployed Maintain Their Identity in a Culture of Consumption?" *European Advances in Consumer Research* 2 (1995): 1–4, quoted on p.3.

63. Lisa R. Szykman and Ronald Paul Hill, "A Consumer-Behavior Investigation of a Prison Economy," *Research in Consumer Behavior* 6 (1993): 231–60.

64. T. Bettina Cornwell and Terrance G. Gabel, "Out of Sight, Out of Mind: An Exploratory Examination of Institutionalization and Consumption," *Journal of Public Policy & Marketing* 15, 2 (Fall 1996): 278–295.

65. Linda Alwitt, "Marketing and the Poor," in ed. Ronald P. Hill, *Marketing and Consumer Research in the Public Interest* (Thousand Oaks, CA: Sage, 1995): 69–86; see also Linda F. Alwitt and Thomas D. Donley, *The Low Income Consumer: Adjusting the Balance of Exchange* (Thousand Oaks, CA: Sage, 1996); Steve London, "A City Magazine for the Poor," *American Demographics* (May 1994): 14 (2 pp.); Cyndee Miller, "The Have-Nots: Firms with the Right Products and Services Succeed among Low-Income Consumers," *Marketing News* (August 1, 1994): 1 (2 pp.); Mark Veverka, "New Stores Planned for Inner City," *Advertising Age* (July 11, 1994): 29.

66. Linda F. Alwitt and Thomas D. Donley, "Retail Stores in Poor Urban Neighborhoods," *The Journal of Consumer Affairs* 31 (1997)1: 108–27.

67. Chad Rubel, "Banks Go Mobile to Serve Low-Income Areas," *Marketing News* (November 20, 1995): 12.

68. Susan Chandler, "Data is Power. Just Ask Fingerhut," *Business Week* (June 3, 1996): 69.

69. Cyndee Miller, "New Line of Barbie Dolls Targets Big, Rich Kids," *Marketing News* (June 17, 1996): 6.

70. Cyndee Miller, "Baubles are Back," *Marketing News* (April 14,1997): 1 (2 pp.).

71. Anita Sharpe, "Magazines for the Rich Rake in Readers," *Wall Street Journal* (February 16, 1996): B1 (2 pp.).

72. "Reading the Buyer's Mind," *U.S. News & World Report* (March 16, 1987): 59.

73. Rebecca Piirto Heath, "Life on Easy Street," *American Demographics* (April 1997): 33–8.

74. *Wealth in America: A Study of Values and Attitudes among the Wealthy Today* (Town & Country, 1994).

75. Paul Fussell, *Class: A Guide through the American Status System* (New York: Summit Books, 1983): 29.

76. Elizabeth C. Hirschman, "Secular Immortality and the American Ideology of Affluence," *Journal of Consumer Research* 17 (June 1990): 31–42.

77. Coleman and Rainwater, *Standing in America:* 150.

78. Fussell, *Class:* 30.

79. M. H. Moore, "Homing in on Russian 'Super Spenders'," *Adweek* (February 28, 1994): 14–16.

80. Jason DeParle, "Spy Anxiety; The Smart Magazine That Makes Smart People Nervous about Their Standing," *Washingtonian Monthly* (February 1989): 10.

81. For a recent examination of retailing issues related to the need for status, see Jacqueline Kilsheimer Eastman, Leisa Reinecke Flynn, and Ronald E. Goldsmith, "Shopping for Status: The Retail Managerial Implications," *Association of Marketing Theory and Practice* (Spring 1994): 125–30.

82. Dennis Rodkin, "Wealthy Attitude Wins over Healthy Wallet: Consumers Prove Affluence Is a State of

Mind," *Advertising Age* (July 9, 1990): S4.

83. John Brooks, *Showing Off in America* (Boston: Little, Brown, 1981): 13.

84. Thorstein Veblen, *The Theory of the Leisure Class* (1899; reprint, New York: New American Library, 1953): 45.

85. Michael Shnayerson, "The Champagne City," *Vanity Fair* (December 1997): 182–202.

86. Quoted in Cyndee Miller, "Baubles are Back," *Marketing News* (April 14, 1997): 1 (2 pp.); Elaine Underwood, "Luxury's Tide Turns," *Brandweek* (March 7, 1994): 18–22.

87. Quoted in Joshua Levine, "Conditional Hedonism," *Forbes*, (February 10, 1997): 154.

88. For examples, see John T. Molloy, *Dress For Success* (New York: Warner Books, 1975); Vicki Keltner and Mike Holsey, *The Success Image* (Houston, TX: Gulf Publishing, 1982); and William Thourlby, *You Are What You Wear* (New York: New American Library, 1978).

89. Brooks, *Showing Off in America*.

90. Brooks, *Showing Off in America*: 31–2.

MARIA, WAKING UP EARLY on Saturday morning, braces herself for a long day of errands and chores. As usual, her mother is at work and expects Maria to do the shopping and then help prepare the food for the big family gathering tonight. Of course, her older brother Roberto would never be asked to do the grocery shopping or help out in the kitchen—these are woman's jobs.

Family gatherings make a lot of work, and Maria wishes that her mother would use prepared foods once in a while, especially on a Saturday when Maria has an errand or two of her own to do. But no, her mother insists on preparing most of her food from scratch; she rarely uses any convenience products to ensure that the meals she serves are of the highest quality.

Resigned, Maria watches a *telenovela* (soap opera) on Univision while she's getting dressed, and then she heads down to the *carnicería* (small grocery store) to buy a newspaper—there are almost 40 different Spanish newspapers published in her area, and she likes to pick up new ones occasionally. Then Maria buys the grocery items her mother wants; the list is full of well-known brand names such as Casera and Goya that she gets all the time, so she's able to finish quickly. With any luck, she'll have a few minutes to go to the *mercado* (shopping center) to pick up that new CD by Gloria Trevi she's been saving to buy. She'll listen to it in the kitchen while she chops, peels, and stirs.

Maria smiles to herself: Despite all the negative publicity, L.A. is a great place to live and what could be better than spending a lively, fun evening with *la familia.* . . .

Ethnic, Racial, and Religious Subcultures

SUBCULTURES AND CONSUMER IDENTITY

Yes, Maria lives in Los Angeles, not Mexico City. One in four Californians is Latino. Demographers predict that by 2010 Southern California essentially will be a Latino "subcontinent," culturally distinct from the rest of the United States.[1]

Hispanic Americans have much in common with members of other racial and ethnic groups who live in the United States. They observe the same national holidays, their expenditures are affected by the country's economic health, and they may join together in rooting for Team USA in the Olympics. Nonetheless, American citizenship may provide the raw material for some consumption decisions, but others are profoundly affected by the enormous variations in the social fabric of the United States. The United States is truly a "melting pot" of hundreds of diverse and interesting groups, from Italian and Irish Americans to Mormons and Seventh Day Adventists. Consider that in some American school systems, including New York City, Chicago, and Los Angeles, more than 100 languages are now spoken![2]

Consumers lifestyles are affected by group memberships *within* the society-at-large. These groups are known as **subcultures,** whose members share beliefs and common experiences that set them apart from others. Every consumer belongs to many subcultures. These memberships can be based on similarities in age, race or ethnic background, place of residence or heritage, or even a strong identification with an activity or art form. Whether "Dead Heads," "Netizens," or skinheads, each group exhibits its own unique set of norms, vocabulary, and product insignias (such as the skulls and roses that signify the Grateful Dead subculture).

These "communities" can even gel around fictional characters and events. Many devotees of *Star Trek,* for example, immerse themselves in a make-believe world of starships, phasers, and Vulcan neck pinches. Gene Roddenberry, *Star Trek's* creator, realized early on that people who identify with the show would also value products that identify them as members of this subculture. Sure enough, sales of *Star Trek* merchandise have topped $1 billion, and approximately three million people attend the more than 3000 *Star Trek* conventions that are held each year. Some Trekkers have even formed more specialized subcultures within the larger one; there is an entire group of fans devoted to the Klingons, an aggressive warrior race that long battled the Federation. These loyal followers boast their own language (*tlhIngan,* which was created by a linguist for one of the *Star Trek* movies), fan `zines, food, and even a summer camp.[3]

ETHNIC AND RACIAL SUBCULTURES

Ethnic and religious identity is often a significant component of a consumer's self-concept. An **ethnic** or **racial subculture** consists of a self-perpetuating group of consumers who are held together by common cultural and/or genetic ties, and is identified both by its members and by others as being a distinguishable category.[4]

In some countries, Japan for instance, ethnicity is almost synonymous with the dominant culture, because most citizens claim the same homogenous cultural ties (although Japan has sizeable minority populations, most notably people of Korean ancestry). In a heterogenous society such as the United States, many different cultures are represented, and consumers may expend great effort to keep their subcultural identification from being submerged into the mainstream of the dominant society.

WHY IT PAYS TO TARGET ETHNIC GROUPS

Marketers can no longer ignore the stunning diversity of cultures that are reshaping mainstream society. Ethnic minorities spend over $600 billion a year on products and services, and firms must devise products and communications strategies tailored to the needs of these subcultures. Almost half of all Fortune 1000 companies now have an ethnic marketing program up and running. For example, AT&T sponsors Chinese Dragon Boat Festival races and Cuban folk festivals, and runs advertisements that are aimed at 30 different cultures, including messages in languages such as Tagalog, spoken by Filipinos, and Twi, a West African dialect. As AT&T's director of multicultural marketing observed, "Marketing today is part anthropology."[5]

ETHNICITY AND MARKETING STRATEGIES

Although some people may feel uncomfortable at the notion that people's racial and ethnic differences should be explicitly taken into account when formulating marketing strategies, the reality is that these subcultural memberships are frequently paramount in shaping people's needs and wants. Membership in these groups is often predictive of consumer variables such as level and type of media exposure, food preferences, wearing distinctive apparel, political behavior, leisure activities, and even willingness to try new products.

Furthermore, research indicates that members of minority groups are more likely to find an advertising spokesperson from their own group to be more trustworthy, and this enhanced credibility in turn translates into more positive brand attitudes.[6] In addition, the way marketing messages should be structured depends on subcultural differences in how meanings are communicated. Sociologists make a distinction between *high-context cultures* and *low-context cultures*. In a high-context culture, group members tend to be tightly knit, and they are likely to infer meanings that go beyond the spoken word. Symbols and gestures, rather than words, carry much of the weight of the message. Compared to Anglos, many minority cultures are high context and have strong oral traditions, so perceivers will be more sensitive to nuances in advertisements that go beyond the message copy.[7]

IS ETHNICITY A MOVING TARGET?

Although ethnic marketing is in vogue with many firms, the process of actually defining and targeting members of a distinct ethnic group is not always so easy in our "melting pot" society. The popularity of golfer Tiger Woods illuminates the complexity of ethnic identity in the United States. Although Woods has been lauded as

MULTICULTURAL DIMENSIONS

Ethnic restaurants are one of the fastest-growing segments of the food industry worldwide. These diverse cuisines are a part of the internationalization of lifestyles, through which consumers reach out for new experiences. The greatest concentration of ethnic restaurants is found in the northeastern and western parts of the United States and in urban areas of Canada. Chinese is the most frequently served ethnic cuisine, followed closely by Mexican and Italian (these three types account for over 70 percent of all ethnic restaurants). A new trend is toward "fusion foods"—traditional dishes from different cuisines mixed to yield interesting results. Recent hits include nacho-flavored Bagel Bites, Southwest egg rolls, Thai Jungle salsa, and southwestern lasagna.[8]

an African American role model, in reality he is a model of multiracialism. His mother is a Thai and he also has Caucasian and Indian ancestry. Other popular cultural figures are also multiracial, including actor Keanu Reeves (Hawaiian, Chinese, Caucasian), singer Mariah Carey (black Venezuelan and white), and Dean Cain of Superman fame (Japanese, Caucasian).[9]

Indeed, it is estimated that 70 to 90 percent of people who call themselves African Americans are actually of mixed lineage, and the same is true of many Caucasians. This trend toward the blurring of ethnic and racial boundaries will only increase over time—more than 2 percent of all American marriages now involve mixed-race couples.[10] Intermarriage rates are highest among people of Asian descent; approximately 12 percent of Asian men and 25 percent of Asian women marry non-Asians.[11]

The steady increase in the number of mixed marriages is creating opportunities for other marketers who wish to meet the needs of children raised in multicultural families. Because many kids are exposed to others from diverse cultural backgrounds, some marketing executives feel that their racial attitudes will be quite different from those of their parents. As a senior MTV executive observed, "Tolerance and diversity is absolutely the number-one shared value" among young adults.

These encounters with diverse cultural traditions create the needs for products and services that allow consumers to celebrate multiple heritages. For example, books such as *Modern Bride Wedding Celebrations* contain information about wedding traditions for different ethnic groups so that interracial couples can mix and match. Magazines with titles such as *Interrace* and *New People* are also springing up to cater to this segment. They feature advertising for interracial-themed toys, books, and dating services.[12]

This "blender culture" led the Miller Brewing Company to *abandon* its sizeable ethnic marketing efforts; the firm instead has decided to develop ads and events that cut across cultural groups with a common denominator of youth, not ethnic background. One motivation behind this decision is the desire to save money by producing fewer ads, each including a pastiche of actors representing different subcultures. Miller's decision is not typical, however; although other companies are also finding that tastes among groups are merging to some extent, most believe that each group still wants to be considered distinct.[13]

As people from different racial and ethnic groups intermarry, it is becoming increasingly difficult for the U.S. Census Bureau and other organizations to classify consumers into neat ethnic and racial categories. Federal agencies currently use four broad racial designations—American Indian or Alaskan Native, Asian or Pacific

Islander, black, and white. However, many people cannot fit neatly into one of these categories, especially if they come from multiracial families. Other people resent the "mushing together" of many diverse groups under these broad headings. For example, Arab Americans are designated on one part of the census survey as "white, non-European," a category that also includes those of Sudanese, Iranian, and Scandinavian backgrounds.

This problem is compounded because the Census Bureau views race and ethnicity as different demographic characteristics, and asks separate questions about them on their surveys. Hispanic origin is viewed as an ethnic, not a racial category. As a result, about 1 in 25 Americans checks a box labeled "other race" instead of choosing one of the four categories provided. About 98 percent of those people then designate themselves as Hispanic on the separate ethnicity questions, indicating that people feel they don't fit neatly into one of the racial categories provided.

This classification issue has implications for marketers and policy makers, because these statistics are used to allocate government funds (and college scholarships!), determine if companies are violating antidiscrimination laws, and to determine marketing budgets for target marketing strategies. The federal government is now considering a modification of the categories it uses to include people who claim a multiracial identity, but this process is likely to be a long and politically painful one.[14]

Products that are marketed with an ethnic appeal are not necessarily intended for consumption only by the ethnic subculture from which they originate. **De-ethnicitization** refers to the process whereby a product formerly associated with a specific ethnic group is detached from its roots and marketed to other subcultures. This process is illustrated by the case of bagels, a bread product formerly associated with Jewish culture and now mass marketed. Recent variations include jalapeño bagels, blueberry bagels, and even a green bagel for St. Patrick's Day. A California company even markets tiny bagels as "bagel seeds."[15] Bagels now account for 3 to 6 percent of all American breakfasts, and bagel franchisers like Bruegger's Corporation and the Einstein/Noah Bagel Corporation are opening hundreds of stores in cities that had never heard of a bagel just a few years ago.[16]

A similar attempt to assimilate ethnic products into mainstream culture is underway by Goya Foods, a major marketer of Hispanic food products. As one company executive noted, "Several food items such as tacos . . . and burritos were once considered the domain of an ethnic group, and now they're mainstream."[17] To underscore this evolution, consider the fact that salsa is now the most popular condiment in the United States, outselling ketchup by $40 million.[18]

THE "BIG THREE" AMERICAN SUBCULTURES

The U.S. Census Bureau estimates that the population of the United States, which numbered 255 million in the 1990 census, will grow to 275 million by the year 2000. Much of this growth will be accounted for by members of non-white ethnic groups, and a substantial portion will be due to the immigration of people from other countries as opposed to citizens who are born in the United States.[19]

Three groups that account for much of America's current growth are African Americans, Hispanic Americans, and Asian Americans. The Hispanic population is projected to surpass the black population in the year 2013, at which time there will be 42.1 million Hispanic Americans and 42 million African Americans. The Asian American population, though smaller in absolute numbers, is the fastest-growing racial group. This growth is largely due to immigration; the number of Asian immigrants who arrive in the United States each year is actually greater than the number who are born in the country.[20]

MULTICULTURAL DIMENSIONS

Just as marketers have discovered that it is a mistake to group together all members of racial minorities, the same wisdom can be applied to Caucasian consumers: "White" is made up of many shades of gray, and there are big differences among ethnic whites. Consider, for example, differences in income levels among subcultures of various European extractions. These differences often reflect the length of time members of a subculture have been settled in the United States; groups who have been here longer have had more time to develop business networks and amass wealth. French Americans are the most likely to be affluent—almost 42 percent have a household income greater than $75,000; whereas Polish Americans have the lowest income among these segments.

Some organizations are beginning to develop campaigns to target various Caucasian ethnic groups. For example, casino gambling is most popular among those of German, Italian, or Portuguese extraction, so some gaming operations are reaching out to them. AT&T discovered that using singer Whitney Houston in its successful "your true voice" campaign did not appeal to Russian Americans, so the company instead used a Russian comedian in commercials it aired on Russian-language television. Even the U.S. Postal Service is trying to target ethnic whites after its research found that European Americans are more likely than others to use money transfer programs and parcel post. The USPS is advertising in foreign language papers and directories to compete with UPS for these customers.[21]

ETHNIC AND RACIAL STEREOTYPES: THE DARK SIDE OF MULTICULTURAL MARKETING

A recent television commercial for Taco Bell illustrates how marketers (intentionally or not) use ethnic and racial stereotypes to craft promotional communications The spot for the restaurant's Wild Burrito featured dark-skinned "natives" with painted faces who danced around in loincloths. Following an uproar in the African American community, the ad was withdrawn.[22]

Many subcultures have powerful stereotypes associated with them. Members of a subgroup are assumed to possess certain traits, even though these assumptions are often erroneous. The same trait can be cast either positively or negatively, depending on the communicator's intentions and biases. For example, the Scottish stereotype in the United States is largely positive, so the supposed frugality of this ethnic group is viewed favorably. Scottish imagery has been used by the 3M company to denote value (e.g., Scotch tape) and also by a motel chain that offers inexpensive lodging. However, invoking the Scottish "personality" might carry quite different connotations to consumers in Britain or Ireland. Thus, one person's "thrifty" is another's "stingy."

Ethnic symbolism has been used in the past by marketers as a shorthand to connote certain product attributes. The images employed were often crude and unflattering. Blacks were depicted as subservient, Mexicans as bandits.[23] As the Civil Rights movement gave more power to minority groups and their rising economic status commanded respect from marketers, these negative stereotypes began to disappear. Frito-Lay responded to protests by the Hispanic community and stopped using the Frito Bandito character in 1971 while Quaker Foods gave Aunt Jemima a makeover in 1989.

The use of subtle (and sometimes not so subtle) ethnic stereotypes in movies illustrates how the media can perpetuate assumptions about ethnic or racial groups. In 1953, the Disney animated feature *Peter Pan* caricatured Native Americans as tomahawk-wielding savages (absurdly led by a blonde, blue-eyed Tiger Lily!), but in the more recent movie *Pocahontas*, the company tried to be more sensitive to stereotypes. Still, objections were raised about the historical accuracy of this feature as well: Disney turned the 12-year-old heroine into a Playmate-type character and made her seem older, because it was felt that a 12-year-old in love with a 27-year-old man would not be well received by modern audiences.[24] Disney also drew fire from the Arab American community about the movie *Aladdin,* and some controversial lyrics were changed when the movie was released on video.

NEW ETHNIC GROUPS

The dominant American culture has historically exerted pressure on immigrants to divest themselves of their origins and become rapidly absorbed into the host culture. As President Theodore Roosevelt put it in the early part of the century, "We welcome the German or the Irishman who becomes an American. We have no use for the German or the Irishman who remains such."[25]

The bulk of American immigrants historically came from Europe, but immigration patterns have shifted dramatically in the latter part of this century. New immigrants are much more likely to be Asian or Hispanic. As these new waves of immigrants settle in the United States, marketers are attempting to track their consumption patterns and adjust their strategies accordingly. These new arrivals—whether Arabs, Asians, Russians, or people of Caribbean descent—are best marketed to in their native languages. They tend to cluster together geographically,

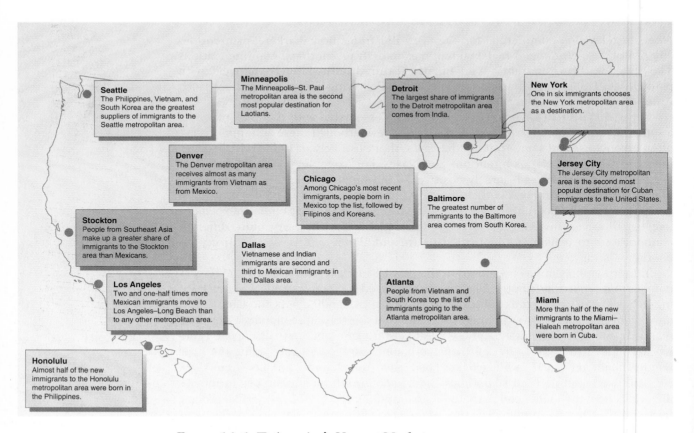

FIGURE 14–1 ■ **America's Newest Markets**
Source: "Newest Markets," *American Demographics* (September 1988): 27. Reprinted with permission, © *American Demographics.*

Tex-Mex cuisine is popular in Scandinavia. This ad appeared in a Swedish magazine.

which makes them easy to reach. The local community is the primary source for information and advice, so word of mouth is especially important (see chapter 11). Figure 14–1 shows how new waves of immigrants are changing the ethnic composition of major American cities.

One striking example is the growing numbers of American consumers who have immigrated from India. This group is relatively affluent and is growing. Many Indian Americans live in urban portions of New York and New Jersey, but the largest number reside in California. The first wave of an immigrant group often consists of relatively well-off people, and that is the case here. In 1990, 30 percent of Indian

MARKETING PITFALL

The mass merchandising of ethnic products is widespread and growing. Aztec Indian designs appear on sweaters, gym shoes are sold trimmed in *kente* cloth from an African tribe, greeting cards bear likenesses of Native American sand paintings. However, many people are concerned about the borrowing—and in some cases, misinterpretation—of distinctive symbolism.

Consider, for example, the storm of protest from the international Islamic community over what started as a simple dress design for the House of Chanel. In a fashion show, supermodel Claudia Schiffer wore a strapless evening gown designed by Karl Lagerfeld. The dress included Arabic letters that the designer believed spelled out a love poem. Instead, the message was a verse from the Koran, the Muslim holy book. To add insult to injury, the word "God" happened to appear over the model's right breast. Both the designer and the model received death threats, and the controversy subsided only after the three versions of the dress that had been made (and priced at almost $23,000) were burned.[26] Some industry experts feel that it's acceptable to appropriate symbols from another culture even if the buyer does not know their original meaning. They argue that even in the host society there is often disagreement about these meanings. What do you think?

Americans were employed in professional specialty occupations, compared to 13 percent of the general population. These consumers also own a large number of businesses, partly because family networks allow the businesses to grow—it is common for residents to pool resources and form associations enabling them to buy in bulk and sell at lower prices. This segment places great value on education and financial security, has a very high savings rate, and buys a lot of insurance. A growing number of Indo-American magazines such as *Masala, Onward,* and *Hum* have sprung up to straddle two cultures and appeal to young people.[27]

AFRICAN AMERICANS

African Americans comprise a significant racial subculture and account for 12 percent of the U.S. population. Although black consumers do differ in important ways from whites, the black market is hardly as homogenous as many marketers seem to believe. Historically, blacks were separated from mainstream society (unfortunately, not by choice). More recently, though, increasing economic success and the many cultural contributions of this group that have been absorbed by mainstream white culture, have in some instances blurred the lines between American blacks and whites.

Indeed, some commentators have argued that black/white differences are largely illusory. Different consumption behaviors are more likely due to differences in income, the relatively high concentration of African Americans in urban areas, and other dimensions of social class than by racial differences. With some exceptions, the overall spending patterns of blacks and whites are roughly similar. Both blacks and white spend about two-thirds of their incomes on housing, transportation, and food.[28]

BLACK/WHITE CONSUMPTION DIFFERENCES

Nonetheless, there clearly are some differences between blacks and whites in consumption priorities and marketplace behaviors that demand marketers' attention.[29] One reason is the vast market potential of this group: If African Americans comprised a separate nation, their buying power would rank twelfth in Western countries.[30] Black spending power increased 54 percent between 1990 and 1997.[31] Because of the growing economic power of this segment, black consumers often represent a fresh opportunity for otherwise saturated markets. Sometimes these differences are subtle but still can be important. When Coffee-Mate discovered that African Americans tend to drink their coffee with sugar and cream much more than do Caucasians, the company mounted a promotional blitz using black media and in return benefited from double-digit increases in sales volume and market share for this segment.[32] The following are some important usage differences in selected product categories.[33]

- African Americans account for only 2 percent of all spending on trucks and vans, whereas they account for almost a quarter of all spending on mass transit. This difference reflects the concentration of African Americans in urban areas.
- African Americans purchase 10 percent of televisions, radios, and sound equipment.
- African Americans buy 17 percent of all encyclopedias and reference books sold.
- African Americans spend 28 percent more than other American consumers on baby products.

- African Americans buy 27 percent more cooking ingredients than average.
- African Americans buy more than one-half of all the cognac sold in the United States.
- African Americans comprise 19 percent of the market for toiletries and cosmetics, and 34 percent for hair care products. African American women spend over $500 a year on health and beauty products—three times the rate of white women.

AFRICAN AMERICANS AND THE MEDIA

African American households watch an average of 10 hours of television a day, a rate 39 percent higher than the average American household. This segment tends to prefer established programming and is less likely to experiment with new offerings. As a result, they are more likely to be loyal to major networks, cable networks, and superstations such as WTBS, which attracts about 10 percent of the black viewing audience. In addition, black readership of local morning daily newspapers (as opposed to major regional papers) is 30 percent higher than for adults overall, and blacks also are more likely to read classified ads and circulars.

AFRICAN AMERICAN REPRESENTATION IN MAINSTREAM MEDIA

Historically, African Americans have not been well represented in mainstream advertising, but this situation is changing. Blacks now account for about one-quarter of the people depicted in ads (a rate even greater than their actual proportion of the overall population), and commercials are increasingly likely to be racially integrated.[34] The more striking and important change, though, is the way African American people are portrayed on television. Unlike earlier shows that presented blacks in stereotyped roles, such as *Sanford and Son* and *The Jeffersons*, most tele-

MARKETING PITFALL

The R.J. Reynolds Tobacco Company ignited a lot of controversy when it announced plans to test-market a menthol cigarette, called Uptown, specifically to black consumers in the Philadelphia area. Although the marketing of cigarettes to minorities is not a novel tactic, it was the first time a company explicitly acknowledged the strategy. Many critics immediately attacked the proposal, arguing that the campaign would exploit poor blacks—especially as black people suffer from a higher incidence of tobacco-related diseases than any other group. The publishers of black-oriented newspapers and magazines were caught in the middle, because they stood to receive substantial advertising revenues from the campaign. For example, approximately 10 percent of *Jet's* advertising revenues come from cigarette advertising. For its part, the Reynolds claimed that its actions were a natural result of shrinking markets and the need to more finely target increasingly small segments.

Unlike other ethnic groups that do not seem to display marked cigarette preferences, the tastes of African American consumers are easy to pinpoint. According to Reynolds, 69 percent of black consumers prefer menthol, more than twice the rate of smokers overall. After market research indicated that blacks tend to open cigarette packs from the bottom, the company decided to pack Uptowns with the filters facing down. Reynolds claimed that the product was not designed specifically for blacks, although it acknowledged that it was likely to attract a disproportionate share of black smokers. Following a storm of criticism by both private health groups and government officials (including the Secretary of Health and Human Services), the company announced that it was canceling its test-marketing plans. It would not comment on the likelihood that the cigarette would ever be introduced.[35]

vision roles created for African Americans now tend to depict them as middle-to-upper-class individuals who also happen to be black (e.g., *Family Matters* or *The Fresh Prince of Bel Air*).[36]

BLACK-ORIENTED MEDIA

Several major magazines, such as *Jet, Ebony, Essence,* and *Black Enterprise,* target this segment exclusively, and with great success. *Jet,* for example, claims to reach over 90 percent of the black male audience.[37] Black media tend to depict consumers in their natural social environment and more positively than in the general media, so it is not surprising that many African Americans gravitate to these magazines and newspapers.[38] A new generation of magazines is springing up to meet the demands of this growing market, including titles such as *The Source, Vibe, Shade,* and *Image.*[39]

In addition, other forms of media are being revamped with an African American spin. One recent development is the introduction of so-called multicultural romance novels, which feature African American heroes and heroines. The basic elements of a romance novel remain, but these books feature numerous references to African American culture, and the heroine is more likely to possess "curly brown locks" than "cascading blond hair."[40]

Retailers also are getting into the act. Sears recently launched its first ad campaign targeting African Americans touting its Mosaic by Alvin Bell line. J.C. Penney has its own magazine for black women, and the catalog industry is developing specialized media such as *Essence by Mail,* which reaches over 11 million households.[41]

The use of African American celebrities and sports figures is also on the rise. However, this strategy does not guarantee success with African American consumers. For example, although Pepsi has used singer Michael Jackson in its ad campaigns, its research showed that he did not appeal to 25- to 40-year-old blacks, who interpreted his plastic surgery and eccentric behavior as a desire to distance himself from his black roots.[42]

HISPANIC AMERICANS

The Hispanic subculture is a sleeping giant, a segment that was until recently largely ignored by many marketers. The growth and increasing affluence of this group has now made it impossible to overlook, and Hispanic consumers like Maria and her family are now diligently courted by many major corporations. Nike made history in 1993 by running the first Spanish-language commercial ever broadcast in prime time on a major American network. The spot, which ran during the All-Star baseball game, featured boys in tattered clothes playing ball in the Dominican Republic, or *La Tierra de Mediocampistas* (the Land of Shortstops). This title refers to the fact that over 70 Dominicans have played for major league ball clubs, many of whom started at the shortstop position. This ground-breaking spot also laid bare some of the issues involved in marketing to Hispanics: Many found the commercial condescending (especially the ragged look of the actors), and felt that it promoted the idea that Hispanics don't really want to assimilate into mainstream Anglo culture.[43]

If nothing else, though, this commercial by a large corporation highlights the indisputable fact that the Hispanic American market is now being taken seriously by major marketers. Some are rushing to sign Hispanic celebrities, such as Daisy Fuentes and Rita Moreno, to endorse their products.[44] Others are developing sep-

MARKETING OPPORTUNITY

The recent proliferation of ethnic dolls in America's toy stores reflects society's growing cultural diversity. Whereas non-Caucasian dolls used to appear only in collections of dolls from around the world, all major manufacturers have now introduced ethnic dolls to the mass market. African Americans spend well over $700 million a year on toys and games, so toy marketers are sitting up and taking notice. The American Girls Collection recently introduced Addy Walker, the first non-white doll in the series. Addy comes packaged with a set of books that describe her daily life and her (fictional) history as a slave: Details were provided by an advisory board of experts who ensured that Addy's experiences were told from a black perspective. The newest American Girl, introduced in 1997, is named Josefina Montoya; she supposedly grew up in New Mexico in the early 1800's.

Other new entrants include Kira, the Asian fashion doll, and Emmy, the African American baby doll. Mattel introduced a trio of dolls named Shani (which means "marvelous" in Swahili), Asha, and Nichelle that represent the range of African American facial features and skin tones (Shani also has a boyfriend named Jamal). Although Mattel has sold a black version of Barbie for over 20 years, it only recently began to promote the doll in television and print campaigns.[45]

arate Spanish-language campaigns, often with entirely different emphases calculated to appeal to the unique characteristics of this market. For example, the California Milk Processor Board discovered that its hugely successful "got milk?" campaign was not well received by Hispanics, because biting, sarcastic humor is not part of the Hispanic culture. In addition, the notion of milk deprivation is not funny to the Hispanic homemaker, because running out of milk means she has failed her family. An alternative targeted to Hispanics features a grandmother who teaches her granddaughter how to drink milk. As she explains to her granddaughter that "*cocinando con amor y con leche*" (she cooks with love and milk), this execution reinforces cultural beliefs that old people are to be revered, a grandmother is sweet, knowledgeable and strong, and the kitchen is a magical place where food is turned into love.[46]

THE ALLURE OF THE HISPANIC MARKET

Demographically, two important characteristics of the Hispanic market are worth noting: First, it is a young market. The median age of Hispanic Americans is 23.6, compared with the U.S. average of 32. That helps to explain why General Mills developed a breakfast cereal called Buñuelitos specifically for this market. The brand name is an adaptation of *buñuelos,* a traditional Mexican pastry served on holidays.[47]

Second, the Hispanic family is much larger than the rest of the population's. The average Hispanic household contains 3.5 people, compared to only 2.7 for other U.S. households. These differences obviously affect the overall allocation of income to various product categories. For example, Hispanic households spend 15 to 20 percent more of their disposable income than the national average on groceries.[48] There are now over 19 million Hispanic consumers in the United States, and a number of factors make this market segment extremely attractive:

● Hispanics tend to be brand loyal, especially to brands from their country of origin. In one study, about 45 percent reported that they always buy their usual brand, whereas only one in five said they frequently switch brands.[49] Another found that Hispanics who strongly identify with their ethnic origin are more likely to seek Hispanic vendors, to be loyal to brands used by family and friends, and to be influenced by Hispanic media.[50]

● Hispanics are highly concentrated geographically by country of origin, which makes them relatively easy to reach. Over 50 percent of all Hispanics live in the Los Angeles, New York, Miami, San Antonio, San Francisco, and Chicago metropolitan areas.[51]

● Education levels are increasing dramatically. In the period between 1984 and 1988, the number of Hispanics with four years of college increased by 51 percent. Although the absolute numbers are still low compared to the general population, the number of Hispanic men in managerial and professional jobs increased by 42 percent, and the corresponding increase of 61 percent for Hispanic women during this period was even more encouraging.[52]

APPEALING TO HISPANIC SUBCULTURES

The behavior profile of the Hispanic consumer includes a need for status and a strong sense of pride. A high value is placed on self-expression and familial devotion. Some campaigns have played to Hispanics' fear of rejection and apprehension about loss of control and embarrassment in social situations. Conventional wisdom recommends creating action-oriented advertising and emphasizing a problem-solving atmosphere. Assertive role models who are cast in nonthreatening situations appear to be effective.[53]

As with other large subcultural groups, marketers are now beginning to discover that the Hispanic market is not homogenous. Subcultural identity is not as much with being Hispanic as it is with the particular country of origin. Mexican Americans, who make up about 62 percent of all Hispanic Americans, are also the fastest-growing subsegment; their population has grown by 40 percent since 1980. Cuban Americans are ʰy far the wealthiest subsegment, but they also are the smallest Hispanic ethnic group.[54] Many Cuban American families with high educational levels fled Fidel Castro's communist regime in the late 1950s and early 1960s, worked hard for many years to establish themselves, and are now firmly entrenched in the Miami political and economic establishment. Because of this affluence, businesses in South Florida now make an effort to target "YUCAs" (young, upwardly mobile Cuban Americans), especially since the *majority* of Miami residents are Hispanic American![55]

MARKETING BLUNDERS

Many initial efforts by Americans to market to Hispanics were, to say the least, counterproductive. Companies bumbled in their efforts to translate advertising adequately or to compose copy that could capture desired nuances. These mistakes do not occur so much anymore as marketers become more sophisticated in dealing with this market and as Hispanics themselves become involved in advertising production. The following are some translation mishaps that have slipped through in the past:[56]

● The Perdue slogan, "It takes a tough man to make a tender chicken," was translated as "It takes a sexually excited man to make a chick affectionate."
● Budweiser was promoted as the "queen of beers."

- A burrito was mistakenly called a *burrada,* which means "big mistake."
- Braniff, promoting its comfortable leather seats, used the headline, *Sentado en cuero,* which was interpreted as "Sit naked."
- Coors beer's slogan to "get loose with Coors" appeared in Spanish as "get the runs with Coors."

UNDERSTANDING HISPANIC IDENTITY

Native language and culture are important components of Hispanic identity and self-esteem (about three-quarters of Hispanics still speak Spanish at home), and these consumers are very sympathetic to marketing efforts that acknowledge and emphasize the Hispanic cultural heritage.[57] More than 40 percent of Hispanic consumers say they deliberately attempt to buy products that show an interest in the Hispanic consumer, and this number jumps to over two-thirds for Cuban Americans.[58]

Many Hispanic Americans are avid consumers of soap operas, called *telenovelas.* Ethnic soap operas, shown on American television, are becoming big business. Univision, the biggest Spanish-language network, airs 10 different ones each day. These shows are produced by Latin American networks, but some viewers have complained that they do not address problems of Hispanic Americans such as illegal immigration, getting a job, or speaking the language.[59]

Since the beginning of the 1990s, Hispanic radio stations have been blossoming—there are now over 390 stations in the United States. This growth is partly due to the increasing size and economic clout of Hispanic consumers. It is also attributable to stations' efforts to attract younger listeners by playing more contemporary musical styles, such as *tejano, banda, ranchera,* and *nortena.* A movie about the shooting death of Selena, a popular young *tejano* singer, has fueled this interest. These new formats feature bilingual disk jockeys, who are developing a patter that some have called "Spanglish."[60]

THE ROLE OF THE CHURCH

Although Hispanics traditionally have been predominantly Catholic, millions of Hispanics are leaving the Catholic Church. It is estimated that about one in five Hispanics now practices some form of evangelical Protestantism. This change is ascribed to two factors: The evangelical Protestants have adopted sophisticated marketing techniques, such as providing local clergy with profiles of Hispanic communities in a campaign to convert large numbers of Hispanic Catholics, and the style of U.S. Catholicism is alien to many Hispanics. It tends to be more rational and bureaucratic and is not viewed by many as being responsive to the more emotional and mystical Hispanic religious experience. For example, the belief in miraculous healing that is prevalent in Latin American Catholicism does not tend to be emphasized in American Catholic churches.[61]

THE ROLE OF THE FAMILY

The importance of the family to Hispanics cannot be overstated. Preferences to spend time with family influence the structure of many consumption activities. As one illustration, the act of going to the movies has a different meaning for many Hispanics, who tend to regard this activity as a family outing. One study found that 42 percent of Hispanic moviegoers attend in groups of three or more, as compared with only 28 percent of Anglo consumers.[62]

Behaviors that underscore one's ability to provide well for the family are reinforced in this subculture. Clothing one's children well is regarded in particular as a matter of pride. In contrast, convenience and a product's ability to save time is not terribly important to the Hispanic homemaker, who is willing to purchase labor-intensive products if it means that her family will benefit.

For this reason, a time-saving appeal short-circuited for Quaker Foods, which found that Hispanic women tend to cook Instant Quaker Oats on the stove, as if it were regular oatmeal, refrigerate it, and serve it later as a pudding.[63] Similarly, telephone company promotions that emphasize cheaper rates for calling family members would offend many Hispanic consumers, who would view deterring a phone call home just to save money as an insult![64] This orientation also explains why generic products do not tend to do well in the Hispanic market; these consumers value the quality promised by well-known brand names.

The pervasiveness of the family theme can be seen in many marketing contexts. When Johnson Wax decided to enter the Hispanic market with Future floor polish, market research revealed that Hispanic consumers cleaned their floors regularly, but did not wax them. As a result of this finding, the company's television commercial depicted a homemaker standing on her dull floor while the voice-over asked, "We know your floors are clean, but do they shine?" Traditional gender roles are then reinforced as the husband leaps into the air, shouting *"resalta!"* (outstanding).[65]

LEVEL OF ACCULTURATION

One important way to distinguish among members of a subculture is to consider the extent to which they retain a sense of identification with their country of origin. **Acculturation** refers to the process of movement and adaptation to one country's cultural environment by a person from another country.[66]

This factor is especially important when considering the Hispanic market, because the degree to which these consumers are integrated into the American way of life varies widely. For instance, about 38 percent of all Hispanics live in *barrios,* or predominantly Hispanic neighborhoods, which tend to be somewhat insulated from mainstream society.[67] Table 14–1 describes a recent attempt to segment Hispanic consumers in terms of degree of acculturation.

The acculturation of Hispanic consumers may be understood in terms of the **progressive learning model.** This perspective assumes that people gradually learn a new culture as they increasingly come in contact with it. Thus, we would expect the consumer behavior of Hispanic Americans to be a mixture of practices taken from their original culture and those of the new or *host culture.*[68]

Research has generally obtained results that support this pattern when factors such as shopping orientation, the importance placed on various product attributes, media preference, and brand loyalty are examined.[69] When the intensity of ethnic identification is taken into account, consumers who retained a strong ethnic identification differed from their more assimilated counterparts in the following ways:[70]

- They had a more negative attitude toward business in general (probably caused by frustration due to relatively low income levels).
- They were higher users of Spanish-language media.
- They were more brand loyal.
- They were more likely to prefer brands with prestige labels.
- They were more likely to buy brands specifically advertised to their ethnic group.

TABLE 14–1 ■ Segmenting the Hispanic American Subculture by Degree of Acculturation

SEGMENT	SIZE	STATUS	DESCRIPTION	CHARACTERISTICS
Established adapters	17%	Upwardly mobile	Older, U.S. born; assimilated into U.S. culture	Relatively low identification with Hispanic culture
Young strivers	16%	Increasingly important	Younger, born in U.S.; highly motivated to succeed; adaptable to U.S. culture	Movement to reconnect with Hispanic roots
Hopeful loyalists	40%	Largest but shrinking	Working class; attached to traditional values	Slow to adapt to U.S. culture; Spanish is dominant language
Recent seekers	27%	Growing	Newest; very conservative with high aspirations	Strongest identification with Hispanic background; little use of non-Hispanic media

Source: Adapted from a report by Yankelovich Clancy Shulman, described in "A Subculture with Very Different Needs," *Adweek* (May 11, 1992): 44. By permission of Yankelovich Partners, Inc.

ATRAVESANDO FRONTERAS: CROSSING TO A NEW LIFE

For many Hispanics, *atravesando fronteras* (border crossings) are a part of life. Thousands of Mexican immigrants cross back and forth between their home country and the United States every year. These journeys highlight the complex processes by which people learn the ways of another culture and develop new patterns of consumption that combine existing practices with new ones, as immigrants forge new identities for themselves in a strange, yet not so strange, land.

Leaving one's culture and family to go to a new place creates many new needs and anxieties about fitting into a new environment. Recent immigrants (both legal and illegal) encounter a strange culture and have often left family members behind. This frightening odyssey was incorporated by AT&T in its campaign to boost international calling volume. In a Spanish-language commercial called "Countryside," a young man says goodbye to his mother and promises to keep in touch. The announcer says, "The decision of leaving the family is based on a promise: Keeping it united."

A recent study of language usage among Hispanics revealed an interesting finding: Although respondents preferred advertising that was in Spanish, the researchers also found that an ad that was done exclusively in Spanish actually created negative feelings. The researchers interpreted this finding to mean that exclusive usage of the Spanish language aroused perceivers' insecurities about fitting into mainstream Anglo culture, which "rubbed off" onto the brand being advertised.[71]

Another study, using the research technique of *ethnography,* probed into the ways that Mexican immigrants undergo an acculturation process as they adapt to life in the United States.[72] Interviews and observations of recent arrivals in natural settings revealed that immigrants feel a lot of ambivalence about their move. On the one hand, they are happy about the improvements in the quality of their lives due to greater job availability, educational opportunities for their children, and so on.

On the other hand, they report bittersweet feelings about leaving Mexico. They miss their friends, their holidays, their food, and the comfort that comes from living in familiar surroundings.

The nature of the transition process is affected by many factors, as shown in Figure 14–2. Individual differences, such as whether the person speaks English, influence how rocky the adjustment will be. The person's contact with **acculturation agents**—people and institutions that teach the ways of a culture, are also crucial. Some of these agents are aligned with the *culture of origin* (in this case, Mexico), including family, friends, the church, local businesses, and Spanish-language media that keep the consumer in touch with his or her country of origin. Other agents are associated with the *culture of immigration* (in this case, America), and help the consumer to learn how to navigate in the new environment. These include public schools, English-language media, and government agencies.

As immigrants adapt to their new surroundings, several processes come into play. *Movement* refers to the factors motivating people to physically uproot themselves from one location and go to another. In this case, people leave Mexico due to the scarcity of jobs and the desire to provide a good education for their children. On arrival, immigrants encounter a need for *translation*. This means attempting to master a set of rules for operating in the new environment, whether learning how to decipher a different currency or figuring out the social meanings of unfamiliar clothing styles. This cultural learning leads to a process of *adaptation,* by which new consumption patterns are formed. For example, some of the Mexican women interviewed started to wear shorts and pants since settling in the United States, although this practice is frowned upon in Mexico.

FIGURE 14–2 ■ A Model of Consumer Acculturation

Source: Adapted from Lisa Teñaloza, "*Atravesando Fronteras*/Border Crossings: Ac Critical Ethnographic Exploration of the Consumer Acculturation of Mexican Immigrants," *Journal of Consumer Research* 21 (June 1994) 1: 32–54. Reprinted by permission of The University of Chicago Press.

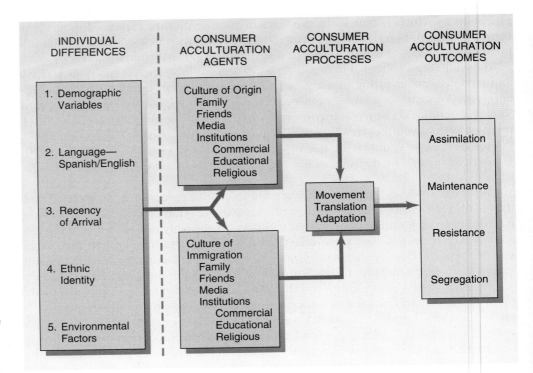

As consumers undergo acculturation, several things happen. Many immigrants undergo (at least to some extent) *assimilation,* whereby they adopt products, habits, and values that are identified with the mainstream culture. At the same time, there is an attempt at *maintenance* of practices associated with the culture of origin. Immigrants stay in touch with people in their country, and many continue to eat Spanish foods and read Spanish newspapers. Their continued identification with Mexican culture may cause *resistance,* as they resent the pressure to submerge their Mexican identities and take on new roles. Finally, immigrants (voluntarily or not) tend to exhibit *segregation;* they are likely to live and shop in places that are physically separated from mainstream Anglo consumers.

These processes illustrate that ethnicity is a fluid concept, and the boundaries of a subculture constantly are being recreated. An *ethnic pluralism* perspective argues that ethnic groups differ from the mainstream in varying degrees, and that adaptation to the larger society occurs selectively. Research evidence refutes the idea that assimilation necessarily involves losing identification with the person's original ethnic group. One study found, for example, that many French Canadians show a high level of acculturation, yet they still retain a strong ethnic affiliation. The best indicator of ethnic assimilation, these researchers argue, is the extent to which members of an ethnic group have social interactions with members of other groups in comparison to their own.[73]

ASIAN AMERICANS

Although their numbers are still relatively small, Asian Americans are the fastest-growing minority group in the United States. Marketers are just beginning to recognize their potential as a unique market segment, and some are beginning to adapt their products and messages to reach this group. For example, WonderBra launched a special line sized for a slimmer Asian body.[74]

This subculture is attractive to marketers because Asian Americans are typically hard working and many have above-average incomes. The average household incomes of Asian Americans are more than $2,000 greater than those of whites and $7,000 to $9,000 higher than those of African Americans and Hispanics. These consumers also place a very high priority on education and send a large percentage of children to college. Of Asian Americans over the age of 25, about a third have completed four or more years of college, twice the graduation rate of whites and more than quadruple that of African Americans and Hispanics.[75]

MARKETING PITFALL

Whereas many corporations are just now waking up to the potential of the Hispanic market, others that sell harmful products such as junk food, cigarettes, and alcohol discovered this market long ago. Critics point to a high concentration of liquor stores and related advertising in Hispanic neighborhoods. Available evidence indicates that Mexican-born men stand a greater chance of dying of cirrhosis of the liver and that Hispanic men are also more likely to die of lung cancer than are Anglos. The smoking rate of fourth- and fifth-grade Hispanic boys is roughly five times that of Anglo boys.[76] In many cities, community action groups and others have begun programs to reverse these trends.

SEGMENTING ASIAN AMERICANS

Despite its potential, this group is hard to market to, because it actually comprises subgroups that are culturally diverse and speak many different languages and dialects. The term Asian refers to 20 ethnic groups, with Chinese being the largest and Filipino and Japanese second and third, respectively.[77] Also, although their birth rate is increasing at almost four times the rate of most other groups, Asian Americans still comprise only about 2 percent of the population, so mass marketing techniques are often not viable to reach them.[78] Finally, Asian Americans save more of their wages and borrow less, preferring to keep large balances in conservative passbook accounts rather than investing their earnings.

On the other hand, as one Asian American advertising executive noted, "Prosperous Asians tend to be very status-conscious and will spend their money on premium brands, such as BMW and Mercedes-Benz, and the best French cognac and Scotch whiskey."[79] This group is also a good market for high-tech products. They spend more than average on products such as VCRs, personal computers, and compact disc players. Advertising that features Asian celebrities can be particularly effective. When Reebok used tennis star Michael Chang in one advertisement, shoe sales among Asian Americans soared.[80]

Long-distance phone companies have already recognized the value of the Asian American market segment. They spend more than $20 million annually on advertising in Asian languages. In a TV commercial, Sprint borrows the Monkey King, an all-wise character from Chinese folklore, to make its pitch. (Christy Fisher, "Marketers Straddle Asia-America Curtain," Advertising Age (November 7, 1994)(: S2 (2 pp.).

Another interesting aspect is that brand loyalty—especially to Asian brands—on the whole is low. In one survey of Chinese residents of San Francisco, a third of the respondents could not name the brand of laundry detergent they used.[81] Finally, these consumers also tend to be fairly conservative: Citibank had to drop a New Year's ad targeted to Chinese customers after people complained about the sexual innuendo of corks popping out of champagne bottles![82]

REACHING THE ASIAN AMERICAN CONSUMER

The problems encountered by American marketers when they first tried to reach the Hispanic market also occurred when targeting Asians and Asian Americans. Some attempts to translate advertising messages and concepts into Asian media have backfired. Coca-Cola's slogan, "Coke Adds Life" was translated as "Coke brings your ancestors back from the dead" in Japanese. One company did attempt to run an ad in Chinese to wish the community a Happy New Year, but the characters were upside down.

Other advertisements have overlooked the complex differences among Asian subcultures (e.g., some advertisements targeted to Koreans have used Japanese models), and some have unknowingly been insensitive to cultural practices. Kentucky Fried Chicken, for example, ran into a problem when it described its chicken as finger-licking good to the Chinese, who don't lick their fingers in appreciation when food is good.[83] In another case, a footwear ad depicted Japanese women performing foot binding, a practice done exclusively in China.[84]

Many marketers are discouraged by the lack of media available to reach Asian Americans.[85] Practitioners generally find that advertising in English works best for broadcast ads, whereas print ads are more effective when executed in Asian languages.[86] Filipinos are the only Asians who predominantly speak English among themselves; most Asians prefer media in their own languages.[87] The most frequently spoken languages among Asian Americans are Mandarin Chinese, Korean, Japanese, and Vietnamese.[88] In an attempt to reach these groups, Pacific Bell produces its brochures in three of these languages.

As with other racial and ethnic subcultures, a crop of new magazines is trying to capture younger Asian Americans. One new offering is *A. Magazine,* which is written for and about affluent Asian Americans aged 18 to 40.[89] Even mass retailer Sears is getting into the act: The company recently became the first major department store to formally target the Asian American market by hiring

MARKETING OPPORTUNITY

Real estate marketers who do business in areas with a high concentration of Asian American buyers are learning to adapt to some unique cultural traditions. Asians are very sensitive to the design and location of a home, especially as these aspects affect the home's *chi*—an invisible energy current that is believed to bring good or bad luck. Asian home buyers are concerned about whether a prospective house offers a good *feng shui* environment (translated literally as "the wind and the water").

One home developer in San Francisco sold up to 80 percent of its homes to Asian customers after making a few minor design changes, such as reducing the number of "T" intersections in the houses and adding rounded rocks to the yards—harmful *chi* travels in a straight line, whereas gentle *chi* travels on a curved path. It is not unusual for specialists to inspect a home or office to ensure that the *chi* is right before a purchase is transacted.[90]

an advertising agency to develop messages targeted to this segment.[91] Finally, the AsiaOne radio network was formed to provide national broadcasting in seven Asian languages.[92]

One of the first companies to realize the potential of the Asian American segment was the Metropolitan Life Insurance Company. Because Asian American consumers tend to be well educated and place a very high priority on education and security for their children, they seemed ideal prospects for insurance products. Qualitative research showed marked differences among Asian subsegments in their attitudes toward insurance. These differences paralleled those between Cuban Americans and Mexican Americans, in that subsegments' degrees of acculturation affect understanding and interest in products and services.

In general, Asians tend to be leery of buying insurance, superstitiously equating its purchase with old age and death. The company found that Chinese consumers emphasize family members' protection and education, so they were more likely to be interested in whole life policies. On the other hand, Vietnamese consumers, many of whom were recent immigrants, tended to be unfamiliar with the concept of insurance. Still, this group is seen as having potential because they are very survival oriented.[93] Based on this research, a Chinese ad campaign stressed the role of insurance in protecting children. As a reward for its efforts, Met Life increased its premiums among Asian Americans by 22 percent in one year.[94]

RELIGIOUS SUBCULTURES

The 1990s witnessed a resurgence of interest in religion and spirituality—including a spate of books, TV shows, and movies about angels. It seems fair to assert that spirituality is in fashion: IBM has ads featuring Catholic nuns and Eastern monks. Nissan uses an aging Asian hero and themes of Eastern mysticism in its marketing messages as the company proclaims, "Life is a Journey, Enjoy the Ride." When the San Diego Padres baseball team went through a losing streak, a campaign asked fans to "Keep the Faith" and the team resurrected its old mascot, a friar, on its new logo. TV spots introduced the "Gospel of Baseball" and since then attendance at Padres games has doubled—now there's a miracle![95]

Also, consider that spirituality oriented books are the fastest-growing segment in adult publishing. The United States now is home to about 400 "megachurches," each serving 2,000 or more congregants and bringing in a combined $1.85 billion annual income. Christian bookstores now make less than 40 percent of their sales in books and Bibles, as consumers buy up religion-oriented merchandise including apparel (such as a clothing line for born-again Christians called Witness Wear that sells over $1 million worth of apparel per year), framed art, and inspirational gifts.[96] In fact, sales of Christian merchandise now exceed $3 billion per year. Clearly, religion is big business.

THE IMPACT OF RELIGION ON CONSUMPTION

Religion per se has not been studied extensively in marketing, possibly because it is seen as a taboo subject.[97] However, the little evidence that has been accumulated indicates that religious affiliation has the potential to be a valuable predictor of consumer behavior.[98] Religious subcultures in particular may exert a significant impact on consumer variables such as personality, attitudes toward sexuality, birthrates and household formation, income, and political attitudes.

One study that examined this issue, for example, found marked differences among Catholic, Protestant, and Jewish college students in preferences for weekend entertainment activities, as well as the criteria used in making these decisions. Price was a relatively more important criterion for Protestants, whereas desire for companionship was highest for Jews. Catholics were most likely to designate dancing as a favored activity than were the other two groups, but much less likely to select sex.[99]

At least on paper, the United States is the most religious Western country. More than 90 percent of Americans say they believe in God, and more than 40 percent claim to have attended church services in a given week. However, recent data comparing reported attendance with actual head counts at services indicate a gap between attitudes and behavior—or at least, reported behavior. These findings show that about half the respondents who tell poll-takers that they go to church services on a regular basis are not telling the truth! Because most people believe that going to church is a socially desirable activity, they are likely to say they do it even when they don't.

A major survey on religious attitudes that included 113,000 respondents sheds some interesting light on the current state of American religions. The study reports that Catholics dominate the New England area, Baptists are pervasive in the South, and Lutherans concentrate in the upper Midwest. Nonbelievers (about 8 percent of American adults) are most likely to be found in the Pacific Northwest and in the Southwestern desert. This survey also highlights the emergence of new religious affiliations. For example, it found that there are more Scientologists than Fundamentalists, and it also found sizable numbers of followers of *wicca* (witchcraft) and New Age faiths.[100] Some of the demographic characteristics of many different religious subcultures are summarized in Figure 14–3.

THE CATHOLIC SUBCULTURE

Approximately one-quarter of Americans are Catholic.[101] The Catholic Church is characterized by a rigid organizational structure centered at the Vatican in Rome. Some observers have concluded that Catholic consumers tend to be fatalistic and are less likely to be innovators.

Catholics have more children than either Protestants or Jews. Officially, sex is seen as functional, in the sense that it is performed for the purpose of procreation rather than recreation. However, there is some evidence that this attitude is changing: As far back as 1975, 50 percent of Catholics endorsed the idea that a husband and wife may engage in sex for pleasure alone, as compared to only 29 percent who said this in 1965.[102]

Members of this religious group traditionally have a lower socioeconomic status than do Jews and Protestants. This deficit may stem from a variety of causes, including historical religious discrimination. Other factors include traditionalism, restricted knowledge seeking, and an emphasis on collective rather than individual initiative. As is the case with all religious subcultures, many of these dimensions are in flux, as younger Catholics search for ways to reconcile their faith with the demands of modern life. In general, more committed Catholics tend to retain a conservative orientation. For example, in a 1993 survey, observant Catholics were only half as likely to favor abortion rights as were all Catholics combined.[103]

THE PROTESTANT SUBCULTURE

About 10 percent of Americans identify themselves as Protestants, which includes members of the "mainline" denominations such as Episcopal, Methodist, Lutheran, and Presbyterian.[104] In contrast to the Catholic emphasis on hierarchy and insti-

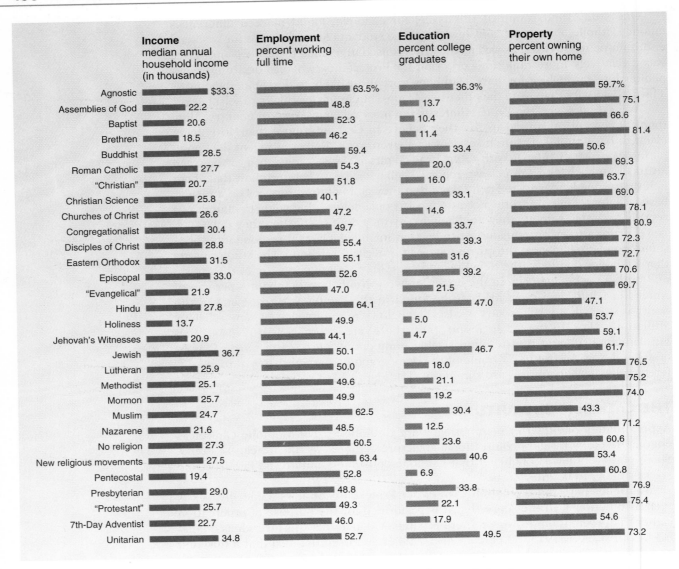

	Income median annual household income (in thousands)	Employment percent working full time	Education percent college graduates	Property percent owning their own home
Agnostic	$33.3	63.5%	36.3%	59.7%
Assemblies of God	22.2	48.8	13.7	75.1
Baptist	20.6	52.3	10.4	66.6
Brethren	18.5	46.2	11.4	81.4
Buddhist	28.5	59.4	33.4	50.6
Roman Catholic	27.7	54.3	20.0	69.3
"Christian"	20.7	51.8	16.0	63.7
Christian Science	25.8	40.1	33.1	69.0
Churches of Christ	26.6	47.2	14.6	78.1
Congregationalist	30.4	49.7	33.7	80.9
Disciples of Christ	28.8	55.4	39.3	72.3
Eastern Orthodox	31.5	55.1	31.6	72.7
Episcopal	33.0	52.6	39.2	70.6
"Evangelical"	21.9	47.0	21.5	69.7
Hindu	27.8	64.1	47.0	47.1
Holiness	13.7	49.9	5.0	53.7
Jehovah's Witnesses	20.9	44.1	4.7	59.1
Jewish	36.7	50.1	46.7	61.7
Lutheran	25.9	50.0	18.0	76.5
Methodist	25.1	49.6	21.1	75.2
Mormon	25.7	49.9	19.2	74.0
Muslim	24.7	62.5	30.4	43.3
Nazarene	21.6	48.5	12.5	71.2
No religion	27.3	60.5	23.6	60.6
New religious movements	27.5	63.4	40.6	53.4
Pentecostal	19.4	52.8	6.9	60.8
Presbyterian	29.0	48.8	33.8	76.9
"Protestant"	25.7	49.3	22.1	75.4
7th-Day Adventist	22.7	46.0	17.9	54.6
Unitarian	34.8	52.7	49.5	73.2

FIGURE 14–3 ■ **The Demographics of Religious Subcultures**
Source: Blumrich, "The Religious Pecking Order," *Newsweek* (November 29, 1993) 80. Copyright ©
1993 by Newsweek, Inc. All rights reserved. Reprinted by permission.

tional faith, Protestant dogma stresses the faith of the individual. This tradition
encourages the acquisition of secular knowledge. Protestants tend to value work and
personal hardship as an avenue toward upward social mobility.

While not all Protestants are wealthy, they appear in disproportionate numbers
in the upper classes. Explanations for this relative affluence include the following:[105]

- An emphasis on industriousness and hard work
- A low fertility rate that facilitates the upward mobility of children
- A U.S. social structure in which Protestants were historically part of the
  power elite

This controversial Benetton ad was rejected by some magazines because of what some perceived to be a disrespectful treatment of religion.

Fleeing religious oppression in Europe, early American colonists were overwhelmingly Protestant, which allowed this group to create the foundations of the American social system and thus create barriers to entry for other groups. The Protestant establishment still dominates leadership positions in the private sector and is also overrepresented in science, education, government, and the military.[106]

The "WASP" (White Anglo-Saxon Protestant) subculture may be thought of as the one ethnic group not acknowledged to be an ethnic group. After all, no one has yet used the term WASP American! Despite this ethnic invisibility, the WASP subculture has been the dominant force in the larger picture of American culture.[107] In fact, the WASP has been a symbol of the American ideal for some time. For many immigrants, the WASP still symbolizes the light at the end of the tunnel: If one desires to assimilate, to make it in America, the WASP is the model.

As a result of this idealized view of the WASP milieu, many of its customs, activities, and values have set the standard in American culture. The formal eating rituals devised by WASPs and propagated by etiquette guides such as Emily Post's are assumed to be the "proper" way to eat and entertain. The leisure activities associated with this subculture (e.g., golfing, yachting, squash) often are seen as socially

MARKETING PITFALL

There are mixed feelings in the Catholic community about the spread of religious imagery in popular culture. On the one hand, the Vatican Museum recently opened its first boutique outside Vatican walls and is now selling silk ties and scarves designed for the Vatican by Salvatore Ferragamo.[108] On the other hand, an ad in a Danish campaign for the French car manufacturer Renault had to be withdrawn after protests from the Catholic community. The ad described a dialogue during confession between a Catholic priest and a repenting man. The man atones for his sins by praying *Ave Maria*s until he confesses to having scratched the paint of the priest's new Renault—then the priest shouts "heathen" and orders the man to pay a substantial penalty to the church.[109]

superior.[110] Marketers have done more than their share to propagate this ideal. Idealized images of the WASP are frequently employed in advertising to epitomize the good life and the amenities associated with old money (see chapter 13).

THE BORN-AGAIN SUBCULTURE

Recent years have seen a dramatic increase in the number of consumers who profess to be born-again Christians, or evangelicals. A Gallup Poll indicates that one-third of American adults say they are born again. Although this movement has reached a variety of social classes and consumer types, it is strongest among women, older adults, and Southerners. It is also a relatively downscale phenomenon: The number of adults who describe themselves as being "born again" steadily decreases as education and income levels rise.[111]

Nevertheless, the born-again movement is exerting a significant impact on American marketing as well as on *demarketing,* which is the discouraging of demand for certain products and services. This community has been influential in altering the content of media programming and advertising that is seen to unduly emphasize sex and violence. It also encourages patronage of local businesses owned by born-agains by encouraging the use of Christian Directories that limit their listings to members of the flock.

The evidence is unclear as to whether the consumption behavior of born-again Christians is radically different from that of other subcultures. In general, these consumers are more likely to endorse traditional sex-role orientations, to be below-average users of credit, and to place relatively low emphasis on purchasing national brands. They are also not as likely as the general public to listen to rock-and-roll music (perhaps due to a perceived emphasis on sex and drugs), preferring gospel and contemporary Christian music. There are no differences in terms of activities such as eating out or attending concerts, but born-again Christians do attend movies less frequently than do other groups.[112]

Christian broadcast media have become a powerful cultural force for many consumers. Approximately 12 percent of all U.S. radio stations have a religious format. In fact, religious programming is now the third most popular kind in the United States. In addition, about 200 local television stations regularly feature religious programming, and television preachers have an estimated audience of over 15 million people. This number represents almost the combined memberships of the United Methodist, Presbyterian, and Episcopal denominations.[113]

THE JEWISH SUBCULTURE

Jewish ethnicity exerts an exceptionally strong influence, because it incorporates both cultural and religious dimensions. American Jews tend to be of relatively high socioeconomic status and average family size is relatively low (with the exception of some Orthodox groups). Although this subculture is well represented in business and the arts, less than 2 percent of the American population is Jewish.[114]

Judaism reinforces individual responsibility for actions and self-education.[115] Jewish consumers have a personality structure characterized by emotionality, individualism, and need for achievement.[116] One study of Jewish versus gentile consumers indeed found that the Jewish respondents were more likely to have been exposed to educational materials in childhood, to use more sources in the process of information search, to be product innovators, and to transfer more consumption information to others.[117]

Some marketers have specifically employed Jewish symbolism in their advertising campaigns. This ad for Sun Maid provides an example of this strategy. The Bank Leumi Trust Company of New York, an Israel-based bank, capitalized on its ethnic ties to try to reach Jewish and gentile customers with the following ad copy used to promote individual retirement accounts: "Some people need a little help getting to the Promised Land. If you dream of retiring to a land of milk and honey, you're going to need plenty of bread." One famous campaign for a bakery company used Chinese, African American, and other spokesmen to tell consumers, "You don't have to be Jewish to love Levy's real Jewish Rye."

THE MUSLIM SUBCULTURE

There are between 3 and 4 million Muslims in America. Although many people equate this subculture with Arabs, the two are not the same. The term Arab refers to an ethnic identity, whereas Muslim is a religious affiliation. Not all Arabs are Muslims, and not all Muslims are Arabs: In fact, one in four Muslims is black. The

MARKETING OPPORTUNITY

One of the most significant Jewish-related marketing developments is the increase in demand for kosher food. Each year, about 500 new kosher products appear on the market to satisfy this demand. This trend is being driven by two developments: The increased religious observance by young Jews, and the belief among many gentiles that kosher food is of higher quality. Seventh-Day Adventists and Muslims have very similar dietary requirements and are good customers for kosher food.[118] It is estimated that less than a third of the 6 million consumers who buy kosher products are Jewish.[119]

The potential of the kosher market has prompted some of the nation's largest manufacturers to get involved. Wise Potato Chips produces kosher chips, and Eagle Snacks also makes kosher snack foods. Of the 330 products made by Pepperidge Farm, Inc., 255 are now kosher.[120] Manischewitz, Inc. has launched about 50 new kosher products including fat-free matzo chips, bagel pretzels, and minestrone soup.[121] In a new twist, one small firm is even selling kosher lipstick—Carmine, a commonly used red pigment, turns out to be nonkosher because it is made from the crushed exoskeletons of insects, a food forbidden to observant Jews![122]

number of people who claim affiliation with this religious subculture is growing; it has been estimated that American Muslims could outnumber American Presbyterians by the year 2000. There are over 1,100 mosques in the United States.

Muslims tend to be conservative, and like many of the other subcultures discussed in this chapter they value a close-knit family structure. The family is the ultimate authority, and bad acts performed by an individual are seen as a reflection on the entire family unit. At this point very little is done by major marketers to target this subculture, though this situation may change as its numbers increase.[123] Certainly, the observance of traditional Islamic practice is growing around the world—stores in the Middle East with names such as High Couture and Propriety and Proper Guidance for Women are springing up to offer fashionable, but Islamically correct, clothing. A shopping mall in Cairo, Egypt even boasts a shopping mall called the Salaam Center for Veiled Women.[124]

- Consumers identify with many groups that share common characteristics and identities. These large groups that exist within a society are *subcultures,* and membership in them often gives marketers a valuable clue about individuals' consumption decisions. A large component of a person's identity is often determined by his or her ethnic origins, racial identity, and religious background. The three largest ethnic/racial subcultures are African Americans, Hispanic Americans, and Asian Americans, but consumers with many diverse backgrounds are beginning to be considered by marketers as well. Indeed, the growing numbers of people who claim multiethnic backgrounds is beginning to blur the traditional distinctions drawn among these subcultures.

- Recently, several minority groups have caught the attention of marketers as their economic power has grown. Segmenting consumers by their *ethnicity* can be effective, but care must be taken not to rely on inaccurate (and sometimes offensive) ethnic stereotypes.

- African Americans are a very important market segment. In some respects the market expenditures of these consumers do not differ that much from whites, but blacks are above-average consumers in such categories as personal care products. In the past, blacks were either ignored or portrayed negatively in mainstream advertising, but such depictions are changing as more blacks actually work on the development of campaigns and as specialized black media increase in importance.

- Hispanic Americans and Asian Americans are other ethnic subcultures that are beginning to be actively courted by marketers. The sizes of both groups are increasing rapidly and in the coming years one or the other will dominate some major markets. Asian Americans on the whole are extremely well educated, and the socioeconomic status of Hispanics is increasing as well.

- Key issues for reaching the Hispanic market are consumers' degree of *acculturation* into mainstream American society and the recognition of important cultural differences among Hispanic subgroups (e.g., Puerto Ricans, Cubans, Mexicans).

- Both Asian Americans and Hispanic Americans tend to be extremely family oriented and are receptive to advertising that understands their heritage and reinforces traditional family values.

- While the impact of religious identification on consumer behavior is not clear, some differences among religious subcultures do emerge. In particular, cultural characteristics of Catholics, Protestants, and Jews result in varied preferences for leisure activities and orientations toward consumption. Some of these factors are closely related to social class. White Anglo-Saxon Protestants (WASPs) in particular have played a dominant role in the formation of American cultural values largely due to their cultural emphasis on achievement and early domination of the American power structure.

- The market power of the growing numbers of Muslims and born-again Christians is uncertain at this point, but opportunities exist to cater to the unique needs of these segments.

KEY TERMS

Acculturation p. 450
Acculturation agents p. 452
De-ethnicitization p. 440

Ethnic subculture p. 438
Progressive learning model
  p. 450

Racial subculture p. 438
Subcultures p. 437

CONSUMER BEHAVIOR CHALLENGE

1. R.J. Reynolds' controversial plan to test-market a cigarette to black consumers raises numerous ethical issues about segmenting subcultures. As one observer noted, "The irony is that if R.J. Reynolds made shoes or shirts and specifically marketed to blacks, they would probably be regarded as progressive and socially positive."[125] Does a company have the right to exploit a subculture's special characteristics, especially to increase sales of a harmful product like cigarettes? What about the argument that virtually every business that follows the marketing concept designs a product to meet the needs and tastes of a preselected segment?

2. Describe the progressive learning model and discuss why this phenomenon is important when marketing to subcultures.

3. Born-again Christian groups have been instrumental in organizing boycotts of products advertised on shows they find objectionable, especially those that they feel undermine family values. Do consumer groups have a right or a responsibility to dictate the advertising a network should carry?

4. Can you locate any current examples of marketing stimuli that depend on an ethnic stereotype to communicate a message? How effective are these appeals?

5. To understand the power of ethnic stereotypes, conduct your own poll. For a set of ethnic groups, ask people to anonymously provide attributes (including personality traits and products) most likely to characterize each group using the technique of free association. How much agreement do you obtain across respondents? To what extent do the characteristics derive from or reflect negative stereotypes? Compare the associations for an ethnic group between actual members of that group and nonmembers.

6. African American singer Gladys Knight took a lot of heat for agreeing to serve as a spokesperson for the Aunt Jemima brand. One commentator said, "You have a famous black singer perpetuating the stereotypes that go along with the trademark. . . ." On the other hand, the singer stated, "What matters to me is what's inside the box. I'm simply saying, 'This is a good product.' "[126] Which side do you take, and why?

7. Locate one or more consumers (perhaps family members) who have immigrated from another country. Interview them about how they adapted to their host culture. In particular, what changes did they make in their consumption practices over time?

NOTES

1. Michael Meyer, "Los Angeles 2010: A Latino Subcontinent," *Newsweek* (November 9, 1992): 32.

2. "The Numbers Game," *Time* (Fall 1993): 17.

3. Erik Davis, "tlhIngan Hol Dajatlh'a' [Do You Speak Klingon?]," *Utne Reader* (March/April 1994): 122–9; additional material provided by personal communication, Prof. Robert V. Kozinets, Northwestern University, October 1997, and adapted from Philip Kotler, Gary Armstrong, Peggy H. Cunningham, and Robert Warren, *Principles of Marketing: Third Canadian Edition* (Scarborough, Ontario: Prentice Hall Canada, 1997): 96.

4. See Frederik Barth, *Ethnic Groups and Boundaries: The Social Organization of Culture Difference* (London: Allen and Unwin, 1969); Janeen A. Costa and Gary J. Bamossy, "Perspectives on Ethnicity, Nationalism, and Cultural Identity," in J.A. Costa and G.J. Bamossy (eds.), *Marketing in a Multicultural World: Ethnicity, Nationalism, and Cultural Identity* (Thousand Oaks, CA: Sage Publications, Inc., 1995): 3–26; Michel Laroche, Annamma Joy, Michael Hui, and Chankon Kim, "An Examination of Ethnicity Measures: Convergent Validity and Cross-Cultural Equivalence," in *Advances in Consumer Research* 18, ed. Rebecca H. Holman and Michael R. Solomon (Provo, Utah: Association for Consumer Research, 1991): 150–157; Melanie Wallendorf and Michael Reilly, "Ethnic Migration, Assimilation, and Consumption," *Journal of Consumer Research* 10 (December 1983): 292–302; Milton J. Yinger, Ethnicity, *Annual Review of Sociology* 11 (1985): 151–80.

5. Thomas McCarroll, "It's a Mass Market No More," *Time* (Fall 1993): 80–1.

6. Rohit Desphandé and Douglas M. Stayman, "A Tale of Two Cities: Distinctiveness Theory and Advertising Effectiveness," *Journal of Marketing Research* 31 (February 1994): 57–64.

7. Steve Rabin, "How to Sell across Cultures," *American Demographics* (March 1994): 56–7.

8. Yumiko Ono, "Marketers Whip up Weird Ethnic Blends," *Wall Street Journal* (November 9, 1994): B1.

9. John Leland and Gregory Beals, "In Living Colors," *Newsweek* (May 5, 1997): 58 (3 pp.).

10. John McCormick, "In Living Color," *Newsweek* (May 5, 1997): 58 (2 pp).

11. Linda Mathews, "More than Identity Rides on a New Racial Category," *New York Times* (July 6, 1996): 1, 7.

12. Gabrielle Sándor, "The 'Other' Americans," *American Demographics* (June 1994): 36–40.

13. Richard Melcher, "United Colors of Miller," *Business Week* (May 19, 1997): 96.

14. Steven A. Holmes, "Federal Government is Rethinking Its System of Racial Classification," *New York Times* (July 8, 1994): A18; Mike McNamee, "Should the Census be Less Black and White?" *Business Week* (July 4, 1994): 40; Sándor, "The 'Other' Americans."

15. Eils Lotozo, "The Jalapeno Bagel and Other Artifacts," *New York Times* (June 26, 1990): C1.

16. Dana Canedy, "The Shmeering of America," *New York Times* (December 26, 1996): D1 (2 pp.).

17. Quoted in Cara S. Trager, "Goya Foods Tests Mainstream Market's Waters," *Advertising Age* (February 9, 1987): S20.

18. Molly O'Neill, "New Mainstream: Hot Dogs, Apple Pie and Salsa," *New York Times* (March 11, 1992): C1.

19. Tom Morganthau, "The Face of the Future," *Newsweek* (January 27, 1997): 58 (3 pp.).

20. Robert Pear, "New Look at the U.S. in 2050; Bigger, Older and Less White," *New York Times* (December 4, 1992): A1.

21. Shelly Reese, "When Whites *Aren't* a Mass Market," *American Demographics* (March 1997): 51–4.

22. Thomas McCarroll, "It's a Mass Market No More," *Time* (Fall 1993): 80–1.

23. Marty Westerman, "Death of the Frito Bandito," *American Demographics* (March 1989): 28.

24. Betsy Sharkey, "Beyond Tepees and Totem Poles," *New York Times* (June 11, 1995): H1 (2 pp.); Paula Schwartz, "It's a Small World . . . and Not Always P.C.," *New York Times* (June 11, 1995): H22.

25. Quoted in Peter Schrag, *The Decline of the WASP* (New York: Simon and Schuster, 1971): 20.

26. Karyn D. Collins, "Culture Clash," *The Asbury Park Press* (October 16, 1994): D1 (2 pp.).

27. Marcia Mogelonsky, "Asian-Indian Americans," *American Demographics* (August 1995): 32–8.

28. William O'Hare, "Blacks and Whites: One Market or Two?" *American Demographics* (March 1987): 44–48.

29. For studies on racial differences in consumption, see Robert E. Pitts, D. Joel Whalen, Robert O'Keefe, and Vernon Murray, "Black and White Response to Culturally Targeted Television Commercials: A Values-based Approach," *Psychology & Marketing* 6 (Winter 1989): 311–28; Melvin T. Stith and Ronald E. Goldsmith, "Race, Sex, and Fashion Innovativeness: A Replication," *Psychology & Marketing* 6 (Winter 1989): 249–62.

30. Monroe Anderson, "Advertising's Black Magic Helping Corporate America Tap a Lucrative Market," *Newsweek* (February 10, 1986): 60.

31. Fred Thompson, "Blacks Spending Potential up 54 Percent since 1990," *Montgomery Advertiser* (May 9, 1997): 1.

32. Bob Jones, "Black Gold," *Entrepreneur* (July 1994): 62–5.

33. Brad Edmonson, "Black Markets," *American Demographics* (November 1987): 20; O'Hare, "Blacks and Whites"; "Older Products Look to Blacks for Rejuvenated Sales Growth," *Wall Street Journal* (February 28, 1985): 1.

34. Robert E. Wilkes and Humberto Valencia, "Hispanics and Blacks in Television Commercials," *Journal of Advertising* 18 (Winter 1989): 19.

35. "Plans for Test Marketing Cigarette Canceled," *The Asbury Park Press* (January 1990): 20; Anthony Ramirez, "A Cigarette Campaign Under Fire," *New York Times* (January 12, 1990): D1; Brad Bennett, "Smoke Signals," *The Asbury Park Press* (July 24, 1994): AA1 (2 pp.).

36. Alvin P. Sanoff, "TV's Disappearing Color Line," *U.S. News & World Report* (July 13, 1987): 56.

37. W. Franklyn Joseph, "Blacks' Ambition Enters the Picture," *Advertising Age* (March 14, 1985): 26.

38. Marie Spadoni, "Marketing to Blacks How Media Segment the Target Audience," *Advertising Age* (November 19, 1984): 43.

39. Michael E. Ross, "At Newsstands, Black is Plentiful," *New York Times* (December 26, 1993): F6.

40. Eleena DeLisser, "Romance Books Get Novel Twist and Go Ethnic," *Wall Street Journal* (September 6, 1994): B1 (2 pp.).

41. Alice Z. Cuneo, "New Sears Label Woos Black Women," *Ad Age* (May 5, 1997): 6; Cyndee Miller, "Catalogers Learn to Take Blacks Seriously," *Marketing News* (March 13, 1995): 8.

42. Westerman, "Death of the Frito Bandito."

43. Michael Janofsky, "A Commercial by Nike Raises Concerns about Hispanic Stereotypes," *New York Times* (July 13, 1993): D19.

44. Kelly Shermach, "Infomercials for Hispanics," *Marketing News* (March 17, 1997): 1 (2 pp.).

45. Kim Foltz, "Mattel's Shift on Barbie Ads," *New York Times* (July 19, 1990): D17; Lora Sharpe, "Dolls in All the Colors of a Child's Dream," *Boston Globe* (February 22, 1991): 42; Barbara Brotman, "Today's Dolls Have Ethnicity That's More Than Skin Deep," *The Asbury Park Press* (November 14, 1993): D6.

46. Roberto Maso-Fleischman, "The Grandmother: A Powerful Symbol for Hispanic Women," *Marketing News* (February 3, 1997): 13–14.

47. Beth Enslow, "General Mills: Baking New Ground," *Forecast* (November/December 1993): 18 (3 pp.).

48. Joe Schwartz, "Hispanic Opportunities," *American Demographics* (May 1987): 56–9.

49. Schwartz, "Hispanic Opportunities."

50. Naveen Donthu and Joseph Cherian, "Impact of Strength of Ethnic Identification on Hispanic Shopping Behavior," *Journal of Retailing* 70 (1994)4: 383–93. For another study that compared shopping behavior and ethnicity influences among six ethnic groups, see Joel Herce and Siva Balasubramanian, "Ethnicity and Shopping Behavior," *Journal of Shopping Center Research* 1 (Fall 1994): 65–80.

51. Howard LaFranchi, "Media and Marketers Discover Hispanic Boom," *Christian Science Monitor* (April 20, 1988): 1.

52. Joe Schwartz, "Rising Status," *American Demographics* (January 10, 1989).

53. " 'Cultural Sensitivity' Required When Advertising to Hispanics," *Marketing News* (March 19, 1982): 45.

54. Schwartz, "Rising Status."

55. David J. Wallace, "How to Sell Yucas to YUCAs," *Advertising Age* (February 13, 1989): 5–6; "1994 Survey of Buying Power," *Sales & Marketing Management* (August 30, 1994): A9.

56. Schwartz, "Hispanic Opportunities."

57. "Dispel Myths before Trying to Penetrate Hispanic Market," *Marketing News* (April 16, 1982): 1.

58. Schwartz, "Hispanic Opportunities."

59. Brad Edmondson, "Mexican Soap," *American Demographics* (January 1989): 18.

60. Andrea Gerlin, "Radio Stations Gain by Going after Hispanics," *Wall Street Journal* (July 18, 1993): B1 (2 pp.).

61. Roberto Suro, "Switch by Hispanic Catholics Changes Face of U.S. Religion," *New York Times* (May 14, 1989): 1.

62. " 'Cultural Sensitivity' Required When Advertising to Hispanics".

63. Westerman, "Death of the Frito Bandito."

64. Stacy Vollmers and Ronald E. Goldsmith, "Hispanic-American Consumers and Ethnic Marketing," *Proceedings of the Atlantic Marketing Association* (1993): 46–50.

65. Kristine Stiven, "Educational Approach Shines," *Advertising Age* (February 13, 1989): S10.

66. See Lisa Peñaloza, "Atravesando Fronteras/Border Crossings: A Critical Ethnographic Exploration of the Consumer Acculturation of Mexican Immigrants," *Journal of Consumer Research* 21 (June 1994)1: 32–54.

67. Sigfredo A. Hernandez and Carol J. Kaufman, "Marketing Research in Hispanic Barrios: A Guide to Survey Research," *Marketing Research* (March 1990): 11–27.

68. Melanie Wallendorf and Michael D. Reilly, "Ethnic Migration, Assimilation, and Consumption," *Journal of Consumer Research* 10 (December 1983): 292–302.

69. Ronald J. Faber, Thomas C. O'Guinn, and John A. McCarty, "Ethnicity, Acculturation and the Importance of Product Attributes," *Psychology & Marketing* 4 (Summer 1987): 121–34; Humberto Valencia, "Developing an Index to Measure Hispanicness," in eds. Elizabeth C. Hirschman and Morris B. Holbrook, *Advances in Consumer Research* 12 (Provo: Association for Consumer Research, 1985); 118–21.

70. Rohit Deshpande, Wayne D. Hoyer, and Naveen Donthu, "The Intensity of Ethnic Affiliation: A Study of the Sociology of Hispanic Consumption," *Journal of Consumer Research* 13 (September 1986): 214–20.

71. Scott Koslow, Prem N. Shamdasani, and Ellen E. Touchstone, "Exploring Language Effects in Ethnic Advertising: A Sociolinguistic Perspective," *Journal of Consumer Research* 20 (March 1994)4: 575–85.

72. Peñaloza, "Atravesando Fronteras/Border Crossings."

73. Michael Laroche, Chankon Kim, Michael K. Hui, and Annamma Joy, "An Empirical Study of Multi-dimensional Ethnic Change: The Case of the French Canadians in Quebec," *Journal of Cross-Cultural Psychology* 27 (January 1996)1: 114–31.

74. Dorinda Elliott, "Objects of Desire," *Newsweek* (February 12, 1996): 41.

75. Richard Kern, "The Asian Market: Too Good to Be True?" *Sales & Marketing Management* (May 1988): 38; Joo Gim Heaney and Ronald E. Goldsmith, "The Asian-American Market Segment: Opportunities and Challenges," *Association of Marketing Theory and Practice* (Spring 1993): 260–5; Betsy Wiesendanger, "Asian-Americans: The Three Biggest Myths," *Sales & Marketing Management* (September 1993): 86 (4 pp.).

76. Fernando Gonzalez, "Study Finds Alcohol, Cigarette Makers Target Hispanics," *Boston Globe* (November 23, 1989): A11.

77. Donald Dougherty, "The Orient Express," *The Marketer* (July/August 1990): 14; Cyndee Miller, " 'Hot' Asian-American Market Not Starting Much of a Fire Yet," *Marketing News* (January 21, 1991): 12.

78. Kern, "The Asian Market."

79. Quoted in Dougherty, "The Orient Express."14.

80. Miller, " 'Hot' Asian-Market Not Starting Much of a Fire Yet."

81. Wiesendanger, "Asian-Americans."

82. McCarroll, "It's a Mass Market No More."

83. Marty Westerman, "Fare East: Targeting the Asian-American Market," *Prepared Foods* (January 1989): 48–51.

84. Eleanor Yu, "Asian-American Market Often Misunderstood," *Marketing News* (December 4, 1989): 11.

85. Marianne Paskowski, "Trailblazing in Asian America," *Marketing and Media Decisions* (October 1986): 75–80.

86. Ellen Schultz, "Asians in the States," *Madison Avenue* (October 1985): 78.

87. Dougherty, "The Orient Express."

88. Westerman, "Fare East: Targeting the Asian-American Market."

89. "A Window on the Fast-Growing Audience of Asian-Americans," *New York Times* (March 22, 1993): D5; Elizabeth Seay, "Two English-Speaking Magazines Target Affluent Asian-Americans," *Wall Street Journal* (October 1, 1993): B5B.

90. Dan Fost, "Asian Homebuyers Seek Wind and Water," *American Demographics* (June 1993): 23–5.

91. Jeanne Whalen, "Sears Targets Asians: Retailer Names Agency to Attract Fast-Growing Segment," *Advertising Age* (October 10, 1994): 1 (2 pp.).

92. "Radio Network Targets Asian-Americans," *Marketing News* (August 29, 1994): 46.

93. Paskowski, "Trailblazing in Asian America."

94. John Schwartz and Dorothy Wang, "Tapping into a Blossoming Asian Market: The Pull of Ethnic Ties," *Newsweek* (September 7, 1987): 47.

95. Jennifer Harrison, "Advertising Joins the Journey of the Soul," *American Demographics* (June 1997): 22 (5 pp.).

96. Tim W. Ferguson and Josephine Lee, "Spiritual Reality," Forbes (January 27, 1997): 70 (4 pp.); Catherine Dressler, "Holy Socks! This Line Sends a Christian Message," *Marketing News* (February 12, 1996): 5.

97. Elizabeth C. Hirschman, "Religious Affiliation and Consumption Processes: An Initial Paradigm," *Research in Marketing* (Greenwich, CT: JAI Press, 1983): 131–70.

98. See, for example, Nejet Delener, "The Effects of Religious Factors on Perceived Risk in Durable Goods Purchase Decisions," *Journal of Consumer Marketing* 7 (Summer 1990): 27–38.

99. Hirschman, "Religious Affiliation and Consumption Processes."

100. Kenneth L. Woodward, "The Rites of Americans," *Newsweek* (November 29, 1993): 80 (3 pp.).

101. "The Numbers Game."

102. Andrew M. Greeley, *The American Catholic* (New York: Basic Books, 1977).

103. Woodward, "The Rites of Americans."

104. "The Numbers Game."

105. C. Wright Mills, *The Power Elite* (New York: Oxford University Press, 1956).

106. Kenneth R. Hardy, "Social Origins of American Scientists and Scholars," *Science* (September 9, 1975): 497–506; Hirschman, "Religious Affiliation and Consumption Processes"; Stanley Verba and Norman H. Nie, *Participation in America: Political Democracy and Social Equality* (New York: Harper & Row, 1972).

107. Peter Schrag, *The Decline of the Wasp* (New York: Simon & Schuster, 1971): 14.

108. "Vatican Opens Boutique Outside Walls," *Montgomery Advertiser* (June 10, 1996): 4A.

109. Markedsføring, 10, 1996, p.22; adapted from Michael R. Solomon, Gary Bamossy, and Soren Askegaard, *Consumer Behavior: A European Perspective* (London: Prentice Hall International, 1998).

110. Elizabeth C. Hirschman, "Upper-Class WASPs as Consumers: A Humanist Inquiry," in eds. Jagdish N. Sheth and Elizabeth C. Hirschman, *Research in Consumer Behavior,* (Greenwich, CT: JAI Press, 1988): 115–48.

111. Brad Edmondson, "Bringing in the Sheaves,"(August 1988): 28.

112. Priscilla LaBarbera, "Consumer Behavior and Born Again Christianity," in eds. Sheth and Hirschman, *Research in Consumer Behavior* 1988: 193–222.

113. LaBarbera, "Consumer Behavior and Born Again Christianity"; Robert Ostling, "Power, Glory and Politics," *Time* (February 17, 1986): 62–9; James B. Kelleher, "Christian Radio Stations, Riding a Wave of Change, Keep Their Popularity," *New York Times* (January 10, 1994): D6.

114. "The Numbers Game."

115. Elizabeth C. Hirschman, "American Jewish Ethnicity: Its Relationship to Some Selected Aspects of Consumer Behavior," *Journal of Marketing* 45 (Summer 1981): 102–10.

116. Hirschman, "Religious Affiliation and Consumption Processes."

117. Hirschman, "American Jewish Ethnicity."

118. Isadore Barmash, "The Drive to Promote Kosher Food," *New York Times* (April 11, 1989): D25.

119. Joan Delaney, "New Kosher Products, from Tacos to Tofu," *New York Times* (December 31, 1989): F13.

120. Delaney, "New Kosher Products, from Tacos to Tofu."

121. Joshua Levine, "You Don't Have to be Jewish ..." Forbes (April 24, 1995): 154 (2 pp.).

122. "Kiss Me, You Kosher Fool," *American Demographics* (May 1994): 17–18.

123. "Understanding Islam in America," *American Demographics* (January 1994): 10.

124. Amy Djockers Marcus, "Veils are Fashion Statement, Not Just a Religious Thing," *Wall Street Journal Interactive Edition* (May 1, 1997).

125. "A Cigarette Campaign under Fire," *New York Times* (January 12, 1990): D1.

126. Quoted in "Knight Knocked," *The Asbury Park Press* (October 3, 1994): A2.

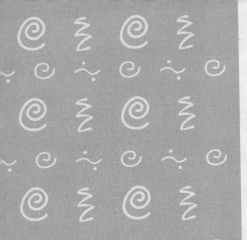

IT'S THE LAST WEEK OF SUMMER VACATION, and Brandon is looking forward to going back to college. It's been a tough summer. He had trouble finding a summer job and seemed to be out of touch with his old friends—and with so much time on his hands just hanging around the house, he and his mother weren't getting along too well. As usual, Brandon is plopped on the couch, aimlessly flipping channels—from *The Grind* on MTV, to *Bewitched* on Nickelodeon, to a Sony beach volleyball tournament on ESPN, back to MTV. . . . Suddenly, Mrs. Boyd walks in, grabs the remote, and switches the channel to public television. Yet another documentary is on about Woodstock (the original one, way back in 1969. . .). When Brandon protests, "Come on Jackie, get a life. . ." his mom snaps back, "Keep your cool. You might actually learn about what it was like to be in college when it really meant something. And what's with the first name stuff? In my day I would never have dreamed of calling my mom or dad by their first name!"

That's when Brandon loses it. He's tired of hearing about the "good old days" of Woodstock, Berkeley, and 20 other places he doesn't care about. Besides, most of his mom's ex-hippie friends now work for the very corporations they used to protest about—who are they to preach to him about doing something meaningful with his life? Because they'd screwed up the economy so much, he'll be lucky to get a job as a bicycle messenger when he finally gets his degree next year.

In disgust, Brandon storms into his room, puts a Prodigy CD into his Discman, and pulls the covers up over his head. So much for a constructive use of time. What's the difference, anyway—they'll probably all be dead from the "greenhouse effect" by the time he graduates . . . .

Tracy in NYC. She said if she spits her gum out from up here and it hit someone below, the force would totally split them in half.

Age
Subcultures

AGE AND CONSUMER IDENTITY

The era in which a consumer is born creates for that person a cultural bond with the millions of others born during the same time period. As we grow older, our needs and preferences changes, often in concert with others who are close to our own age. For this reason, a consumer's age exerts a significant influence on his or her identity. All things being equal, we are more likely to have things in common with others of our own age than not. As Brandon found out, this identity may become even stronger when the actions and goals of one generation conflict with those of others—an age-old battle.

A marketer needs to recognize this, and to figure out how to communicate with members of an age group in their own language. For example, Sony finally figured out that it had to sponsor events like beach volleyball to get the attention of young people. When the electronics giant first entered the U.S. car stereo market, it simply hammered on its usual themes of technical prowess and quality. This got nothing but yawns from the 16- to 24-year-olds who make up half of the consumers who buy these products, and Sony ranked a pitiful seventh in the market after ten years. Finally, the company got the picture—it totally revamped its approach and by 1997 car stereo revenues had more than doubled.[1] In this chapter, we'll explore some of the important characteristics of some key age groups, and consider how marketing strategies must be modified to appeal to diverse age subcultures.

AGE COHORTS: "MY GENERATION"

An **age cohort** consists of people of similar ages who have undergone similar experiences. They share many common memories about cultural heroes (e.g., John Wayne versus Brad Pitt, or Frank Sinatra versus Kurt Cobain), important historical events (e.g., the 1969 moon landing versus the 1997 Mars mission), and so on. Although there is no universally accepted way to divide up people into age cohorts, each of us seems to have a pretty good idea of what we mean when we refer to "my generation." Figure 15–1 presents one reasonable scheme for defining generations.

Marketers often target products and services to one or more specific age cohorts. As shown in Figure 15–2, although middle-aged people make the most money, there's plenty of market potential attached to other age groups as well. The same offering will probably not appeal to people of different ages, nor will the language and images used to reach them. In some cases separate campaigns are developed to attract consumers of different ages. For example, Norelco found that younger men are far less likely to use electric shavers than are its core customer

THE DEPRESSION COHORT
(the G.I. generation)

Born 1912–21   Age in '95: 74 to 83
% of Adult Population: 7% (13 million)
Money Motto: Save for a rainy day.
Sex Mindset: Intolerant
Favorite Music: Big Band

People who were starting out in the Depression era were scarred in ways that remain with them today—especially when it comes to financial matters like spending, saving, and debt. The Depression cohort was also the first to be truly influenced by contemporary media: such as radio and especially motion pictures.

THE WORLD WAR II COHORT
(the Depression generation)

Born 1922–27   Age in '95: 68 to 73
% of Adult Population: 6% (11 million)
Money Motto: Save a lot, spend a little.
Sex Mindset: Ambivalent
Favorite Music: Swing

People who came of age in the Forties were unified by the shared experience of a common enemy and a common goal. Consequently, this group became intensely romantic. A sense of self-denial that long outlived the war is especially strong among the 16 million veterans and thier families

THE POSTWAR COHORT
(the silent generation)

Born 1928–45   Age in '95: 50 to 67
% of Adult Population: 21% (41 million)
Money Motto: Save some, spend some.
Sex Mindset: Repressive
Favorite Music: Frank Sinatra

Members of this 18-year cohort, the war babies, benefited from a long period of economic growth and relative social tranquillity. But global unrest and the threat of nuclear attack sparked a need to alleviate uncertainty in everyday life. The youngest subset, called the cool generation, were the first to dig folk rock.

THE BOOMERS COHORT
(the Woodstock generation)

Born 1946–54   Age in '95: 41 to 49
% of Adult Population: 17% (33 million)
Money Motto: Spend, borrow, spend.
Sex Mindset: Permissive
Favorite Music: Rock & roll

Vietnam is the demarcation point between leading-edge and trailing-edge boomers. The Kennedy and King assassinations signaled an end to the status quo and galvanized this vast cohort. Still, early boomers continued to experience good times and want a lifestyle at least as good as their predecessors'.

THE BOOMERS II COHORT
(zoomers)

Born 1955–65   Age in '95: 30 to 40
% of Adult Population: 25% (49 million)
Money Motto: Spend, borrow, spend.
Sex Mindset: Permissive
Favorite Music: Rock & roll

It all changed after Watergate. The idealistic fervor of youth disappeared. Instead, the later boomers exhibited a narcissistic preoccupation that manifested itself in things like the self-help movement. In this dawning age of downward mobility, debt as a means of maintaining a lifestyle made sense.

THE GENERATION X COHORT
(baby-busters)

Born 1966–76   Age in '95: 19 to 29
% of Adult Population: 21% (41 million)
Money Motto: Spend? Save? What?
Sex Mindset: Confused
Favorite Music: Grunge, rap, retro

The slacker set has nothing to hang on to. The latchkey kids of divorce and day care are searching for anchors with their seemingly contradictory "retro" behavior: the resurgence of proms, coming-out parties, and fraternities. Their political conservatism is motivated by a "What's in it for me?" cynicism.

FIGURE 15–1 ■ **Fortune Magazine Cohorts**
Source: "Generation Cohorts", *Fortune* (June 26, 1995): 110.

base of older men. The company launched a two-pronged effort to convince younger men on the one hand to switch from wet shaving to electric, and on the other hand to maintain loyalty among its older following. Ads for Norelco's Speedrazor, aimed at males aged 18 to 35, ran on late-night TV and in *GQ* and *Details* magazines. Messages about the company's triple-head razors, geared to men over 35, ran in such traditional publications as *Time* and *Newsweek*.

THE APPEAL OF NOSTALGIA

Because consumers within an age group confront crucial life changes at roughly the same time, the values and symbolism used to appeal to them can evoke powerful feelings of nostalgia (see chapter 3). Adults over 30 are particularly susceptible to

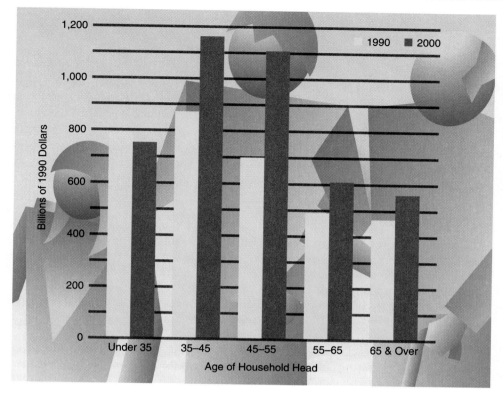

FIGURE 15–2 ■
Household Income by Age
Source: Fabian Linden, *Consumer Affluence: The Next Wave* (New York: The Conference Board, Inc., 1994).

this phenomenon.[2] However, young people as well as old are influenced by references to their past. In fact, research indicates that some people are more disposed to be nostalgic than others, regardless of age. A scale that has been used to measure the impact of nostalgia on individual consumers appears in Table 15–1.

TABLE 15–1 ■ The Nostalgia Scale

SCALE ITEMS
● They don't make 'em like they used to.
● Things used to be better in the good old days.
● Products are getting shoddier and shoddier.
● Technological change will ensure a brighter future (reverse coded).
● History involves a steady improvement in human welfare (reverse coded).
● We are experiencing a decline in the quality of life.
● Steady growth in GNP has brought increased human happiness (reverse coded).
● Modern business constantly builds a better tomorrow (reverse coded).

Note: Items are presented on a nine-point scale ranging from strong disagreement (1) to strong agreement (9), and responses are summed.

Source: Morris B. Holbrook and Robert M. Schindler, "Age, Sex, and Attitude toward the Past as Predicters of Consumers' Aesthetic Tastes for Cultural Products," *Journal of Marketing Research* 31 (August 1994): 416. Reprinted by permission of the American Marketing Association.

MARKETING OPPORTUNITY

A reunion is an event based on a shared age cohort. People who were not necessarily fond of each other in high school or college nonetheless get together to celebrate the common experience of having been together at the same time and place. It is estimated that more than 150,000 reunions are held in the United States each year, attended by 22 million people (the 10-year high school reunion is the most heavily attended). In addition to the boon this nostalgia provides to caterers and professional reunion organizers, some marketers realize that the people who attend reunions often represent a valuable customer base. They are self-selected to be fairly successful, because the "failures" tend not to show up. Some companies use reunion-goers to test new products, and travel-related businesses interview attendees about their trips or provide special promotional packages for returning.[3]

Chapter 3 noted that product sales can be dramatically affected by linking a brand to vivid memories and experiences, especially for items associated with childhood or adolescence. As observed by the maker of a candy bar called the Big Hunk, which has been on the market since 1950, "Adults turn back into children when they bite into candy. . . . If you remember buying a Big Hunk every Saturday when you went to the movies, you're going to buy the memory every time you buy the product."[4]

Many advertising campaigns have played on the collective memories of consumers by resuscitating old pop classics. Michelob's "The Night Belongs to Michelob" campaign sponsored heroes of classic rock such as Eric Clapton, Steve Winwood, and Roger Daltrey; and Ford Mercury commercials are produced against a background of classic songs. *Memories* magazine, which was founded to exploit the nostalgia boom, even offers advertisers a discount if they run old ads next to their current ones.

THE TEEN MARKET: IT TOTALLY RULES

In 1956, the label "teenage" first entered the general American vocabulary, as Frankie Lymon and the Teenagers became the first pop group to identify themselves with this new subculture. The concept of a teen is a fairly new cultural construction; throughout most of history a person simply made the transition from child to adult (often accompanied by some sort of ritual or ceremony, as we'll see in the next chapter). The magazine *Seventeen,* born in 1944, was based on the revelation that young women didn't want to look just like Mom. Following World War II, the teenage conflict between rebellion and conformity began to unfold, pitting Elvis Presley with his slicked hair and suggestive swivels against the wholesome Pat Boone with his white bucks (see Figure 15–3). Now, this rebellion is often played out by acting detached from the adult world, as exemplified by Beavis and Butthead or the confused, sullen teens appearing daily on Ricki Lake and other daytime talk shows.[5]

TEEN VALUES AND CONFLICTS

As anyone who has been there knows, the process of puberty and adolescence can be both the best of times and the worst of times. Many exciting changes happen as individuals leave the role of child and prepare to assume the role of adult. These changes create a lot of uncertainty about the self, and the need to belong and to find

U.S. RESIDENT POPULATION,
13 TO 19 YEARS OLD,
1950–2010

THE '60s

THE '70s

THE '80s

THE '90s

THE YEARS
2000 TO 2010

1976
29.85
Million

1991
24.01
Million

2010
30.81
Million*

1950
14.93
Million

THE '50s

*Projections for 1994–2010
Data: U.S. Census Bureau Current Population Estimates

FIGURE 15–3 ■ The U.S. Teen Population
Source: Business Week (April 11, 1994): 78–79. Photos from left to right courtesy of Brooks Kraft, Sygma; Sunset Boulevard, Sygma; Michael Childers, Sygma; Sunset Boulevard, Sygma; AP/Wide World Photos.

one's unique identity as a person becomes extremely important. At this age, choices of activities, friends, and "looks" are often crucial to social acceptance. Teens actively search for cues from their peers and from advertising for the "right" way to look and behave. Advertising geared to teens is typically action-oriented and depicts a group of "in" teens using the product.

Teens use products to express their identities, to explore the world and their new-found freedoms in it, and also to rebel against the authority of their parents and other socializing agents. Marketers often do their best to assist in this process. In 1996, for example, PepsiCo capitalized on the surge of teens wearing beepers (presumably to facilitate drug sales) by distributing the devices as part of a sales promotion—participants were beeped weekly with messages from sports and music stars advertising Pepsi and other teen products.[6]

Teenagers in every culture grapple with fundamental developmental issues as they make the transition from childhood to adult. According to research by the Saatchi & Saatchi advertising agency, there are four themes of conflict common to all teens:

1. *Autonomy versus belonging:* Teens need to acquire independence so they try to break away from their families. On the other hand, they need to attach themselves to a support structure, such as peers, to avoid being alone. A thriving Internet subculture has developed among many teens to serve this purpose. The net is the preferred method of communication for many young people, because its anonymity makes it easier to talk to people of the opposite sex, or of different ethnic and racial groups.[7]

2. *Rebellion versus conformity:* Teens need to rebel against social standards of appearance and behavior, yet they still need to fit in and be accepted by others. Cult products that cultivate a rebellious image are prized for this reason. Hot Topic, a retail chain based in Pomona, California, caters to this need by selling

$44 million per year of such "in your face" items as nipple rings, tongue barbells, purple hair dye, and Marilyn Manson T-shirts.[8] Skeleteens, a line of natural soft drinks in flavors like Brain Wash, Black Lemonade, and DOA, is developing a substantial following due to its "dangerous" mystique. This underground product was first discovered by California bikers, who were drawn to the images of skulls and crossbones on the labels.[9]

3. *Idealism versus pragmatism:* Teens tend to view adults as hypocrites, whereas they see themselves as being sincere. They have to struggle to reconcile their view of how the world should be with the realities they perceive around them.

4. *Narcissism versus intimacy:* Teens are often obsessed with their own appearance and needs. On the other hand, they also feel the desire to connect with others on a meaningful level.[10]

Teenagers throughout history have had to cope with insecurity, parental authority, and peer pressure. In the 1990s, however, these issues are compounded by concerns about the environment, racism, AIDS, and other pressing social problems. According to Teenage Research Unlimited, the five most important social issues for teens are AIDS, race relations, child abuse, abortion, and the environment. Today's teens often have to cope with additional family responsibilities as well, especially if they live in nontraditional families in which they must take significant responsibility for shopping, cooking, and housework. It's hard work being a teen in the modern world.

APPEALING TO THE TEEN MARKET

Consumers in this age subculture have a number of needs, including experimentation, belonging, independence, responsibility, and approval from others. Product usage is a significant medium through which to express these needs. This age group is growing nearly twice as fast as the general population, and is expected to number 30 million by 2005, and teens spend an average of $3,000 per year.[11] Much of this money goes toward "feel-good" products: cosmetics, posters, and fast food—with the occasional nose ring thrown in as well. Because they are so interested in many different products and have the resources to obtain them, the teen market is avidly courted by many marketers.

Because modern teens were raised on TV and tend to be much more "savvy" than older generations, marketers must tread lightly in attempts to reach them. In particular, the messages must be seen as authentic and not condescending. As one

MARKETING PITFALL

Calvin Klein's strategy of using adolescent sexuality to sell the company's products dates way back to 1980, when Brooke Shields proclaimed that "Nothing comes between me and my Calvins." Later, ads featuring singer Marky Mark in his underwear sparked a new fashion craze. In 1995, though, Klein took this approach one very daring step further, when the company unveiled a very controversial advertising campaign featuring young-looking models in situations dripping with sexual innuendo. In one spot, an old man with a gravelly voice says to a scantily clad young boy, "You got a real nice look. How old are you? Are you strong? You think you could rip that shirt off of you? That's a real nice body. You work out? I can tell." The campaign ended when the chairman of Dayton Hudson asked that the stores' names be removed from the ads, and *Seventeen* refused to carry them.[12] By that time, of course, Klein had reaped invaluable volumes of free publicity as teens and adults debated the appropriateness of these images.

researcher observed, ". . . they have a B.S. alarm that goes off quick and fast. . . . They walk in and usually make up their minds very quickly about whether it's phat or not phat, and whether they want it or don't want it. They know a lot of advertising is based on lies and hype."[13] This wisdom formed the basis for Coca-Cola's introduction of OK soda, a beverage targeted to teens. After a year of field research, the company found that teens responded better to a product that did not overpromise—it's just "OK."[14]

Marketers view teens as "consumers-in-training," because brand loyalty often is developed during this age. A teenager who is committed to a brand may continue to purchase it for many years to come. Such loyalty creates a barrier-to-entry for other brands that were not chosen during these pivotal years. Thus, advertisers sometimes try to "lock in" consumers to certain brands so that in the future they will buy these brands more or less automatically. As one teen magazine ad director observed, "We . . . always say it's easier to start a habit than stop it."[15]

Teens also exert a big influence on the purchase decisions of their parents (see chapter 12).[16] Sixty percent of teens, for instance, say they influence the vacation choices of their families.[17] In addition to providing "helpful" advice to parents, teens are increasingly buying products on behalf of the family. The majority of mothers are now employed outside the home and have less time to shop for the family. In fact, seven out of ten mothers of teens work, and five of those seven are employed full-time.[18]

This fundamental change in family structure has altered the way marketers must conceive of teenage consumers. Although teens are still a good market for discretionary items, in recent years their spending on such "basics" as groceries is even larger than for nonessentials. A market research firm specializing in this segment has gone so far as to label teens "skippies"—school kids with income and purchasing power.[19] One survey of 16- to 17-year-old girls found that over a three-month period a significant proportion of them had purchased staple items such as cereal, frozen meals, cheese, yogurt, and salad dressing.[20] Marketers are beginning to respond to these changes. The number of pages devoted to food advertising in *Seventeen* magazine increased by 31 percent in one year.

BABY BUSTERS: "GENERATION X"

The cohort of consumers born between 1960 and 1976 consists of 46 million Americans like Brandon who will be a powerful force. This group, has been labeled **"Generation X,"** (popularized by the bestselling 1991 novel of that name) "slackers," or "baby busters." So-called baby busters include many people, both in and out of college, whose tastes and priorities are beginning to be felt in fashion, popular culture, politics, and marketing.[21] Their (supposed) sense of alienation is echoed by their choices in music (e.g., the Satanic-oriented group Marilyn Manson), media (e.g., shows with an "attitude" like *The Real World* or *Jerry Springer*), and in fashion (e.g., body piercings and prominent tattoos). Even Pepsi-Cola got into the act with its 1997–1998 advertising theme, "Generation Next."

MARKETING TO BUSTERS OR MARKETING BUST?

Although the income of this age cohort is below expectations, they still constitute a formidable market segment—partly because so many still live at home and have more discretionary income. Busters in their twenties are estimated to have an annual spending power of $125 billion, and their purchases are essential to the fortunes of such product categories as beer, fast food, and cosmetics (see Figure 15–4).

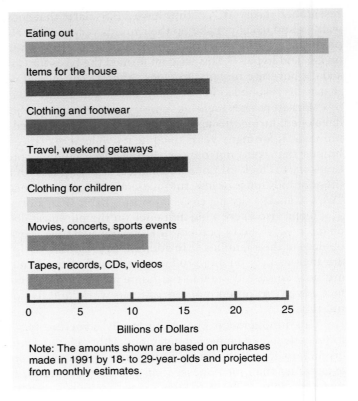

Figure 15–4 ■ **The Spending Power of an Emerging Market Force— Young Adults**
Source: Laura Zinn, "Move Over Boomers," *Business Week* (December 14, 1992): 75. Reprinted by special permission, copyright © 1992 by McGraw-Hill, Inc.

Note: The amounts shown are based on purchases made in 1991 by 18- to 29-year-olds and projected from monthly estimates.

Toyota hopes that the list of slang words in this ad will appeal to young people.

Because many busters have been exposed to commercial messages and doing the family shopping for a long time, marketers are finding that they are much more sophisticated about evaluating products. They are turned off by advertising that either contains a lot of hype or takes itself too seriously. They see advertising as a form of entertainment but are turned off by overcommercialization. As the vice-president of marketing for MTV put it, "You must let them know that you know who they are, that you understand their life experiences. You want them to feel you're talking directly to them."[22]

Nike, for example, took a soft-sell approach to woo younger buyers of its athletic shoes. Its ads show little of the product, focusing instead on encouraging readers to improve themselves through exercise. Other ads make fun of advertising: An ad created for a Maybelline eye shadow depicts supermodel Christy Turlington coolly posing in a glamorous setting. She then suddenly appears on her living room couch, where she laughs and says, "Get over it."

Advertisers have been falling all over themselves trying to create messages that will not turn off the worldly Generation X cohort. Many of these efforts have involved references to old TV shows like *Gilligan's Island,* or vignettes featuring disheveled actors in turned-around baseball caps doing their best to appear blasé. This approach actually does turn off a lot of busters, because it implies that they have nothing else to do but sit around and watch old television reruns.

One of the first commercials of this genre was created for Subaru. It showed a sloppily dressed young man who described the Impreza model as "like punk rock," while denouncing the competition as "boring and corporate." The commercial did not play well with its intended audience, and Subaru eventually switched agencies. In contrast, the campaign for Chrysler Neon was successful, because it appealed to value rather than working too hard to be "cutting edge."

Perhaps one reason marketers' efforts to appeal to Xers with messages of alienation, cynicism, and despair have not succeeded is that many people in their twenties aren't so depressed after all! Generation Xers actually are quite a diverse group—they don't all wear reversed baseball caps and work as burger flippers. Despite the birth of dozens of magazines with names such as *Axcess, Project X,* and *KGB* catering to "riot grrrls" and other angry Xers, the most popular magazine for twentysomething women is *Cosmopolitan.* What seems to make this age cohort the angriest is constantly being labeled angry by the media![23]

The advertising agency Saatchi & Saatchi sent teams of psychologists and cultural anthropologists into the field to study the buster subculture. These researchers identified four key segments:

1. *Cynical Disdainers:* the most pessimistic and skeptical about the world.
2. *Traditional Materialists:* the most like baby boomers in their thirties and forties, these young people are upbeat, optimistic about the future, and actively striving for what they continue to view as the American Dream of material prosperity.
3. *Hippies Revisited:* This group tends to espouse the nonmaterialistic values of the Sixties. Their priorities are expressed through music (e.g., many continue to be Dead Heads despite the death of Jerry Garcia), retro fashion, and a strong interest in spirituality.
4. *Fifties Machos:* These consumers tend to be young Republicans. They believe in traditional gender roles, are politically conservative, and they are the least accepting of multiculturalism.[24]

MULTICULTURAL DIMENSIONS

Images of American consumption bombarding teens on TV screens around the world are rapidly creating a global youth culture. Some Japanese teenagers are so enamored of American culture that they have been known to cruise down the main streets of Tokyo with surfboards on the roofs of their cars.

Spending time with friends and watching TV tie as teens' favorite pastimes, but eight of the ten top teen activities are media related. Middle Easterners watch the most television (3.6 hours per day), North Americans watch 2.9 hours per day, and Western Europeans log in at 2.5 hours. MTV reaches over 239 million viewers in 68 countries. Despite differences in cultures, middle-class youth world-wide can be spotted wearing their cherished Levi's and Nikes (the Japanese call this style *Amekaji,* or American casual); identification with these products helps to form tangible bonds among young people around the world. Many of these young consumers learn about the United States (or rather, the idealized version of it shown to us by television producers) by watching American television. The soap opera *Santa Barbara* is the most popular show among kids ages 11 to 17 in Russia, whereas Brazilian teens are avid followers of the hospital drama *E.R.*[25] Some visitors to American soil are a bit surprised to find that not all American teens share the lifestyle of the stars of *Beverly Hills 90210.*

BIG (WO)MAN ON CAMPUS: THE COLLEGE MARKET

Advertisers spend more than $100 million a year to influence the purchases of college students, who buy about $20 billion worth of products a year. After paying for books, board, and tuition, the average student has about $200 per month to spend, so this interest is not surprising. As one marketing executive observed, "This is the time of life where they're willing to try new products. . . . This is the time to get them in your franchise."[26]

Many college students are away from home for the first time, and they must make many buying decisions that used to be made for them by parents, such as the purchase of routine personal care products or of cleaning supplies. Some marketers are attracted by this lack of experience. As one executive put it, "Advertisers look at the college student as someone who can be more easily influenced than someone who has developed brand preferences."[27]

Advertisers spend more than $140 million on college campuses to woo students, whose combined purchasing power is estimated at $30 billion. Credit card companies are now the biggest spenders (54 percent of students have at least one card), replacing beer marketers who have reduced their presence in this market due to political and social pressures.[28]

Nevertheless, college students pose a special challenge for marketers, since they are hard to reach via conventional media. Students watch less television than other people, and when they do watch, they are much more likely to do so after midnight. Students also do not read newspapers as much. AT&T and other large companies have found that the best way to reach students is through their college newspapers; about 90 percent of students read their college paper at least one day a week, which explains why $17 million a year is spent on advertising in college newspapers.[29]

Other strategies to reach students include the widespread distribution of sampler boxes containing a variety of personal care products in student centers and dormitories and the use of posters (termed *wall media*). In addition, a growing number of marketers are capitalizing on the ritual of Spring Break to reach college students; it is estimated that about 40 percent of students now make the annual trek to points

South. Beach promotions used to be dominated by suntan lotion and beer companies, but many others now are well represented, including Chanel, Hershey, Chevrolet, Procter & Gamble, and Columbia Pictures.[30]

BABY BOOMERS

The **baby boomers** age segment is the source of many fundamental cultural and economic changes. The reason: power in numbers. As GIs returned after World War II, they began to establish families and careers at a record pace. Birthrates soared. To appreciate the impact of this sense in the population, imagine a large python that has swallowed a mouse; the mouse moves down the length of the python, creating a moving bulge as it goes. So it is with baby boomers as seen in Figure 15–5.

THE CULTURAL IMPACT OF BOOMERS

As teenagers in the 1960s and 1970s, the "Woodstock Generation" created a revolution in style, politics, and consumer attitudes. As they have aged, their collective will has been behind cultural events as diverse as the Free Speech movement and hippies in the 1960s to Reaganomics and yuppies in the 1980s. Now that they are older, they continue to influence popular culture in important ways.

ECONOMIC POWER:
HE WHO PAYS THE PIPER, CALLS THE TUNE

Because of the size and buying power of the boomer group over the last 20 years, marketers have focused most of their attention on the youth market. The popular slogan at the time, "Don't trust anyone over 30," also meant that people over 30 had

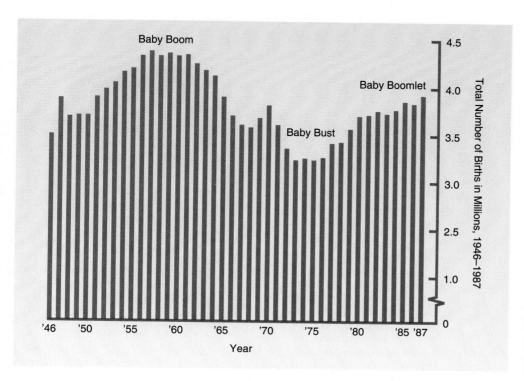

FIGURE 15–5 ■ The Origins of the Baby Boomer Age Cohort
Source: National Center for Health Services.

trouble finding products appropriate to their age groups. Times have changed, and again it is the baby boomers who have changed them. For example, boomers tend to have different emotional and psychological needs than did those who came before them. Domain, a high-fashion furniture chain, found that its core boomer clientele is as concerned about self-improvement as it is about home decoration. The company launched a series of in-store seminars dealing with themes such as women's issues and how to start a business, and found its repeat business doubled since beginning the program.[31]

This "mouse in the python" has moved into its mid-thirties to fifties, and this age group is now the one that exerts the most impact on consumption patterns. Most of the growth in the market will be accounted for by people who are moving into their peak earning years. As one commercial for VH1, the music-video network that caters to those who are a bit too old for MTV pointed out, "The generation that dropped acid to escape reality . . . is the generation that drops antacid to cope with it."

Levi Strauss faced the challenge of keeping aging baby boomers in their franchise, even though these men now bought less of their traditional products. They answered this challenge by creating a new product category, "new casuals," that would be more formal than jeans but less casual than dress slacks. The target audience was men aged 25–49 with higher than average education and income, who worked in white collar jobs in major metropolitan areas. The Dockers line was born.[32]

Consumers aged 35 to 44 spend the most on housing, cars, and entertainment. In addition, consumers aged 45 to 54 spend the most of any age category on food (30 percent above average), apparel (38 percent above average), and retirement programs (57 percent above average). To appreciate the impact middle-aged consumers have and will have on our economy, consider this: At current spending levels, a 1 percent increase in the population of householders aged 35 to 54 results in an additional $8.9 billion in consumer spending.

In addition to the direct demand for products and services created by this age group, these consumers have also created a new baby boom of their own to keep

The baby boomer age cohort has had an enormous impact on our culture. This Pepsi ad, which trumpets the emphasis on youth brought about by this group, first appeared in 1962.

now it's Pepsi-for those who think young
Thinking young is a wholesome attitude, an enthusiastic outlook. It means getting the most out of life, and everyone can join in. This is the life for Pepsi —light, bracing, clean-tasting Pepsi. Think young. Say "Pepsi, please!"

marketers busy in the future. Because fertility rates have dropped, this new boom is not as big as the one that created the baby boom generation; the new upsurge in the number of children born in comparison can best be described as a **baby boomlet.**

Many couples postponed getting married and having children because of the new opportunities and options for women. They began having babies in their late twenties and early thirties, resulting in fewer (but perhaps more pampered) children per family. Couples in the 25 to 34 age group account for 22 percent of all married couples, but for 35 percent of married couples with children. This new emphasis on children and the family has created opportunities for products such as cars (e.g., the success of the "minivan" concept), services (e.g., the day care industry, as exemplified by the KinderCare chain), and media (e.g., magazines such as *Working Mother* and local magazines for parents that exist in more than 70 American cities).[33]

THE GRAY MARKET

The old woman sits alone in her dark apartment, while the television blares out a soap opera. Once every couple of days, she slowly and painfully opens her triple-locked door with arthritic hands and ventures out to the corner store to buy essentials like tea, milk, and cereal, always being sure to pick the least expensive brand. Most of the time she sits in her rocking chair, thinking sadly of her dead husband and the good times she used to have.

Is this the image you have of a typical elderly consumer? Until recently, many marketers did. As a result, they largely neglected the elderly in their feverish pursuit of the baby boomer market. But as our population ages and people are living longer and healthier lives, the game is rapidly changing. A lot of businesses are beginning to replace the old stereotype of the poor recluse. The newer, more accurate image is of an older person who is active, interested in what life has to offer, and is an enthusiastic consumer with the means and willingness to buy many goods and services.

MARKETING OPPORTUNITY

As the oldest members of the baby boom generation move into their fifties, businesses are cashing in. Female menopause begins on average at the age of 51, and a new frankness about this life change has led to a boom in self-help books, estrogen supplements, and exercise classes.[34]

Men are not immune from life changes, either, as many fall prey to so-called "male menopause." As humorist Dave Barry notes, this is a period when a man wears ". . . enormous pleated pants and designer fragrances, encases his pale porky body in tank tops, and buys a boat shaped like a sexual aid. He then abandons his attractive, intelligent wife to live with a 19-year-old aerobics instructor who once spent an entire summer reading a single magazine article called 'Ten Tips for 'Terrific Toenails'."

Marketers are eager to provide solutions to "menopausal" men's social anxieties. The Hair Club for Men has about 40,000 members who have received new heads of hair with the help of "hair-replacement engineers." Plastic surgeons also report a sharp rise in the number of men electing to have cosmetic surgery, including nose jobs and liposuction. On the other hand, Dave Barry maintains all these efforts are futile: "Regardless of how many gallons of Oil of Olay you smear on yourself," he warns, "you're going to start aging faster than a day-old bagel on a hot dumpster."[35]

GRAY POWER: SHATTERING STEREOTYPES

People over the age of 65 currently head over 18 million households in the United States. By the year 2010, one of every seven Americans will be 65 or older. Older adults control over 50 percent of discretionary income and spend over $60 billion annually in the United States alone.[36] In many cases they spend this money at an even greater rate than other age groups: Householders aged 55 to 64 spend 15 percent more than average per capita. They spend 56 percent more than the average consumer on women's clothing, and as new grandparents they actually spend more than people aged 25 to 44 on pets, toys, and playground equipment.[37]

The Bureau of Labor Statistics estimates that the mature market will grow by 62 percent between 1987 and 2015, compared to a 19 percent rate of growth for the overall U.S. population.[38] This increase makes the mature market the second fastest growing market segment in the United States, lagging only behind the baby boomers. Such dramatic growth can largely be explained by healthier lifestyles and improved medical diagnoses and treatment, and the resulting increase in life expectancy.

Most older people lead more active, multidimensional lives than we assume. Nearly 60 percent engage in volunteer activities, one in four seniors aged 65 to 72 still works, and over 14 million are involved in daily care of a grandchild.[39] Still, outdated images of mature consumers persist. The editors of *Modern Maturity* reject about a third of the ads submitted to them because they portray older people in a negative light. In one survey, one-third of consumers over age 55 reported that they deliberately did *not* buy a product because of the way an older person was stereotyped in the product's advertising.[40]

SENIORS' ECONOMIC CLOUT

There is abundant evidence that the economic health of older consumers is good and getting better. Some of the important areas that stand to benefit from the surging **gray market** include exercise facilities, cruises and tourism, cosmetic surgery and skin treatments, and "how-to" books and university courses that offer enhanced learning opportunities.

MARKETING OPPORTUNITY

A few marketers are beginning to recognize the vast potential of the senior market and are designing products and services to cater to its specific needs.

- General Motors is redesigning some Oldsmobiles to include bigger buttons and clearer dashboard displays, and a Cadillac's rearview mirrors automatically dim when hit with headlights. The Lincoln Town Car (the average age of a Lincoln driver is 67) features two sets of radio and AC controls, one on the dashboard and one on the steering wheel, because older drivers have trouble shifting attention from controls to the road. Chrysler engineers are experimenting with collision control systems, which sound an alarm when a driver is too close to another car.[41]

- Domain, the furniture chain that developed a special program for baby boomers, also launched a new furniture series especially for its older customers that includes features such as narrow sofas designed to provide more back support.[42]

- By hiring older people as greeters, Wal-Mart makes seniors feel welcome. Similarly, Home Savings of America, a California bank, opened branches catering to seniors. The bank supplies coffee and donuts, and encourages its older customers to think of the branches as a convenient meeting place and a venue for social interaction.[43]

It is crucial to remember that income alone does not express the spending power of this group. Older consumers are finished with many of the financial obligations that siphon off the income of younger consumers. Eighty percent of consumers past age 65 own their own homes, and 80 percent of those homes are owned outright. In addition, child-rearing costs are over with. As evidenced by the popularity of the bumper sticker that proudly proclaims "We're Spending Our Children's Inheritance," many seniors now are more inclined to spend money on themselves rather than skimping for the sake of children and grandchildren.

KEY VALUES OF SENIORS

Researchers have identified a set of key values that are relevant to older consumers. For marketing strategies to succeed, they should be related to one or more of these factors:[44]

- *Autonomy:* Mature consumers want to lead active lives and to be self-sufficient. The advertising strategy for Depends, undergarments for incontinent women made by Kimberly-Clark, is centered around actress June Allyson who plays golf and goes to parties without worrying about her condition.

- *Connectedness:* Mature consumers value the bonds they have with friends and family. Quaker Oats successfully tapped into this value with its ads featuring actor Wilford Brimley, who dispenses grandfatherly advice about eating right to the younger generation.

- *Altruism:* Mature consumers want to give something back to the world. Thrifty Car Rental found in a survey that over 40 percent of older consumers would

Several hotel chains targeted the mature market. Choice Hotels International made adjustments to some of its brands' pricing, structure, room design, and promotional strategy. New rooms—all on the first floor for easier access—offered brighter lighting and larger buttons on phones and TV remote controls. Choice's RODEWAY® hotel brand offered travelers over the age of 50 a 30 percent discount on rooms. This ad for RODEWAY INN® hotels shows this strategy.

select a rental car company if it sponsored a program that gives van discounts to senior citizens centers. Based on this research, the company launched its highly successful program, "Give a Friend a Lift."

● *Personal growth:* Mature consumers are very interested in trying new experiences and developing their potential. In some of its ads for health care products, Prudential tried to appeal to this value by emphasizing the late-in-life accomplishments of Clara Barton, Benjamin Franklin, and Noah Webster.

PERCEIVED AGE: YOU'RE ONLY AS OLD AS YOU FEEL

Market researchers who work with older consumers often comment that people think of themselves as being 10 to 15 years younger than they actually are. In fact, research confirms the popular wisdom that age is more a state of mind than of body. A person's mental outlook and activity level has a lot more to do with his or her longevity and quality of life than does *chronological age,* or the actual number of years lived.

A better yardstick to categorize seniors is **perceived age,** or how old a person feels. Perceived age can be measured on several dimensions, including "feel-age"

No. 2 in a series on how to advertise to Mature America.

Take off 15 years. At least.

They look and act years younger than their mothers and fathers did in their maturity. Proper nutrition, a zest for fitness and an active lifestyle have handed many of them a whole new lease on life. The lesson to marketers? Talk to a person, not a birth date. Enjoy their continuing youth with them. They love a pistachio ice cream cone, have a great time "umping" a Little League game. How do you cast them in advertising? Looking and acting 10 to 15 years younger than preceding generations at the same age. A just completed Yankelovich study* commissioned by Modern Maturity reveals that Americans 50 and over are as vain about the way they look, eat as much fun food, are as likely to bike or hike as people a decade younger. The magazine that understands how young they feel, that even helps them feel that way, is Modern Maturity. A circulation of 17.4 million makes Modern Maturity the second largest magazine in America, and the fastest growing of the big three. For more insights into Mature America and its magazine, call Peter Hanson at (212) 599-1880. **Modern Maturity**

The beginning of a new lifetime.

A ROCKING CHAIR IS A PIECE OF FURNITURE.
NOT A STATE OF MIND.

We know people whose lust for life has not and will not diminish because it's the morning after their 65th birthday. They're too busy putting the finishing touches on a book of poems. Tutoring underprivileged kids with their math. Learning the tango. Or taking acting classes. It's an outlook that works rather well with ours. Whether it's annuities, 401(k)s, IRAs, mutual funds or life insurance for your family, we've packaged a unique set of tools to help you realize your life's next great exploit. Which comes naturally when retirement isn't viewed as merely an end. But rather the way you've been living all along: passionately. For a free brochure, call 1-800-AETNA-60 or visit us at http://www.aetna.com.

Build for Retirement. Manage for Life.

Ætna
Retirement Services

Echoing the saying, "You're only as old as you feel," these ads remind us that a person's perceptual age often does not correspond to his or her chronological age.

MARKETING PITFALL

Some marketing efforts targeted to older adults have backfired because they reminded people of their age or presented their age group in an unflattering way. One of the more infamous blunders was committed by Heinz. A company analyst found that many older people were buying baby food because of the small portions and easy chewing consistency, so Heinz introduced a line of "Senior Foods" made especially for denture wearers. Needless to say, the product failed. Consumers did not want to admit that they required strained foods (even to the supermarket cashier). They preferred to purchase baby foods, which they could pretend they were buying for a grandchild.

(i.e., how old a person feels) and "look-age" (i.e., how old a person looks).[45] The older consumers get, the younger they feel relative to actual age. For this reason, many marketers emphasize product benefits rather than age-appropriateness in marketing campaigns, because many consumers will not relate to products targeted to their chronological age.[46]

SEGMENTING SENIORS

The senior subculture represents an extremely large market: The number of Americans 65 and older exceeds the entire population of Canada.[47] Because this group is so large, it is helpful to think of the mature market as actually consisting of four subsegments: an "older" group (aged 55–64), an "elderly" group (aged 65–74), an "aged" group (aged 75–84), and finally a "very old" group (85 and up).[48]

The elderly market is well suited for segmentation. Older consumers are easy to identify by age and stage in the family life cycle. Most receive Social Security benefits so they can be located without much effort, and many belong to organizations like The American Association of Retired Persons, which boasts over 12 million

Jockey Apparel is one of many advertisers that is increasingly featuring attractive older models in its ads.

dues-paying members. Its main publication, *Modern Maturity,* has the largest circulation of any American magazine. For example, one ad agency devised a segmentation scheme for American women over the age of 65 using two dimensions: self-sufficiency and perceived opinion leadership.[49] The study yielded many important differences among the groups. The self-sufficient group was found to be more independent, cosmopolitan, and outgoing. Compared to the other seniors, these women were more likely to read a book, attend concerts and sporting events, and dine out.

Several segmentation approaches begin with the premise that a major determinant of elderly marketplace behavior is the way a person deals with being old.[50] *Social aging theories* try to understand how society assigns people to different roles across the life span. For example, when someone retires he/she may reflect society's expectations for someone at this life stage—this is a major transition point when people exit from many relationships.[51] Some people become depressed, withdrawn, and apathetic as they age; some are angry and resist the thought of aging; and some appear to accept the new challenges and opportunities this period of life has to offer. Table 15-2 summarizes some selected findings from one current segmentation approach called **gerontographics** that divides the mature market into groups based on both level of physical well-being and social conditions such as becoming a grandparent or losing a spouse.

A number of specialty magazines have been introduced in recent years that focus on the active lifestyles of today's elderly, such as *Modern Maturity* and *50 Plus.* In addition, television is a very important medium, because older adults often rely on it as a window onto society—they watch 60 percent more television than

TABLE 15–2 ■ Gerontographics: Selected Characteristics

SEGMENT	% OF 55+ POPULATION	PROFILE	MARKETING RAMIFICATIONS
Healthy Indulgers	18%	Have experienced the fewest events related to aging, such as retirement or widowhood, and are most likely to behave like younger consumers. Main focus is on enjoying life.	Looking for independent living and are good customers for discretionary services like home cleaning and answering machines.
Healthy Hermits	36%	React to life events like the death of a spouse by becoming withdrawn. Resent that they are expected to behave like old people.	Emphasize conformity. They want to know their appearance is socially acceptable, and tend to be comfortable with well-known brands.
Ailing Outgoers	29%	Maintain positive self-esteem despite adverse life events. They accept limitations but are still determined to get the most out of life.	Have health problems that may require a special diet. Special menus and promotions will bring these people in to restaurants seen as catering to their needs.
Frail Recluses	17%	Have adjusted their lifestyles to accept old age, but have chosen to cope with negative events by becoming spiritually stronger.	Like to stay put in the same house where they raised their families. Good candidates for remodeling, also for emergency-response systems.

Source: Adapted from George P. Moschis, "Life Stages of the Mature Market," *American Demographics* (September 1996): 44–50.

MARKETING PITFALL

Many consumer products will encounter a more sympathetic reception from seniors if products and the packages they come in are redesigned to be sensitive to physical limitations. Even though aesthetically appealing, packages are often awkward and difficult to manage, especially for those who are frail or arthritic. Also, many serving sizes are not geared to smaller families, widows, and other people living alone, and coupons tend to be for family-sized products, rather than for single servings.

Seniors have difficulty with pull-tab cans and push-open milk cartons. Ziploc packages and clear plastic wrap also are difficult to handle. Packages need to be easier to read and should be made lighter and smaller. Finally, designers need to pay attention to contrasting colors. A slight yellowing of the eye's lens as one ages makes it harder to see background colors on packages. Discerning between blues, greens, and violets becomes especially difficult. The closer identifying type colors are to the package's or advertisement's background color, the less visibility and attention they will command.

average households and prefer programs that provide news and current events as a way to keep up. They also watch more golf, baseball, and bowling on television than the average consumer. They tend to listen to radio news at all times of the day and are above the norm in readership of news magazines.

In general, older adults have been shown to respond positively to ads that provide an abundance of information. Unlike other age groups, these consumers usually are not amused, or persuaded, by imagery-oriented advertising. A more successful strategy involves the construction of advertising that depicts the aged as well-integrated, contributing members of society, with emphasis on their expanding their horizons rather than clinging precariously to life.

Some basic guidelines have been suggested for effective advertising to the elderly. These include the following:[52]

- Keep language simple.
- Use clear, bright pictures.
- Use action to attract attention.
- Speak clearly, and keep the word count low.
- Use a single sales message, and emphasize brand extensions to tap consumers' familiarity.
- Avoid extraneous stimuli (i.e., excessive pictures and graphics can detract from the message).

CHAPTER SUMMARY

- People have many things in common with others merely because they are about the same age or live in the same part of the country. Consumers who grew up at the same time share many cultural memories, so they may respond to marketers' *nostalgia appeals* that remind them of these experiences.

- Four important age cohorts are teens, college students, baby boomers, and older adults. Teenagers are making a transition from childhood to adulthood, and their self-concepts tend to be unstable. They are receptive to products that help them to be accepted and enable them to assert their independence. Because many teens earn money but have few financial obligations, they are a particularly important segment for many nonessential or expressive products, ranging from chewing gum to clothing fashions and music. Because of changes in family structure, many teens also are taking more responsibility for their families' day-to-day shopping and routine purchase decisions. College students are an important but hard-to-reach market. In many cases, they are living alone for the first time, so they are making important decisions about setting up a household.

- Baby boomers are the most powerful age segment because of their size and economic clout. As this group ages, its interests have changed and marketing priorities have changed as well. The needs and desires of baby boomers affect demands for housing, child care, automobiles, clothing, and many other products.

- As the population ages, the needs of older consumers will become increasingly influential. Many marketers traditionally ignored seniors because of the stereotype that they are too inactive and spend too little. This stereotype is no longer accurate. Many older adults are healthy, vigorous, and interested in new products and experiences—and they have the income to purchase them. Marketing appeals to this age subculture should focus on consumers' self-concepts and perceived ages, which tend to be more youthful than their chronological ages. Marketers also should emphasize concrete benefits of products, because this group tends to be skeptical of vague, image-related promotions. Personalized service is of particular importance to this segment.

1. What are some possible marketing opportunities present at reunions? What effects might attending such an event have on consumers' self-esteem, body image, affect, and so on?

2. What are some of the positives and negatives of targeting college students? Identify some specific marketing strategies that you feel have either been successful or unsuccessful at appealing to this segment. What characteristics distinguish the successes from the failures?

3. Why have baby boomers had such an important impact on consumer culture in the second half of the twentieth century?

4. How has the baby boomlet changed attitudes toward child-rearing practices and created demand for different products and services?

5. "Kids these days seem content to just hang out, surf the net, and watch mindless TV shows all day." How accurate is this statement?

6. Is it practical to assume that people age 55 and older constitute one large consumer market? What are some approaches to further segmenting this age subculture?

7. What are some important variables to keep in mind when tailoring marketing strategies to older adults?

8. Find good and bad examples of advertising targeted to older consumers. To what degree does advertising stereotype the elderly? What elements of ads or other promotions appear to determine their effectiveness in reaching and persuading this group?

NOTES

1. Shelly Reese, "The Lost Generation," *Marketing Tools* (April 1997): 50 (4 pp.).
2. Bickley Townsend, *"Ou sont les reiges d'antan? (Where are the snows of yesteryear?),"* *American Demographics* (October 1988): 2.
3. Paula Mergenhagen, "The Reunion Market," *American Demographics* (April 1996): 30–4.
4. "Chuckles' Rebirth," *American Demographics* (May 1987): 23.
5. Stephen Holden, "After the War the Time of the Teen-Ager," *New York Times* (May 7, 1995): E4.
6. Mary Kuntz and Joseph Weber, "The New Hucksterism," *Business Week* (July 1, 1996): 75 (7 pp.).
7. Scott McCartney, "Society's Subcultures Meet by Modem," *Wall Street Journal* (December 8, 1994): B1 (2 pp.).
8. Mary Beth Grover, "Teenage Wasteland," *Forbes* (July 28, 1997): 44–5.
9. Sara Olkon, "Black Soda with Skulls on Label Isn't Aimed at the Pepsi Generation," *Wall Street Journal* (May 24, 1995): B1.
10. Junu Bryan Kim, "For Savvy Teens: Real Life, Real Solutions," *Advertising Age* (August 23, 1993): S1 (3 pp.).
11. Grover, "Teenage Wasteland."
12. Margaret Carlson, "Where Calvin Crossed the Line," *Time* (September 11, 1995): 64.
13. Quoted in Cyndee Miller, "Phat is Where It's At for Today's Teen Market," *Marketing News* (August 15, 1994): 6 (2 pp.).
14. Laurie M. Grossman, "Coke Hopes 'OK,' New Drink, Will be the Toast of Teens," *Wall Street Journal* (April 21, 1994): B7.
15. Ellen Goodman, "The Selling of Teenage Anxiety," *Washington Post* (November 24, 1979).
16. Ellen R. Foxman, Patriya S. Tansuhaj, and Karin M. Ekstrom, "Family Members' Perceptions of Adolescents' Influence in Family Decision Making," *Journal of Consumer Research* 15 (March 1989): 482–91.
17. Andrew Malcolm, "Teen-Age Shoppers: Desperately Seeking Spinach," *New York Times* (November 29, 1987): 10.
18. Malcolm, "Teen-Age Shoppers."
19. John Blades, "Tracking Skippies: TRU Researches Habits of Elusive Groups—Teens," *The Asbury Park Press* (March 2, 1991): C1.
20. Malcolm, "Teen-Age Shoppers."
21. Laura Zinn, "Move Over, Boomers," *Business Week* (December 14, 1992) 7.
22. Quoted in T. L. Stanley, "Age of Innocence . . . Not," *PROMO* (February 1997): 28–33, quoted on p. 30.
23. Scott Donaton, "The Media Wakes Up to Generation X," *Advertising Age* (February 1, 1993): 16 (2 pp.); Laura E. Keeton, "New Magazines Aim to Reach (and Rechristen) Generation X," *Wall Street Journal* (October 17, 1994): B1.
24. Faye Rice, "Making Generational Marketing Come of Age," *Fortune* (June 26, 1995): 110–14.
25. Chip Walker, "Can TV Save the Planet?" *American Demographics* (May 1996): 42–50.
26. Quoted in Fannie Weinstein, "Time to Get Them in Your Franchise," *Advertising Age* (February 1, 1988): S6.
27. Quoted in "Advertisers Target College Market," *Marketing News* (October 23, 1987).
28. Eben Shapiro, "New Marketing Specialists Tap College Consumers," *New York Times* (February 27, 1992): D16.
29. Beth Bogart, "Word of Mouth Travels Fastest," *Advertising Age* (February 6, 1989): S6; Janice Steinberg, "Media 101," *Advertising Age* (February 6, 1989): S4.
30. Stuart Elliott, "Beyond Beer and Sun Oil: The Beach-Blanket Bazaar," *New York Times* (March 18, 1992): D17.
31. Rice, "Making Generational Marketing Come of Age."
32. Kevin Keller, *Strategic Marketing Management* (Upper Saddle River, NJ: Prentice Hall, 1998.
33. Albert Scardino, "The New Baby Boom Spurs Local Magazines for Parents," *New York Times* (June 26, 1989): D1.
34. Patricia Braus, "Facing Menopause," *American Demographics* (March 1993): 44 (5 pp.).
35. Quoted in Blayne Cutler, "Marketing to Menopausal Men," *American Demographics* (March 1993): 49.
36. Catherine A. Cole and Nadine N. Castellano, "Consumer Behavior," in ed. James E. Binnen, *Encyclopedia of Gerontology,* vol. 1 (San Diego: Academic Press 1996): 329–39.
37. Cheryl Russell, "The Ungraying of America," *American Demographics* (July 1997): 12 (3 pp.).
38. William Lazer and Eric H. Shaw, "How Older Americans Spend Their Money," *American Demographics* (September 1987): 36; see also Charles D. Schewe and Anne L. Balazs, "Role Transitions in Older Adults: A Marketing Opportunity," *Psychology & Marketing* 9 (March/April 1992): 85–99.
39. Rick Adler, "Stereotypes Won't Work with Seniors Anymore," *Advertising Age* (November 11, 1996): 32.
40. Melinda Beck, "Going for the Gold," *Newsweek* (April 23, 1990): 74.
41. Daniel McGinn and Julie Edelson Halpert, "Driving Miss Daisy—and Selling Her the Car," *Newsweek* (February 3, 1997): 14.
42. Rice, "Making Generational Marketing Come of Age."
43. Paco Underhill, "Seniors & Stores," *American Demographics* (April 1996): 44–8.
44. David B. Wolfe, "Targeting the Mature Mind," *American Demographics* (March 1994): 32–6.
45. Benny Barak and Leon G. Schiffman, "Cognitive Age: A Nonchronological Age Variable," in ed. Kent B. Monroe, *Advances in Consumer Research* 8 (Provo, UT: Association for Consumer Research, 1981): 602–6.
46. David B. Wolfe, "An Ageless Market," *American Demographics* (July 1987): 27–55.
47. Lenore Skenazy, "These Days, It's Hip to be Old," *Advertising Age* (February 15, 1988):
48. Lazer and Shaw, "How Older Americans Spend Their Money."
49. Ellen Day, Brian Davis, Rhonda Dove, and Warren A. French, "Reaching the

Senior Citizen Market(s)," *Journal of Advertising Research* (December/January 1987/88): 23–30.

50. Day et al., "Reaching the Senior Citizen Market(s)"; Warren A. French and Richard Fox, "Segmenting the Senior Citizen Market," *Journal of Consumer Marketing* 2 (1985): 61–74; Jeffrey G. Towle and Claude R. Martin Jr., "The Elderly Consumer: One Segment or Many?" in ed. Beverlee B. Anderson, *Advances in Consumer Research* 3 (Provo, UT: Association for Consumer Research, 1976): 463.

51. Catherine A. Cole and Nadine N. Castellano, "Consumer Behavior," *Encyclopedia of Gerontology*, vol. 1 (1996): 329–39.

52. J. Ward, "Marketers Slow to Catch Age Wave," *Advertising Age* (May 22, 1989): S-1.

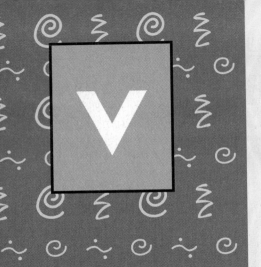

CONSUMERS AND CULTURE

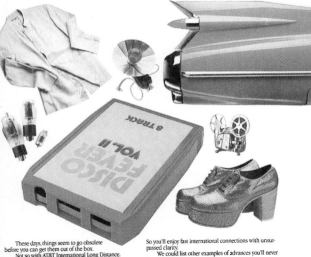

There's one thing AT&T international long distance customers will never have to worry about.

These days, things seem to go obsolete before you can get them out of the box.

Not so with AT&T International Long Distance. We're continually upgrading our Worldwide Intelligent Network, before you have time to even think about it.

When we saw that global events were affecting telephone traffic, we expanded our Network Operations Center. Now events are continually monitored 24 hours a day, and traffic is routed accordingly.

We also anticipated the growing demand for international voice, data and fax transmission, by developing the first transpacific and transatlantic fiber-optic cable systems.

So you'll enjoy fast international connections with unsurpassed clarity.

We could list other examples of advances you'll never have to think about.

But why not call 1 800 222-0400 ext.1277, and let the innovations speak for themselves.

AT&T
The right choice.

© 1989 AT&T

The final section of this book looks at consumers as members of a broad cultural system, and reminds us that even everyday, mundane consumption activities often are rooted in deeper meanings. Chapter 16 looks at some of the basic building blocks of culture and the impact that such underlying processes as myths and rituals exert on "modern" consumers. Chapter 17 focuses on the ways that products spread throughout the members of a culture, and across cultures as well. This final chapter considers the process by which some consumer products succeed and others don't, and also examines how successful Western products influence the consumption practices of people around the world.

SECTION OUTLINE

Chapter 16
Cultural Influences on Consumer Behavior

Chapter 17
The Creation and Diffusion of Consumer Culture

493

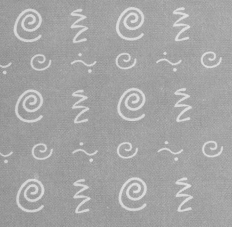

WHITNEY IS AT HER wits' end. It's bad enough that she has a deadline looming on that new Christmas promotion for her gift shop. Now, there's trouble on the home front as well: Her son Stephen had to go and flunk his drivers' license road exam, and now he's just about suicidal because he feels he can't be a "real man" without successfully obtaining his license. To top things off, now her much-anticipated vacation to Disney World with her younger stepchildren will have to be postponed because she just can't find the time to get away.

When Whitney meets up with her buddy Gabrielle at their local Starbucks for their daily "retreat," though, her mood starts to brighten. Somehow the calm of the cafe rubs off as she savors her *grande cappuccino*. Gab consoles her with her usual assurances, and then she prescribes the ultimate remedy to defeat the blues: Go home, take a nice long bath, and then consume a quart of Starbucks Espresso Swirl ice cream. Yes, that's the ticket. It's amazing how the little things in life can make such a big difference. As she strolls out the door, Whitney makes a mental note to get Gab a really nice Christmas gift this year—she's earned it . . .

Cultural Influences on Consumer Behavior

UNDERSTANDING CULTURE

Whitney's daily coffee "fix" is mimicked in various forms around the globe, as people participate in activities that allow them to take a break and affirm their relationships with others. Of course, the products that are consumed in the process can range from black Turkish coffee to Indian tea, or from lager beer to hashish.

The Starbucks Corporation has experienced phenomenal success by turning the coffee break into a cultural event that for many has assumed almost cultlike status. The average Starbucks customer visits 18 times a month, and 10 percent of the clientele stop by twice a day.[1] Part of the appeal is that the retail outlets provide an oasis from the hectic world. Indeed, one of the advertising themes the firm is considering underscores the idea that a visit to a Starbucks is like a visit to a sacred, magical island of calm: "A little sanity, conveniently located."[2] Americans are discovering a secret that Europeans have known for years: Life is too short to spend the *whole* day behind a desk.

Culture, a concept crucial to the understanding of consumer behavior, may be thought of as a society's personality. It includes both abstract ideas, such as values and ethics, as well as the material objects and services, such as automobiles, clothing, food, art, and sports, that are produced or valued by a society. Put another way, **culture** is the accumulation of shared meanings, rituals, norms, and traditions among the members of an organization or society.

Consumption choices simply cannot be understood without considering the cultural context in which they are made: Culture is the "lens" through which people view products. Ironically, the effects of culture on consumer behavior are so powerful and far-reaching that this importance is sometimes difficult to grasp or appreciate. Like a fish immersed in water, we do not always appreciate this power until we encounter a different environment, in which suddenly many of the assumptions we had taken for granted about the clothes we wear, the food we eat, the way we address others, and so on no longer seem to apply. The effect of encountering such differences can be so great the term "culture shock" is not an exaggeration.

The importance of these cultural expectations is often only discovered when they are violated. For example, while on tour in New Zealand, the popular group The Spice Girls created a stir among New Zealand's indigenous Maoris by performing a war dance only men are supposed to do. A tribal official indignantly stated, "It is not

acceptable in our culture, and especially by girlie pop stars from another culture."[3] Sensitivity to cultural issues, whether by rock stars or by brand managers, can only come by understanding these underlying dimensions—that is the goal of this chapter.

CONSUMER BEHAVIOR AND CULTURE: A TWO-WAY STREET

A consumer's culture determines the overall priorities he or she attaches to different activities and products. It also mandates the success or failure of specific products and services. A product that provides benefits consistent with those desired by members of a culture at any point in time has a much better chance of attaining acceptance in the marketplace. For example, American culture started to emphasize the concept of a fit, trim body as an ideal of appearance in the mid-1970s. The premium placed on this goal, which stemmed from underlying values like mobility, wealth, and a focus on the self, greatly contributed to the success of Miller Lite beer at that time. However, when Gablinger introduced a low-cal beer seven years earlier, in 1968, the product failed. This product was "ahead of its time," because American consumers were not interested in this benefit in the 1960s.

The relationship between consumer behavior and culture is a two-way street. On the one hand, products and services that resonate with the priorities of a culture at any given time have a much better chance of being accepted by consumers. On the other hand, the study of new products and innovations in product design successfully produced by a culture at any point in time provides a window onto the dominant cultural ideals of that period. Consider, for example, some American products that reflect underlying cultural processes at the time they were introduced:

- The TV dinner, which hinted at changes in family structure and the onset of a new informality in American home life.
- Cosmetics made of natural materials and not animal-tested, which reflected consumers' apprehensions about pollution, waste, and animal rights.
- Condoms marketed in pastel carrying cases for female buyers, which signaled changes in attitudes toward sexual responsibility and frankness.

ASPECTS OF CULTURE

Culture is not static. It is continually evolving, synthesizing old ideas with new ones. A cultural system consists of three functional areas:[4]

1. *Ecology:* the way in which a system is adapted to its habitat. This area is shaped by the technology used to obtain and distribute resources (e.g., industrialized societies versus Third World countries). The Japanese, for example, greatly value products that are designed for efficient use of space because of the cramped conditions in that island nation.[5]

2. *Social structure:* the way in which orderly social life is maintained. This includes the domestic and political groups that are dominant within the culture (e.g., the nuclear family versus the extended family; representative government versus dictatorship).

3. *Ideology:* the mental characteristics of a people and the way in which they relate to their environment and social groups. This revolves around the notion that members of a society possess a common **worldview.** They share certain ideas about principles of order and fairness. They also share an **ethos,** or a set of moral and aesthetic principles.

Although every culture is different, four dimensions appear to account for much of this variability:[6]

1. *Power distance:* the way in which interpersonal relationships form when differences in power are perceived. Some cultures emphasize strict, vertical relationships (e.g., Japan), whereas others, such as the United States, stress a greater degree of equality and informality.

2. *Uncertainty avoidance:* the degree to which people feel threatened by ambiguous situations and have beliefs and institutions that help them to avoid this uncertainty (e.g., organized religion).

3. *Masculinity/femininity:* the degree to which sex roles are clearly delineated (see chapter 5). Traditional societies are more likely to possess very explicit rules about the acceptable behaviors of men and women, such as who is responsible for certain tasks within the family unit.

4. *Individualism:* the extent to which the welfare of the individual versus that of the group is valued (see chapter 11). Cultures differ in their emphasis on individualism versus collectivism. In **collectivist cultures,** people subordinate their personal goals to those of a stable in-group. In contrast, consumers in **individualist cultures** attach more importance to personal goals, and people are more likely to change memberships when the demands of the group (e.g., workplace, church, etc.) become too costly. Whereas a collectivist society will stress values (see chapter 4) such as self-discipline and accepting one's position in life, people in individualist cultures emphasize personal enjoyment, excitement, equality, and freedom. Some strongly individualistic cultures include the United States, Australia, Great Britain, Canada, and the Netherlands. Venezuela, Pakistan, Taiwan, Thailand, Turkey, Greece, and Portugal are some examples of strongly collectivist cultures.[7]

Values are very general ideas about good and bad goals. From these flow **norms,** or rules dictating what is right or wrong, acceptable or unacceptable. Some norms, called *enacted norms,* are explicitly decided on, such as the rule that a green traffic light means "go" and a red one means "stop." Many norms, however, are much more subtle. These *crescive norms* are embedded in a culture and are only discovered through interaction with other members of that culture. Crescive norms include the following:[8]

- A **custom** is a norm handed down from the past that controls basic behaviors, such as division of labor in a household or the practice of particular ceremonies.
- A **more** ("mor-ay") is a custom with a strong moral overtone. A more often involves a taboo, or forbidden behavior, such as incest or cannibalism. Violation of a more often meets with strong sanctions from other members of a society.
- **Conventions** are norms regarding the conduct of everyday life. These rules deal with the subtleties of consumer behavior, including the "correct" way to furnish one's house, wear one's clothes, host a dinner party, and so on.

All three types of crescive norms may operate to completely define a culturally appropriate behavior. For example, a more may tell us what kind of food is permissible to eat. Note that mores vary across cultures, so a meal of dog may be taboo in the United States, Hindus would shun a steak, and Muslims would avoid pork products. A custom dictates the appropriate hour at which the meal should be served.

Conventions tell us how to eat the meal, including such details as the utensils to be used, table etiquette, and even the appropriate apparel to be worn at dinnertime.

We often take these conventions for granted, assuming that they are the "right" things to do (again, until we travel to a foreign country!). It is good to remember that much of what we know about these norms is learned *vicariously* (see chapter 3), as we observe the behaviors of actors and actresses in television commercials, sitcoms, print ads, and other popular culture media. In the long run, marketers have an awful lot to do with influencing consumers' enculturation!

MYTHS AND RITUALS

Every culture develops stories and practices that help its members to make sense of the world. When we examine these activities in other cultures, they often seem strange or even unfathomable. Yet, our *own* cultural practices appear quite normal—even though a visitor may find them equally bizarre!

To appreciate how "primitive" belief systems that some may consider bizarre, irrational, or superstitious continue to influence our supposedly "modern," rational society, consider the avid interest of many American consumers in magic. Marketers of health foods, antiaging cosmetics, exercise programs, and gambling casinos, often imply that their offerings have "magical" properties that will ward off sickness, old age, poverty, or just plain bad luck. People by the millions play their "lucky numbers" in the lottery, carry rabbits' feet and other amulets to ward off "the evil eye," and many have "lucky" clothing or other products that they believe will bring them good fortune. Software developers even supply "wizards" that help to guide the unitiated through the arcane layers of their programs!

An interest in the occult tends to be popular when members of a society feel overwhelmed or powerless—magical remedies simplify our lives by giving us "easy" answers. Even a computer is regarded with awe by many consumers as a sort of "electronic magician," with the ability to solve our problems (or in other cases to cause data to magically disappear!).[9] This section will discuss myths and rituals, two aspects of culture common to all societies, from the ancients to the modern world.

MYTHS

Every society possesses a set of myths that define that culture. A **myth** is a story containing symbolic elements that expresses the shared emotions and ideals of a culture. The story often features some kind of conflict between two opposing forces, and its outcome serves as a moral guide for people. In this way, a myth reduces anxiety because it provides consumers with guidelines about their world.

An understanding of cultural myths is important to marketers, who in some cases (most likely unconsciously) pattern their strategy along a mythic structure. Consider, for example, the way that McDonald's takes on "mythical" qualities.[10] The "golden arches" are a universally recognized symbol, one that is virtually synonymous with American culture. They offer sanctuary to Americans around the world, who know exactly what to expect once they enter. Basic struggles involving good versus evil are played out in the fantasy world created by McDonald's advertising, as when Ronald McDonald confounds the Hamburglar. McDonald's even has a "seminary" (Hamburger University) where inductees go to learn appropriate behavior.

THE FUNCTIONS AND STRUCTURE OF MYTHS

Myths serve four interrelated functions in a culture:[11]

1. *Metaphysical:* They help to explain the origins of existence.
2. *Cosmological:* They emphasize that all components of the universe are part of a single picture.
3. *Sociological:* They maintain social order by authorizing a social code to be followed by members of a culture.
4. *Psychological:* They provide models for personal conduct.

Myths can be analyzed by examining their underlying structures, a technique pioneered by the French anthropologist Claude Lévi-Strauss (no relation to the blue jeans company). Lévi-Strauss noted that many stories involve **binary opposition,** by which two opposing ends of some dimension are represented (e.g., good versus evil, nature versus technology).[12] Characters, and in some cases, products, are often defined by what they are *not* rather than what they *are* (e.g., "This is not your father's Oldsmobile," "I can't believe it's not butter").

Recall from the discussion of Freudian theory in chapter 6 that the ego functions as a kind of "referee" between the opposing needs of the id and the superego. In a similar fashion, the conflict between mythical opposing forces is sometimes resolved by a *mediating figure* who can link the opposites by sharing characteristics of each. For example, many myths contain animals that have human abilities (e.g., a talking snake) to bridge the gap between humanity and nature, just as cars (technology) are often given animal names (nature) like Cougar, Cobra, or Mustang.

MYTHS ABOUND IN MODERN POPULAR CULTURE

We generally associate myths with the ancient Greeks or Romans, but modern myths are embodied in many aspects of modern popular culture, including comic books, movies, holidays, and yes, even commercials.

Comic book superheroes demonstrate how myths can be communicated to consumers of all ages. Indeed, some of these fictional figures represent a **monomyth,** a myth that is common to many cultures.[13] The most prevalent monomyth involves a hero who emerges from the everyday world with supernatural powers and wins a decisive victory over evil forces. He then returns with the power to bestow good things on his fellow men. The recent success of the Disney movie *Hercules* reminds us that these stories are often timeless and have appealed to people through the ages.

Comic book heroes are familiar to most consumers, and they even may be more credible and effective than real-life celebrity endorsers. Not even counting movie spinoffs or licensing deals, comic books today are a $300 million-a-year industry. The American version of the monomyth is perhaps best epitomized by Superman, a godlike figure who renounces worldly temptations and restores harmony to his community. This imagery is sometimes borrowed by marketers—currently, PepsiCo is trying to enhance its position in the Japanese market by using a figure called "Pepsiman," a muscle-bound caricature of an American superhero in a skin-tight uniform, to promote the drink. Pepsiman even appears in a Sega game called Fighting Vipers.[14]

Many "blockbuster" movies and hit TV shows draw directly on mythic themes. Although dramatic special effects or attractive stars certainly don't hurt, a number of these movies perhaps also owe their success to their presentation of characters and plot structures that follow mythic patterns. Three examples of these mythic blockbusters are:[15]

- *Gone with the Wind.* Myths are often set in times of upheaval, such as wars. In this story, the North (which represents technology and democracy) is pitted again the South (which represents nature and aristocracy). The movie depicts a romantic era (the antebellum South) where love and honor were virtues. This era is replaced by the newer forces of materialism and industrialization (i.e., modern consumer culture). The movie depicts a lost era in which man and nature existed in harmony.

- *E.T.: The Extraterrestrial.* E.T. represents a familiar myth involving messianic visitation. The gentle creature from another world visits Earth and performs miracles (e.g., reviving a dying flower). His "disciples" are neighborhood children, who help him combat the forces of modern technology and an unbelieving secular society. The metaphysical function of myth is served by teaching that the humans chosen by God are pure and unselfish.

- *Star Trek:* The television series and movies documenting the adventures of the starship Enterprise are also linked to myths, such as the story of the New England Puritans exploring and conquering a new continent—"the final frontier." Encounters with the Klingons mirror skirmishes with Native Americans. In addition, the quest for paradise was a theme employed in at least 13 out of the original 79 episodes filmed.[16]

Commercials can also be analyzed in terms of the underlying mythic themes they represent. For example, commercials for Pepperidge Farm ask consumers to "remember" the good old days (lost paradise) when products were wholesome and natural. The theme of the underdog prevailing over the stronger foe (i.e., David and Goliath) has been used by Chrysler and Avis.[17]

RITUALS

A **ritual** is a set of multiple, symbolic behaviors that occur in a fixed sequence and that tend to be repeated periodically.[18] Although bizarre tribal ceremonies, perhaps involving animal or human sacrifice, may come to mind when people think of ritu-

This Italian ad for Volkswagen plays on the myth of the Garden of Eden, a classic struggle between virtue and temptation. The copy reads, "Whoever said that you have to pay dearly for giving in to temptation?"

als, in reality many contemporary consumer activities are ritualistic. Just think of Whitney's daily "mental health" trip to Starbucks.

Rituals can occur at a variety of levels, as noted in Table 16–1. Some affirm broad cultural or religious values, whereas others occur in small groups or even in isolation. Market researchers discovered, for example, that for many people (like Whitney) the act of late-night ice cream eating has ritualistic elements, often involving a favorite spoon and bowl![19] Rituals can even be invented or modified to bring about changes in consumer behavior. In Fiji, a group of visiting doctors who were concerned about the pervasiveness of smoking (60 percent of adult men indulge) created a tobacco taboo in one village by devising a ritual involving kava, a sacred potion that is mildly hallucinogenic. After convincing the villagers that the evil spirits of cigarettes can be exorcised by using the drug, the village has become a smoke-free oasis in a tobacco-happy society.[20]

Many businesses owe their livelihoods to their ability to supply **ritual artifacts,** or items used in the performance of rituals, to consumers. Birthday candles, diplomas, specialized foods and beverages (e.g., wedding cakes, ceremonial wine, or even hot dogs at the ball park), trophies and plaques, band uniforms, greeting cards, retirement watches, and now espresso makers are all used in consumer rituals. In addition, consumers often employ a *ritual script,* which identifies the artifacts, the sequence in which they are used, and who uses them. Examples include graduation programs, fraternity manuals, and etiquette books.

GROOMING RITUALS

Whether brushing one's hair 100 strokes a day or talking to oneself in the mirror, virtually all consumers have private grooming rituals. These are sequences of behaviors that aid in the transition from the private self to the public self or back again. These rituals serve various purposes, ranging from inspiring confidence before confronting the world to cleansing the body of dirt and other impure materials.

When consumers talk about their grooming rituals, some of the dominant themes that emerge from these stories reflect the almost mystical qualities attributed to grooming products and behaviors. Many people emphasize a before-and-

TABLE 16–1 ■ Types of Ritual Experience

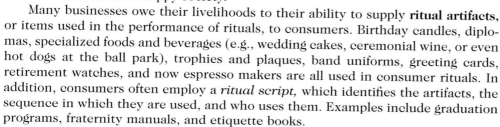

PRIMARY BEHAVIOR SOURCE	RITUAL TYPE	EXAMPLES
Cosmology	Religious	Baptism, meditation, mass
Cultural values	Rites of passage	Graduation, marriage
	Cultural	Festivals, holidays (Valentine's Day), Super Bowl
Group learning	Civic	Parades, elections, trials
	Group	Fraternity initiation, business negotiations, office luncheons
	Family	Mealtimes, bedtimes, birthdays, Mother's Day, Christmas
Individual aims and emotions	Personal	Grooming, household rituals

Source: Dennis W. Rook, "The Ritual Dimension of Consumer Behavior," *Journal of Consumer Research* 12 (December 1985): 251–64. Reprinted with permission of The University of Chicago Press.

after phenomenon, whereby the person feels magically transformed after using certain products (similar to the Cinderella myth).[21]

Two sets of binary oppositions that are expressed in personal rituals are *private/public* and *work/leisure*. Many beauty rituals, for instance, reflect a transformation from a natural state to the social world (as when a woman "puts on her face") or vice versa. In these daily rituals, women reaffirm the value placed by their culture on personal beauty and the quest for eternal youth.[22] This focus is obvious in ads for Oil of Olay Beauty Cleanser, which proclaim ". . . And so your day begins. The Ritual of Oil of Olay." Similarly, the bath is viewed as a sacred, cleansing time, a way to wash away the "sins" of the profane world.[23]

GIFT-GIVING RITUALS

The promotion of appropriate gifts for every conceivable holiday and occasion provides an excellent example of the influence consumer rituals can exert on marketing phenomena. In the **gift-giving ritual**, consumers procure the perfect object (artifact), meticulously remove the price tag and carefully wrap it (symbolically changing the item from a commodity to a unique good), and deliver it to the recipient.[24]

Gift giving is primarily viewed by researchers as a form of *economic exchange*, whereby the giver transfers an item of value to a recipient, who in turn is somehow obligated to reciprocate. However, gift giving also can involve *symbolic exchange*, whereby a giver such as Whitney wants to acknowledge her friend Gabrielle's intan-

Nivea is well-known for its numerous skin care products. Research conducted for the company as it sought to develop a more consistent brand image for all of its lines in the 1990s confirmed the important, yet intangible, functions played by these items for women as they conduct their private grooming rituals. The company found that consumers associated the Nivea image with scenes depicting moistures, freshness, and relaxation.[1]
1. Kevin Keller, *Strategic Marketing Management* (Upper Saddle River, NJ: Prentice Hall 1998).

gible support and companionship. Some research indicates that gift giving evolves as a form of social expression; it is more exchange-oriented (instrumental) in the early stages of a relationship, but becomes more altruistic as the relationship develops.[25]

Every culture prescribes certain occasions and ceremonies for giving gifts, whether for personal or professional reasons. The giving of birthday presents alone is a major undertaking. Each American on average buys about six birthday gifts a year—about one billion gifts in total.[26] Business gifts are an important component in defining professional relationships. Expenditures on business gifts exceed $1.5 billion per year, and great care is often taken to ensure that the appropriate gifts are purchased.

The gift-giving ritual can be broken down into three distinct stages.[27] During *gestation,* the giver is motivated by an event to procure a gift. This event may be either *structural* (i.e., prescribed by the culture, as when people buy Christmas presents) or *emergent* (i.e., the decision is more personal and idiosyncratic). The second stage is *presentation,* or the process of gift exchange. The recipient responds to the gift (either appropriately or not), and the donor evaluates this response.

In the third stage, known as *reformulation,* the bonds between the giver and receiver are adjusted (either looser or tighter) to reflect the new relationship that emerges after the exchange is complete. Negativity can arise if the recipient feels the gift is inappropriate or of inferior quality. The donor may feel the response to the gift was inadequate or insincere or a violation of the **reciprocity norm,** which obliges people to return the gesture of a gift with one of equal value.[28] Both participants may feel resentful for being "forced" to participate in the ritual.[29]

In addition to expressing their feelings toward others through consumption, people commonly find (or devise) reasons to give themselves something as well. It is common for consumers to purchase **self-gifts** as a way to regulate their behavior. This ritual provides a socially acceptable way of rewarding themselves for good deeds, consoling themselves after negative events, or motivating themselves to accomplish some goal.[30] Indeed, retailers report that it is becoming increasingly

MULTICULTURAL DIMENSIONS

The importance of gift-giving rituals is underscored by considering Japanese customs, in which the wrapping of a gift is as important (if not more so) than the gift itself. The economic value of a gift is secondary to its symbolic meaning.[31] To the Japanese, gifts are viewed as an important aspect of one's duty to others in one's social group. Giving is a moral imperative (known as *giri*).

Highly ritualized gift giving occurs during the giving of both household/personal gifts and company/professional gifts. Each Japanese has a well-defined set of relatives and friends with which he or she shares reciprocal gift-giving obligations (*kosai*).[32]

Personal gifts are given on social occasions, such as at funerals, to people who are hospitalized, to mark move-ments from one life stage to another (e.g., weddings, birthdays), and as greetings (e.g., when one is meeting a visitor). Company gifts are given to commemorate the anniversary of a corporations' founding or the opening of a new building, as well as being a routine part of doing business, as when rewards are given at trade meetings to announce new products.

Some of the items most desired by Japanese consumers to receive as gifts include gift coupons, beer, and soap.[33] In keeping with the Japanese emphasis on saving face, presents are not opened in front of the giver, so that it will not be necessary to hide one's possible disappointment with the present.

common for people to treat themselves while they are ostensibly searching for goodies for others. As one shopper admitted recently, "It's one for them, one for me, one for them."[34]

Figure 16–1 is a projective stimulus similar to ones used in research on this phenomenon. Consumers are asked to tell a story based on a picture, and their responses are analyzed to discover the reasons people view as legitimate for rewarding themselves with self-gifts. For example, one recurring story that might emerge is that Mary, the woman pictured, had a particularly grueling day at the office and needs a pick-me-up in the form of a new fragrance. This theme could then be incorporated into the promotional campaign for a perfume.

HOLIDAY RITUALS

On holidays consumers step back from their everyday lives and perform ritualistic behaviors unique to those times.[35] Holiday occasions are filled with ritual artifacts and scripts and are increasingly cast as a time for giving gifts by enterprising marketers. The Thanksgiving holiday is bursting with rituals for Americans; these scripts include serving (in gluttonous portions) foods such as turkey and cranberry sauce that may only be consumed on that day, complaints about how much one has eaten (yet rising to the occasion to somehow find room for dessert), and (for many) a postmeal trip to the couch for the obligatory football game. On Valentine's Day, standards regarding sex and love are relaxed or altered as people express feelings that may be hidden during the rest of the year.

In addition to established holidays, new occasions are invented to capitalize on the need for cards and other ritual artifacts that will then have to be acquired.[36] These cultural events often originate with the greeting card industry, precisely to stimulate demand for more of its products. Some recently invented holidays include Secretaries' Day and Grandparents' Day.

FIGURE 16–1 ■
Projective Drawing to Study the Motivations Underlying the Giving of Self-Gifts.
Source: Based on David G. Mick, Michelle DeMoss and Ronald J. Faber, "Latent Motivations and Meanings of Self-Gifts: Implications for Retail Management" (research report, Center for Retailing Education and Research, University of Florida, 1990).

MARKETING PITFALL

Bride magazine reports that a newly married couple receives an average of 171 wedding gifts, many of which they don't want or need.[37] Just about everyone has at one time or another received a ghastly gift; this "dark side" of gift giving was highlighted in a recent study by an economist, who calculated that of the $40 billion spent yearly on holiday gifts, roughly $4 billion is a "deadweight loss." This refers to the difference between the amount spent on a gift and the value the recipient assigns to it; a gift's "yield" is regarded as its perceived value compared to its true value. For example, if a tie cost $10 but you feel it's worth only $8 to you, its yield is 80 percent. The study computed the average yield of a gift to be 94.1 percent. Based on a survey of students at five universities, these yields were reported (100 percent means the gift has an intrinsic value equal to its actual value):[38]

CDs 104.4%
Books 91%
Socks, underwear 87.7%
Cosmetics 85.7%

Most cultural holidays are based on a myth, and often an historical (e.g., Miles Standish on Thanksgiving) or imaginary (e.g., Cupid on Valentine's Day) character is at the center of the story. These holidays persist because their basic elements appeal to consumers' deep-seated needs.[39] Two of our holidays that are especially rich both in cultural symbolism and in consumption meanings are Christmas and Hallowe'en:

- The Christmas holiday is bursting with myths and rituals, from adventures at the North Pole to those that occur under the mistletoe. The meaning of Christmas has evolved quite dramatically over the last few hundred years, particularly in the United States. In colonial times, Christmas celebrations resembled carnivals and were most noted for public rowdiness, including the tradition of "wassailing," in which packs of poor young people would lay siege to the rich, demanding food and drink. By the end of the 1800s, the mobs were so unruly that Protestant America invented a tradition of families having Christmas gatherings around a tree, a practice "borrowed" from early, pagan rites.

  In a 1822 poem, Clement Clarke Moore, the wealthy son of New York's Episcopal bishop, invented the modern-day myth of Santa Claus and the Christmas ritual slowly changed to a focus on children.[40] One of the most important holiday rituals still involves Santa Claus, a mythical figure eagerly awaited by children the world over. In opposition to Christ, Santa is a champion of materialism. Perhaps it is no coincidence, then, that he appears in stores and shopping malls—secular temples of consumption. Whatever his origins, the Santa Claus myth serves the purpose of socializing children by teaching them to expect a reward when they are good and that members of society get what they deserve.

- Hallowe'en is a holiday that has evolved from a pagan religious observance to a secular event. However, in contrast to Christmas, the rituals of Hallowe'en (e.g., trick-or-treating and costume parties) primarily involve nonfamily members. Hallowe'en is an unusual holiday, because its rituals are the opposite of many other cultural occasions. In contrast to Christmas, it celebrates evil instead of good and death rather than birth, and it encourages revelers to extort treats with veiled threats of "tricks" rather than rewarding only the good. Because of these oppositions, Hallowe'en has been described as an *antifestival*, in which

The Coca-Cola Company claims credit for inventing the modern image of Santa, which it distributed in its advertising in 1931. Until that time (the company claims), Santa was pictured as a cartoonlike elf. More likely, the modern image of Santa Claus was shaped by the 19th century cartoonist Thomas Nast, whose rendering of Santa was related to his other drawings of "fat cats" such as Boss Tweed and the Robber Barons, greedy capitalists who exploited the poor and lived in useless luxury. This Thomas Nast cartoon was published in 1881. Despite this figure's resemblance to Santa Claus, it is actually a caricature of a "fat cat" Robber Baron who had accumulated a horde of worldly possessions.

the symbols associated with other holidays are distorted. For example, the Hallowe'en witch can be viewed as an inverted mother figure. The holiday also parodies the meaning of Easter by stressing the resurrection of ghosts and of Thanksgiving by transforming the wholesome symbolism of the pumpkin pie into the evil jack-o-lantern.[41] Furthermore, Hallowe'en provides a ritualized, and therefore socially sanctioned, context in which people can act out uncharacteristic behaviors and try on new roles: Children can go outside after dark, stay up late, and eat all the candy they like for a night; the otherwise geeky guy who always sits in the back of class comes dressed as Elvis and turns out to be the life of the party.

RITES OF PASSAGE

What does a dance for recently divorced people have in common with a fraternity Hell Week? Both are examples of modern **rites of passage**, or special times marked by a change in social status. Every society, both primitive and modern, sets aside times at which such changes occur. Some of these changes may occur as a natural part of consumers' life-cycles (e.g., puberty or death), whereas others are more individual in nature (e.g., getting divorced and reentering the dating market). As Whitney's son discovered, when he bombed his driving test, the importance of a rite of passage becomes more obvious when one fails to undergo it at the prescribed time.

Some marketers attempt to reach consumers on occasions in which their products can enhance a transition from one stage of life to another.[42] For example, a chain of fur stores ran a series of ads positioning a fur coat as a way to celebrate "all of life's moments." Suggested moments included a thirtieth birthday, a raise, a second marriage, and even a "divorce-is-final" fur coat: "Shed the tears and slip into a fur," reads the ad.[43]

Much like the metamorphosis of a caterpillar into a butterfly, consumers' rites of passage consist of three phases.[44] The first stage, *separation,* occurs when the individual is detached from his or her original group or status (e.g., the college freshman leaves home). *Liminality* is the middle stage, in which the person is literally

MARKETING PITFALL

Hallowe'en observances among adults are booming, changing the character of this holiday. Hallowe'en is now the second most popular party night for adults (after New Year's Eve), and one in four grown-ups wears a costume.[45] The holiday is now becoming trendy in Europe as well, where the French in particular have discovered it as an occasion for festivities, dancing, and the chance to show off new fashions.[46]

The shift in the Hallowe'en ritual has been attributed to adult fears aroused by stories of children receiving tampered candy containing poison, razor blades, and so on, which encouraged people to plan supervised parties rather than send their children out trick-or-treating.[47] Another factor accounting for the popularity of Hallowe'en among adults is that, unlike other holidays, one does not require a family to celebrate it, which permits single people to participate without feeling lonely or left out.[48]

The liquor industry has come under fire for attempting to reinforce the idea that Hallowe'en is as much an occasion to drink as St. Patrick's Day or New Year's Eve.[49] Miller Brewing Company, Anheuser-Busch, Coors, and Jack Daniels are some companies that have seized on Hallowe'en as an opportunity to stimulate sales during a normally slow season. A public advocacy group has complained that ". . . beer companies try to make drinking a part of every celebration . . . these types of promotions are clearly attractive to young consumers.[50]

Halloween is evolving from a children's festival to an opportunity for adults to experiment with fantasy roles—and party.

in-between statuses (e.g., the new arrival on campus tries to figure out what is happening during orientation week). The last stage, *aggregation,* takes place when the person reenters society after the rite of passage is complete (e.g., the student returns home for Christmas vacation as a college "veteran").

Rites of passage mark many consumer activities, as exemplified by fraternity pledges, recruits at boot camp, or novitiates becoming nuns. A similar transitional state can be observed when people are prepared for certain occupational roles. For example, athletes and fashion models typically undergo a "seasoning" process. They are removed from their normal surroundings (e.g., athletes are taken to training camps; young models are often moved to Paris), indoctrinated into a new subculture, and then returned to the real world in their new roles.

MARKETING OPPORTUNITY

Hold the starch: Although many rituals are strongly ingrained, sometimes pressure arises to adapt them to modern times. This is the case regarding the custom of throwing rice, which symbolizes fertility, at a wedding. In recent years many newlyweds have substituted soap bubbles or jingling bells because of the tendency of birds to eat the rice, which can then expand inside their bodies and cause injury or death. Some enterprising businesses are springing up to work around this problem. The Hole-in-Hand Butterfly Farm in Pennsylvania ships newly hatched butterflies at $100 a dozen. They arrive in dark, cool envelops that keep them in a resting stage until the package is opened, when they fly out in a crescendo of wagging wings. Another company sells a product called Bio Wedding Rice; this is reconstituted rice that dissolves in water and doesn't harm birds.[51]

Even rites of passage associated with death support an entire industry. Survivors must make fairly expensive purchase decisions, often on short notice and driven by emotional and superstitious concerns. The funeral industry is beginning to be more aggressive in its marketing practices and is even targeting younger consumers who are worried about arranging for their aging parents. (The prepayment of funeral and burial expenses is euphemistically known in the industry as "preneed".) Perhaps because of the emotional tone many of these appeals take, women tend to initiate these purchases.[52]

Funeral ceremonies help the living to organize their relationships with the deceased, and action tends to be tightly scripted, down to the costumes (e.g., the ritual black attire, black ribbons for mourners, the body in its best clothes) and specific behaviors (e.g., sending condolence cards or holding a wake). Mourners "pay their last respects," and seating during the ceremony is usually dictated by mourners' closeness to the individual. Even the *cortege* (the funeral motorcade) is accorded special status by other motorists, who recognize its separate, sacred nature by not cutting in as it proceeds to the cemetery.[53]

SACRED AND PROFANE CONSUMPTION

As we saw when considering the structure of myths, many types of consumer activity involve the demarcation, or binary opposition, of categories, such as good versus bad, male versus female—or even regular versus diet. One of the most important of these sets of categories is the distinction between the sacred and the profane. **Sacred consumption** involves objects and events that are "set apart" from normal activities and are treated with some degree of respect or awe. They may or may not be associated with religion, but most religious items and events tend to be regarded as sacred. **Profane consumption** involves consumer objects and events that are ordinary, everyday objects and events that do not share the "specialness" of sacred ones. (Note that profane does not mean vulgar or obscene in this context.)

DOMAINS OF SACRED CONSUMPTION

Sacred consumption events permeate many aspects of consumers' experiences. We find ways to "set apart" a variety of places, people, and events. In this section, we'll consider some examples of ways that "ordinary" consumption is sometimes not so ordinary after all.

SACRED PLACES

Sacred places have been "set apart" by a society because they have religious or mystical significance (e.g., Bethlehem, Mecca, Stonehenge) or because they commemorate some aspect of a country's heritage (e.g., the Kremlin, the Emperor's Palace in Tokyo, the Statue of Liberty). The sacredness of these places is due to the property of **contamination**—that is, something sacred happened on that spot, so the place itself takes on sacred qualities.

Still other places are created from the profane world and imbued with sacred qualities. Graumann's Chinese Theater in Hollywood, where movie stars leave their footprints in concrete for posterity, is one such place. Even the modern shopping mall can be regarded as a secular "cathedral of consumption," a special place to which community members come to practice shopping rituals. Theme parks are a form of mass-produced fantasy that take on aspects of sacredness. In particular, Disney World and Disneyland (and their outposts in Europe and Japan) are destinations for pilgrimages from consumers around the globe. Disney World displays many characteristics of more traditional sacred places. It is even regarded by some as having healing powers. A trip to the park is the most common "last wish" for terminally ill children.[54]

In many cultures, the home is a particularly sacred place. It represents a crucial distinction between the harsh, external world and consumers' "inner space." Americans spend more than $50 billion a year on interior decorators and home furnishings, and the home is a central part of consumers' identities.[55] "Home is where the heart is." Consumers all over the world go to great lengths to create a special environment that allows them to create the quality of "homeyness." This effect is created by personalizing the home as much as possible, using devices such as door wreaths, mantle arrangements, and a "memory wall" for family photos.[56] Even public places, such as Starbucks cafes, strive for a homelike atmosphere that shelters customers from the harshness of the outside world.

SACRED PEOPLE

People themselves can be sacred, when they are idolized and set apart from the masses. Souvenirs, memorabilia, and even mundane items touched or used by sacred people take on special meanings and acquire value in their own right. Indeed, many businesses thrive on consumers' desire for products associated with famous people. There is a thriving market for celebrity autographs and objects once owned by celebrities, whether Princess Diana's gowns or John Lennon's guitars, are often sold at auction for astronomical prices. One entrepreneur dug dirt from the lawns of Johnny Carson, Shirley MacLaine, Katharine Hepburn, and 43 other stars. He sold 20,000 vials of celebrity dirt in three years, at $1.95 a vial. A store called "A Star is Worn" sells items donated by celebrities—a black bra autographed by Cher went for $575. As one observer commented about the store's patrons, "They want something that belonged to the stars, as if the stars have gone into sainthood and the people want their shrouds."[57]

SACRED EVENTS

Many consumers' activities have also taken on a special status. Public events in particular resemble sacred, religious ceremonies, as exemplified by the recitation of the "Pledge of Allegiance" before a game or the reverential lighting of matches at the end of a rock concert.[58]

For many people, the world of sports is sacred, and almost assumes the status of a religion. The roots of modern sports events can be found in ancient religious

The quest to memorialize Elvis has become an industry—about 20,000 people make a pilgrimage to Graceland each year to "worship" his memory. There is an official Elvis site: www.elvis-presley.com/, and many other websites devoted to him, such as one just for Elvis impersonators: http://members.aol.com/nude elvis/index.html. Some of the sites are in somewhat poorer taste, such as a Shockwave game called Gimme That Dang Pill, where the object is to flush the Quaaludes down the toilet before Elvis eats them in order to win a virtual fried peanut butter sandwich, (his favorite meal).[1]
1. "Elvis Evermore," *Newsweek* (August 11, 1997): 12.

rites, such as fertility festivals (e.g., the original Olympics).[59] Indeed, it is not uncommon for teams to join in prayer prior to a game. The sports pages are like the scriptures (and we describe ardent fans as reading them "religiously"), the stadium is a house of worship, and the fans are members of the congregation. Devotees engage in group activities, such as tailgate parties and the "Wave." The athletes that fans come to see are godlike; they are reputed to have almost superhuman powers (especially superstars like Michael Jordan, who is accorded the ability to fly in his Air Nikes).

MARKETING PITFALL

The public's fascination with the images of celebrities, living or dead, endures. The images of dead stars are frequently brought back to life to endorse products. James Dean hawks for Jack Purcell sneakers, and Babe Ruth sells Zenith products. Licensing fees for dead celebrities now average about $100 million per year.[60]

The sacredness of some celebrities has spawned a secondary industry—celebrity look-alikes and sound-alikes. The simulated voice of Louis Armstrong has appeared in ads for the Hershey Food Corporation, Canada Dry, and Milk Bones.[61] Elvis Presley has imitators around the world. By one estimate, about 100 women make their living impersonating Marilyn Monroe.[62] This type of advertising is so pervasive that several lawsuits have been brought by stars (e.g., Woody Allen) to prevent doubles from using their likenesses.[63] Nonetheless, look-alikes continue to be used, with disclaimer notices appearing in the ad.[64]

Athletes are central figures in a common cultural myth, the hero tale. As exemplified by the heroic performance of gymnast Kerri Strug in the 1996 Olympics, often the person must prove him- or herself under strenuous circumstances and victory is achieved only through sheer force of will. One extremely popular Coke commercial, which featured the football player Mean Joe Greene and an admiring little boy, followed the same plot structure as the fairy tale of *The Lion and the Mouse*. The injured hero has his confidence restored by the humble mouse/boy, allowing his heroic persona to be rejuvenated. He then shows his gratitude to his benefactor.[65]

Tourism is another example of a sacred, nonordinary experience of extreme importance to marketers. When people travel on vacation, they occupy sacred time and space. The tourist is continually in search of "authentic" experiences that differ from his or her normal world (think of Club Med's motto, "The antidote to civilization").[66] This traveling experience involves binary oppositions between work and leisure and being "at home" versus "away," and often norms regarding appropriate behavior are modified as tourists scramble after illicit or adventurous experiences they would not dream of engaging in at home.

The desire of travelers to capture these sacred experiences in objects forms the bedrock of the souvenir industry, which may be said to be in the business of selling sacred memories. Whether a personalized matchbook from a wedding or New York City salt-and-pepper shakers, souvenirs represent a tangible piece of the consumer's sacred experience.[67] In addition to personal mementos, such as ticket stubs saved from a favorite concert, the following are other types of sacred souvenir icons:[68]

- Local products (e.g., wine from California)
- Pictorial images (e.g., post cards)
- "Piece of the rock" (e.g., seashells, pine cones)
- Symbolic shorthand in the form of literal representations of the site (e.g., a miniature Statue of Liberty)
- Markers (e.g., Hard Rock Cafe T-shirts)

Souvenirs, tacky or otherwise, allow consumers to tangibilize sacred (i.e., out of the ordinary) experiences accumulated as tourists.

FROM SACRED TO PROFANE, AND BACK AGAIN

Just to make life interesting, in recent times many consumer activities have moved from one sphere to the other: Some things that were formerly regarded as sacred have moved into the realm of the profane; whereas other, everyday phenomena now are regarded as sacred.[69] Both of these processes are relevant to our understanding of contemporary consumer behavior.

DESACRALIZATION

Desacralization occurs when a sacred item or symbol is removed from its special place or is duplicated in mass quantities, becoming profane as a result. For example, souvenir reproductions of sacred monuments such as the Washington Monument or the Eiffel Tower, artworks such as the Mona Lisa or Michelangelo's *David,* or adaptations of important symbols such as the American flag by clothing designers, eliminate their special aspects by turning them into unauthentic commodities, produced mechanically with relatively little value.[70]

Religion itself has to some extent been desacralized. Religious symbols, such as stylized crosses or New Age crystals, have moved into the mainstream of fashion jewelry.[71] Religious holidays, particularly Christmas, are regarded by many (and criticized by some) as having been transformed into secular, materialistic occasions devoid of their original sacred significance.

Even the clergy are increasingly adopting secular marketing techniques. Televangelists rely upon the power of television, a secular medium, to convey their messages. The Catholic Church generated a major controversy after it hired a prominent public relations firm to promote its antiabortion campaign.[72] Nonetheless, many religious groups have taken the secular route. The Mormons sponsored a $12 million campaign in *Readers Digest,* and *Newsweek: On Campus* featured the comedian Father Guido Sarducci in a humorous ad designed to recruit college students as padres.[73]

This jeans style borrows "sacred" imagery and applies it in a "profane" context.

SACRALIZATION

Sacralization occurs when ordinary objects, events, and even people, take on sacred meaning to a culture or to specific groups within a culture. For example, events such as the Super Bowl and people such as Elvis Presley have become sacralized to some consumers.

Objectification occurs when sacred qualities are attributed to mundane items. One way that this process can occur is through *contamination,* by which objects associated with sacred events or people become sacred in their own right. This reason explains the desire by many fans for items belonging to, or even touched by, famous people. Even the Smithsonian Institution in Washington, D.C., maintains a display featuring such "sacred items" as the ruby slippers from *The Wizard of Oz,* a phaser from *Star Trek,* and Archie Bunker's chair from the television show *All in the Family*—all reverently protected behind sturdy display glass.

In addition to museum exhibits displaying rare objects, even mundane, inexpensive things may be set apart in *collections,* where they are transformed from profane items to sacred ones. Name an item, and the odds are that a group of collectors is lusting after it. The contents of collections range from movie memorabilia, rare books, and autographs to GI Joe dolls, Elvis memorabilia, and even junk mail.[74] The 1,200 members of the McDonald's collectors' club collect "prizes" such as sandwich wrappers and Happy Meal trinkets—rare ones like the 1987 Potato Head Kids Toys sell for $25.[75] Consumers often are ferociously attached to their collections; this passion is exemplified by the comment made in one study by a woman who collects teddy bears: "If my house ever burns down, I won't cry over my furniture, I'll cry over the bears."[76]

An item is sacralized as soon as it enters a collection, and it takes on special significance to the collector that, in some cases, may be hard to comprehend by the outsider. **Collecting** refers to the systematic acquisition of a particular object or set of objects, and this widespread activity can be distinguished from hoarding, which is merely unsystematic collecting.[77] Collecting typically involves both rational and emotional components; collectors are often obsessed by their objects but they also carefully organize and exhibit them.[78]

In the early 1990s, "Swatch fever" infected many people. The company made more than 500 different models, some of which were special editions designed by artists. Collectors' interest made a formerly mundane product into a rare piece of art (e.g., a "Jelly Fish" that originally sold for $30 was sold at auction for $17,000). Although thousands of people still collect the watches, the frenzy began to fade by around 1993.[1]
1. "A Feeding Frenzy for Swatches," *New York Times* (August 29, 1991): C3; Patricia Leigh Brown, "Fueling a Frenzy: Swatch," *New York Times* (May 10, 1992): 1,9; Mary M. Long and Leon G. Schiffman, "Swatch Fever: An Allegory for Understanding the Paradox of Collecting," *Psychology & Marketing* 14 (August 1997)5: 495–509.

Some consumer researchers feel that collectors are motivated to acquire their "prizes" in order to gratify a high level of materialism in a socially acceptable manner. By systematically amassing a collection, the collector is allowed to "worship" material objects without feeling guilty or petty. Another perspective is that collecting is actually an aesthetic experience; for many collectors the pleasure emanates from being involved in creating the collection, rather than from passively admiring the items one has scavenged or bought. Whatever the motivation, hard-core collectors often devote a great deal of time and energy to maintaining and expanding their collections, so for many this activity becomes a central component of their extended selves (see chapter 5).[79]

MARKETING OPPORTUNITY

Marketers continue to find new ways to indulge consumers' passions for collecting. For example, many children and adults are avid collectors of sports trading cards—people spend about $1.5 billion a year on these cards. Now, in addition to grabbing up photos and stats of baseball, football, and basketball players, consumers can also collect trading cards featuring advertisements and product information for such companies as Sears, Harley-Davidson, Coca-Cola, and even the Hooters restaurant chain. The Sears cards feature photos of "classic" Craftsman tools, including such "valuable" items as reversible ratchets and drill presses.

Some of the hottest new collectibles are phone cards; sales of these prepaid cards are projected to reach around $3 billion by the year 2000. One company, called Future Call, has licensing agreements with *Star Trek, Melrose Place,* and the *Mighty Morphin Power Rangers* and is issuing MCI cards with these images. The attractiveness of these cards to the phone companies is magnified because many of them will never actually be redeemed as they are far more valuable to collectors if they are "virgins."[80]

Another "must have" for kids are Beanie Babies, a series of stuffed animals that come with distinctive names like Bubbles and Stinky and are released periodically. Ty, Inc. is doing a good job of following industry guidelines for creating collectible product lines, which include limiting the number of items available, numbering and dating each one, and offering a range to encourage people to collect the entire set.[81] Virtually no advertising is done, other than the provision of a Web site (http://www.ty.com) that gives information about the latest releases.[82] As any parent of a young girl can attest, no further encouragement is needed!

- A society's *culture* includes its values, ethics, and the material objects produced by its members. It is the accumulation of shared meanings and traditions among members of a society. A culture can be described in terms of *ecology* (the way people adapt to their habitat), its *social structure,* and its *ideology* (including people's moral and aesthetic principles).

- *Myths* are stories containing symbolic elements that express the shared ideals of a culture. Many myths involve a *binary opposition,* whereby values are defined in terms of what they are and what they are not (e.g., nature versus technology). Modern myths are transmitted through advertising, movies, and other media.

- A *ritual* is a set of multiple, symbolic behaviors that occur in a fixed sequence and that tend to be repeated periodically. Ritual is related to many consumption activities that occur in popular culture. These include holiday observances, gift giving, and grooming.

- A *rite of passage* is a special kind of ritual that involves the transition from one role to another. These passages typically entail the need to acquire products and services, called *ritual artifacts,* to facilitate the transition. Modern rites of passage include graduations, fraternity initiations, weddings, debutante balls, and funerals.

- Consumer activities can be divided into *sacred* and *profane* domains. Sacred phenomena are "set apart" from everyday activities or products. People, events, or objects can become sacralized. *Objectification* occurs when sacred qualities are ascribed to products or items owned by sacred people. *Sacralization* occurs when formerly sacred objects or activities become part of the everyday, as when "one-of-a-kind" works of art are reproduced in large quantities. *Descralization* occurs when objects that previously were considered sacred become commercialized and integrated into popular culture.

CHAPTER SUMMARY

KEY TERMS

Binary opposition p. 499
Collecting p. 513
Collectivist cultures p. 497
Contamination p. 509
Convention p. 497
Culture p. 495
Custom p. 497
Desacralization p. 512

Ethos p. 496
Gift-giving ritual p. 502
Individualist cultures p. 497
Monomyth p. 499
More p. 497
Myth p. 497
Norms p. 497
Profane consumption p. 508

Rites of passage p. 506
Ritual p. 500
Ritual artifacts p. 501
Sacralization p. 513
Sacred consumption p. 508
Self-gifts p. 503
Worldview p. 496

CONSUMER BEHAVIOR CHALLENGE

1. Culture can be thought of as a society's personality. If your culture were a person, how would you describe its personality traits?

2. What is the difference between an enacted norm and a crescive norm? Identify the set of crescive norms operating when a man and woman in your culture go out for dinner on a first date. What products and services are affected by these norms?

3. How do the consumer decisions involved in gift giving differ from other purchase decisions?

4. The chapter argues that not all gift giving is positive. In what ways can this ritual be unpleasant or negative?

5. What are some of the major motivations for the purchase of self-gifts? Discuss some marketing implications of these.

6. Describe the three stages of the rite of passage associated with graduating from college.

7. Identify the ritualized aspects of football that are employed in advertising.

8. "Christmas has become just another opportunity to exchange gifts and stimulate the economy." Do you agree? Why or why not?

NOTES

1. Bill McDowell, "Starbucks is Ground Zero in Today's Coffee Culture," *Advertising Age* (December 9, 1996): 1 (2 pp.).

2. Seanna Browder, "Starbucks Does Not Live by Coffee Alone," *Business Week* (August 5, 1996): 76; for a discussion of the act of coffee drinking as ritual, see Susan Fournier and Julie L. Yao, "Reviving Brand Loyalty: A Reconceptualization within the Framework of Consumer–Brand Relationships" (working paper 96-039, Harvard Business School, 1996).

3. "Spice Girls Dance into Culture Clash," *Montgomery Advertiser* (April 29, 1997): 2A.

4. Clifford Geertz, *The Interpretation of Cultures* (New York: Basic Books, 1973); Marvin Harris, *Culture, People and Nature* (New York: Crowell, 1971); John F. Sherry Jr., "The Cultural Perspective in Consumer Research," in ed. Richard J. Lutz, *Advances in Consumer Research* 13 (Provo, UT: Association for Consumer Research, 1985): 573–5.

5. William Lazer, Shoji Murata, and Hiroshi Kosaka, "Japanese Marketing: Towards a Better Understanding," *Journal of Marketing* 49 (Spring 1985): 69–81.

6. Geert Hofstede, *Culture's Consequences* (Beverly Hills, CA: Sage, 1980); see also Laura M. Milner, Dale Fodness, and Mark W. Speece, "Hofstede's Research on Cross-Cultural Work-Related Values: Implications for Consumer Behavior," in eds. W. Fred van Raaij and Gary J. Bamossy, *European Advances in Consumer Research* (Amsterdam: Association for Consumer Research, 1993): 70–76.

7. Daniel Goleman, "The Group and the Self: New Focus on a Cultural Rift," *New York Times* (December 25, 1990): 37; Harry C. Triandis, "The Self and Social Behavior in Differing Cultural Contexts," *Psychological Review* 96 (July 1989): 506; Harry C. Triandis, Robert Bontempo, Marcelo J. Villareal, Masaaki Asai, and Nydia Lucca, "Individualism and Collectivism: Cross-Cultural Perspectives on Self-Ingroup Relationships," *Journal of Personality and Social Psychology* 54 (February 1988): 323.

8. George J. McCall and J. L. Simmons, *Social Psychology: A Sociological Approach* (New York: The Free Press, 1982).

9. Molly O'Neill, "As Life Gets More Complex, Magic Casts a Wider Spell," *New York Times* (June 13, 1994): A1 (2 pp.).

10. Conrad Phillip Kottak, "Anthropological Analysis of Mass Enculturation," in ed. Conrad P. Kottak, *Researching American Culture* (Ann Arbor, MI: University of Michigan Press, 1982): 40–74.

11. Joseph Campbell, *Myths, Dreams, and Religion* (New York: E. P. Dutton, 1970).

12. Claude Lévi-Strauss, *Structural Anthropology* (Harmondsworth: Peregrine, 1977).

13. Jeffrey S. Lang and Patrick Trimble, "Whatever Happened to the Man of Tomorrow? An Examination of the American Monomyth and the Comic Book Superhero," *Journal of Popular Culture* 22 (Winter 1988): 157.

14. Yumiko Ono, "PepsiCo's 'American' Superhero in Japanese Ads is Alien to U.S.," *WSJ Interactive Edition* (May 23, 1997).

15. Elizabeth C. Hirschman, "Movies as Myths: An Interpretation of Motion Picture Mythology," in ed. Jean Umiker-Sebeok, *Marketing and Semiotics: New Directions in the Study of Signs for Sale* (Berlin: Mouton de Gruyter, 1987): 335–74.

16. See William Blake Tyrrell, "Star Trek as Myth and Television as Mythmaker," in eds. Jack Nachbar, Deborah Weiser, and John L. Wright, *The Popular Culture Reader* (Bowling Green, OH: Bowling Green University Press, 1978): 79–88.

17. Bernie Whalen, "Semiotics: An Art or Powerful Marketing Research Tool?" *Marketing News* (May 13, 1983): 8.

18. See Dennis W. Rook, "The Ritual Dimension of Consumer Behavior," *Journal of Consumer Research* 12 (December 1985): 251–64; Mary A. Stansfield Tetreault and Robert E. Kleine III, "Ritual, Ritualized Behavior, and Habit: Refinements and Extensions of the Consumption Ritual Construct," in eds. Marvin Goldberg, Gerald Gorn, and Richard W. Pollay, *Advances in Consumer Research* 17 (Provo, UT: Association

19. Kim Foltz, "New Species for Study: Consumers in Action," *New York Times* (December 18, 1989): A1.

20. Christina Duff, "Fijian Village, Surfing Doctors Invoke Taboo Against Tobacco," *WSJ Interactive Edition* (May 19, 1997).

21. Dennis W. Rook and Sidney J. Levy, "Psychosocial Themes in Consumer Grooming Rituals," in eds. Richard P. Bagozzi and Alice M. Tybout, *Advances in Consumer Research* 10 (Provo, UT: Association for Consumer Research, 1983): 329–33.

22. Diane Barthel, *Putting on Appearances: Gender and Attractiveness* (Philadelphia: Temple University Press, 1988).

23. Quoted in Barthel, *Putting on Appearances: Gender and Advertising.*

24. Russell W. Belk, Melanie Wallendorf, and John F. Sherry, Jr., "The Sacred and the Profane in Consumer Behavior: Theodicy on the Odyssey," *Journal of Consumer Research* 16 (June 1989): 1–38.

25. Russell W. Belk and Gregory S. Coon, "Gift Giving as Agapic Love: An Alternative to the Exchange Paradigm Based on Dating Experiences," *Journal of Consumer Research* 20 (December 1993)3: 393–417.

26. Monica Gonzales, "Before Mourning," *American Demographics* (April 1988): 19.

27. John F. Sherry Jr., "Gift Giving in Anthropological Perspective," *Journal of Consumer Research* 10 (September 1983): 157–68.

28. Daniel Goleman, "What's Under the Tree? Clues to a Relationship," *New York Times* (December 19, 1989): C1.

29. John F. Sherry Jr., Mary Ann McGrath, and Sidney J. Levy, "The Dark Side of the Gift," *Journal of Business Research* (1993): 225–244.

30. David Glen Mick and Michelle DeMoss, "Self-Gifts: Phenomenological Insights from Four Contexts," *Journal of Consumer Research* 17 (December 1990): 327; John F. Sherry, Jr., Mary Ann McGrath, and Sidney J. Levy, "Monadic Giving: Anatomy of Gifts Given to the Self," in *Contemporary Marketing and Consumer Behavior: An Anthro-*

pological Sourcebook, ed. John F. Sherry, Jr. (New York: Sage, 1995): 399–432.

31. Colin Camerer, "Gifts as Economics Signals and Social Symbols," *American Journal of Sociology* 94 (Supplement 1988): 5180–214.

32. Robert T. Green and Dana L. Alden, "Functional Equivalence in Cross-Cultural Consumer Behavior: Gift Giving in Japan and the United States," *Psychology & Marketing* 5 (Summer 1988): 155–68.

33. Hiroshi Tanaka and Miki Iwamura, "Gift Selection Strategy of Japanese Seasonal Gift Purchasers: An Explorative Study" (paper presented at the Association for Consumer Research, Boston, October 1994).

34. Quoted in Cynthia Crossen, "Holiday Shoppers' Refrain: 'A Merry Christmas to Me,'" *The Wall Street Journal Interactive Edition* (December 11, 1997).

35. See, for example, Russell W. Belk, "Halloween: An Evolving American Consumption Ritual," in eds. Richard Pollay, Jerry Gorn, and Marvin Goldberg, *Advances in Consumer Research* 17 (Provo, UT: Association for Consumer Research, 1990): 508–17; Melanie Wallendorf and Eric J. Arnould, "We Gather Together: The Consumption Rituals of Thanksgiving Day," *Journal of Consumer Research* 18 (June 1991): 13–31.

36. Rick Lyte, "Holidays, Ethnic Themes Provide Built-In F&B Festivals," *Hotel & Motel Management* (December 14, 1987): 56; Megan Rowe, "Holidays and Special Occasions: Restaurants Are Fast Replacing 'Grandma's House' as the Site of Choice for Special Meals," *Restaurant Management* (November 1987): 69; Judith Waldrop, "Funny Valentines," *American Demographics* (February 1989): 7.

37. Quoted in Cyndee Miller, "Nix the Knick-Knacks; Send Cash," *Marketing News* (May 26, 1997): 1, 13.

38. Hubert B. Herring, "Dislike Those Suspenders? Don't Complain, Quantify!" *New York Times* (December 25, 1994): F3.

39. Bruno Bettelheim, *The Uses of Enchantment: The Meaning and Importance of Fairy Tales* (New York: Alfred A. Knopf, 1976).

40. Kenneth L. Woodward, "Christmas Wasn't Born Here, Just Invented," *Newsweek* (December 16, 1996): 71.

41. Theodore Caplow, Howard M. Bahr, Bruce A. Chadwick, Reuben Hill, and Margaret M. Williams, *Middletown Families: Fifty Years of Change and Continuity* (Minneapolis, MN: University of Minnesota Press, 1982).

42. Michael R. Solomon and Punam Anand, "Ritual Costumes and Status Transition: The Female Business Suit as Totemic Emblem," in eds. Elizabeth C. Hirschman and Morris Holbrook, *Advances in Consumer Research* 12 (Washington, D.C.: Association for Consumer Research, 1985): 315–18.

43. "Divorce Can be Furry," *American Demographics* (March 1987): 24.

44. Arnold Van Gennep, *The Rites of Passage*, trans. Maika B. Vizedom and Gabrielle L. Caffee (London: Routledge and Kegan Paul, 1960; orig. published 1908); Solomon and Anand, "Ritual Costumes and Status Transition."

45. Andrea Adelson, "A New Spirit for Sales of Halloween Merchandise," *New York Times* (October 31, 1994): D1 (2 pp.).

46. Anne Swardson, "Trick or Treat? In Paris, It's Dress, Dance, Eat," *International Herald Tribune* (October 31, 1996): 2.

47. N. R. Kleinfeld, "The Weird, the Bad and the Scary," *New York Times* (October 15, 1989): 4.

48. Georgia Dullea, "It's the Year's No. 2 Night to Howl," *New York Times* (October 30, 1988): 20.

49. Paul Fahri, "Brewing up More Spirits; Liquor Firms Promoting Halloween for Adults," *The Washington Post* (October 31,1989): D1.

50. Quoted in Thomas R. King, "Brewers Hope for Treat from Promotion Tricks," *Wall Street Journal* (1989): B1.

51. Joyce Cohen, "Here Comes the Bride; Get Ready to Release a Swarm of Live Insects," *Wall Street Journal* (January 22, 1996): B1.

52. Kelly Shermach, "Pay Now, Die Later: Consumers Urged Not to Delay That Final Decision," *Marketing News* (October 24, 1994): 1 (2 pp.).

53. Walter W. Whitaker III, "The Contemporary American Funeral Ritual," in ed. Ray B. Browne, *Rites and Ceremonies in Popular Culture* (Bowling Green, OH: Bowling Green University Popular Press, 1980): 316–25; for a recent examination of

funeral rituals, see Larry D. Compeau and Carolyn Nicholson, "Funerals: Emotional Rituals or Ritualistic Emotions" (paper presented at the Association of Consumer Research, Boston, October 1994).

54. Conrad Phillip Kottak, "Anthropological Analysis of Mass Enculturation," in ed. Conrad P. Kottak, *Researching American Culture* (Ann Arbor, MI: University of Michigan Press, 1982): 40–74.

55. Joan Kron, *Home-Psych: The Social Psychology of Home and Decoration* (New York: Clarkson N. Potter, 1983); Gerry Pratt, "The House as an Expression of Social Worlds," in ed. James S. Duncan, *Housing and Identity: Cross-Cultural Perspectives* (London: Croom Helm, 1981): 135–79; Michael R. Solomon, "The Role of the Surrogate Consumer in Service Delivery," *The Service Industries Journal* 7 (July 1987): 292–307.

56. Grant McCracken, "'Homeyness': A Cultural Account of One Constellation of Goods and Meanings," in ed. Elizabeth C. Hirschman, *Interpretive Consumer Research* (Provo, UT: Association for Consumer Research, 1989): 168–84.

57. James Hirsch, "Taking Celebrity Worship to New Depths," *New York Times* (November 9, 1988): C1.

58. Emile Durkheim, *The Elementary Forms of the Religious Life* (New York: Free Press, 1915).

59. Susan Birrell, "Sports as Ritual: Interpretations from Durkheim to Goffman," *Social Forces* 60 (1981)2: 354–76; Daniel Q. Voigt, "American Sporting Rituals," in *Rites and Ceremonies in Popular Culture*.

60. Mindy Weinstein, "Dead Stars are In," *Advertising Age* (August 14, 1989): 44.

61. Judann Dagnoli, "Ads Trumpet Satchmo's Immortality," *Advertising Age* (April 30, 1990): 26.

62. Bob Greene, "Some Like It Hot," *Esquire* (October 1987): 59.

63. Fred Kirby, "Woody Allen Wins Lawsuit to Stymie National Video Lookalike," *Variety* (May 22, 1985): 84.

64. James P. Forkan, "Send in the Clones: Ads Must ID Celeb Doubles," *Advertising Age* (May 20, 1985): 2.

65. Alf Walle, "The Epic Hero," *Marketing Insights* (Spring 1990): 63.

66. Dean MacCannell, *The Tourist: A New Theory of the Leisure Class* (New York: Shocken Books, 1976).

67. Belk et al., "The Sacred and the Profane in Consumer Behavior."

68. Beverly Gordon, "The Souvenir: Messenger of the Extraordinary," *Journal of Popular Culture* 20 (1986)3: 135–46.

69. Belk et al., "The Sacred and the Profane in Consumer Behavior."

70. Belk et al., "The Sacred and the Profane in Consumer Behavior."

71. Deborah Hofmann, "In Jewelry, Choices Sacred and Profane, Ancient and New," *New York Times* (May 7, 1989):

72. "Public Relations Firm to Present Anti-Abortion Effort to Bishops," *New York Times* (August 14, 1990): A12.

73. Martin E. Marty, "Sunday Mass and the Media: There's a Fine Line in Religious Advertising Between Tasteful and Tacky," *Across the Board* 24 (May 1987): 55.

74. For an extensive bibliography on collecting, see Russell W. Belk, Melanie Wallendorf, John F. Sherry Jr., and Morris B. Holbrook, "Collecting in a Consumer Culture," in ed. Russell W. Belk, *Highways and Buyways* (Provo, UT: Association for Consumer Research, 1991): 178–215. See also Russell W. Belk, "Acquiring, Possessing, and Collecting: Fundamental Processes in Consumer Behavior," in eds. Ronald F. Bush and Shelby D. Hunt, *Marketing Theory: Philosophy of Science Perspectives* (Chicago: American Marketing Association, 1982): 85–90; Werner Muensterberg, *Collecting: An Unruly Passion* (Princeton, NJ: Princeton University Press, 1994); Melanie Wallendorf and Eric J. Arnould, " 'My Favorite Things': A Cross-Cultural Inquiry into Object Attachment, Possessiveness, and Social Linkage," *Journal of Consumer Research* 14 (March 1988): 531–47.

75. Calmetta Y. Coleman, "Just Any Old Thing from McDonald's Can be a Collectible," *Wall Street Journal* (March 29, 1995): B1 (2 pp.).

76. Quoted in Ruth Ann Smith, "Collecting as Consumption: A Grounded Theory of Collecting Behavior" (unpublished manuscript, Virginia Polytechnic Institute and State University, 1994): 14.

77. Dan L. Sherrell, Alvin C. Burns, and Melodie R. Phillips, "Fixed Consumption Behavior: The Case of Enduring Acquisition in a Product Category," in ed. Robert L. King, *Developments in Marketing Science* 14 (1991): 36–40.

78. Belk, "Acquiring, Possessing, and Collecting: Fundamental Processes in Consumer Behavior," cf 74.

79. For a discussion of these perspectives, see Smith, "Collecting as Consumption."

80. Glenn J. Kalinoski, "Collecting Sales," *PROMO: The Magazine of Promotion Marketing* (May 1996): 41–7.

81. Kalinoski, "Collecting Sales."

82. Christy Ellis, *My First Greenbook: The First, Original Complete Guide to Ty Beanie Babies* (East Setauket, NY: Greenbook, 1997).

AS AMANDA IS BROWSING through the racks at her local Limited store in Wichita, Kansas, her friend Alexandra yells to her, "Amanda, check this out! These baggy jeans are just too phat! You'll look totally awesome in them!"

As Amanda takes the jeans to the cash register, she's looking forward to wearing them to school the next day. All of her girlfriends in junior high compete with each other to dress just like the singers in En Vogue and other groups—her friends just won't believe their eyes when they see her tomorrow. Maybe some of the younger kids in her school might even think she was fresh off the mean streets of New York City! Even though she has never been east of the Mississippi, Amanda just knows she would fit right in with all of the Bronx "sistahs" she reads about in her magazines. . . .

The Creation and Diffusion of Consumer Culture

THE CREATION OF CULTURE

The Yankelovich African American Monitor reports that its hip-hopper segment includes 27 percent of African Amercians. They are largely single, urban residents who put a high priority on being fashionably dressed, and they favor grassroots apparel brands such as Mecca, Boss Jeans, and Phat Farm.[1] Even though inner-city teens represent only 8 percent of all people in that age group and have incomes significantly lower than their white suburban counterparts, their influence on young people's musical and fashion tastes is much greater than these numbers would suggest. Turn on MTV, and it won't be long before a rap video fills the screen. Go to the newsstand, and magazines like *Vibe* are waiting for you. There are even numerous Web sites devoted to hip-hop culture, including www.vibe.com.

Americans always have been fascinated by outsider heroes—whether John Dillinger, Marlon Brando, or Dennis Rodman—who achieve money and fame without being hemmed in by societal constraints. As one executive of a firm that researches urban youth noted, "People resonate with the strong antioppression messages of rap, and the alienation of blacks."[2]

Ironically, the only "oppression" Amanda has experienced is being grounded by her parents after her mom found a half-smoked cigarette in her room. She lives in a white middle-class area in the Midwest, but she is able to "connect" symbolically with millions of other young consumers by wearing styles that originated far away—even though the original meanings of those styles have little relevance to her. As a privileged member of "white bread" society, her hip-hop clothes have a very different meaning in her suburban world than they would to street kids in New York City or L.A. The fact that she's wearing a style might even be interpreted by these "cutting-edge" types as a sign that this item is no longer in fashion, and it is time to move on to something else. Perhaps that explains why the baggy jeans that have become a part of the "cool" uniform for suburban teens have already started to fade from "real" hip-hop culture.

At least for now, big corporations are working hard to capture the next killer fashion being incubated in black urban culture—what is called "flavor" on the streets. For example, Fila, which started as an Italian underwear maker in 1926, initially broke into sportswear by focusing on "lily-white" activities such as skiing and tennis, and first made a splash by signing Swedish tennis sensation Bjorn Borg as an endorser. Ten years later, the tennis fad faded, but company executives noticed that rap stars such as Heavy D were wearing Fila sweatsuits to symbolize their idealized vision of life in white country clubs. Fila switched gears and went with the flow, and is now the third-leading sneaker marketer with U.S. revenues of $575 million wholesale.[3] While some big companies are treading a bit lightly due to the negative publicity caused by events such as the violent deaths of rappers Notorious B.I.G. and Tupac Shakur, hip-hop's outlaw image continues to appeal to teens the world over.

How did rap music and fashions, which began as forms of expression in the black urban subculture, make it to mainstream America? Here's a brief chronology:

- 1968: Hip-hop is invented in the Bronx by DJ Kool Herc.
- 1973–1978: Urban block parties feature break-dancing and graffiti.
- 1979: A small record company named Sugar Hill becomes the first rap label.
- 1980: Graffiti artists are featured in Manhattan art galleries.
- 1981: Blondie's song *Rapture* hits #1 on the charts.
- 1985: Columbia Records buys the Def Jam label.
- 1988: MTV begins "Yo! MTV Raps," featuring Fab 5 Freddy.
- 1990: Hollywood gets into the act with the hip-hop film *House Party*; Ice-T's rap album is a big hit on college radio stations; amid controversy, white rapper Vanilla Ice hits the big time; NBC launches a new sitcom, *Fresh Prince of Bel Air.*
- 1991: Mattel introduces its Hammer doll (a likeness of the rap star Hammer, formerly known as M.C. Hammer); designer Karl Lagerfeld shows shiny vinyl raincoats and chain belts in his Chanel collection; designer Charlotte Neuville sells gold vinyl suits with matching baseball caps for $800; Isaac Mizrahi features wide-brimmed caps and take-offs on African medallions (including an oversized gold Star of David); Bloomingdale's launches Anne Klein's rap-inspired clothing line by featuring a rap performance in its Manhattan store.
- 1992: Rappers start to abandon this look, turning to low-fitting baggy jeans, sometimes worn backwards; white rapper Marky Mark appears in a national campaign wearing Calvin Klein underwear, exposed above his hip-hugging pants; composer Quincy Jones launches a new magazine for people who are into hip-hop, and it gains a significant white readership.[4]
- 1993: Hip-hop fashions and slang continue to cross over into mainstream consumer culture. An outdoor ad for Coca-Cola proclaims, "Get Yours 24–7." The company is confident that many viewers in its target market will know that the phrase is urban slang for "always" (24 hours a day, 7 days a week).[5]
- 1994: Designers persevere in their adaptations of street fashion. The (now deceased) Italian designer Versace, among others, pushes oversized overalls favored by urban kids. In one ad, he asks, "Overalls with an oversize look, something like what rappers and homeboys wear. Why not a sophisticated version?"[6]
- 1996: Tommy Hilfiger, a designer who was the darling of the preppie set, turns hip-hop. He gives free wardrobes to rap artists such as Grand Puba and Chef Raekwon, and in return finds his name mentioned in rap songs—the ultimate endorsement. The September 1996 issue of *Rolling Stone* features The Fugees, with the Hilfiger logo prominently displayed by several band members. In the same year the designer uses rap stars Method Man and Treach of Naughty by Nature as runway models. Hilfiger's new Tommy Girl perfume plays on his name but also is a reference to the New York hip-hop record label Tommy Boy.[7]
- 1997: Coca-Cola features rapper LL Cool J in a commercial that debuts in the middle of the sitcom *In the House*, a TV show starring the singer.[8]

It's quite common for mainstream culture to modify symbols identified with "cutting-edge" subcultures and present these to a larger audience. As this occurs, these cultural products undergo a process of **cooptation,** by which their original meanings are transformed by outsiders. In this case, rap music was to a large extent divorced from its original connection with the struggles of young African Americans and is now used as an entertainment format for other fans.[9] One hip-hop writer sees the white part of the "hip-hop nation" as a series of concentric rings. In the center are those who actually know blacks and understand their culture. The next ring consists of those who have contact with these symbols via friends or relatives, but who don't actually rap, spray paint or break dance. Then, there are those a bit further out who simply play hip-hop between other types of music. Finally come the more suburban "wiggers" who are simply trying to catch on to the next popular craze.[10] The spread of hip-hop fashions and music is just one example of what happens when the meanings created by some members of a culture are interpreted and produced for mass consumption.

This chapter considers how the culture in which we live creates the meaning of everyday products and how these meanings move through a society to consumers. As Figure 17–1 shows, meaning transfer is largely accomplished by such marketing vehicles as the advertising and fashion industries, which associate functional products with symbolic qualities. These goods, in turn, impart their meanings to consumers as these products are used by them to create and express their identities in their daily lives.[11] Thus, this closing chapter brings us full circle back to the issues regarding the diverse meanings of consumption we considered in chapter 1.

CULTURAL SELECTION

The Artist Formerly Known as Prince. Nipple rings. Platform shoes. Sushi. High-tech furniture. Postmodern architecture. Chat rooms. Double decaf cappuccino with a hint of cinnamon. We inhabit a world brimming with different styles and possibilities. The food we eat, the cars we drive, the clothes we wear, the places we live and work, the music we listen to—all are influenced by the ebb and flow of popular culture and fashion.

Consumers may at times feel overwhelmed by the sheer number of choices in the marketplace. A person trying to decide on something as routine as a necktie has many hundreds of alternatives to choose from. Despite this seeming abundance, however, the options available to consumers at any point in time actually represent only a small fraction of the total set of possibilities.

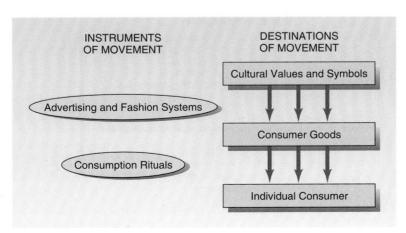

FIGURE **17–1** ■ **The Movement of Meaning**
Source: Adapted from Grant McCracken, "Culture and Consumption: A Theoretical Account of the Structure and Movement of the Cultural Meaning of Consumer Goods," *Journal of Consumer Research* 13 (June 1986): 72. Reprinted with permission of The University of Chicago Press.

The selection of certain alternatives over others—whether automobiles, dresses, computers, recording artists, political candidates, religions, or even scientific methodologies—is the culmination of a complex filtration process resembling a funnel, as depicted in Figure 17–2. Many possibilities initially compete for adoption, and these are steadily winnowed out as they make their way down the path from conception to consumption in a process of **cultural selection.**

Our tastes and product preferences are not formed in a vacuum. Choices are driven by the images presented to us in mass media, our observations of those around us, and even by our desires to live in the fantasy worlds created by marketers. These options are constantly evolving and changing. A clothing style or type of cuisine that is "hot" one year may be "out" the next.

Amanda's emulation of hip-hop style illustrates some of the characteristics of fashion and popular culture:

● Styles are often a reflection of deeper societal trends (e.g., politics and social conditions).
● Styles usually originate as an interplay between the deliberate inventions of designers and business people and spontaneous actions by ordinary consumers. Designers, manufacturers, and merchandisers who can anticipate

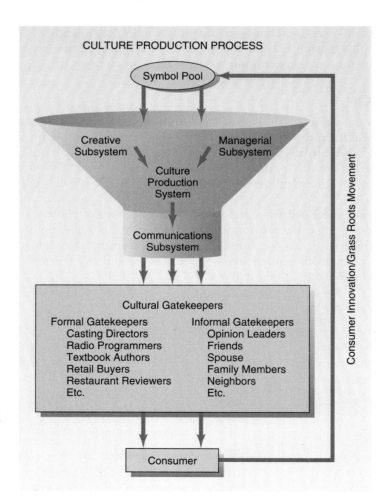

FIGURE 17–2 ■ **The Culture Production Process**
Source: Adapted from Michael R. Solomon, "Building Up and Breaking Down: The Impact of Cultural Sorting on Symbolic Consumption," in ed. J. Sheth and E. C. Hirschman, *Research in Consumer Behavior* (Greenwich, CT: JAI Press, 1988): 325–51.

There's one thing AT&T international long distance customers will never have to worry about.

These days, things seem to go obsolete before you can get them out of the box.

Not so with AT&T International Long Distance. We're continually upgrading our Worldwide Intelligent Network, before you have time to even think about it.

When we saw that global events were affecting telephone traffic, we expanded our Network Operations Center. Now events are continually monitored 24 hours a day, and traffic is routed accordingly.

We also anticipated the growing demand for international voice, data and fax transmission, by developing the first transpacific and transatlantic fiber-optic cable systems.

So you'll enjoy fast international connections with unsurpassed clarity.

We could list other examples of advances you'll never have to think about.

But why not call 1 800 222-0400 ext. 1277, and let the innovations speak for themselves.

AT&T
The right choice.

© 1989 AT&T

As this AT&T ad demonstrates, many product styles are doomed to become obsolete.

what consumers want will succeed in the marketplace. In the process, they also help to fuel the fire by encouraging mass distribution of the item.

- These cultural products can travel widely, often between countries and across continents. Influential people in the media play a large role in deciding which will succeed.

- A style begins as a risky or unique statement by a relatively small group of people, then spreads as others increasingly become aware of the style and feel confident about trying it.

- Most styles eventually wear out, as people continually search for new ways to express themselves and marketers scramble to keep up with these desires.

CULTURE PRODUCTION SYSTEMS

No single designer, company, or advertising agency is totally responsible for creating popular culture. Every product, whether a hit record, a car, or a new clothing style, requires the input of many different participants. The set of individuals and organizations responsible for creating and marketing a cultural product is a **culture production system (CPS)**.[12]

The nature of these systems helps to determine the types of products that eventually emerge from them. Factors such as the number and diversity of competing systems and the amount of innovation versus conformity that is encouraged are important. For example, an analysis of the country/western music industry has shown that the hit records it produces tend to be similar to one another during time periods when the industry is dominated by a few large companies, whereas there is more diversity when a greater number of producers are competing within the same market.[13]

The different members of a CPS may not necessarily be aware of or appreciate the roles played by other members, yet many diverse agents work together to create popular culture.[14] Each member does his or her best to anticipate which particular images will be most attractive to a consumer market. Of course, those who are able to consistently forecast consumers' tastes most accurately will be successful over time.

COMPONENTS OF A CPS

A culture production system has three major subsystems: (1) a *creative subsystem* responsible for generating new symbols and/or products; (2) a *managerial subsystem* responsible for selecting, making tangible, mass producing, and managing the distribution of new symbols and/or products; and (3) a *communications subsystem* responsible for giving meaning to the new product and providing it with a symbolic set of attributes that are communicated to consumers.

An example of the three components of a culture production system for a record would be (1) a singer (e.g., Coolio, a creative subsystem); (2) a company (e.g., Tommy Boy Music, which manufactures and distributes Coolio's CDs, a managerial subsystem); and (3) the advertising and publicity agencies hired to promote the albums (a communications subsystem). Table 17–1 illustrates some of the many *cultural specialists* who are required to create a hit CD.

TABLE 17–1 ■ Cultural Specialists in the Music Industry

SPECIALIST	FUNCTIONS
Songwriter(s)	Compose music and lyrics; must reconcile artistic preferences with estimates of what will succeed in the marketplace
Performer(s)	Interpret music and lyrics; may be formed spontaneously, or may be packaged by an agent to appeal to a predetermined market (e.g., The Monkees, Menudo, and New Kids on the Block)
Teachers and coaches	Develop and refine performers' talents
Agent	Represent performers to record companies
A&R (artist & repertoire) executive	Acquire artists for the record label
Publicists, image consultants, designers, stylists	Create an image for the group that is transmitted to the buying public
Recording technicians, producers	Create a recording to be sold
Marketing executives	Make strategic decisions regarding performer's appearances, ticket pricing, promotional strategies, and so on
Video director	Interpret the song visually to create a music video that will help to promote the record
Music reviewers	Evaluate the merits of a recording for listeners
Disc jockeys, radio program directors	Decide which records will be given airplay and/or placed in the radio stations' regular rotations
Record store owner	Decide which of the many records produced will be stocked and/or promoted heavily in the retail environment

CULTURAL GATEKEEPERS

Many judges or "tastemakers" influence the products that are eventually offered to consumers. These **cultural gatekeepers** are responsible for filtering the overflow of information and materials intended for consumers. Gatekeepers include movie, restaurant, and car reviewers, interior designers, disc jockeys, retail buyers, and magazine editors. Collectively, this set of agents is known as the *throughput sector.*[15]

HIGH CULTURE AND POPULAR CULTURE

Do Beethoven and Coolio have anything in common? Although both the famous composer and the rap singer are associated with music, many would argue that the similarity stops there. Culture production systems create many kinds of products, but some basic distinctions can be offered regarding their characteristics.

ARTS AND CRAFTS

One distinction can be made between arts and crafts.[16] An **art product** is viewed primarily as an object of aesthetic contemplation without any functional value. A **craft product,** in contrast, is admired because of the beauty with which it performs some function (e.g., a ceramic ashtray or hand-carved fishing lures). A piece of art is original, subtle, and valuable, and is associated with the elite of society. A craft tends to follow a formula that permits rapid production. According to this framework, elite culture is produced in a purely aesthetic context and is judged by reference to recognized classics. It is high culture—"serious art."[17]

HIGH ART VERSUS LOW ART

The distinction between high and low culture is not as clear as it may first appear. In addition to the possible class bias that drives such a distinction (i.e., we assume that the rich have culture but the poor do not), high and low culture are blending together in interesting ways. Popular culture reflects the world around us; these phenomena touch rich and poor. In Europe, for example, advertising is widely

These Absolut ads featuring popular artists help to blur the boundaries between marketing activities and popular culture.

appreciated as an art form. Some advertising executives are public figures in Great Britain. For over 10 years, people in France have paid up to $30 to watch an all-night program in a movie theater consisting of nothing but television commercials.[18]

The arts are big business. Americans alone spend more than $2 billion per year to attend arts events.[19] All cultural products that are transmitted by mass media become a part of popular culture.[20] Classical recordings are marketed in much the same way as Top 40 albums, and museums use mass marketing techniques to sell their wares. The Metropolitan Museum of Art has branch gift stores across the United States.

Marketers often incorporate high art imagery to promote products. They may feature works of art on shopping bags or sponsor artistic events to build public goodwill.[21] When observers from Toyota watched customers in luxury car showrooms, the company found that these consumers tended to view a car as an art object. This theme was then used in an ad for the Lexus with the caption, "Until now, the only fine arts we supported were sculpture, painting, and music."[22]

CULTURAL FORMULAE

Mass culture, in contrast, churns out products specifically for a mass market. These products aim to please the average taste of an undifferentiated audience and are predictable because they follow certain patterns. As illustrated in Table 17–2, many popular art forms, such as detective stories or science fiction, generally follow a **cultural formula**, in which certain roles and props often occur consistently.[23] Romance novels are an extreme case of a cultural formula. Computer programs even allow users to "write" their own romances by systematically varying certain set elements of the story.

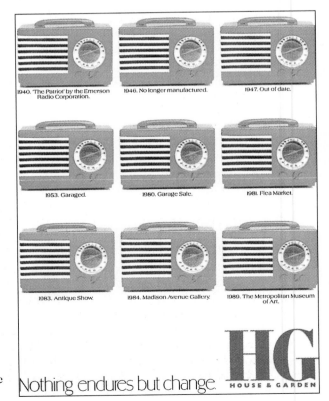

This *House & Garden* ad illustrates the life cycle of an Emerson radio to show how ideas about a mass-produced cultural product can change over time and create a classic and valuable collector's item.

TABLE 17–2 ■ Cultural Formulae in Public Art Forms

ART FORM/ GENRE	CLASSIC WESTERN	SCIENCE FICTION	HARD-BOILED DETECTIVE	FAMILY SITCOM
Time	1800s	Future	Present	Anytime
Location	Edge of civilization	Space	City	Suburbs
Protagonist	Cowboy (lone individual)	Astronaut	Detective	Father (figure)
Heroine	Schoolmarm	Spacegal	Damsel in distress	Mother (figure)
Villain	Outlaws, killers	Aliens	Killer	Boss, neighbor
Secondary characters	Townfolk, Indians	Technicians in spacecraft	Cops, underworld	Kids, dogs
Plot	Restore law and order	Repel aliens	Find killer	Solve problem
Theme	Justice	Triumph of humanity	Pursuit and discovery	Chaos and confusion
Costume	Cowboy hat, boots, etc.	High-tech uniforms	Raincoat	Regular clothes
Locomotion	Horse	Spaceship	Beat-up car	Station wagon
Weaponry	Sixgun, riffle	Rayguns	Pistol, fists	Insults

Source: Arthur A. Berger, *Signs in Contemporary Culture: An Introduction to Semiotics* (New York: Longman, 1984): 86. Copyright © 1984. Reissued 1989 by Sheffield Publishing Company, Salem, Wisconsin. Reprinted with permission of the publisher.

Reliance on these formulae also leads to a *recycling* of images, as members of the creative subsystem reach back through time for inspiration. Thus, young people watch retro shows like Gilligan's Island and remakes of The Brady Bunch, designers modify styles from Victorian England, colonial Africa, and other historical periods, hip hop DJ's sample sound bits from past songs and combine them in new ways, and we see Gap clothing store ads featuring icons such as Humphrey Bogart, Gene Kelly, and Pablo Picasso dressed in khaki pants. And, the regeneration of images in the postmodern world (see Chapter 1) is accelerating, as the technology of borrowing becomes more available. With easy access to VCRs, CD-ROMs, digital cameras and imaging software, and copying machines, virtually anyone can "remix" the past.[24]

AESTHETIC MARKET RESEARCH

Creators of aesthetic products are increasingly adapting conventional marketing methods to fine-tune their mass market offerings. Market research is used, for example, to test audience reactions to movie concepts. Although testing cannot account for such intangibles as acting quality or cinematography, it can determine if the basic themes of the movie strike a responsive chord in the target audience. This type of research is most appropriate for blockbuster movies, which usually follow one of the formulae described earlier.

Even the content of movies is sometimes influenced by consumer research. Typically, free invitations to prescreenings are handed out in malls and movie theaters. Attendees are asked a few questions about the movie, then some are selected to participate in focus groups. Although groups' reactions usually result in only minor editing changes, occasionally more drastic effects result. When initial reaction to the ending of *Fatal Attraction* was negative, Paramount Pictures spent an additional $1.3 million to shoot a new one.[26]

REALITY ENGINEERING

Many of the environments in which we find ourselves, whether shopping malls, sports stadiums, or theme parks, are composed at least partly of images and characters drawn from products, marketing campaigns, or the mass media. **Reality engineering** occurs as elements of popular culture are appropriated by marketers and converted to vehicles for promotional strategies.[27] These elements include sensory and spatial aspects of everyday existence, whether in the form of products appearing in movies, scents pumped into offices and stores, billboards, theme parks, video monitors attached to shopping carts, and so on.

Marketing sometimes seems to exert a "self-fulfilling prophecy" on popular culture. As commercial influences on popular culture increase, marketer-created symbols make their way into our daily lives to a greater degree. Historical analyses of Broadway plays, best-selling novels, and the lyrics of hit songs, for example, clearly show large increases in the use of brand names over time.[28]

The melding of marketing activity with popular culture is also evident in other countries. A British coffee ad recently borrowed the words from the Beatles' song *A Day in the Life* and went so far as to include a shot of John Lennon's signature round glasses sitting on a table. The British Boy Scouts announced that they would begin accepting corporate sponsorships for merit badges. The Lost City, a new resort in South Africa, blurs the boundaries even further; it has created a "fake" Africa for affluent guests. The complex is drought-proof and disease-proof, and it features a three-story water slide, an "ocean" with a panic button that will stop the wave motion on command, and a nightly volcanic eruption complete with "nonallergenic" smoke.[30]

Reality engineering is accelerating due to the current popularity of product placements by marketers. It is quite common to see real brands prominently displayed or to hear them discussed in movies and on television. In many cases, these "plugs" are no accident. **Product placement** refers to the insertion of specific products and/or the use of brand names in movie and TV scripts. Perhaps the greatest product placement success story was Reese's Pieces; sales jumped by 65 percent after the candy appeared in the film *E.T.*[31]

Since that time, products are popping up everywhere: a Chrysler Dodge Ram is featured in the movie *Twister,* the basketball team in *Eddie* wears Knicks uniforms, and an Apple PowerBook can clearly be seen in *Mission:Impossible* (in return, Apple underwrote a television advertising campaign for the movie, and also created an on-line Web site for the release free of charge). Sometimes, these placements even result in changes to the show itself. For example, the movie *Flipper* was filmed with a Coke can in one scene. When producers signed a marketing deal with Pizza Hut (which is owned by PepsiCo), they had to spend about $40,000 to digitally change the drink label to Pepsi.[32]

Product placement refers to the insertion of specific products and/or the use of brand names in movie and TV scripts. The popular sitcom *Seinfeld* includes blatant references to numerous products, from Junior Mints and Kenny Rogers Fried Chicken to Snapple and Pez.

Traditionally, networks demanded that brand names be "greeked" or changed before they could appear in a show, as when a Nokia cell phone is changed to Nokio on *Melrose Place*.[33] Nowadays, though, real products pop up everywhere. Still, to bypass Federal Communications Commission regulations requiring the disclosure of promotional deals, marketers typically don't pay for placements. They pay product placement firms that work with set decorators looking for free props and realism. As a result, Al on the show *Home Improvement* models a Detroit Lions jacket, and Jamie on *Mad About You* splashes on Bijan fragrances.[34]

Some critics argue that the practice of product placement has gotten out of hand: Shows are created with the purpose of marketing products rather than for their entertainment value. Some children's shows have been berated for essentially being extended commercials for a toy. One major film company sent a letter to large consumer products companies to solicit product placements for an upcoming movie production and even provided a fee scale: $20,000 for the product to be seen in the movie, $40,000 for an actor to mention the product by name, and $60,000 for the actor to actually use the product.[35] The director of strategic planning at Saatchi & Saatchi New York predicts, ". . . any space you can take in visually, anything you hear in the future will be branded, I believe. It's not going to be the Washington Monument. It's going to be the Washington Post Monument."[36]

Media images appear to significantly influence consumers' perceptions of reality, affecting viewers' notions about such issues as dating behavior, racial stereotypes, and occupational status.[37] Studies of the **cultivation hypothesis,** which relates to media's ability to distort consumers' perceptions of reality, have shown that heavy television viewers tend to overestimate the degree of affluence in the country, and these effects also extend to areas such as perceptions of the amount of violence in one's culture.[38] The media also tend to exaggerate or distort the frequency of behaviors such as drinking or smoking. For example, one study found that characters in movies smoke at a much higher rate than do people in real life.[39]

THE DIFFUSION OF INNOVATIONS

An **innovation** is any product or service that is perceived to be new by consumers (even if it has long been used by others in other places). These new products or services occur in both consumer and industrial settings. Innovations may take the form of a clothing style (e.g., skirts for men), a new manufacturing technique, or a novel way to deliver a service. If an innovation is successful (most are not), it spreads through the population. First it is bought and/or used by only a few people, and then more and more consumers decide to adopt it, until, in some cases, it seems that almost everyone has bought or tried the innovation. **Diffusion of innovations** refers to the process whereby a new product, service, or idea spreads through a population.[40]

ADOPTING INNOVATIONS

A consumer's adoption of an innovation resembles the decision-making sequence discussed in chapter 9. The person moves through the stages of awareness, information search, evaluation, trial, and adoption, although the relative importance of each stage may differ depending on how much is already known about a product, as well as on cultural factors that may affect people's willingness to try new things.[41]

However, even within the same culture, not all people adopt an innovation at the same rate. Some do so quite rapidly, and others never do at all. Consumers can be placed into approximate categories based on their likelihood of adopting an innovation. The categories of adopters, shown in Figure 17–3, can be related to phases of the product life-cycle concept used widely by marketing strategists.

As can be seen in Figure 17–3, roughly one-sixth of the population (innovators and early adopters) are very quick to adopt new products, and one-sixth of the people (**laggards**) are very slow. The other two-thirds, so-called **late adopters,** are somewhere in the middle, and these adopters represent the mainstream public. These consumers are interested in new things, but they do not want them to be *too* new. In some cases, people deliberately wait to adopt an innovation because they assume that its technological qualities will be improved or that its price will fall after it has been on the market awhile.[42] Keep in mind that the proportion of consumers falling into each category is an estimate; the actual size of each depends on such factors as the complexity of the product, its cost, and so on.

Even though **innovators** represent only about 2.5 percent of the population, marketers are always interested in identifying them. These are the brave souls who are always on the lookout for novel developments and will be the first to try a new offering. Just as generalized opinion leaders do not appear to exist, innovators tend to be category-specific, as well. A person who is an innovator in one area may even be a laggard in another. For example, a gentleman who prides himself as being on the cutting edge of fashion may have no conception of new developments in recording technology and may still stubbornly cling to his antique phonograph albums even as he searches for the latest avant-garde clothing styles in obscure boutiques. Despite this qualification, some generalizations can be offered regarding the profile of innovators.[43] Not surprisingly, for example, they tend to have more favorable attitudes toward taking risks. They also are likely to have higher educational and income levels, and to be socially active.

Early adopters share many of the same characteristics as innovators, but an important difference is their degree of concern for social acceptance, especially with regard to expressive products, such as clothing, cosmetics, and so on. Generally speaking, an early adopter is receptive to new styles because he or she is involved in the product category and also places high value on being in fashion. What appears on the surface to be a fairly high-risk adoption (e.g., wearing a skirt three inches above the knee when most people are wearing them below the knee) is actually not

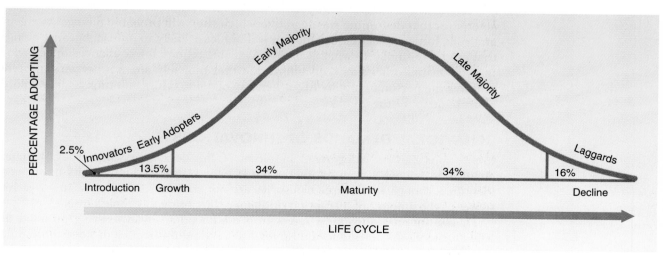

FIGURE 17–3 ■ **Types of Adopters**

MARKETING OPPORTUNITY

The race to uncover the preferences of innovators is heating up. Some companies are even hiring *coolhunters* to scout out the latest trends and report back to headquarters. For example, the Steven Rifkind Co. sends its "street teams," an army of 80 kids in 28 cities, into local clubs, record stores, and other hangouts as part of an urban intelligence network on behalf of Nike, Tommy Hilfiger, Miramax Films, and other corporate clients. These soldiers of cool hand out free samples of product prototypes to kids they identify as trendsetters, and then get their feedback regarding what's cool and what isn't. When client Converse was developing its model of Dennis Rodman sneakers, they were tested by coolhunters. The shoe got good marks for overall "badness," but the innovators didn't like the design of the bottom of the sole, which was half-white fading into black. The word on the street said this style would be much cooler in black and red, so Converse switched colors before introducing the shoe to the mass market.[44]

that risky. The style change has already been "field-tested" by innovators, who truly took the fashion risk. Early adopters are likely to be found in "fashion-forward" stores featuring the latest "hot" designers. In contrast, true innovators are more likely to be found in small boutiques featuring as-yet-unknown designers.

TYPES OF INNOVATIONS

Innovations can occur in different forms. A **symbolic innovation** communicates a new social meaning (e.g., a new hairstyle or car design), whereas a **technological innovation** involves some functional change (e.g., central air conditioning or car air bags).[45] Obviously, these innovations usually involve very different types of companies and of consumers who are interested in them. The Backer Spielvogel Bates advertising agency found that one in five American adults is what it terms a *techthusiast*, a person who is most likely to buy new technology or subscribe to new services. These 37 million adults are more affluent, younger, and better educated than the average American. They tend to live in cities that have major universities and technology industries, such as Boston, Houston, San Diego, and Seattle. In contrast, *technophobes* have a fear of technology—they outnumber techthusiasts by 2:1.[46]

Whether symbolic or functional, new products, services, and ideas have characteristics that determine the degree to which they will probably diffuse. As a general rule, innovations that are more novel are least likely to diffuse, because things that are fairly similar to what is already available require fewer changes in behavior to use. On the other hand, an innovation that radically alters a person's lifestyle requires the person to modify his or her way of doing things and thus requires more effort to adapt to the change.

BEHAVIORAL DEMANDS OF INNOVATIONS

Innovations can be categorized in terms of the degree to which they demand changes in behavior from adopters. Three major types of innovations have been identified, though these three categories are not absolutes. They refer, in a relative sense, to the amount of disruption or change they bring to people's lives.

A **continuous innovation** refers to a modification of an existing product, as when General Mills introduced a Honey Nut version of Cheerios or Levi's promoted shrink-to-fit jeans. This type of change may be used to set one brand apart from its competitors. Most product innovations are of this type; that is, they are evolutionary rather than revolutionary. Small changes are made to position the product, add line extensions, or merely to alleviate consumer boredom.

Consumers may be lured to the new product, but adoption represents only minor changes in consumption habits, because innovation perhaps adds to the product's convenience or to the range of choices available. A typewriter company, for example, many years ago modified the shape of its product to make it more "user friendly" to secretaries. One simple change was making the tops of the keys concave, a convention that is carried over on today's computer keyboards. The reason for the change was that secretaries had complained about the difficulty of typing with long fingernails on the flat surfaces.

A **dynamically continuous innovation** is a more pronounced change in an existing product, as represented by self-focusing 35 mm cameras or touch-tone telephones. These innovations have a modest impact on the way people do things, requiring some behavioral changes. When introduced, the IBM Selectric typewriter, which uses a typing ball rather than individual keys, permitted secretaries to instantly change the typeface of manuscripts by replacing one Selectric ball with another.

A **discontinuous innovation** creates major changes in the way we live. Major inventions, such as the airplane, the car, the computer, and TV have radically changed modern lifestyles. The personal computer has, in many cases, supplanted the typewriter, and it has created the phenomenon of "telecommuters" by allowing many consumers to work from their homes. Of course, the cycle continues, as new continuous innovations (e.g., new versions of software) are constantly being made for computers; dynamically continuous innovations, such as the "mouse," compete for adoption, and discontinuous innovations like wristwatch personal computers loom on the horizon.

PREREQUISITES FOR SUCCESSFUL ADOPTION

Regardless of how much behavioral change is demanded by an innovation, several factors are desirable for a new product to succeed.[47]

Compatibility. The innovation should be compatible with consumers' lifestyles. As one illustration, a manufacturer of personal care products tried unsuccessfully several years ago to introduce a cream hair remover for men as a substitute for razors and shaving cream. This formulation was similar to that used widely by women to remove hair from their legs. Although the product was simple and convenient to use, it failed because men were not interested in a product they perceived to be too feminine and thus threatening to their masculine self-concepts.

Trialability. Because an unknown is accompanied by high perceived risk, people are more likely to adopt an innovation if they can experiment with it prior to making a commitment. To reduce this risk, companies often choose the expensive strategy of distributing free "trial-size" samples of new products.

Complexity. The product should be low in complexity. A product that is easier to understand and use will be chosen over a competitor. This strategy requires less effort from the consumer, and it also lowers perceived risk. Manufacturers of videocassette recorders, for example, have put a lot of effort into simplifying VCR usage (e.g., on-screen programming) to encourage adoption.

Observability. Innovations that are easily observable are more likely to spread, because this quality makes it more likely that other potential adopters will become aware of its existence. The rapid proliferation of fanny packs (pouches worn around the waist in lieu of wallets or purses) was due to their high visibility. It was easy for others to see the convenience offered by this alternative.

Relative Advantage. Most importantly, the product should offer relative advantage over other alternatives. The consumer must believe that its use will provide a benefit other products cannot offer. Two popular new products demonstrate the importance of possessing a perceived relative advantage vis-à-vis existing products: Energizer Green Power Batteries are promoted as being better for the environment because they contain less mercury, and the Bugchaser is a wristband containing insect repellent. Mothers with young children have liked it because it is nontoxic and nonstaining. In contrast, the Crazy Blue Air Freshener, which was added to windshield wiper fluid and emitted a fragrance when the wipers were turned on, fizzled: People didn't see the need for the product and felt there were simpler ways to freshen their cars if they cared to.

THE FASHION SYSTEM

The **fashion system** is an integral part of symbolic innovation. It consists of all those people and organizations involved in creating symbolic meanings and transferring these meanings to cultural goods. Although people tend to equate fashion with clothing, it is important to keep in mind that fashion processes affect *all* types of cultural phenomena, including music, art, architecture, and even science (i.e., certain research topics and scientists are "hot" at any point in time). Even business practices are subject to the fashion process; they evolve and change depending on which management techniques are "in vogue," such as total quality management or just-in-time inventory control.

Fashion can be thought of as a *code,* or language, that helps us to decipher these meanings.[48] Unlike a language, however, fashion is *context-dependent.* The same

MARKETING PITFALL

The issue of what exactly constitutes a "new" product is quite important to many businesses. It is said that "imitation is the sincerest form of flattery," and decisions regarding how much (if at all) one's product should resemble those of competitors are often the centerpiece of marketing strategy (e.g., packaging of "me-too" or look-alike products). On the other hand, the product cannot be an exact duplicate; patent law is concerned with the precise definition of what is a new product and protecting that invention from illegal imitation.

A **knockoff** is a style that has been deliberately copied and modified, often with the intent to sell to a larger or different market. For example, *haute couture* clothing styles presented by top designers in Paris and elsewhere are commonly "knocked off" by other designers and sold to the mass market. It is difficult to legally protect a design (as opposed to a technological feature), but pressure is building in many industries to do just that. Manufacturers argue that a distinctive curve on a car bumper, say, is as important to the integrity of the car as is a mechanical innovation. Legislation is being considered to protect new designs with a 10-year copyright (clothing would be exempt).[49]

A related problem is pirated versions of legitimate products that diffuse through a market. For example, software piracy is a practice that increases its user base over time. Ironically, though, pirates may actually influence others to adopt the software—and actually buy it. A British study suggests that though six of every seven software users had pirated copies, these pirates actually generated more than 80 percent of new software buyers![50]

item can be interpreted differently by different consumers and in different situations.[51] In semiotic terms (see chapter 1), the meaning of fashion products often is *undercoded*—that is, there is no one precise meaning, but rather plenty of room for interpretation among perceivers.

At the outset, it may be helpful to distinguish among some confusing terms. **Fashion** is the process of social diffusion by which a new style is adopted by some group(s) of consumers. In contrast, *a fashion* (or style) refers to a particular combination of attributes. And, to be *in fashion* means that this combination is currently positively evaluated by some reference group. Thus, the term *Danish Modern* refers to particular characteristics of furniture design (i.e., a fashion in interior design); it does not necessarily imply that Danish Modern is a fashion that is currently desired by consumers.[52]

CULTURAL CATEGORIES

The meaning that does get imparted to products reflects underlying **cultural categories,** which correspond to the basic ways we characterize the world.[53] Our culture makes distinctions between different times, between leisure and work, between genders, and so on. The fashion system provides us with products that signify these categories. For example, the apparel industry gives us clothing to denote certain times (e.g., evening wear, resort wear), it differentiates between leisure clothes and work clothes, and it promotes masculine and feminine styles.

These cultural categories affect many different products and styles. As a result, it is common to find that dominant aspects of a culture at any point in time tend to

This *House & Garden* ad demonstrates how different products represent the same cultural categories over time.

be reflected in the design and marketing of very different products. This concept is a bit hard to grasp, because on the surface a clothing style, say, has little in common with a piece of furniture or with a car. However, an overriding concern with a value such as achievement or environmentalism can determine the types of products likely to be accepted by consumers at any point in time. These underlying or latent themes then surface in various aspects of design. A few examples of this interdependence will help to demonstrate how a dominant fashion *motif* reverberates across industries.

- Costumes worn by political figures or movie and rock stars can affect the fortunes of the apparel and accessory industries. A movie appearance by actor Clark Gable without a T-shirt (unusual at that time) dealt a severe setback to the men's apparel industry, and Jackie Kennedy's famous "pillbox hat" prompted a rush for hats by women in the 1960s. Other cross-category effects include the craze for ripped sweatshirts instigated by the movie *Flashdance,* a boost for cowboy boots from the movie *Urban Cowboy,* and singer Madonna's legitimation of lingerie as an acceptable outerwear clothing style.

- The Louvre in Paris was recently remodeled to include a controversial glass pyramid at the entrance designed by the architect I. M. Pei. Shortly thereafter, several designers unveiled pyramid-shaped clothing at Paris fashion shows.[54]

- In the 1950s and 1960s, much of America was preoccupied with science and technology. This concern with "space-age" mastery was fueled by the Russians' launching of the Sputnik satellite, which prompted fears that America was falling behind in the technology race. The theme of technical mastery of nature and of futuristic design became a motif that cropped up in many aspects of American popular culture—from car designs with prominent tailfins to high-tech kitchen styles.

A cultural emphasis on science in the 1950s and 1960s affected product designs, as seen in the design of automobiles with large tail fins (to resemble rockets).

COLLECTIVE SELECTION

Fashions tend to "sweep" the country; it seems that all of a sudden "everyone" is doing the same thing or wearing the same styles. Some sociologists view fashion as a form of *collective behavior,* or a wave of social conformity. How do so many people get "tuned in" to the same phenomenon, as happened with hip-hop styles?

Remember that creative subsystems within a culture production system attempt to anticipate the tastes of the buying public. Despite their unique talents, members of this subsystem are also members of mass culture. Cultural gatekeepers are drawing from a common set of ideas and symbols, and are influenced by the same cultural phenomena as the eventual consumers of their products.

The process by which certain symbolic alternatives are chosen over others has been termed **collective selection.**[55] As with the creative subsystem, members of the managerial and communications subsystems also seem to develop a common frame of mind. Although products within each category must compete for acceptance in the marketplace, they can usually be characterized by their adherence to a dominant theme or motif—be it "The Western Look," "New Wave," "Danish Modern," or "Nouvelle Cuisine."

BEHAVIORAL SCIENCE PERSPECTIVES ON FASHION

Fashion is a very complex process that operates on many levels. At one extreme, it is a macro, societal phenomenon affecting many people simultaneously. At the other, it exerts a very personal effects on individual behavior. A consumer's purchase decisions are often motivated by his or her desire to be in fashion. Fashion products also are aesthetic objects, and their origins are rooted in art and history. For this reason, there are many perspectives on the origin and diffusion of fashion. Although these cannot be described in detail here, some major approaches can be briefly summarized.[56]

PSYCHOLOGICAL MODELS OF FASHION

Many psychological factors help to explain why people are motivated to be in fashion. These include conformity, variety seeking, personal creativity, and sexual attraction. For example, many consumers seem to have a "need for uniqueness": They want to be different, but not too different.[57] For this reason, people often conform to the basic outlines of a fashion, but try to improvise and make a personal statement within these general guidelines.

One of the earliest theories of fashion proposed that "shifting **erogenous zones**" (sexually arousing areas of the body) accounted for fashion changes, and that different zones become the object of interest because they reflect societal trends. J. C. Flugel, a disciple of Freud, proposed in the 1920s that sexually charged areas wax and wane in order to maintain interest, and that clothing styles change to highlight or hide these parts. For example, it was common for Renaissance-era women to drape their abdomens in fabrics in order to give a swollen appearance—successful childbearing was a priority in the disease-ridden fourteenth and fifteenth centuries. Interest in the female leg in the 1920s and 1930s coincided with women's new mobility and independence, and the exposure of breasts in the 1970s signaled a renewed interest in breast-feeding. Breasts were deemphasized in the 1980s as women concentrated on careers, but some analysts have theorized that a larger bust size is now more popular as women try to combine professional activity with child rearing. Some contemporary fashion theorists suggest that the current prevalence

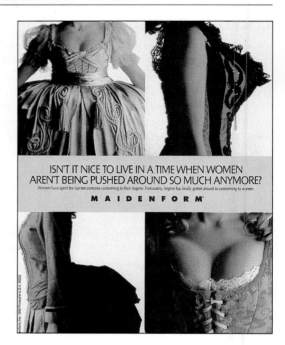

This ad for Maidenform illustrates that fashions have accentuated different parts of the female anatomy throughout history. Copyright © 1990 by Maidenform, Inc.

of the exposed midriff reflects the premium our society places on fitness.[58] (Note: Until very recently, the study of fashion focused almost exclusively on its impact on women. Hopefully, this concentration will broaden as scholars and practitioners begin to appreciate that men are affected by many of the same fashion influences.)

ECONOMIC MODELS OF FASHION

Economists approach fashion in terms of the model of supply and demand. Items that are in limited supply have high value, whereas those readily available are less desirable. Rare items command respect and prestige.

Veblen's notion of conspicuous consumption proposed that the wealthy consume to display their prosperity, for example by wearing expensive (and at times impractical) clothing. As noted in chapter 12, this approach is somewhat outdated; upscale consumers often engage in *parody display,* by which they deliberately adopt formerly low status or inexpensive products, such as jeeps or jeans. Other factors also influence the demand curve for fashion-related products. These include a *prestige-exclusivity effect,* in which high prices still create high demand, and a *snob effect,* whereby lower prices actually reduce demand ("If it's that cheap, it can't be any good").[59]

SOCIOLOGICAL MODELS OF FASHION

The collective selection model discussed previously is an example of a sociological approach to fashion. In addition, much attention has been focused on the relationship between product adoption and class structure.

Trickle-down theory, first proposed in 1904 by Georg Simmel, has been one of the most influential approaches to understanding fashion. It states that there are two conflicting forces that drive fashion change. First, subordinate groups try to adopt the status symbols of the groups above them as they attempt to climb up the ladder of social mobility. Dominant styles thus originate with the upper classes and *trickle-down* to those below. However, this is where the second force kicks in: Those people in the superordinate groups are constantly looking below them on the ladder to ensure that they are not imitated. They respond to the attempts of lower classes to "impersonate" them by adopting even newer fashions.. These two processes create a self-perpetuating cycle of change—the machine that drives fashion.[60]

The trickle-down theory was quite useful for understanding the process of fashion changes when applied to a society with a stable class structure, which permitted the easy identification of lower- versus upper-class consumers. This task is not so easy in modern times. In contemporary Western society, then, this approach must be modified to account for new developments in mass culture.[61]

- A perspective based on class structure cannot account for the wide range of styles that are simultaneously made available in our society. Modern consumers have a much greater degree of individualized choice than in the past because of advances in technology and distribution. Just as an adolescent like Amanda is almost instantly aware of the latest style trends by watching MTV, *elite fashion* has been largely replaced by *mass fashion,* because media exposure permits many groups to become aware of a style at the same time.

- Consumers tend to be more influenced by opinion leaders who are similar to them. As a result each social group has its own fashion innovators who determine fashion trends. It is often more accurate to speak of a *trickle-across effect,* whereby fashions diffuse horizontally among members of the same social group.[62]

- Finally, current fashions often originate with the lower classes and *trickle up.* Grassroots innovators typically are people who lack prestige in the dominant culture (e.g., urban youth). Since they are less concerned with maintaining the status quo, they are more free to innovate and take risks.[63]

MARKETING PITFALL

Large companies that try to stay on top of hot fashion trends face a disturbing paradox: Young consumers are drawn to happening street fashions such as those produced by small entrepreneurs. For example, when Dinah Mohajer was a student at USC in 1995, she needed blue nail polish to go with her blue platform shoes and mixed up her own batch. Her friends loved the idea, and she started Hard Candy with a loan from her parents. Soon Drew Barrymore, Cher, and even Antonio Banderas were wearing Hard Candy colors such as Trailer Trash, Jail Bait, and Fiend.[64]

But, as soon as these styles are "discovered" and mass produced, they are no longer cool. In the old days, couture houses and major retailers set the styles, but with the advent of the Web and numerous small 'zines produced by individuals or small companies, the big guys no longer have the final say on what is cool, and big brand names are distrusted. One way around this is dilemma is to spin off a separate division and try to distance it from the parent company, as Levi-Strauss did with its Silver Tab boutique label and Miller did with its boutique brewery called Red Dog.

Philip Morris took a similar tack with Dave's, a new discount cigarette. While "Dave" is is described as ". . . an entrepreneur who believes in the value of homemade products," in reality the brand is made by Philip Morris Companies, even though the tobacco giant's name is nowhere to be found on the package. Retailers are asked to exhibit Dave's anywhere but next to other PM cigarettes (like Marlboro). According to promotional materials, "Dave's homegrown smokes don't mix with the 'corporate' cigarettes."[65]

Sometimes this strategy backfires, as when a watered-down version of a product gets foisted on the market—for instance, jeans that have an underwearlike band of cloth sewn into them to simulate the look of real underwear sticking out of slouchy pants.[66] Furthermore, there is a fine line between using upstart companies' ideas as "inspiration" and blatant imitation. Another small company called Urban Decay found this out when it was forced to sue Revlon over a line of nail polishes. Its colors included Oil Slick, Rust, and Pallor, and shortly thereafter Revlon introduced Tar, Blood, Rusty, Gun Metal, and other selections.[67]

CYCLES OF FASHION ADOPTION

In the early 1980s, Cabbage Patch dolls were all the rage among American children. Faced with a limited supply of the product, some retailers reported near-riots among adults as they tried desperately to buy the dolls for their children. A Milwaukee disc jockey jokingly announced that people should bring catcher's mitts to a local stadium because 2,000 dolls were going to be dropped from an airplane. Listeners were instructed to hold up their American Express cards so their numbers could be aerially photographed. More than two dozen anxious parents apparently didn't get the joke; they showed up in subzero weather, mitts in hand.[68]

Although the Cabbage Patch craze lasted for a couple of seasons, it eventually died out and consumers moved on to other things, such as Teenage Mutant Ninja Turtles, which grossed more than $600 million in 1989.[69] The Mighty Morphin Power Rangers in turn replaced the Turtles, and they in turn were deposed by Beanie Babies and Giga Pets in 1998—what will be next?

FASHION LIFE-CYCLES

Although the longevity of a particular style can range from a month to a century, fashions tend to flow in a predictable sequence. The **fashion life-cycle** is quite similar to the more familiar product life-cycle. An item or idea progresses through basic stages from birth to death, as shown in Figure 17–4.

The diffusion process discussed earlier in the chapter is intimately related to the popularity of fashion-related items. To illustrate how this process works, consider how the **fashion acceptance cycle** works in the popular music business. In the *introduction stage,* a song is listened to by a small number of music innovators. It may be played in clubs or on "cutting-edge" college radio stations, which is exactly how "grunge rock" groups such as Nirvana got their start. During the *acceptance stage,* the song enjoys increased social visibility and acceptance by large segments of the population. A record may get wide airplay on Top 40 stations, steadily rising up the charts "like a bullet."

In the *regression stage,* the song reaches a state of social saturation as it becomes overused, and eventually it sinks into decline and obsolescence as new

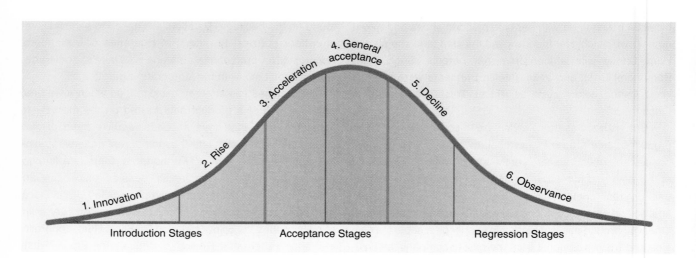

FIGURE 17–4 ■ **A Normal Fashion Cycle**
Source: Reprinted with the permission of Macmillan College Publishing Company from *The Social Psychology of Clothing* by Susan Kaiser. Copyright © 1985 by Macmillan College Publishing Company, Inc.

You always come back to the basics.

This Jim Beam ad illustrates
the cyclical nature of fashion.
Courtesy of Jim Beam Brand, Inc.

songs rise to take its place. A hit record may be played once an hour on a Top 40
station for several weeks. At some point, though, people tend to get sick of it and
focus their attention on newer releases. The former hit record eventually winds up
in the discount rack at the local record store.

Figure 17–5 illustrates that fashions are characterized by slow acceptance at the
beginning, which (if the fashion is to "make it") rapidly accelerates, peaks, and then
tapers off. Different classes of fashion can be identified by considering the relative
length of the fashion acceptance cycle. Many fashions exhibit a moderate cycle, taking several years to work their way through the stages of acceptance and decline;
others are extremely long lived or short lived.

A **classic** is a fashion with an extremely long acceptance cycle. It is in a sense
"antifashion," because it guarantees stability and low risk to the purchaser for a long
period of time. Keds sneakers, introduced in 1917, have been successful because
they appeal to those who are turned off by the high fashion, trendy appeal of L.A.
Gear, Reebok, and others. When consumers in focus groups were asked to project
what kind of building Keds would be, a common response was a country house with
a white picket fence. In other words, the shoes are seen as a stable, classic product.
In contrast, Nikes were often described as steel-and-glass skyscrapers, reflecting
their more modern image.[70]

A **fad** is a very short-lived fashion. Fads are usually adopted by relatively few
people. Adopters may all belong to a common subculture, and the fad "trickles
across" members but rarely breaks out of that specific group. Some successful fad
products include hula hoops, snap bracelets, and "pet rocks." Streaking was a fad
that hit college campuses in the mid-1970s. This term referred to students running

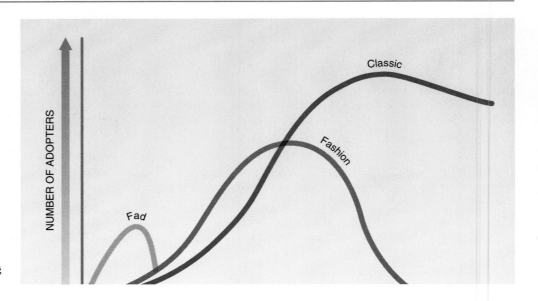

FIGURE 17–5 ■
Comparison of the Acceptance Cycles of Fads, Fashions, and Classics.
Source: Reprinted with the permission of Macmillan College Publishing Company from *The Social Psychology of Clothing* by Susan Kaiser. Copyright © 1985 by Macmillan College Publishing Company, Inc.

naked through classrooms, cafeterias, dorms, and sports venues. Although the practice quickly spread across many campuses, it was primarily restricted to college settings. Streaking highlights several important characteristics of fads.[71]

- The fad is nonutilitarian—that is, it does not perform any meaningful function.
- The fad is often adopted on impulse; people do not undergo stages of rational decision making before joining in.
- The fad diffuses rapidly, gains quick acceptance, and is short lived.

FAD OR TREND?

In 1988, a company called Clearly Canadian began testing a clear soft drink, and over the next few years others jumped on board. Colgate-Palmolive spent $6 million developing a clear version of Palmolive dishwashing liquid, by 1992 Colgate was selling clear soap, Coors introduced a clear malt beverage called Zima, and consumers could even choose clear gasoline for their cars. Clear products were so ubiquitous that they were spoofed on Saturday Night Live in a fake commercial for Crystal Gravy: "You can see your meat!" It was clear that the beginning of the end was in sight and the novelty was wearing off the clear fad. The comments of one 25-year-old research participant in a study about clear drinks sums up the problem: "When I first started drinking them, I thought they were interesting. But once it became a fad I thought, 'this isn't cool anymore'."[72]

The first company to identify a trend and act on it has an advantage, whether the firm is Starbucks (gourmet coffee), Nabisco (Snackwell's low-fat cookies and crackers), or Taco Bell (value pricing). Nothing is certain, but some guidelines help to predict if the innovation will endure as a long-term trend or is just a fad, destined to go the way of hula hoops, Pet Rocks, and Wally Wallwalkers:[73]

- Does it fit with basic lifestyle changes? If a new hairstyle is hard to care for, this innovation will not be consistent with women's increasing time demands. On the other hand, the movement to shorter-term vacations is more likely to last because this innovation makes trip planning easier for harried consumers.

MULTICULTURAL DIMENSIONS

The Japanese have a weakness for gadgets, and local companies produce toys for adults that may strike others as somewhat, well, bizarre. One recent fad is a hit series of Japanese software called *Princess Maker*, targeted to adult men. The player controls the activities, hobbies, and clothing of a girl character he "raises" from childhood. The game probably would be frowned on in the West, because this virtual daughter can be programmed to dress in lingerie or sunbathe naked. The player names her, picks her birthday, and even chooses her blood type, which some Japanese believe determines character traits. His choice of activities for her affects her future success in life (and his score). For example, choosing painting lessons increases the score, whereas dressing her in provocative clothing reduces her moral standing and lowers the score. If a player winds up with a really low score, the daughter may face a future as a bar hostess—when this happens, she giggles while holding up a slinky dress.[74]

Another Japanese fad has now invaded American shores. It's a hand-held chicken video game—a *tamagotchi,* or "cute little egg." The keychain computer game unfolds as an egg hatches on the display screen. The owner uses three tiny buttons to feed the baby chick, play with it, clean up after it, and discipline it. The game can go on for several days if the chick is cared for properly, but if the owner forgets to feed it he or she hears a loud "peep, peep, peep" and eventually the chick grows sickly and dies. Nearly 2,000 people showed up at store when word leaked out a new shipment had been received, with many sleeping outside in the cold.[75] In late 1997, the concept invaded the United States, with about 6 million units of American versions such as Microchimp and Compu Kitty pre-ordered in anticipation of the next craze for these "giga pets."[76]

- **What are the benefits?** The switch to poultry and fish from beef came about because these meats are healthier, so a real benefit is evident.

- **Can it be personalized?** Enduring trends tend to accommodate a desire for individuality, whereas styles such as mohawk haircuts or the grunge look are inflexible and don't allow people to express themselves.

- **Is it a trend or a side effect?** An increased interest in exercises is part of a basic trend toward health consciousness, although the specific form of exercise that is "in" at any given time will vary (e.g., low-impact aerobics versus in-line skating).

- **What other changes have occurred in the market?** Sometimes the popularity of products is influenced by *carryover effects.* The miniskirt fad in the 1960s brought about a major change in the hosiery market, as sales of pantyhose and tights grew from 10 percent of this product category to more than 80 percent in two years. Now, sales of these items are declining due to the casual emphasis in dressing.

- **Who has adopted the change?** If the innovation is not adopted by working mothers, baby boomers, or some other important market segment, it is not likely to become a trend.

TRANSFERRING PRODUCT MEANINGS TO OTHER CULTURES

Innovations know no country boundaries; in modern times they travel across oceans and desserts with blinding speed. Just as Marco Polo brought noodles from China and colonial settlers introduced Europeans to the "joys" of tobacco, today multinational firms seeking to expand their markets are constantly working to conquer new markets and convince legions of foreign consumers to desire their offerings.

As if understanding the dynamics of one's culture weren't hard enough, these issues get even more complicated when we take on the daunting—but essential—task of learning about the practices of other cultures. The consequences of ignoring cultural sensitivities can be costly. This oversight became evident, for example, during the 1994 soccer World Cup. Both McDonald's and Coca-Cola made the mistake of reprinting the Saudi Arabian flag, which includes sacred words from the Koran, on disposable packaging used in promotions. Despite their delight at having a Saudi team in contention for the cup, Muslims around the world protested this borrowing of sacred imagery, and both companies had to scramble to rectify the situation.[77]

In this section, we'll consider some of the issues confronting consumer researchers seeking to understand the cultural dynamics of other countries. We'll also consider the consequences of the "Americanization" of global culture, as U.S. (and to some extent, Western European) marketers continue to export Western popular culture to a globe full of increasingly affluent consumers, many of whom are eagerly waiting to replace their traditional products and practices with the likes of McDonald's, Levi's, and MTV.

THINK GLOBALLY, ACT LOCALLY

As corporations increasingly find themselves competing in many markets around the world, the debate has intensified regarding the necessity of developing separate marketing plans for each culture. A lively debate has ensured regarding the need to "fit in" to the local culture. Let's briefly consider each viewpoint.

ADOPTING A STANDARDIZED STRATEGY
Proponents of a standardized marketing strategy argue that many cultures, especially those of relatively industrialized countries, have become so homogenized that the same approach will work throughout the world. By developing one approach for multiple markets, a company can benefit from economies of scale, because it does not have to incur the substantial time and expense of developing a separate strategy for each culture.[78] This viewpoint represents an **etic perspective,** which focuses on commonalities across cultures. An etic approach to a culture is objective and analytical; it reflects impressions of a culture as viewed by outsiders.

MULTICULTURAL DIMENSIONS

The etic approach has been chosen by many companies who have adopted a standardized strategy for marketing products in Europe. Although the unification of the European Economic Community has not happened as smoothly as many predicted, the prospect of many separate economies eventually being massed into one market of 325 million consumers has led many companies to begin to standardize their prices, brand names, and advertising.[79]

Many companies are responding to this dramatic change by consolidating the different brands sold in individual countries into common *Eurobrands.* In the United Kingdom and France, for example, the Marathon candy bar sold by Mars, Inc. is becoming the Snickers bar (a somewhat risky move, considering that the British refer to women's underwear as "knickers").[80]

Companies that have "gone global" include Merrill Lynch, Xerox, and Chase Manhattan Bank. After testing four campaigns in seven countries, Seagram's Chivas Regal Scotch chose a series of 24 ads, each featuring a Chivas crest and the theme line, "There will always be a Chivas Regal."[81]

ADOPTING A LOCALIZED STRATEGY

On the other hand, many marketers endorse an **emic perspective**, which focuses on variations within a culture. They feel that each culture is unique, with its own value system, conventions, and regulations. This perspective argues that each country has a *national character,* a distinctive set of behavior and personality characteristics.[82] An effective strategy must be tailored to the sensibilities and needs of each specific culture. An emic approach to a culture is subjective and experiential; it attempts to explain a culture as it is experienced by insiders.

Sometimes this strategy involves modifying a product or the way it is positioned to make it acceptable to local tastes. For example, consider the challenge faced by the brewing industry in the Middle East. Alcohol-free beers are growing in popularity, and Saudi market leader Moussey has been doing business there for over 20 years. Still, selling such a product in a country where alcohol consumption is punishable by flogging can be tricky. These drinks are called malt beverages instead of beer, and they can only be marketed through special promotions. Stroh's Schlitz No-Alcohol brand is touted vaguely as "The famous American beverage."[83]

In other contexts adaptation demands more than wordplay. Consumers in some cultures simply do not like some tastes, for example, that are popular elsewhere. Snapple failed in Japan because consumers there didn't like the drink's cloudy appearance or stuff floating in the bottles. Similarly, Frito-Lay, Inc. stopped selling Ruffles potato chips (too salty) and Cheetos (the Japanese didn't appreciate having their fingers turn orange after eating a handful).[84] Cheetos are being made in China, but the local version doesn't contain any cheese, which is not a staple of the Chinese diet. Instead, local flavors will be available in varieties like Savory American Cream and Japanese Steak.[85] Even the venerable McDonald's, which has won Big Mac fans the world over, is finding the need to make changes in order to meet local competition in The Phillipines offered by the Jobilee Foods Corporation. This chain, which has 46 percent of the Filipino market compared to McDonald's 16 percent, caters to the local preference for sweet and spicy flavors, and offers rice with its entrees, similar to what a Filipino mother would cook at home. In response, McDonald's was forced to offer its own version of spicy burgers, one of the few times it has actually changed the composition of its regular burger patty.[86]

CULTURAL DIFFERENCES RELEVANT TO MARKETERS

So, which perspective is correct—the emic or the etic? Perhaps it will be helpful to consider some of the ways that cultures vary in terms of their product preferences and norms regarding what types of products are appropriate or desirable.

Given the sizeable variations in tastes within the United States alone, it is hardly surprising that people around the world have developed their own unique preferences. Unlike Americans, for example, Europeans favor dark chocolate over milk chocolate, which they regard as suitable only for children. Sara Lee sells its pound cake with chocolate chips in the United States, raisins in Australia, and coconut in Hong Kong. Whisky is considered a "classy" drink in France and Italy, but not in England. Crocodile handbags are popular in Asia and Europe, but not in the United States. Americans' favorite tie colors are red and blue, whereas the Japanese prefer olive, brown, and bronze.[87]

Consumers are also accustomed to different forms of advertising. In general, ads that focus on universal values such as love of family travel fairly well, but those with a focus on specific lifestyles do not. In some cases, advertising content is regulated by the local government. For example, pricing in Germany is controlled, and special sales can be held only for a particular reason, such as going out of business or the end of the season. Advertising also focuses more on the provision of factual information rather than on the aggressive hard sell. Indeed, it is illegal to mention the names of competitors.[88] A similar emphasis on facts can be found in Spain and Denmark. In contrast, the British and the Japanese regard advertising as a form of entertainment. Compared to the United States, British television commercials contain less information,[89] and Japanese advertising is more likely to feature emotional appeals while avoiding comparative messages, which are considered impolite.[90]

Marketers must be aware of a culture's norms regarding sensitive topics such as taboos and sexuality. Opals signify bad luck to the British, whereas hunting dog or pig emblems are offensive to Muslims. The Japanese are superstitious about the number four. *Shi*, the word for four, is also the word for death. For this reason, Tiffany sells glassware and china in sets of five in Japan.

Cultures vary sharply in the degree to which reference to sex and bodily functions is permitted. Many American consumers pride themselves on their sophistication. However, some would blush at much European advertising, in which sexuality is more explicit. On the other hand, Muslim countries tend to be quite puritanical.

DOES GLOBAL MARKETING WORK?

So, after briefly considering some of the many differences one encounters across cultures, does global marketing work? Perhaps the more appropriate question is, "*When* does it work?"

Although the argument for a homogenous world culture is appealing in principle, in practice it has met with mixed results. One reason for the failure of global

 # MULTICULTURAL DIMENSIONS

Strongly held values can make life very difficult for marketers, especially when selling sensitive products. This is the case with tampons; 70 percent of American women use them, but only 100 million out of a potential market of 1.7 billion eligible women around the world do. Resistance to the product posed a major problem for Tambrands, which does not make other products and must expand its customer base to remain viable.

The company has found it difficult to sell its feminine hygiene products in some cultures such as Brazil, where many young women fear they will lose their virginity if they use a tampon. A commercial developed for this market included an actress who says in a reassuring voice, "Of course, you're not going to lose your virginity," and a second woman adds, "That will happen, in a much more romantic way."

To counteract this problem prior to launching a new global advertising campaign for Tampax in 26 countries, the firm's advertising agency conducted research and divided the world into three clusters based on residents' resistance to using tampons (resistance was so intense in Muslim countries that the agency didn't even attempt to reach women in those places!):

In Cluster One (including the United States, the United Kingdom, and Australia), women felt comfortable with the idea and offered little resistance. A teaser ad was developed to encourage more frequency of use: "Should I sleep with it, or not?"

In Cluster Two (including France, Israel, and South Africa), about 50 percent of women use the product, but some concerns about virginity remain. To counteract these objections, the marketing strategy focused on obtaining the endorsements of gynecologists within each country.

In Cluster Three (including Brazil, China, and Russia), the greatest resistance was encountered. To try to make inroads in these countries, the researchers found that the first priority is simply to explain how to use the product without making women feel squeamish—a challenge they still are trying to puzzle out.[91]

marketing is that consumers in different countries have different conventions and customs, so they simply do not use products the same way. Kellogg, for example, discovered that in Brazil big breakfasts are not traditional—cereal is more commonly eaten as a dry snack.

In fact, significant cultural differences can even show up within the *same* country: Advertisers in Canada, for example, know that when they target consumers in French-speaking Quebec, their messages must be much different from those addressed to their fellow countrymen who live in English Canada. Ads in Montreal tend to be a lot racier than those in Toronto, reflecting differences in attitudes toward sexuality between consumers with French versus British roots.[92]

Some large corporations, such as Coca-Cola, have been successful in crafting a single, international image. Still, even Coca-Cola must make minor modifications to the way it presents itself in each culture. Although Coke commercials are largely standardized, local agencies are permitted to edit them to highlight close-ups of local faces.[93]

As the world's borders fade due to advances in communications, many companies continue to develop global advertising campaigns. In some cases they are encountering obstacles to acceptance, especially in less-developed countries or in those areas, such as Eastern Europe, that are only beginning to embrace Western-style materialism as a way of life.[94] To maximize the chances of success for these multicultural efforts, marketers must locate consumers in different countries who nonetheless share a common worldview. This is more likely to be the case among people whose frame of reference is relatively more international or cosmopolitan, and/or who receive much of their information about the world from sources that incorporate a worldwide perspective.

Who is likely to fall into this category? Two consumer segments are particularly good candidates: (1) affluent people who are "global citizens" and who are exposed to ideas from around the world through their travels, business contacts, and media experiences, and (2) young people whose tastes in music and fashion are strongly

MARKETING PITFALL

The language barrier is one problem confronting marketers who wish to break into foreign markets. Local product names often raise eyebrows to visiting Americans, who may be surprised to stumble on a Japanese coffee creamer called Creap, a Mexican bread named Bimbo, or even a Scandinavian liquid called Super Piss that unfreezes car locks.[95] Chapter 14 noted some gaffes made by U.S. marketers when advertising to ethnic groups in their own country. Imagine how these mistakes are compounded outside of the United States! One technique that is used to avoid this problem is **back-translation,** in which a translated ad is retranslated into the original language by a different interpreter to catch errors. Some specific translation obstacles that have been encountered around the world include the following:[96]

- Fresca (a soft drink) is Mexican slang for lesbian.
- When rendered phonetically, Esso means "stalled car" in Japan.
- Ford had several problems in Spanish markets. The company discovered that a truck model it called Fiera means "ugly old woman" in Spanish. Its Caliente model, sold in Mexico, is slang for a streetwalker. In Brazil, Pinto is a slang term meaning "small male appendage."
- When Rolls-Royce introduced its Silver Mist model in Germany, it found that the word "mist" is translated as excrement. Similarly, Sunbeam's hair curling iron, called the Mist-Stick, translated as manure wand. To add insult to injury, Vicks is German slang for sexual intercourse, so that company's name had to be changed to Wicks in this market.

influenced by MTV and other media that broadcast many of the same images to multiple countries. For example, viewers of MTV Europe in Rome or Zurich can check out the same "buzz clips" as their counterparts in London or Luxembourg.[97] Benetton, the Italian clothing manufacturer, has been at the forefront in creating vivid (and often controversial) messages about AIDS, racial equality, war, and so on that transcend national boundaries.[98]

THE DIFFUSION OF WESTERN CONSUMER CULTURE

The allure of Western consumer culture has spread throughout the world, as people in other societies slowly but surely fall under the spell of far-reaching advertising campaigns, contact with tourists, and the desire to form attachments with other parts of the world. The process of **creolization** occurs when foreign influences are absorbed and integrated with local meanings—just as modern Christianity incorporated the pagan Christmas tree into its own rituals. This attraction sometimes results in bizarre permutations of products and services, as they are modified to be compatible with local customs. Consider these events, for example:[99]

- In Peru, Indian boys can be found carrying rocks painted to look like transistor radios.
- In highland Papua New Guinea, tribesmen put Chivas Regal wrappers on their drums and wear Pentel pens instead of nosebones.
- Bana tribesmen in the remote highlands of Kako, Ethiopia, pay to watch *Pluto the Circus Dog* on a Viewmaster.
- When a Swazi princess marries a Zulu king, she wears red touraco wing feathers around her forehead and a cape of windowbird feathers and oxtails. He is wrapped in a leopard skin. All is recorded on a Kodak movie camera while the band plays "The Sound of Music."
- In addition to traditional gifts of cloth, food, and cosmetics, Nigerian Hausa brides, although they cannot tell time, receive cheap quartz watches.

"I'D LIKE TO BUY THE WORLD A COKE . . ."

As indicated by these examples, many formerly isolated cultures now incorporate Western objects into their traditional practices. In the process, the meanings of these objects are transformed and adapted to local tastes in ways that a Western visitor might not recognize. Sometimes the process enriches local cultures; sometimes it produces painful stresses and strains the local fabric.

The West (and especially the United States) is a net exporter of popular culture. Western symbols in the form of images, words, and products have diffused throughout the world. This influence is eagerly sought by many consumers, who have learned to equate Western lifestyles in general and the English language in particular with modernization and sophistication. As a result, people around the world are being exposed to a blizzard of American products and media that are attempting to become part of local lifestyles.

For example, American-inspired TV game shows are popular around the world: *Geh Aufs Ganze* (Let's Make a Deal) is one of Germany's top shows. Although *The Dating Game* went off the air in The United States in 1989, it is now seen in 10 foreign countries and is top in its time period in Poland, Finland, and England. In Singapore a cult has formed around locally produced broadcasts of *The $25,000 Pyramid*, and in France *Le Juste Prix* (The Price is Right) attracts almost half of the country's viewers. Not everyone in these countries is happy with the Western influence—producers of the *The Dating Game* in Turkey received death threats from Muslim fundamentalists.[100]

The American appeal is so strong that some non-U.S. companies go out of their way to create an American image. A British ad for Blistex lip cream, for example, includes a fictional woman named "Miss Idaho Lovely Lips" who claims Blistex is "America's best-selling lip cream."[101] Recent attempts by American marketers to "invade" other countries include:

- Kellogg Co. is trying to carve out a market for breakfast cereal in India, even though currently only about 3 percent of Indian households consume such products. Most middle-class Indians eat a traditional hot breakfast that includes such dishes as *chapatis* (unleavened bread) and *dosas* (a fried pancake), but the company is confident that it can entice them to make the switch to Corn Flakes, Froot Loops, and other American delicacies.[102]

- The National Basketball Association is fast becoming the first truly global sports league. Nearly $500 million of licensed merchandise was sold *outside* of the United States in 1996. A survey of 28,000 teens in 45 countries conducted by the DMB&B advertising agency found that Michael Jordan is by far the world's favorite athlete. In China, his Chicago Bulls team (translated as "The Red Oxen") is virtually everyone's favorite.[103]

- The British are avid tea drinkers, but how will they react to American-style iced tea? U.S. companies such as Snapple are hoping they can convince the British that iced tea is more than hot tea that's gotten cold. These firms may have a way to go, based on the reactions of one British construction worker who tried a canned iced tea for the first time, "It was bloody awful."[104]

- Pizza Hut is invading, of all places, Italy. The country will be exposed to the American mass-produced version, quite a different dish from the local pizza, which is often served on porcelain dishes and eaten with a knife and fork. On the other hand, one of Pizza Hut's top performing restaurants is now located in Paris, a center of fine cuisine, so only time will tell if Italians will embrace pizza "American-style."[105]

THE U.S. INVADES ASIA

Although a third of the world's countries have a gross national product of less than $500 per capita, people around the world now have access to Western media, on which they can watch reruns of shows such as *Lifestyles of the Rich and Famous* and *Dallas,* idealized tributes to the opulence of Western lifestyles. To illustrate the impact of this imagery around the world, it is interesting to compare its impact in two very different Asian countries, China and Japan.

As the People's Republic of China endorses some aspects of capitalism and has taken over Hong Kong (a mecca of materialism), its material expectations have escalated. Twenty years ago, the Chinese strove to attain what they called the "three bigs": bikes, sewing machines, and wristwatches. This wish list was later modified to become the "new big six," adding refrigerators, washing machines, and TVs. At last count, the ideal is now the "eight new things." The list now includes color TVs, cameras, and video recorders.[106] Chinese women are starting to demand Western cosmetics costing up to a quarter of their salaries, ignoring domestically produced competitors. As one Chinese executive noted, "Some women even buy a cosmetic just because it has foreign words on the package."[107]

In contrast to China, the Japanese are already accustomed to a bounty of consumer goods. Still, the Japanese are also particularly enthusiastic borrowers of Western culture. Some Japanese pay the equivalent of one-half million dollars for shrunken versions of U.S. homes, and the more avid Americophiles have been known to stage cookouts around imported brick barbecues and trade in their Toyotas for expensive imports such as Chevy vans.[108]

One of the latest fads is *Bassu Boomu*. Inspired by the popularity of the American film *A River Runs Through It*, thousands of Japanese are dressing up like American fishermen and heading for the water. Some years ago a wealthy businessman imported American black bass to Japan, and they spread through the country but were considered a pest until now. According to one importer of expensive fishing gear, "To consumers, bass fishing is equal to America." Sixteen million foreign fishing rods were imported in one year, and magazines such as *Basser* and *LureFreak* have sprung up to meet the needs of Japanese hooked on American outdoor culture.[109]

The Japanese often use Western words as a shorthand for anything new and exciting, even if they do not understand their meaning. The resulting phenomenon is known as "Japlish," in which new Western sounding words are merged with Japanese. Cars are given names such as Fairlady, Gloria, and Bongo Wagon. Consumers buy *deodoranto* (deodorant) and *appuru pai* (apple pie). Ads urge shoppers to *stoppu rukku* (stop and look), and products are claimed to be *yuniku* (unique).[110] Coca-Cola cans say, "I feel Coke & sound special," and a company called Cream Soda sells products with the slogan, "Too old to die, too young to happy."[111] Other Japanese products with English names include Mouth Pet (breath freshener), Pocari Sweat ("refreshment water"), Armpit (electric razor), Brown Gross Foam (hair-coloring mousse), Virgin Pink Special (skin cream), Cow Brand (beauty soap), and Mymorning Water (canned water).[112]

EMERGING CONSUMER CULTURES IN TRANSITIONAL ECONOMIES

In the early 1980s the American TV show *Dallas* was broadcast by the Romanian Communist government to show off the decadence of Western capitalism. This strategy backfired, and instead the devious (but rich!) J. R. became a revered icon in parts of Eastern Europe and the Middle East—to the extent that a tourist attraction outside of Bucharest includes a big white log gate that announces (in English) the name, "South Fork Ranch."[113] Western "decadence" appears to be infectious.[114]

After the downfall of communism, Eastern Europeans emerged from a long winter of deprivation into a springtime of abundance. The picture is not all rosy, however, because attaining consumer goods is not easy for many in *transitional economies*, in which the economic system is still "neither fish now fowl," and governments ranging from China to Portugal struggle with the difficult adaptation from a controlled, centralized economy to a free-market system. These problems stem from factors such as the unequal distribution of income among citizens, as well as striking rural–urban differences in expectations and values. The key aspect of a transitional economy is the rapid change required on social, political, and economic dimensions as the populace suddenly is exposed to global communications and market external market pressures.[115]

Some of the consequences of the transition to capitalism include a loss of confidence and pride in the local culture, as well as alienation, frustration, and an increase in stress as leisure time is sacrificed to work ever harder to buy consumer goods. The yearning for the trappings of Western material culture is perhaps most evident in parts of Eastern Europe, where citizens who threw off the shackles of communism now have direct access to coveted consumer goods from the United States and Western Europe—if they can afford them. One analyst observed, ". . . as former subjects of the Soviet empire dream it, the American dream has very little to do with liberty and justice for all and a great deal to do with soap operas and the Sears Catalogue."[116]

In 1990 well over 60 countries had a gross national product of less than $10 billion, an amount exceeded by the revenues of more than 135 transnational companies. The dominance of these marketing powerhouses has helped to create a *globalized consumption ethic;* as people the world over are increasingly surrounded by goods and tempting images of them, a material lifestyle becomes more important to attain. Shopping evolves from a wearying, task-oriented struggle to locate even basic necessities to a leisure activity, and possessing luxury items becomes a mechanism to display one's status (see chapter 13)—often at great personal sacrifice. In Romania, for example, Kent cigarettes became an underground currency, even though the cost of smoking a pack a day of foreign cigarettes would cost the average Romanian his or her entire yearly salary. As the global consumption ethic spreads, the products wished for in different cultures become homogenized—for example, Christmas is now celebrated among some urbanites in Muslim Turkey, though gift giving even on birthdays is not customary in many parts of the country.

Does this mean that in time consumers who live in Nairobi, New Guinea, or the Netherlands will all be indistinguishable from those in New York or Nashville? Probably not—as we saw at the beginning of this section, it's common for the meanings of consumer goods to be adapted to local customs and needs. For example, in Turkey some urban women use ovens to dry clothes and dishwashers to wash muddy spinach. Or, a traditional clothing style such as a *bilum* worn in Papua New Guinea may be combined with Western items such as Mickey Mouse shirts or baseball caps.[117] These processes make it unlikely that global homogenization will overwhelm local cultures, but rather that there will be multiple consumer cultures, each blending global icons such as Nike's pervasive "swoosh," with indigenous products and meanings.

Globalization has become an integral part of the marketing strategy of many, if not most, major corporations.

CREEPING AMERICANISM: A NEGATIVE BACKLASH

Despite the proliferation of Western culture around the world, there are signs that this invasion is slowing. Japanese consumers, for example, are beginning to exhibit waning interest in foreign products as the health of their country's economy declines. Some of the latest "hot" products in Japan now include green tea and *yukata*, traditional printed cotton robes donned after the evening bath.[118] Several locally made products are catching on in parts of Eastern Europe due to their lower prices, improved quality, and the problem that sometimes the imported products are inferior versions. Some Muslims are rejecting Western symbols as they adhere to a green Islam philosophy that includes using natural, traditional products.[119]

Critics in other countries deplore the creeping Americanization of their cultures. Debates continue in many countries on the imposition of quotas that limit American television programming.[120] The conflict created by exporting American culture was brought to a head in trade negotiations on GATT (the global trade agreement), which deadlocked over the export of American movies to Europe (the United States share of the European cinema market is about 75 percent). As one French official put it, "French films are the cinema of creation. American films are products of marketing."[121]

The French have been the most outspoken opponents of creeping Americanization. They have even tried to ban the use of such "Franglish" terms as *le drugstore, le fast food,* and even *le marketing,* though this effort was recently ruled unconstitutional.[122] The French debate over cultural contamination was brought to a head by the 1992 opening of Euro Disney in a Paris suburb. In addition to the usual attractions, hotels with names like The Hotel New York, The Newport Bay Club, and The Hotel Cheyenne attempt to recreate portions of America. The park appears to have rebounded after a shaky start, but some Europeans have been less than enthusiastic about the cultural messages being sent by the Disney organization. One French critic described the theme park as "a horror made of cardboard, plastic, and appalling colors—a construction of hardened chewing gum and idiotic folklore taken straight out of a comic book written for obese Americans."[123]

MARKETING PITFALL

Cigarettes are among the most successful of Western exports. Asian consumers alone spend $90 billion a year on cigarettes, and U.S. tobacco manufacturers continue to push relentlessly into these markets. Cigarette advertising, often depicting glamorous Western models and settings, is found just about everywhere, on billboards, buses, storefronts, and clothing, and many major sports and cultural events are sponsored by tobacco companies. Some companies even hand out cigarettes and gifts in amusement areas, often to preteens.

A few countries have taken steps to counteract this form of Westernization. Singapore bans all promotions that mention a product's name. Hong Kong has prohibited cigarette ads from appearing on radio and TV. Japan and South Korea do not allow ads to appear in women's magazines. Industry executives argue that they are simply competing in markets that do little to discourage smoking (e.g., Japan issues health warnings like "Please don't smoke too much"), often against heavily subsidized local brands with names such as Long Life (Taiwan). The warnings and restrictions are likely to increase, however; smoking-related deaths have now overtaken communicable diseases for the "honor" of being Asia's #1 killer.[124]

- The styles prevalent in a culture at any point in time often reflect underlying political and social conditions. The set of agents responsible for creating stylistic alternatives is termed a *culture production system (CPS)*. Factors such as the types of people involved in this system and the amount of competition by alternative product forms influence the choices that eventually make their way to the marketplace for consideration by end consumers.

- Culture is often described in terms of high (or elite) forms and low (or popular) forms. Products of popular culture tend to follow a *cultural formula* and contain predictable components. On the other hand, these distinctions are blurring in modern society as imagery from "high art" is increasingly being incorporated into marketing efforts.

- *Reality engineering* occurs as elements of popular culture are appropriated by marketers and converted to vehicles for promotional strategies. These elements include sensory and spatial aspects of everyday existence, whether in the form of products appearing in movies, scents pumped into offices and stores, billboards, theme parks, and video monitors attached to shopping carts.

- *Diffusion of innovations* refers to the process whereby a new product, service, or idea spreads through a population. *Innovators* and *early adopters* are quick to adopt new products, and *laggards* are very slow. A consumer's decision to adopt a new product depends on his or her personal characteristics as well as on characteristics of the innovation itself. Products stand a better change of being adopted if they demand relatively little change in behavior from users, are easy to understand, and they provide a relative advantage compared to existing products.

- The *fashion system* includes everyone involved in the creation and transference of symbolic meanings. Meanings that express common *cultural categories* (e.g., gender distinctions) are conveyed by many different products. New styles tend to be adopted by many people simultaneously in a process known as *collective selection*. Perspectives on motivations for adopting new styles include psychological, economic, and sociological models of fashion.

- Fashions tend to follow cycles that resemble the product life-cycle. The two extremes of fashion adoption, *classics* and *fads*, can be distinguished in terms of the length of this cycle.

- Because a consumer's culture exerts such a big influence on his or her lifestyle choices, marketers must learn as much as possible about differences in cultural norms and preferences when marketing in more than one country. One important issue is to the extent to which marketing strategies must be tailored to each culture versus standardized across cultures. Followers of an *etic perspective* believe that the same universal messages will be appreciated by people in many cultures. Believes in an *emic perspective* argue that individual cultures are too unique to permit such standardization; marketers must instead adapt their approaches to be consistent with local values and practices. Attempts at global marketing have met with mixed success; in many cases this approach is more likely to work if the messages appeal to basic values and/or if the target markets consist of consumers who are more internationally rather than locally oriented.

- The United States is a net exporter of popular culture. Consumers around the world have eagerly adopted American products, especially entertainment vehicles and items that are linked symbolically to a uniquely American lifestyle (e.g., Marlboro cigarettes, Levi's jeans). Despite the continuing "American-ization" of world culture, some consumers are alarmed by this influence, and are instead emphasizing a return to local products and customs. In other cases, they are integrating these products with existing cultural practices in a process known as **creolization.**

KEY TERMS

Art product p. 527
Back-translation p. 549
Classic p. 543
Collective selection p. 539
Continuous innovation
    p. 543
Cooptation p. 523
Craft product p. 527
Creolization p. 556
Cultivation hypothesis
    p. 532
Cultural categories p. 537
Cultural formula p. 528
Cultural gatekeepers p. 527
Cultural selection p. 524
Culture production system
    (CPS) p. 525

Diffusion of innovations
    p. 532
Discontinuous innovation
    p. 535
Dynamically continuous
    innovation p. 535
Early adopter p. 533
Emic perspective p. 547
Erogenous zones p. 539
Etic perspective p. 546
Fad p. 543
Fashion p. 537
Fashion acceptance cycle
    p. 542
Fashion life-cycle p. 542
Fashion system p. 536
Innovation p. 532

Innovators p. 533
Knockoff p. 536
Laggards p. 533
Late adopters p. 533
Product placement p. 531
Reality engineering p. 530
Symbolic innovation p. 534
Technological innovation
    p. 534
Trickle-down theory p. 540

CONSUMER BEHAVIOR CHALLENGE

1. Is it appropriate for large corporations to market small boutique brands (e..g., Dave's cig-arettes) and hide the true origins of these products?

2. Some consumers complain that they are "at the mercy" of designers: They are forced to buy whatever styles are in fashion, because nothing else is available. Do you agree that there is such a thing as a "designer conspiracy?"

3. What are the basic differences between a fad, a fashion, and a classic? Provide examples of each.

4. What is the difference between an art and a craft? Where would you characterize adver-tising within this framework?

5. The chapter mentions some instances in which market research findings influenced artistic decisions, as when a movie ending was reshot to accommodate consumers' pref-erences. Many people would most likely oppose this practice, claiming that books, movies, records, or other artistic endeavors should not be designed to merely conform to what people want to read, see, or hear. What do you think?

6. Due to increased competition and market saturation, marketers in industrialized coun-tries are increasingly trying to develop Third World markets by encouraging people in underdeveloped countries to desire Western products. Should this practice be encour-aged, even if the products being marketed may be harmful to consumers' health (e.g., cig-arettes) or divert needed money away from the purchase of essentials? If you were a trade or health official in a Third World country, what guidelines, if any, might you sug-gest to regulate the import of luxury goods from advanced economies?

7. Comment on the growing practices described as reality engineering. Do marketers "own" our culture, and should they?

NOTES

1. Marc Spiegler, "Marketing Street Culture: Bringing Hip-Hop Style to the Mainstream," *American Demographics* (November 1996): 29–34.
2. Quoted in Spiegler, "Marketing Street Culture: Bringing Hip-Hop Style to the Mainstream.": 30.
3. Joshua Levine, "Badass Sells," *Forbes* (April 21, 1997): 142 (6 pp.).
4. Nina Darnton, "Where the Homegirls Are," *Newsweek* (June 17, 1991): 60; "The Idea Chain," *Newsweek* (October 5, 1992): 32.
5. Cyndee Miller, "X Marks the Lucrative Spot, But Some Advertisers Can't Hit Target," *Marketing News* (August 2, 1993): 1.
6. Ad appeared in *Elle* (September 1994).
7. Spiegler, "Marketing Street Culture: Bringing Hip-Hop Style to the Mainstream."; Levine, "Badass Sells."
8. Jeff Jensen, "Hip, Wholesome Image Makes a Marketing Star of Rap's LL Cool J," *Advertising Age* (August 25, 1997): 1 (2 pp.).
9. Elizabeth M. Blair, "Commercialization of the Rap Music Youth Subculture," *Journal of Popular Culture* 27 (Winter 1993): 21–34; Basil G. Englis, Michael R. Solomon, and Anna Olofsson, "Consumption Imagery in Music Television: A Bi-Cultural Perspective," *Journal of Advertising* 22 (December 1993): 21–34.
10. Spiegler, "Marketing Street Culture: Bringing Hip-Hop Style to the Mainstream."
11. Grant McCracken, "Culture and Consumption: A Theoretical Account of the Structure and Movement of the Cultural Meaning of Consumer Goods," *Journal of Consumer Research* 13 (June 1986): 71–84.
12. Richard A. Peterson, "The Production of Culture: A Prolegomenon," in ed. Richard A. Peterson, *The Production of Culture*, Sage Contemporary Social Science Issues, (Beverly Hills, CA: Sage, 1976)33: 7–22.
13. Richard A. Peterson and D. G. Berger, "Entrepreneurship in Organizations: Evidence from the Popular Music Industry," *Administrative Science Quarterly* 16 (1971): 97–107.
14. Elizabeth C. Hirschman, "Resource Exchange in the Production and Distribution of a Motion Picture," *Empirical Studies of the Arts* 8 (1990)1: 31–51; Michael R. Solomon, "Building Up and Breaking Down: The Impact of Cultural Sorting on Symbolic Consumption," in eds. J. Sheth and E. C. Hirschman, *Research in Consumer Behavior* (Greenwich, CT: JAI Press, 1988), 325–51.
15. See Paul M. Hirsch, "Processing Fads and Fashions: An Organizational Set Analysis of Cultural Industry Systems," *American Journal of Sociology* 77 (1972)4: 639–59; Russell Lynes, *The Tastemakers* (New York: Harper and Brothers, 1954); Michael R. Solomon, "The Missing Link: Surrogate Consumers in the Marketing Chain," *Journal of Marketing* 50 (October 1986): 208–19.
16. Howard S. Becker, "Arts and Crafts," *American Journal of Sociology* 83 (January 1987): 862–89.
17. Herbert J. Gans, "Popular Culture in America: Social Problem in a Mass Society or Social Asset in a Pluralist Society?" in ed. Howard S. Becker, *Social Problems: A Modern Approach* (New York: Wiley, 1966).
18. Peter S. Green, "Moviegoers Devour Ads," *Advertising Age* (June 26, 1989): 36.
19. John P. Robinson, "The Arts in America," *American Demographics* (September 1987): 42.
20. Michael R. Real, *Mass-Mediated Culture* (Upper Saddle River, NJ: Prentice Hall, 1977).
21. Annetta Miller, "Shopping Bags Imitate Art: Seen the Sacks? Now Visit the Museum Exhibit," *Newsweek* (January 23, 1989): 44.
22. Kim Foltz, "New Species for Study: Consumers in Action," *New York Times* (December 18, 1989): A1.
23. Arthur A. Berger, *Signs in Contemporary Culture: An Introduction to Semiotics* (New York: Longman, 1984).
24. Michiko Kakutani, "Art is Easier the 2d Time Around," *The New York Times* (October 30, 1994):E4.
25. Robin Givhan, "Designers Caught in a Tangled Web," *The Washington Post* (April 5, 1997): C1 (2 pp.).
26. Helene Diamond, "Lights, Camera . . . Research!" *Marketing News* (September 11, 1989): 10.
27. Michael R. Solomon and Basil G. Englis, "Reality Engineering: Blurring the Boundaries between Marketing and Popular Culture," *Journal of Current Issues and Research in Advertising* 16 (Fall 1994)2: 1–17.
28. T. Bettina Cornwell and Bruce Keillor, "Contemporary Literature and the Embedded Consumer Culture: The Case of Updike's Rabbit," in eds. Roger J. Kruez and Mary Sue MacNealy, *Empirical Approaches to Literature and Aesthetics: Advances in Discourse Processes* 52 (Norwood, NJ: Ablex, 1996): 559–72; Monroe Friedman, "The Changing Language of a Consumer Society: Brand Name Usage in Popular American Novels in the Postwar Era," *Journal of Consumer Research* 11 (March 1985): 927–37; Monroe Friedman, "Commercial Influences in the Lyrics of Popular American Music of the Postwar Era," *Journal of Consumer Affairs* 20 (Winter 1986): 193.
29. Suzanne Alexander Ryan, "Companies Teach All Sorts of Lessons with Educational Tools They Give Away," *Wall Street Journal* (April 19, 1994): B1 (2 pp.); Cyndee Miller, "Marketers Find a Seat in the Classroom," *Marketing News* (June 20, 1994): 2.
30. Bill Keller, "For Rich Tourists (and Not Too African)," *New York Times* (December 3, 1992)2: A1.
31. Benjamin M. Cole, "Products That Want to Be in Pictures," *Los Angeles Herald Examiner* (March 5, 1985): 36; see also Stacy M. Vollmers and Richard W. Mizerski, "A Review and Investigation into the Effectivenss of Product Placements in Films," in ed. Karen Whitehill King, *Proceedings of the 1994 Conference of the American Academy of Advertising* 97–102; Solomon and Englis, "Reality Engineering: Blurring the Boundaries Between Marketing and Popular Culture."
32. David Leonhardt, "Cue the Soda Can," *Business Week* (June 24, 1996): 64 (2 pp.).
33. Fara Warner, "Why It's Getting Harder to Tell the Shows from the

Ads," *Wall Street Journal* (June 15, 1995): B1 (2 pp.).

34. Warner, "Why It's Getting Harder to Tell the Shows from the Ads."

35. Randall Rothenberg, "Is it a Film? Is it an Ad? Harder to Tell?" *New York Times* (March 13, 1990): D23.

36. Quoted in Mary Kuntz and Joseph Weber, "The New Hucksterism," *Business Week* (July 1, 1996): 75, 7 pp., quoted on p. 78.

37. George Gerbner, Larry Gross, Nancy Signorielli, and Michael Morgan, "Aging with Television: Images on Television Drama and Conceptions of Social Reality," *Journal of Communication* 30 (1980): 37–47.

38. Stephen Fox and William Philber, "Television Viewing and the Perception of Affluence," *Sociological Quarterly* 19 (1978): 103–12; W. James Potter, "Three Strategies for Elaborating the Cultivation Hypothesis," *Journalism Quarterly* 65 (Winter 1988): 930–9; Gabriel Weimann, "Images of Life in America: The Impact of American T.V. in Israel," *International Journal of Intercultural Relations* 8 (1984): 185–97.

39. "Movie Smoking Exceeds Real Life," *The Asbury Park Press* (June 20, 1994): A4.

40. The new science of memetics, which tries to explain how beliefs gain acceptance and predict their progress, was spurred by Richard Dawkins, who in the 1970s proposed culture as a Darwinian struggle among "memes" or mind viruses—see Geoffrey Cowley, "Viruses of the Mind: How Odd Ideas Survive," *Newsweek* (April 14, 1997): 14.

41. Eric J. Arnould, "Toward a Broadened Theory of Preference Formation and the Diffusion of Innovations: Cases from Zinder Province, Niger Republic," *Journal of Consumer Research* 16 (September 1989): 239–67; Susan B. Kaiser, *The Social Psychology of Clothing* (New York: Macmillan, 1985); Thomas S. Robertson, *Innovative Behavior and Communication* (New York: Holt, Rinehart and Winston, 1971).

42. Susan L. Holak, Donald R. Lehmann, and Fareena Sultan, "The Role of Expectations in the Adoption of Innovative Consumer Durables: Some Preliminary Evidence," *Journal of Retailing* 63 (Fall 1987): 243–59.

43. Hubert Gatignon and Thomas S. Robertson, "A Propositional Inventory for New Diffusion Research," *Journal of Consumer Research* 11 (March 1985): 849–67.

44. Joshua Levine, "The Streets Don't Lie," *Forbes* (April 21, 1997): 145.

45. Elizabeth C. Hirschman, "Symbolism and Technology as Sources of the Generation of Innovations," in ed. Andrew Mitchell, *Advances in Consumer Research* 9 (Provo, UT: Association for Consumer Research): 537–41.

46. Susan Mitchell, "Technophiles and Technophobes," *American Demographics* (February 1994): 36–9.

47. Everett M. Rogers, *Diffusion of Innovations*, 3rd ed. (New York: The Free Press 1983).

48. Umberto Eco, *A Theory of Semiotics* (Bloomington, IN: Indiana University Press, 1979).

49. Edmund L. Andrews, "When Imitation Isn't the Sincerest Form of Flattery," *New York Times* (August 9, 1990): 20.

50. Moshe Givon, Vijay Mahajan, and Eitan Muller, "Software Piracy: Estimation of Lost Sales and the Impact on Software Diffusion," *Journal of Marketing* 59 (January 1995)1: 29–37.

51. Fred Davis, "Clothing and Fashion as Communication," in ed. Michael R. Solomon, *The Psychology of Fashion* (Lexington, MA: Lexington Books, 1985): 15–28.

52. Melanie Wallendorf, "The Formation of Aesthetic Criteria through Social Structures and Social Institutions," in ed. Jerry C. Olson, *Advances in Consumer Research* 7 (Ann Arbor, MI: Association for Consumer Research, 1980): 3–6.

53. Grant McCracken, "Culture and Consumption: A Theoretical Account of the Structure and Movement of the Cultural Meaning of Consumer Goods," *Journal of Consumer Research* 13 (June 1986): 71–84.

54. "The Eternal Triangle," *Art in America* (February 1989): 23.

55. Herbert Blumer, *Symbolic Interactionism: Perspective and Method* (Upper Saddle River, NJ: Prentice Hall, 1969); Howard S. Becker, "Art as Collective Action," *American Sociological Review* 39 (December 1973); Richard A. Peterson, "Revitalizing the Culture Concept," *Annual Review of Sociology* 5 (1979): 137–66.

56. For more details, see Kaiser, *The Social Psychology of Clothing*; George B. Sproles, "Behavioral Science Theories of Fashion," in ed. Michael R. Solomon, *The Psychology of Fashion*, (Lexington, MA: Lexington Books, 1985): 55–70.

57. C. R. Snyder and Howard L. Fromkin, *Uniqueness: The Human Pursuit of Difference* (New York: Plenum Press, 1980).

58. Linda Dyett, "Desperately Seeking Skin," *Psychology Today* (May/June 1996): 14; Alison Lurie, *The Language of Clothes* (New York: Random House, 1981).

59. Harvey Leibenstein, *Beyond Economic Man: A New Foundation for Microeconomics* (Cambridge, MA: Harvard University Press, 1976).

60. Georg Simmel, "Fashion," *International Quarterly* 10 (1904): 130–55.

61. Grant D. McCracken, "The Trickle-Down Theory Rehabilitated," in ed. Michael R. Solomon, *The Psychology of Fashion* (Lexington, MA: Lexington Books, 1985): 39–54.

62. Charles W. King, "Fashion Adoption: A Rebuttal to the 'Trickle-Down' Theory," in ed. Stephen A. Greyser, *Toward Scientific Marketing* (Chicago: American Marketing Association, 1963): 108–25.

63. Alf H. Walle, "Grassroots Innovation," *Marketing Insights* (Summer 1990): 44–51.

64. Gregory Beals and Leslie Kaufman, "The Kids Know Cool," *Newsweek* (March 31, 1997): 48–9.

65. Suein L. Hwang, "Philip Morris Makes Dave's—but Sh! Don't Tell," *Wall Street Journal* (March 22, 1995): B1 (2 pp.).

66. Spiegler, "Marketing Street Culture: Bringing Hip-Hop Style to the Mainstream."

67. Beals and Kaufman, "The Kids Know Cool."

68. "Cabbage-Hatched Plot Sucks in 24 Doll Fans," *New York Daily News* (December 1, 1983).

69. "Turtlemania," *The Economist* (April 21, 1990): 32.

70. Anthony Ramirez, "The Pedestrian Sneaker Makes a Comeback," *New York Times* (October 14, 1990): F17.

71. B. E. Aguirre, E. L. Quarantelli, and Jorge L. Mendoza, "The Collective Behavior of Fads: The Characteristics, Effects, and Career of Streaking," *American Sociological Review* (August 1989): 569.

72. Quoted in Kathleen Deveny," Anatomy of a Fad: How Clear Products Were Hot and Then Suddenly Were Not," *Wall Street Journal* (March 15, 1994): B1 (2 pp.), quoted on p. B8.

73. Martin G. Letscher, "How to Tell Fads from Trends," *American Demographics* (December 1994): 38–45.

74. The Associated Press, "Hit Japanese Software Lets Players Raise 'Daughter'," *Montgomery Advertiser* (April 7, 1996): 14A.

75. "Japanese Flock to Stores for Virtual Chicken Game," *Montgomery Advertiser* (January 27, 1997): 6A.

76. Joseph Pereira, "Retailers Bet Virtual Pets Will be the Next Toy Craze," *Wall Street Journal Interactive Edition* (May 2, 1997).

77. "Packaging Draws Protest," *Marketing News* (July 4, 1994): 1.

78. Theodore Levitt, *The Marketing Imagination* (New York: The Free Press, 1983).

79. Kevin Cote, "The New Shape of Europe," *Advertising Age* (November 9, 1988): 98.

80. Steven Prokesch, "Selling in Europe: Borders Fade," *New York Times* (May 31, 1990): D1.

81. Gary Levin, "Ads Going Global," *Advertising Age* (July 22, 1991): 4; Dagmar Mussey and Anika Michalowska, "Wella Unifies Image," *Advertising Age* (March 11, 1991): 22.

82. Terry Clark, "International Marketing and National Character: A Review and Proposal for an Integrative Theory," *Journal of Marketing* 54 (October 1990): 66–79.

83. Tara Parker-Pope, "Nonalcoholic Beer Hits the Spot in Mideast," *Wall Street Journal* (December 6, 1995): B1 (2 pp.).

84. Norihiko Shirouzu, "Snapple in Japan: How a Splash Dried Up," *Wall Street Journal* (April 15 1996): B1 (2 pp.).

85. Glenn Collins, "Chinese to Get a Taste of Cheese-Less Cheetos," *New York Times* (September 2, 1994): D4.

86. Hugh Filman, "Happy Meals for a McDonald's Rival," *Business Week* (July 29, 1996): 77.

87. Julie Skur Hill and Joseph M. Winski, "Goodbye Global Ads: Global Village is Fantasy Land for Marketers," *Advertising Age* (November 16, 1987): 22.

88. Matthias D. Kindler, Ellen Day, and Mary R. Zimmer, "A Cross-Cultural Comparison of Magazine Advertising in West Germany and the U.S." (unpublished manuscript, The University of Georgia, Athens, 1990).

89. Marc G. Weinberger and Harlan E. Spotts, "A Situational View of Information Content in TV Advertising in the U.S. and U.K.," *Journal of Marketing* 53 (January 1989): 89–94; see also Abhilasha Mehta, "Global Markets and Standardized Advertising: Is It Happening? An Analysis of Common Brands in USA and UK," in *Proceedings of the 1992 Conference of the American Academy of Advertising* (1992): 170.

90. Jae W. Hong, Aydin Muderrisoglu, and George M. Zinkhan, "Cultural Differences and Advertising Expression: A Comparative Content Analysis of Japanese and U.S. Magazine Advertising," *Journal of Advertising* 16 (1987): 68.

91. Yumiko Ono, "Tambrands Ads Try to Scale Cultural, Religious Obstacles," *Wall Street Journal Interactive Edition* (March 17, 1997).

92. Clyde H. Farnsworth, "Yoked in Twin Solitudes: Canada's Two Cultures," *New York Times* (September 18, 1994): E4.

93. Hill and Winski, "Goodbye Global Ads."

94. See, for example, Russell W. Belk and Güliz Ger, "Problems of Marketization in Romania and Turkey," *Research in Consumer Behavior* 7 (JAI Press, 1994): 123–55.

95. Steve Rivkin, "The Name Game Heats Up," *Marketing News* (April 22, 1996): 8.

96. David A. Ricks, "Products That Crashed into the Language Barrier," *Business and Society Review* (Spring 1983): 46–50.

97. MTV Europe, personal communication, 1994.; see also Teresa J. Domzal and Jerome B. Kernan, "Mirror, Mirror: Some Postmodern Reflections on Global Advertising," *Journal of Advertising* 22 (December 1993)4: 1–20; Douglas P. Holt, "Consumers' Cultural Differences as Local Systems of Tastes: A Critique of the Personality-Values Approach and an Alternative Framework," *Asia Pacific Advances in Consumer Research* 1 (1994): 1–7.

98. Roberto Grandi, "Benetton's Advertising: A Case History of Postmodern Communication" (unpublished manuscript, Center for Modern Culture & Media, University of Bologna, 1994).

99. Eric J. Arnould and Richard R. Wilk, "Why Do the Natives Wear Adidas: Anthropological Approaches to Consumer Research," in *Advances in Consumer Research* 12 (Provo, UT: Association for Consumer Research, 1985): 748–52.

100. Robert LaFranco, "Long-Lived Kitsch," *Forbes* (February 26, 1996): 68.

101. Dana Milbank, "Made in America Becomes a Boast in Europe," *Wall Street Journal*, January 19, 1994, B1 (2 pp.).

102. Suman Dubey, "Kellogg Invites India's Middle Class to Breakfast of Ready-to-Eat Cereal," *Wall Street Journal* (August 29, 1994): B3B.

103. "They All Want to be Like Mike," *Fortune* (July 21, 1997): 51–3.

104. Tara Parker-Pope, "Will the British Warm UP to Iced Tea? Some Big Marketers are Counting on It," *Wall Street Journal* (August 22, 1994): B1 (2 pp.).

105. John Tagliabue, "Proud Palaces of Italian Cusine Await Pizza Hut," *New York Times* (September 1, 1994): A4.

106. David K. Tse, Russell W. Belk, and Nan Zhou, "Becoming a Consumer Society: A Longitudinal and Cross-Cultural Content Analysis of Print Ads from Hong Kong, the People's Republic of China, and Taiwan," *Journal of Consumer Research* 15 (March 1989): 457–72; see also Annamma Joy, "Marketing in Modern China: an Evolutionary Perspective," *CJAS* (June 1990): 55–67, for a review of changes in Chinese marketing practices since the economic reforms of 1978.

107. Quoted in Sheryl WuDunn, "Cosmetics from the West Help to Change the Face of China," *New York Times* (May 6, 1990): 16.

108. Michael Williams and Miho Inada, "Japanese Families Learn to Play House the American Way," *Wall Street Journal* (January 16, 1995): A1 (2 pp.).

109. Steve Glain, "Japan's Big Fish Tale: It's Hip to Emulate American Anglers," *Wall Street Journal Europe* (March 27,1997): 1–2.

110. John F. Sherry Jr. and Eduardo G. Camargo, "'May Your Life be Marvelous': English Language Labeling and the Semiotics of Japanese Promotion," *Journal of Consumer Research* 14 (September 1987): 174–88.

111. Bill Bryson, "A Taste for Scrambled English," *New York Times* (July 22, 1990): 10; Rose A. Horowitz, "California Beach Culture Rides Wave of Popularity in Japan," *Journal of Commerce* (August 3, 1989): 17; Elaine Lafferty, "American Casual Seizes Japan: Teenagers Go for N.F.L. Hats, Batman and the California Look," *Time* (November 13, 1989): 106.

112. Lucy Howard and Gregory Cerio, "Goofy Goods," *Newsweek* (August 15, 1994): 8.

113. Prof. Russell Belk, University of Utah, personal communication, July 25, 1997.

114. Material in this section adapted from Güliz Ger and Russell W. Belk, "I'd Like to Buy the World a Coke: Consumptionscapes of the 'Less Affluent World'," *Journal of Consumer Policy* 19 (1996)3: 271–304; Russell W. Belk, "Romanian Consumer Desires and Feelings of Deservingness," in ed. Lavinia Stan, *Romania in Transition* (Hanover, NH: Dartmouth Press, 1997): 191–208; see also Güliz Ger, "Human Development and Humane Consumption: Well Being Beyond the Good Life," *Journal of Public Policy and Marketing,* 16 (1997): 110–125.

115. Prof. Güliz Ger, Bilkent University, Turkey, personal communication, July 25, 1997.

116. Erazim Kohák, "Ashes, Ashes . . . Central Europe After Forty Years," *Daedalus* 121 (Spring 1992): 197–215, quoted on p. 209, quoted in Belk, "Romanian Consumer Desires and Feelings of Deservingness."

117. This example courtesy of Prof. Russell Belk, University of Utah, personal communication, July 25, 1997.

118. Jennifer Cody, "Now Marketers in Japan Stress the Local Angle," *Wall Street Journal* (February 23, 1994): B1 (2 pp.).

119. Ger and Belk, "I'd Like to Buy the World a Coke: Consumptionscapes of the 'Less Affluent World'."

120. Steven Greenhouse, "The Television Europeans Love, and Love to Hate," *New York Times* (August 13, 1989): 24.

121. Charles Goldsmith and Charles Fleming, "Film Industry in Europe Seeks Wider Audience," *Wall Street Journal* (December 6, 1993): B1 (2 pp.).

122. Sherry and Camargo, "May Your Life Be Marvelous"; "French Council Eases Language Ban," *New York Times* (July 31, 1994): 12.

123. Quoted in Alan Riding, "Only the French Elite Scorn Mickey's Debut," *New York Times* (1992)2: A1.

124. Mike Levin, "U.S. Tobacco Firms Push Eagerly into Asian Market," *Marketing News* (January 21, 1991) Volume 2: 2.

Glossary

ABC model of attitudes a multidimensional perspective stating that attitudes are jointly defined by affect, behavior, and cognition

Absolute threshold the minimum amount of stimulation that can be detected on a given sensory channel

Accommodative purchase decision the process using bargaining, coercion, compromise, and the wielding of power to achieve agreement among group members who have different preferences or priorities

Acculturation the process of learning the beliefs and behaviors endorsed by another culture

Acculturation agents friends, family, local businesses, and other reference groups that facilitate the learning of cultural norms

Activation models of memory approaches to memory stressing different levels of processing that occur and activate some aspects of memory rather than others, depending on the nature of the processing task

Actual self a person's realistic appraisal of his or her qualities

Adaptation the process that occurs when a sensation becomes so familiar that it no longer commands attention

Affect the way a consumer feels about an attitude object

Affinity marketing a strategy that allows a consumer to emphasize his or her identification with some organization, as, for example, when organizations issue credit cards with their names on them

Age cohort a group of consumers of approximately the same age who have undergone similar experiences

Agentic goals an emphasis on self-assertion and mastery, often associated with traditional male gender roles

AIOs (activities, interests, and opinions) the psychographic variables used by researchers in grouping consumers

Androgyny the possession of both masculine and feminine traits

Animism cultural practices whereby inanimate objects are given qualities that make them somehow alive

Anticonsumption the actions taken by consumers that involve the deliberate defacement or mutilation of products

Archetype a universally shared idea or behavior pattern, central to Carl Jung's conception of personality; archetypes involve themes—such as birth, death, or the devil—that appear frequently in myths, stories, and dreams

Art product a creation viewed primarily as an object of aesthetic contemplation without any functional value

Atmospherics the use of space and physical features in store design to evoke certain effects in buyers

Attention the assignment of processing activity to selected stimuli

Attitude a lasting, general evaluation of people (including oneself), objects, or issues

Attitude object (A_o) anything toward which one has an attitude

Attitude toward the act of buying (A_{act}) the perceived consequences of a purchase

Attitude toward the advertisement (A_{ad}) a predisposition to respond favorably or unfavorably to a particular advertising stimulus during a particular exposure occasion

Autocratic decisions those purchase decisions that are made almost exclusively by one or the other spouse

Baby boomers a large cohort of people born between the years of 1946 and 1964 who are the source of many important cultural and economic changes

baby boomlet a modest surge of children born to baby boomers, who have until recently delayed having children and are less likely to have large families in comparison to their parents

Back-translation to ensure accurate translation of research materials or advertising messages, a process whereby a translated message is again translated back into its original language to verify its correctness

Balance theory a theory that considers relations among elements a person might perceive as belonging together, and people's tendency to change relations among elements in order to make them consistent or "balanced"

Behavior a consumer's actions with regard to an attitude object

Behavioral economics the study of the behavioral determinants of economic decisions

Behavioral influence perspective the view that consumer decisions are learned responses to environmental cues

Behavioral learning theories the perspectives on learning that assume that it takes place as the result of responses to external events

Binary opposition a defining structural characteristic of many myths, in which two opposing ends of some dimension are represented (e.g., good versus evil, nature versus technology)

Body cathexis a person's feelings about aspects of his or her body

Body image a consumer's subjective evaluation of his or her physical self

Boomerang kids grown children who return to their parents' home to live

Brand equity a brand that has strong positive associations in a consumer's memory and commands a lot of loyalty as a result

Brand loyalty a pattern of repeat product purchases, accompanied by an underlying positive attitude toward the brand

Business ethics rules of conduct that guide actions in the marketplace

Business-to-business marketers specialists in meeting the needs of organizations such as corporations, government agencies, hospitals, and retailers

Buyclass theory of purchasing classification scheme that divides organizational buying decisions into types based on the complexity and effort required to make them

Buying center the part of an organization charged with making purchasing decisions

Classic a fashion with an extremely long acceptance cycle

Classical conditioning the learning that occurs when a stimulus eliciting a response is paired with another stimulus that initially does not elicit a response on its own but will cause a similar response over time because of its association with the first stimulus

Closure principle the gestalt principle that describes a person's tendency to supply missing information in order to perceive a holistic image

Co-consumers the other people present in a consumption situation; their presence or absence or specific characteristics may influence evaluations of that situation and the products or services consumed therein

Cognition the beliefs a consumer has about an attitude object

Cognitive learning theory approaches that stress the importance of internal mental processes. This perspective views people as problem solvers who actively use information from the world around them to master their environment

Cognitive structure the set of factual knowledge, or beliefs about a product, and the way these beliefs are organized

Collecting the systematic acquisition of a particular object or set of objects

Collective selection the process by which certain symbolic alternatives tend to be jointly chosen over others by members of a society

Collectivist cultures cultural orientation that encourages people to subordinate their personal goals to those of a stable in-group; values such as self-discipline and group accomplishment are stressed

Communal goals an emphasis on affiliation and the fostering of harmonious rela-

tions, often associated with traditional female gender-roles

Communications model a framework specifying that a number of elements are necessary for communication to be achieved, including a source, message, medium, receivers, and feedback

Comparative advertising a strategy in which a message compares two or more specifically named or recognizably presented brands and makes a comparison of them in terms of one or more specific attributes

Comparative influence the process whereby a reference group influences decisions about specific brands or activities

Compensatory decision rules a set of rules that allow information about attributes of competing products to be averaged in some way; poor standing on one attribute can potentially be offset by good standing on another

Compulsive consumption the process of repetitive, often excessive, shopping used to relieve tension, anxiety, depression, or boredom

Conformity a change in beliefs or actions as a reaction to real or imagined group pressure

Consensual purchase decision a decision in which the group agrees on the desired purchase and differs only in terms of how it will be achieved

Conspicuous consumption the purchase and prominent display of luxury goods to provide evidence of a consumer's ability to afford them

Consumed consumers those people who are used or exploited, whether willingly or not, for commercial gain in the marketplace

Consumer a person who identifies a need or desire, makes a purchase, and/or disposes of the product

Consumer addiction a physiological and/or psychological dependency on products or services

Consumer behavior the processes involved when individuals or groups select, purchase, use, or dispose of products, services, ideas, or experiences to satisfy needs and desires

Consumer confidence the state of mind of consumers relative to their optimism or pessimism about economic conditions; people tend to make more discretionary purchases when their confidence in the economy is high

Consumer desire a feeling of longing for goods or services not presently possessed

Consumer satisfaction/dissatisfaction (CS/D) the overall attitude a person has about a product after it has been purchased

Consumer socialization the process by which people acquire skills that enable them to function in the marketplace

Consumption constellations a set of products and activities used by consumers to define, communicate, and perform social roles

Consumption situation factors over and above characteristics of the person and of the product that influence the buying and/or using of products and services, such as the nature of the environment in which the decision is being made.

Contamination when a place or object takes on sacred qualities due to its association with another sacred person or event

Continuous innovation a product change or new product that requires relatively little adaptation by the adopter

Convention norms regarding the conduct of everyday life

Cooptation a cultural process by which the original meanings of a product or other symbol associated with a subculture are modified by members of mainstream culture

Craft product a creation valued because of the beauty with which it performs some function; this type of product tends to follow a formula that permits rapid production, and it is easier to understand than an art product

Creolization foreign influences are absorbed and integrated with local meanings

Cultivation hypothesis a perspective emphasizing media's ability to distort consumers' perceptions of reality

Cultural categories the grouping of ideas and values that reflect the basic ways members of a society characterize the world

Cultural formula a sequence of media events in which certain roles and props tend to occur consistently

Cultural gatekeepers individuals who are responsible for determining the types of messages and symbolism to which members of mass culture are exposed

Cultural resistance the process whereby subcultures of consumers who are alienated from mainstream society (e.g., juvenile delinquents) single out objects that represent the values of the larger group and modify them as an act of rebellion or self-expression

Cultural selection the process by which some alternatives are selected over others by cultural gatekeepers

Culture the values, ethics, rituals, traditions, material objects, and services produced or valued by the members of a society

Culture jamming the defacement or alteration of advertising materials as a form of political expression

Culture production system (CPS) the set of individuals and organizations responsible for creating and marketing a cultural product

Custom a norm that is derived from a traditional way of doing things

Database marketing tracking consumers' buying habits very closely, and crafting products and messages tailored precisely to people's wants and needs based on this information

Decay structural changes in the brain produced by learning decrease over time

Decision polarization the process whereby individuals' choices tend to become more extreme (polarized), in either a conservative or risky direction, following group discussion of alternatives

De-ethnicitization the process whereby a product formerly associated with a specific ethnic group is detached from its roots and marketed to other subcultures

Deindividuation the process whereby individual identities get submerged within a group, reducing inhibitions against socially inappropriate behavior

Demographics the observable measurements of a population's characteristics, such as birthrate, age distribution, and income

Desacralization the process that occurs when a sacred item or symbol is removed from its special place, or is duplicated in mass quantities, and becomes profane as a result

Differential threshold the ability of a sensory system to detect changes or differences among stimuli

Diffusion of innovation the process whereby a new product, service, or idea spreads through a population

Discontinuous innovation a product change or new product that requires a significant amount of behavioral adaptation on the part of the adopter

Discretionary income the money available to a household over and above that required for necessities

Drive the desire to satisfy a biological need in order to reduce physiological arousal

Dynamically continuous innovation a product change or new product that requires a moderate amount of behavioral adaptation on the part of the adopter

Early adopters people who are receptive to new products and adopt them relatively soon, though they are motivated more by social acceptance and being in style than by the desire to try risky new things

Ego the system that mediates between the id and the superego

Elaborated codes the ways of expressing and interpreting meanings that are more complex and depend on a more sophisticated worldview, which tend to be used by the middle and upper classes

Elaboration likelihood model (ELM) the approach that one of two routes to persuasion (central versus peripheral) will be followed, depending on the personal relevance of a message; the route taken determines the relative importance of message contents versus other characteristics, such as source attractiveness

Emic perspective an approach to studying (or marketing to) cultures that stresses the unique aspects of each culture

Encoding the process in which information from short-term memory enters into long-term memory in a recognizable form

Enculturation the process of learning the beliefs and behaviors endorsed by one's own culture

Erogenous zones areas of the body considered by members of a culture to be foci of sexual attractiveness

Ethnic subculture a self-perpetuating group of consumers held together by common cultural ties

Ethnocentrism the belief in the superiority of one's own country's practices and products

Ethos a set of moral, aesthetic, and evaluative principles

Etic perspective an approach to studying (or marketing to) cultures that stresses commonalities across cultures

Evaluative criteria the dimensions used by consumers to compare competing product alternatives

Evoked set those products already in memory plus those prominent in the retail environment that are actively considered during a consumer's choice process

Exchange a transaction where two or more organizations or people give and receive something of value

Exchange theory the perspective that every interaction involves an exchange of value

Expectancy disconfirmation model the perspective that consumers form beliefs about product performance based upon prior experience with the product and/or communications about the product that imply a certain level of quality; their actual satisfaction depends on the degree to which performance is consistent with these expectations

Expectancy theory the perspective that behavior is largely "pulled" by expectations of achieving desirable outcomes, or positive incentives, rather than "pushed" from within

Experiential perspective an approach stressing the gestalt or totality of the product or service experience, focusing on consumers' affective responses in the marketplace

Expert power authority derived from possessing a specific knowledge or skill

Exposure an initial stage of perception during which some sensations come within range of consumers' sensory receptors

Extended family traditional family structure in which several generations live together

Extended problem solving an elaborate decision-making process, often initiated by a motive that is fairly central to the self-concept and accompanied by perceived risk; the consumer tries to collect as much information as possible, and carefully weighs product alternatives

Extended self the definition of self created by the external objects with which one surrounds oneself

Extinction the process whereby a learned connection between a stimulus and response is eroded so that the response is no longer reinforced

Fad a very short-lived fashion

Family financial officer (FFO) the individual in the family who is in charge of making financial decisions

Family household a housing unit containing at least two people who are related by blood or marriage

Family life-cycle (FLC) a classification scheme that segments consumers in terms of changes in income and family composition and the changes in demands placed on this income

Fantasy a self-induced shift in consciousness, often focusing on some unattainable or improbable goal; sometimes fantasy is a way of compensating for a lack of external stimulation or for dissatisfaction with the actual self

Fashion the process of social diffusion by which a new style is adopted by some group(s) of consumers

Fashion acceptance cycle the diffusion process of a style through three stages: introduction, acceptance, and regression

Fashion life-cycle the "career" or stages in the life of a fashion as it progresses from introduction to obsolescence

Fashion system those people and organizations involved in creating symbolic meanings and transferring these meanings to cultural goods

Fear appeal an attempt to change attitudes or behavior through the use of threats or by highlighting negative consequences of noncompliance with the request

Felt ethnicity the extent to which a person's ethnic identity influences his or her self-image and behavior at any point in time

Fertility rate a rate determined by the number of births per year per 1,000 women of child-bearing age

Figure–ground principle the gestalt principle whereby one part of a stimulus configuration dominates a situation, while other aspects recede into the background

Foot-in-the-door technique based on the observation that a consumer is more likely to comply with a request if he or she has first agreed to comply with a smaller request

Frequency marketing a marketing technique that reinforces regular purchasers by giving them prizes with values that increase along with the amount purchased

Functional theory of attitudes a pragmatic approach that focuses on how attitudes facilitate social behavior; attitudes exist because they serve some function for the person

Generation X a widely-used term to describe "twentysomething" consumers who are (stereotypically) characterized as being confused, alienated, and depressed

Geodemography techniques that combine consumer demographic information with geographic consumption patterns to permit precise targeting of consumers with specific characteristics

Gerontographics a segmentation approach divides the mature market into groups based on both level of physical well-being and social conditions such as becoming a grandparent or losing a spouse

Gestalt meaning derived from the totality of a set of stimuli, rather than from any individual stimulus

Gift-giving ritual the events involved in the selection, presentation, acceptance, and interpretation of a gift

Goal a consumer's desired end state

Gray market the economic potential created by the increasing numbers of affluent elderly consumers

Green marketing a marketing strategy involving an emphasis on protecting the natural environment

Habitual decision making the consumption choices that are made out of habit, without additional information search or deliberation among products

Hedonic consumption the multisensory, fantasy, and emotional aspects of consumers' interactions with products

Heuristics the mental rules-of-thumb that lead to a speedy decision

Hierarchy of effects a fixed sequence of steps that occurs during attitude formation; this sequence varies depending on such factors as the consumer's level of involvement with the attitude object

Homeostasis the state of being in which the body is in physiological balance; goal-oriented behavior attempts to reduce or eliminate an unpleasant motivational state and return to a balanced one

Hyperreality the becoming real of what is initially simulation or "hype"

Id the system oriented toward immediate gratification

Ideal of beauty a model, or exemplar, of appearance valued by a culture

Ideal self a person's conception of how he or she would like to be

Impulse buying a process that occurs when the consumer experiences a sudden urge to purchase an item that he or she cannot resist

Individualist cultures a cultural orientation that encourages people to attach more importance to personal goals than to group goals; values such as personal enjoyment and freedom are stressed

Inept set the product alternatives that the consumer is aware of but would not consider buying during the choice process

Inert set the product alternatives of which the consumer is not aware and therefore, are not even included in the consumer's choice process

Inertia the process whereby purchase decisions are made out of habit because the consumer lacks the motivation to consider alternatives

Information power power of knowing something others would like to know

Information search the process whereby a consumer searches for appropriate information to make a reasonable decision

Informational social influence the conformity that occurs because the group's behavior is taken as evidence about reality

Innovation a product or style that is perceived as new by consumers

Innovators people who are always on the lookout for novel developments and will be the first to try a new offering

Instrumental conditioning also known as *operant conditioning,* occurs as the individual learns to perform behaviors that produce positive outcomes and to avoid those that yield negative outcomes

Instrumental values goals endorsed because they are needed to achieve desired end states, or terminal values

Interference a process whereby additional learned information displaces the earlier information, resulting in memory loss for the item learned previously

Interpretant the meaning derived from a sign or symbol

Interpretation the process whereby meanings are assigned to stimuli

Interpretivism as opposed to the dominant positivist perspective on consumer behavior, instead stresses the importance of symbolic, subjective experience, and the idea that meaning is in the mind of the person rather than existing "out there" in the objective world

Invidious distinction the display of wealth or power to inspire envy in others

Involvement the motivation to process product-related information

J.N.D. (just noticeable difference) the minimum difference between two stimuli that can be detected by a perceiver

Kin-network system the rituals intended to maintain ties among family members both immediate and extended

Knockoff a style that has been deliberately copied and modified, often with the intent to sell to a larger or different market

Knowledge structures organized systems of concepts relating to brands, stores, and other concepts

Laddering a technique for uncovering consumers' associations between specific attributes and general consequences

Laggards consumers who are exceptionally slow to adopt innovations

Late adopters the majority of consumers who are moderately receptive to adopting innovations

Latitudes of acceptance and rejection formed around an attitude standard; ideas that fall within a latitude will be favorably received, whereas those falling outside this zone will not

Lateral cycling a process in which already-purchased objects are sold to others or exchanged for other items

Learning a relatively permanent change in a behavior caused by experience

Legitimate power the power granted to people by virtue of social agreements

Lifestyle a set of shared values or tastes exhibited by a group of consumers, especially as these are reflected in consumption patterns

Limited problem solving a problem-solving process in which consumers are not motivated to search for information or to rigorously evaluate each alternative; instead they use simple decision rules to arrive at a purchase decision

Long-term memory the system that allows us to retain information for a long period of time

Looking-glass self the process of imagining the reaction of others toward oneself

Market beliefs the specific beliefs or decision rules pertaining to marketplace phenomena

Market maven a person who often serves as a source of information about marketplace activities

Market segmentation the process of identifying groups of consumers who are similar to one another in one or more ways, and then devising marketing strategies that appeal to one or more of these groups

Mass customization a basic product or service is modified to meet the needs of an individual

Match-up hypothesis a celebrity's image and that of the product he or she endorses should be similar to maximize the credibility and effectiveness of the communication

Materialism the importance consumers attach to worldly possessions

Memory a process of acquiring information and storing it over time so that it will be available when– needed

Metaphor the use of an explicit comparison ("A" is "B") between a product and some other person, place, or thing

Modified rebuy in the context of the buyclass framework, a task that requires a modest amount of information search and evaluation, often focused on identifying the appropriate vendor

Monomyth a myth with basic characteristics that are found in many cultures

More a custom with strong moral overtones

Motivation an internal state that activates goal-oriented behavior

Motivational research a qualitative research approach, based on psychoanalytic (Freudian) interpretations, with a heavy emphasis on unconscious motives for consumption

Multiattribute attitude models those models that assume that a consumer's attitude (evaluation) of an attitude object depends on the beliefs he or she has about several or many attributes of the object; the use of a multiattribute model implies that an attitude toward a product or brand can be predicted by identifying these specific beliefs and combining them to derive a measure of the consumer's overall attitude

Myth a story containing symbolic elements that expresses the shared emotions and ideals of a culture

Negative reinforcement the process whereby the environment weakens responses to stimuli so that inappropriate behavior is avoided

New task in the context of the buyclass framework, a task that requires a great degree of effort and information search

Noncompensatory decision rules a set of simple rules used to evaluate competing alternatives; a brand with a low standing on one relevant attribute is eliminated from the consumer's choice set

Normative influence the process in which a reference group helps to set and enforce fundamental standards of conduct

Normative social influence the conformity that occurs when a person alters his or her behavior to meet the expectations of a person or group

Norms the informal rules that govern what is right or wrong

Nostalgia a bittersweet emotion; the past is viewed with sadness and longing; many "classic" products appeal to consumers' memories of their younger days

Nuclear family a contemporary living arrangement composed of a married couple and their children

Object in semiotic terms, the product that is the focus of a message

Observational learning the process in which people learn by watching the actions of others and noting the reinforcements they receive for their behaviors

Opinion leaders those people who are knowledgeable about products and who are frequently able to influence others' attitudes or behaviors with regard to a product category

Organizational buyers people who purchase goods and services on behalf of companies for use in the process of manufacturing, distribution, or resale

Paradigm a widely accepted view or model of phenomena being studied; the perspective that regards people as rational information processors is currently the dominant paradigm, though this approach is now being challenged by a new wave of research that emphasizes the frequently subjective nature of consumer decision making

Parental yielding the process that occurs when a parental decision maker is influenced by a child's product request

Parody display the deliberate avoidance of widely used status symbols, whereby a person seeks status by mocking it

Perceived age how old a person feels as compared to his or her true chronological age

Perceived risk the belief that use of a product has potentially negative consequences, either physical or social

Perception the process by which stimuli are selected, organized, and interpreted

Perceptual map a research tool used to understand how a brand is positioned in consumers' minds relative to competitors

Perceptual defense the tendency for consumers to avoid processing stimuli that are threatening to them

Perceptual selection process by which people attend to only a small portion of the stimuli to which they are exposed

Perceptual vigilance the tendency for consumers to be more aware of stimuli that relate to their current needs

Personality a person's unique psychological makeup, which consistently influences the way the person responds to his or her environment

Persuasion an active attempt to change attitudes

Pleasure principle the belief that behavior is guided by the desire to maximize pleasure and avoid pain

Point-of-purchase stimuli (POP) the promotional materials that are deployed in stores or other outlets to influence consumers' decisions at the time products are purchased

Popular culture the music, movies, sports, books, celebrities, and other forms of entertainment consumed by the mass market

Positioning strategy an organization's use of elements in the marketing mix to influence the consumer's interpretation of a product's meaning vis-à-vis competitors

Positive reinforcement the process whereby rewards provided by the environment strengthen responses to stimuli and appropriate behavior is learned

Positivism a research perspective that relies on principles of the "scientific method" and assumes that a single reality exists; events in the world can be objectively measured; and the causes of behavior can be identified, manipulated, and predicted

Principle of cognitive consistency the belief that consumers value harmony among their thoughts, feelings, and behaviors and that they are motivated to maintain uniformity among these elements

Principle of similarity the gestalt principle that describes how consumers tend to group objects that share similar physical characteristics

Problem recognition the process that occurs whenever the consumer sees a significant difference between his or her current state of affairs and some desired or ideal state; this recognition initiates the decision-making process

Product complementarity the view that products in different functional categories have symbolic meanings that are related to one another

Product placement the process of obtaining exposure for a product by arranging for it to be inserted into a movie, television show, or some other medium

Profane consumption the process of consuming objects and events that are ordinary or of the everyday world

Progressive learning model the perspective that people gradually learn a new culture as they increasingly come in contact with it; consumers assimilate into a new culture, mixing practices from their old and new environments to create a hybrid culture

Psychographics the use of psychological, sociological, and anthropological factors to construct market segments

Psychophysics the science that focuses on how the physical environment is integrated into the consumer's subjective experience

Punishment the learning that occurs when a response is followed by unpleasant events

Racial subculture a self-perpetuating group of consumers who are held together by common genetic ties

Rational perspective a view of the consumer as a careful, analytical decision maker who tries to maximize utility in purchase decisions

Reactance a "boomerang effect" that sometimes occurs when consumers are threatened with a loss of freedom of choice; they respond by doing the opposite of the behavior advocated in a persuasive message

Reality engineering the process whereby elements of popular culture are appropriated by marketers and become integrated into marketing strategies

Reality principle the ego seeks ways that will be acceptable to society to gratify the id

Reference group an actual or imaginary individual or group that has a significant effect on an individual's evaluations, aspirations, or behavior

Referent power the power of prominent people to affect others' consumption behaviors by virtue of product endorsements, distinctive fashion statements, or championing of causes

Relationship marketing the strategic perspective that stresses the long-term, human side of buyer–seller interactions

Repositioning a marketing strategy that involves a modification of a product's original market to update the product's image or to appeal to a different market segment

Resonance a literary device, frequently used in advertising, that uses a play on words (a double meaning) to communicate a product benefit

Response bias a form of contamination in survey research in which some factor, such as the desire to make a good impression on the experimenter, leads respondents to modify their true answers

Restricted codes the ways of expressing and interpreting meanings that focus on the content of objects and tend to be used by the working class

Retrieval the process whereby desired information is recovered from long-term memory

Rites of passage sacred times marked by a change in social status

Ritual a set of multiple, symbolic behaviors that occur in a fixed sequence and that tend to be repeated periodically

Ritual artifacts items (consumer goods) used in the performance of rituals

Role theory the perspective that much of consumer behavior resembles actions in a play

Sacralization a process that occurs when ordinary objects, events, or people take on sacred meaning to a culture or to specific groups within a culture

Sacred consumption the process of consuming objects and events that are set apart from normal life and treated with some degree of respect or awe

Savings rate the amount of money saved for later use that is influenced by consumers' pessimism or optimism about their personal circumstances, world events, and cultural attitudes toward saving

Schema an organized collection of beliefs and feelings represented in a cognitive category

Self-concept the beliefs a person holds about his or her own attributes and how he or she evaluates these qualities

Self-gifts the products or services bought by consumers for their own use as a reward or consolation

Self-image congruence models the approaches based on the prediction that products will be chosen when their attributes match some aspect of the self

Self-perception theory an alternative (to cognitive dissonance) explanation of dissonance effects; it assumes that people use observations of their own behavior to infer their attitudes toward some object

Semiotics a field of study that examines the correspondence between signs and symbols and the meaning or meanings they convey

Sensation the immediate response of sensory receptors (eyes, ears, nose, mouth, fingers) to such basic stimuli as light, color, sound, odors, and textures

Sensory memory the temporary storage of information received from the senses

Sex-typed traits characteristics that are stereotypically associated with one gender or the other

Shopping orientation a consumer's general attitudes and motivations regarding the act of shopping

Short-term memory the mental system that allows us to retain information for a short period of time

Shrinkage the loss of money or inventory from shoplifting and/or employee theft

Sign the sensory imagery that represents the intended meanings of the object

Single-source data a compilation of information that includes different aspects of consumption and demographic data for a common consumer segment

Situational self-image a person's self-concept at a particular point in time, which is influenced by the specific role he or she is playing at that time

Sleeper effect the process whereby differences in attitude change between positive and negative sources seem to diminish over time

Social class the overall rank of people in a society; people who are grouped within the same social class are approximately equal in terms of their income, occupations, and lifestyles

Social comparison theory the perspective that people compare their outcomes with others' as a way to increase the stability of their own self-evaluation, especially when physical evidence is unavailable

Social judgment theory the perspective that people assimilate new information about attitude objects in light of what they already know or feel; the initial attitude acts as a frame of reference, and new information is categorized in terms of this standard

Social marketing the promotion of causes and ideas (social products), such as energy conservation, charities, and population control

Social mobility the movement of individuals from one social class to another

Social power the capacity of one person to alter the actions or outcome of another

Social stratification the process in a social system by which scarce and valuable resources are distributed unequally to status positions that become more or less permanently ranked in terms of the share of valuable resources each receives

Social trends broad changes in people's attitudes and behaviors

Sociometric methods the techniques for measuring group dynamics that involve tracing communication patterns in and among groups

Source attractiveness the dimensions of a communicator that increase his or her persuasiveness; these include expertise and attractiveness

Source credibility a communications source's perceived expertise, objectivity, or trustworthiness

Stage of cognitive development the ability to comprehend concepts of increasing complexity as a person ages

Status crystallization the extent to which different indicators of a person's status (income, ethnicity, occupation) are consistent with one another

Status hierarchy a ranking of social desirability in terms of consumers' access to resources such as money, education, and luxury goods

Status symbols products that are purchased and displayed to signal membership in a desirable social class

Stimulus discrimination the process that occurs when behaviors caused by two stimuli are different, as when consumers learn to differentiate a brand from its competitors

Stimulus generalization the process that occurs when the behavior caused by a reaction to one stimulus occurs in the presence of other, similar stimuli

Storage the process that occurs when knowledge in long-term memory is integrated with what is already in memory and "warehoused" until needed

Store image a store's "personality," composed of such attributes as location, merchandise suitability, and the knowledge and congeniality of the sales staff

Straight rebuy in the context of the buy-class framework, the type of buying decision that is virtually automatic and requires little deliberation

Subculture a group whose members share beliefs and common experiences that set them apart from other members of a culture

Subliminal perception the processing of stimuli presented below the level of the consumer's awareness

Superego the system that internalizes society's rules and that works to prevent the id from seeking selfish gratification

Surrogate consumer a professional who is retained to evaluate and/or make purchases on behalf of a consumer

Symbolic innovation an innovation that communicates a new social meaning

Symbolic interactionism a sociological approach stressing that relationships with other people play a large part in forming the self; people live in a symbolic environment, and the meaning attached to any situation or object is determined by a person's interpretation of these symbols

Symbolic self-completion theory the perspective that people who have an incomplete self-definition in some context will compensate by acquiring symbols associated with a desired social identity

Syncratic decisions those purchase decisions that are made jointly by both spouses

Synoptic ideal a model of spousal decision making in which the husband and wife take a common view and act as joint decision makers, assigning each other well-defined roles and making mutually beneficial decisions to maximize the couple's joint utility

Taste culture a group of consumers who share aesthetic and intellectual preferences

Technological innovation an innovation that involves some functional change to the product

Terminal values end states desired by members of a culture

Theory of cognitive dissonance theory based on the premise that a state of tension is created when beliefs or behaviors conflict with one another; people are motivated to reduce this inconsistency (or dissonance) and thus eliminate unpleasant tension

Theory of reasoned action an updated version of the Fishbein multiattribute attitude theory that considers factors such as social pressure and A_{act} (the attitude toward the act of buying a product), rather than attitudes toward just the product itself

Trait the identifiable characteristics that define a person

Trickle-down theory of fashion the perspective that fashions spread as the result of status symbols associated with the upper classes "trickling down" to other social classes as these consumers try to emulate those with greater status

80/20 principle a rule-of-thumb in volume segmentation, which says that about 20 percent of consumers in a product category (the heavy users) account for about 80 percent of sales

Two-factor theory the perspective that two separate psychological processes are operating when a person is repeatedly exposed to an ad: *repetition* increases familiarity and thus reduces uncertainty about the product but over time *boredom* increases with each exposure, and at some point the amount of boredom incurred begins to exceed the amount of uncertainty reduced, resulting in wear-out

Uses and gratifications theory views consumers as an active, goal-directed audience that draws on mass media as a resource to satisfy needs

VALS (Values and Lifestyles) a psychographic segmentation system used to categorize consumers into clusters, or "VALS Types"

Value a belief that some condition is preferable to its opposite

Value system a culture's ranking of the relative importance of values

Want the particular form of consumption chosen to satisfy a need

Weber's Law the principle that the stronger the initial stimulus, the greater its change must be for it to be noticed

Word-of-mouth communication (WOM) product information transmitted by individual consumers on an informal basis

Worldview the ideas shared by members of a culture about principles of order and fairness

Indexes

PRODUCT INDEX

SUBJECT INDEX